506 Best SMALL Home Plans

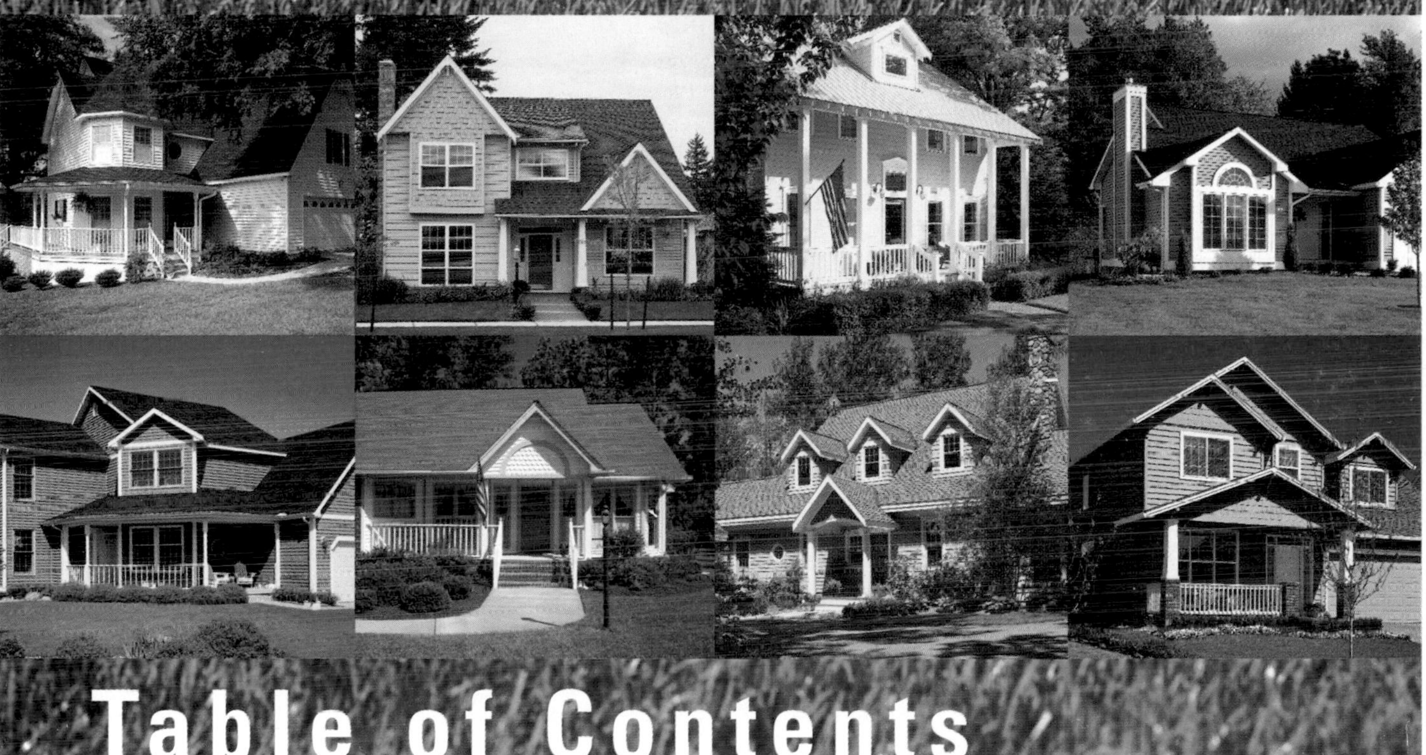

Table of Contents

506 Best SMALL Home Plans

800 to 2,400 square feet

A comprehensive collection
of the best small home plans available today.

506 Best Small Home Plans

Printed and bound in the USA.

Steve Culpepper, Editorial Director
Christopher Berrien, Art Director
Debra Novitch, Art Production Manager
Debbie Cochran, Managing Editor
Gia C. Manalio, Associate Editor
Andrew Russell, Graphic Artist
Kevin Degutis, Melani Gonzalez, Cindy King, Production Artists

The photographed homes may have been modified to suit individual tastes.

Submit all Canadian plan orders
to the following address:
Garlinghouse Company, 102 Ellis Street, Penticton, BC V2A 4L5

Library of Congress: 99-76717
ISBN: 1-893536-08-4

2536

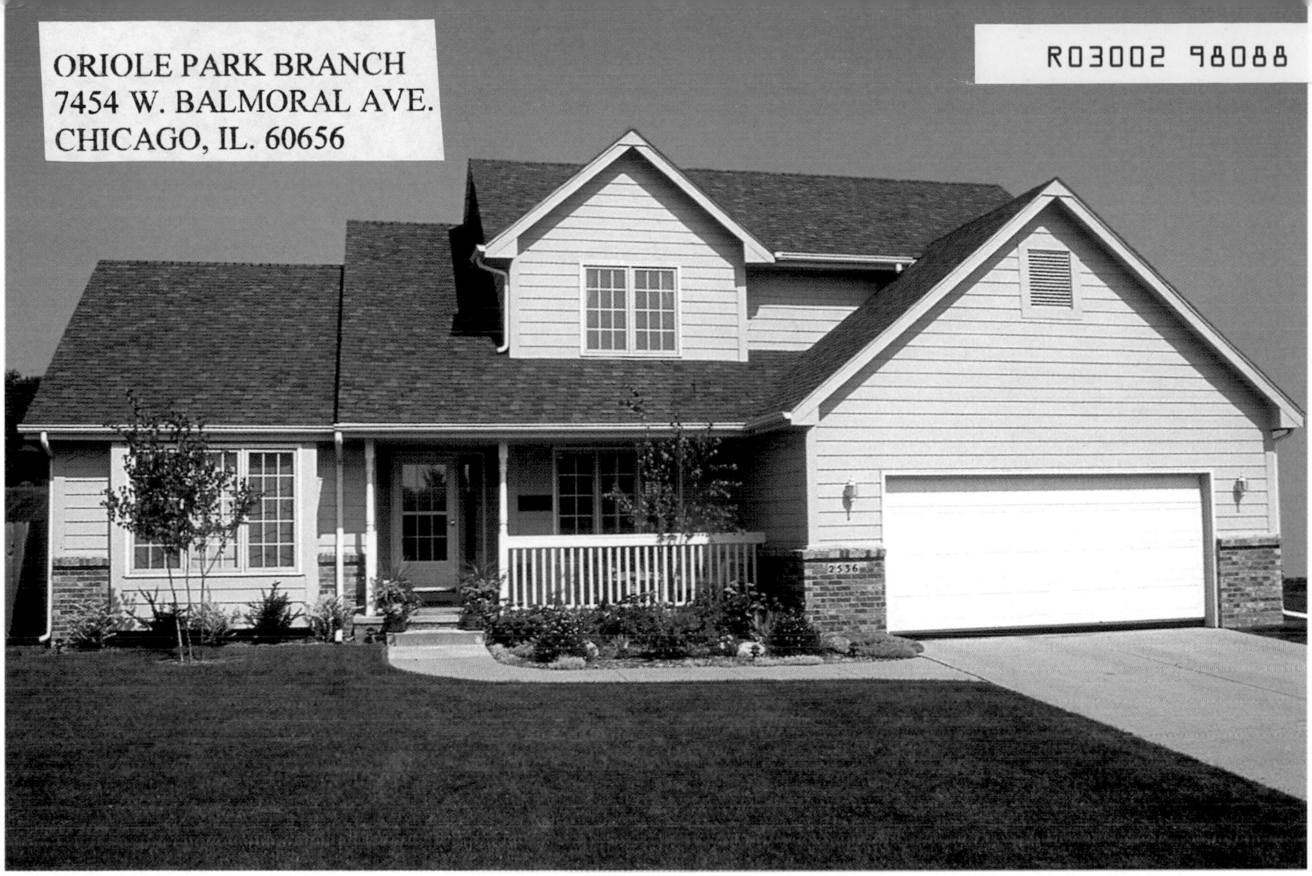

PHOTOGRAPHY: COURTESY OF THE DESIGNER

above The center gable nicely sets off the gabled garage. The covered porch and triple windows add curb appeal.

compact and PLEASING

design 99420

Units	Single
Price Code	B
Total Finished	1,694 sq. ft.
First Finished	1,298 sq. ft.
Second Finished	396 sq. ft.
Basement Unfinished	1,298 sq. ft.
Garage Unfinished	513 sq. ft.
Dimensions	54'x45'4"
Foundation	Basement
Bedrooms	3
Full Baths	2
Half Baths	1
Max Ridge Height	23'9"
Roof Framing	Stick
Exterior Walls	2x4

The main entry leads directly into the formal dining room to the right, past the stairs leading to the second floor, and into the great-room. The breakfast room, with a built-in desk, shares a snack bar with the kitchen, which is almost completely enclosed by its ample counters. The laundry room is a few steps away, beside the door to the spacious garage. In the opposite wing of the first floor is the master suite. The second floor is reserved for two secondary bedrooms and a full bath. A linen closet makes use of what could have been wasted space. This home is designed with a basement foundation. Alternate foundation options available at an additional charge. Please call 1-800-235-5700 for more information.

Please note: The photographed home may have been modified to suit homeowner preferences. If you order plans, have a builder or design professional check them against the photographs to confirm actual construction details.

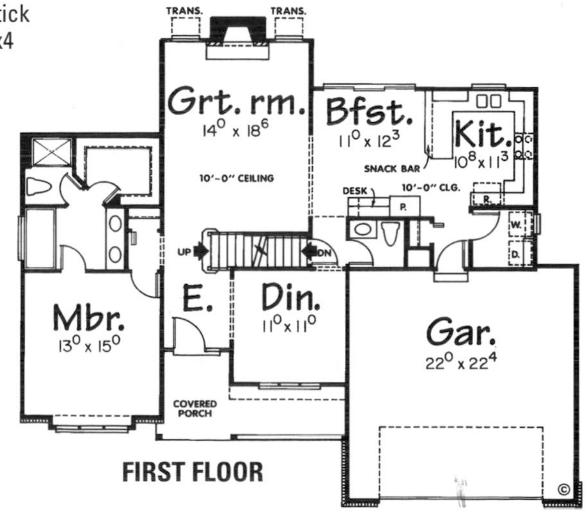

TRANS.
TRANS.
Grt. rm.
14⁰ x 18⁶
10'-0" CEILING
Bfst.
11⁰ x 12³
SNACK BAR
Kit.
10⁸ x 11³
DESK
10'-0" CLG.
R.
P.
W.
D.
UP
DN
Mbr.
13⁰ x 15⁰
E.
Din.
11⁰ x 11⁰
Gar.
22⁰ x 22⁴
COVERED PORCH
©

FIRST FLOOR

DN
LINEN
Br. 3
11⁰ x 10⁰
Br. 2
10⁴ x 11⁰

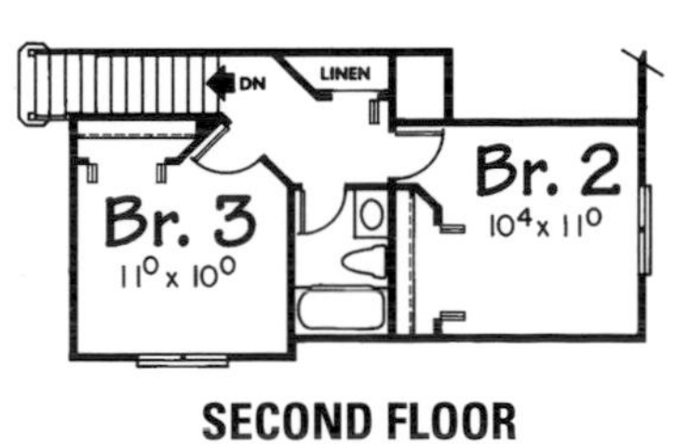

SECOND FLOOR

PHOTOGRAPHY: STEPHEN CRIDLAND

traditional DETAILS

above A mix of clapboard and cedar-shake siding, simple but elegant gables, eave brackets, and tapered pillars establish timeless appeal.

below To the right of the foyer is the formal dining room. Columns on half walls add a touch of elegance to its entry.

Sometimes it's the simple details that make the biggest statement. Such is the case with this house, whose gable roofline, cedar-shake siding accents, and simple but elegant tapered pillars showcase the classic details of traditional design. The living and dining rooms flank the entry. The kitchen features a center island with a cooktop. The second-floor master suite includes a tub, shower, dual-sink vanity, and a walk-in closet. The main level has 1,211 square feet, and the upper level has 867 square feet. This home is designed with a crawlspace foundation.

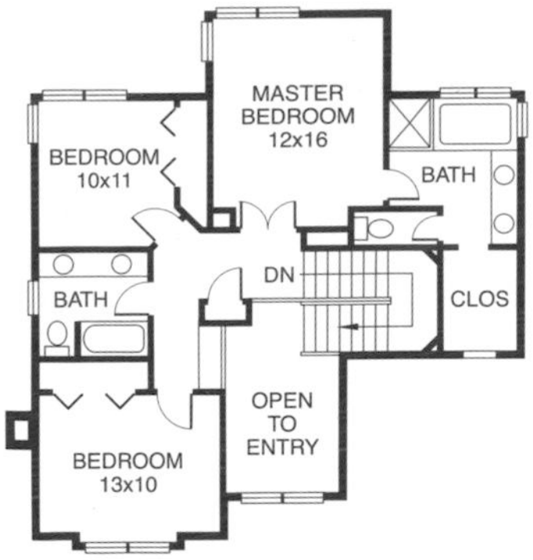

SECOND FLOOR

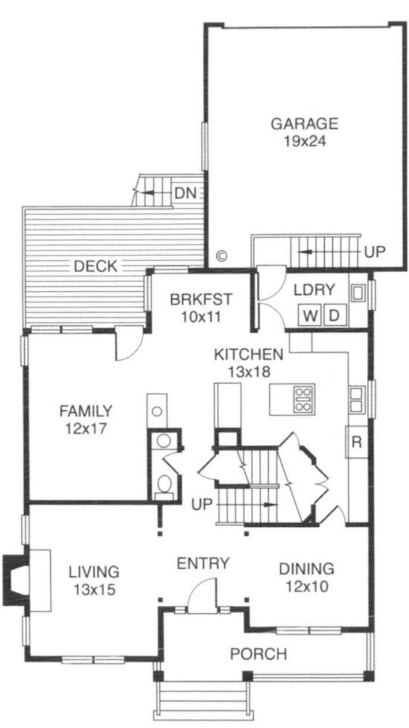

FIRST FLOOR

Design Number 32049

Units	Single
Price Code	D
Total Finished	2,078 sq. ft.
First Finished	1,211 sq. ft.
Second Finished	867 sq. ft.
Dimensions	40'6"x65'
Foundation	Crawlspace
Bedrooms	3
Full Baths	2
Half Baths	1
Max Ridge Height	34'
Roof Framing	Stick
Exterior Walls	2x6

Please note: The photographed home may have been modified to suit homeowner preferences. If you order plans, have a builder or design professional check them against the photographs to confirm actual construction details.

below The formal living room sits to the left of the foyer, delineated by columns and half walls. Notice the symmetry of the view, including the distant windows and recessed lights.

PHOTOGRAPHY: JOHN EHRENCLOU

above A tall gable adds an interesting architectural focal point to this classic design.

separate formal SPACES

The tiled foyer leads to the private dining room on the left and to the isolated living room on the right. Straight ahead is the vast family room, which features a fireplace on one end and built-in bookshelves on the other. Take a left into the window-lined breakfast nook that shares a peninsula snack bar with the efficient kitchen. The handy laundry room is just steps away. On the second floor, two secondary bedrooms, with walk-in closets, share a full bath. The master suite, with two walk-in closets and a full bath with dressing area, fills the right wing. An unfinished area to the left supplies 350 square feet of future space. This home is designed with basement, slab, and crawlspace foundation options.

Design Number 34825

Units	Single
Price Code	D
Total Finished	2,242 sq. ft.
First Finished	1,212 sq. ft.
Second Finished	1,030 sq. ft.
Bonus Unfinished	350 sq. ft.
Basement Unfinished	1,212 sq. ft.
Garage Unfinished	521 sq. ft.
Dimensions	55'x34'4"
Foundation	Basement Crawlspace Slab
Bedrooms	3
Full Baths	2
Half Baths	1
Max Ridge Height	29'
Roof Framing	Stick
Exterior Walls	2x4, 2x6

CRAWLSPACE/SLAB FOUNDATION OPTION

FIRST FLOOR

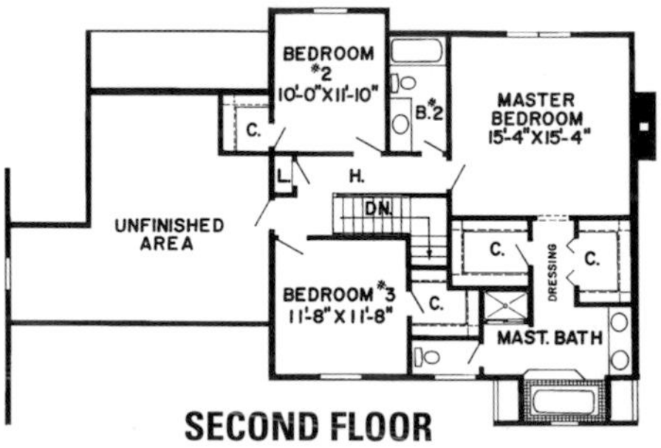

BEDROOM #2 10'-0"X11'-10"

B.#2

MASTER BEDROOM 15'-4"X15'-4"

C.

H.

L.

DN.

UNFINISHED AREA

BEDROOM #3 11'-8"X11'-8"

C.

C.

DRESSING

C.

MAST. BATH

SECOND FLOOR

Please note: The photographed home may have been modified to suit homeowner preferences. If you order plans, you may wish to have a builder or design professional check them against the photographs to confirm construction details.

PHOTOGRAPHY: JOHN EHRENCLOU

above An octagonal turret, long, railed porch, and brick facing give this traditional design some extra style.

classic DESIGN

Design Number 34043

Units	Single
Price Code	B
Total Finished	1,583 sq. ft.
Main Finished	1,583 sq. ft.
Basement Unfinished	1,573 sq. ft.
Garage Unfinished	484 sq. ft.
Dimensions	70'x46'
Foundation	Basement Crawlspace Slab
Bedrooms	3
Full Baths	2
Main Ceiling	8'
Max Ridge Height	20'
Roof Framing	Stick
Exterior Walls	2x4, 2x6

This convenient plan is perfect for the modern family with a taste for classic design. Traditional Victorian touches in this three-bedroom beauty include a romantic, railed porch and an intriguing breakfast tower just off the kitchen. The arrangement of the kitchen between the breakfast and formal dining rooms is nothing less than efficient and the wide-open living room, which opens out to the deck, rounds out the common areas.

In the private wing, the master suite enjoys a skylit bath, while two secondary bedrooms boast ample closet space. The third bedroom would also make an ideal den. This home is designed with basement, slab, and crawlspace foundation options.

Please note: The photographed home may have been modified to suit homeowner preferences. If you order plans, have a builder or design professional check them against the photographs to confirm actual construction details.

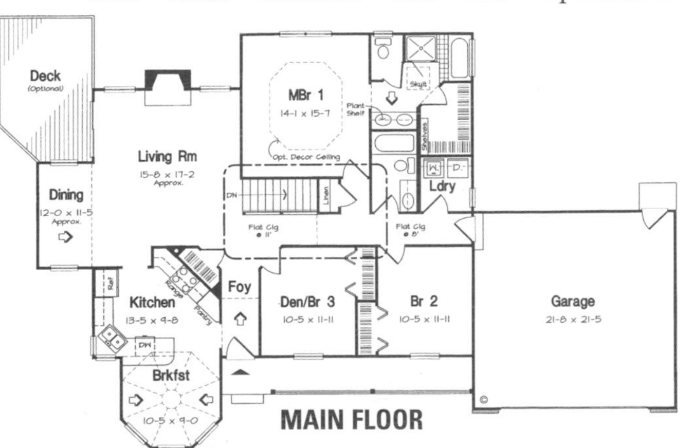

MAIN FLOOR

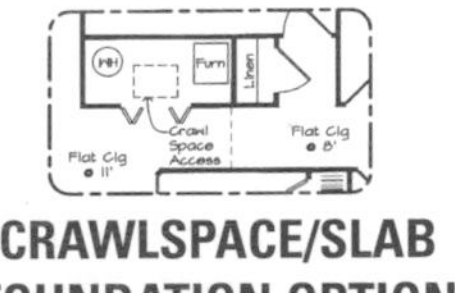

CRAWLSPACE/SLAB FOUNDATION OPTION

PHOTOGRAPHY: MARK ENGLUND

homey HABITAT

above Gables, a Palladian window, and a sheltering entry combine to present a welcoming facade on this well-planned design.

Family-friendly describes this design with its open community areas and core of bedrooms. The vaulted ceilings topping the master suite, living, and dining rooms add grand scale. The centralized kitchen boasts ample counter space and easy access to the dining area. Made for the growing family, or one that expects a lot of guests, the design includes a den that can be easily converted into a third bedroom. A corner of windows, a large closet, and a convenient private bath make a comfortable master suite. Meanwhile, a corner of windows and ample closet space spruce up the second bedroom. This home is designed with a basement foundation.

design 51020

Price Code	A
Total Finished	1,252 sq. ft.
Main Finished	1,252 sq. ft.
Basement Unfinished	1,252 sq. ft.
Garage Unfinished	420 sq. ft.
Deck Unfinished	120 sq. ft.
Dimensions	44'8"x50'8"
Foundation	Basement
Bedrooms	3
Full Baths	2
Main Ceiling	8'
Max Ridge Height	21'6"
Roof Framing	Truss
Exterior Walls	2x4

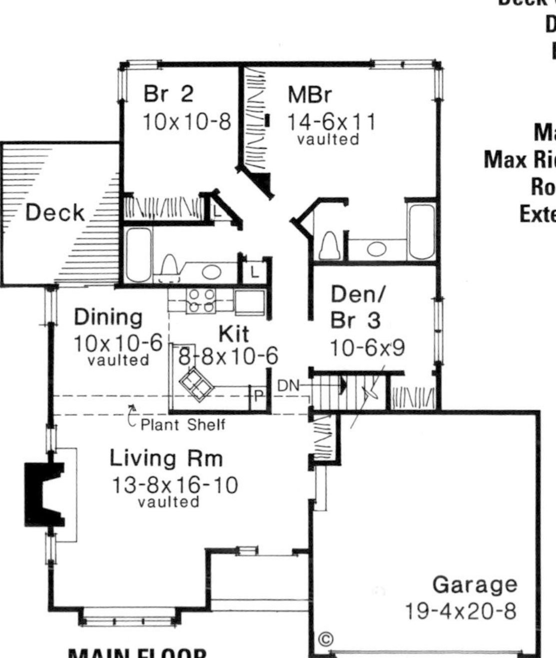

MAIN FLOOR

Please note: The photographed home may have been modified to suit homeowner preferences. If you order plans, have a builder or design professional check them against the photographs to confirm actual construction details.

PHOTOGRAPHY: MARK ENGLUND

perfectly DETAILED

above Stacked rooflines and a covered entry add a touch of understated charm to the exterior.

High ceilings, a sunken living room, and built-in plant shelves are just some of the pleasant details embellishing this home's interior. All of these features are highlighted by the abundance of windows that brighten every room.

A fireplace in the living room and one in the country kitchen help create warm and welcoming spaces for family to gather. For quieter times, the bedrooms are isolated in the left wing. A deck completes the plan, extending comfortable living area outdoors. This home is designed with a basement foundation.

design 51017

Units	Single
Price Code	C
Total Finished	1,993 sq. ft.
Main Finished	1,993 sq. ft.
Basement Unfinished	1,993 sq. ft.
Garage Unfinished	521 sq. ft.
Deck Unfinished	180 sq. ft.
Dimensions	60'x48'4"
Foundation	Basement
Bedrooms	3
Full Baths	2
Main Ceiling	8'
Max Ridge Height	23'3"
Roof Framing	Truss
Exterior Walls	2x4

Please note: The photographed home may have been modified to suit homeowner preferences. If you order plans, have a builder or design professional check them against the photographs to confirm actual construction details.

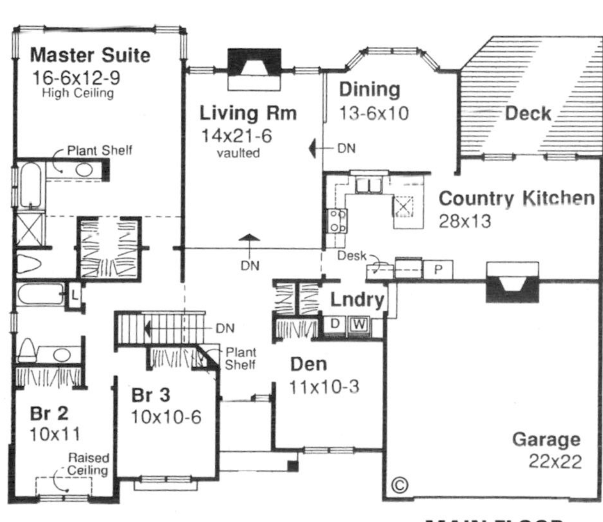

MAIN FLOOR

PHOTOGRAPHY: ED GOHLICH

cottage DELIGHT

above Efficient zoning of space includes shared, private, and outdoor areas.

Love of nature and love of home walk side-by-side in this delightful cottage that's perfect for a starter family or empty nesters who still want room for family, friends, or grown children to visit. A deep front porch set into the floor plan is an ideal spot for visiting with neighbors or just watching the world go by. This cottage home provides all the necessary spaces, both private and shared. Its central 340-square-foot living area includes a deep rear bay that's large enough to hold a dining table and chairs. The open living space forms an "L" that wraps around back to enfold the efficient kitchen. A diagonal countertop juts out toward the dining bay and holds the kitchen sink. The door off the back of this space leads to the rear yard. Opposite the kitchen, in its own discrete space, is a laundry facility. The home's two bedrooms are on opposite sides of the house. Each bedroom is large and includes two good-sized closets in the hall that connects to the full bath. Plenty of windows throughout provide all the natural light and views you'll need while exposed rafters and ridges complete the cozy cottage experience. This home is designed with a crawlspace foundation.

Please note: The photographed home may have been modified to suit homeowner preferences. If you order plans, you may wish to have a builder or design professional check them against the photographs to confirm construction details.

Design Number 32323

Units	Single
Price Code	A
Total Finished	1,200 sq. ft.
Main Finished	1,200 sq. ft.
Porch Unfinished	200 sq. ft.
Dimensions	51'4"x34'
Foundation	Crawlspace
Bedrooms	2
Full Baths	2
Main Ceiling	8'
Vaulted Ceiling	12'4"
Max Ridge Height	16'4"
Roof Framing	Stick
Exterior Walls	2x4

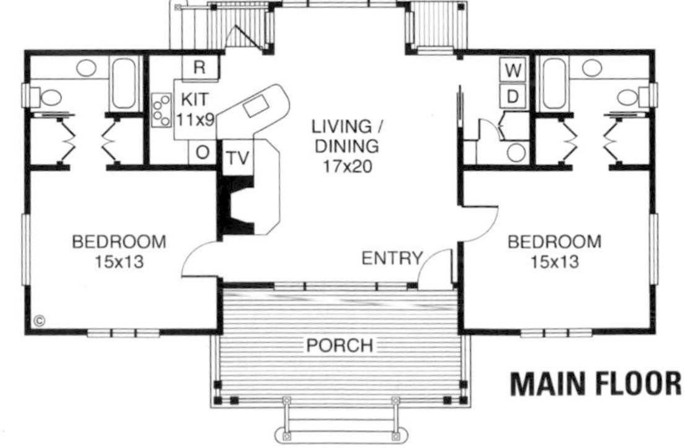

MAIN FLOOR

above With its efficient design, the living room supplies all the shared space necessary for the full enjoyment of cottage living. A cheery fireplace with built-in television nook is set into the corner that leads into the kitchen.

left Exposed rafters add a touch of tradition while big windows, in the front and back, draw light deep into the living room's interior.

perfect use of SPACE

above Clean, classic lines define the style of this compact beauty that's packed with big features.

Two front porches, which expand living space outdoors, will delight the nature lover. Inside, each room is distinctly separate, allowing for multifunctional use. Counter space, including a casual eating bar, abounds in the kitchen. A separate dining area, featuring sliding glass doors to the backyard, offers an atmosphere for more formal dining. In the main section of the house, two bedrooms offer generous closet space, with extra closet space in the hallway. The laundry is tucked away in the large full bath. This home is designed with a basement foundation.

design 65019

Units	Single
Price Code	A
Total Finished	920 sq. ft.
Main Finished	920 sq. ft.
Dimensions	40'x28'
Foundation	Basement
Bedrooms	2
Full Baths	1
Exterior Walls	2x4

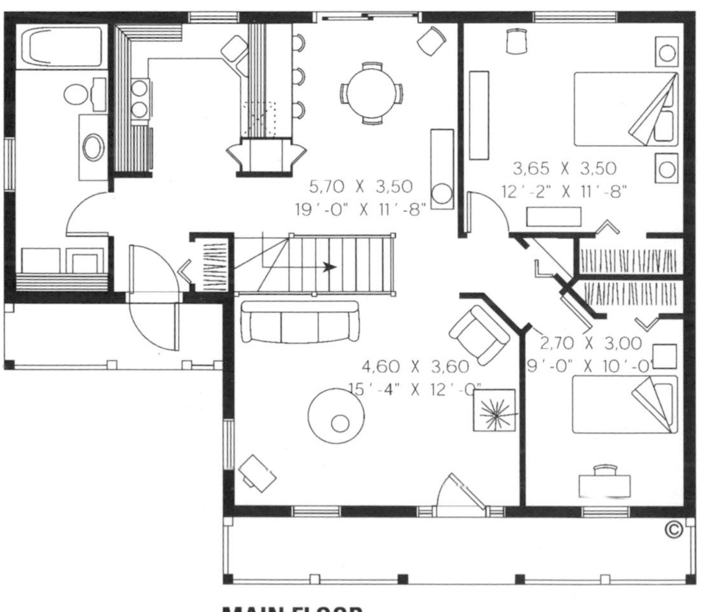

MAIN FLOOR

PHOTOGRAPHY: SUSAN GILMORE

above and below Traditional farmhouse good looks wrap up a carefully laid out interior plan.

clean LINES

Basic elements of design—one larger rectangle and two smaller rectangles topped by triangular gables—allow this attractive home to be built very cost effectively. Soaring ceilings, open spaces, and carefully positioned windows work together to make this home seem larger than it is. The front porch welcomes guests into an air-lock vestibule, which maintains inside heat during cold weather and air conditioning during hot weather. The vestibule opens to the great-room, which has a cathedral ceiling and a prominent fireplace. The great-room is large enough to accommodate a dining area and opens to the sunroom on one side and kitchen on the other. Stairs lead down from this area to the bedrooms on the walk-out lower level, which also holds a full bath and a walk-in closet. Stairs lead up to the master suite, which includes a private study. This home is designed with a basement foundation.

design 32056

Units	Single
Price Code	D
Total Finished	2,035 sq. ft.
Main Finished	1,015 sq. ft.
Upper Finished	510 sq. ft.
Lower Finished	510 sq. ft.
Basement Unfinished	840 sq. ft.
Garage Unfinished	672 sq. ft
Dimensions	81'x52'
Foundation	Basement
Bedrooms	3
Full Baths	2
Max Ridge Height	26'
Roof Framing	Truss
Exterior Walls	2x6

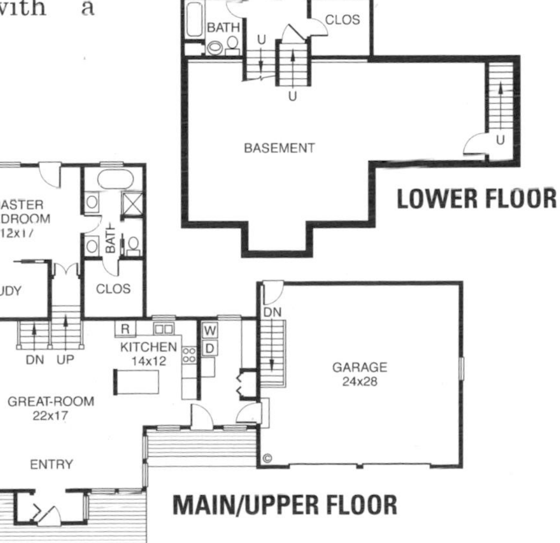

Please note: The photographed home may have been modified to suit homeowner preferences. If you order plans, you may wish to have a builder or design professional check them against the photographs to confirm construction details.

PHOTOGRAPHY: JAMES YOCHUM PHOTOGRAPHY

farmhouse FAVORITE

above The covered porch and center gable draw attention to the front of this cozy home.

opposite top This homeowner has chosen the master bath option with the extra closet in the bedroom and double vanity in the bath.

opposite right The angled sink sits under two windows, creating a well-lit and comfortable place to work.

All the right spaces in all the right places are packed into this efficient beauty, including formal and informal living spaces as well as three bedrooms, all in just 1,550 square feet.

A simple footprint makes the design extremely cost efficient to build. The front porch (not shown on the floor plan) leads into the living room, which feels more spacious because it opens to the dining room. The U-shape kitchen maximizes space and seems larger than it is because it opens into the breakfast area and den, which can include a fireplace. A laundry area and powder room complete the 775-square-foot main level. On the upper level, double doors open to the master suite. An optional master bath design offers a dual-sink vanity and a third closet. Two secondary bedrooms round out the floor. This home is designed with a basement foundation.

Design Number 32229

Units	Single
Price Code	B
Total Finished	1,550 sq. ft.
First Finished	775 sq. ft.
Second Finished	775 sq. ft.
Basement Unfinished	775 sq. ft.
Deck Unfinished	112 sq. ft.
Porch Unfinished	150 sq. ft.
Dimensions	25'x37'
Foundation	Basement
Bedrooms	3
Full Baths	2
Half Baths	1
First Ceiling	8'
Second Ceiling	8'
Max Ridge Height	30'3"
Roof Framing	Truss
Exterior Walls	2x4

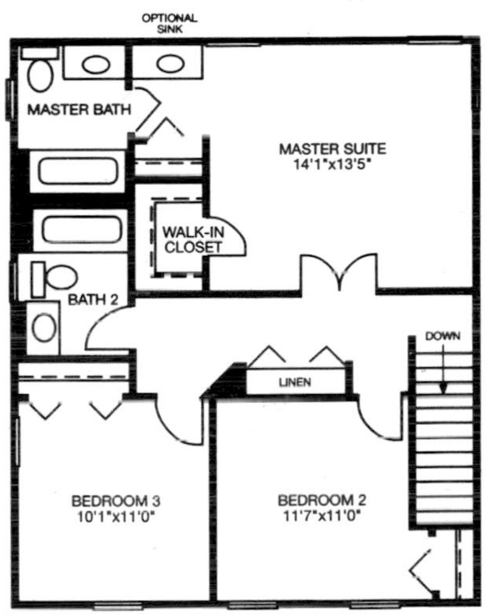

SECOND FLOOR

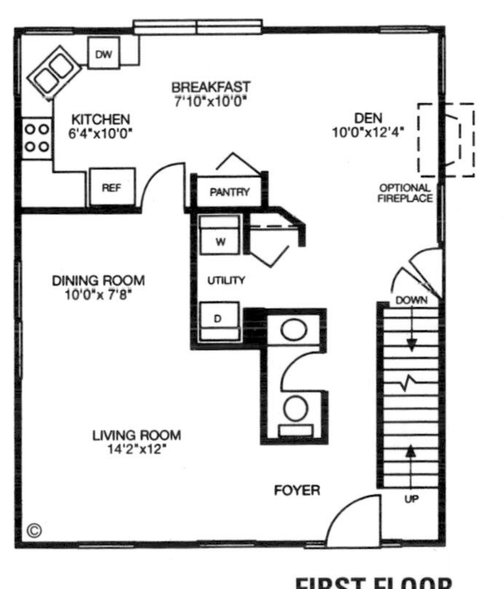

FIRST FLOOR

MASTER BATH
OPTIONAL SHOWER

MASTER BATH OPTION

Please note: The photographed home may have been modified to suit homeowner preferences. If you order plans, you may wish to have a builder or design professional check them against the photographs to confirm construction details.

above Exquisite detailing wraps this compact home in style that's big enough for a home twice its size.

compact GEM

The foyer of this home contains a convenient coat closet and leads directly into the living room, which opens to the dining area and kitchen. A bay window draws sunlight into the dining area, which divides the open kitchen from the living room area. Counters, an eating area, and a wall of sliding glass doors define the kitchen. The two bedrooms share the left wing of the home and a full bath. Two hall closets add more storage space, while the garage is extra deep for additional storage. This home is designed with a basement foundation.

design 65241

Units	Single
Price Code	A
Total Finished	1,068 sq. ft.
Main Finished	1,068 sq. ft.
Basement Unfinished	1,068 sq. ft.
Garage Unfinished	245 sq. ft.
Dimensions	30'8"x48'
Foundation	Basement
Bedrooms	2
Full Baths	1
Main Ceiling	8'
Max Ridge Height	22'1"
Roof Framing	Truss
Exterior Walls	2x6

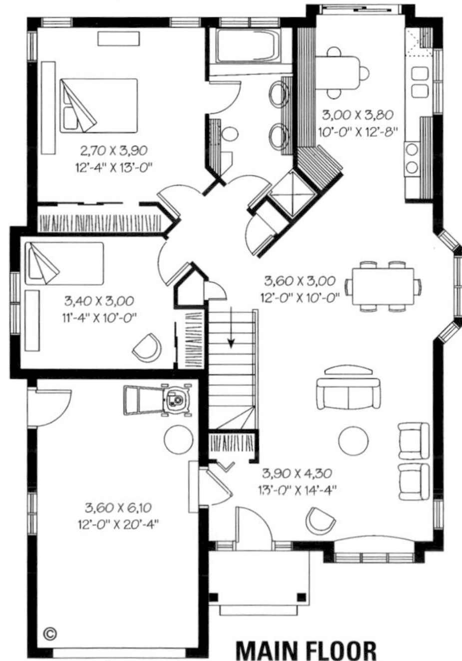

above White trim, keystones, subtle arches, and clapboard siding add character and appeal.

dollhouse DELIGHT

Design 81037

Units	Single
Price Code	A
Total Finished	1,275 sq. ft.
Main Finished	1,275 sq. ft.
Garage Unfinished	440 sq. ft.
Dimensions	40'x58'
Foundation	Crawlspace
Bedrooms	3
Full Baths	1
3/4 Baths	1
Main Ceiling	9'
Max Ridge Height	26'
Roof Framing	Truss
Exterior Walls	2x6

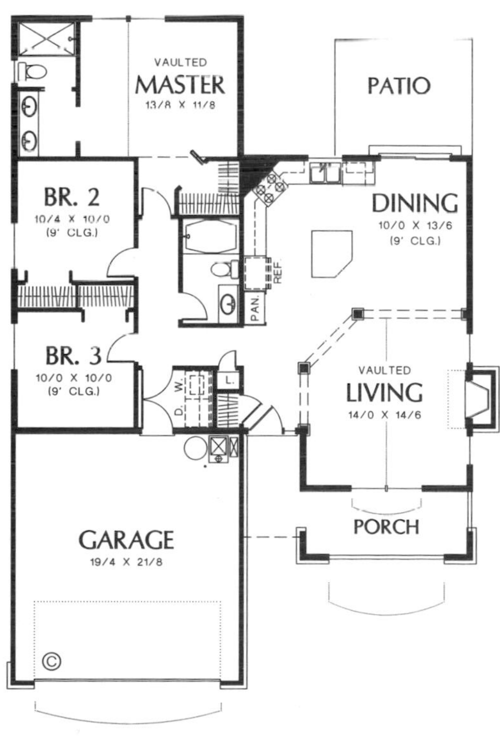

MAIN FLOOR

Victorian detailing sets this home apart in any neighborhood. Reminiscent of the carriage house of old, right down to the stone fireplace and facade base, this home contains all the neccessary ingredients for a comfortable lifestyle.

The front porch leads to the formal living room, which is set off by a dramatic vaulted ceiling and angled openings connected by columns. The shared kitchen/dining area is roomy enough for a center island and pantry. In the left wing, two secondary bedrooms share a full hall bath, while the pleasing master suite has a full bath of its own, as well as a walk-in closet. This home is designed with a crawlspace foundation.

PHOTOGRAPHY: COURTESY OF THE DESIGNER

perfect RETREAT

above A quartet of gables topping a covered porch give this home classic bungalow appeal.

The bungalow-style facade of this home harkens back to the early 20th century when compact four-squares were favored over rambling Victorians and Colonials. Like its predecessors, this floor plan packs a lot of living into its stylish square footage.

Much of the first floor is unobstructed by walls, with arch-and-column configurations serving as the sole delineation for the dining area. The great-room and eat-in kitchen are backed by abundant windows, which allow light to stream in unhindered. French doors and custom built-ins characterize the den.

The second floor features an expansive bonus room over the garage, perfect for games, exercise equipment, or a home office. This home is designed with a crawlspace foundation.

design 81033

Units	Single
Price Code	C
Total Finished	1,946 sq. ft.
First Finished	1,082 sq. ft.
Second Finished	864 sq. ft.
Bonus Unfinished	358 sq. ft.
Garage Unfinished	620 sq. ft.
Porch Unfinished	120 sq. ft.
Dimensions	40'x52'
Foundation	Crawlspace
Bedrooms	3
Full Baths	2
Half Baths	1
First Ceiling	9'
Second Ceiling	8'
Max Ridge Height	27'
Roof Framing	Stick/Truss
Exterior Walls	2x6

Please note: The photographed home may have been modified to suit homeowner preferences. If you order plans, have a builder or design professional check them against the photographs to confirm actual construction details.

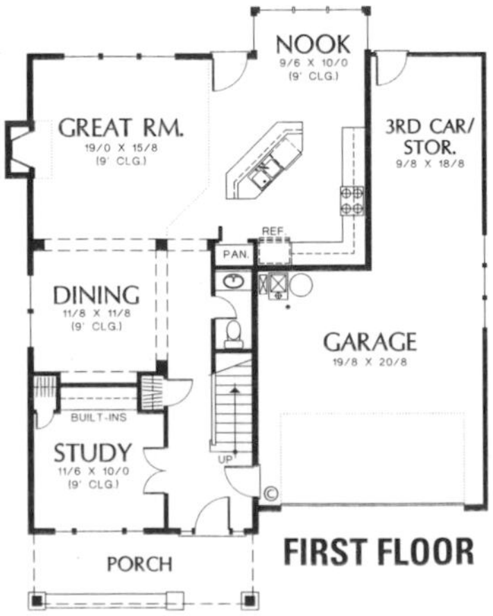

NOOK
GREAT RM.
3RD CAR/STOR.
DINING
GARAGE
BUILT-INS
STUDY
PORCH
FIRST FLOOR

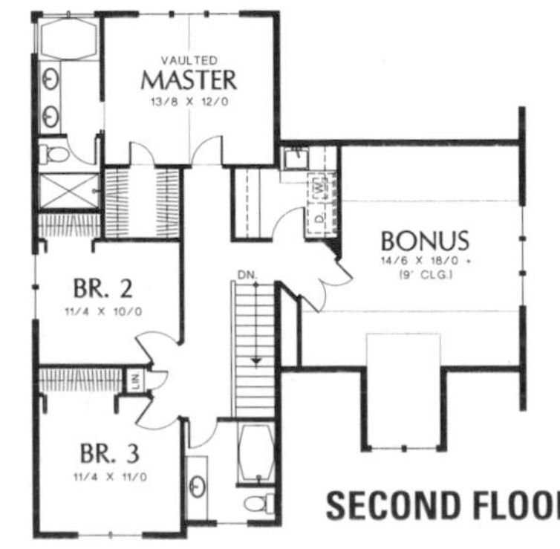

PHOTOGRAPHY: MIKE MORELAND

above Days and warm nights can be spent enjoying the cool breeze or summer stars on this home's front porch.

family getaway LODGE

SECOND FLOOR

Design 19422

Units	Single
Price Code	B
Total Finished	1,695 sq. ft.
First Finished	1,290 sq. ft.
Second Finished	405 sq. ft.
Garage Unfinished	513 sq. ft.
Porch Unfinished	152 sq. ft.
Dimensions	50'8"x61'8"
Foundation	Basement Crawlspace
Bedrooms	2
Full Baths	2
First Ceiling	9'
Second Ceiling	8'
Max Ridge Height	29'
Roof Framing	Stick/Truss
Exterior Walls	2x4

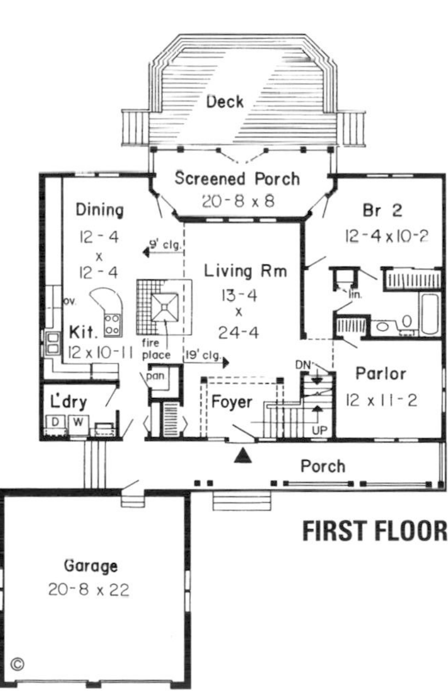

FIRST FLOOR

Please note: The photographed home may have been modified to suit homeowner preferences. If you order plans, you may wish to have a builder or design professional check them against the photographs to confirm construction details.

The features of this plan include a unique fireplace that is centrally located and shared by the living room, kitchen, and dining room. A parlor in the front of the design provides an ideal spot for quieter pursuits and entertaining. For added convenience, a pantry and laundry room help keep the whole family well fed and well organized. A first-floor secondary bedroom, connected to a full bath, rounds out the floor. The second floor is reserved for the master suite, full of amenities including a luxurious bath, makeup area, walk-in closet, and private balcony with a storage closet. This home is designed with a basement foundation.

above A wraparound porch, balcony, decorative windows, and farmhouse gables lend this simple home a taste of the Victorian era.

simple CHARM

Decorative columns, glass doors, and arch windows add to the welcoming design of this home and make seeing what's inside hard to resist. The kitchen is brightly lit with natural light, which adds to the ambiance when serving guests at the island snack bar or at the dinner table. Two bedrooms on the second floor share a convenient corner bathroom. The larger bedroom includes a spacious walk-in closet and French doors that open to a small balcony with wooden railing. This home is designed with a basement foundation.

design 65013

Units	Single
Price Code	A
Total Finished	1,298 sq. ft.
First Finished	678 sq. ft.
Second Finished	620 sq. ft.
Basement Unfinished	678 sq. ft.
Garage Unfinished	228 sq. ft.
Porch Unfinished	416 sq. ft.
Dimensions	28'x40'
Foundation	Basement
Bedrooms	3
Full Baths	1
Half Baths	1
First Ceiling	8'
Second Ceiling	8'
Max Ridge Height	25'4"
Roof Framing	Truss
Exterior Walls	2x6

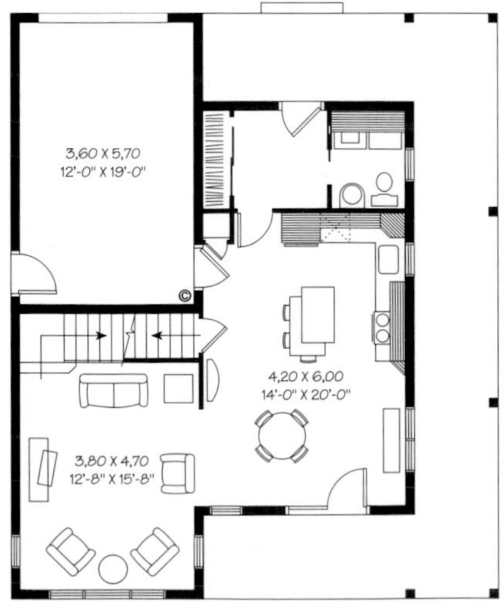

FIRST FLOOR

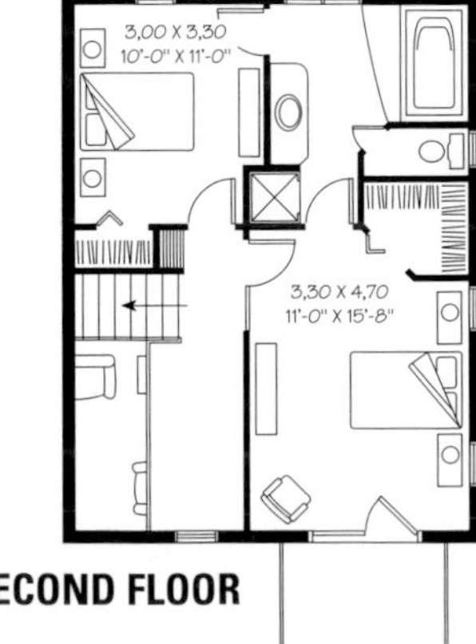

SECOND FLOOR

above Adorned with Victorian-style millwork and topped with a prominent gable dormer set into a steeply pitched roofline, this home is an immediate attention grabber.

romantic CHARMER

Design 24706

Units	Single
Price Code	A
Total Finished	1,470 sq. ft.
First Finished	1,035 sq. ft.
Second Finished	435 sq. ft.
Basement Unfinished	1,018 sq. ft.
Deck Unfinished	240 sq. ft.
Porch Unfinished	192 sq. ft.
Dimensions	35'x42'
Foundation	Basement Crawlspace Slab
Bedrooms	3
Full Baths	2
First Ceiling	8'
Second Ceiling	8'
Max Ridge Height	27'
Roof Framing	Stick
Exterior Walls	2x4, 2x6

The warm glow from the fireplace will comfort you and your guests as you relax in the living room of this storybook home. Two first-floor bedrooms share a bath and the convenience of a nearby galley kitchen for late night snacks. The upstairs master bedroom is a private haven from the shared spaces downstairs. Set apart from the lower level and accessed through two sets of stairs and a small landing, the master bedroom has its own bathroom and walk-in closet. This home is designed with basement, slab, and crawlspace foundation options.

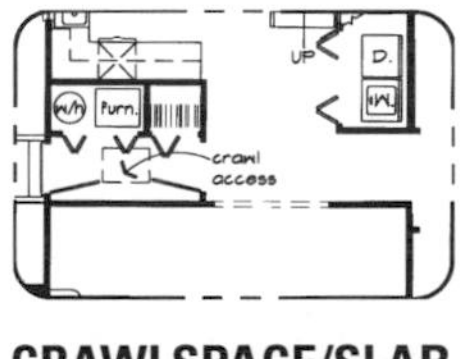

CRAWLSPACE/SLAB OPTION

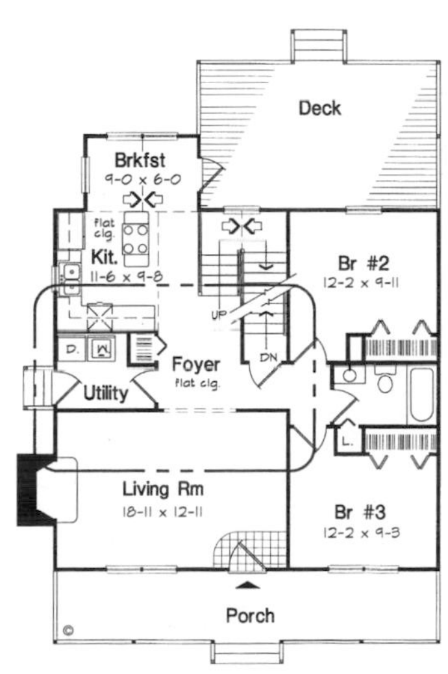

FIRST FLOOR

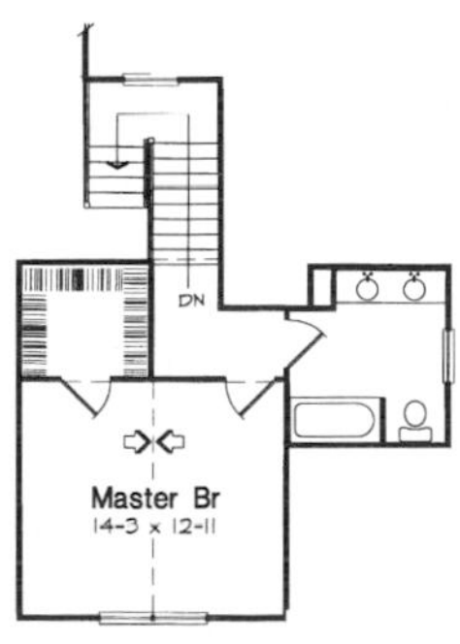

SECOND FLOOR

distinctive SHINGLE & STONE

The shingle and stone exterior, with its angles and peaks and generous porch, sets the stage for an attractively designed interior. The vaulted ceilings in the center rooms, and corner fireplace in the great-room, create a relaxing, welcoming atmosphere. The split-bedroom design allows privacy for every member of the family, while the master bath and shared hall bath offer convenience for the whole family. This home abounds with convenient features, such as a separate laundry room and an abundance of counter space and cabinets in the kitchen. This home is designed with a basement foundation.

above From its white trim, to its wide dormer, to its arched porch, this home boasts fine details inside and out.

design 50021

Units	Single
Price Code	B
Total Finished	1,651 sq. ft.
Main Finished	1,651 sq. ft.
Basement Unfinished	1,651 sq. ft.
Garage Unfinished	430 sq. ft.
Porch Unfinished	212 sq. ft.
Dimensions	60'9"x49'
Foundation	Basement
Bedrooms	3
Full Baths	2
Main Ceiling	8'
Max Ridge Height	23'6"
Roof Framing	Truss
Exterior Walls	2x4

Master Bedroom 12' x 16'2"
Dressing
Porch
Laun.
Walk-in Closet
Hall
Sloped Ceiling
Dining Area 12'8" x 13'
Great Room 16'4" x 16'6"
Bedroom 11'6" x 10'6"
Bath
Kitchen 13'9" x 11'
Foyer
Garage 20' x 23'
Porch
Bedroom 11'4" x 10'6"

MAIN FLOOR

above Tall windows, an angled porch, and a welcoming gable lend a classic feel.

something for ALL

Design 81036

Units	Single
Price Code	B
Total Finished	1,557 sq. ft.
Main Finished	1,557 sq. ft.
Garage Unfinished	434 sq. ft.
Porch Unfinished	137 sq. ft.
Dimensions	50'x50'
Foundation	Basement Crawlspace Slab
Bedrooms	3
Full Baths	2
Main Ceiling	9'
Max Ridge Height	24'
Roof Framing	Truss
Exterior Walls	2x6

The neat front exterior with its tall, elegant windows and front porch provides a warm welcome. This design features vaulted ceilings in the great-room, dining room, and master bedroom, adding space to the generously sized rooms. Ideal for the seasoned chef or the beginner, the wraparound kitchen counter provides ample work area, while the desk and pantry are good for storage. Built-ins and a large closet enhance one secondary bedroom, while the other, an optional den, features an optional French door location as well as its own large closet. This home is designed with basement, slab, and crawlspace foundation options.

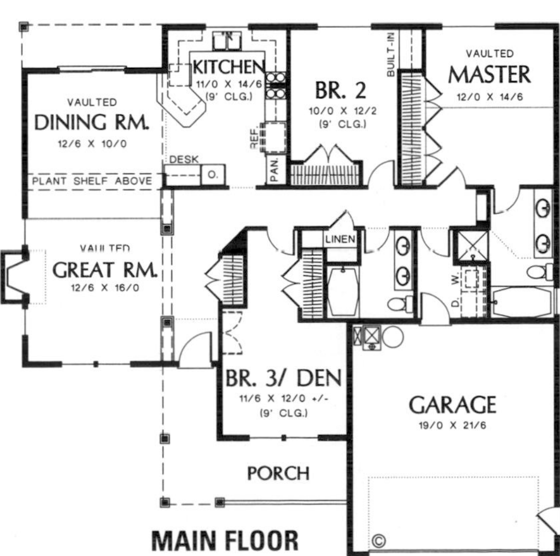

PHOTOGRAPHY: JAMES YOCHUM PHOTOGRAPHY

above This home is angled to catch light at every turn, thanks to its ample supply of windows, including the clerestory above the entry.

decked OUTDOORS

This home is a medley of shapes and angles beautifully orchestrated to take advantage of the outdoor splendor that surrounds it. Hundreds of square feet of porch and deck, both covered and open, make it a nature lover's delight. A sense of openness suffuses the 1,213-square-foot first floor. The dining room and kitchen are likewise open and airy, visually open to the living room through the screen porch. The octagonal living room rises up two stories and its wall of windows offer dazzling vistas. The master suite enjoys its own private corner on the first floor, separated from the two upstairs bedrooms, one of which includes a pair of casement windows that open into the upper regions of the living room. This home is designed with a basement foundation.

design 32109

Units	Single
Price Code	D
Total Finished	2,038 sq. ft.
First Finished	1,213 sq. ft.
Second Finished	825 sq. ft.
Basement Unfinished	1,213 sq. ft.
Deck Unfinished	535 sq. ft.
Porch Unfinished	144 sq. ft.
Dimensions	46'4"x37'8"
Foundation	Basement
Bedrooms	3
Full Baths	2
Half Baths	1
First Ceiling	9'
Second Ceiling	8'
Max Ridge Height	24'8"
Roof Framing	Stick/Truss
Exterior Walls	2x6

Please note: The photographed home may have been modified to suit homeowner preferences. If you order plans, have a builder or design professional check them against the photographs to confirm actual construction details.

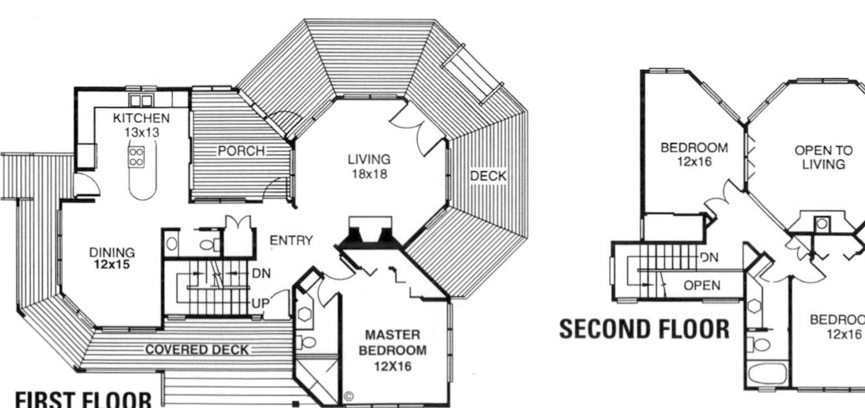

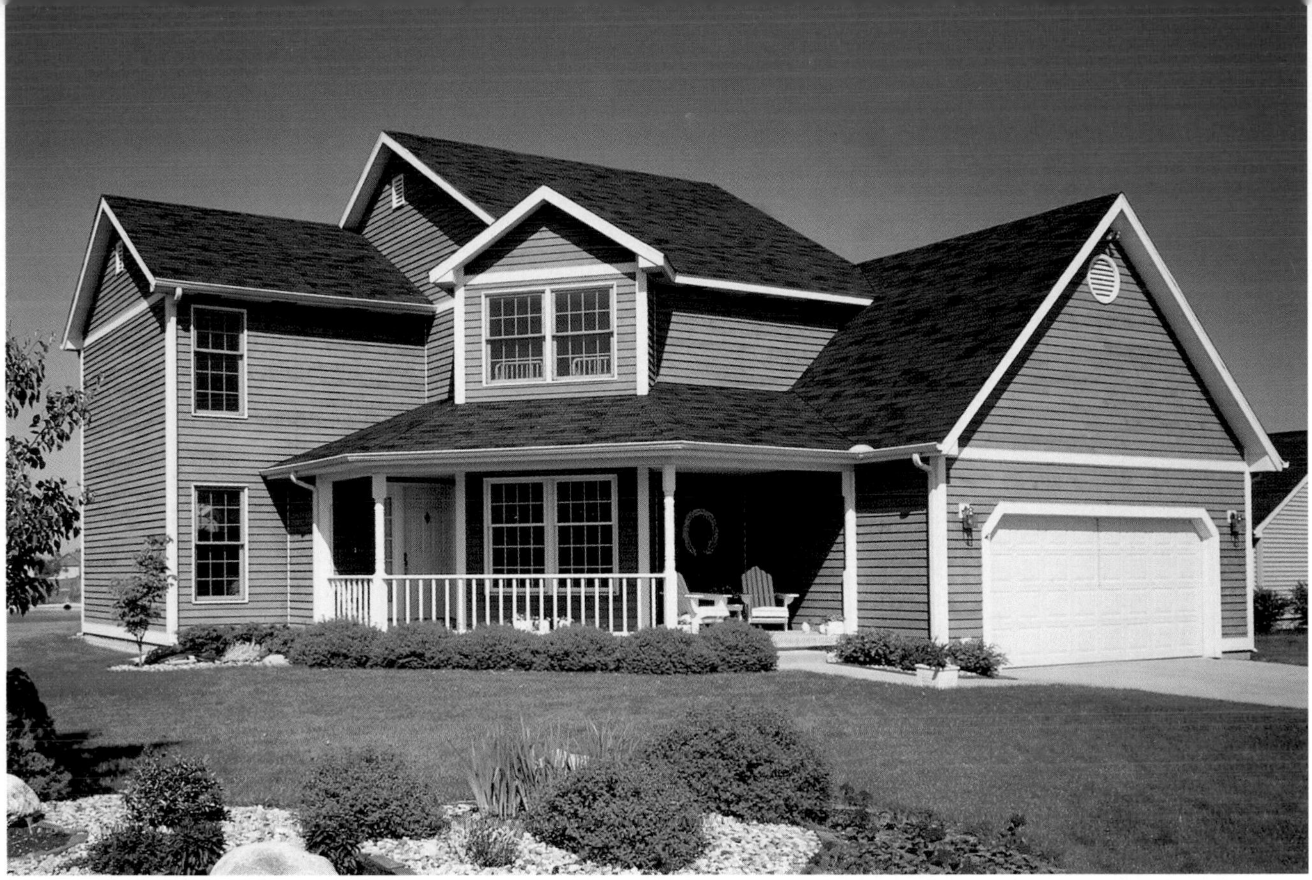

PHOTOGRAPHY: LAURIE SOLOMON

above A covered porch shades the tall windows that line the dining room and keeps the front entry out of the elements.

a new ANGLE

design 34901

Units	Single
Price Code	C
Total Finished	1,763 sq. ft.
First Finished	909 sq. ft.
Second Finished	854 sq. ft.
Basement Unfinished	899 sq. ft.
Garage Unfinished	491 sq. ft.
Dimensions	48'x44'
Foundation	Basement Crawlspace Slab
Bedrooms	3
Full Baths	1
3/4 Baths	1
Half Baths	1
First Ceiling	8'
Second Ceiling	8'
Tray Ceiling	9'
Maximum Ridge Height	29'
Roof Framing	Stick
Exterior Walls	2x4, 2x6

The appeal of this home begins at the curb, when you get a look at the angled porch, gable, and entryway. The dining room, with a large bump-out window, has a recessed ceiling. The living room includes a large fireplace, which is flanked by a window on one side and a door to the backyard deck on the other. The kitchen has plenty of workspace, a pantry and a double sink overlooking the deck. All three bedrooms are on the second floor. The master suite features a large bath with walk-in closet; the two secondary bedrooms share a bath. This home is designed with basement, slab, and crawlspace foundation options.

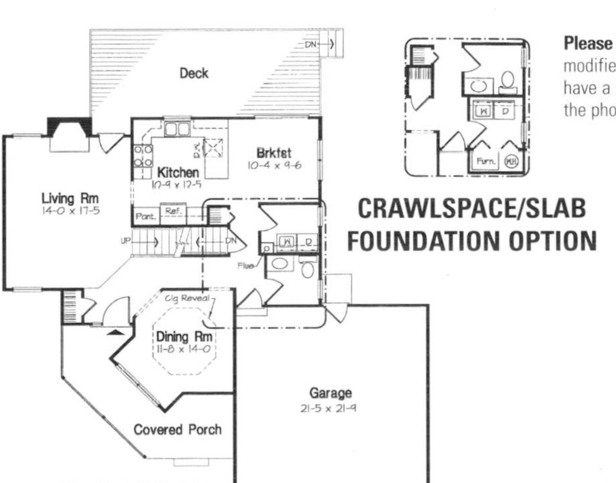

Please note: The photographed home may have been modified to suit homeowner preferences. If you order plans, have a builder or design professional check them against the photographs to confirm actual construction details.

FIRST FLOOR

CRAWLSPACE/SLAB FOUNDATION OPTION

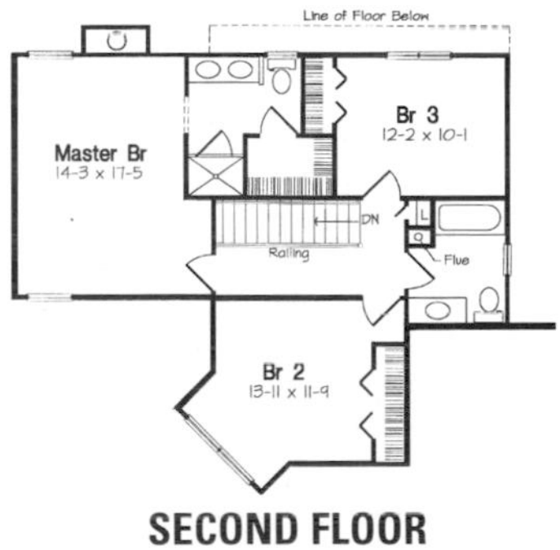

SECOND FLOOR

PHOTOGRAPHY: BETH SINGER

three GABLES

above Traditional shingle siding and elegant arched window and door openings provide classic appeal.

below Three gables and a covered porch add visual interest to the rear elevation of this home.

Roomy and light-filled, this home provides great shared spaces. The 936-square-foot first floor also includes an ample sunroom set just behind the living room.

Exposed trusses in the living room provide evidence of the home's strength and create a subtle lattice work pattern against the tall vaulted ceiling. A lowered ceiling in the dining area and kitchen create a subtle change of mood from the open living room, establishing a clear distinction of function. The comfortable kitchen is fully equipped with storage. The home's laundry is conveniently located behind the kitchen. A detached two-car garage rounds out the home's first floor.

The 916-square-foot second floor holds the master suite, two secondary bedrooms, and a bath. This home is designed with crawlspace and pier/post foundation options.

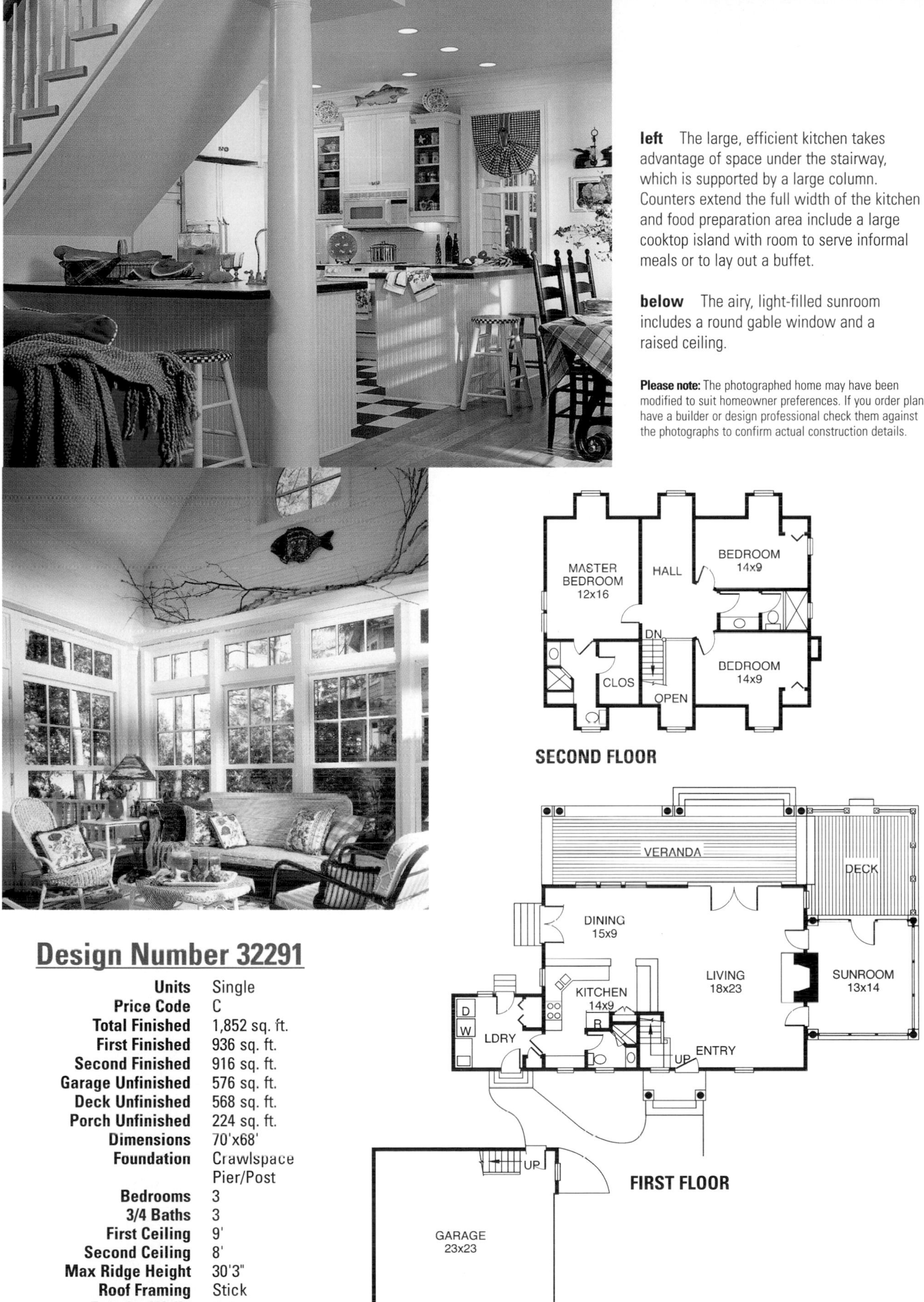

left The large, efficient kitchen takes advantage of space under the stairway, which is supported by a large column. Counters extend the full width of the kitchen and food preparation area include a large cooktop island with room to serve informal meals or to lay out a buffet.

below The airy, light-filled sunroom includes a round gable window and a raised ceiling.

Please note: The photographed home may have been modified to suit homeowner preferences. If you order plans, have a builder or design professional check them against the photographs to confirm actual construction details.

Design Number 32291

Units	Single
Price Code	C
Total Finished	1,852 sq. ft.
First Finished	936 sq. ft.
Second Finished	916 sq. ft.
Garage Unfinished	576 sq. ft.
Deck Unfinished	568 sq. ft.
Porch Unfinished	224 sq. ft.
Dimensions	70'x68'
Foundation	Crawlspace Pier/Post
Bedrooms	3
3/4 Baths	3
First Ceiling	9'
Second Ceiling	8'
Max Ridge Height	30'3"
Roof Framing	Stick
Exterior Walls	2x6

PHOTOGRAPHY: JAMES YOCHUM PHOTOGRAPHY

tropical FLAVOR

above The two-story porch lets light into the upper level, but keeps out the sun during the hottest times of the year. Metal roofing and exposed rafter tails suggest the design's tropical roots.

below Shallow but long, the porch provides just enough space for a group of neighbors to relax.

Created for any climate, but steeped in the regional architecture of Key West, this compact home makes the most of its 1,129 square feet and does it with style. Defining the home is a basic Cape Cod-style shape: a central gable structure with porches front and back. Outside, the home's wide trim, crown moldings, and deep sills create a vintage look. Inside, a sense of spaciousness is projected that reaches beyond the modest-sized home's actual dimensions. To maximize space, hallways are kept at a minimum and the living room, dining area, and kitchen all flow together around a central powder room. Out back is a long screen porch and wraparound deck. On the second floor, a smaller porch leads to a small deck off the rear. The secondary bedroom and master bedroom share the full bath. This home is designed with a crawlspace foundation. 🏛

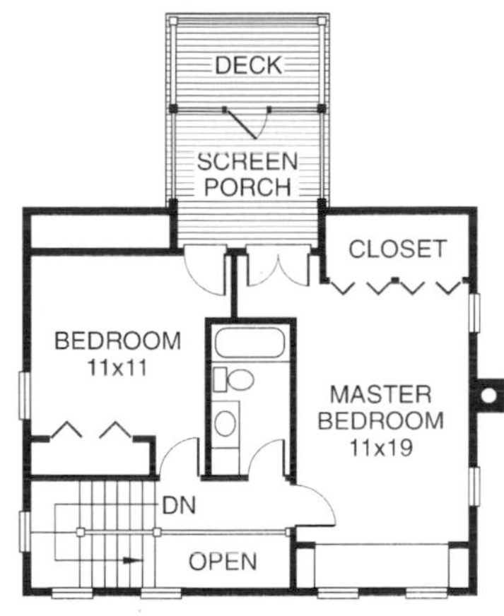

SECOND FLOOR

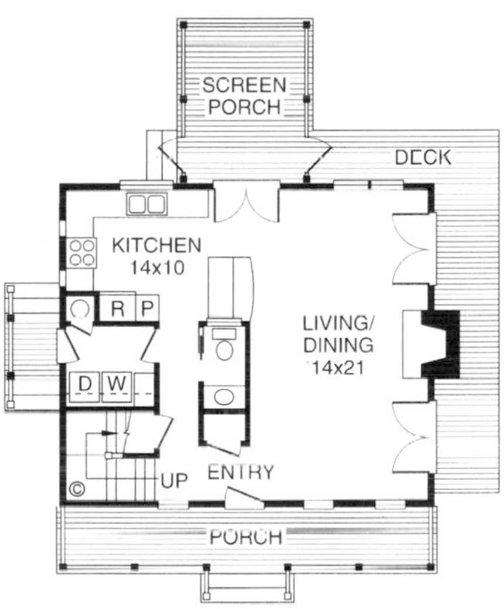

FIRST FLOOR

Design Number 32399

Units	Single
Price Code	A
Total Finished	1,129 sq. ft.
First Finished	576 sq. ft.
Second Finished	553 sq. ft.
Deck Unfinished	230 sq. ft.
Porch Unfinished	331 sq. ft.
Dimensions	36'8"x36'
Foundation	Crawlspace
Bedrooms	2
Full Baths	1
Half Baths	1
First Ceiling	8'
Second Ceiling	8'
Max Ridge Height	25'4"
Roof Framing	Stick
Exterior Walls	2x4

Please note: The photographed home may have been modified to suit homeowner preferences. If you order plans, have a builder or design professional check them against the photographs to confirm actual construction details.

top Sharing a fireplace with the living room and surrounded by windows, the dining area can host both casual and formal meals.

above Nestled into the trees, the first-floor screen porch provides a shaded place to enjoy the backyard in privacy.

compact and COZY

above Small size doesn't mean lack of style as the well-designed front facade of this home proves.

A covered porch and a carport add outdoor living area to this home. Inside, the plan packs a lot of living in less than 1,000 square feet. The large, open common area encompasses the family room, kitchen, and dining area. The kitchen makes the most of its space with L-shape counters and a peninsula snack bar. A central pantry is convenient to all three rooms. A closet near the bedrooms is handy for storing linens. The two bedrooms share the right wing with a full bath, which has everything from a window-lined soaking tub to a laundry facility. This home is designed with a basement foundation.

design 65009

Units	Single
Price Code	A
Total Finished	947 sq. ft.
Main Finished	947 sq. ft.
Basement Unfinished	947 sq. ft.
Dimensions	34'x30'
Foundation	Basement
Bedrooms	2
Full Baths	1
Main Ceiling	8'2"
Max Ridge Height	16'10"
Roof Framing	Truss
Exterior Walls	2x6

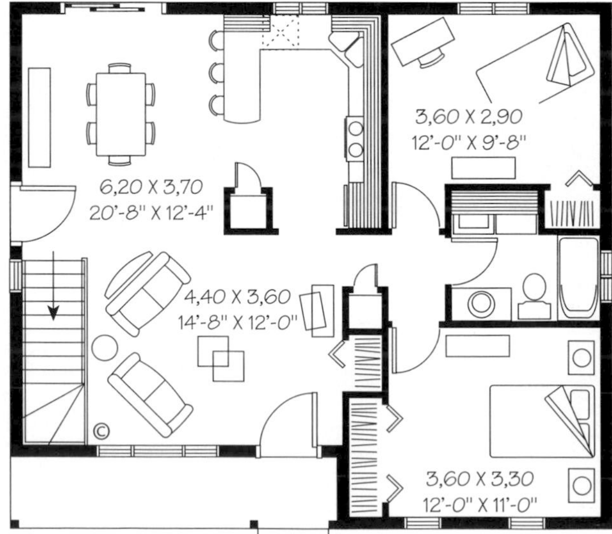

MAIN FLOOR

above Outdoor living area is a key element in the design of this home, which includes a large wraparound deck and a balcony.

balcony and PORCHES

design 65004

Units	Single
Price Code	E
Total Finished	2,300 sq. ft.
First Finished	1,067 sq. ft.
Second Finished	1,233 sq. ft.
Basement Unfinished	1,067 sq. ft.
Dimensions	58'x33'
Foundation	Basement
Bedrooms	3
Full Baths	2
Half Baths	1
First Ceiling	9'2"
Second Ceiling	8'2"
Max Ridge Height	24'6"
Roof Framing	Truss
Exterior Walls	2x6

There are several entrances to this 2,300-square-foot home. From the wraparound porch, you can enter the foyer, the dining room, and the family room. The garage has its own entrance in the rear of the home. Once inside, the foyer hallway opens into the kitchen. The peninsula snack bar is ideal for casual meals, while the nearby dining area is great for more formal times. A step away is the living room, which is just open enough between the rooms. On the second floor are two secondary bedrooms, a full bath, a sitting area, and a luxurious master suite with a fireplace. The balcony, adds outdoor living space to the second floor. This home is designed with a basement foundation.

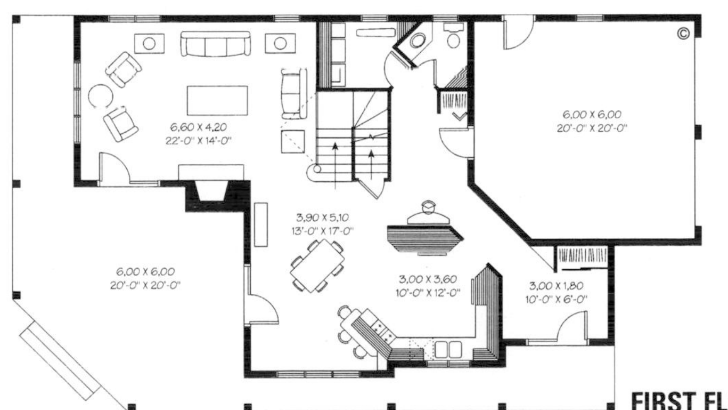

FIRST FLOOR

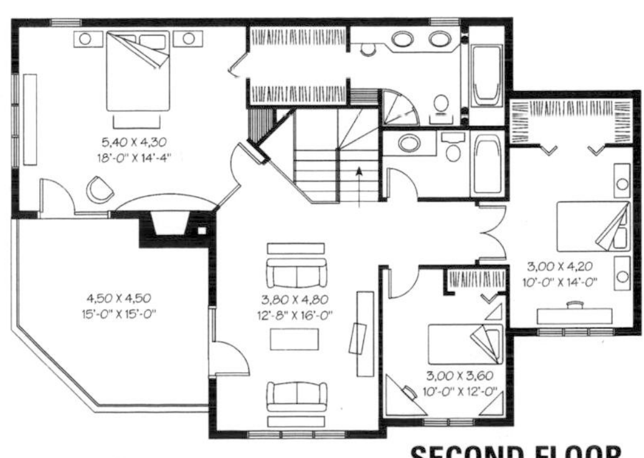

SECOND FLOOR

PHOTOGRAPHY: JOHN EHRENCLOU

above The unique style of this home, includes a turret, wraparound porch, and multiple tall gables.

sweet and STYLISH

The charming architectural elements of the exterior welcome family and friends. Inside, the tiled foyer opens into the kitchen/breakfast area to the left, and to a powder room to the right. Straight ahead lie the formal dining room, topped with a decorative ceiling, and the living room, which is warmed by a fireplace and illuminated by skylights. A large center island and abundant built-ins make the kitchen space attractive and efficient. The second floor was designed with privacy in mind; it contains two secondary bedrooms, which share a full hall bath. The impressive master suite, with private bath and large walk-in closet, rounds out this floor. This home is designed with a basement foundation.

design 20093

Units	Single
Price Code	D
Total Finished	2,001 sq. ft.
First Finished	1,027 sq. ft.
Second Finished	974 sq. ft.
Basement Unfinished	978 sq. ft.
Garage Unfinished	476 sq. ft.
Dimensions	43'x56'
Foundation	Basement
Bedrooms	3
Full Baths	2
Half Baths	1
Max Ridge Height	34'
Roof Framing	Stick
Exterior Walls	2x6

Please note: The photographed home may have been modified to suit homeowner preferences. If you order plans, have a builder or design professional check them against the photographs to confirm actual construction details.

above The deck continues around the rear, embracing the dining room and leading to the living room.

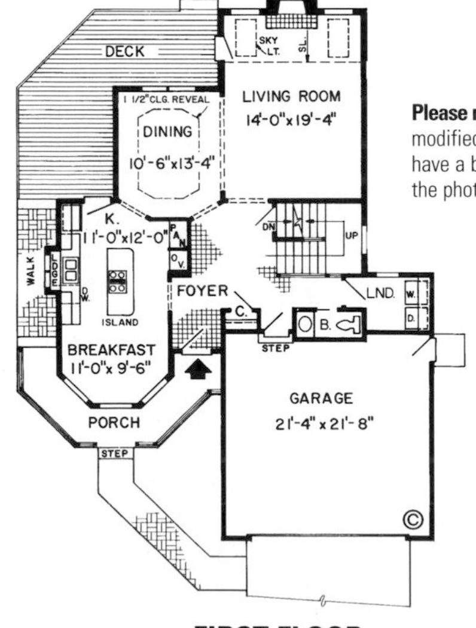

FIRST FLOOR

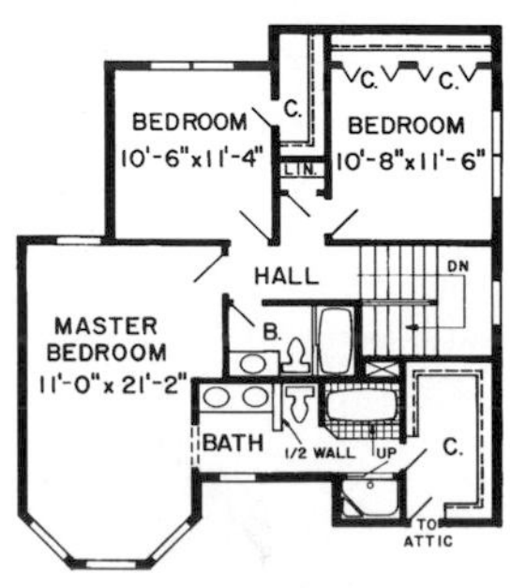

SECOND FLOOR

Design 65162

Units	Single
Price Code	A
Total Finished	784 sq. ft.
Main Finished	784 sq. ft.
Garage Unfinished	46 sq. ft.
Dimensions	28'x28'
Foundation	Slab
Bedrooms	1
Full Baths	1
Main Ceiling	8'
Max Ridge Height	18'
Roof Framing	Truss

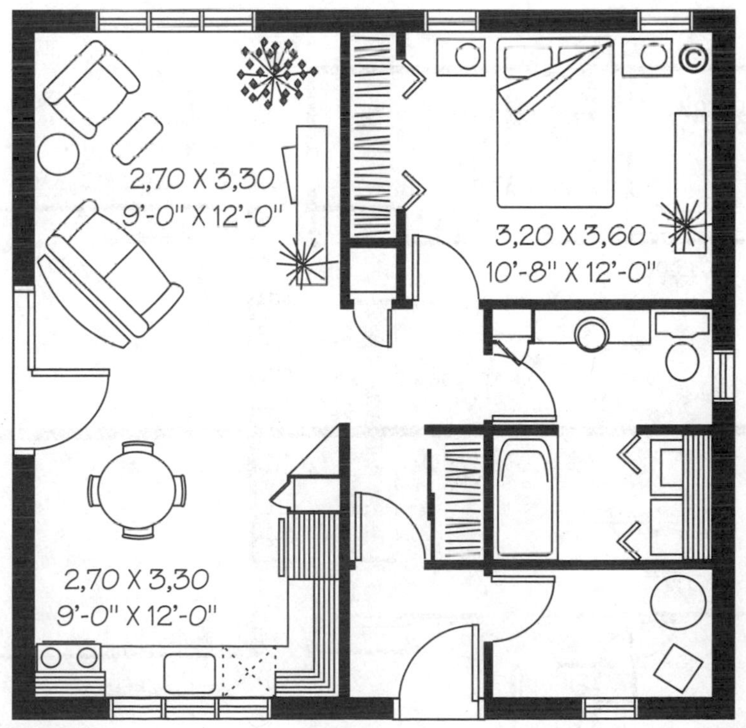

MAIN FLOOR

Design 99799

Units	Duplex
Price Code	G
Total Finished	828 sq. ft.
Main Finished	828 sq. ft.
Dimensions	56'x48'
Foundation	Crawlspace
Bedrooms	4
Full Baths	2
Max Ridge Height	15'
Roof Framing	Stick/Truss
Exterior Walls	2x6

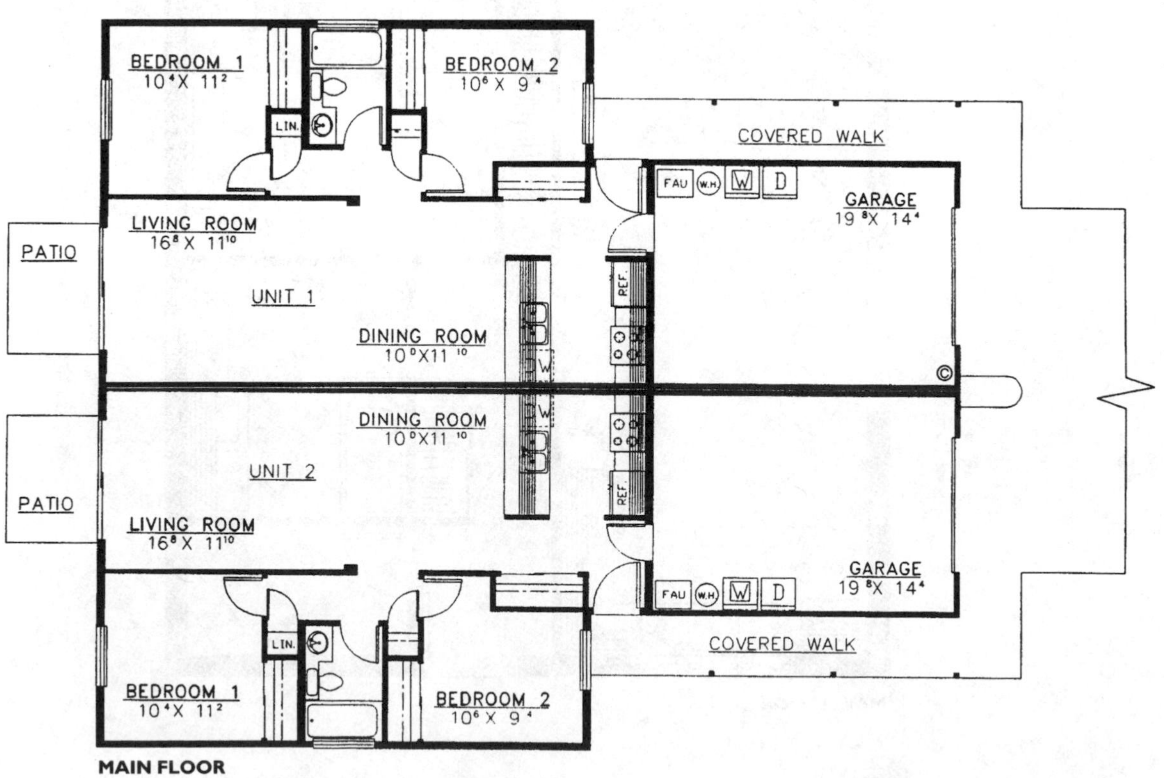

MAIN FLOOR

Design 65259

Units Single
Price Code A
Total Finished 832 sq. ft.
Main Finished 832 sq. ft.
Dimensions 26'x32'
Foundation Basement
Bedrooms 2
Full Baths 1
Exterior Walls 2x4

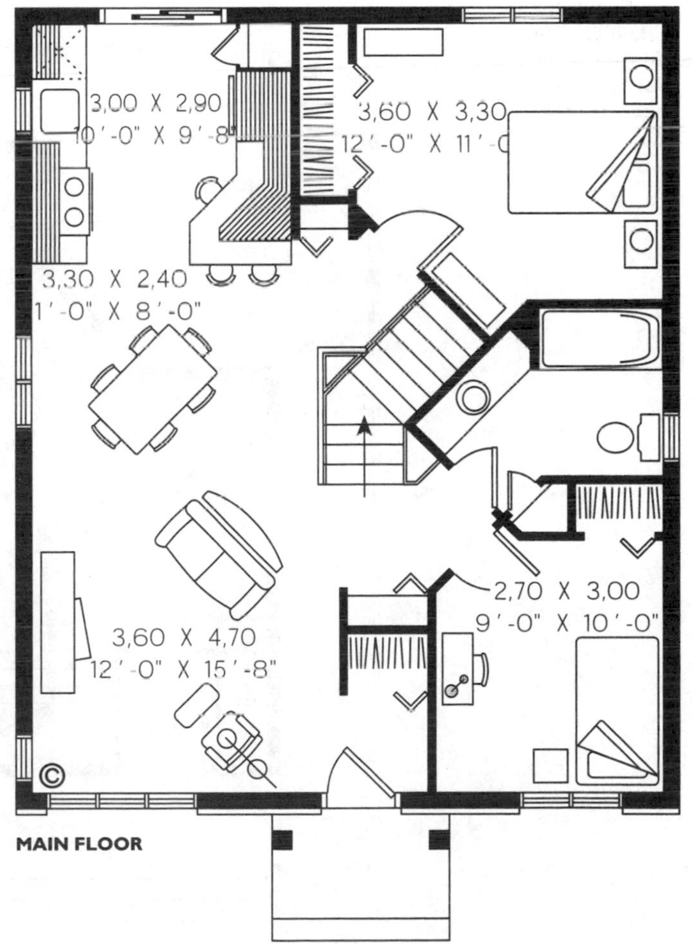

MAIN FLOOR

Design 65263

Units	Single
Price Code	A
Total Finished	840 sq. ft.
Main Finished	840 sq. ft.
Porch Unfinished	466 sq. ft.
Dimensions	33'x31'
Foundation	Basement
Bedrooms	1
Full Baths	1
Main Ceiling	8'
Max Ridge Height	22'11"
Roof Framing	Truss
Exterior Walls	2x6

4,80 X 4,80
16'-0" X 16'-0"

4,40 X 3,30
14'-8" X 11'-0"

2,70 X 3,90
9'-0" X 13'-0"

2,40 X 3,90
8'-0" X 13'-0"

3,60 X 3,50
12'-0" X 11'-8"

©

MAIN FLOOR

Design 65045

Units Single
Price Code A
Total Finished 860 sq. ft.
Main Finished 860 sq. ft.
Dimensions 30'x30'
Foundation Basement
Bedrooms 2
Full Baths 1
Roof Framing Stick

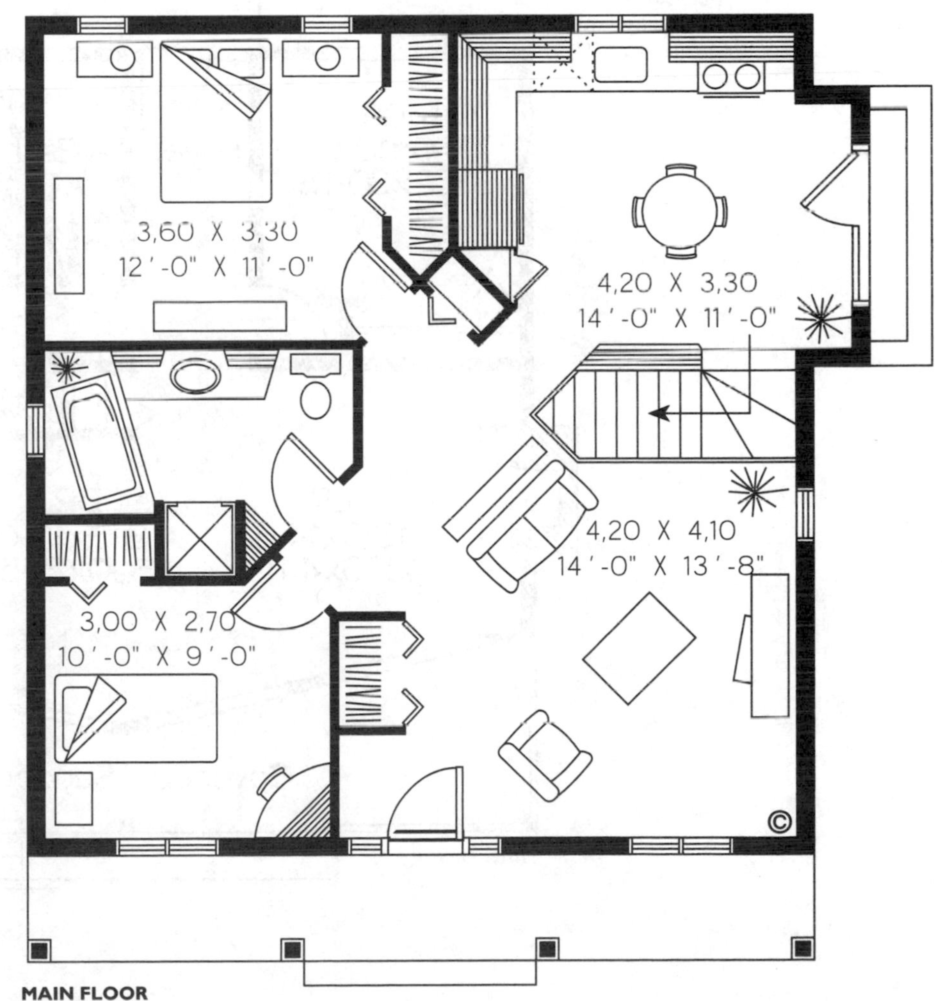

MAIN FLOOR

Design 90934

Units	Single
Price Code	A
Total Finished	884 sq. ft.
Main Finished	884 sq. ft.
Dimensions	34'x28'
Foundation	Slab
Bedrooms	2
Full Baths	1
Main Ceiling	8'
Max Ridge Height	15'

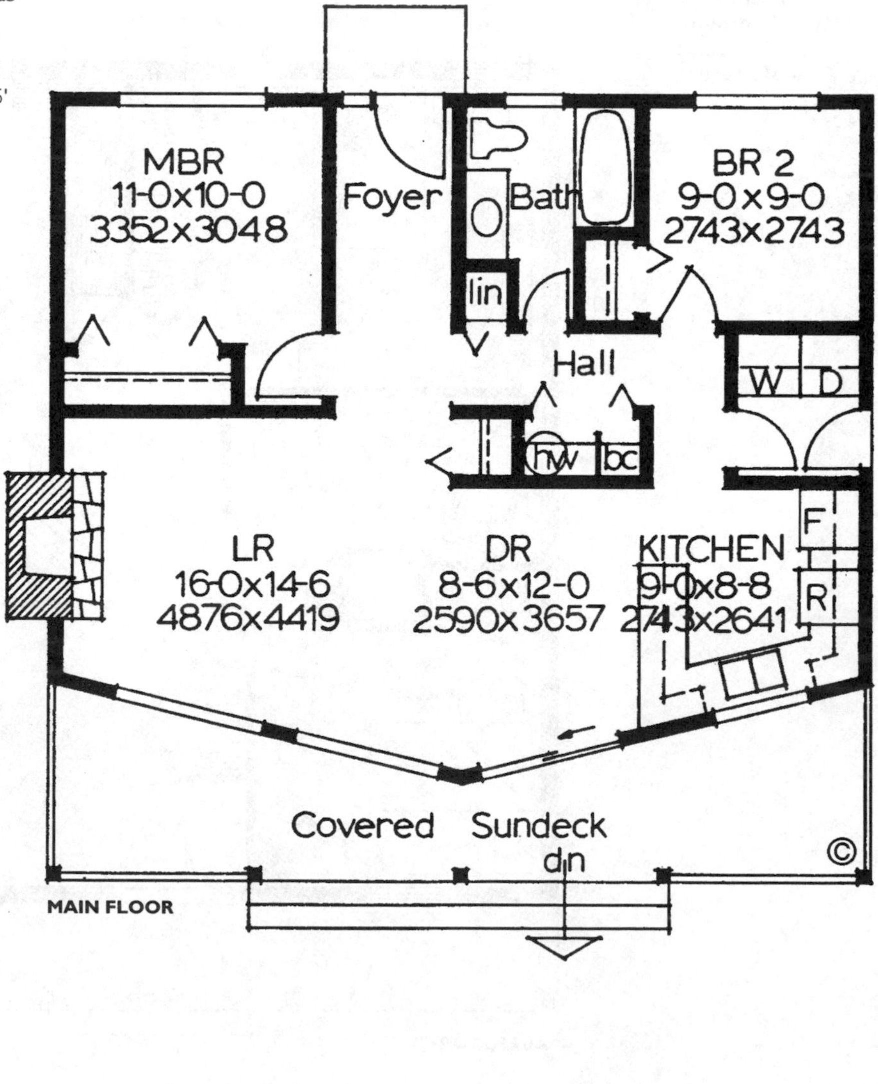

MBR
11-0x10-0
3352x3048

Foyer

Bath

lin

BR 2
9-0x9-0
2743x2743

Hall

W D

hw bc

F

R

LR
16-0x14-6
4876x4419

DR
8-6x12-0
2590x3657

KITCHEN
9-0x8-8
2743x2641

Covered Sundeck
dn

©

MAIN FLOOR

Design 61093

Units	Single
Price Code	A
Total Finished	930 sq. ft.
Main Finished	930 sq. ft.
Porch Unfinished	102 sq. ft.
Dimensions	35'x28'6'
Foundation	Basement Crawlspace Slab
Bedrooms	3
Full Baths	1
Main Ceiling	8'
Roof Framing	Stick
Exterior Walls	2x4

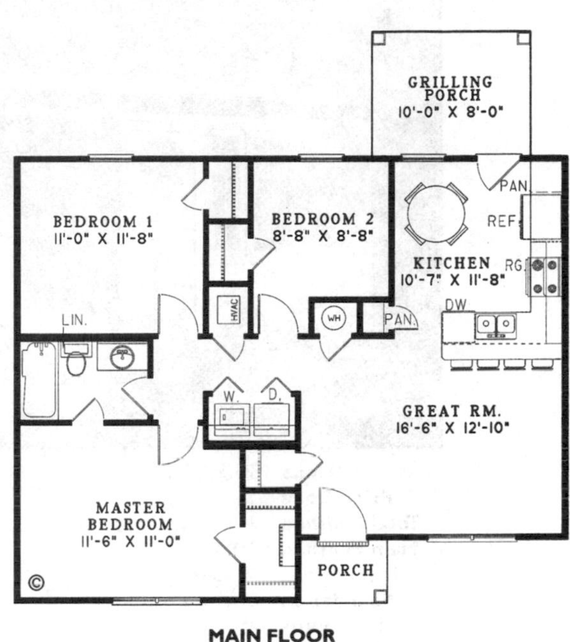

MAIN FLOOR

Design 65366

Units	Single
Price Code	A
Total Finished	923 sq. ft.
Main Finished	923 sq. ft.
Basement Unfinished	923 sq. ft.
Dimensions	30'x31'
Foundation	Basement
Bedrooms	2
Full Baths	1
Main Ceiling	8'
Max Ridge Height	22'1"

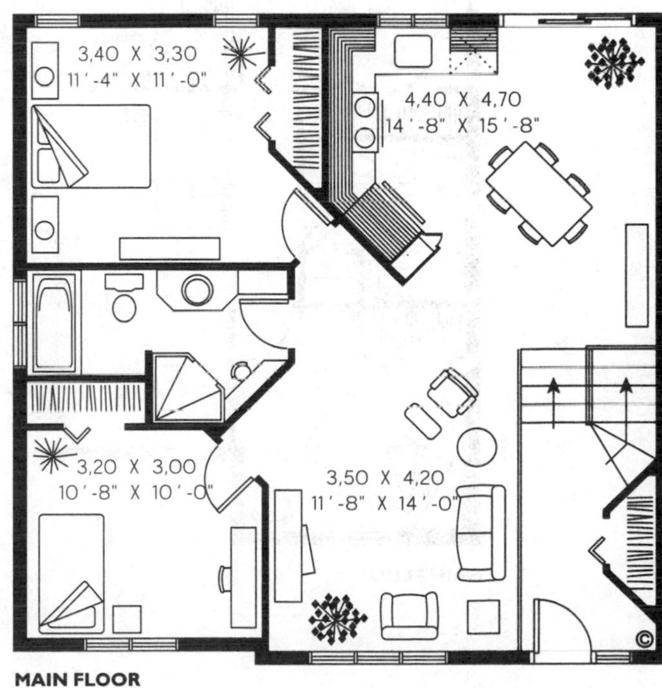

MAIN FLOOR

Design 65387

Units Single
Price Code A
Total Finished 948 sq. ft.
Main Finished 948 sq. ft.
Dimensions 30'x34'
Foundation Basement
Bedrooms 2
Full Baths 1
Roof Framing Stick

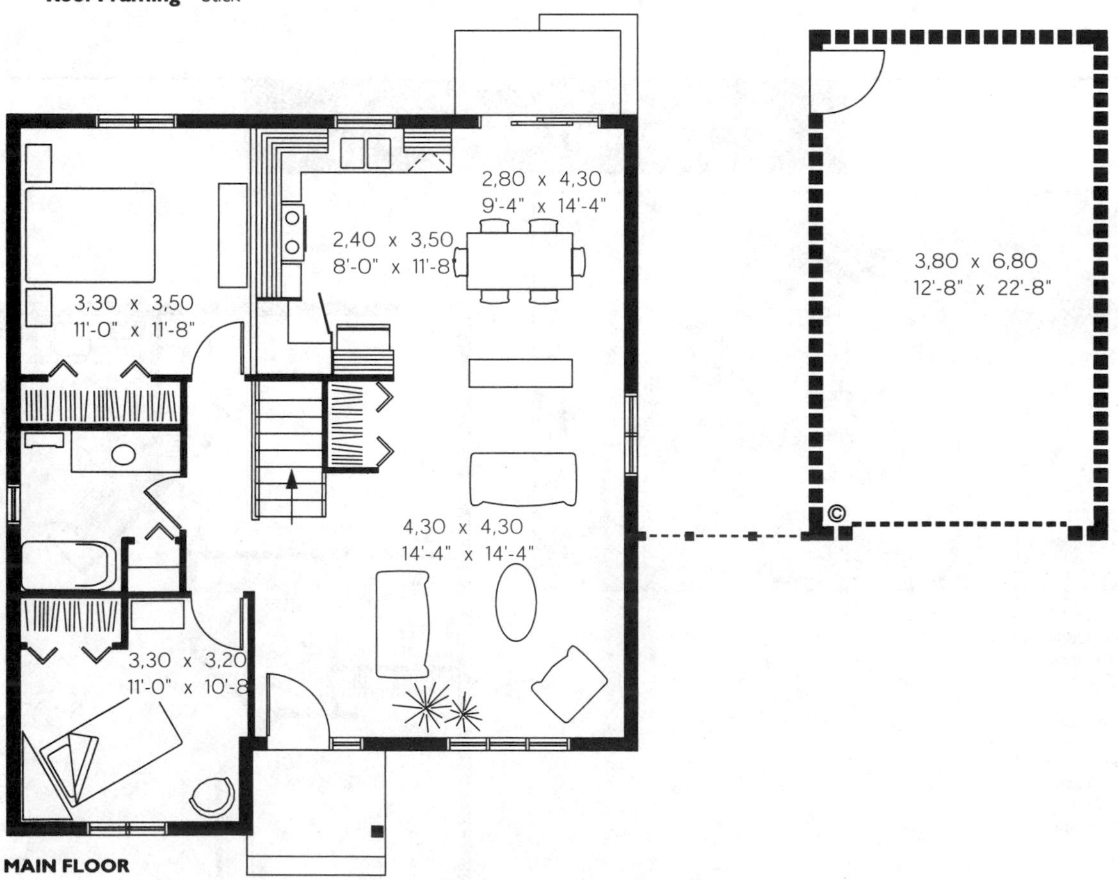

Design 65005

Units	Single
Price Code	A
Total Finished	972 sq. ft.
Main Finished	972 sq. ft.
Basement Unfinished	972 sq. ft.
Dimensions	30'x35'
Foundation	Basement
Bedrooms	2
Full Baths	1
Main Ceiling	8'2"
Max Ridge Height	17'6"
Exterior Walls	2x6

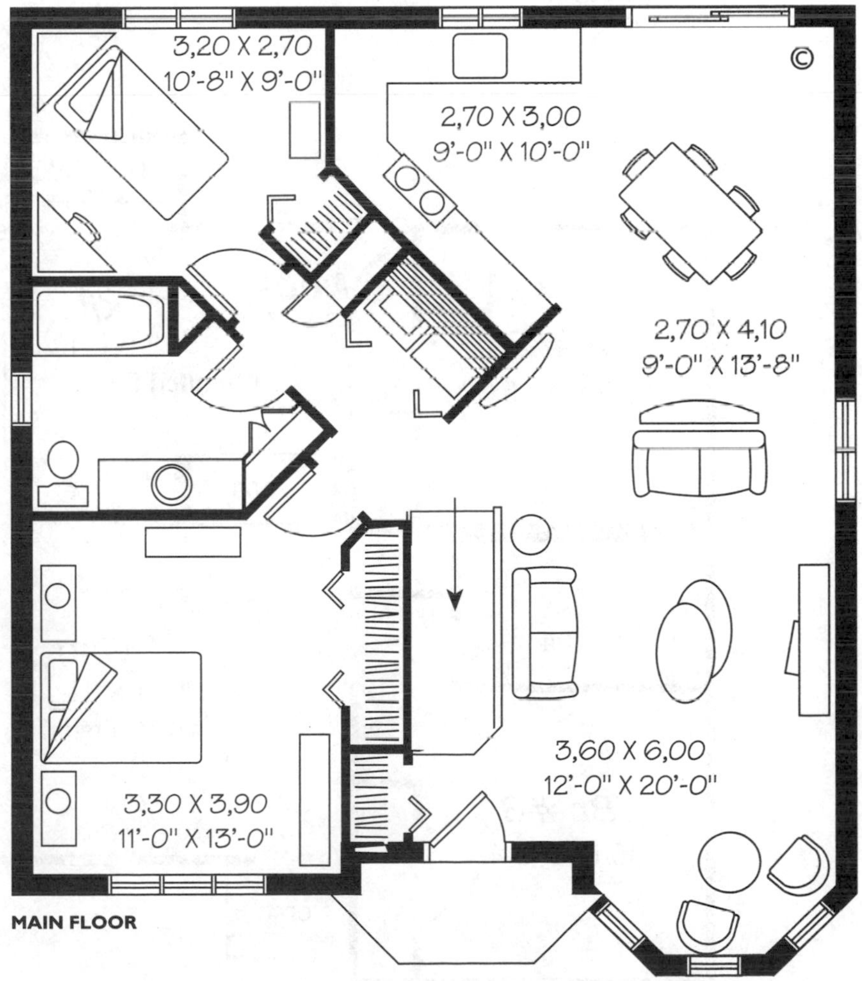

MAIN FLOOR

Design 91147

Units	Single
Price Code	A
Total Finished	975 sq. ft.
Main Finished	975 sq. ft.
Dimensions	39'4"x31'2"
Foundation	Slab
Bedrooms	3
Full Baths	2

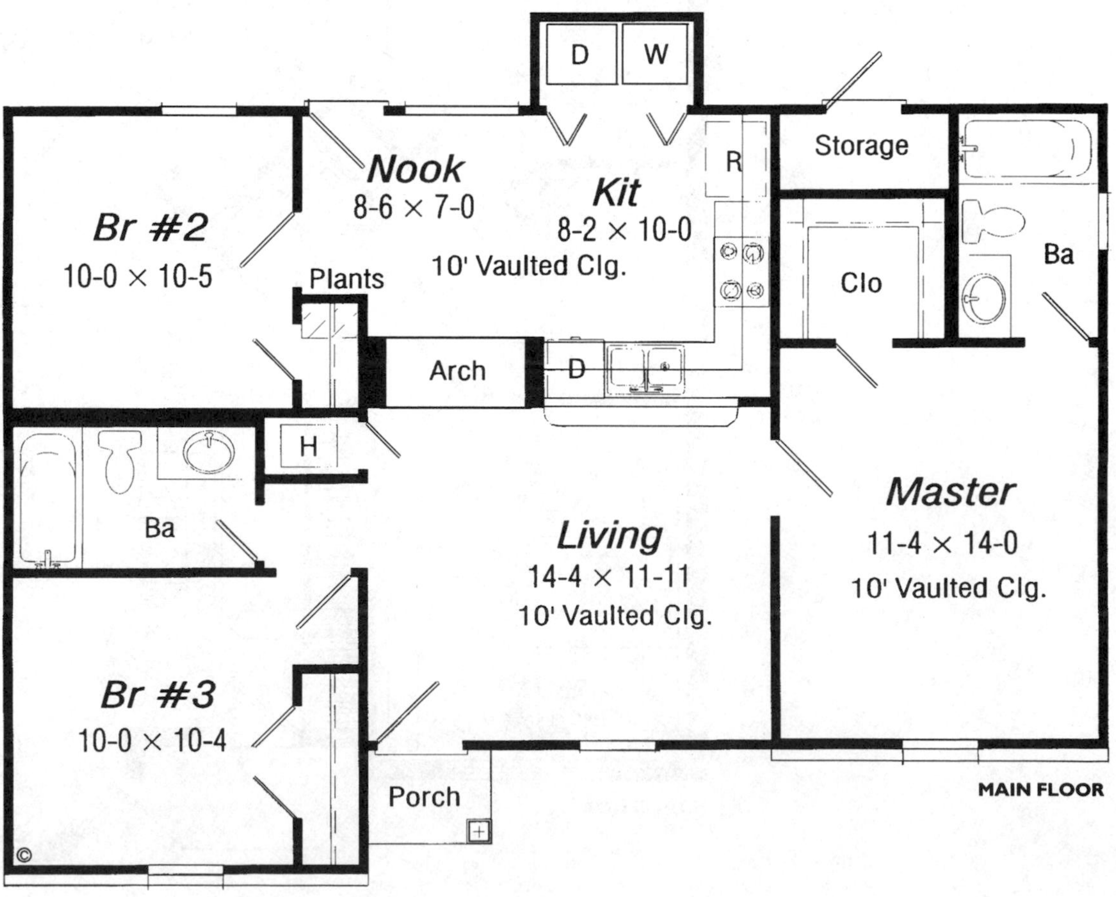

Design 65003

Units	Single
Price Code	A
Total Finished	976 sq. ft.
First Finished	593 sq. ft.
Second Finished	383 sq. ft.
Basement Unfinished	593 sq. ft.
Dimensions	22'8"x26'8"
Foundation	Crawlspace
Bedrooms	2
Full Baths	1
3/4 Baths	1
First Ceiling	8'
Second Ceiling	8'
Max Ridge Height	22'8"
Roof Framing	Truss
Exterior Walls	2x6

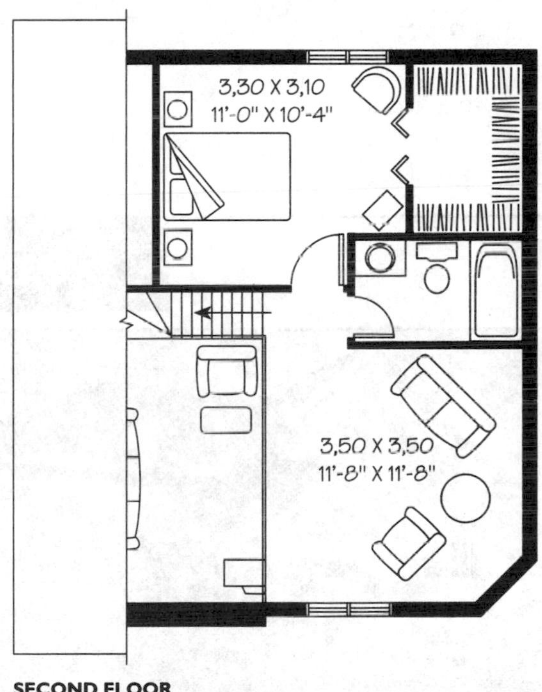

SECOND FLOOR

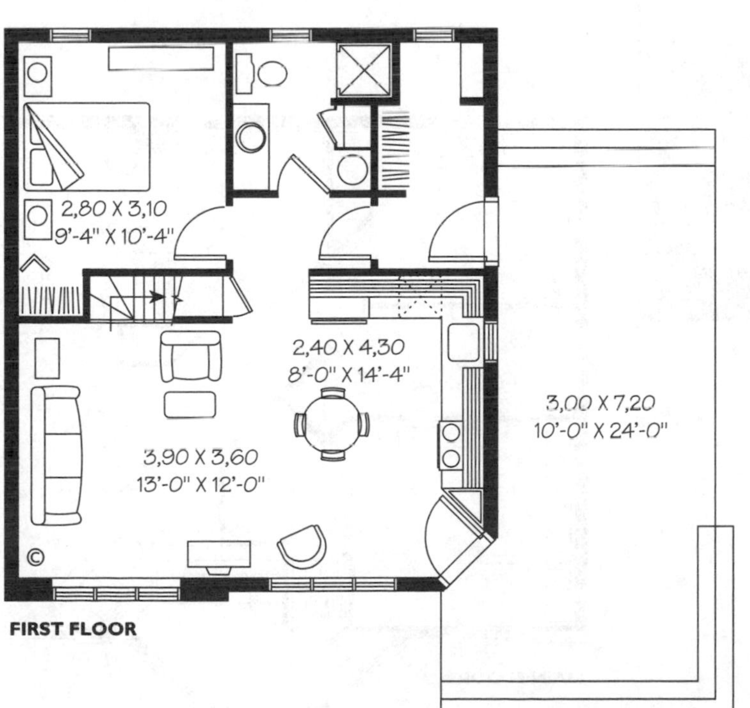

FIRST FLOOR

Design 65643

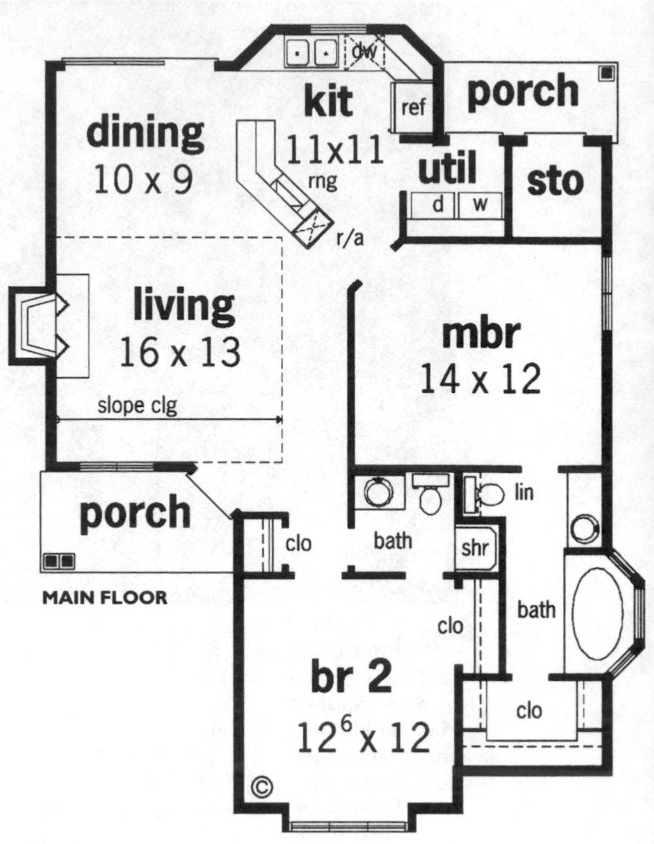

Units	Single
Price Code	A
Total Finished	984 sq. ft.
Main Finished	984 sq. ft.
Dimensions	33'9"x43'
Foundation	Crawlspace Slab
Bedrooms	2
Full Baths	1
3/4 Baths	1
Max Ridge Height	26'
Exterior Walls	2x6

Design 65260

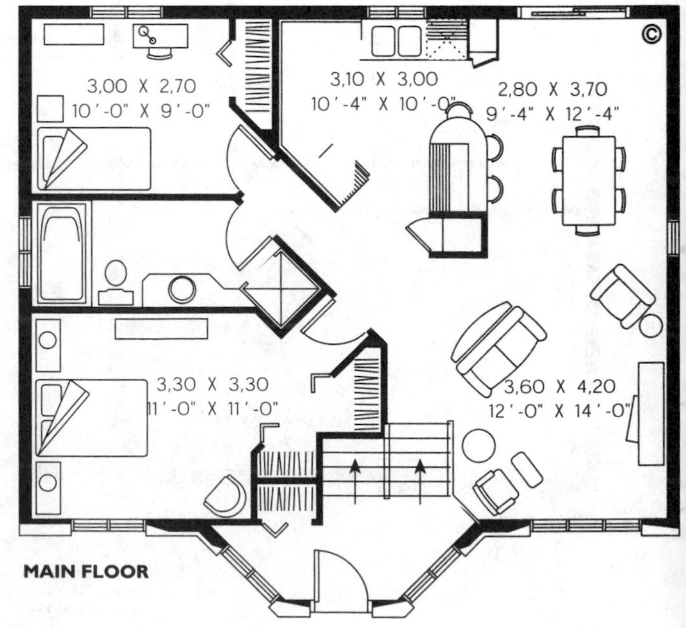

Units	Single
Price Code	A
Total Finished	996 sq. ft.
Main Finished	996 sq. ft.
Dimensions	34'x32'4"
Foundation	Basement
Bedrooms	2
Full Baths	1
Exterior Walls	2x4

Design 65642

Units	Single
Price Code	A
Total Finished	998 sq. ft.
Main Finished	998 sq. ft.
Dimensions	48'x29'
Foundation	Crawlspace Slab
Bedrooms	3
Full Baths	1
Main Ceiling	8'
Max Ridge Height	26'
Roof Framing	Stick
Exterior Walls	2x4

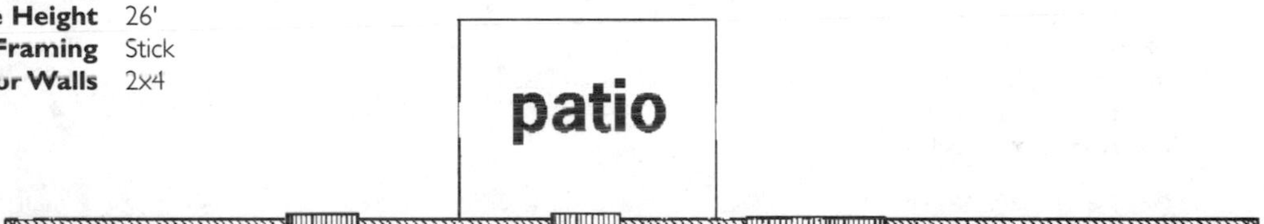

patio
shvs
clo
mbr
12 x 12
bath
lin
bar
rg
ref
kit
dining
12 x 10
W.H.
sto
wash
12 x 7
clo
divider
carport
20 x 12
HEAT & A/C
clo
br 2
13 x 10
br 3
11 x 10
living
15 x 13
clo
©

MAIN FLOOR

Design 98469

Units	Single
Price Code	A
Total Finished	1,042 sq. ft.
Main Finished	1,042 sq. ft.
Basement Unfinished	1,042 sq. ft.
Garage Unfinished	400 sq. ft.
Dimensions	60'x30'
Foundation	Basement Crawlspace
Bedrooms	3
Full Baths	2
Main Ceiling	9'
Max Ridge Height	22'
Roof Framing	Stick
Exterior Walls	2x4

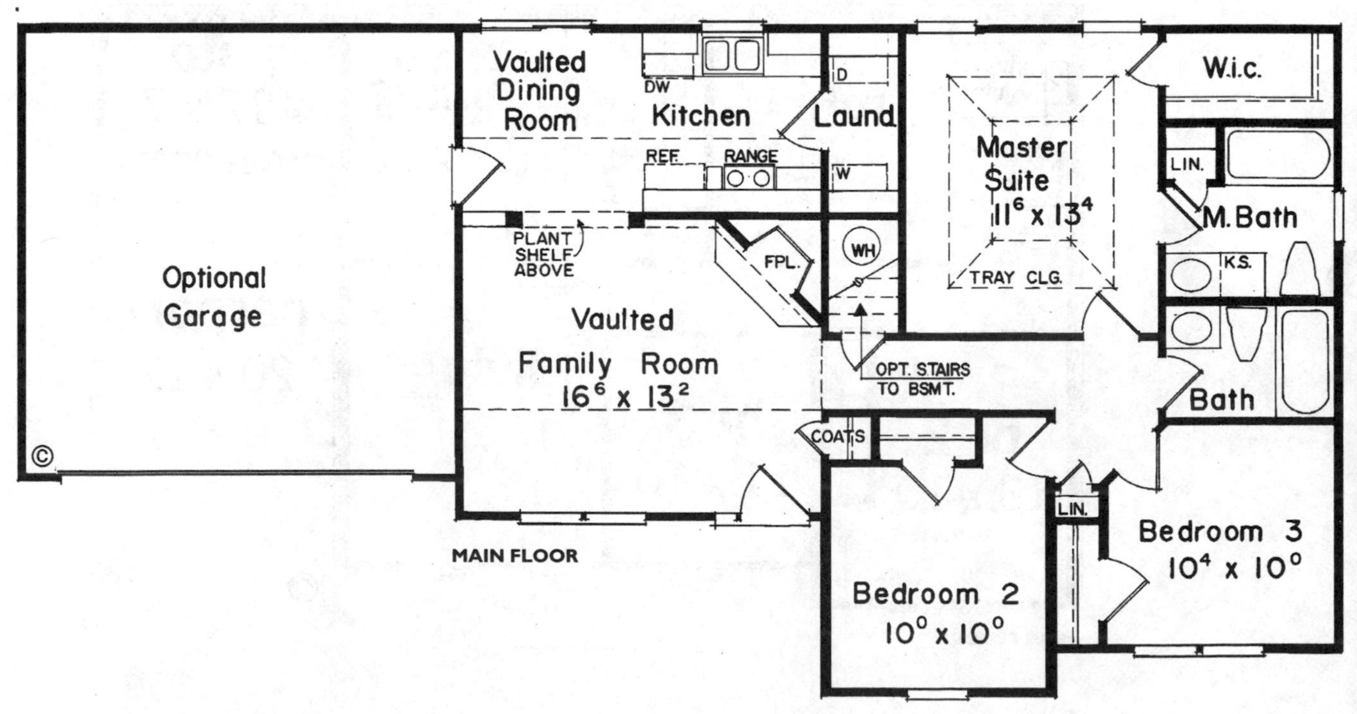

MAIN FLOOR

Design 65036

Units	Single
Price Code	A
Total Finished	1,052 sq. ft.
Main Finished	1,052 sq. ft.
Basement Unfinished	1,052 sq. ft.
Dimensions	32'8"x36'
Foundation	Basement
Bedrooms	2
Full Baths	1
Main Ceiling	8'
Max Ridge Height	17'6"
Roof Framing	Truss
Exterior Walls	2x6

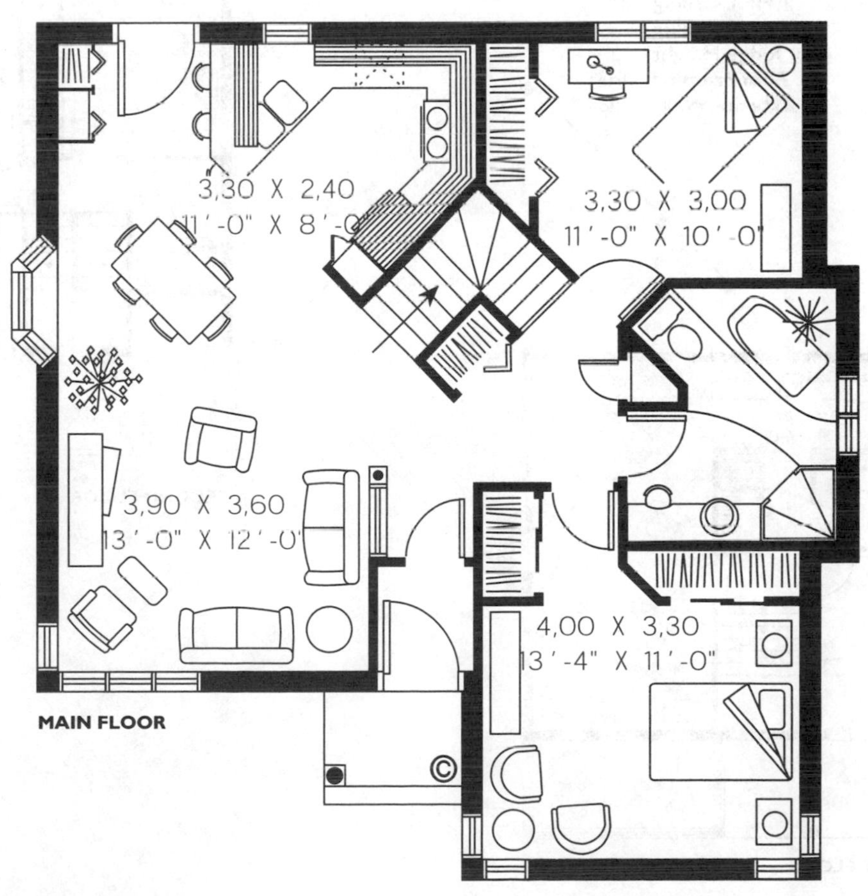

MAIN FLOOR

Design 65161

Units	Single
Price Code	A
Total Finished	1,056 sq. ft.
First Finished	576 sq. ft.
Second Finished	480 sq. ft.
Basement Unfinished	576 sq. ft.
Deck Unfinished	315 sq. ft.
Porch Unfinished	45 sq. ft.
Dimensions	24'x30'
Foundation	Basement
Bedrooms	2
Full Baths	1
Half Baths	1
First Ceiling	8'
Second Ceiling	8'
Max Ridge Height	23'
Roof Framing	Truss
Exterior Walls	2x6

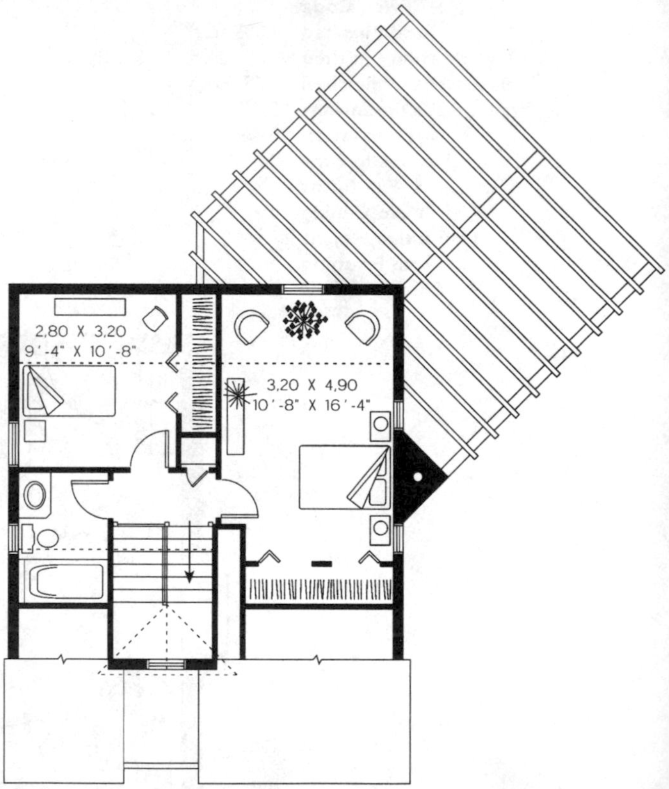

2,80 X 3,20
9'-4" X 10'-8"

3,20 X 4,90
10'-8" X 16'-4"

SECOND FLOOR

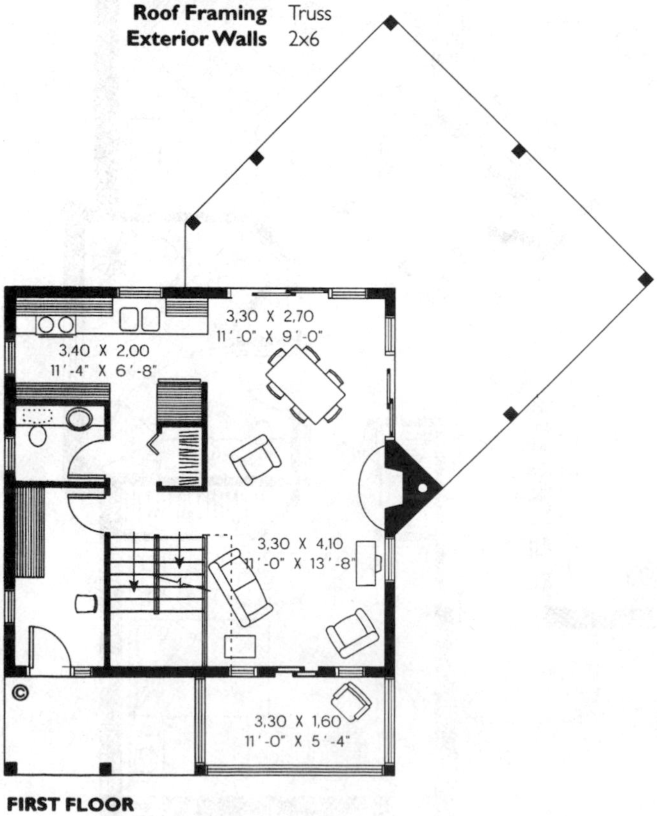

3,30 X 2,70
11'-0" X 9'-0"

3,40 X 2,00
11'-4" X 6'-8"

3,30 X 4,10
11'-0" X 13'-8"

©

3,30 X 1,60
11'-0" X 5'-4"

FIRST FLOOR

Design 98413

Units	Single
Price Code	A
Total Finished	1,070 sq. ft.
Main Finished	1,070 sq. ft.
Basement Unfinished	1,090 sq. ft.
Garage Unfinished	400 sq. ft.
Dimensions	48'x36'
Foundation	Basement Crawlspace Slab
Bedrooms	3
Full Baths	2
Main Ceiling	9'
Max Ridge Height	22'
Roof Framing	Stick
Exterior Walls	2x4

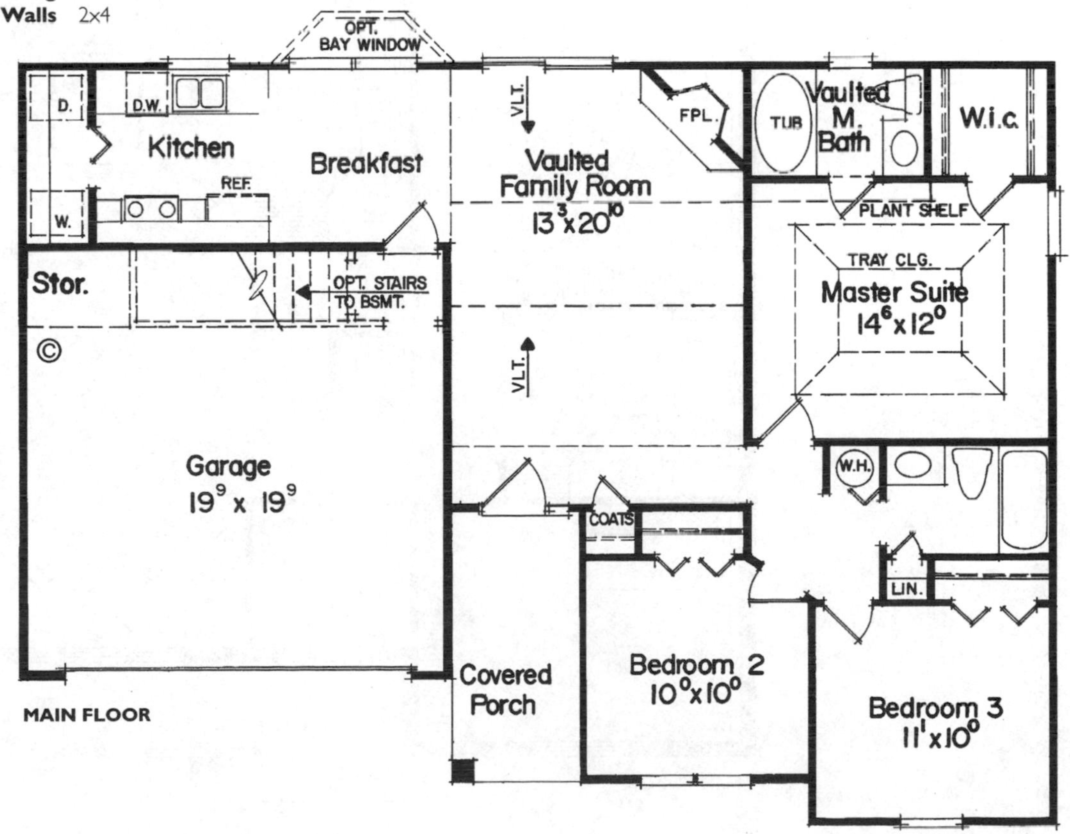

MAIN FLOOR

Design 65149

Units	Single
Price Code	A
Total Finished	1,079 sq. ft.
Main Finished	1,079 sq. ft.
Dimensions	34'x34'
Foundation	Basement
Bedrooms	2
Full Baths	1
Max Ridge Height	22'6"
Roof Framing	Truss
Exterior Walls	2x6

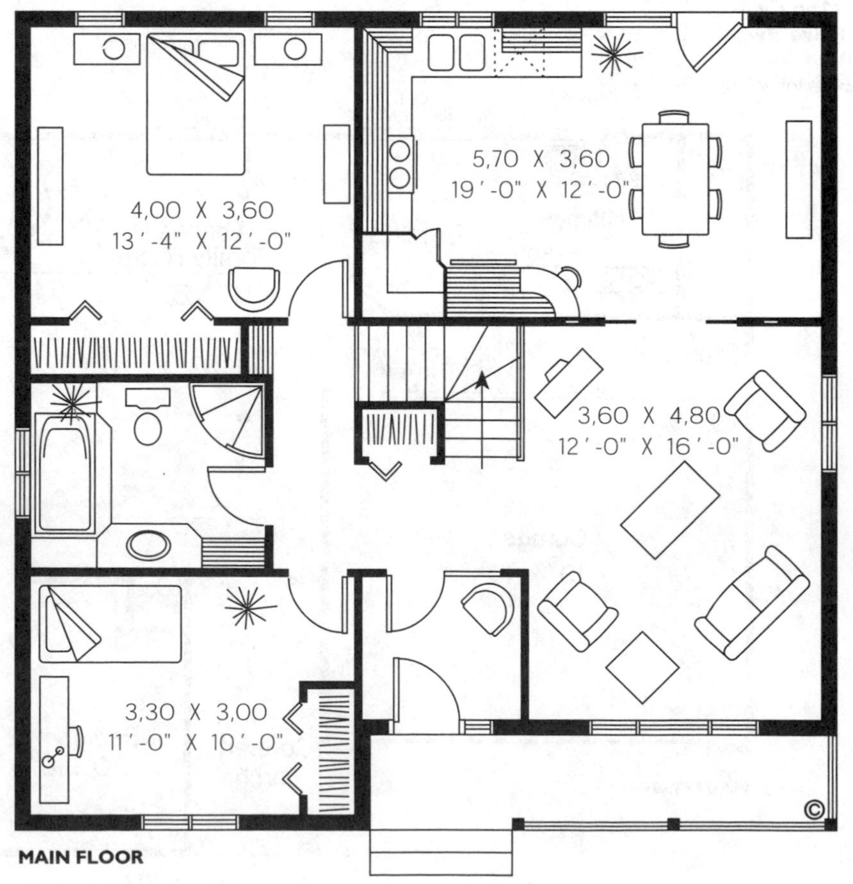

MAIN FLOOR

Design 65093

Units	Single
Price Code	A
Total Finished	1,087 sq. ft.
Main Finished	1,087 sq. ft.
Dimensions	46'x40'4"
Foundation	Basement
Bedrooms	2
Full Baths	1

MAIN FLOOR

Design 65640

Units	Single
Price Code	A
Total Finished	1,088 sq. ft.
Main Finished	1,088 sq. ft.
Bonus Unfinished	580 sq. ft.
Dimensions	34'x44'
Foundation	Crawlspace Slab
Bedrooms	2
Full Baths	1
Main Ceiling	8'
Second Ceiling	8'
Max Ridge Height	30'
Roof Framing	Stick
Exterior Walls	2x6

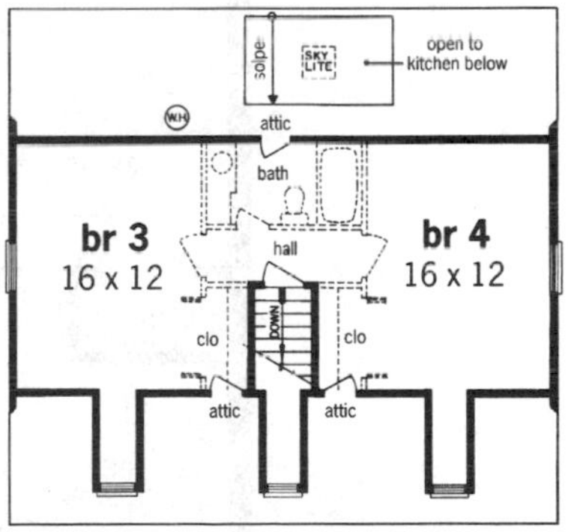

BONUS

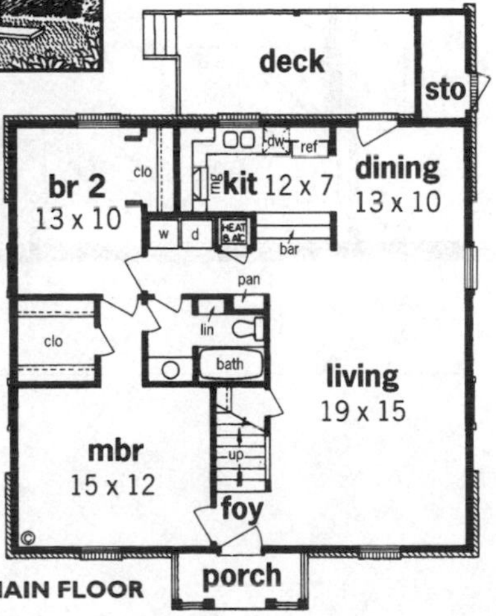

MAIN FLOOR

Design 65383

Units	Single
Price Code	A
Total Finished	1,092 sq. ft.
Main Finished	1,092 sq. ft.
Dimensions	42'x26'
Foundation	Basement
Bedrooms	3
Full Baths	1

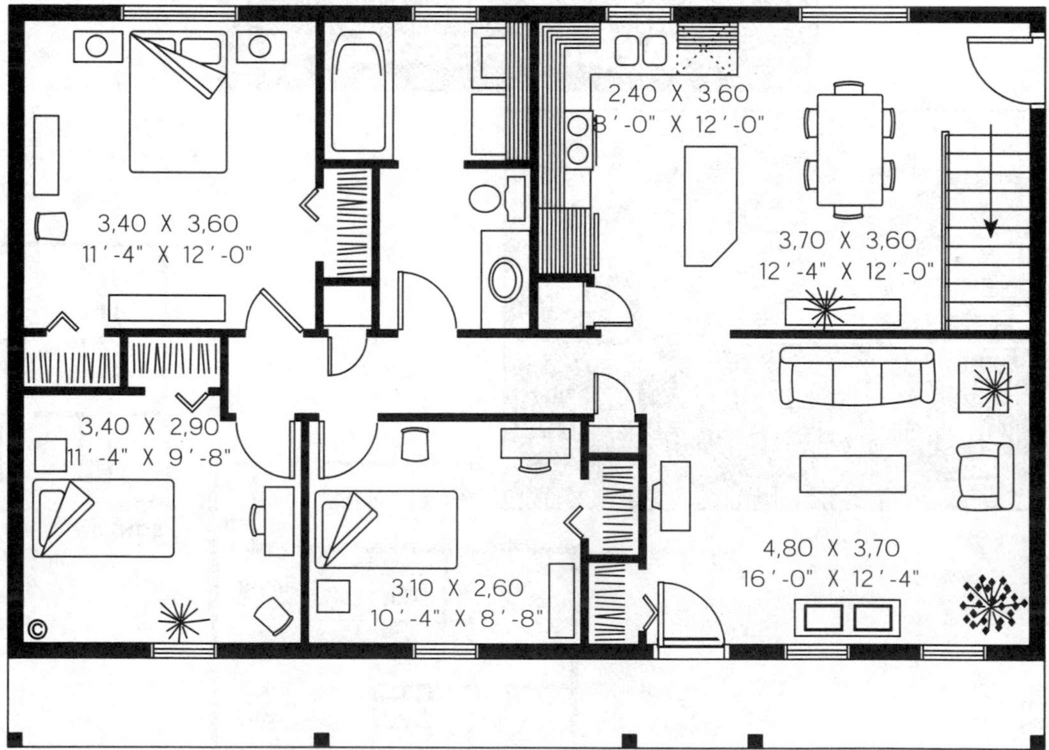

MAIN FLOOR

Design 24723

Units	Single
Price Code	A
Total Finished	1,112 sq. ft.
Main Finished	1,112 sq. ft.
Garage Unfinished	563 sq. ft.
Dimensions	64'x33'
Foundation	Crawlspace Slab
Bedrooms	3
Full Baths	2
Main Ceiling	8'-9'
Max Ridge Height	21'6"
Roof Framing	Stick
Exterior Walls	2x4

MAIN FLOOR

Design 65091

Units	Single
Price Code	A
Total Finished	1,122 sq. ft.
Main Finished	1,122 sq. ft.
Garage Unfinished	294 sq. ft.
Dimensions	32'x48'
Foundation	Basement
Bedrooms	2
Full Baths	1

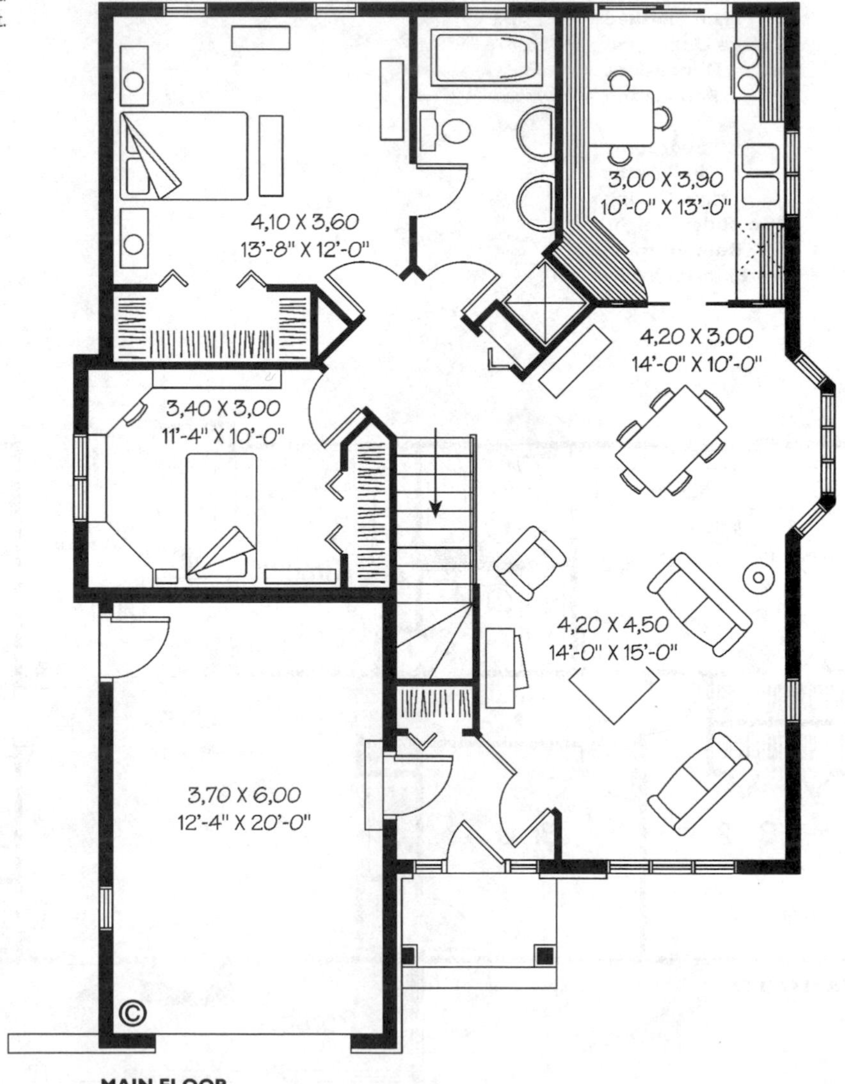

MAIN FLOOR

Design 98498

Units	Single
Price Code	A
Total Finished	1,135 sq. ft.
Main Finished	1,135 sq. ft.
Garage Unfinished	460 sq. ft.
Dimensions	60'x33'6"
Foundation	Crawlspace
Bedrooms	3
Full Baths	2
Main Ceiling	9'
Max Ridge Height	20'6"
Roof Framing	Stick
Exterior Walls	2x4

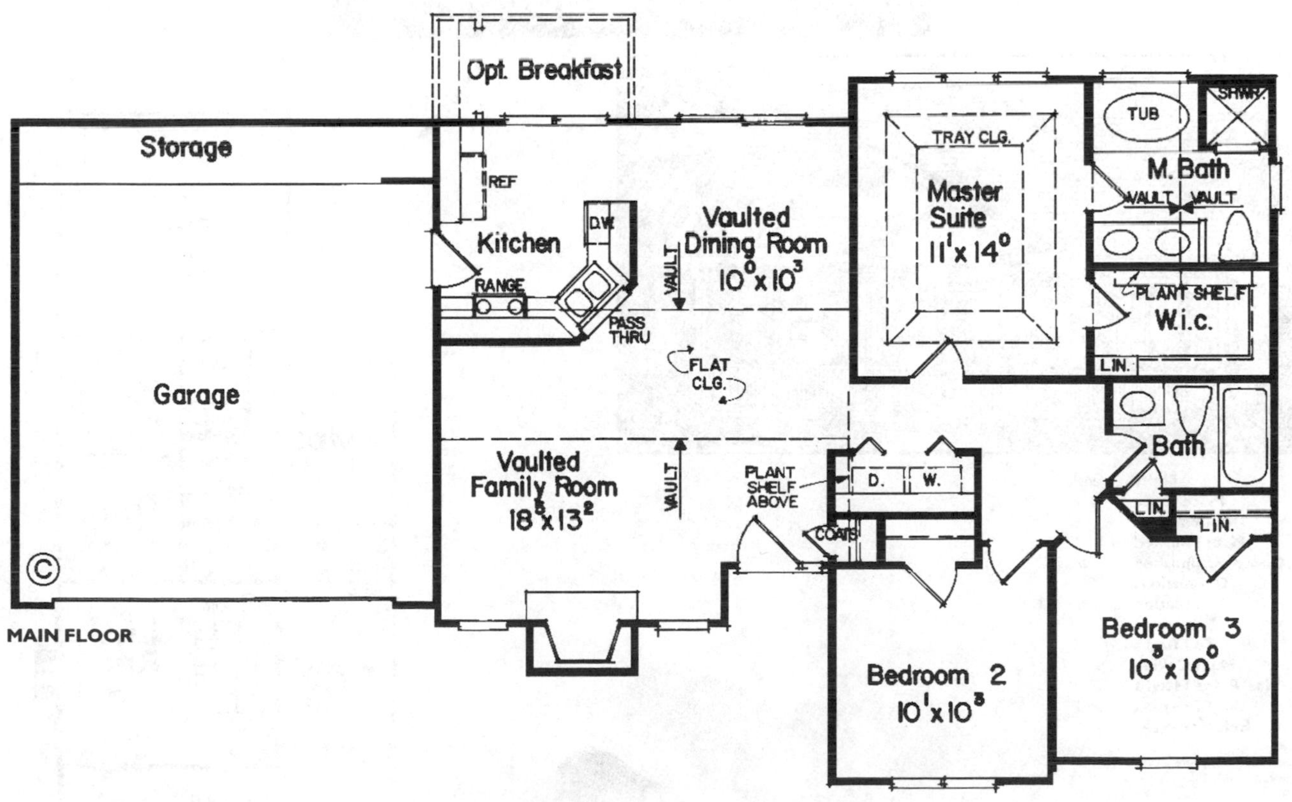

MAIN FLOOR

Design 65376

Units	Single
Price Code	A
Total Finished	1,142 sq. ft.
Main Finished	1,142 sq. ft.
Garage Unfinished	400 sq. ft.
Dimensions	46'x38'
Foundation	Basement
Bedrooms	2
Full Baths	1

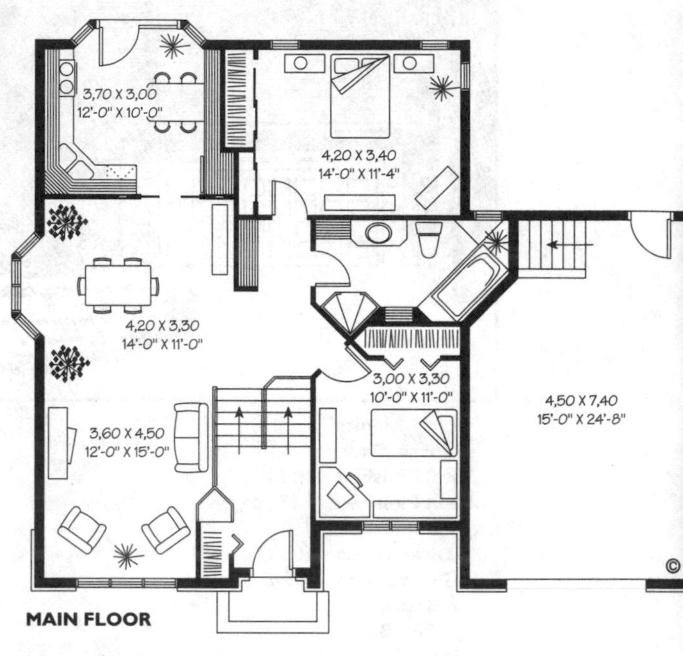

Design 68093

Units	Single
Price Code	A
Total Finished	1,142 sq. ft.
Main Finished	1,142 sq. ft.
Garage Unfinished	435 sq. ft.
Dimensions	30'4"x64'8"
Foundation	Basement
Bedrooms	2
Full Baths	2
Main Ceiling	9'
Max Ridge Height	20'3"
Roof Framing	Stick
Exterior Walls	2x4

* Alternate foundation options available at an additional charge. Please call 1-800-235-5700 for more information.

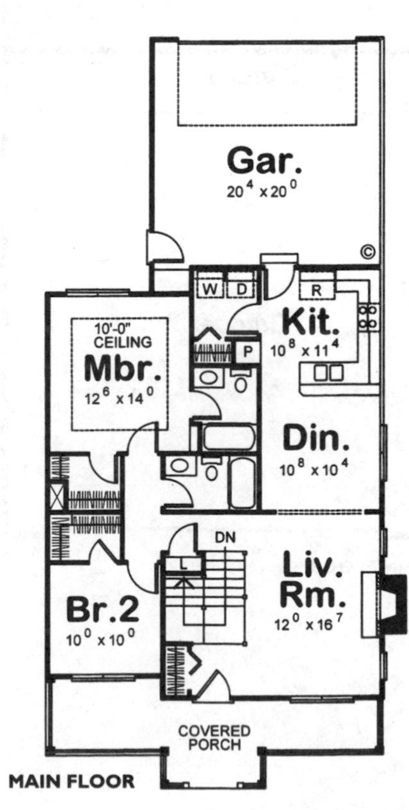

Design 65365

Units	Single
Price Code	A
Total Finished	1,146 sq. ft.
First Finished	726 sq. ft.
Second Finished	420 sq. ft.
Basement Unfinished	728 sq. ft.
Porch Unfinished	187 sq. ft.
Dimensions	28'x26'
Foundation	Basement
Bedrooms	1
Full Baths	1
Half Baths	1
First Ceiling	8'
Second Ceiling	8'
Max Ridge Height	29'8"
Exterior Walls	2x6

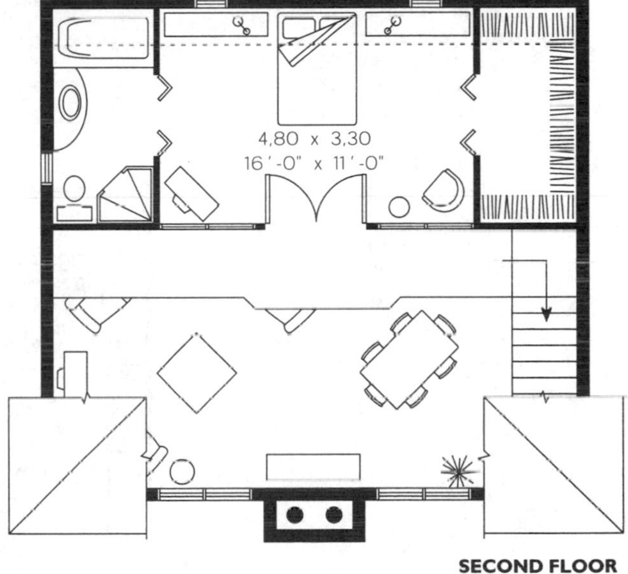

SECOND FLOOR

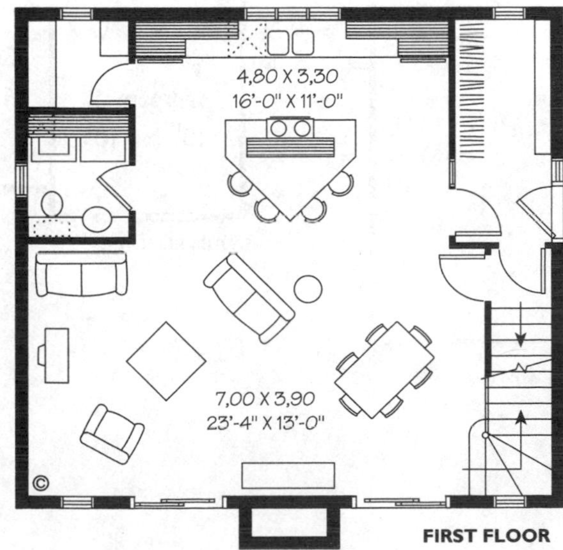

FIRST FLOOR

Design 60112

Units	Single
Price Code	A
Total Finished	1,149 sq. ft.
Main Finished	1,149 sq. ft.
Basement Unfinished	1,166 sq. ft.
Garage Unfinished	422 sq. ft.
Dimensions	47'6"x42'4"
Foundation	Basement
Bedrooms	3
Full Baths	2
Main Ceiling	9'
Max Ridge Height	21'10"
Roof Framing	Stick
Exterior Walls	2x4

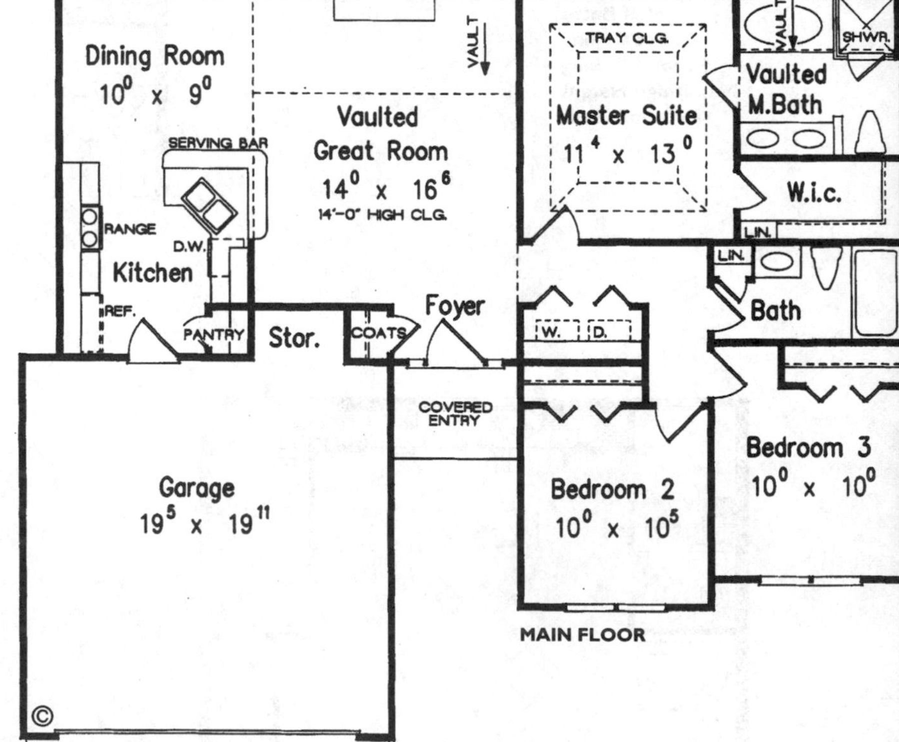

MAIN FLOOR

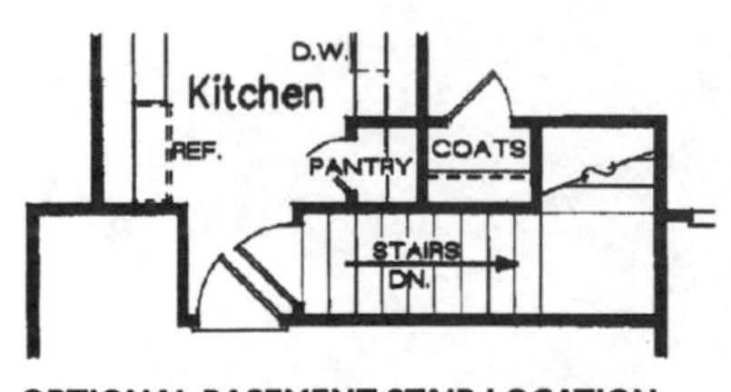

OPTIONAL BASEMENT STAIR LOCATION

Design 93006

Units	Single
Price Code	A
Total Finished	1,163 sq. ft.
Main Finished	1,163 sq. ft.
Garage Unfinished	449 sq. ft.
Porch Unfinished	19 sq. ft.
Dimensions	39'2"x55'10"
Foundation	Slab
Bedrooms	3
Full Baths	1
3/4 Baths	1
Max Ridge Height	19'
Roof Framing	Stick
Exterior Walls	2x4

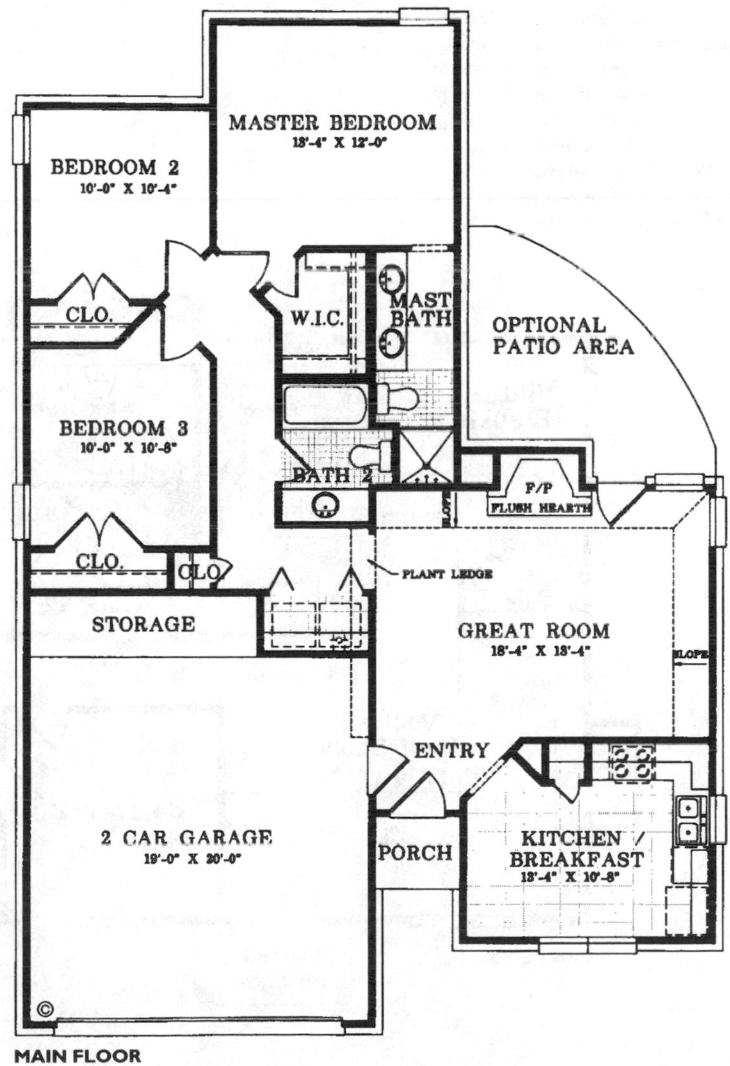

MAIN FLOOR

Design 97296

Units	Single
Price Code	A
Total Finished	1,166 sq. ft.
Main Finished	1,166 sq. ft.
Basement Unfinished	1,166 sq. ft.
Dimensions	43'4"x34'
Foundation	Basement
Bedrooms	3
Full Baths	2
Max Ridge Height	22'3"
Roof Framing	Stick
Exterior Walls	2x4

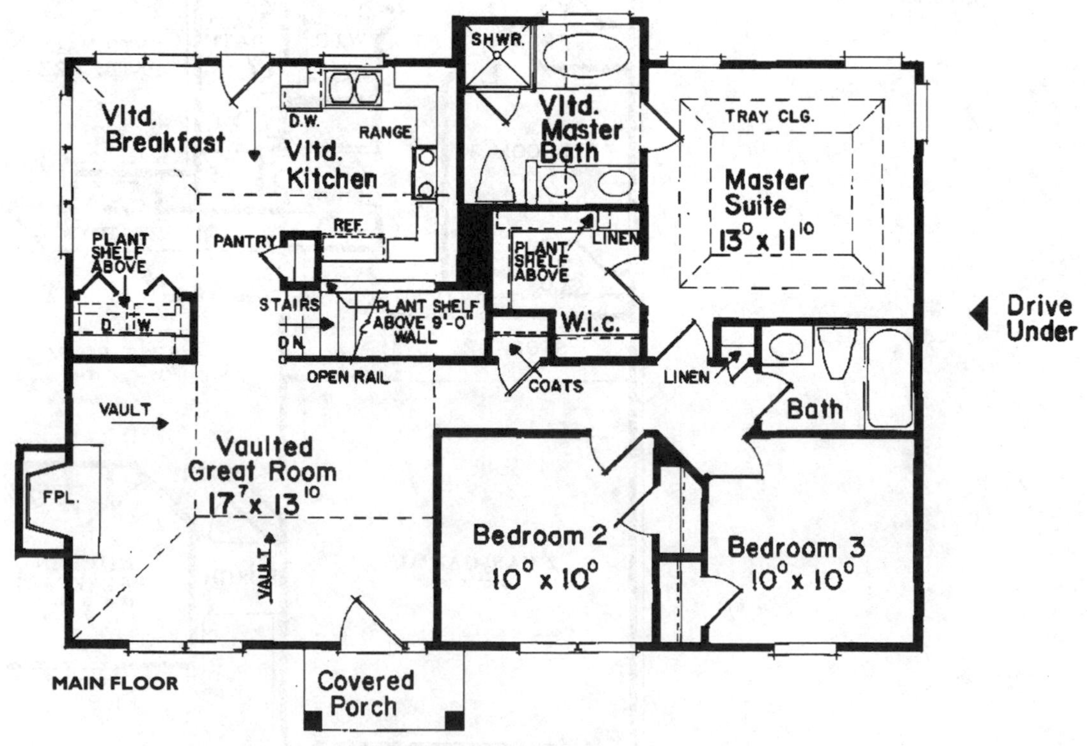

Design 98497

Units	Single
Price Code	A
Total Finished	1,169 sq. ft.
Main Finished	1,169 sq. ft.
Basement Unfinished	1,194 sq. ft.
Garage Unfinished	400 sq. ft.
Dimensions	40'x49'6"
Foundation	Basement Crawlspace Slab
Bedrooms	3
Full Baths	2
Main Ceiling	9'
Max Ridge Height	21'
Roof Framing	Stick
Exterior Walls	2x4

Breakfast
D
W
REF.
Kitchen
RANGE
D.W.
PANTRY
PASS THRU
FPL.
Vaulted Family Room 14^6x18^0
SHWR
PLANT LEDGE ABOVE
Vaulted M.Bath
W.i.c.
TRAY CLG.
Master Suite 14^0x12^0
Bedroom 3 10^4x10^2
WH
HVAC
COATS
LIN
OPT. STAIRS TO BASEMENT
Vaulted Foyer
Bath
Garage
Bedroom 2 10^2x10^2
©

MAIN FLOOR

Design 65075

Units	Single
Price Code	A
Total Finished	1,176 sq. ft.
Main Finished	1,176 sq. ft.
Basement Unfinished	1,176 sq. ft.
Garage Unfinished	401 sq. ft.
Porch Unfinished	110 sq. ft.
Dimensions	58'x28'
Foundation	Basement
Bedrooms	3
Full Baths	1
Max Ridge Height	18'10"
Roof Framing	Truss
Exterior Walls	2x6

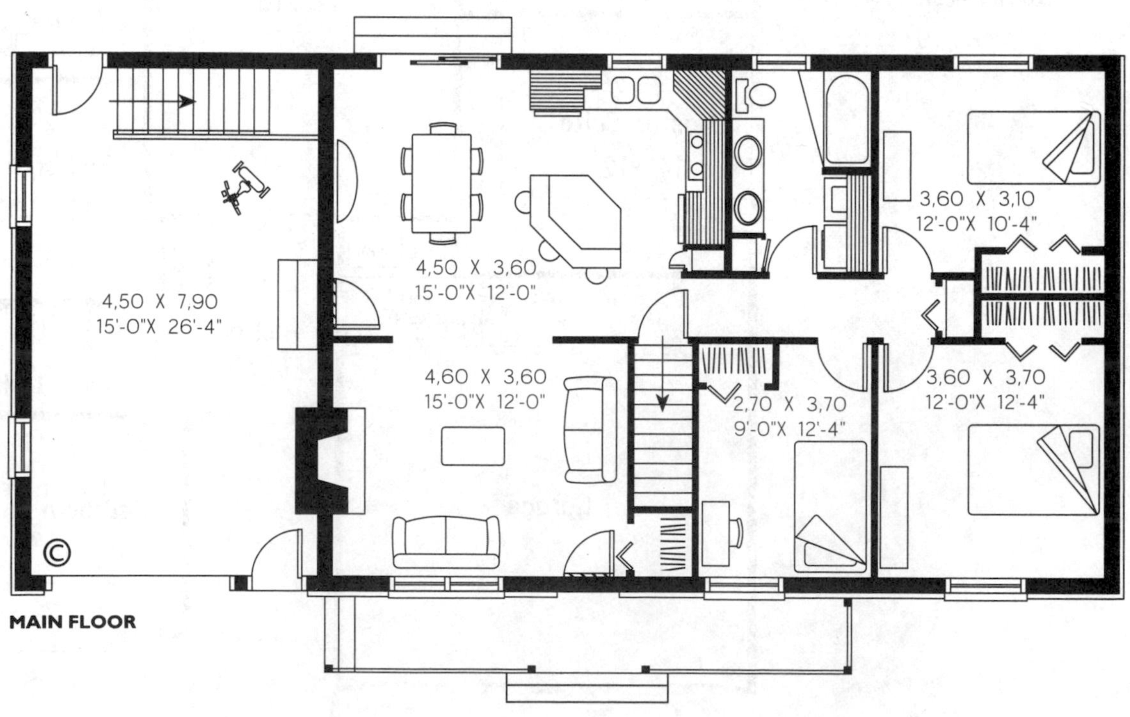

MAIN FLOOR

Design 97338

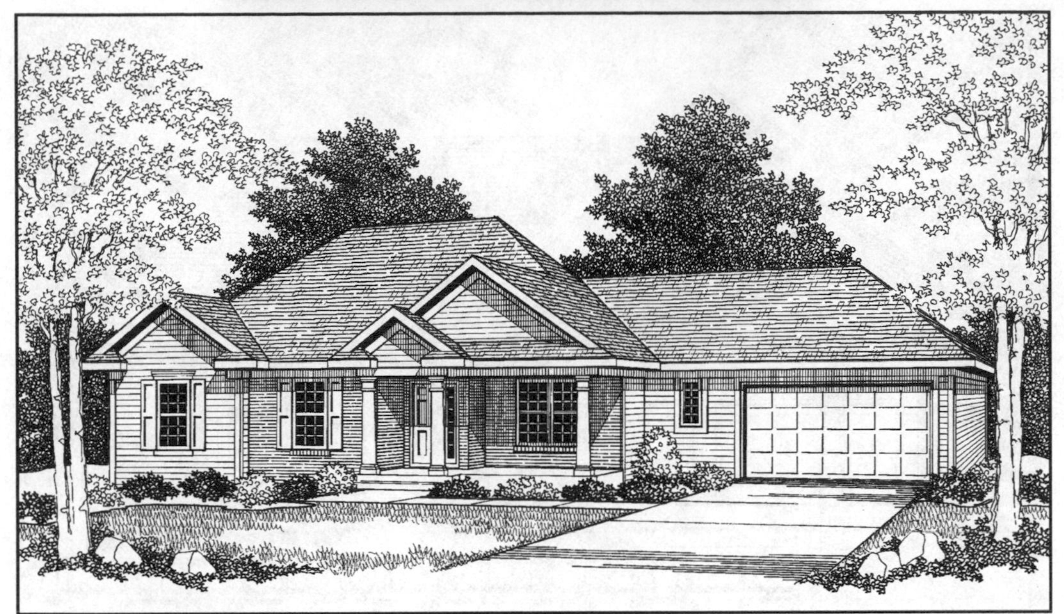

Units	Single
Price Code	A
Total Finished	1,186 sq. ft.
Main Finished	1,186 sq. ft.
Basement Unfinished	1,186 sq. ft.
Garage Unfinished	419 sq. ft.
Dimensions	66'4"x32'
Foundation	Basement
Bedrooms	3
Full Baths	1
Main Ceiling	9'
Max Ridge Height	20'8"
Roof Framing	Truss
Exterior Walls	2x6

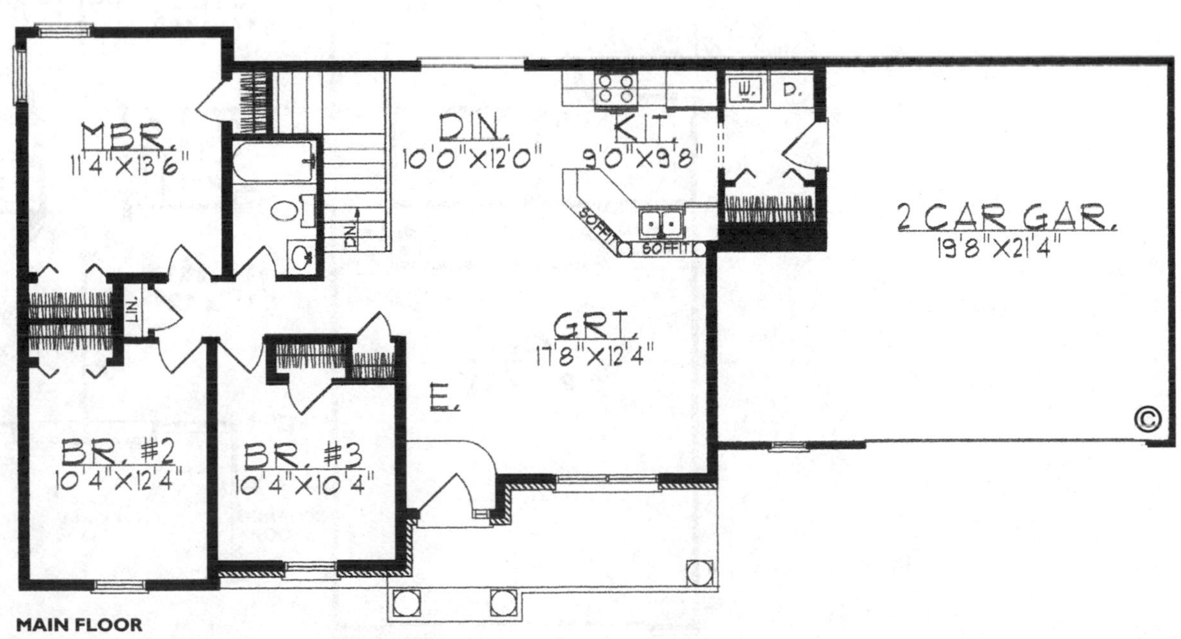

MAIN FLOOR

Design 97467

Units	Single
Price Code	A
Total Finished	1,191 sq. ft.
Main Finished	1,191 sq. ft.
Garage Unfinished	492 sq. ft.
Deck Unfinished	321 sq. ft.
Dimensions	48'4"x43'8"
Foundation	Basement
Bedrooms	3
Full Baths	2
Main Ceiling	9'
Max Ridge Height	23'3"
Roof Framing	Stick
Exterior Walls	2x4

* Alternate foundation options available at an additional charge. Please call 1-800-235-5700 for more information.

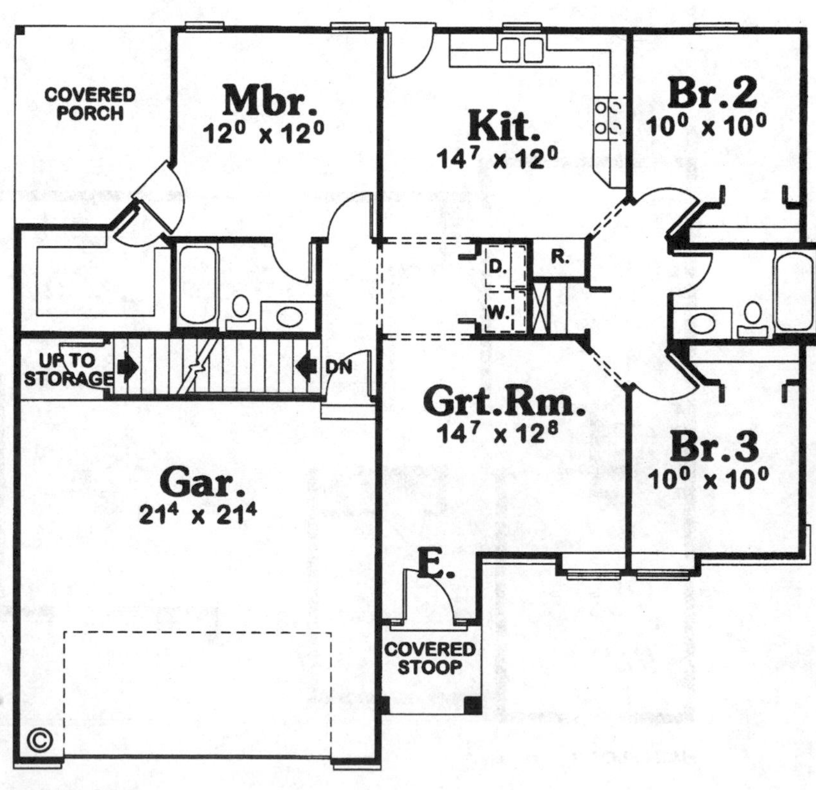

MAIN FLOOR

Design 61004

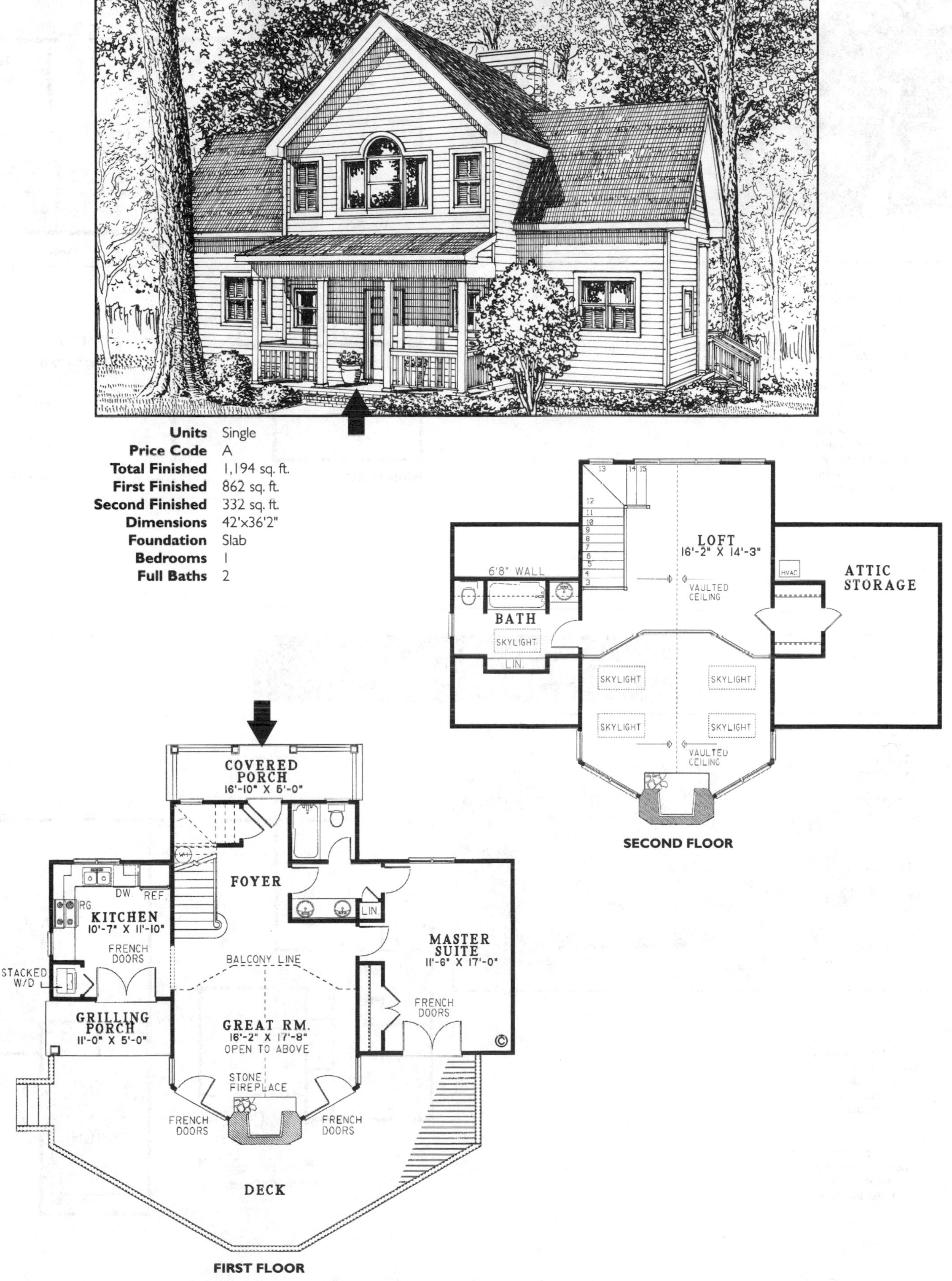

Units Single
Price Code A
Total Finished 1,194 sq. ft.
First Finished 862 sq. ft.
Second Finished 332 sq. ft.
Dimensions 42'x36'2"
Foundation Slab
Bedrooms 1
Full Baths 2

Design 91107

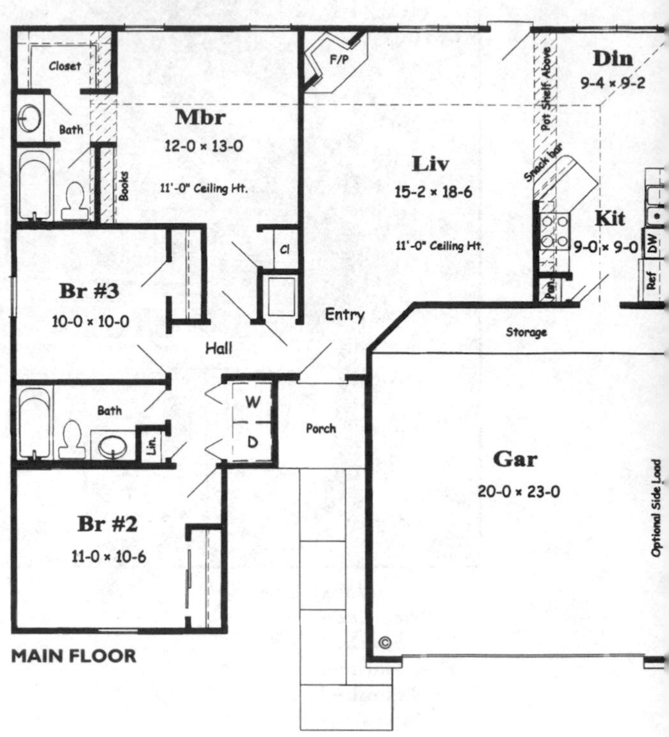

Units	Single
Price Code	A
Total Finished	1,199 sq. ft.
Main Finished	1,199 sq. ft.
Garage Unfinished	484 sq. ft.
Porch Unfinished	34 sq. ft.
Dimensions	44'2"x42'6¾"
Foundation	Slab
Bedrooms	3
Full Baths	2
Main Ceiling	8'
Vaulted Ceiling	11'
Max Ridge Height	18'
Roof Framing	Stick
Exterior Walls	2x4

Design 93073

OPTIONAL GARAGE DOOR LOCATION
SLOPE CLG
FP
MSTR BDRM 11-0x13-8 10 FT CLG
LIVING 13-0x17-8 10 FT CLG
GARAGE
MSTR BATH
BATH 2
LIN
STOR
BDRM 3 10-10x11-6
FOYER 9 FT CLG
STORAGE
BDRM 2 10-4x10-2
DINING 11-0x9-2 9 FT CLG
DESK
COVERED PORCH
KITCH 11-6x 8-0 9 FT CLG
MAIN FLOOR

Units	Single
Price Code	A
Total Finished	1,202 sq. ft.
Main Finished	1,202 sq. ft.
Garage Unfinished	482 sq. ft.
Porch Unfinished	147 sq. ft.
Dimensions	51'x43'10"
Foundation	Crawlspace Slab
Bedrooms	3
Full Baths	2
Max Ridge Height	21'6"
Roof Framing	Stick
Exterior Walls	2x4

Design 97341

Units	Single
Price Code	A
Total Finished	1,206 sq. ft.
Main Finished	1,206 sq. ft.
Basement Unfinished	1,206 sq. ft.
Garage Unfinished	455 sq. ft.
Dimensions	56'4"x40'
Foundation	Basement
Bedrooms	3
Full Baths	1
Main Ceiling	9'
Max Ridge Height	21'4"
Roof Framing	Truss
Exterior Walls	2x4

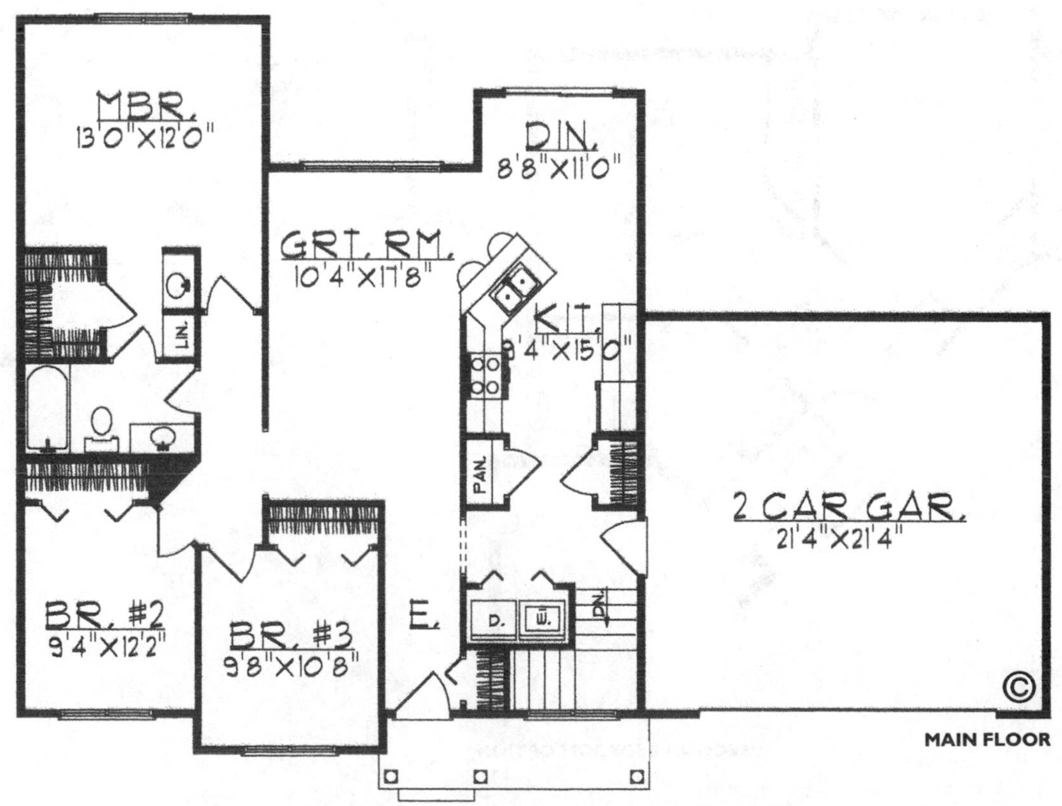

MAIN FLOOR

Design 65084

Units	Single
Price Code	A
Total Finished	1,208 sq. ft.
Main Finished	1,208 sq. ft.
Garage Unfinished	278 sq. ft.
Dimensions	41'x45'
Foundation	Basement
Bedrooms	1
Full Baths	1
Main Ceiling	8'
Max Ridge Height	26'22"
Roof Framing	Truss
Exterior Walls	2x6

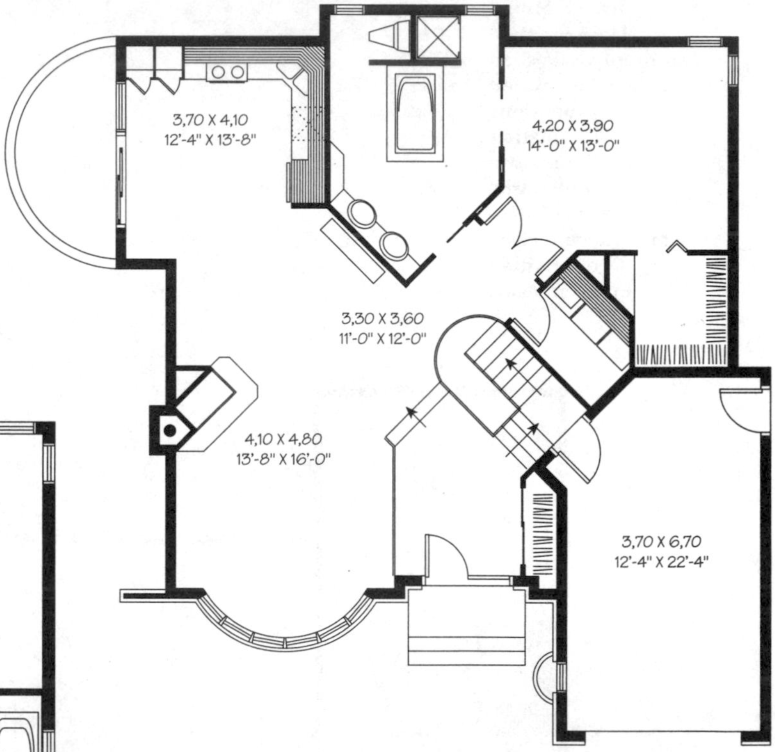

3,70 X 4,10
12'-4" X 13'-8"

4,20 X 3,90
14'-0" X 13'-0"

3,30 X 3,60
11'-0" X 12'-0"

4,10 X 4,80
13'-8" X 16'-0"

3,70 X 6,70
12'-4" X 22'-4"

MAIN FLOOR

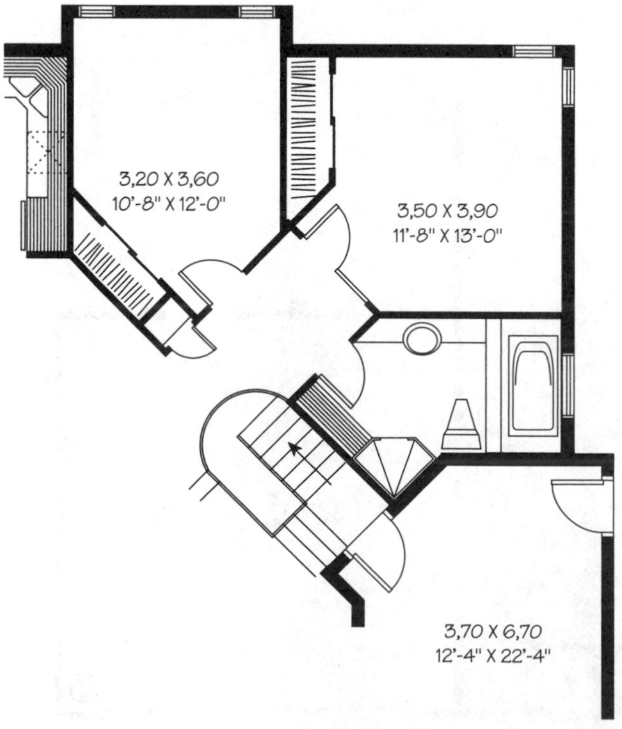

3,20 X 3,60
10'-8" X 12'-0"

3,50 X 3,90
11'-8" X 13'-0"

3,70 X 6,70
12'-4" X 22'-4"

SECOND BEDROOM OPTION

Design 98925

Units	Single
Price Code	A
Total Finished	1,208 sq. ft.
Main Finished	1,208 sq. ft.
Basement Unfinished	760 sq. ft.
Garage Unfinished	448 sq. ft.
Deck Unfinished	100 sq. ft.
Porch Unfinished	40 sq. ft.
Dimensions	50'4"x29'
Foundation	Basement
Bedrooms	3
Full Baths	2
Max Ridge Height	25'
Roof Framing	Truss
Exterior Walls	2x4

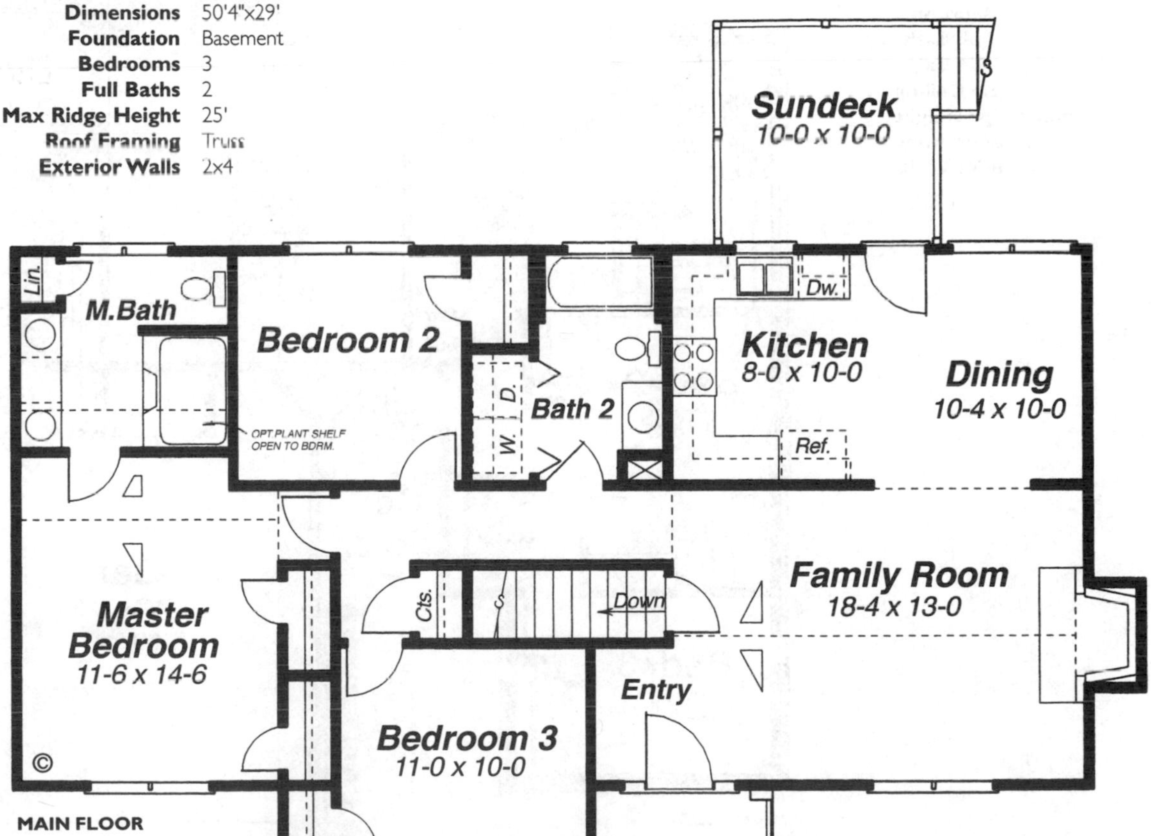

Sundeck
10-0 x 10-0

Lin.
M.Bath
Bedroom 2
OPT PLANT SHELF OPEN TO BDRM.
D.
W.
Bath 2
Dw.
Kitchen
8-0 x 10-0
Ref.
Dining
10-4 x 10-0
Family Room
18-4 x 13-0
Cts.
Down
Master Bedroom
11-6 x 14-6
Entry
Bedroom 3
11-0 x 10-0
©

MAIN FLOOR

Design 97836

Units	Single
Price Code	A
Total Finished	1,225 sq. ft.
Main Finished	1,225 sq. ft.
Garage Unfinished	415 sq. ft.
Porch Unfinished	100 sq. ft.
Dimensions	45'x42'
Foundation	Slab
Bedrooms	3
Full Baths	1
3/4 Baths	1
Main Ceiling	8'
Max Ridge Height	17'
Roof Framing	Stick
Exterior Walls	2x4

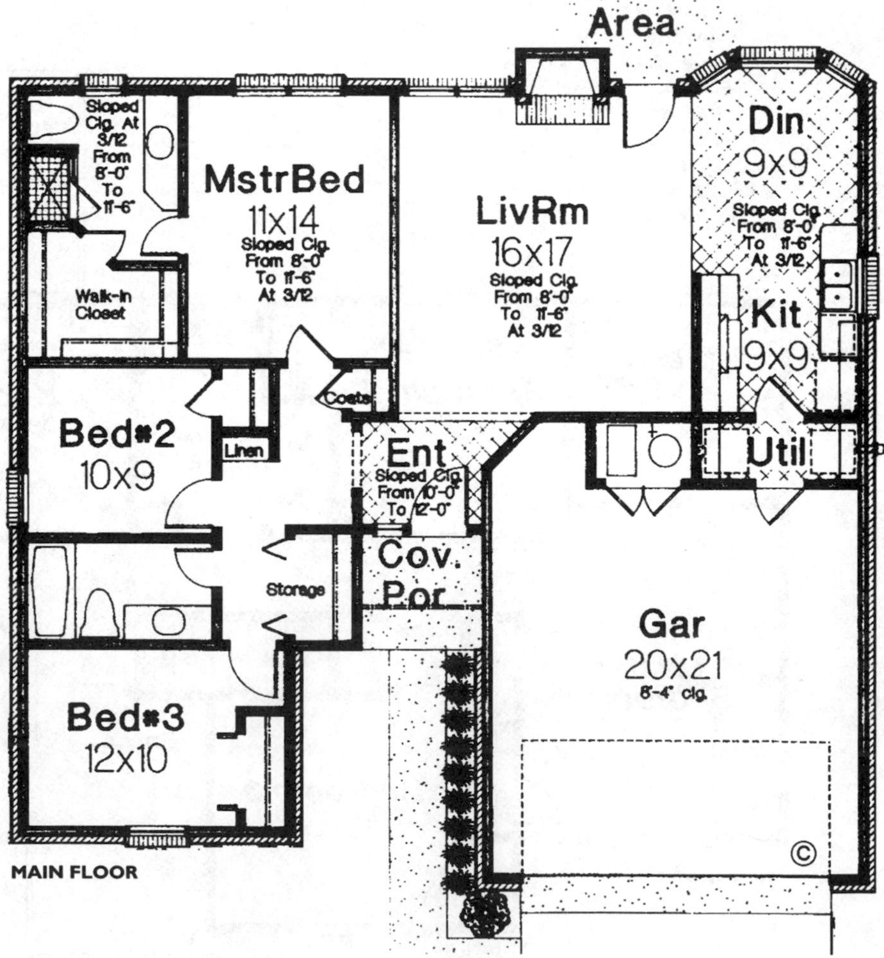

Design 97339

Units	Single
Price Code	A
Total Finished	1,233 sq. ft.
Main Finished	1,233 sq. ft.
Basement Unfinished	1,233 sq. ft.
Garage Unfinished	419 sq. ft.
Dimensions	57'x39'
Foundation	Basement
Bedrooms	3
Full Baths	1
Main Ceiling	9'
Max Ridge Height	23'1"
Roof Framing	Truss
Exterior Walls	2x6

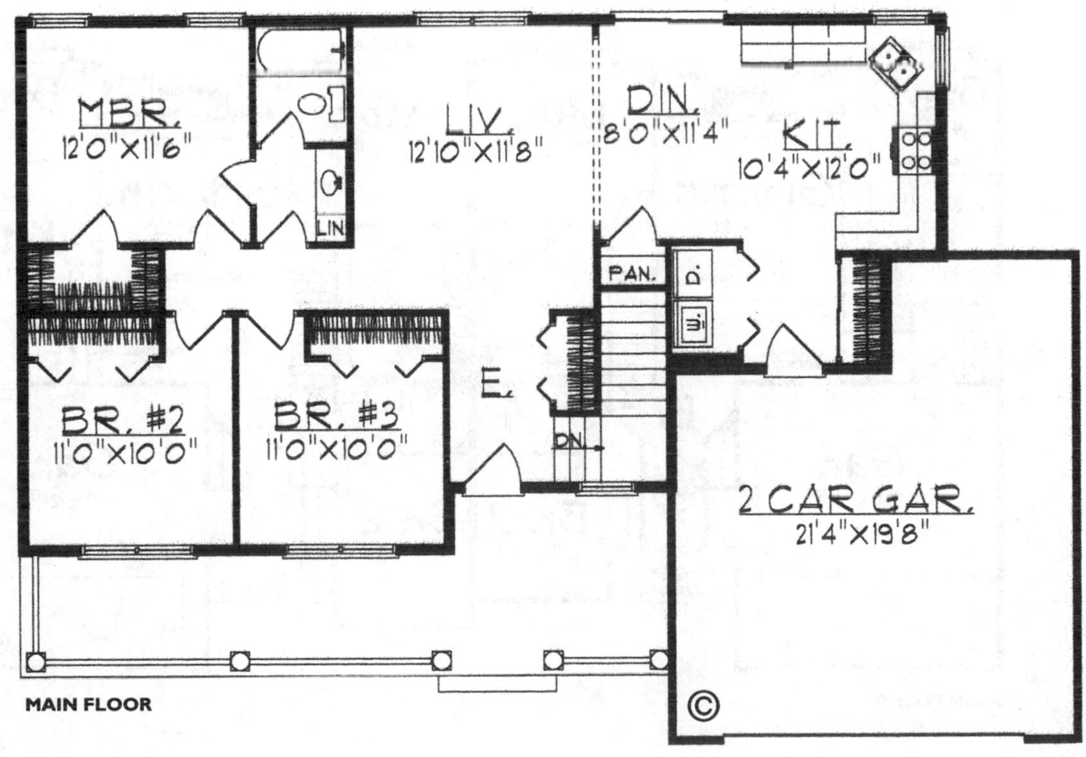

MAIN FLOOR

Design 99428

Units	Duplex
Price Code	G
Total Finished	1,233 sq. ft.
Main Finished	1,233 sq. ft.
Basement Unfinished	1,233 sq. ft.
Garage Unfinished	448 sq. ft.
Dimensions	80'x47'8"
Foundation	Basement
Bedrooms	2
Full Baths	1
Max Ridge Height	19'
Roof Framing	Stick
Exterior Walls	2x4

* Alternate foundation options available at an additional charge.
Please call 1-800-235-5700 for more information.

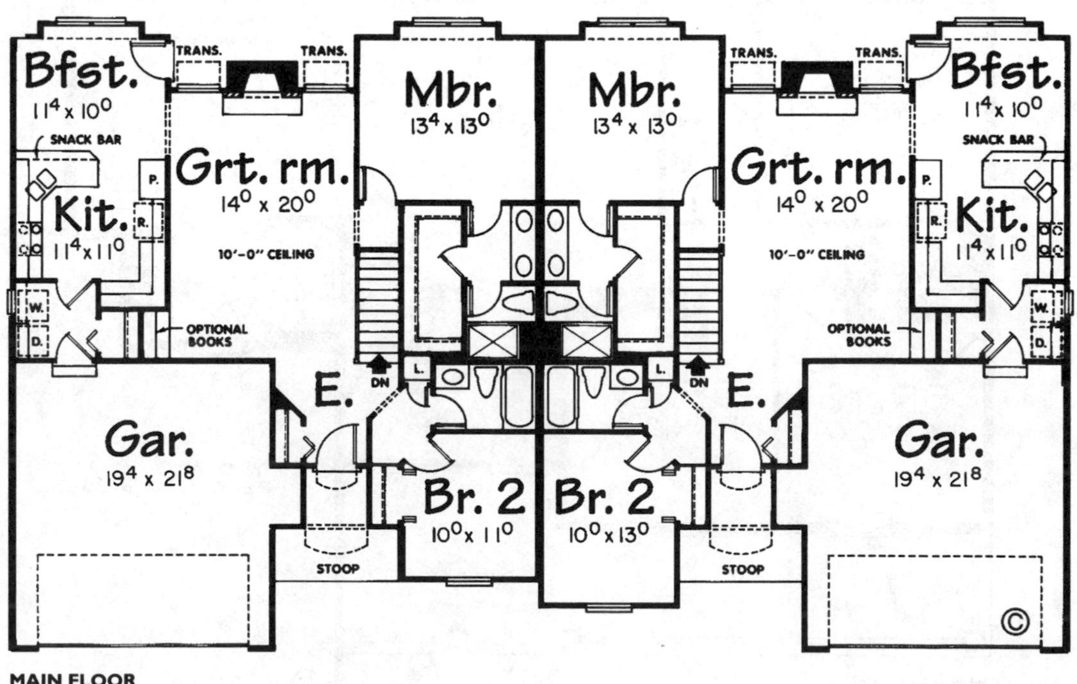

MAIN FLOOR

Design 90682

Units	Single
Price Code	A
Total Finished	1,243 sq. ft.
Main Finished	1,243 sq. ft.
Basement Unfinished	1,103 sq. ft.
Garage Unfinished	490 sq. ft.
Dimensions	66'4"x30'4"
Foundation	Basement Slab
Bedrooms	3
Full Baths	2
Max Ridge Height	16'
Roof Framing	Stick
Exterior Walls	2x4

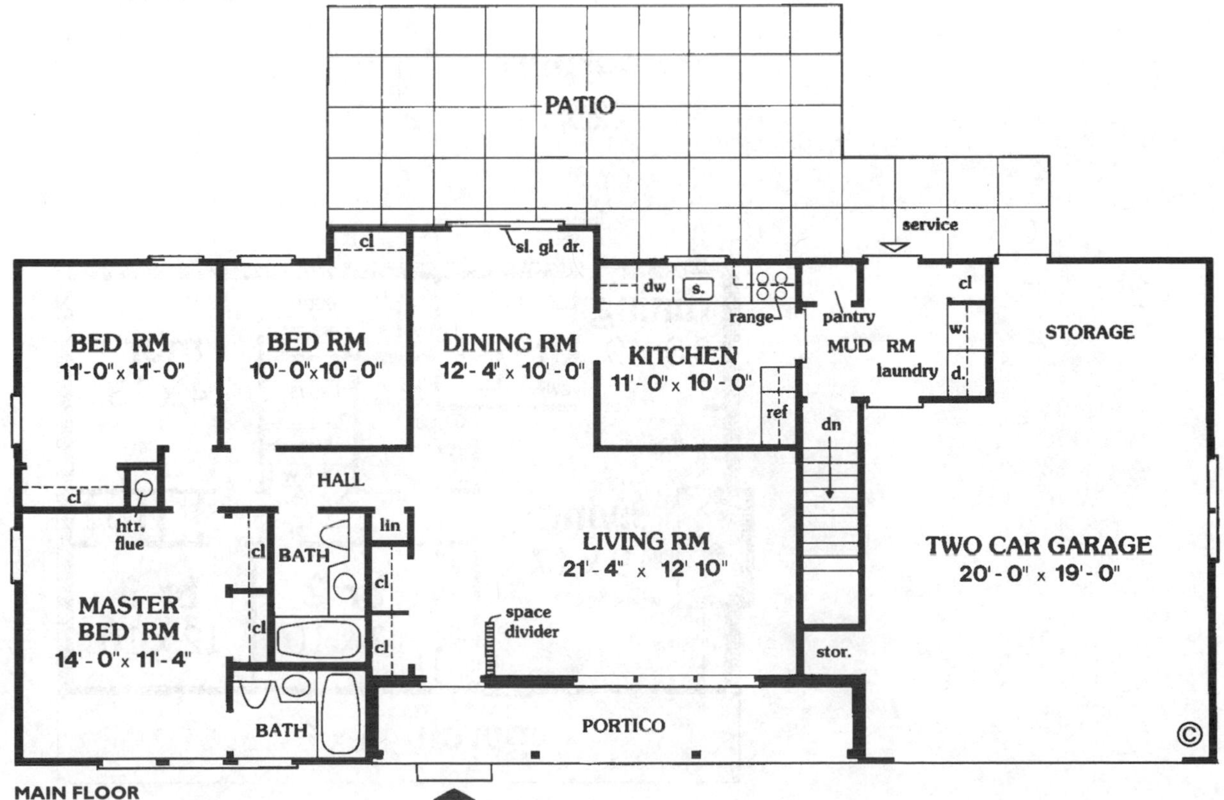

MAIN FLOOR

Design 65638

Units	Single
Price Code	A
Total Finished	1,244 sq. ft.
Main Finished	1,244 sq. ft.
Dimensions	44'x62'
Foundation	Crawlspace Slab
Bedrooms	3
Full Baths	2
Main Ceiling	8'
Max Ridge Height	26'
Roof Framing	Stick
Exterior Walls	2x6

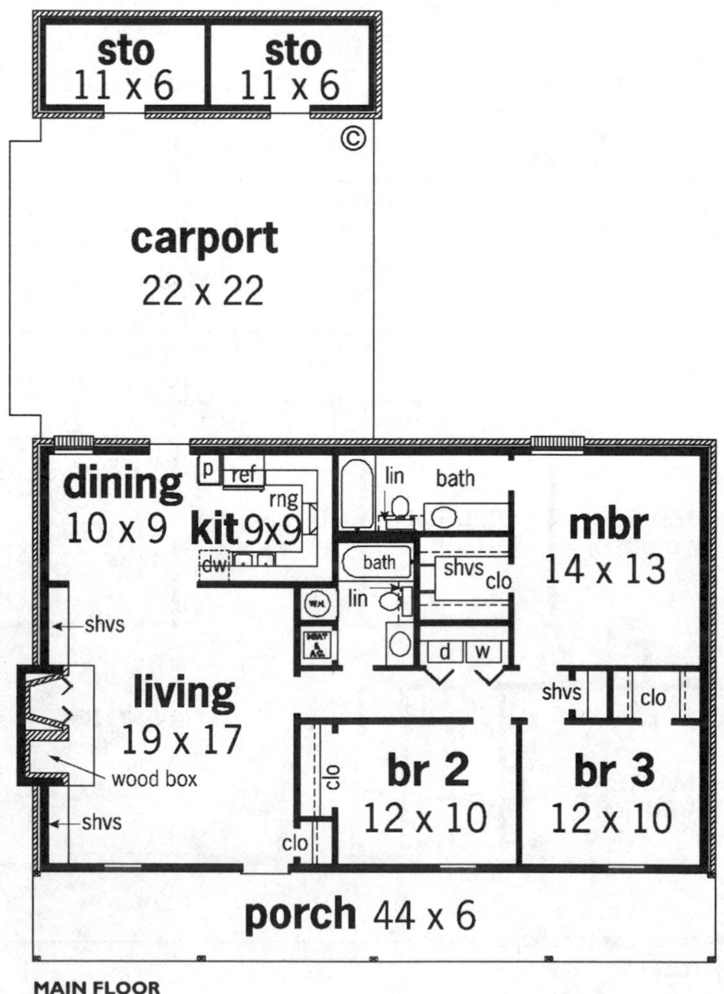

MAIN FLOOR

Design 96511

Units	Single
Price Code	A
Total Finished	1,247 sq. ft.
Main Finished	1,247 sq. ft.
Garage Unfinished	512 sq. ft.
Dimensions	43'x60'
Foundation	Crawlspace Slab
Bedrooms	3
Full Baths	2
Main Ceiling	8'
Max Ridge Height	19'
Roof Framing	Stick
Exterior Walls	2x4

GARAGE 19 × 22
DECK
PORCH
REFG
RNG
KITCHEN 11 × 11
D/W
BAR
DINING 11 × 11
BATH
MASTER SUITE 12 × 14
FAN
BATH
WASH DRY
CLOSET
LIVING RM 15 × 18
F/P
FAN
LIN
A/C
CLOS
BEDRM 11 × 10
CLOS
BEDRM 11 × 12
CLO
PORCH

MAIN FLOOR

Design 91120

Units	Single
Price Code	A
Total Finished	1,249 sq. ft.
Main Finished	1,249 sq. ft.
Porch Unfinished	23 sq. ft.
Dimensions	29'x54'10"
Foundation	Slab
Bedrooms	2
Full Baths	2
Max Ridge Height	19'3"
Roof Framing	Truss
Exterior Walls	2x4

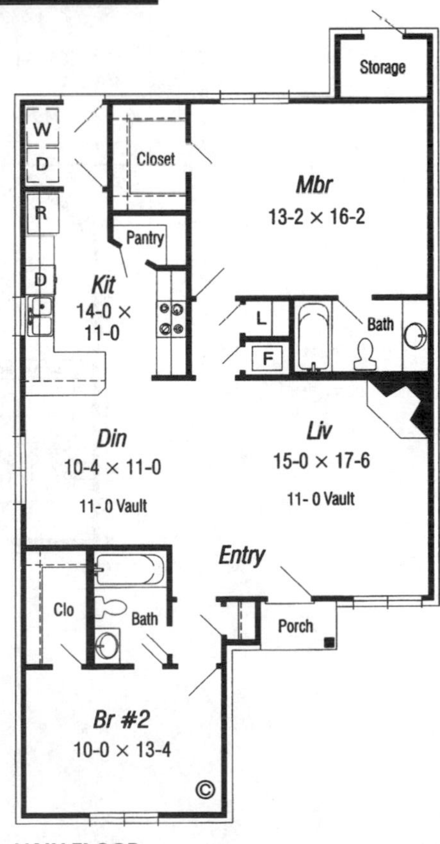

MAIN FLOOR

Design 93023

Units	Single
Price Code	A
Total Finished	1,249 sq. ft.
Main Finished	1,249 sq. ft.
Porch Unfinished	263 sq. ft.
Dimensions	38'6"x46'
Foundation	Crawlspace Slab
Bedrooms	3
Full Baths	2
Max Ridge Height	22'
Roof Framing	Stick
Exterior Walls	2x4

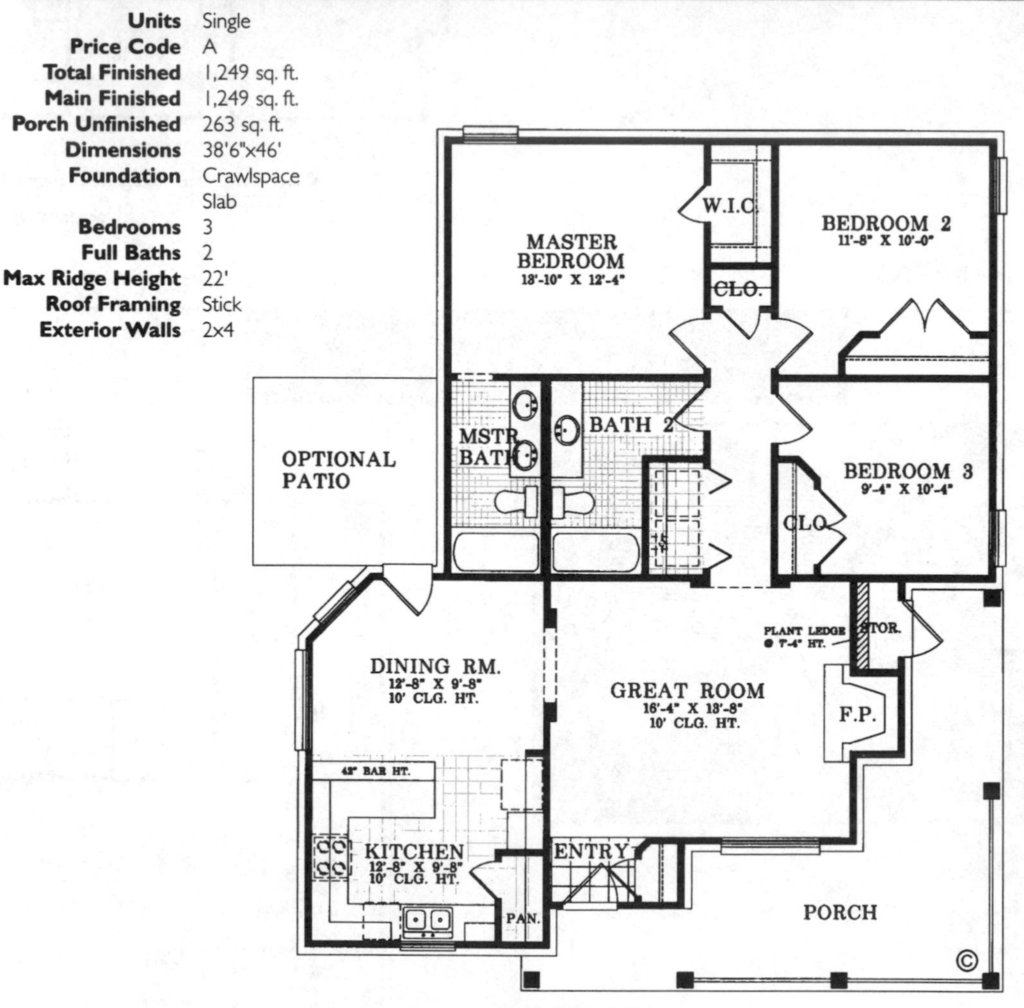

MAIN FLOOR

Design 93449

Units	Single
Price Code	A
Total Finished	1,253 sq. ft.
Main Finished	1,253 sq. ft.
Garage Unfinished	486 sq. ft.
Porch Unfinished	208 sq. ft.
Dimensions	61'3"x40'6"
Foundation	Crawlspace Slab
Bedrooms	3
Full Baths	2
Main Ceiling	8'
Max Ridge Height	19'6"
Roof Framing	Stick
Exterior Walls	2x4

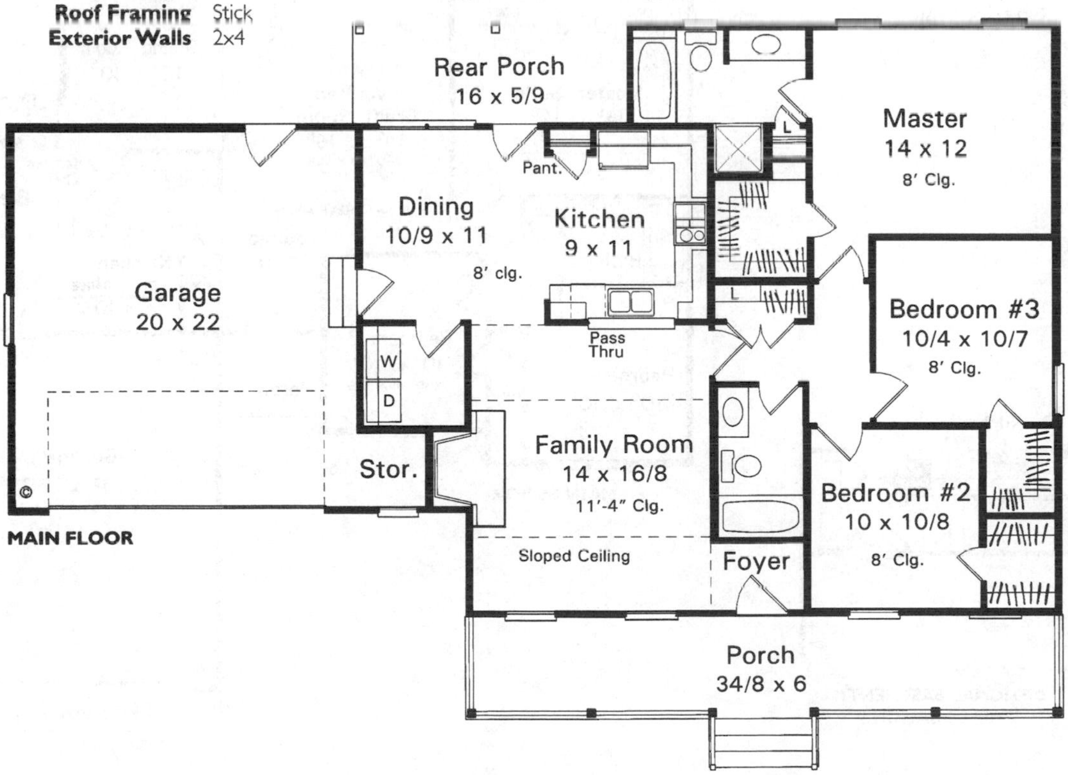

Rear Porch
16 x 5/9

Master
14 x 12
8' Clg.

Dining
10/9 x 11
8' clg.

Pant.

Kitchen
9 x 11

Garage
20 x 22

L

L

Pass Thru

W

D

Bedroom #3
10/4 x 10/7
8' Clg.

Stor.

Family Room
14 x 16/8
11'-4" Clg.

Bedroom #2
10 x 10/8
8' Clg.

Sloped Ceiling

Foyer

MAIN FLOOR

Porch
34/8 x 6

Design 97260

Units	Single
Price Code	A
Total Finished	1,259 sq. ft.
Main Finished	1,259 sq. ft.
Basement Unfinished	1,282 sq. ft.
Garage Unfinished	450 sq. ft.
Dimensions	49'x51'6"
Foundation	Basement Crawlspace
Bedrooms	3
Full Baths	2
Max Ridge Height	21'
Roof Framing	Stick
Exterior Walls	2x4

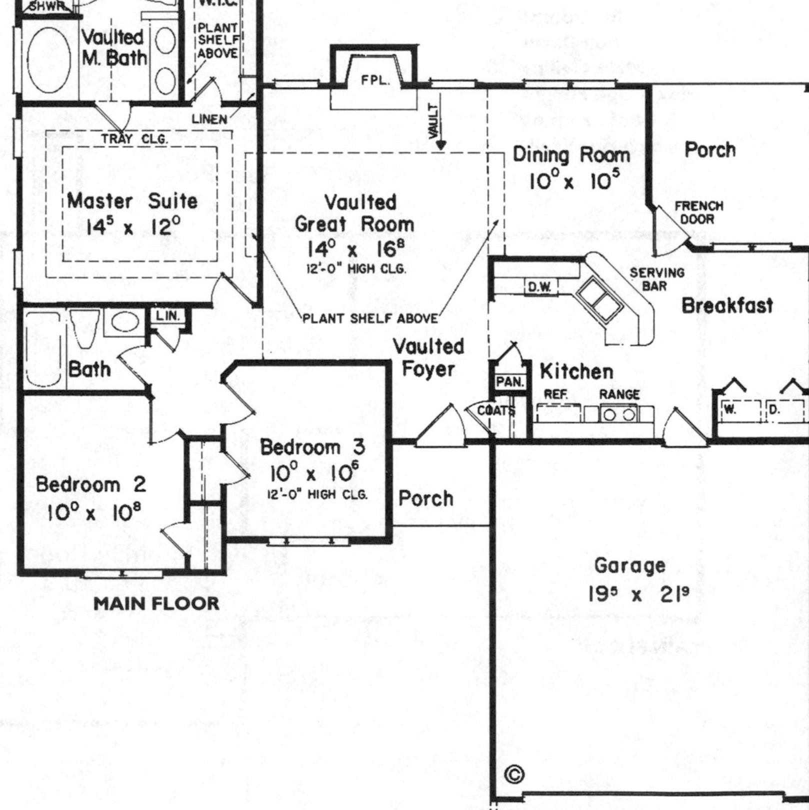

MAIN FLOOR

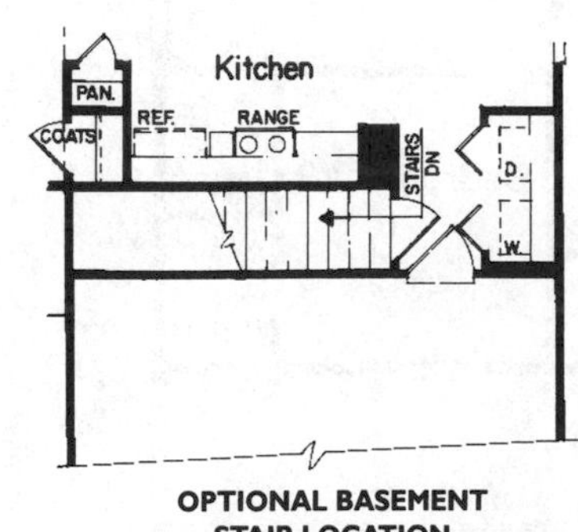

OPTIONAL BASEMENT STAIR LOCATION

 To order blueprints, call **800-235-5700** or visit us on the web, **familyhomeplans.com**

Design 94927

Units	Single
Price Code	A
Total Finished	1,271 sq. ft.
Main Finished	1,271 sq. ft.
Garage Unfinished	433 sq. ft.
Dimensions	50'x46'
Foundation	Basement Slab
Bedrooms	3
Full Baths	1
3/4 Baths	1
Max Ridge Height	16'
Roof Framing	Stick
Exterior Walls	2x4

* Alternate foundation options available at an additional charge. Please call 1-800-235-5700 for more information.

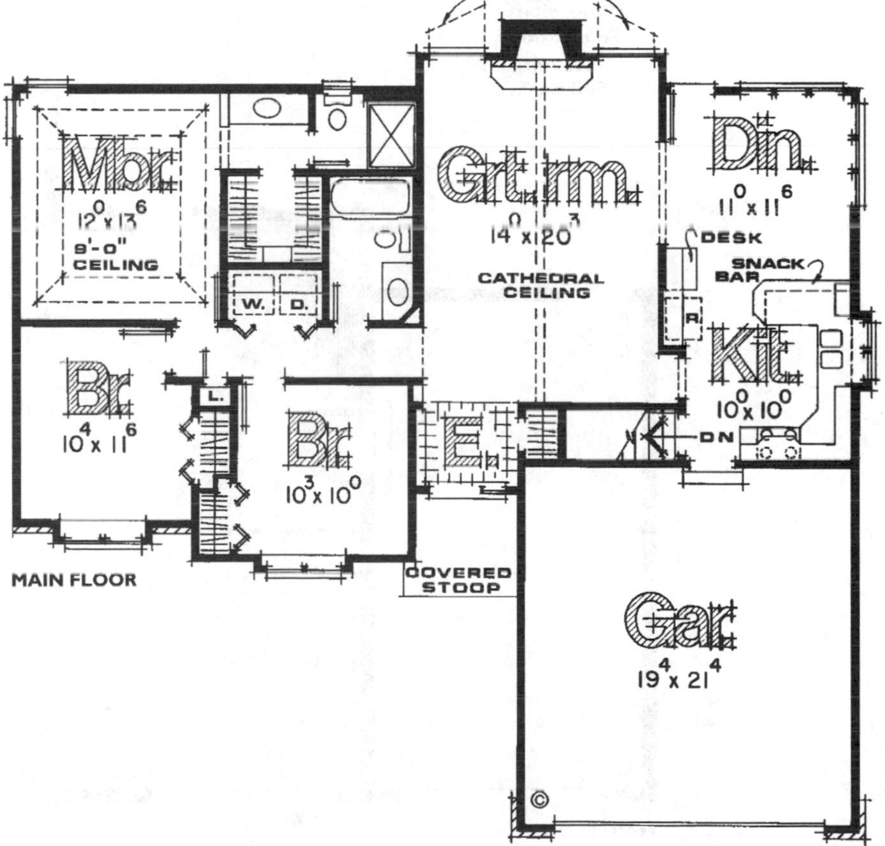

Units	Single
Price Code	A
Total Finished	1,272 sq. ft.
Main Finished	1,272 sq. ft.
Garage Unfinished	274 sq. ft.
Dimensions	42'x42'
Foundation	Basement
Bedrooms	3
Full Baths	1

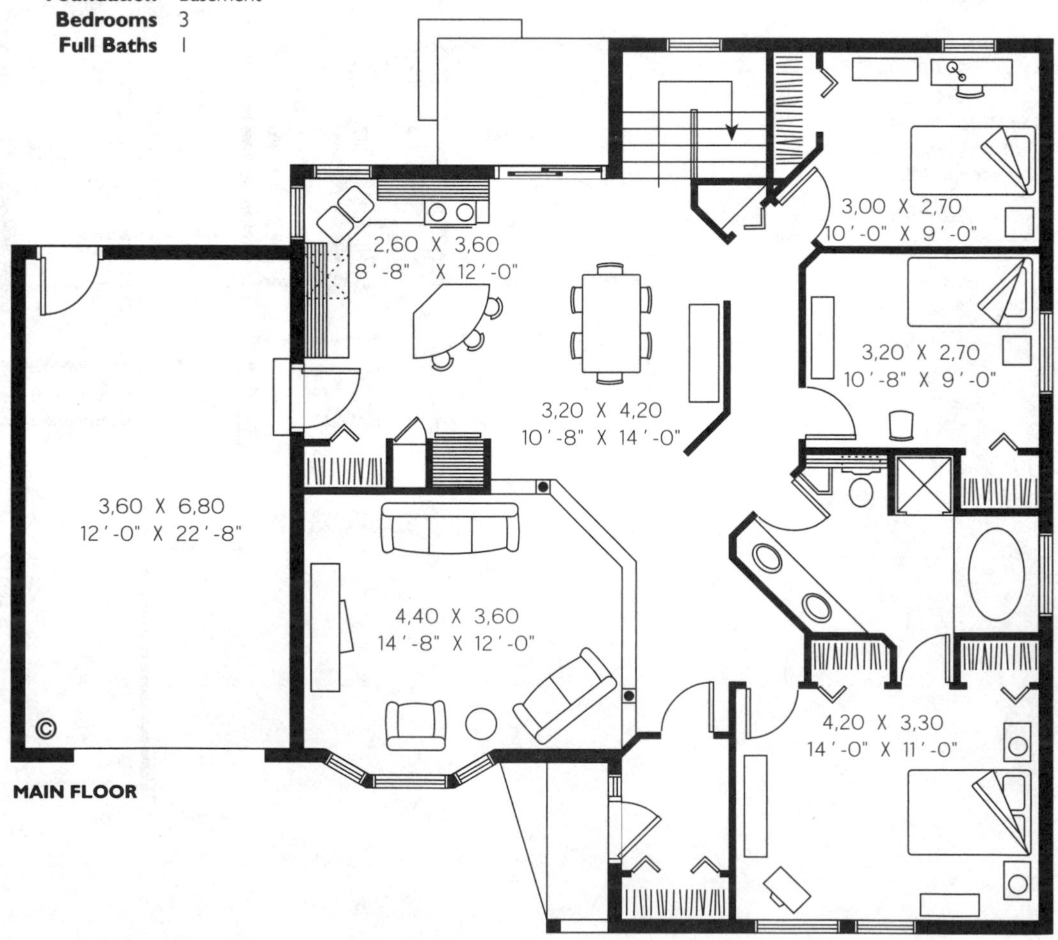

Design 97337

Units	Single
Price Code	A
Total Finished	1,274 sq. ft.
Main Finished	1,274 sq. ft.
Basement Unfinished	1,274 sq. ft.
Garage Unfinished	380 sq. ft.
Dimensions	51'x46'
Foundation	Basement
Bedrooms	3
Full Baths	2
Main Ceiling	9'
Second Ceiling	8'
Max Ridge Height	20'2"
Roof Framing	Truss
Exterior Walls	2x6

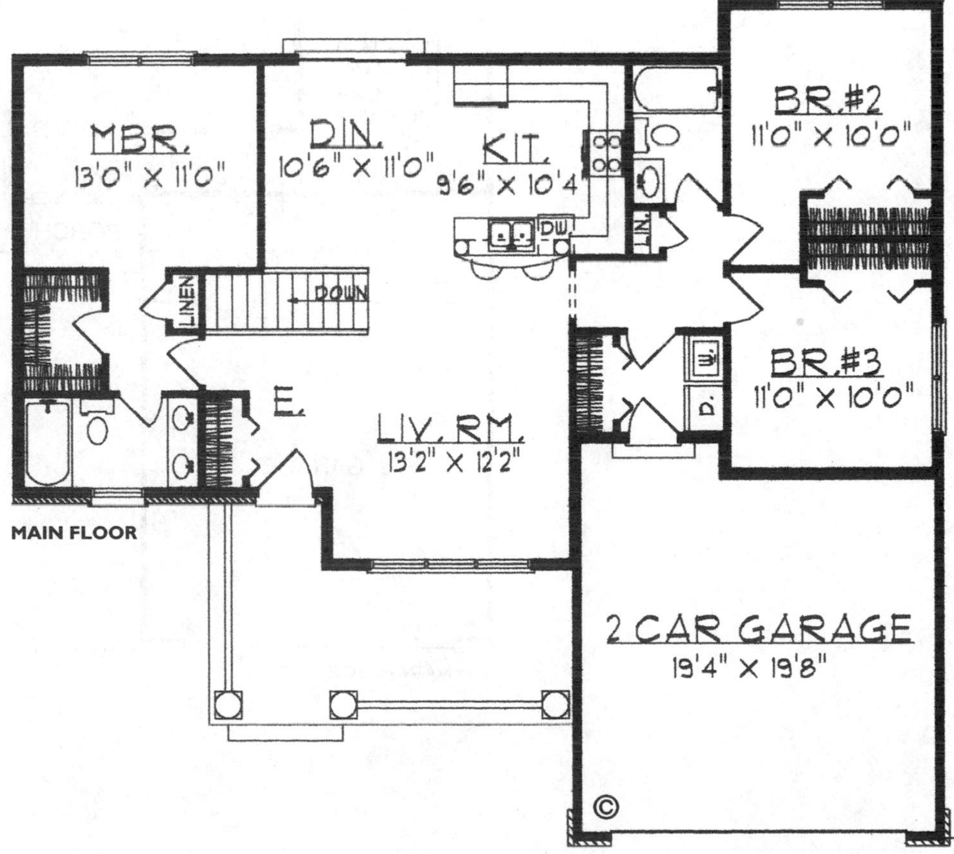

MAIN FLOOR

Units	Single
Price Code	A
Total Finished	1,282 sq. ft.
Main Finished	1,282 sq. ft.
Garage Unfinished	501 sq. ft.
Dimensions	48'10"x52'6"
Foundation	Crawlspace Slab
Bedrooms	3
Full Baths	2
Max Ridge Height	20'
Roof Framing	Stick
Exterior Walls	2x4

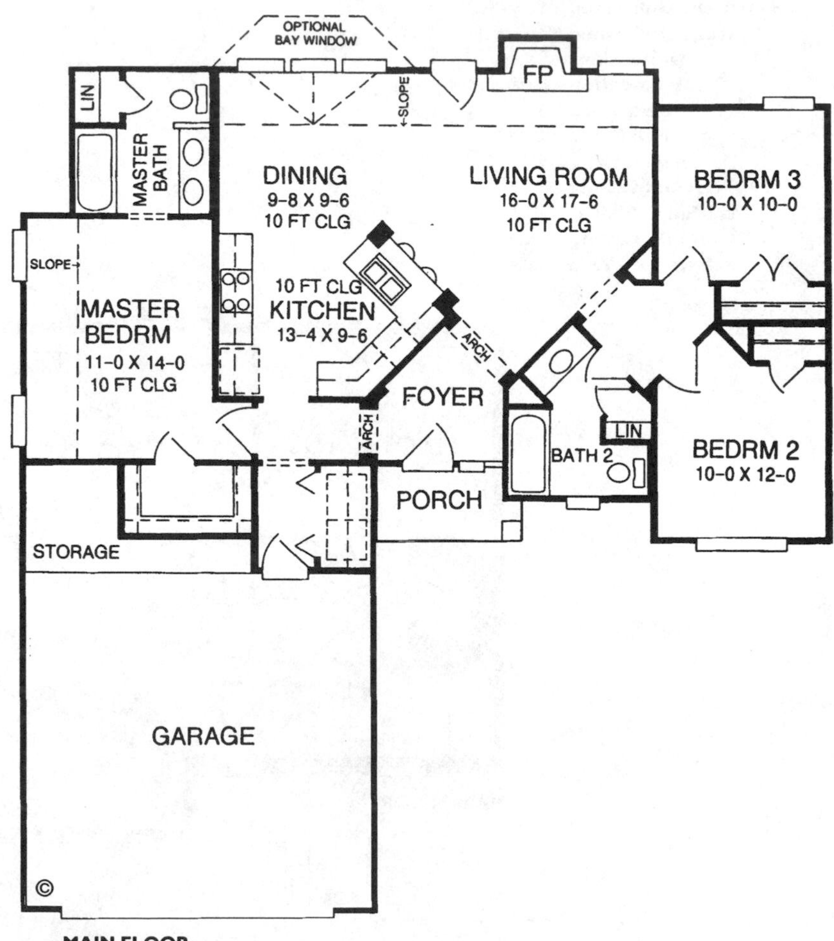

MAIN FLOOR

Design 10643

Units	Single
Price Code	A
Total Finished	1,285 sq. ft.
Main Finished	1,285 sq. ft.
Garage Unfinished	473 sq. ft.
Dimensions	62'x40'
Foundation	Crawlspace
Bedrooms	3
Full Baths	1
3/4 Baths	1
Max Ridge Height	26'
Roof Framing	Stick
Exterior Walls	2x6

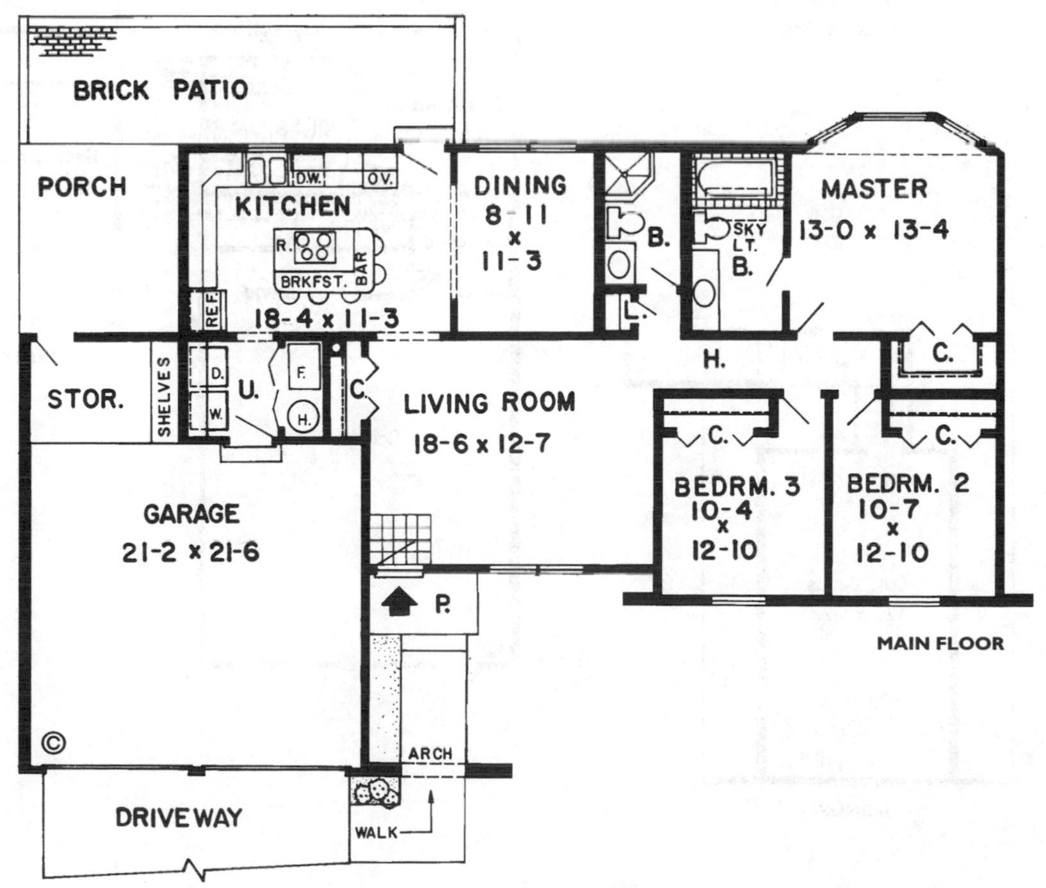

MAIN FLOOR

Design 97614

Units	Single
Price Code	A
Total Finished	1,287 sq. ft.
Main Finished	1,287 sq. ft.
Bonus Unfinished	312 sq. ft.
Basement Unfinished	1,287 sq. ft.
Garage Unfinished	516 sq. ft.
Dimensions	50'x55'10"
Foundation	Basement Crawlspace
Bedrooms	3
Full Baths	2
Max Ridge Height	24'
Roof Framing	Stick
Exterior Walls	2x4

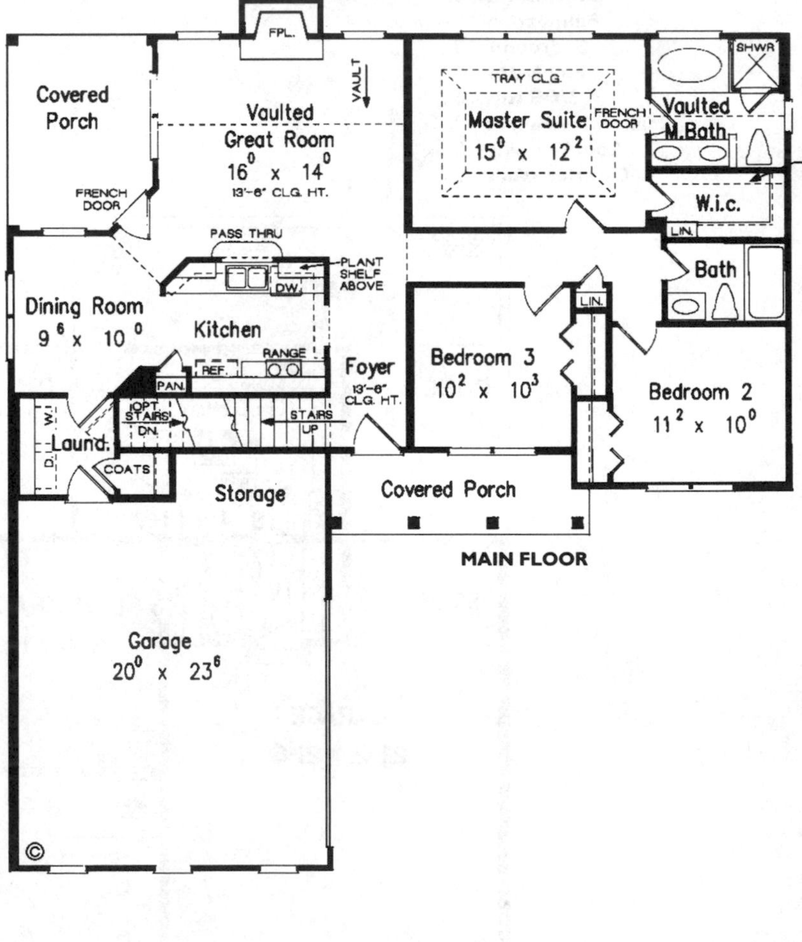

MAIN FLOOR

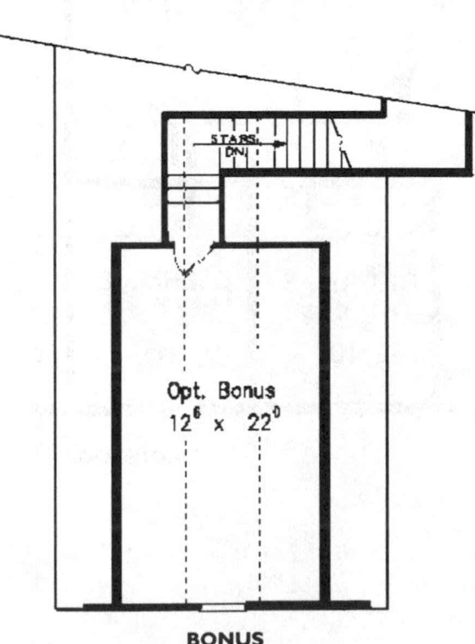

BONUS

Design 97334

Units	Single
Price Code	A
Total Finished	1,295 sq. ft.
Main Finished	1,295 sq. ft.
Basement Unfinished	1,295 sq. ft.
Garage Unfinished	386 sq. ft.
Dimensions	46'x47'4"
Foundation	Basement
Bedrooms	3
Full Baths	1
3/4 Baths	1
Main Ceiling	9'
Max Ridge Height	19'11"
Roof Framing	Truss
Exterior Walls	2x4

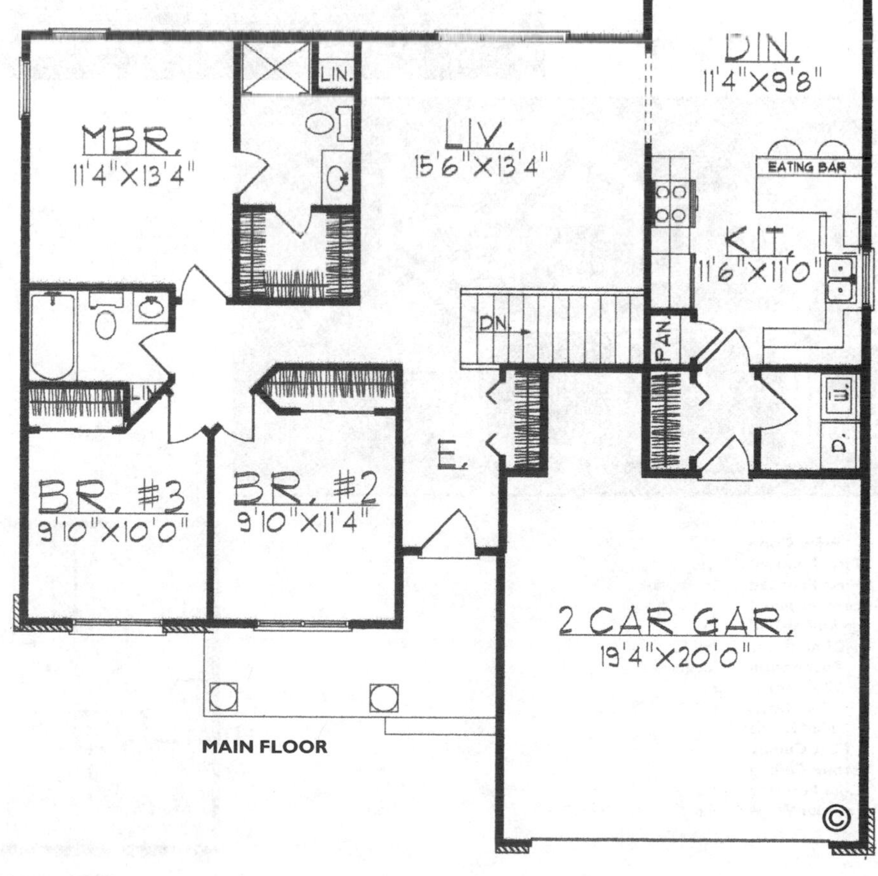

MAIN FLOOR

Design 97476

3 SEASON PORCH
Kit. 9^0 x 9^2
Din. 11^7 x 12^2
Gar. 20^4 x 23^4
Liv.Rm. 13^0 x 13^0
COVERED PORCH
FIRST FLOOR

Units	Single
Price Code	A
Total Finished	1,297 sq. ft.
First Finished	603 sq. ft.
Second Finished	694 sq. ft.
Bonus Unfinished	354 sq. ft.
Garage Unfinished	478 sq. ft.
Deck Unfinished	160 sq. ft.
Dimensions	42'x43'
Foundation	Basement
Bedrooms	3
Full Baths	2
Half Baths	1
First Ceiling	9'
Max Ridge Height	25'8"
Exterior Walls	2x4

* Alternate foundation options available at an additional charge. Please call 1-800-235-5700 for more information.

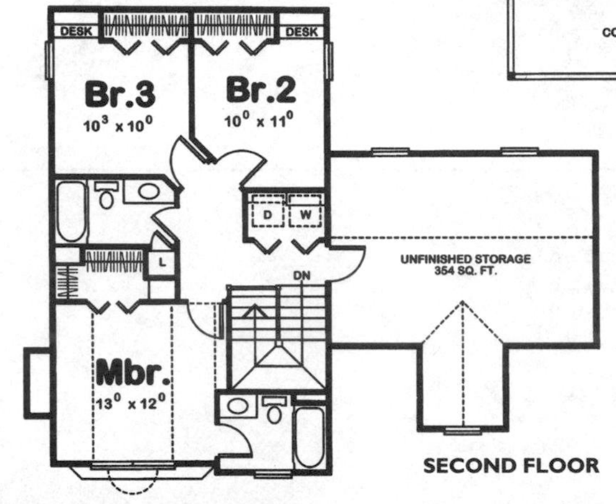

SECOND FLOOR

Design 65134

Units	Single
Price Code	A
Total Finished	1,304 sq. ft.
First Finished	681 sq. ft.
Second Finished	623 sq. ft.
Garage Unfinished	260 sq. ft.
Dimensions	28'x40'
Foundation	Basement
Bedrooms	2
Full Baths	1
Half Baths	1
First Ceiling	8'
Second Ceiling	8'
Roof Framing	Truss
Exterior Walls	2x6

3,30 X 4,70
11'-0" X 15'-8"
3,00 X 3,30
10'-0" X 11'-0"
SECOND FLOOR

3,80 X 4,70
12'-8" X 15'-8"
4,20 X 6,00
14'-0" X 20'-0"
3,60 X 5,70
12'-0" X 19'-0"
FIRST FLOO

Design 63046

Units	Single
Price Code	A
Total Finished	1,309 sq. ft.
Main Finished	1,309 sq. ft.
Garage Unfinished	383 sq. ft.
Dimensions	30'x60'
Foundation	Slab
Bedrooms	3
Full Baths	2
Main Ceiling	8'
Vaulted Ceiling	11'10"
Max Ridge Height	15'11"
Roof Framing	Truss

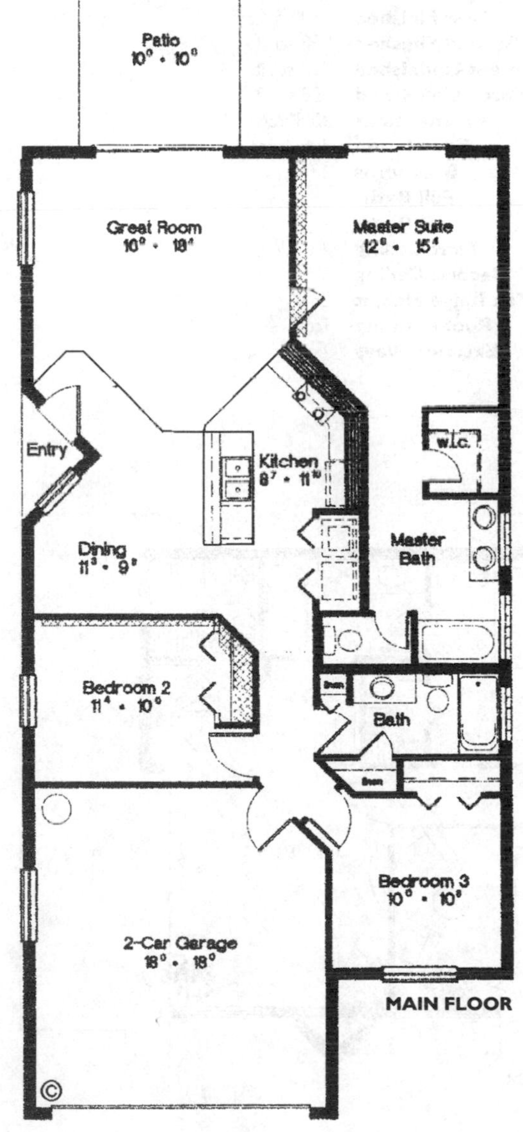

MAIN FLOOR

Design 65173

Units	Single
Price Code	A
Total Finished	1,311 sq. ft.
First Finished	713 sq. ft.
Second Finished	598 sq. ft.
Basement Unfinished	713 sq. ft.
Porch Unfinished	158 sq. ft.
Dimensions	30'8"x26'
Foundation	Basement
Bedrooms	2
Full Baths	1
3/4 Baths	1
First Ceiling	8'
Second Ceiling	8'
Max Ridge Height	28'4"
Roof Framing	Truss
Exterior Walls	2x6

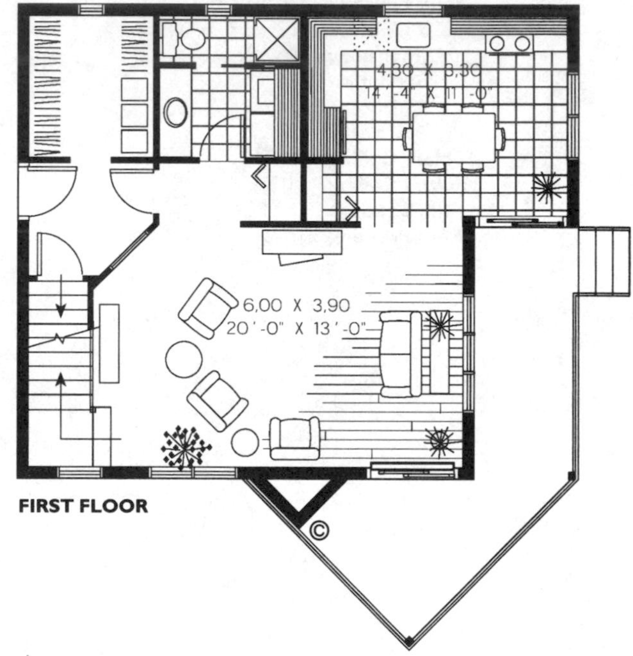

FIRST FLOOR

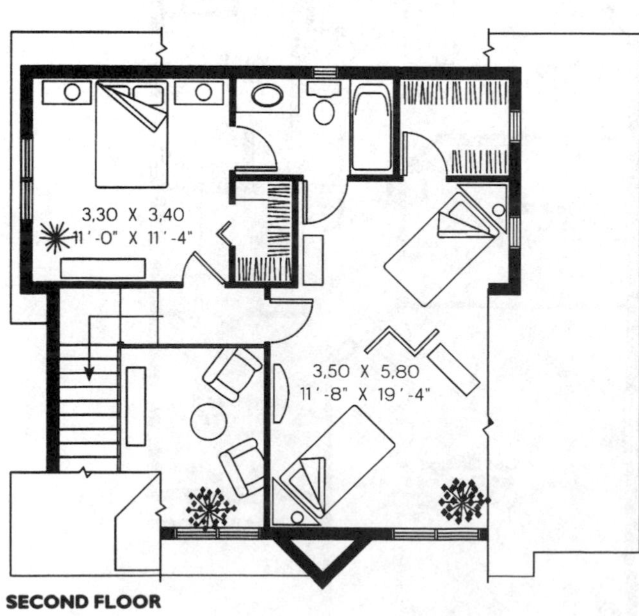

SECOND FLOOR

Design 68096

Units	Single
Price Code	A
Total Finished	1,311 sq. ft.
Main Finished	1,311 sq. ft.
Garage Unfinished	439 sq. ft.
Deck Unfinished	112 sq. ft.
Dimensions	34'8"x58'4"
Foundation	Crawlspace Slab
Bedrooms	3
Full Baths	2
Main Ceiling	9'
Max Ridge Height	22'6"
Exterior Walls	2x4

* Alternate foundation options available at an additional charge. Please call 1-800-235-5700 for more information.

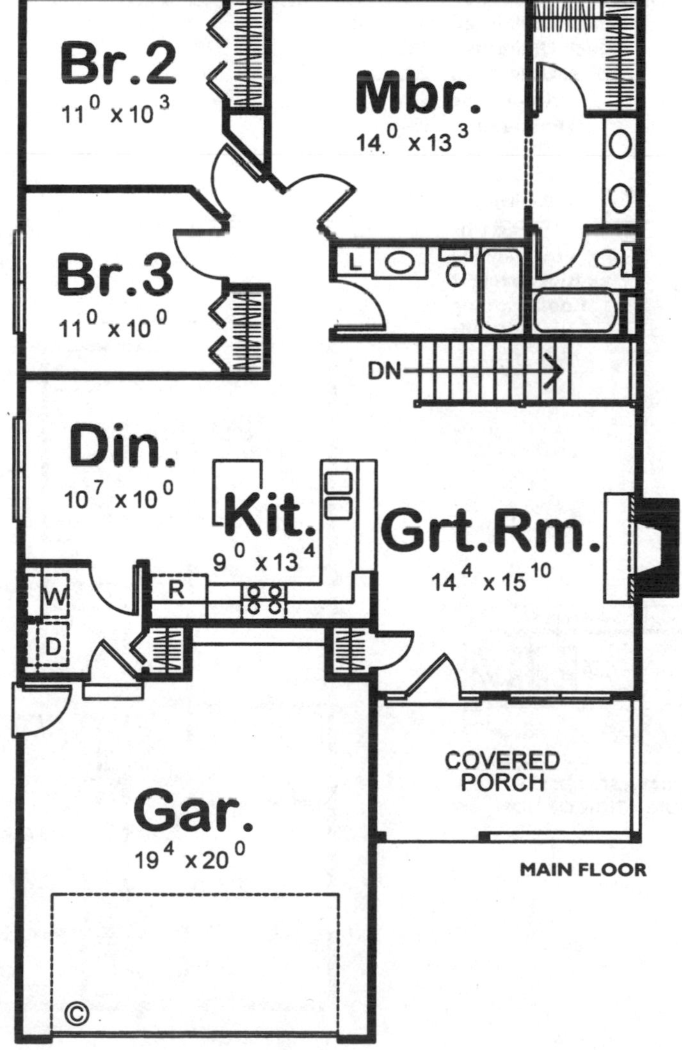

MAIN FLOOR

Design 24700

Units	Single
Price Code	A
Total Finished	1,312 sq. ft.
Main Finished	1,312 sq. ft.
Basement Unfinished	1,293 sq. ft.
Garage Unfinished	459 sq. ft.
Deck Unfinished	185 sq. ft.
Porch Unfinished	84 sq. ft.
Dimensions	50'x40'
Foundation	Basement Crawlspace Slab
Bedrooms	3
Full Baths	2
Main Ceiling	8'
Max Ridge Height	20'
Roof Framing	Stick
Exterior Walls	2x6

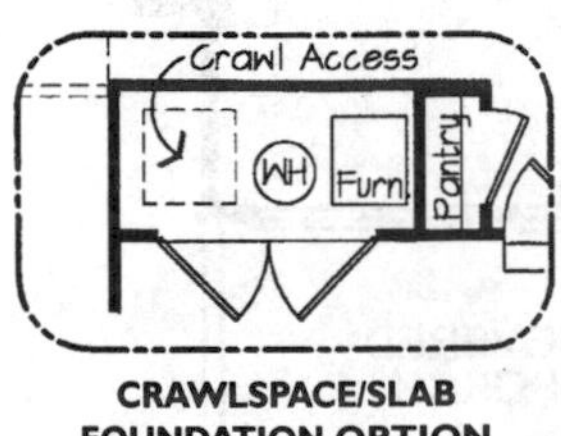

CRAWLSPACE/SLAB FOUNDATION OPTION

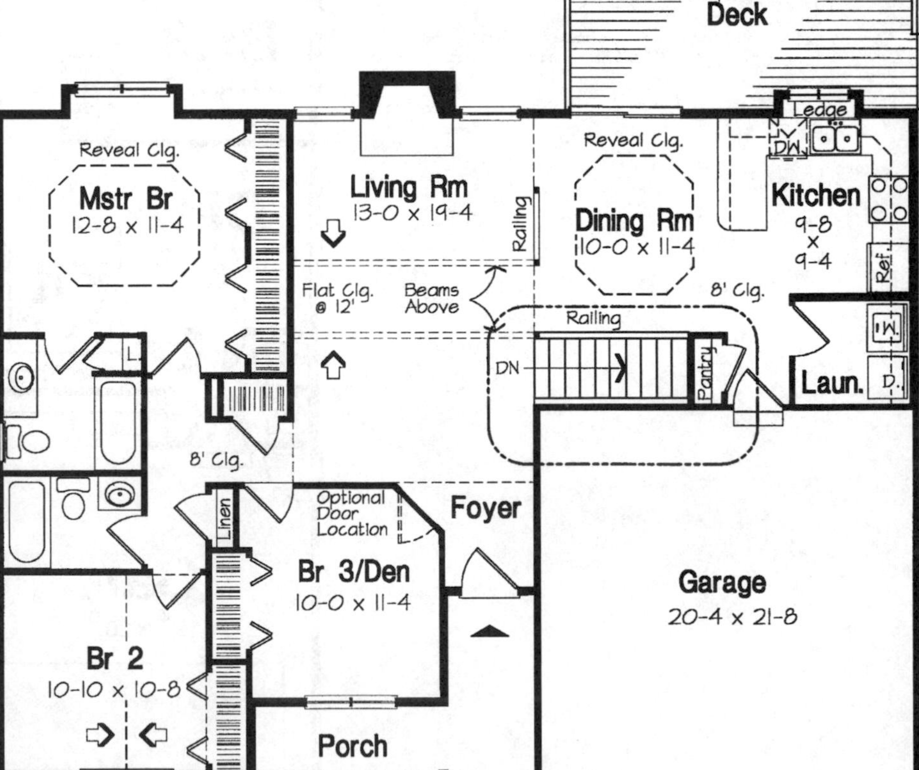

MAIN FLOOR

 To order blueprints, call **800-235-5700** or visit us on the web, **familyhomeplans.com**

Design 97731

Units	Single
Price Code	A
Total Finished	1,315 sq. ft.
Main Finished	1,315 sq. ft.
Basement Unfinished	1,315 sq. ft.
Garage Unfinished	488 sq. ft.
Porch Unfinished	75 sq. ft.
Dimensions	50'x54'8"
Foundation	Basement
Bedrooms	3
Full Baths	2
Main Ceiling	0'
Max Ridge Height	18'
Roof Framing	Truss
Exterior Walls	2x4

Design 82044

Units	Single
Price Code	A
Total Finished	1,317 sq. ft.
Main Finished	1,317 sq. ft.
Garage Unfinished	412 sq. ft.
Porch Unfinished	163 sq. ft.
Dimensions	46'x54'10"
Foundation	Basement Crawlspace Slab
Bedrooms	3
Full Baths	2
Main Ceiling	9'
Roof Framing	Stick
Exterior Walls	2x4

MAIN FLOOR

Design 65284

Units	Single
Price Code	A
Total Finished	1,324 sq. ft.
First Finished	737 sq. ft.
Second Finished	587 sq. ft.
Dimensions	26'x33'
Foundation	Basement
Bedrooms	2
Full Baths	1
Half Baths	1
First Ceiling	8'
Second Ceiling	8'
Max Ridge Height	34'9"
Roof Framing	Truss
Exterior Walls	2x6

2,40 X 2,70
8'-0" X 9'-0"

3,30 X 5,70
11'-0" X 19'-0"

4,20 X 4,80
14'-0" X 16'-0"

FIRST FLOOR

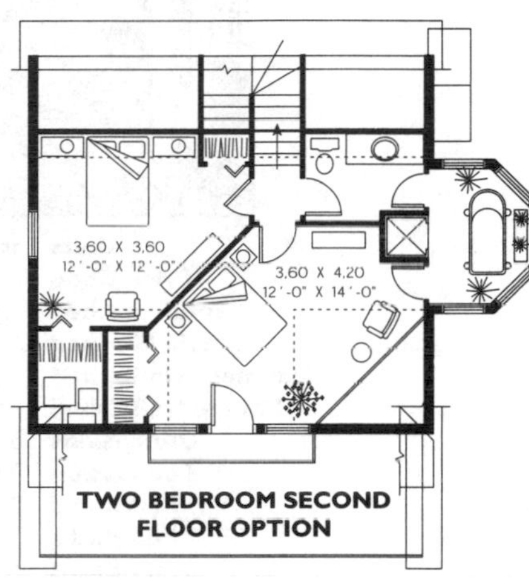

Design 93453

Units	Single
Price Code	A
Total Finished	1,333 sq. ft.
Main Finished	1,333 sq. ft.
Garage Unfinished	520 sq. ft.
Dimensions	55'6"x64'3"
Foundation	Crawlspace Slab
Bedrooms	3
Full Baths	2
Main Ceiling	8'
Max Ridge Height	19'5"
Roof Framing	Stick
Exterior Walls	2x4

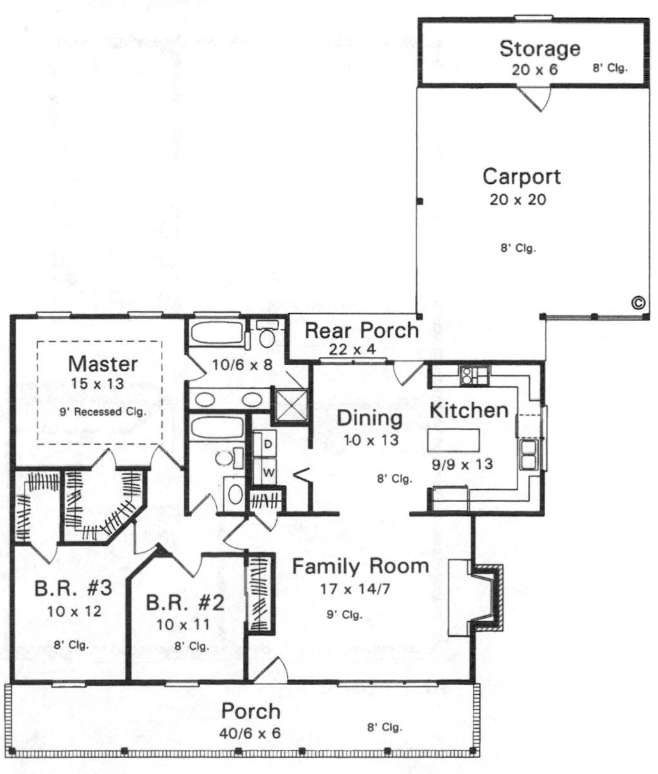

MAIN FLOOR

Design 97332

Units	Single
Price Code	A
Total Finished	1,340 sq. ft.
Main Finished	1,340 sq. ft.
Basement Unfinished	1,340 sq. ft.
Garage Unfinished	419 sq. ft.
Dimensions	51'x40'
Foundation	Basement
Bedrooms	3
Full Baths	1
3/4 Baths	1
Main Ceiling	9'
Max Ridge Height	19'11"
Roof Framing	Truss
Exterior Walls	2x4

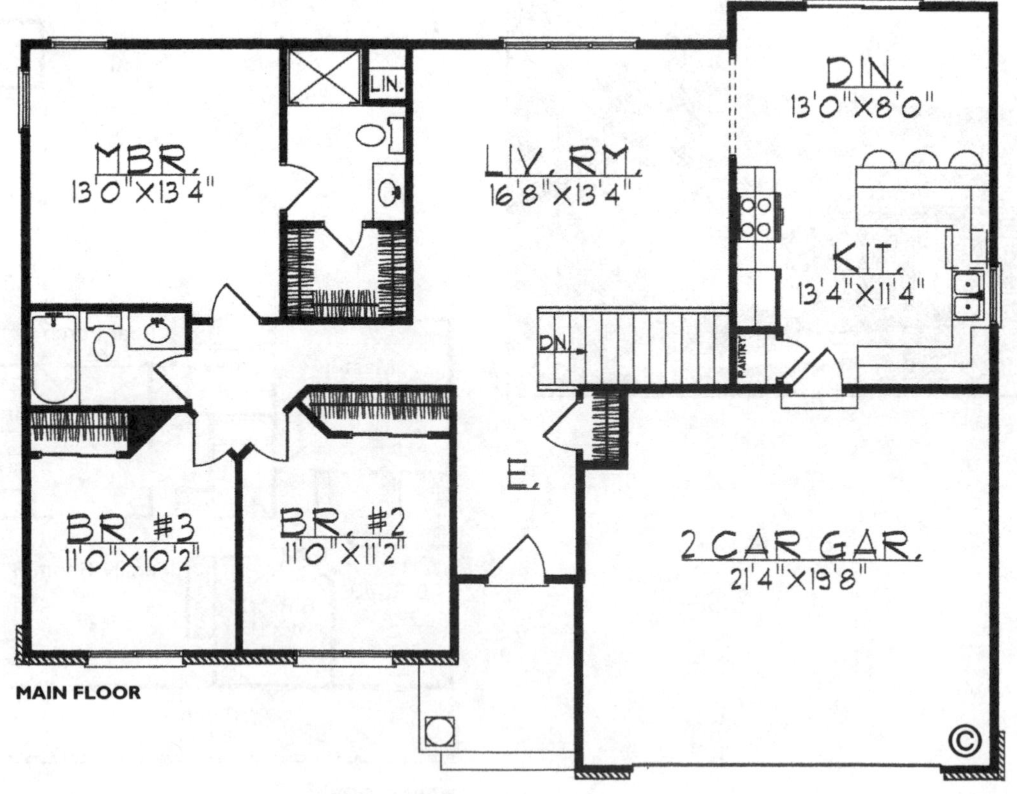

MAIN FLOOR

Design 97331

Units	Single
Price Code	A
Total Finished	1,342 sq. ft.
Main Finished	1,342 sq. ft.
Basement Unfinished	1,342 sq. ft.
Garage Unfinished	416 sq. ft.
Dimensions	57'x45'
Foundation	Basement
Bedrooms	3
Full Baths	2
Main Ceiling	9'
Max Ridge Height	23'5"
Roof Framing	Truss
Exterior Walls	2x6

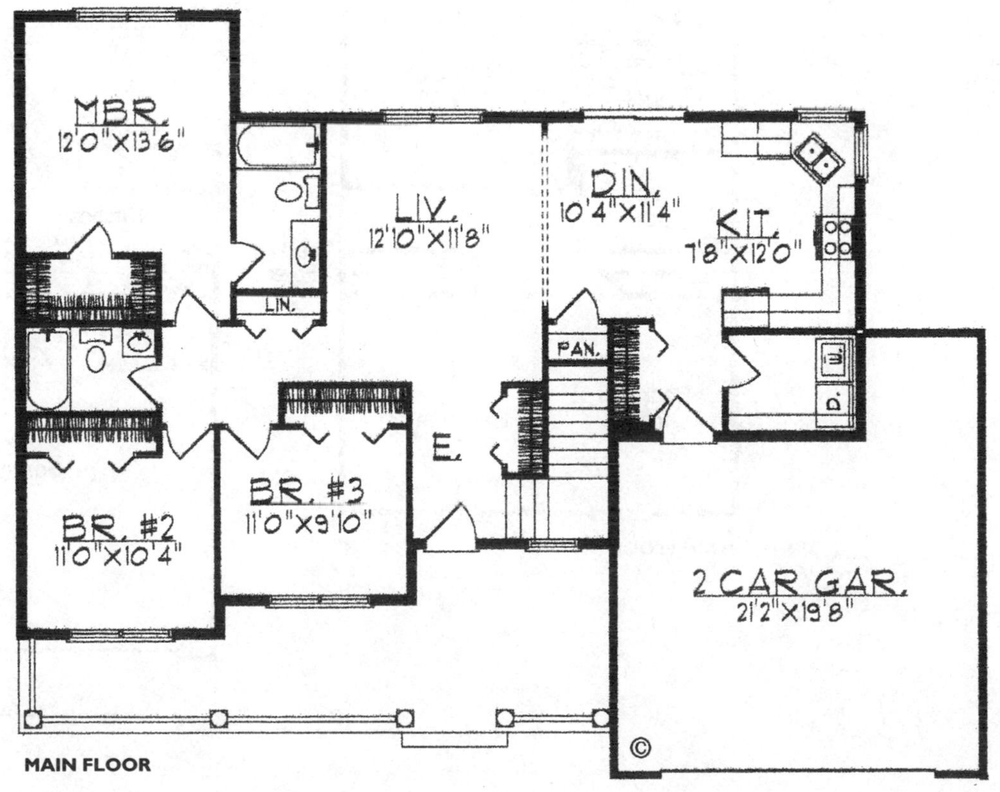

MAIN FLOOR

Design 97202

Units	Single
Price Code	A
Total Finished	1,344 sq. ft.
Main Finished	1,344 sq. ft.
Basement Unfinished	1,363 sq. ft.
Garage Unfinished	409 sq. ft.
Dimensions	48'x44'10"
Foundation	Basement Crawlspace Slab
Bedrooms	3
Full Baths	2
Main Ceiling	9'
Max Ridge Height	22'6"
Roof Framing	Stick
Exterior Walls	2x4

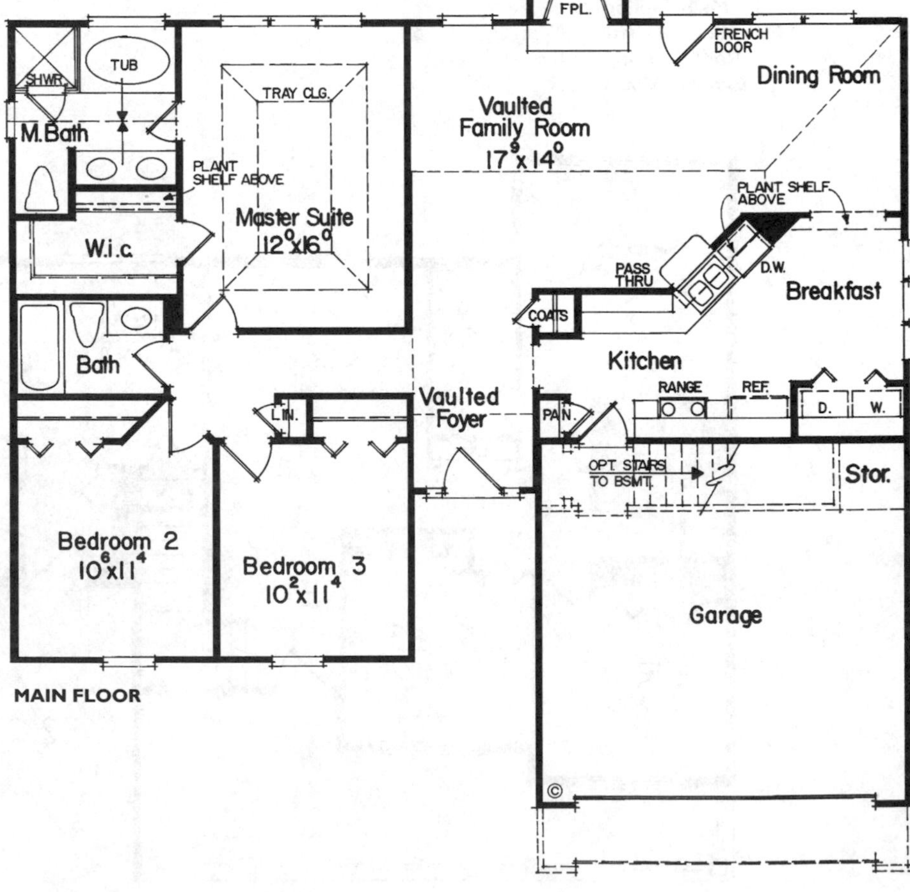

MAIN FLOOR

Design 98912

Units	Single
Price Code	A
Total Finished	1,345 sq. ft.
Main Finished	1,325 sq. ft.
Lower Finished	20 sq. ft.
Basement Unfinished	556 sq. ft.
Garage Unfinished	724 sq. ft.
Deck Unfinished	157 sq. ft.
Porch Unfinished	216 sq. ft.
Dimensions	52'x42'
Foundation	Basement
Bedrooms	3
Full Baths	2
Main Ceiling	8'
Max Ridge Height	19'
Roof Framing	Stick
Exterior Walls	2x4

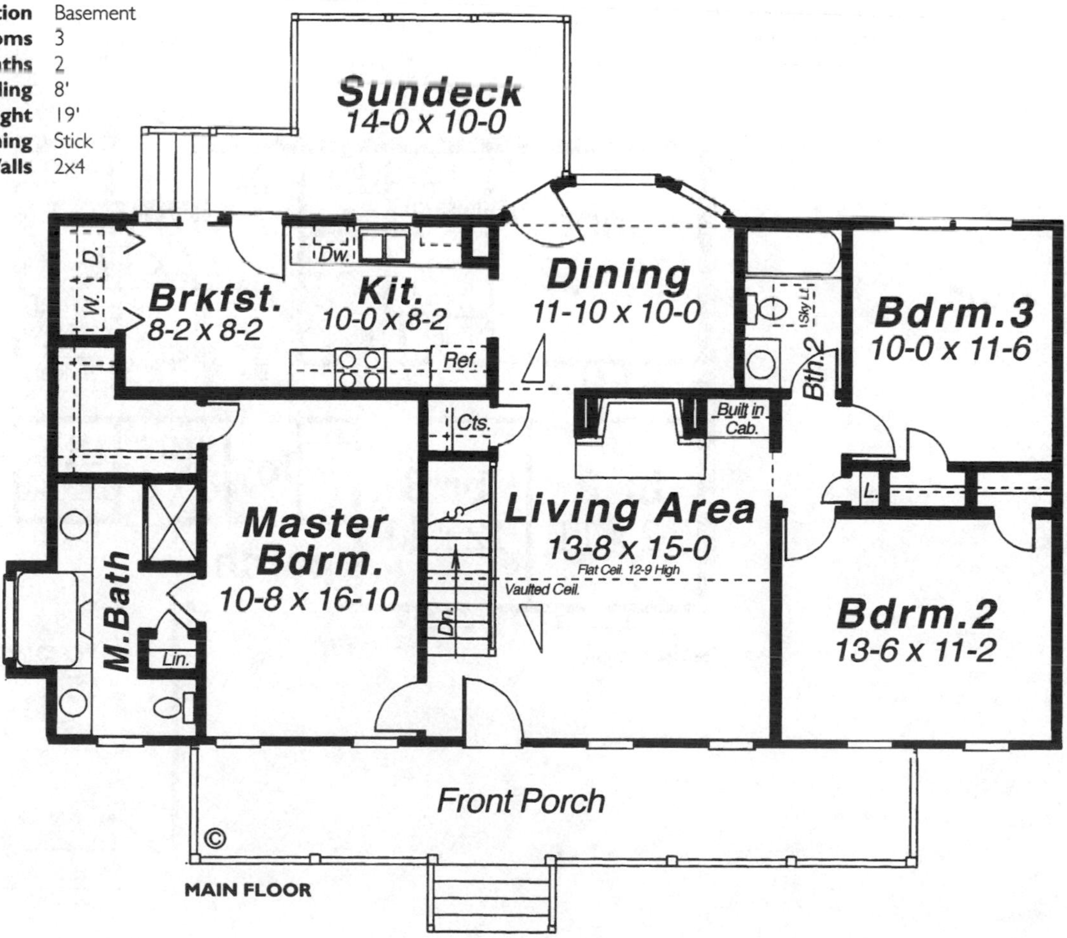

Sundeck
14-0 x 10-0

W. D.
Brkfst.
8-2 x 8-2
Dw.
Kit.
10-0 x 8-2
Ref.
Dining
11-10 x 10-0
Sky Lt.
Bth.2
Bdrm.3
10-0 x 11-6
Cts.
Built in Cab.
L.
Master Bdrm.
10-8 x 16-10
M.Bath
Lin.
Dn.
Living Area
13-8 x 15-0
Flat Ceil. 12-9 High
Vaulted Ceil.
Bdrm.2
13-6 x 11-2
Front Porch
©

MAIN FLOOR

Design 65644

Units	Single
Price Code	A
Total Finished	1,346 sq. ft.
Main Finished	1,346 sq. ft.
Dimensions	54'x44'6"
Foundation	Crawlspace Slab
Bedrooms	3
Full Baths	2
Main Ceiling	8'
Max Ridge Height	25'
Roof Framing	Stick
Exterior Walls	2x4

patio

mbr
15 x 13

bath
dress rm
clo
bath
clo
lin

living
17^6 x 17
vault
vault
false beams
post
turned wood post divider

dining
12 x 11
floor raised 8"
bar

ov
ct
kit
11^6 x 11
dw
ref

clo
r/a

br 2
12 x 11

br 3
12 x 11

clo
foy
sto
6^9 x 6^6
util
w d

porch

garage
21 x 21

©

MAIN FLOOR

Design 65176

Units	Single
Price Code	A
Total Finished	1,352 sq. ft.
First Finished	676 sq. ft.
Second Finished	676 sq. ft.
Basement Unfinished	676 sq. ft.
Deck Unfinished	32 sq. ft.
Dimensions	26'x26'
Foundation	Basement
Bedrooms	3
Full Baths	1
3/4 Baths	1
First Ceiling	8'
Second Ceiling	8'
Max Ridge Height	28'1"
Roof Framing	Truss
Exterior Walls	2x6

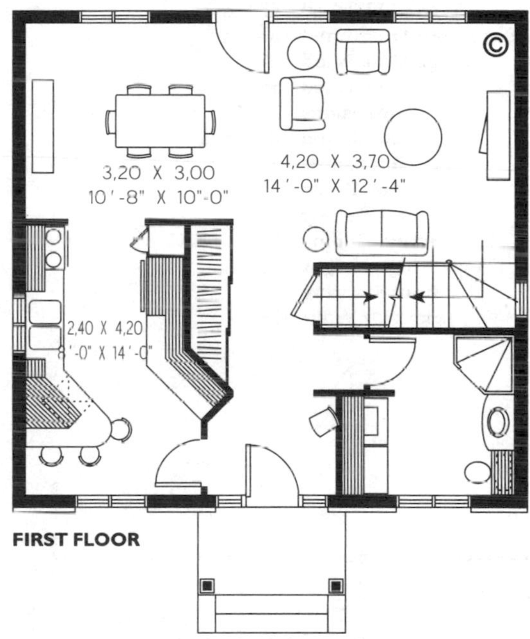

FIRST FLOOR

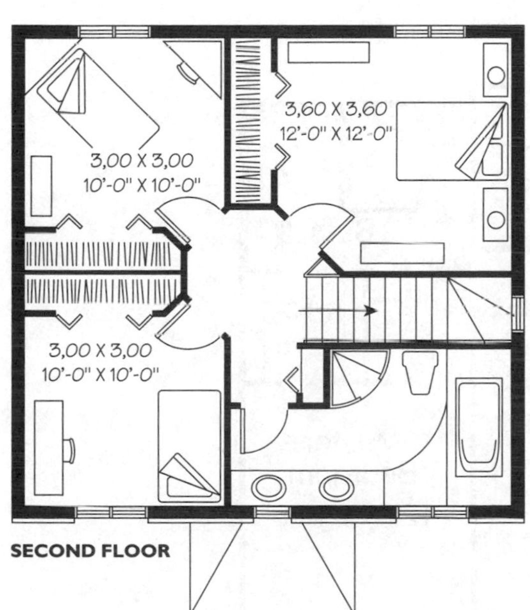

SECOND FLOOR

Design 50035

Units	Single
Price Code	A
Total Finished	1,354 sq. ft.
First Finished	873 sq. ft.
Second Finished	481 sq. ft.
Basement Unfinished	873 sq. ft.
Garage Unfinished	253 sq. ft.
Porch Unfinished	95 sq. ft.
Dimensions	51'6"x31'8"
Foundation	Basement
Bedrooms	3
Full Baths	2
First Ceiling	8'
Second Ceiling	8'
Max Ridge Height	23'
Roof Framing	Stick
Exterior Walls	2x4

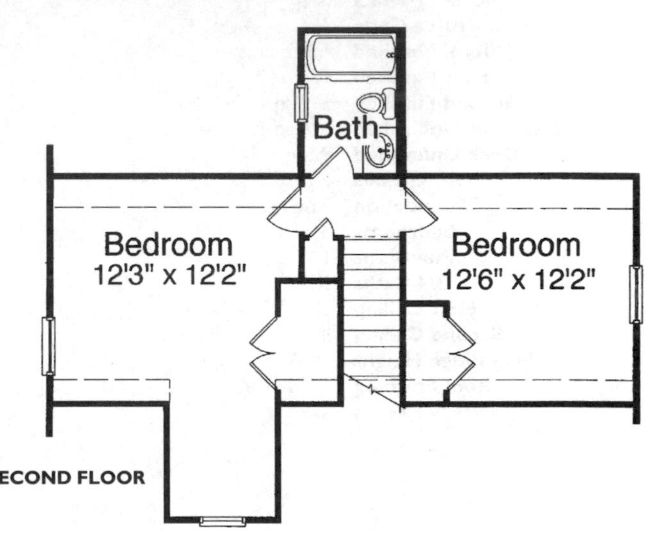

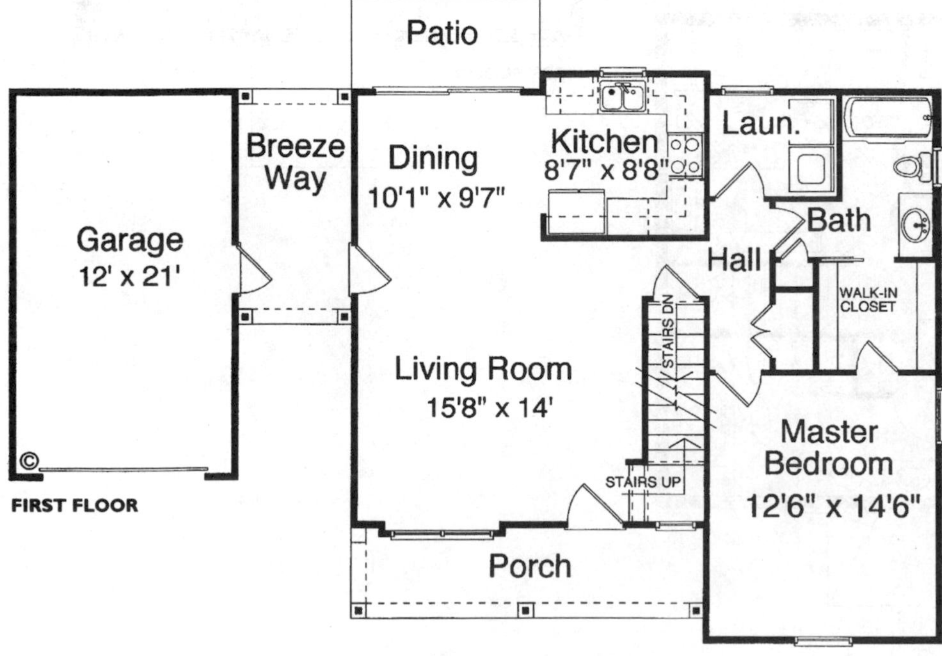

Design 97272

Units	Single
Price Code	A
Total Finished	1,354 sq. ft.
Main Finished	1,354 sq. ft.
Basement Unfinished	1,390 sq. ft.
Garage Unfinished	434 sq. ft.
Dimensions	47'x46'
Foundation	Basement Crawlspace
Bedrooms	3
Full Baths	2
Main Ceiling	9'
Max Ridge Height	24'2"
Roof Framing	Stick
Exterior Walls	2x4

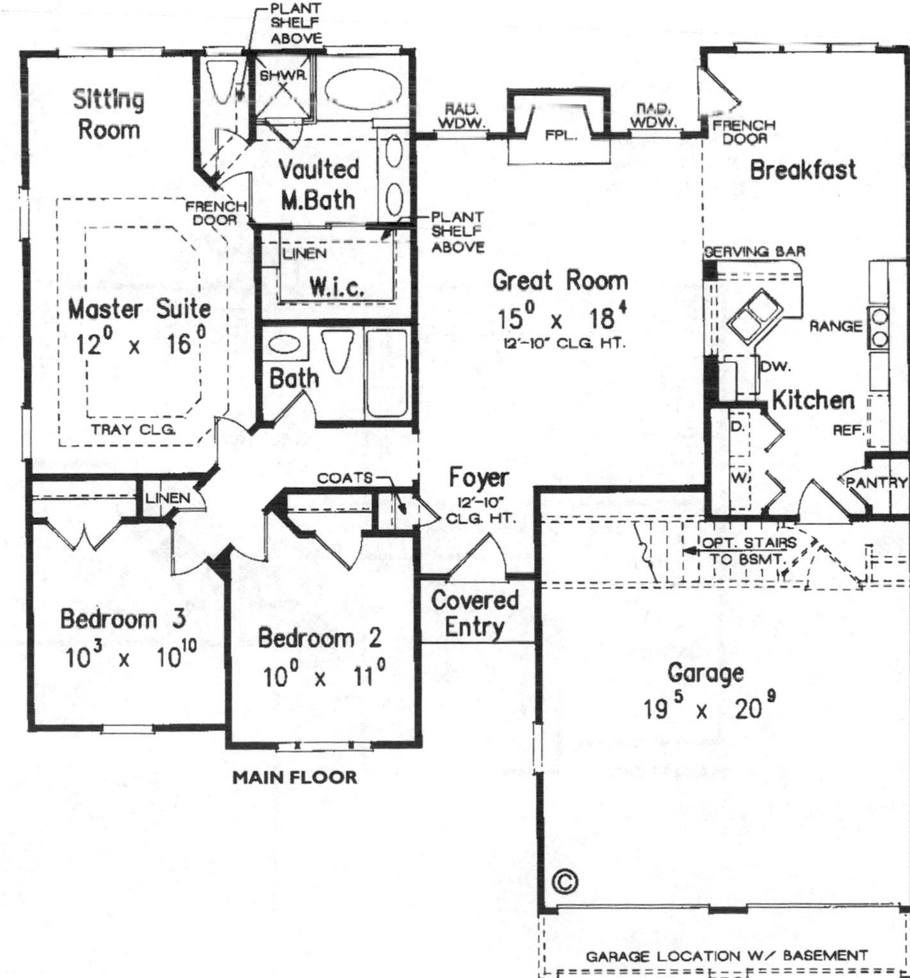

MAIN FLOOR

Design 97678

Units	Single
Price Code	A
Total Finished	1,354 sq. ft.
Main Finished	1,354 sq. ft.
Bonus Unfinished	246 sq. ft.
Basement Unfinished	1,354 sq. ft.
Garage Unfinished	450 sq. ft.
Dimensions	51'x48'4"
Foundation	Basement Crawlspace
Bedrooms	3
Full Baths	2
Main Ceiling	8'
Second Ceiling	8'
Max Ridge Height	22'
Roof Framing	Stick
Exterior Walls	2x4

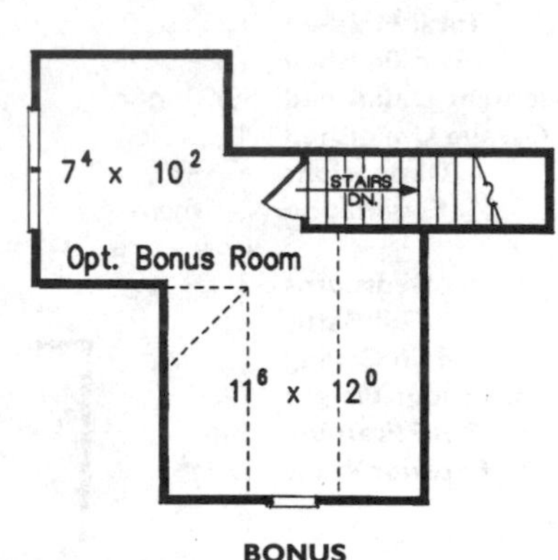

BONUS

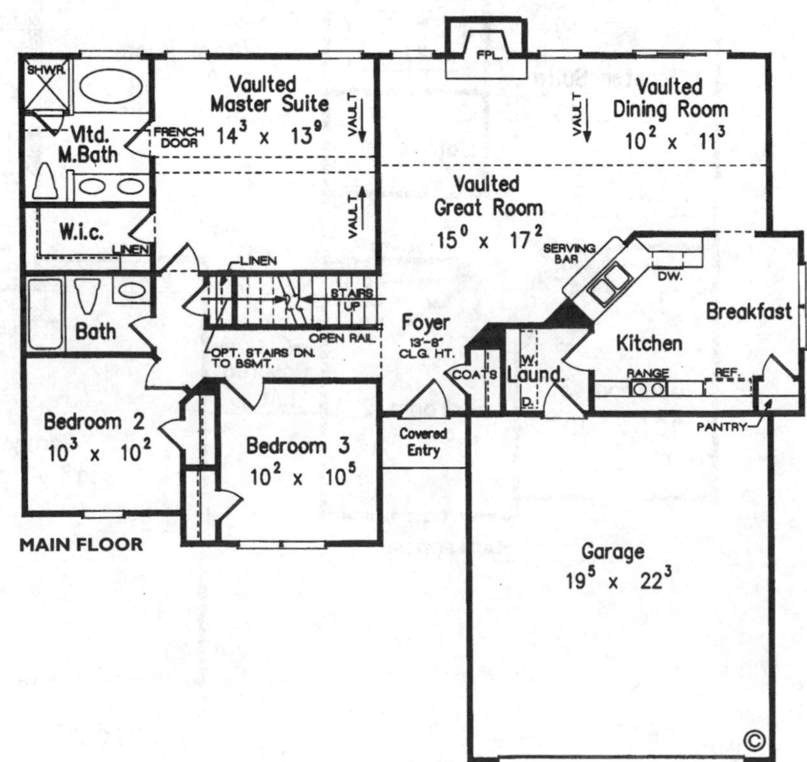

MAIN FLOOR

Design 97336

Units	Single
Price Code	A
Total Finished	1,356 sq. ft.
Main Finished	1,356 sq. ft.
Basement Unfinished	750 sq. ft.
Garage Unfinished	429 sq. ft.
Dimensions	48'x46'
Foundation	Basement
Bedrooms	3
Full Baths	1
3/4 Baths	1
Main Ceiling	9'
Max Ridge Height	23'2"
Roof Framing	Truss
Exterior Walls	2x6

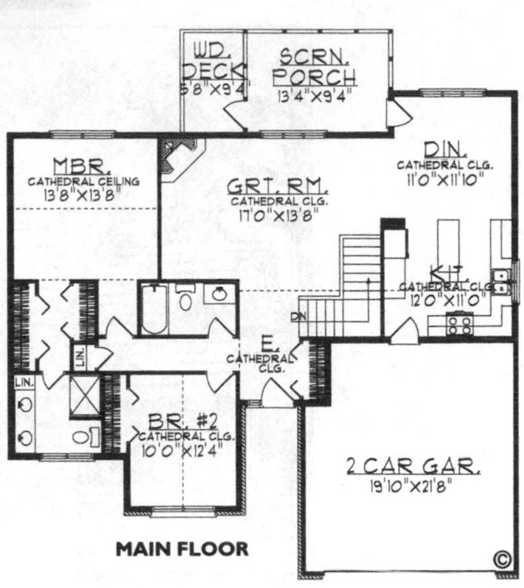

MAIN FLOOR

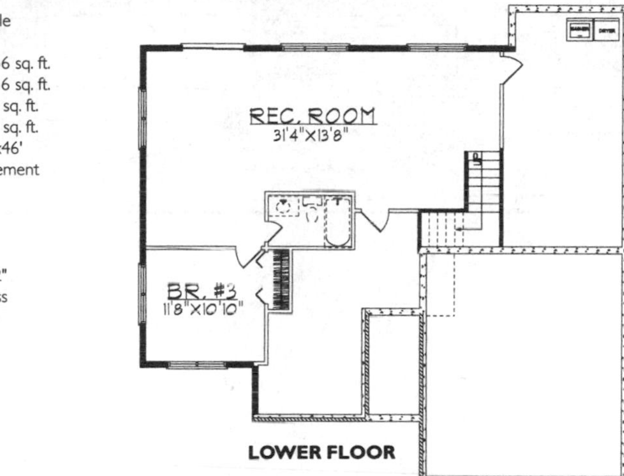

LOWER FLOOR

Design 65015

Units	Single
Price Code	A
Total Finished	1,360 sq. ft.
First Finished	858 sq. ft.
Second Finished	502 sq. ft.
Basement Unfinished	858 sq. ft.
Dimensions	35'x29'8"
Foundation	Basement
Bedrooms	3
Full Baths	2
First Ceiling	8'
Second Ceiling	8'
Max Ridge Height	26'6"
Roof Framing	Truss
Exterior Walls	2x6

3,00 X 3,30
10'-0" X 11'-0"
4,50 X 3,30
15'-0" X 11'-0"

SECOND FLOOR

6,00 X 4,20
20'-0" X 14'-0"
3,60 X 3,60
12'-0" X 12'-0"
4,20 X 3,90
14'-0" X 13'-0"
3,90 X 2,70
13'-0" X 9'-0"

FIRST FLOOR

Design 94982

Units	Single
Price Code	A
Total Finished	1,360 sq. ft.
Main Finished	1,360 sq. ft.
Garage Unfinished	544 sq. ft.
Dimensions	52'x46'
Foundation	Basement
Bedrooms	3
Full Baths	2
Max Ridge Height	18'
Roof Framing	Stick
Exterior Walls	2x4

* Alternate foundation options available at an additional charge. Please call 1-800-235-5700 for more information.

TRANS.
TRANS.
Mbr. $12^0 \times 14^0$
Grt. rm. $14^0 \times 17^3$
10'-0" CEILING
DN
Bfst. $10^0 \times 9^0$
SNACK BAR
P.
R.
Kit. $10^0 \times 10^3$
L.
E.
W.
D.
Br. 3 $10^0 \times 10^0$
Br. 2 $10^0 \times 12^0$
COVERED STOOP
Gar. $21^4 \times 26^0$
©
MAIN FLOOR

Design 99639

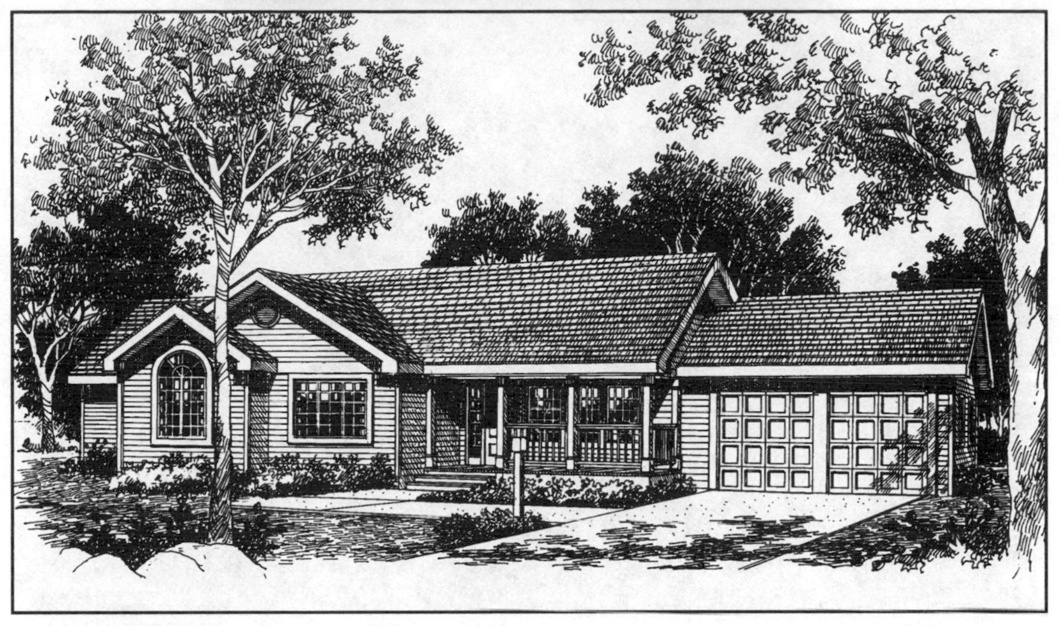

Units	Single
Price Code	A
Total Finished	1,367 sq. ft.
Main Finished	1,367 sq. ft.
Basement Unfinished	1,267 sq. ft.
Garage Unfinished	431 sq. ft.
Dimensions	71'4"x33'10"
Foundation	Basement Slab
Bedrooms	3
Full Baths	2
Main Ceiling	8'
Vaulted Ceiling	11'
Max Ridge Height	20'
Roof Framing	Stick
Exterior Walls	2x6

MAIN FLOOR

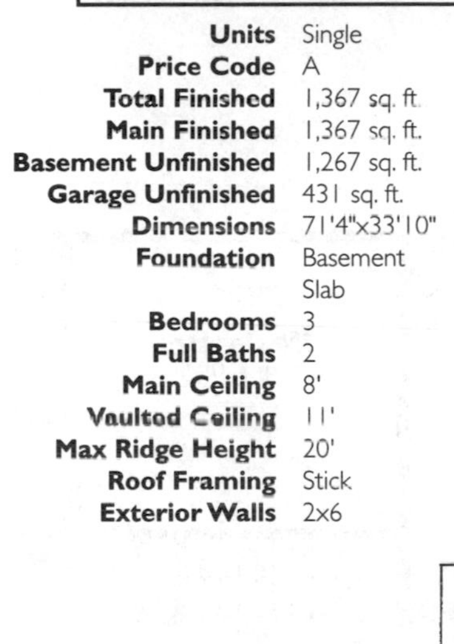

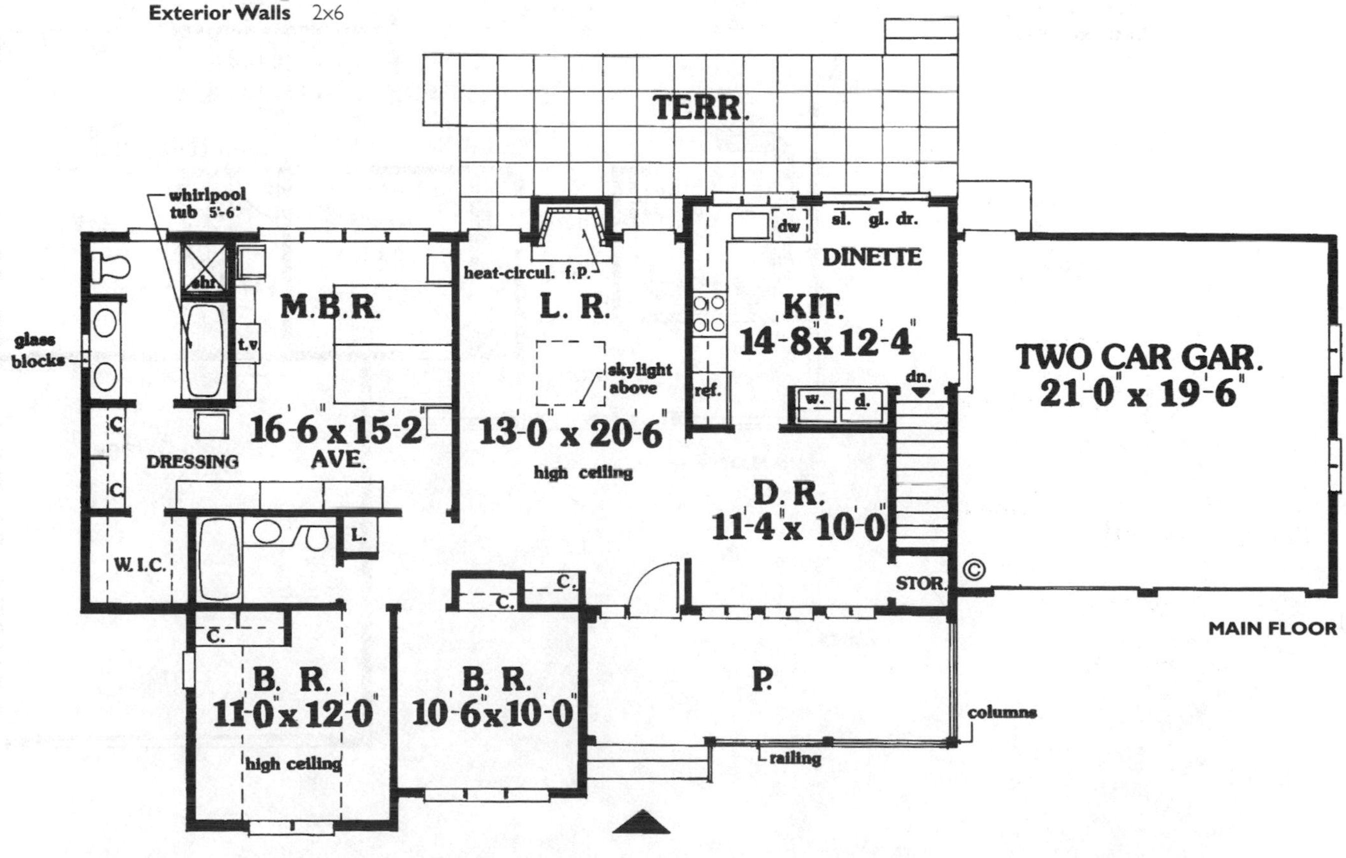

Design 99930

Units	Single
Price Code	A
Total Finished	1,368 sq. ft.
Main Finished	1,368 sq. ft.
Basement Unfinished	1,360 sq. ft.
Garage Unfinished	462 sq. ft.
Deck Unfinished	80 sq. ft.
Porch Unfinished	128 sq. ft.
Dimensions	46'x54'
Foundation	Basement
Bedrooms	3
Full Baths	2
Main Ceiling	8'
Tray Ceiling	11'6"
Max Ridge Height	19'
Roof Framing	Truss
Exterior Walls	2x6

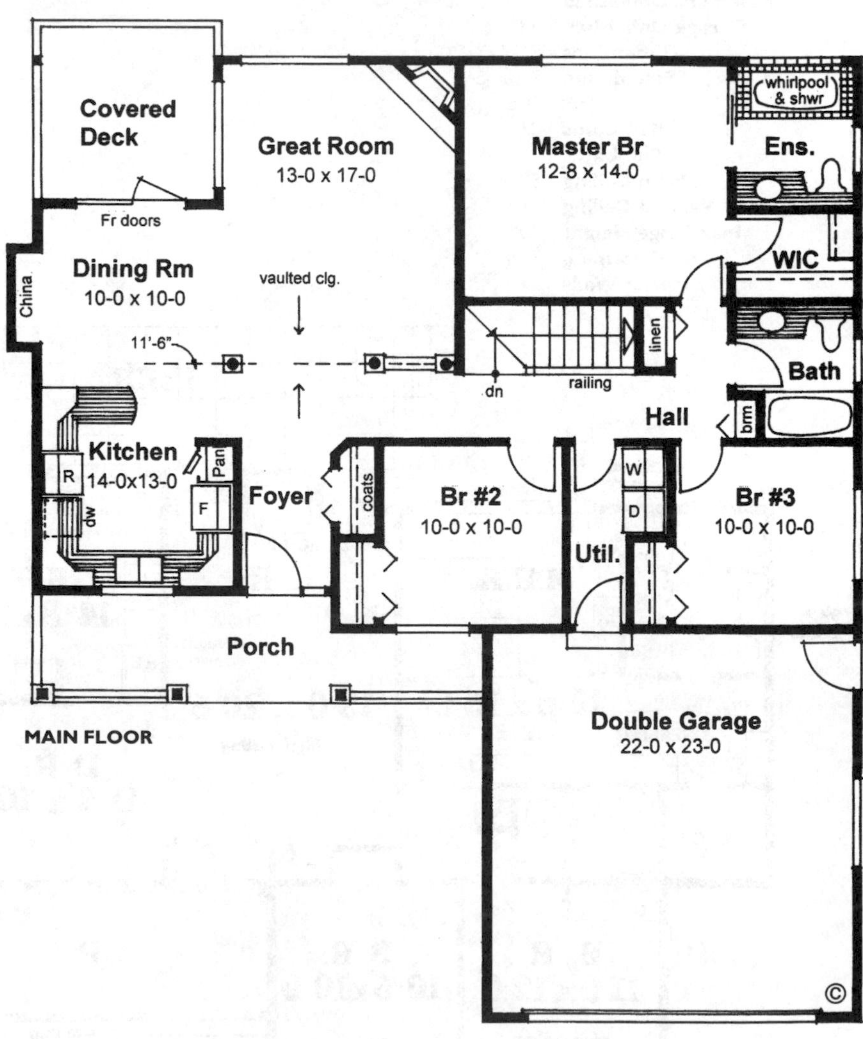

Design 96510

Units	Single
Price Code	A
Total Finished	1,372 sq. ft.
Main Finished	1,372 sq. ft.
Garage Unfinished	465 sq. ft.
Porch Unfinished	136 sq. ft.
Dimensions	38'x65'
Foundation	Crawlspace Slab
Bedrooms	3
Full Baths	2
Main Ceiling	8'
Max Ridge Height	19'
Roof Framing	Stick
Exterior Walls	2x4

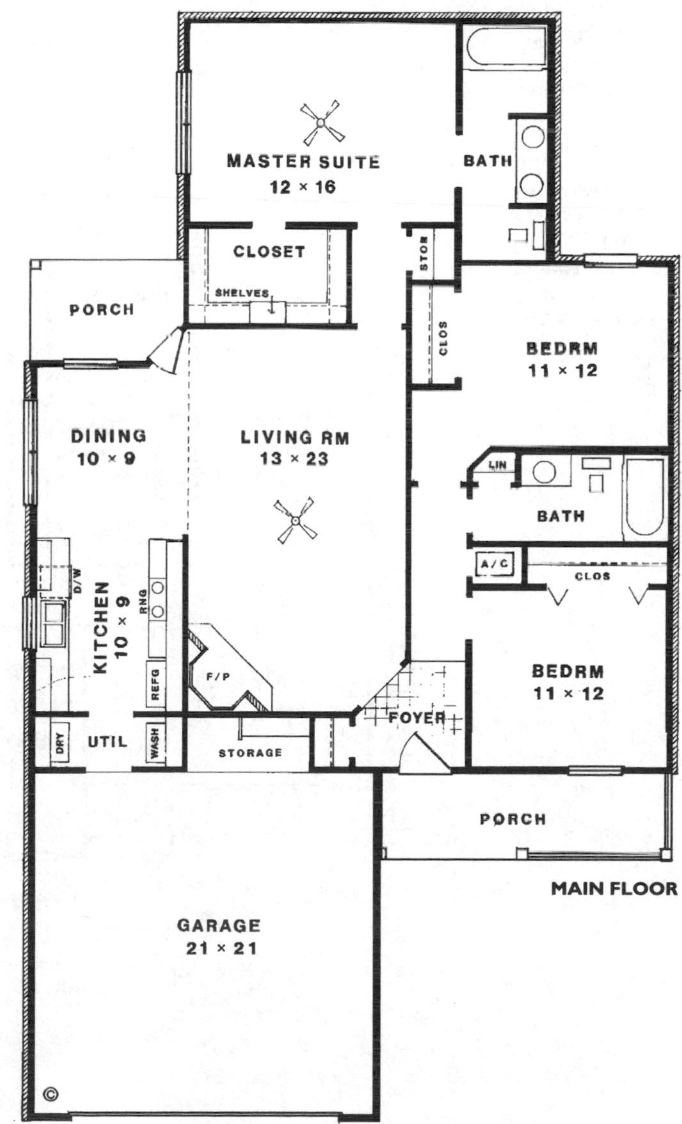

MAIN FLOOR

Design 97638

Units	Single
Price Code	A
Total Finished	1,374 sq. ft.
Main Finished	1,374 sq. ft.
Basement Unfinished	1,391 sq. ft.
Garage Unfinished	460 sq. ft.
Dimensions	50'4"x46'
Foundation	Basement Crawlspace
Bedrooms	3
Full Baths	2
Main Ceiling	9'
Max Ridge Height	24'
Roof Framing	Stick
Exterior Walls	2x4

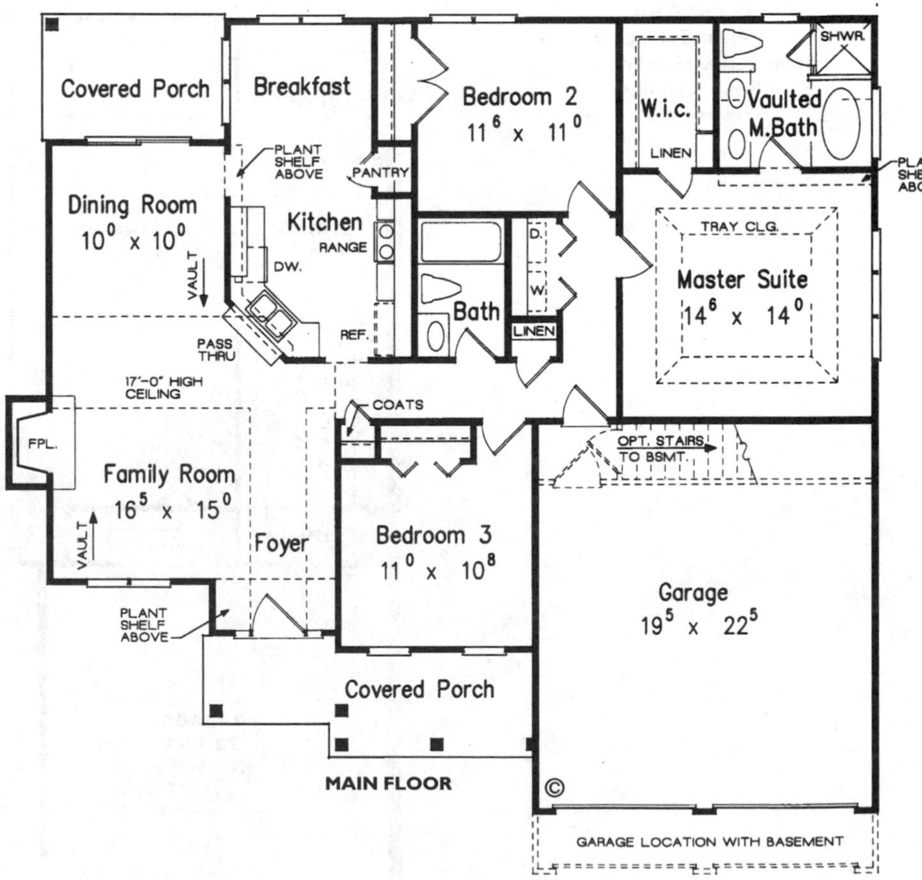

Design 65617

Units	Single
Price Code	A
Total Finished	1,375 sq. ft.
Main Finished	1,375 sq. ft.
Dimensions	61'x35'
Foundation	Crawlspace Slab
Bedrooms	3
Full Baths	2
Main Ceiling	8'
Max Ridge Height	24'
Roof Framing	Stick
Exterior Walls	2x4

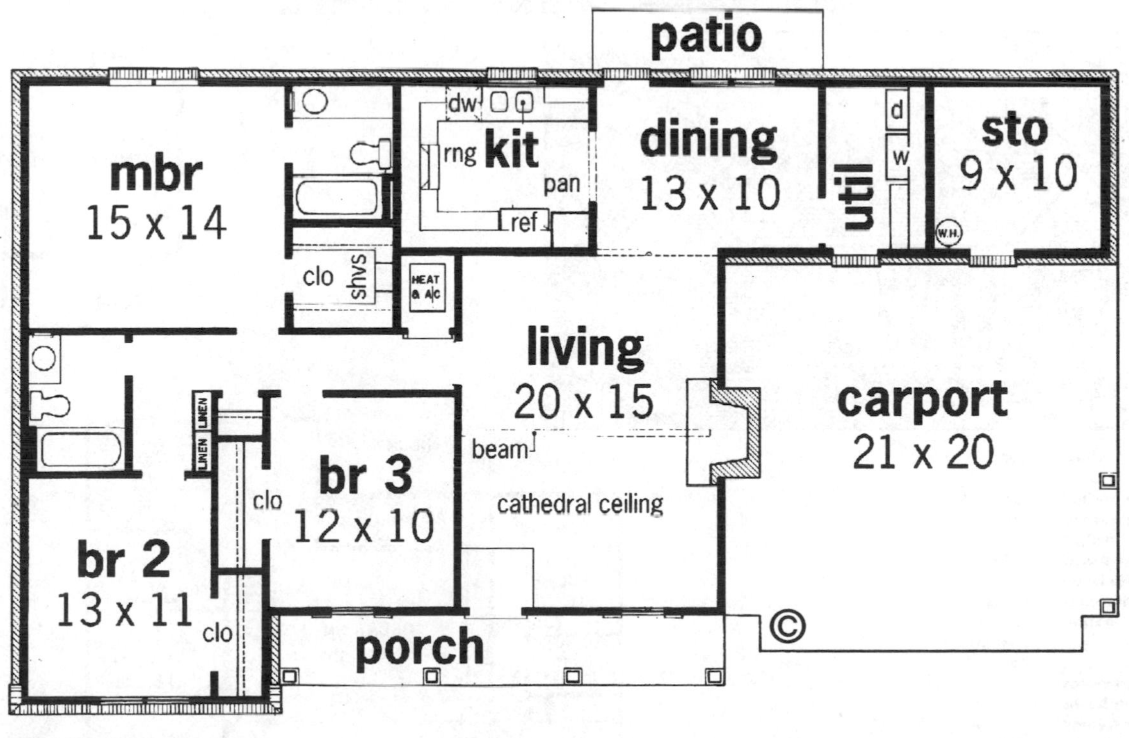

MAIN FLOOR

Design 94304

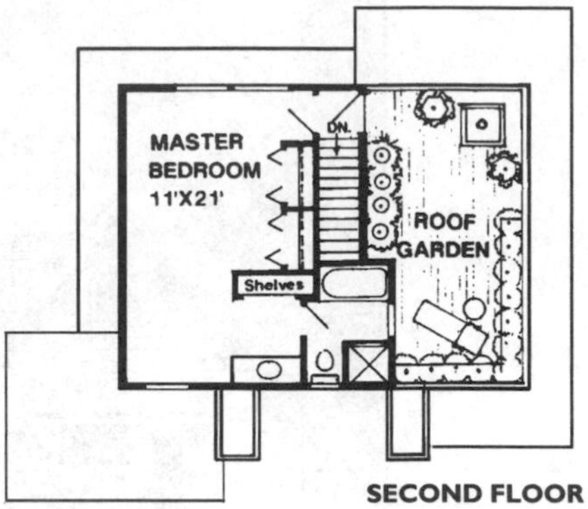

SECOND FLOOR

FIRST FLOOR

Units	Single
Price Code	A
Total Finished	1,377 sq. ft.
First Finished	981 sq. ft.
Second Finished	396 sq. ft.
Dimensions	40'x50'
Foundation	Basement
Bedrooms	3
Full Baths	2
First Ceiling	8'
Second Ceiling	8'
Roof Framing	Truss
Exterior Walls	2x4

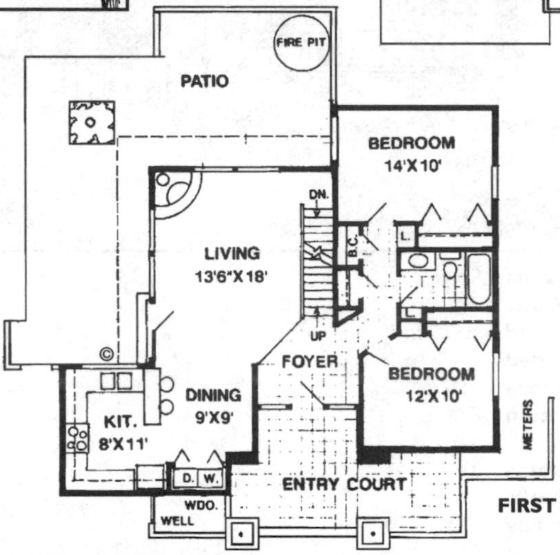

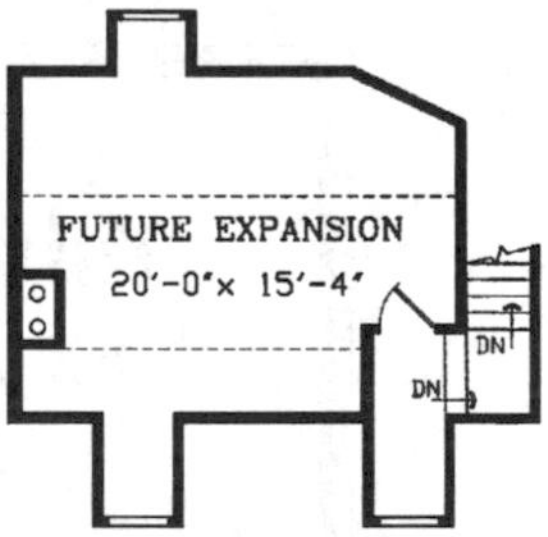

BONUS

MAIN FLOOR

Units	Single
Price Code	A
Total Finished	1,380 sq. ft.
Main Finished	1,380 sq. ft.
Bonus Unfinished	372 sq. ft.
Basement Unfinished	1,380 sq. ft.
Garage Unfinished	427 sq. ft.
Dimensions	48'x43'4"
Foundation	Basement Crawlspace Slab
Bedrooms	3
Full Baths	2
Main Ceiling	8'
Max Ridge Height	24'2"
Exterior Walls	2x4

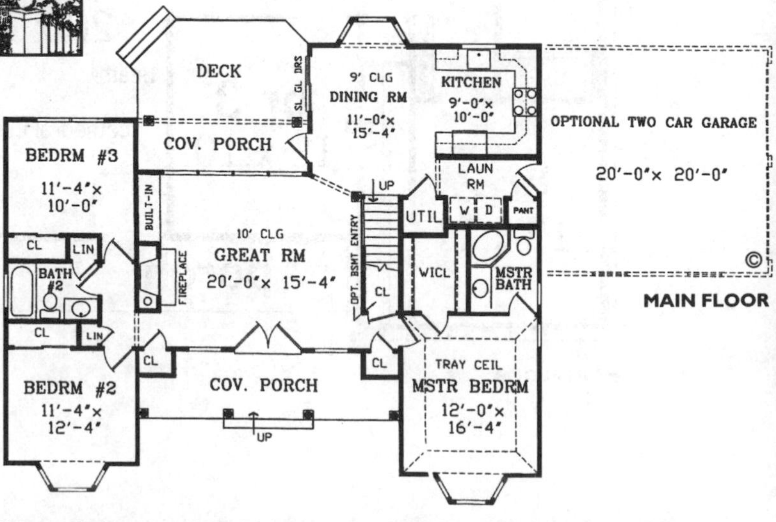

Design 96924

Units	Single
Price Code	A
Total Finished	1,383 sq. ft.
Main Finished	1,383 sq. ft.
Basement Unfinished	1,460 sq. ft.
Garage Unfinished	416 sq. ft.
Deck Unfinished	120 sq. ft.
Porch Unfinished	79 sq. ft.
Dimensions	50'x40'
Foundation	Basement Crawlspace Slab
Bedrooms	3
Full Baths	2
Main Ceiling	9'
Max Ridge Height	20'6"
Roof Framing	Truss
Exterior Walls	2x4

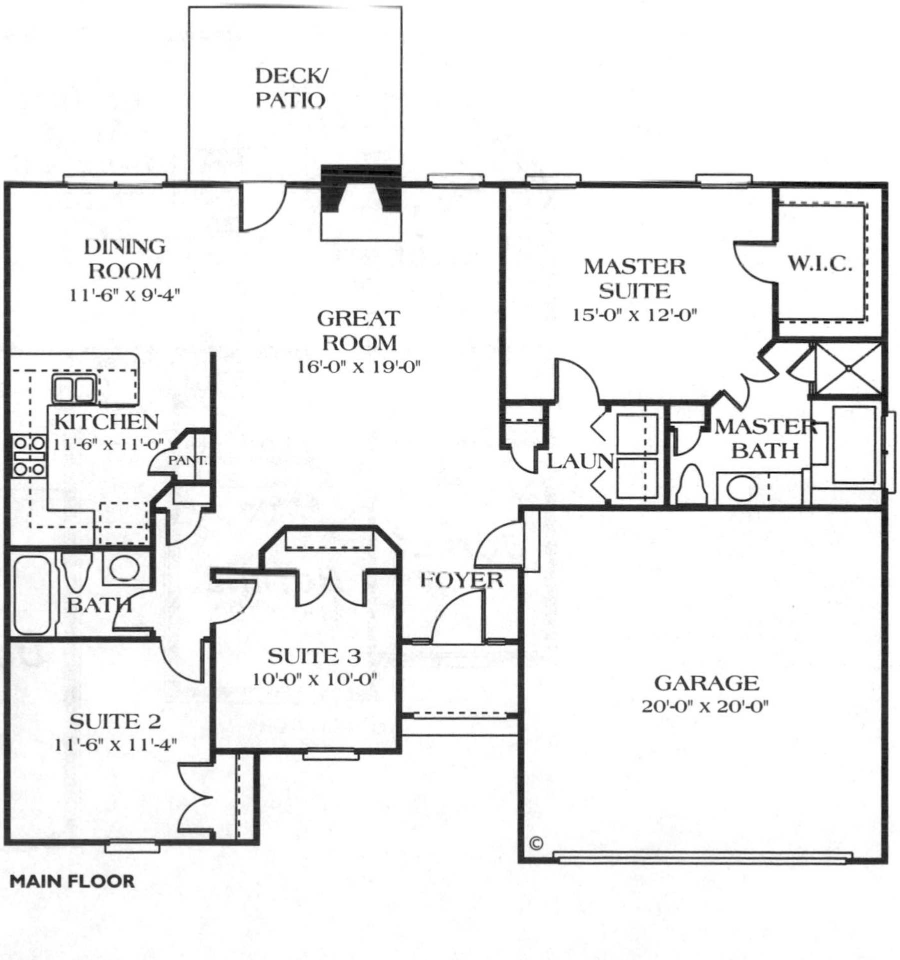

DECK/ PATIO

DINING ROOM 11'-6" x 9'-4"

GREAT ROOM 16'-0" x 19'-0"

MASTER SUITE 15'-0" x 12'-0"

W.I.C.

KITCHEN 11'-6" x 11'-0"

PANT.

LAUN

MASTER BATH

BATH

FOYER

SUITE 3 10'-0" x 10'-0"

GARAGE 20'-0" x 20'-0"

SUITE 2 11'-6" x 11'-4"

©

MAIN FLOOR

Design 93279

Units	Single
Price Code	A
Total Finished	1,388 sq. ft.
Main Finished	1,388 sq. ft.
Garage Unfinished	400 sq. ft.
Dimensions	48'x46'
Foundation	Crawlspace Slab
Bedrooms	3
Full Baths	2
Main Ceiling	8'
Max Ridge Height	18'
Roof Framing	Truss
Exterior Walls	2x4

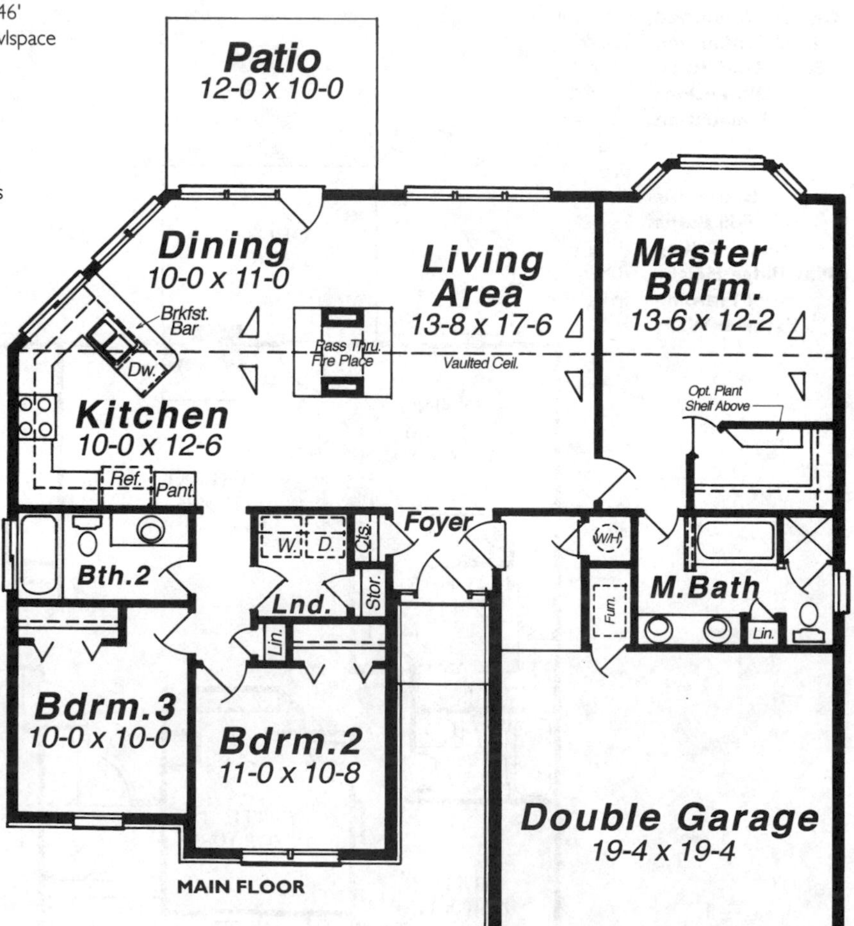

Patio
12-0 x 10-0

Dining
10-0 x 11-0

Brkfst. Bar

Dw.

Living Area
13-8 x 17-6

Pass Thru. Fire Place

Vaulted Ceil.

Master Bdrm.
13-6 x 12-2

Opt. Plant Shelf Above

Kitchen
10-0 x 12-6

Ref.

Pant.

Bth.2

W. D.

Cls.

Foyer

W/H

Lnd.

Stor.

Furn.

M.Bath

Lin.

Lin.

Bdrm.3
10-0 x 10-0

Bdrm.2
11-0 x 10-8

Double Garage
19-4 x 19-4

©

MAIN FLOOR

Design 97604

Units	Single
Price Code	A
Total Finished	1,392 sq. ft.
Main Finished	1,392 sq. ft.
Basement Unfinished	1,414 sq. ft.
Garage Unfinished	415 sq. ft.
Dimensions	49'x49'4"
Foundation	Basement Crawlspace
Bedrooms	3
Full Baths	2
Main Ceiling	9'
Max Ridge Height	23'
Roof Framing	Stick
Exterior Walls	2x4

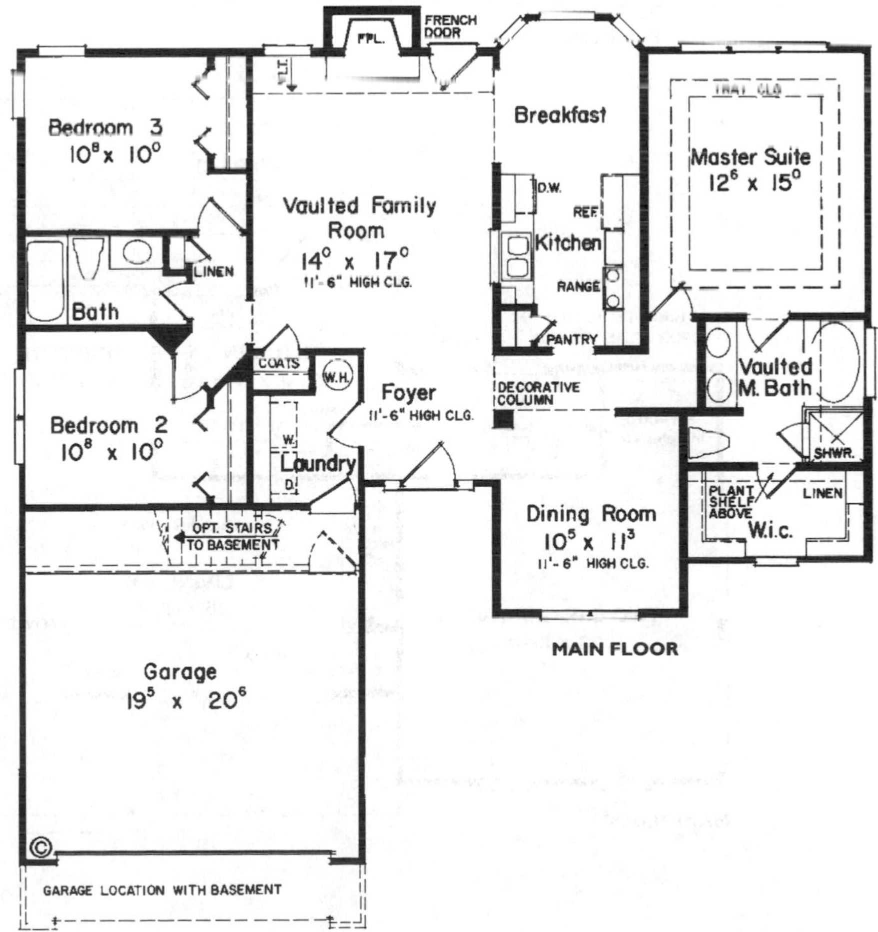

Design 90680

Units	Single
Price Code	A
Total Finished	1,393 sq. ft.
Main Finished	1,393 sq. ft.
Basement Unfinished	1,393 sq. ft.
Garage Unfinished	542 sq. ft.
Porch Unfinished	195 sq. ft.
Dimensions	72'4"x36'8"
Foundation	Basement Slab
Bedrooms	3
Full Baths	2

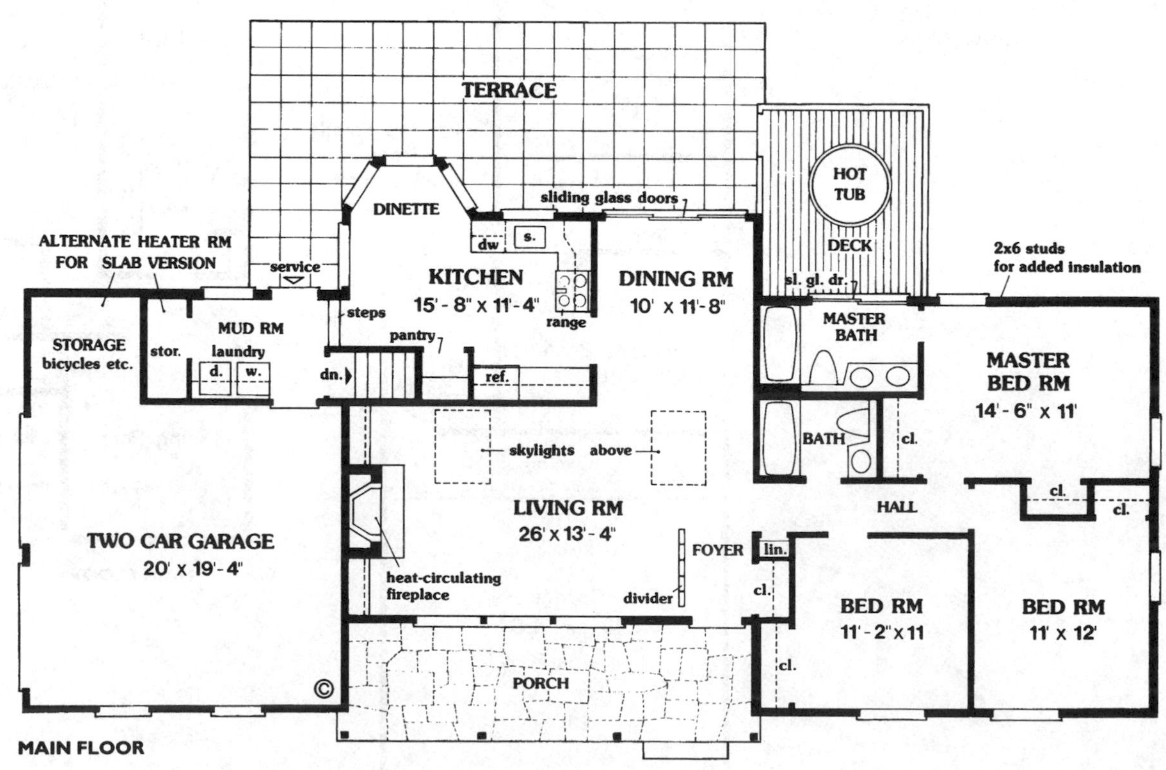

MAIN FLOOR

Design 34054

Units	Single
Price Code	A
Total Finished	1,400 sq. ft.
Main Finished	1,400 sq. ft.
Basement Unfinished	1,400 sq. ft.
Garage Unfinished	528 sq. ft.
Dimensions	50'x28'
Foundation	Basement Crawlspace Slab
Bedrooms	3
Full Baths	2
Main Ceiling	8'
Max Ridge Height	17'
Roof Framing	Stick
Exterior Walls	2x4, 2x6

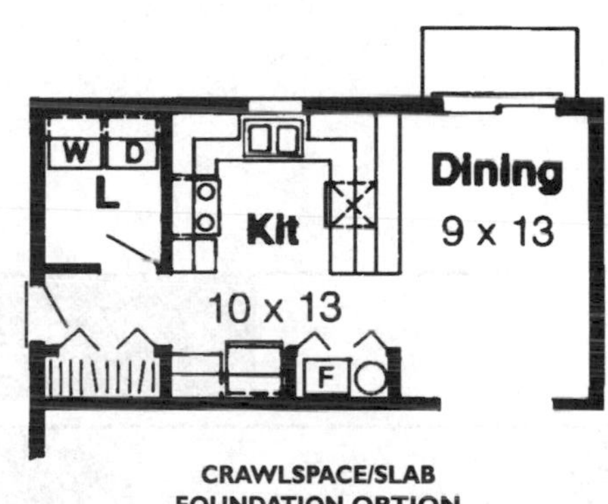

CRAWLSPACE/SLAB FOUNDATION OPTION

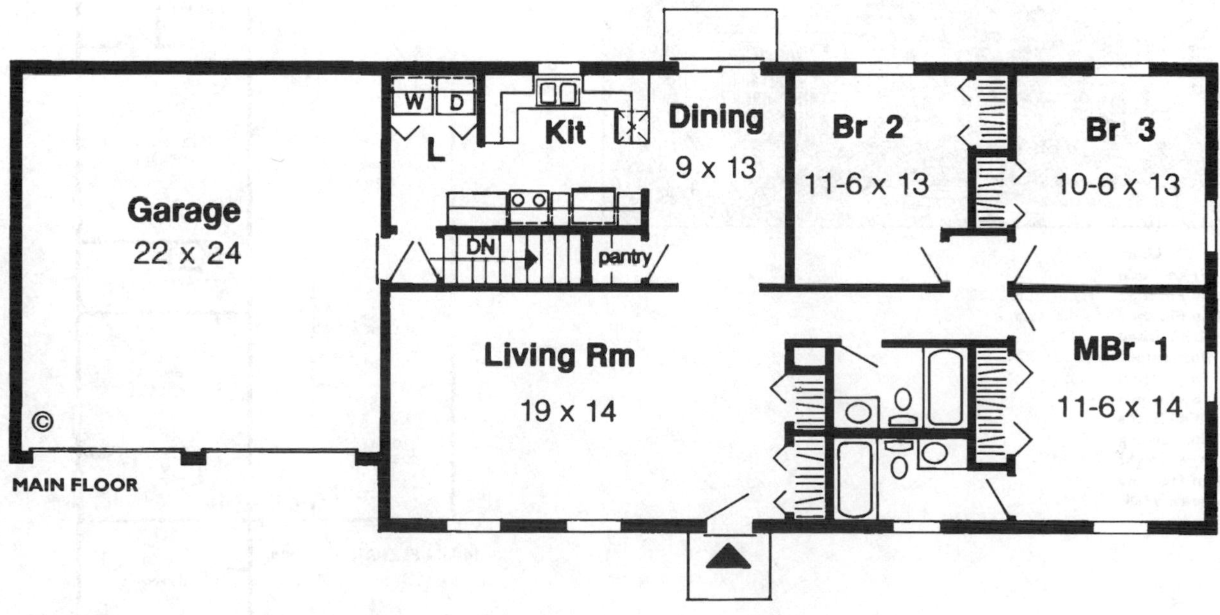

MAIN FLOOR

Design 62024

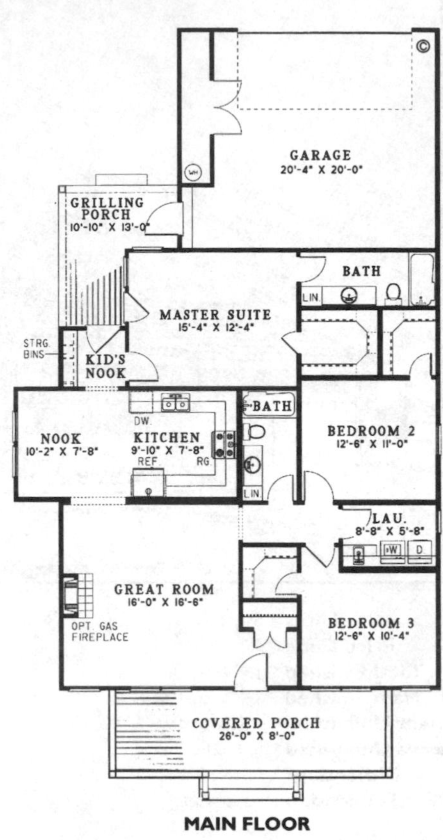

MAIN FLOOR

Units	Single
Price Code	A
Total Finished	1,401 sq. ft.
Main Finished	1,401 sq. ft.
Garage Unfinished	488 sq. ft.
Porch Unfinished	314 sq. ft.
Dimensions	39'x70'6"
Foundation	Crawlspace Slab
Bedrooms	3
Full Baths	2
Main Ceiling	9'
Roof Framing	Stick
Exterior Walls	2x6

Design 94690

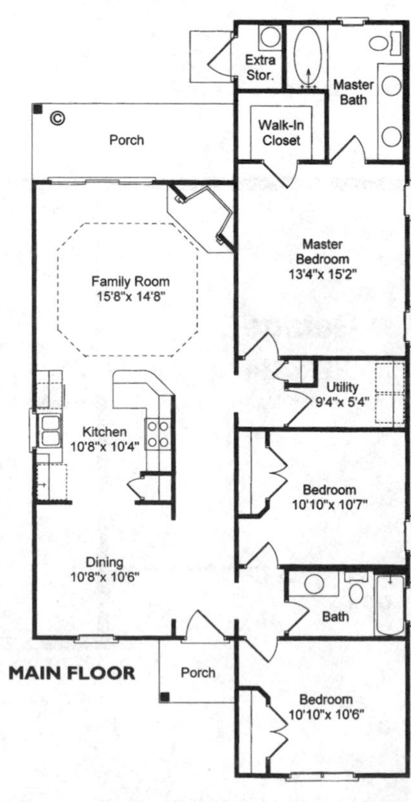

MAIN FLOOR

Units	Single
Price Code	A
Total Finished	1,401 sq. ft.
Main Finished	1,401 sq. ft.
Porch Unfinished	137 sq. ft.
Dimensions	30'x59'10"
Foundation	Slab
Bedrooms	3
Full Baths	2
Main Ceiling	9'
Max Ridge Height	20'6"
Roof Framing	Stick
Exterior Walls	2x4

Design 94689

Units	Single
Price Code	A
Total Finished	1,405 sq. ft.
Main Finished	1,405 sq. ft.
Dimensions	42'x51'
Foundation	Slab
Bedrooms	3
Full Baths	2
Main Ceiling	8'
Max Ridge Height	19'4"
Roof Framing	Stick
Exterior Walls	2x4

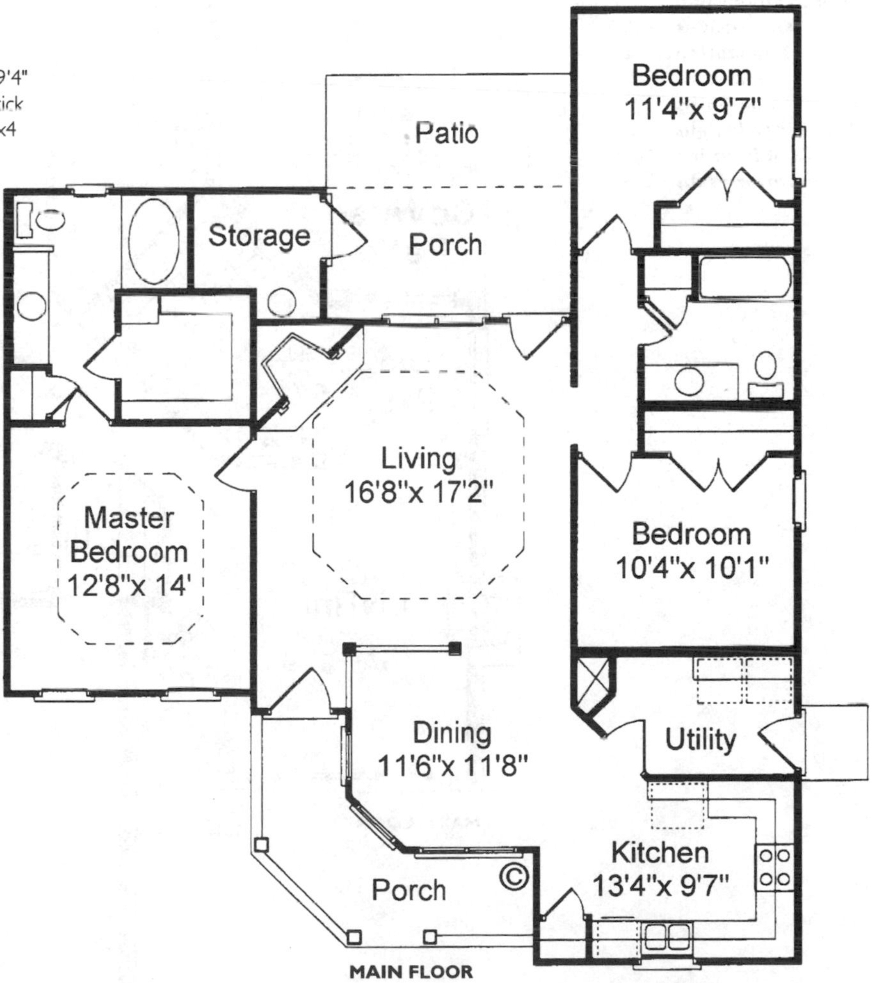

Bedroom 11'4"x 9'7"
Patio
Storage
Porch
Living 16'8"x 17'2"
Master Bedroom 12'8"x 14'
Bedroom 10'4"x 10'1"
Utility
Dining 11'6"x 11'8"
Kitchen 13'4"x 9'7"
Porch
©

MAIN FLOOR

Units	Single
Price Code	A
Total Finished	1,405 sq. ft.
Main Finished	1,405 sq. ft.
Garage Unfinished	440 sq. ft.
Deck Unfinished	160 sq. ft.
Porch Unfinished	28 sq. ft.
Dimensions	40'x60'
Foundation	Slab
Bedrooms	3
Full Baths	2
Max Ridge Height	21'3"
Roof Framing	Stick
Exterior Walls	2x4

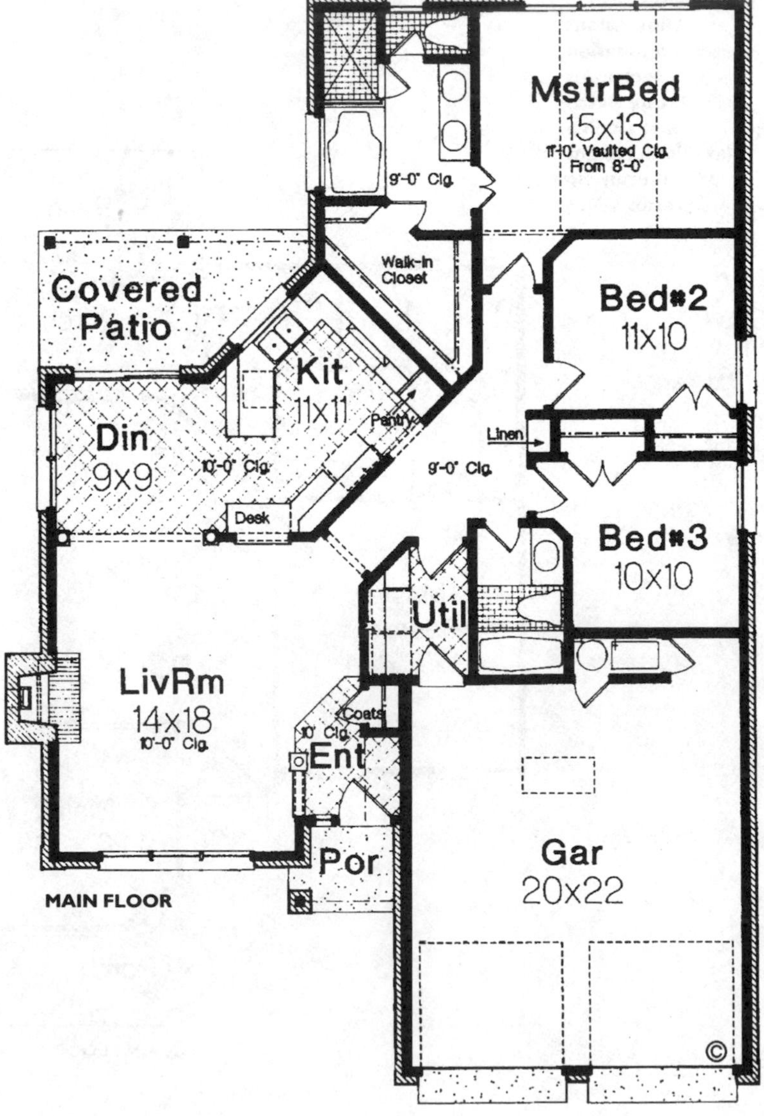

 To order blueprints, call **800-235-5700** or visit us on the web, **familyhomeplans.com**

Design 98970

Units	Single
Price Code	A
Total Finished	1,410 sq. ft.
Main Finished	1,396 sq. ft.
Lower Finished	14 sq. ft.
Garage Unfinished	646 sq. ft.
Deck Unfinished	120 sq. ft.
Dimensions	50'4"x31'
Foundation	Basement
Bedrooms	3
Full Baths	2
Main Ceiling	8'
Max Ridge Height	26'
Roof Framing	Stick
Exterior Walls	2x4

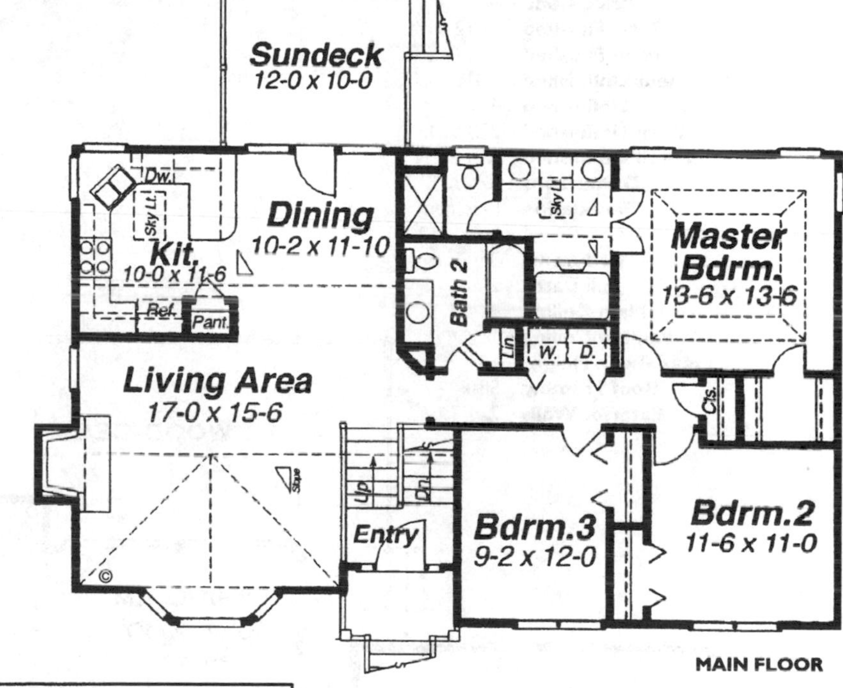

MAIN FLOOR

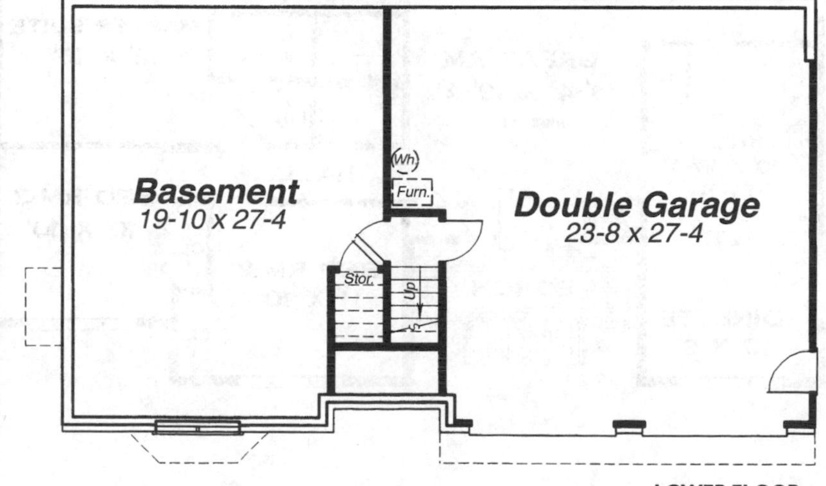

LOWER FLOOR

Design 99669

Units	Single
Price Code	A
Total Finished	1,412 sq. ft.
Main Finished	1,412 sq. ft.
Basement Unfinished	1,412 sq. ft.
Garage Unfinished	441 sq. ft.
Deck Unfinished	370 sq. ft.
Porch Unfinished	65 sq. ft.
Dimensions	72'x30'8"
Foundation	Basement Slab
Bedrooms	3
Full Baths	2
Main Ceiling	8'
Vaulted Ceiling	11'
Max Ridge Height	18'
Roof Framing	Stick
Exterior Walls	2x4

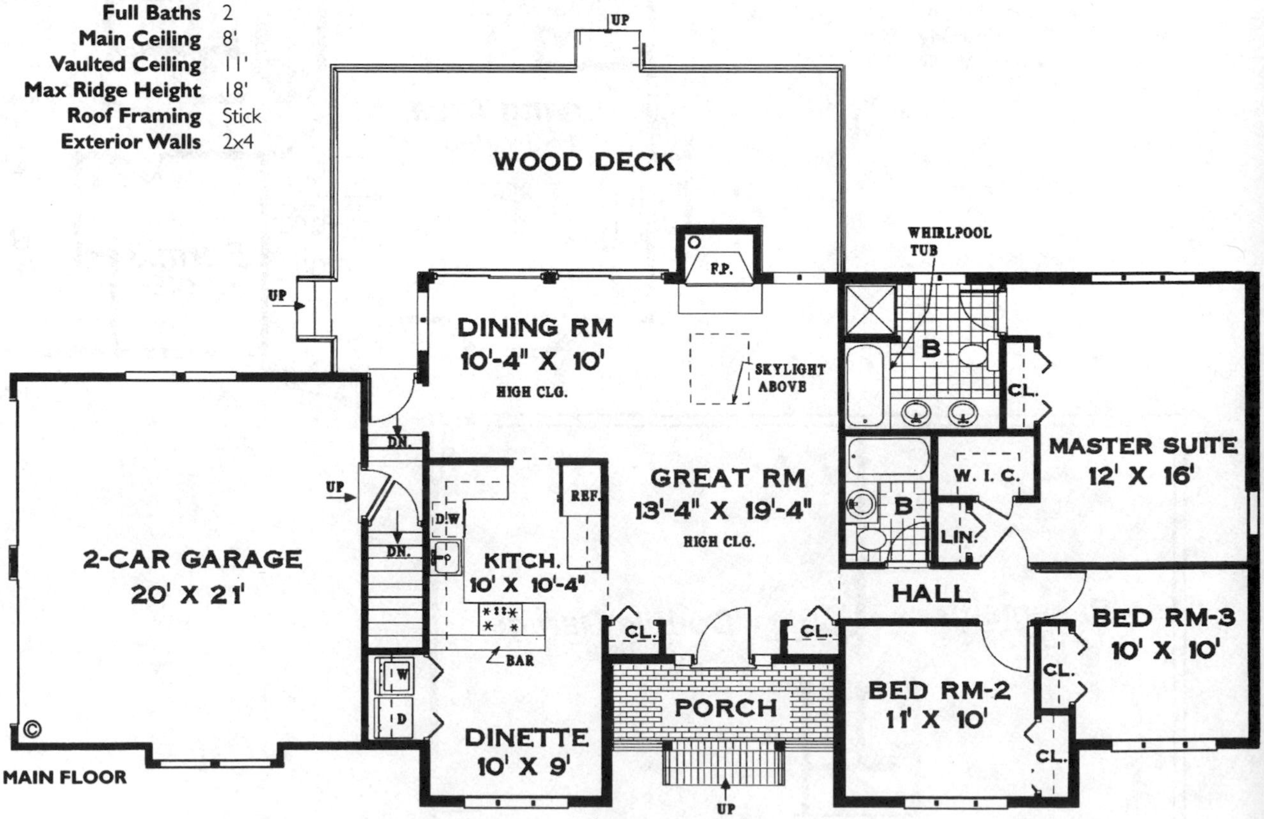

UP
WOOD DECK
UP
F.P.
WHIRLPOOL TUB
DINING RM
10'-4" X 10'
HIGH CLG.
SKYLIGHT ABOVE
B
CL.
DN.
UP
REF.
D/W
DN.
KITCH.
10' X 10'-4"
GREAT RM
13'-4" X 19'-4"
HIGH CLG.
W. I. C.
B
LIN.
MASTER SUITE
12' X 16'
2-CAR GARAGE
20' X 21'
HALL
BED RM-3
10' X 10'
CL.
CL.
CL.
BAR
W
D
PORCH
BED RM-2
11' X 10'
CL.
CL.
DINETTE
10' X 9'
UP
©
MAIN FLOOR

Design 65618

Units	Single
Price Code	A
Total Finished	1,415 sq. ft.
Main Finished	1,415 sq. ft.
Dimensions	56'x50'
Foundation	Crawlspace Slab
Bedrooms	3
Full Baths	2
Main Ceiling	8'
Max Ridge Height	26'
Roof Framing	Stick
Exterior Walls	2x6

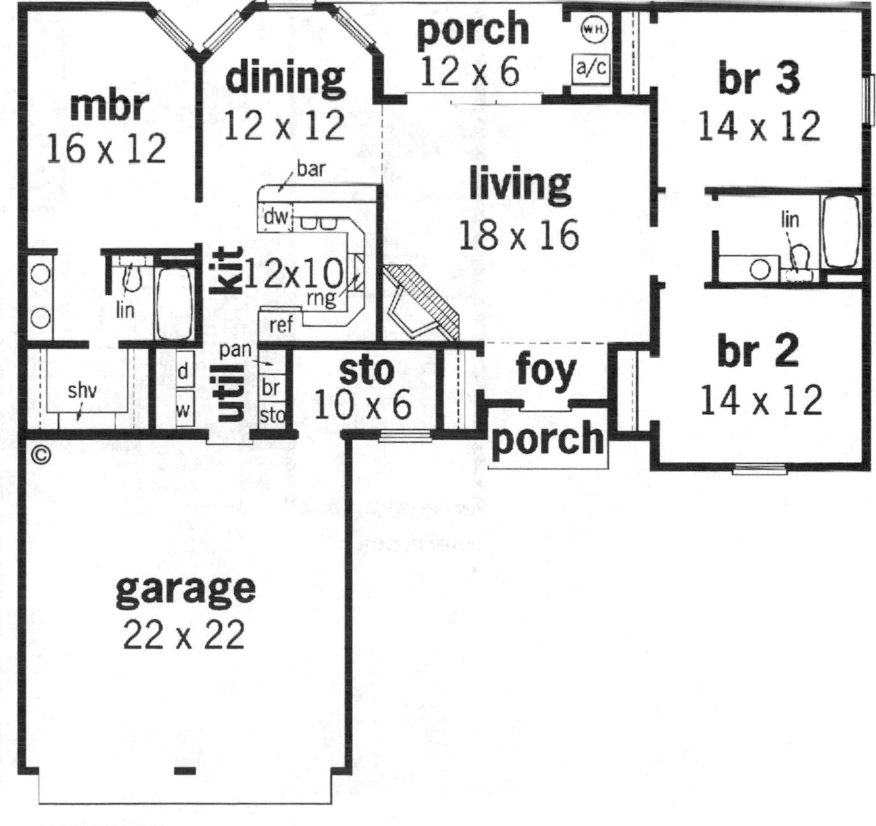

MAIN FLOOR

Design 97113

Units	Single
Price Code	A
Total Finished	1,416 sq. ft.
Main Finished	1,416 sq. ft.
Basement Unfinished	1,416 sq. ft.
Dimensions	48'x55'4"
Foundation	Basement
Bedrooms	3
Full Baths	2
Max Ridge Height	21'8"
Roof Framing	Truss
Exterior Walls	2x6

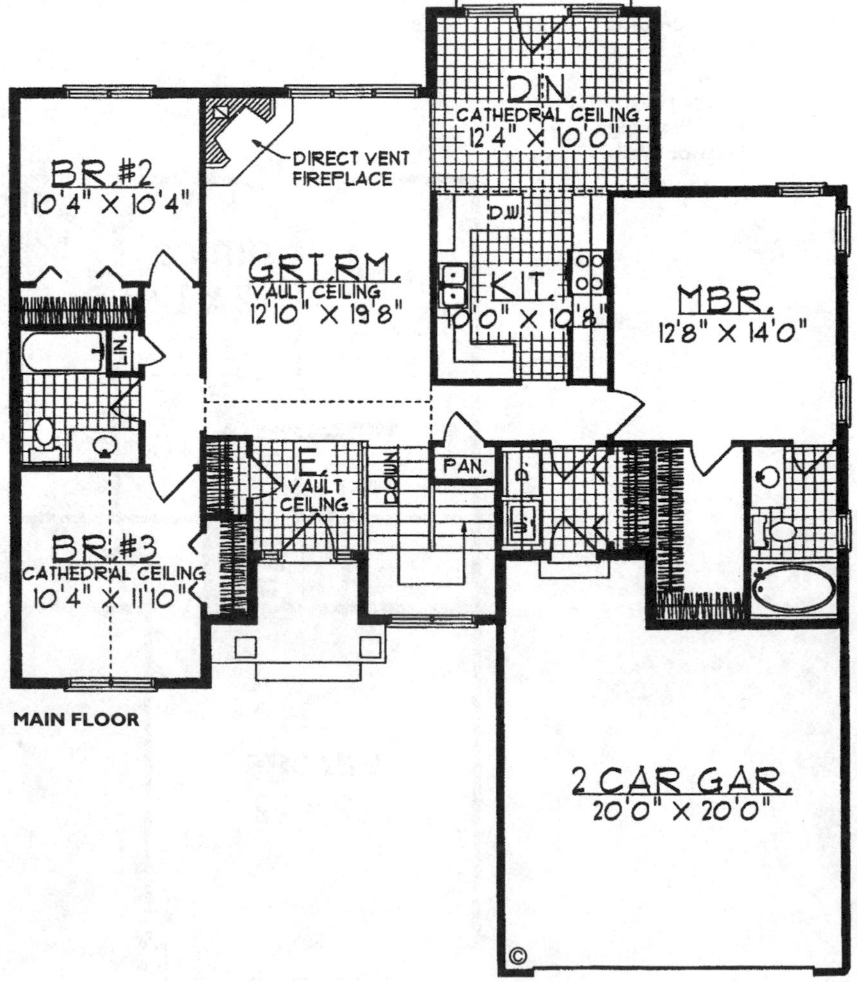

MAIN FLOOR

Design 65636

high wood privacy fence
bath
vanity
shws
lin
mbr
15 x 14
br 2
13 x 12
porch
10 x 10
dining
12 x 10
lin
bath
living
18 x 16
kit
12x10
dw
rng
ref
d
w
sto 12x6
br 3
13 x 12
slope
slope
por 12x6
ht a/c
garage
22 x 21
©
MAIN FLOOR

Units	Single
Price Code	A
Total Finished	1,420 sq. ft.
Main Finished	1,420 sq. ft.
Lower Finished	1,420 sq. ft.
Dimensions	52'x56'
Foundation	Crawlspace Slab
Bedrooms	3
Full Baths	2
Max Ridge Height	28'
Roof Framing	Stick
Exterior Walls	2x6

Design 10567

Units	Single
Price Code	A
Total Finished	1,421 sq. ft.
First Finished	1,046 sq. ft.
Second Finished	375 sq. ft.
Basement Unfinished	1,046 sq. ft.
Garage Unfinished	472 sq. ft.
Dimensions	50'x48'
Foundation	Basement
Bedrooms	3
Full Baths	2
Max Ridge Height	26'
Roof Framing	Stick
Exterior Walls	2x6

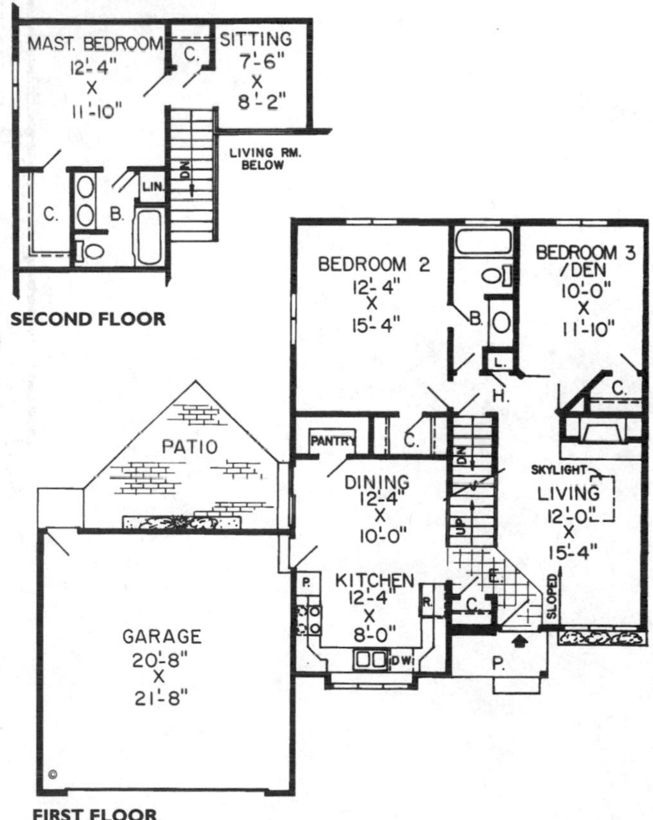

Design 97493

Units	Single
Price Code	A
Total Finished	1,422 sq. ft.
Main Finished	1,422 sq. ft.
Garage Unfinished	566 sq. ft.
Dimensions	50'x58'
Foundation	Basement
Bedrooms	3
Full Baths	2
Main Ceiling	8'
Max Ridge Height	21'3"
Roof Framing	Stick
Exterior Walls	2x4

* Alternate foundation options available at an additional charge. Please call 1-800-235-5700 for more information.

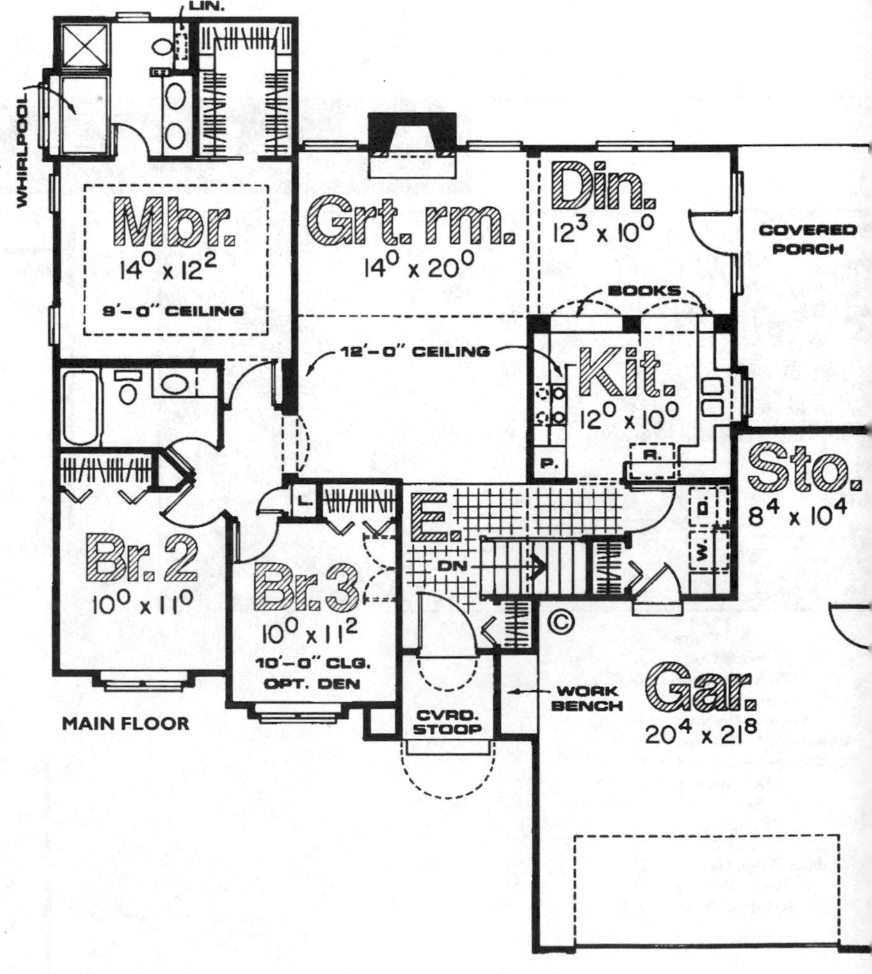

Design 90990

Units	Single
Price Code	A
Total Finished	1,423 sq. ft.
Main Finished	1,423 sq. ft.
Basement Unfinished	1,423 sq. ft.
Garage Unfinished	399 sq. ft.
Dimensions	54'x49'
Foundation	Basement
Bedrooms	3
Full Baths	1
3/4 Baths	1
Exterior Walls	2x6

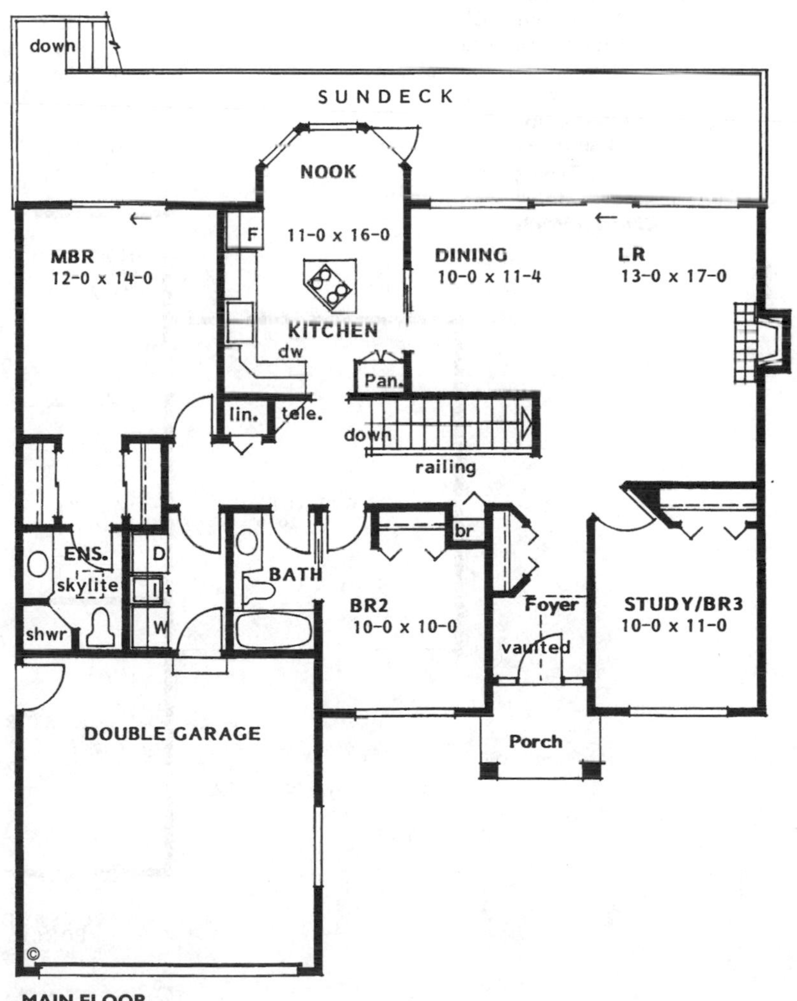

Design 82043

Units	Single
Price Code	A
Total Finished	1,425 sq. ft.
Main Finished	1,425 sq. ft.
Garage Unfinished	353 sq. ft.
Porch Unfinished	137 sq. ft.
Dimensions	45'x64'10"
Foundation	Basement Crawlspace Slab
Bedrooms	3
Full Baths	2
Main Ceiling	9'
Roof Framing	Stick
Exterior Walls	2x4

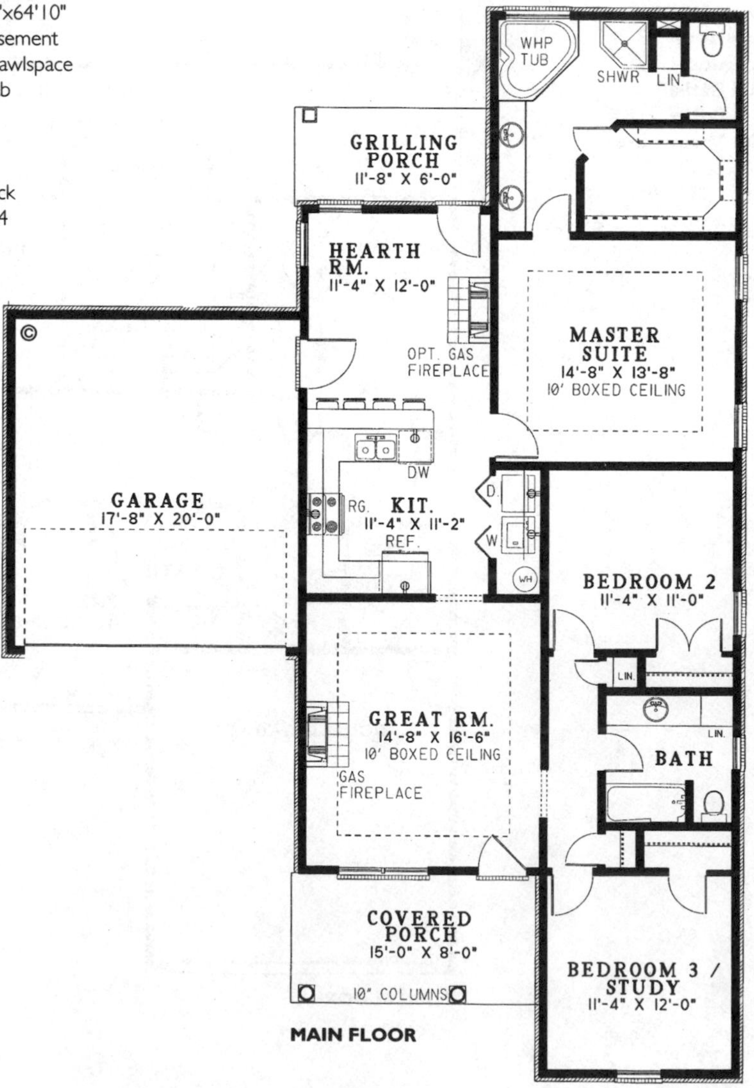

WHP TUB
SHWR
LIN
GRILLING PORCH
11'-8" X 6'-0"
HEARTH RM.
11'-4" X 12'-0"
OPT. GAS FIREPLACE
MASTER SUITE
14'-8" X 13'-8"
10' BOXED CEILING
GARAGE
17'-8" X 20'-0"
DW
D
W
RG.
KIT.
11'-4" X 11'-2"
REF.
WH
BEDROOM 2
11'-4" X 11'-0"
LIN.
GREAT RM.
14'-8" X 16'-6"
10' BOXED CEILING
GAS FIREPLACE
LIN.
BATH
COVERED PORCH
15'-0" X 8'-0"
10" COLUMNS
BEDROOM 3 / STUDY
11'-4" X 12'-0"

MAIN FLOOR

Design 92056

Units	Single
Price Code	A
Total Finished	1,425 sq. ft.
Main Finished	1,425 sq. ft.
Basement Unfinished	1,425 sq. ft.
Dimensions	50'x47'
Foundation	Basement
Bedrooms	3
Full Baths	1
3/4 Baths	1
Max Ridge Height	18'6"
Roof Framing	Stick
Exterior Walls	2x4

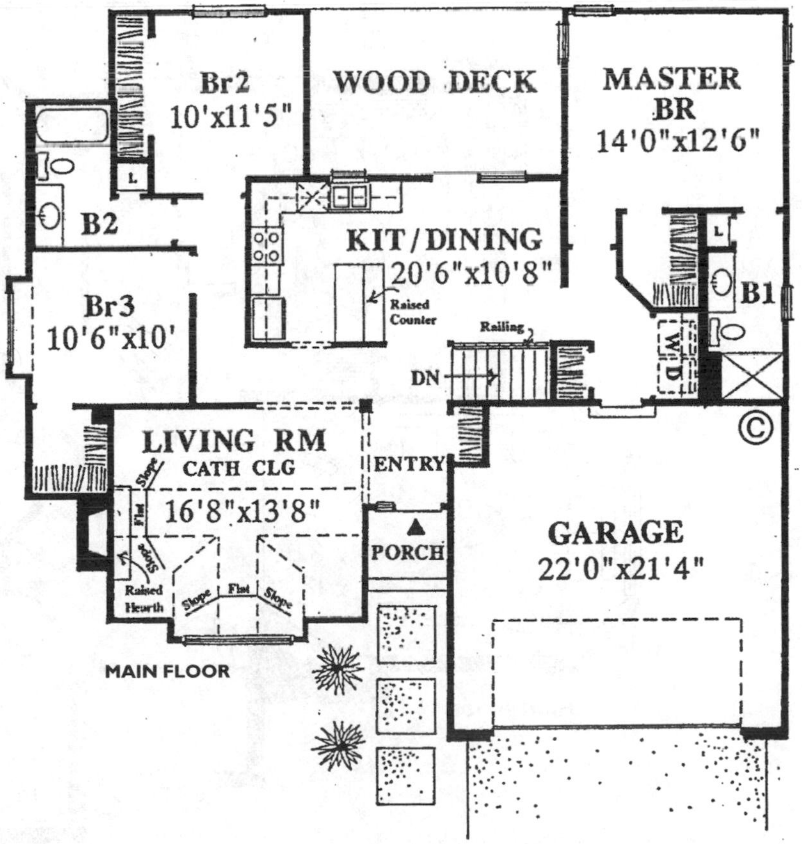

Br2
10'x11'5"
WOOD DECK
MASTER
BR
14'0"x12'6"
L
B2
KIT/DINING
20'6"x10'8"
Raised
Counter
L
B1
Br3
10'6"x10'
Railing
W
D
DN
©
LIVING RM
CATH CLG
ENTRY
Slope
Flat
16'8"x13'8"
GARAGE
22'0"x21'4"
PORCH
Slope
Raised
Hearth
Slope
Flat
Slope

MAIN FLOOR

Units	Single
Price Code	A
Total Finished	1,426 sq. ft.
Main Finished	1,426 sq. ft.
Dimensions	41'4"x42'
Foundation	Basement
Bedrooms	3
Full Baths	1
Main Ceiling	8'
Exterior Walls	2x6

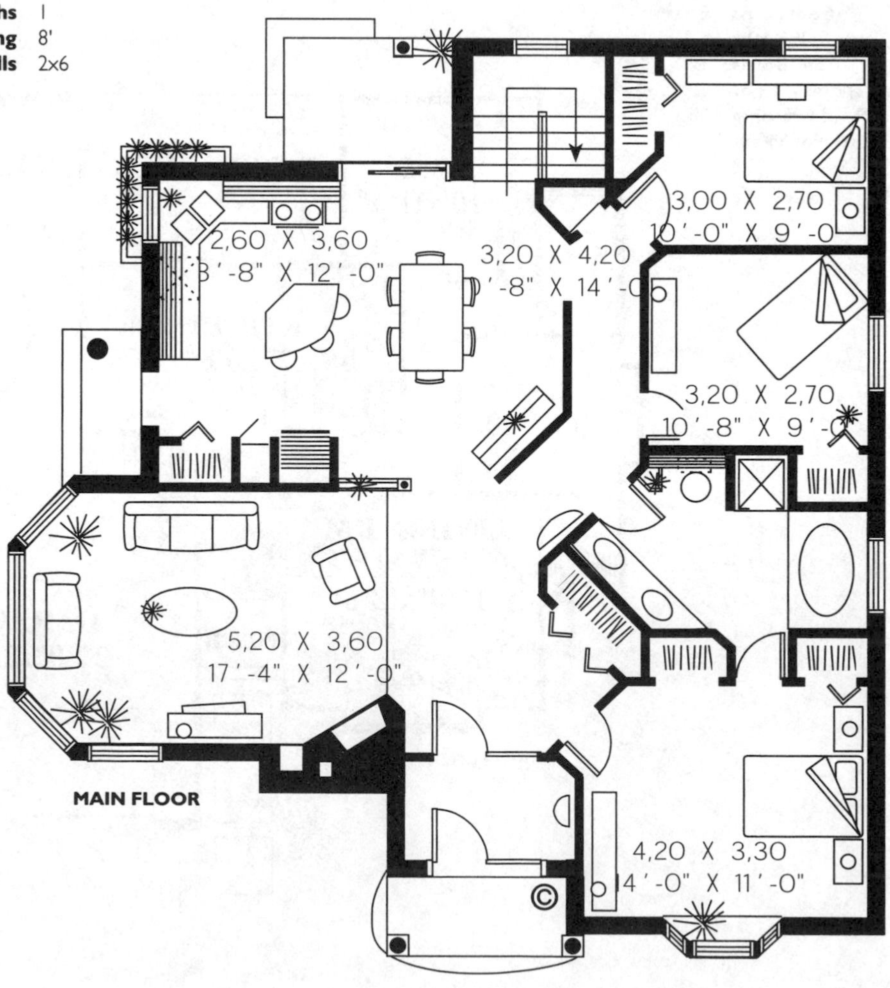

2,60 X 3,60
8'-8" X 12'-0"

3,20 X 4,20
10'-8" X 14'-0"

3,00 X 2,70
10'-0" X 9'-0"

3,20 X 2,70
10'-8" X 9'-0"

5,20 X 3,60
17'-4" X 12'-0"

4,20 X 3,30
14'-0" X 11'-0"

©

MAIN FLOOR

Design 97609

Units	Single
Price Code	A
Total Finished	1,430 sq. ft.
Main Finished	1,430 sq. ft.
Basement Unfinished	1,510 sq. ft.
Garage Unfinished	400 sq. ft.
Dimensions	47'x52'4"
Foundation	Basement Crawlspace Slab
Bedrooms	3
Full Baths	2
Max Ridge Height	23'6"
Roof Framing	Stick
Exterior Walls	2x4

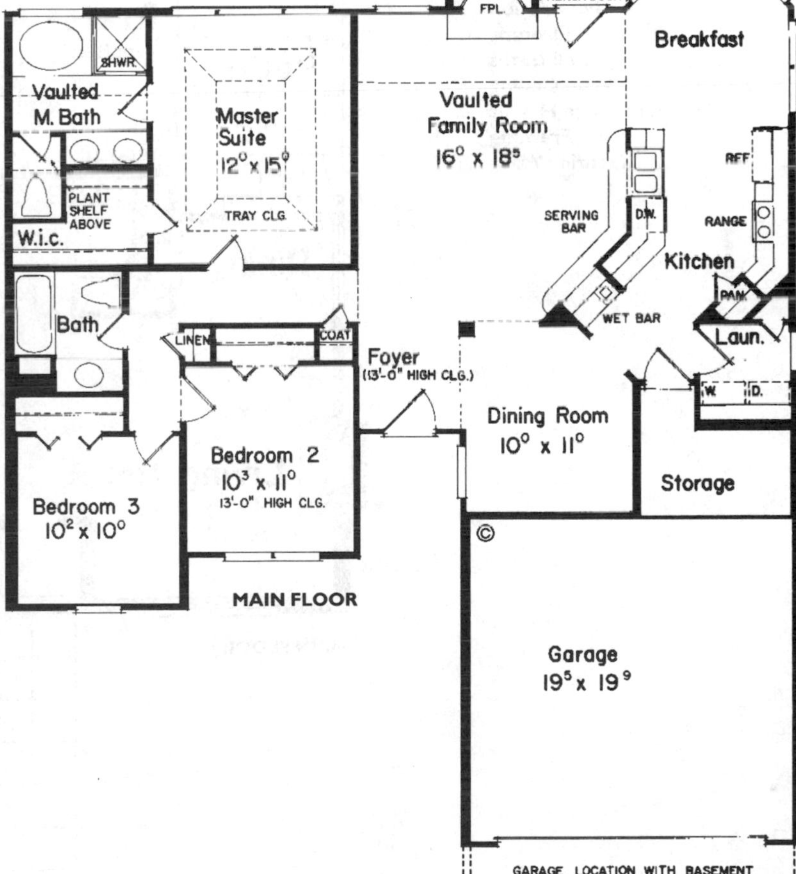

MAIN FLOOR

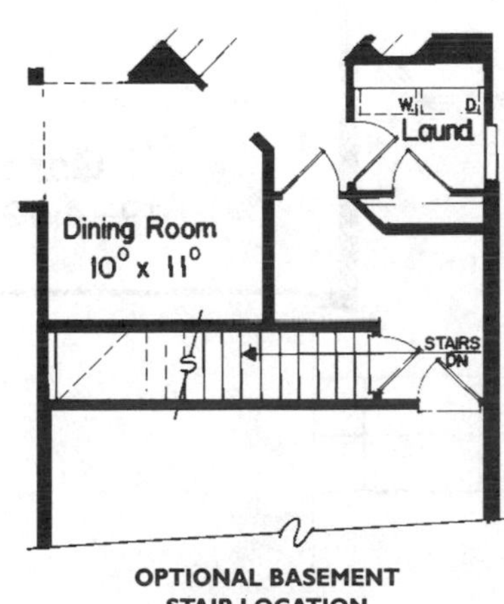

OPTIONAL BASEMENT STAIR LOCATION

Design 98354

Units	Single
Price Code	A
Total Finished	1,431 sq. ft.
Main Finished	1,431 sq. ft.
Basement Unfinished	1,431 sq. ft.
Garage Unfinished	410 sq. ft.
Dimensions	53'x43'8"
Foundation	Basement
Bedrooms	3
Full Baths	2
Main Ceiling	8'
Max Ridge Height	21'
Roof Framing	Truss
Exterior Walls	2x6

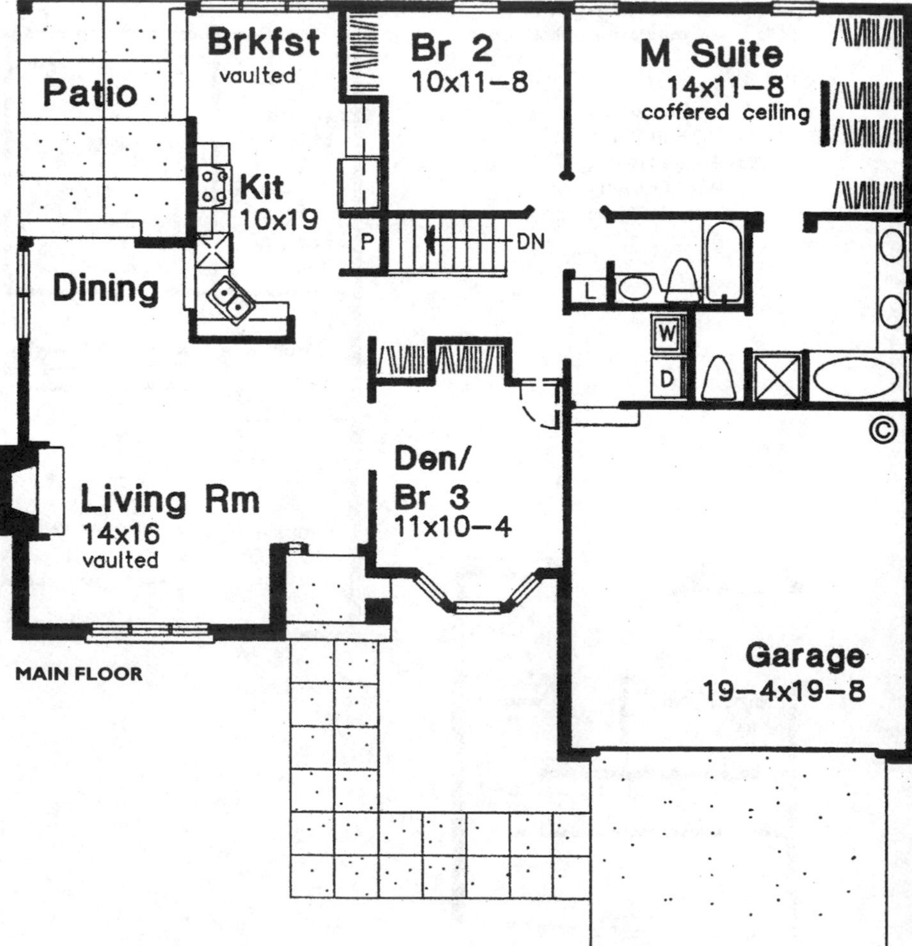

MAIN FLOOR

Design 98549

Units	Single
Price Code	A
Total Finished	1,431 sq. ft.
Main Finished	1,431 sq. ft.
Garage Unfinished	410 sq. ft.
Deck Unfinished	110 sq. ft.
Dimensions	44'x57'1"
Foundation	Slab
Bedrooms	3
Full Baths	2
Max Ridge Height	23'2"
Roof Framing	Stick
Exterior Walls	2x4

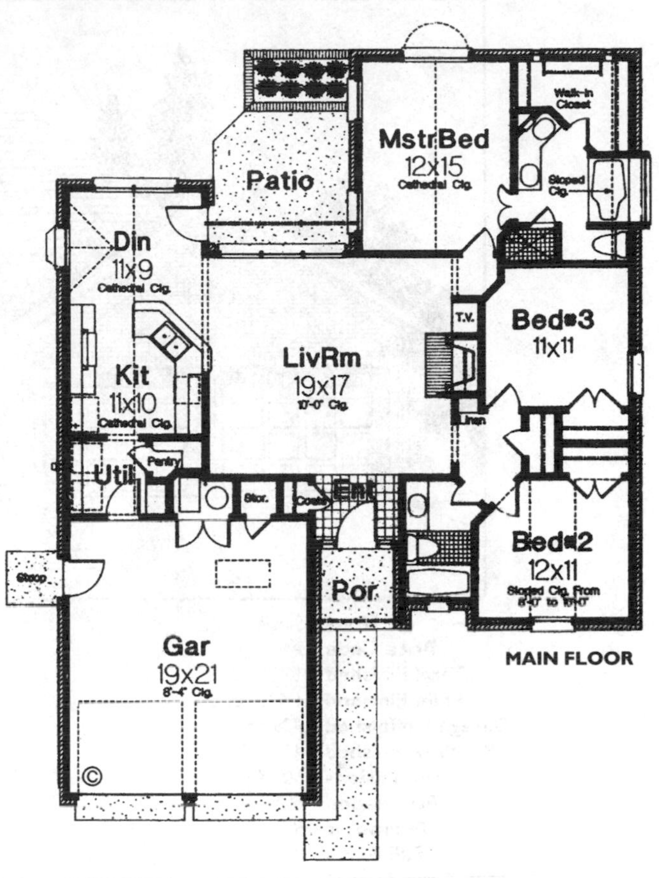

Design 65181

Units	Single
Price Code	A
Total Finished	1,432 sq. ft.
First Finished	756 sq. ft.
Second Finished	676 sq. ft.
Basement Unfinished	657 sq. ft.
Porch Unfinished	148 sq. ft.
Dimensions	26'x32'
Foundation	Basement
Bedrooms	3
Full Baths	1
3/4 Baths	1
First Ceiling	8'
Second Ceiling	8'
Roof Framing	Truss
Exterior Walls	2x6

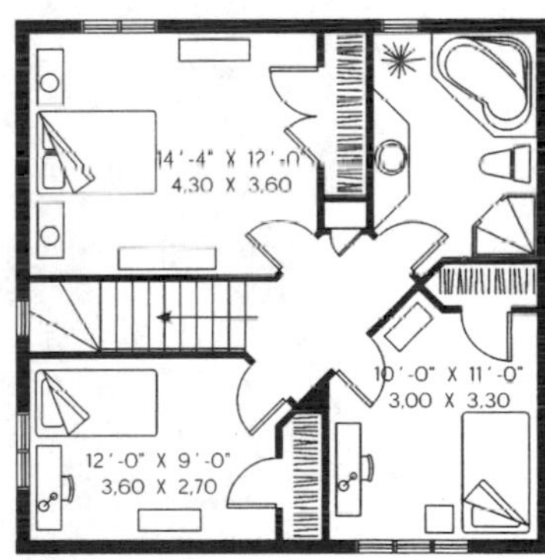

SECOND FLOOR

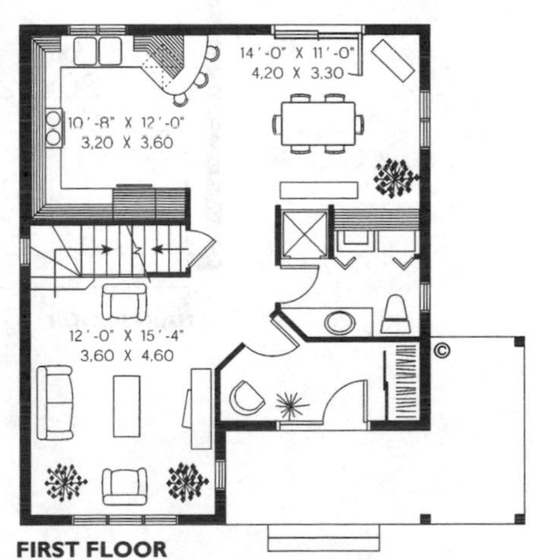

Units	Single
Price Code	A
Total Finished	1,432 sq. ft.
Main Finished	1,432 sq. ft.
Garage Unfinished	409 sq. ft.
Porch Unfinished	42 sq. ft.
Dimensions	50'x49'2"
Foundation	Slab
Bedrooms	3
Full Baths	2
Max Ridge Height	21'
Roof Framing	Stick
Exterior Walls	2x4

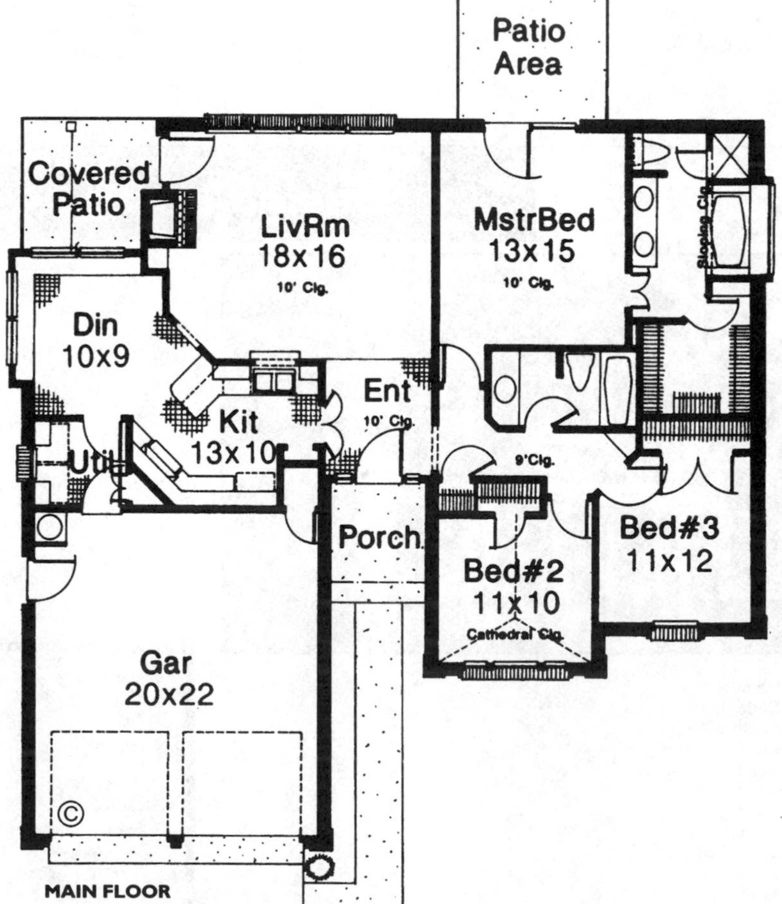

Design 96802

Units	Single
Price Code	A
Total Finished	1,433 sq. ft.
Main Finished	1,433 sq. ft.
Basement Unfinished	1,433 sq. ft.
Garage Unfinished	456 sq. ft.
Dimensions	54'x41'
Foundation	Basement Crawlspace Slab
Bedrooms	3
Full Baths	2
Main Ceiling	8'
Vaulted Ceiling	11'9"
Max Ridge Height	19'9"
Roof Framing	Truss
Exterior Walls	2x4

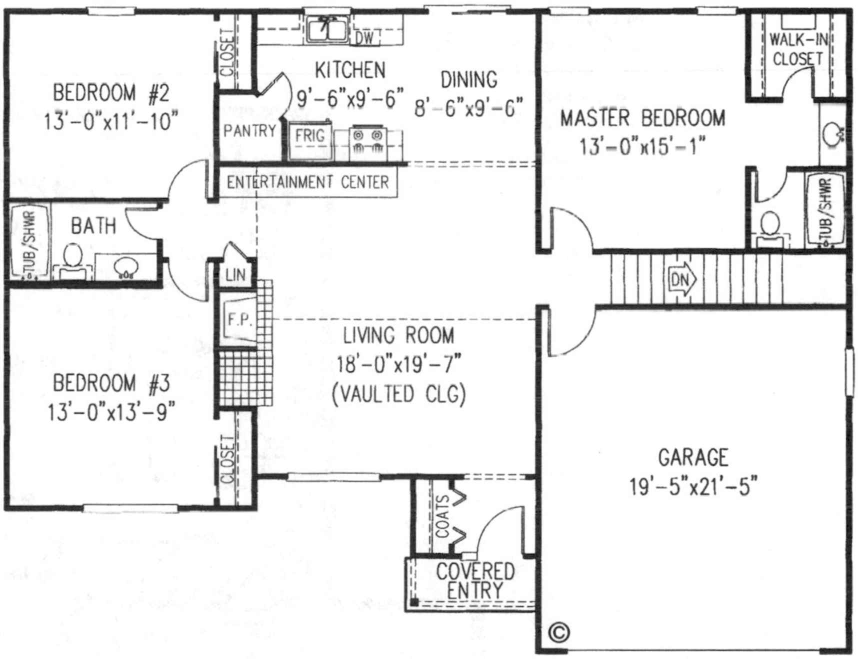

BEDROOM #2
13'-0"x11'-10"
CLOSET
DW
KITCHEN
9'-6"x9'-6"
DINING
8'-6"x9'-6"
PANTRY
FRIG
WALK-IN CLOSET
MASTER BEDROOM
13'-0"x15'-1"
ENTERTAINMENT CENTER
TUB/SHWR
BATH
TUB/SHWR
LIN
DN
F.P.
LIVING ROOM
18'-0"x19'-7"
(VAULTED CLG)
BEDROOM #3
13'-0"x13'-9"
CLOSET
GARAGE
19'-5"x21'-5"
COATS
COVERED ENTRY
©

MAIN FLOOR

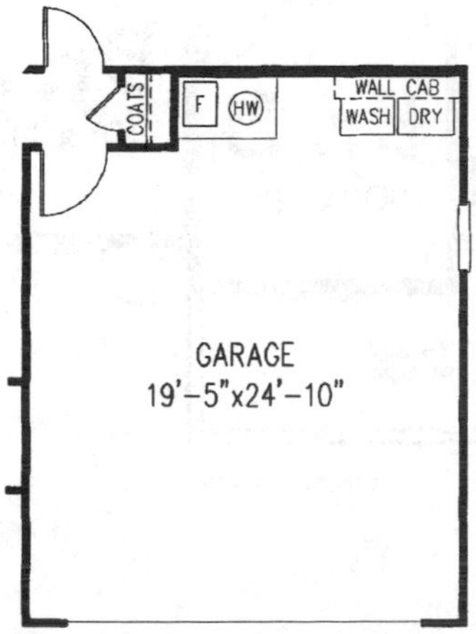

COATS
F
HW
WALL CAB
WASH
DRY
GARAGE
19'-5"x24'-10"

CRAWLSPACE/SLAB FOUNDATION OPTION

Design 97443

Units	Single
Price Code	A
Total Finished	1,433 sq. ft.
Main Finished	1,433 sq. ft.
Garage Unfinished	504 sq. ft.
Dimensions	50'x58'
Foundation	Basement
Bedrooms	3
Full Baths	2
Main Ceiling	8'
Max Ridge Height	19'4"
Roof Framing	Stick
Exterior Walls	2x4

* Alternate foundation options available at an additional charge. Please call 1-800-235-5700 for more information.

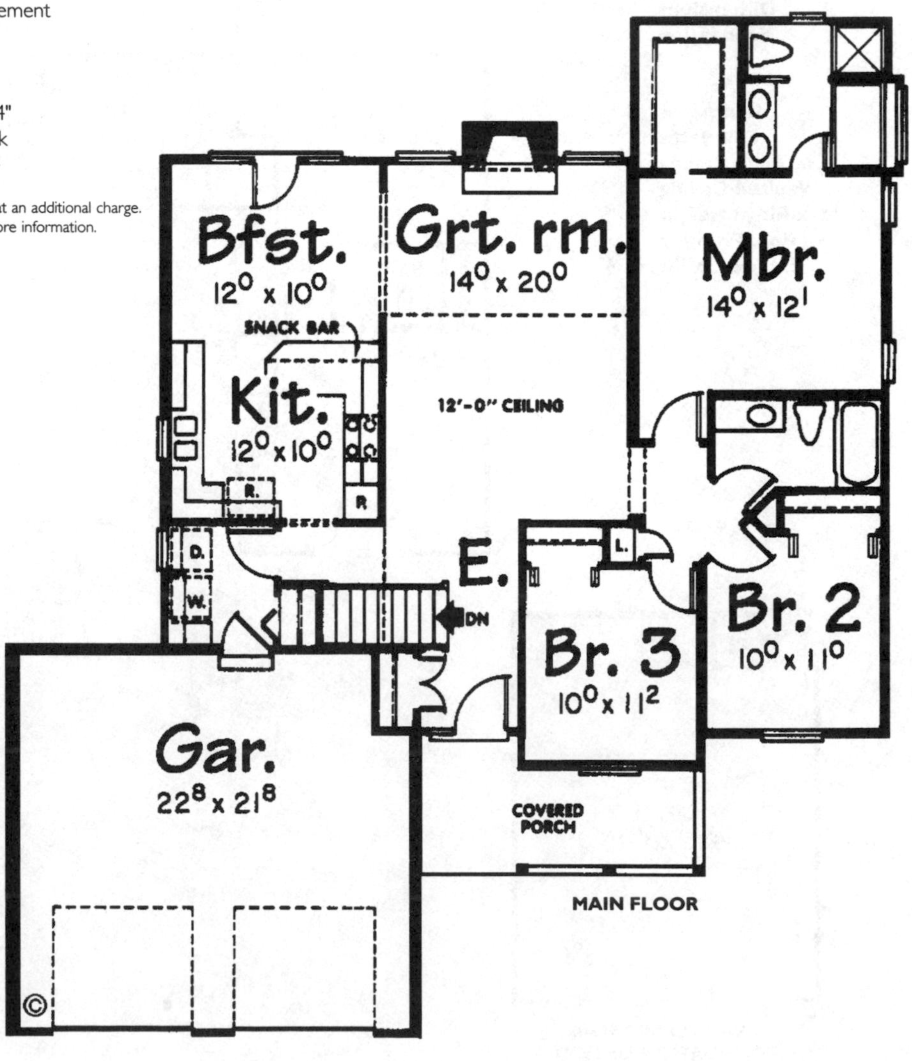

Bfst.
12^{0} x 10^{0}

Grt. rm.
14^{0} x 20^{0}

Mbr.
14^{0} x 12^{1}

SNACK BAR

Kit.
12^{0} x 10^{0}

12'-0" CEILING

R.

R

D.

W.

E.

L.

DN

Br. 3
10^{0} x 11^{2}

Br. 2
10^{0} x 11^{0}

Gar.
22^{8} x 21^{8}

COVERED PORCH

MAIN FLOOR

©

Design 96509

Units	Single
Price Code	A
Total Finished	1,438 sq. ft.
Main Finished	1,438 sq. ft.
Garage Unfinished	486 sq. ft.
Deck Unfinished	282 sq. ft.
Porch Unfinished	126 sq. ft.
Dimensions	54'x57'
Foundation	Crawlspace Slab
Bedrooms	3
Full Baths	2
Max Ridge Height	19'
Roof Framing	Stick
Exterior Walls	2x4

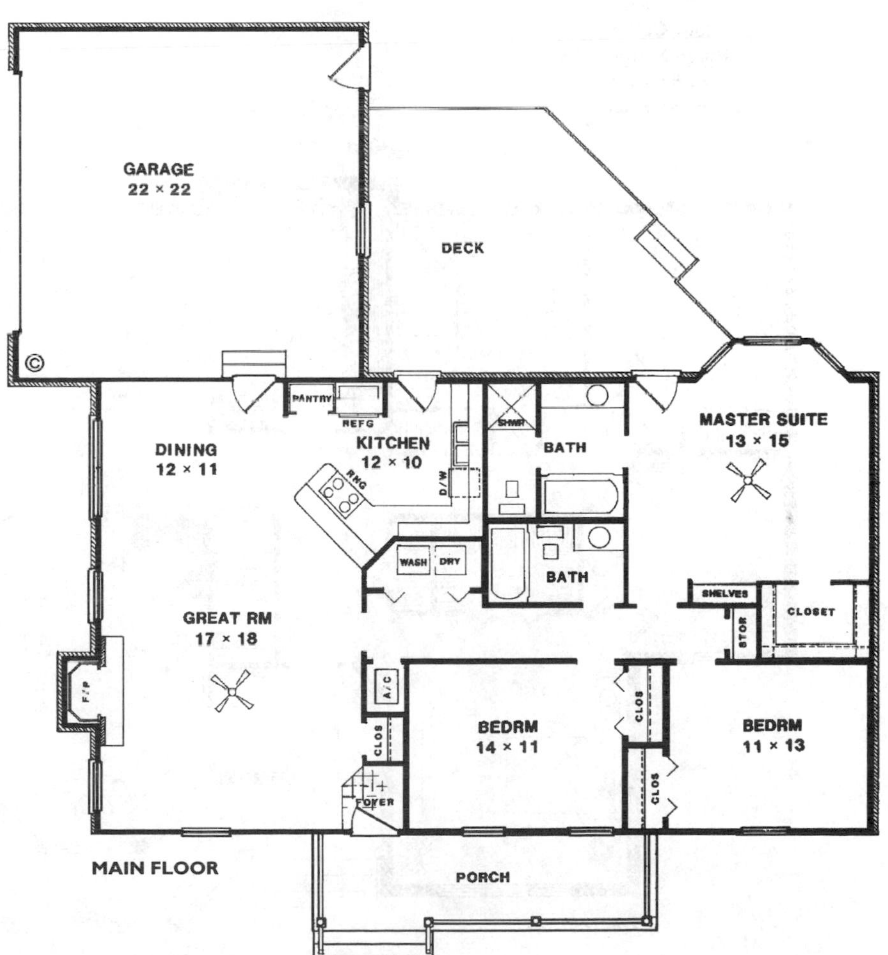

Units	Single
Price Code	A
Total Finished	1,440 sq. ft.
Main Finished	1,440 sq. ft.
Basement Unfinished	1,440 sq. ft.
Garage Unfinished	332 sq. ft.
Dimensions	58'x36'
Foundation	Basement
Bedrooms	3
Full Baths	1
Main Ceiling	8'
Max Ridge Height	26'
Roof Framing	Truss
Exterior Walls	2x6

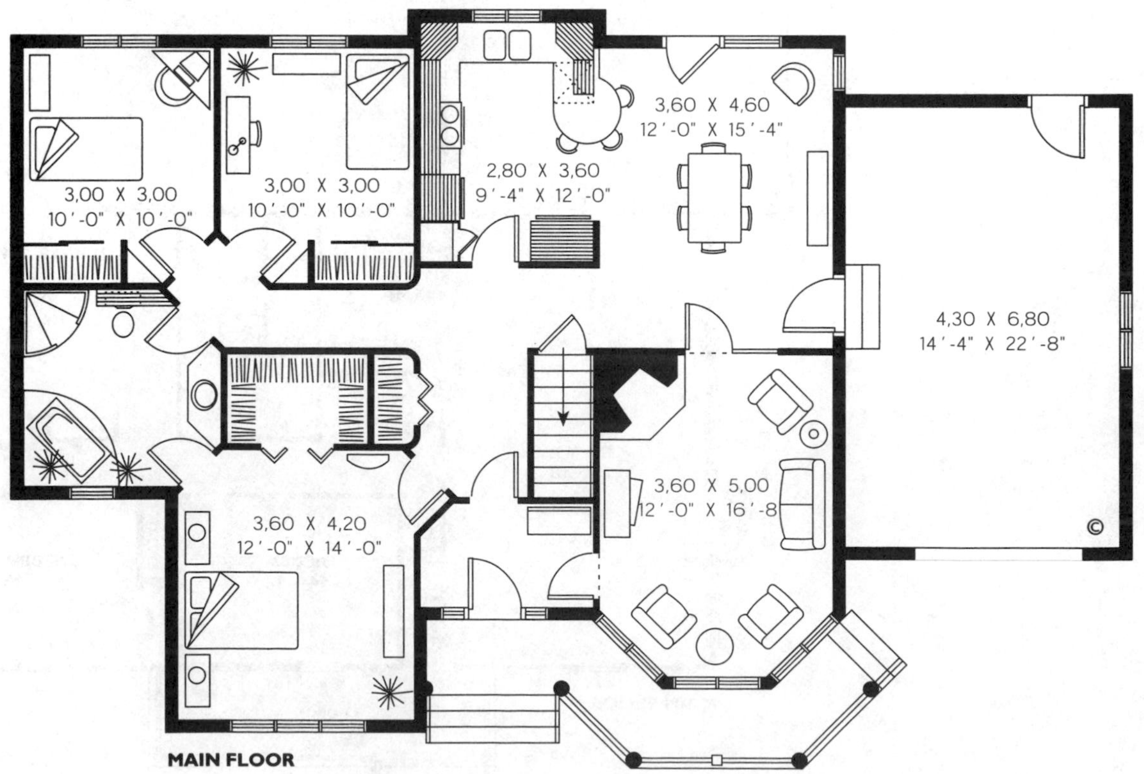

MAIN FLOOR

Design 62025

Units	Single
Price Code	A
Total Finished	1,442 sq. ft.
Main Finished	1,442 sq. ft.
Garage Unfinished	417 sq. ft.
Porch Unfinished	172 sq. ft.
Dimensions	34'8"x71'
Foundation	Crawlspace Slab
Bedrooms	3
Full Baths	2
Main Ceiling	9'
Exterior Walls	2x4

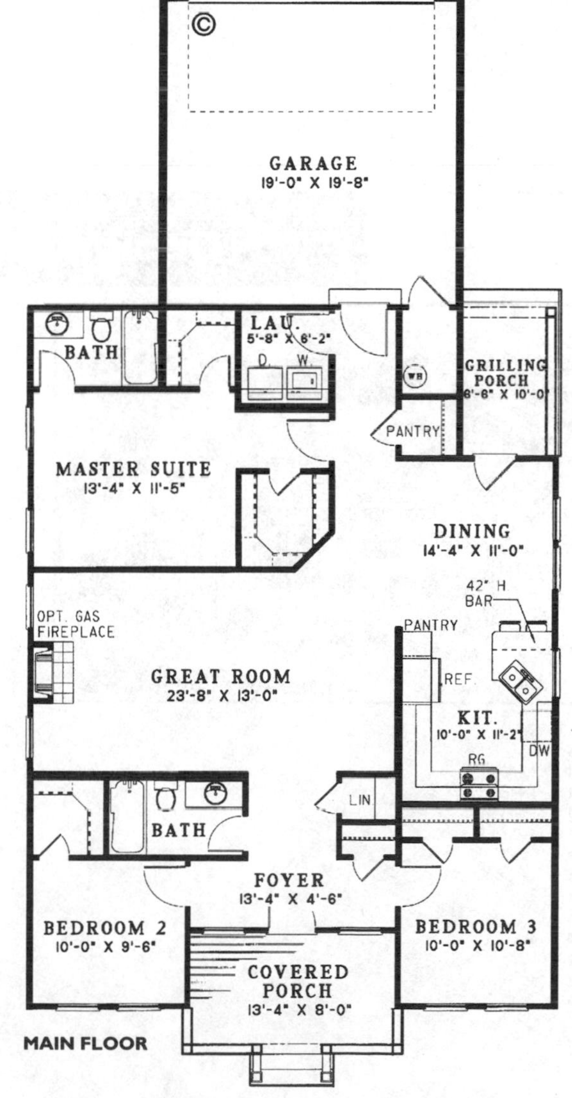

MAIN FLOOR

Design 82049

Units	Single
Price Code	A
Total Finished	1,447 sq. ft.
Main Finished	1,447 sq. ft.
Garage Unfinished	342 sq. ft.
Porch Unfinished	284 sq. ft.
Dimensions	44'x71'2"
Foundation	Crawlspace Slab
Bedrooms	3
Full Baths	2
Main Ceiling	9'
Roof Framing	Stick
Exterior Walls	2x4

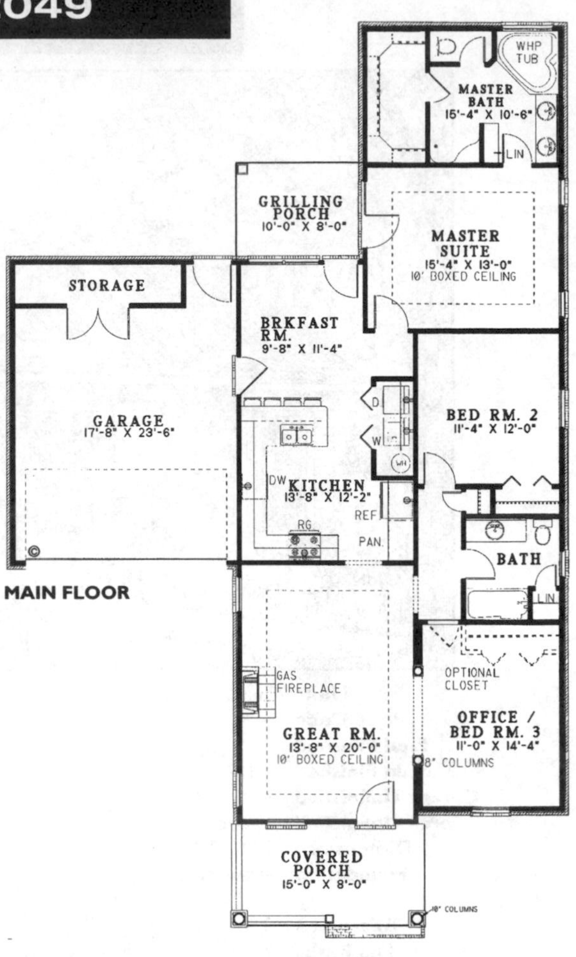

Design 97172

Units	Single
Price Code	A
Total Finished	1,448 sq. ft.
Main Finished	1,448 sq. ft.
Basement Unfinished	1,448 sq. ft.
Garage Unfinished	440 sq. ft.
Dimensions	38'x59'
Foundation	Basement
Bedrooms	3
Full Baths	1
3/4 Baths	1
Main Ceiling	8'
Roof Framing	Truss
Exterior Walls	2x6

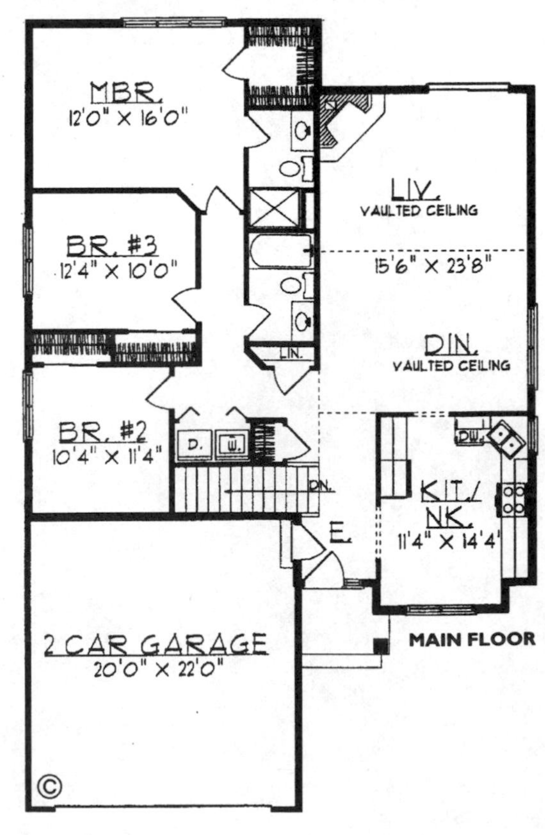

Design 65179

Units	Single
Price Code	A
Total Finished	1,450 sq. ft.
First Finished	918 sq. ft.
Second Finished	532 sq. ft.
Basement Unfinished	918 sq. ft.
Dimensions	26'4"x37'
Foundation	Basement
Bedrooms	3
Full Baths	1
3/4 Baths	1
First Ceiling	8'
Second Ceiling	8'
Max Ridge Height	27'4"
Roof Framing	Truss
Exterior Walls	2x6

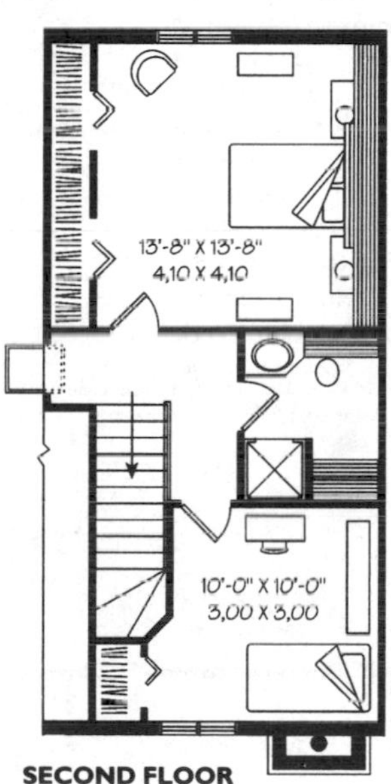

SECOND FLOOR

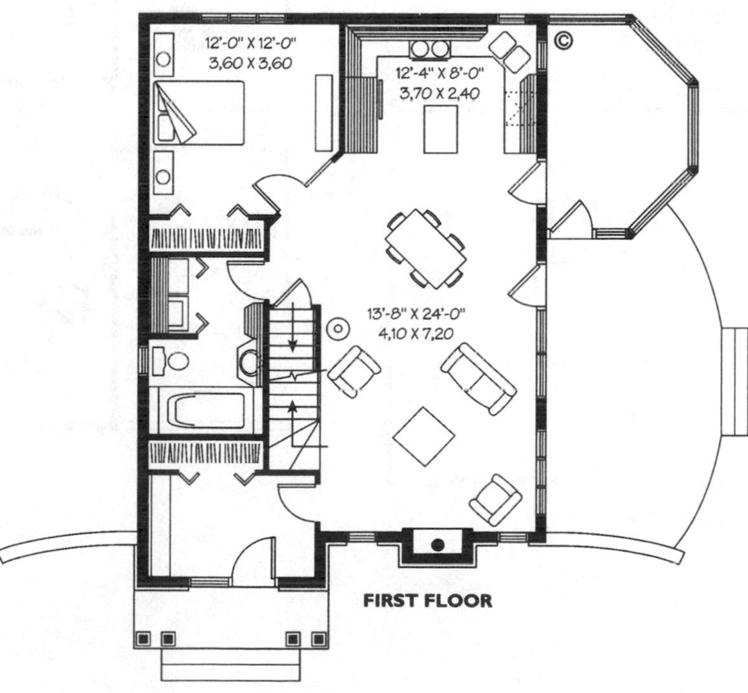

FIRST FLOOR

Design 94914

Units	Single
Price Code	A
Total Finished	1,453 sq. ft.
Main Finished	1,453 sq. ft.
Basement Unfinished	1,453 sq. ft.
Garage Unfinished	481 sq. ft.
Dimensions	48'8"x44'
Foundation	Basement
Bedrooms	3
Full Baths	2
Main Ceiling	8'
Max Ridge Height	18'6"
Roof Framing	Stick
Exterior Walls	2x4

* Alternate foundation options available at an additional charge. Please call 1-800-235-5700 for more information.

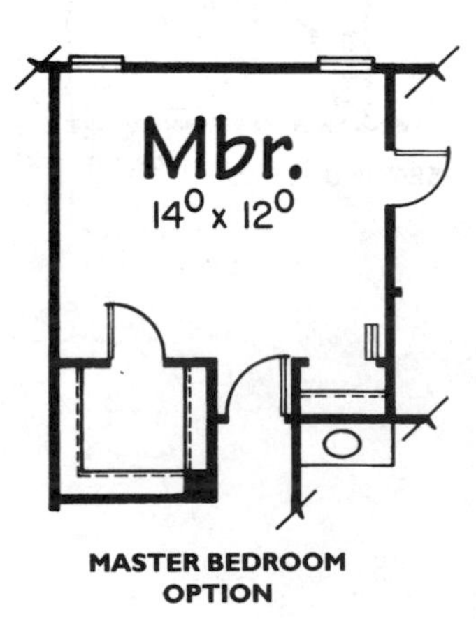

MASTER BEDROOM OPTION

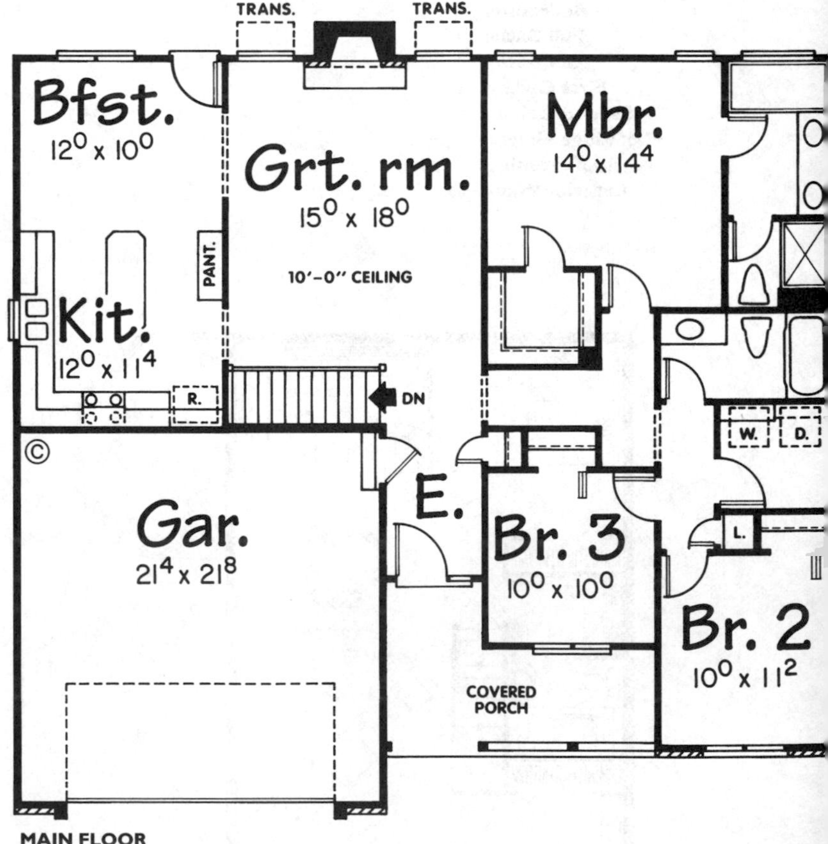

MAIN FLOOR

Design 97137

Units	Single
Price Code	A
Total Finished	1,461 sq. ft.
Main Finished	1,461 sq. ft.
Garage Unfinished	458 sq. ft.
Deck Unfinished	200 sq. ft.
Dimensions	56'x42'
Foundation	Basement
Bedrooms	3
Full Baths	2
Main Ceiling	8'
Max Ridge Height	21'5"
Roof Framing	Truss
Exterior Walls	2x6

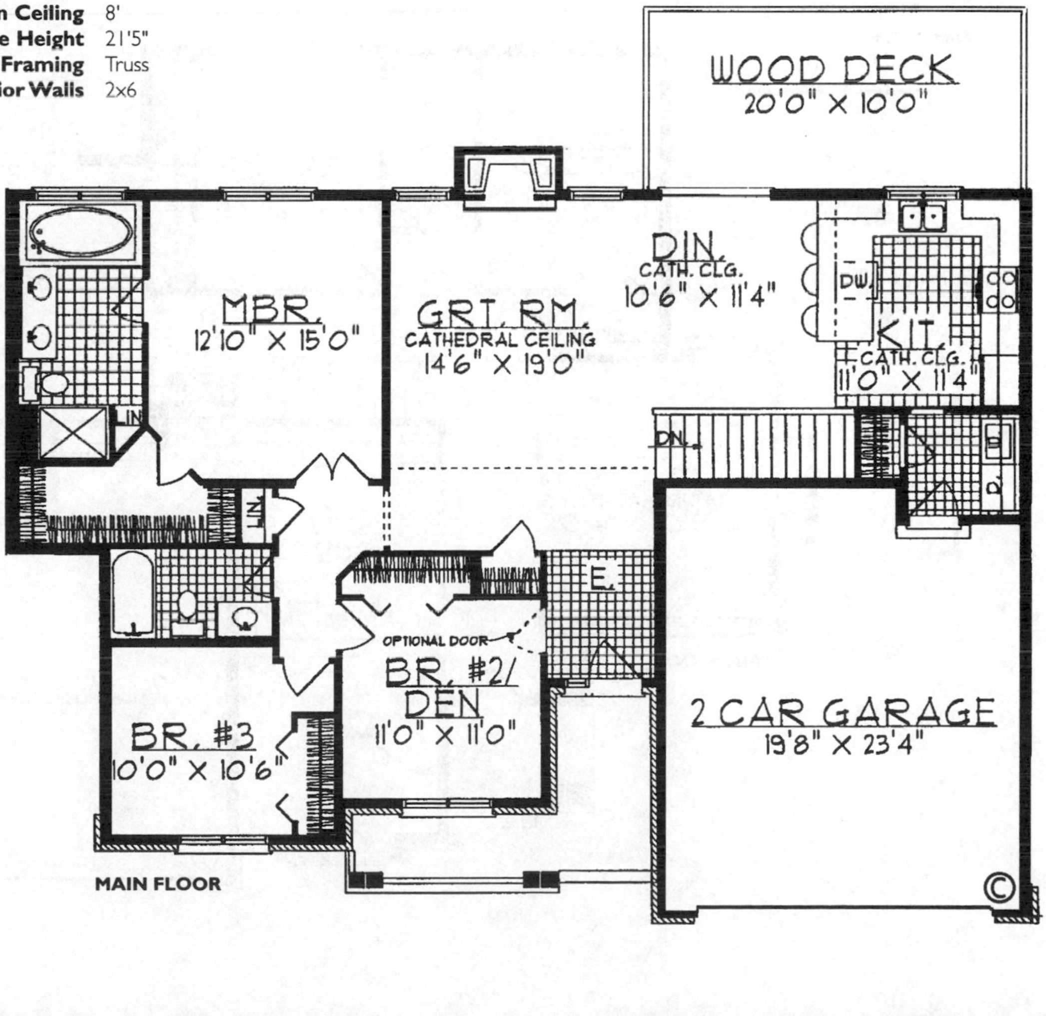

WOOD DECK
20'0" X 10'0"
DIN.
CATH. CLG.
10'6" X 11'4"
DW.
KIT.
CATH. CLG.
11'0" X 11'4"
MBR.
12'10" X 15'0"
GRT. RM.
CATHEDRAL CEILING
14'6" X 19'0"
LIN.
DN.
LIN.
E.
OPTIONAL DOOR
BR. #2/
DEN
11'0" X 11'0"
BR. #3
10'0" X 10'6"
2 CAR GARAGE
19'8" X 23'4"
D.
©

MAIN FLOOR

Design 97176

Units	Single
Price Code	A
Total Finished	1,462 sq. ft.
Main Finished	1,462 sq. ft.
Basement Unfinished	1,462 sq. ft.
Garage Unfinished	400 sq. ft.
Dimensions	52'x46'
Foundation	Basement
Bedrooms	3
Full Baths	2
Main Ceiling	8'
Max Ridge Height	24'10"
Roof Framing	Truss
Exterior Walls	2x6

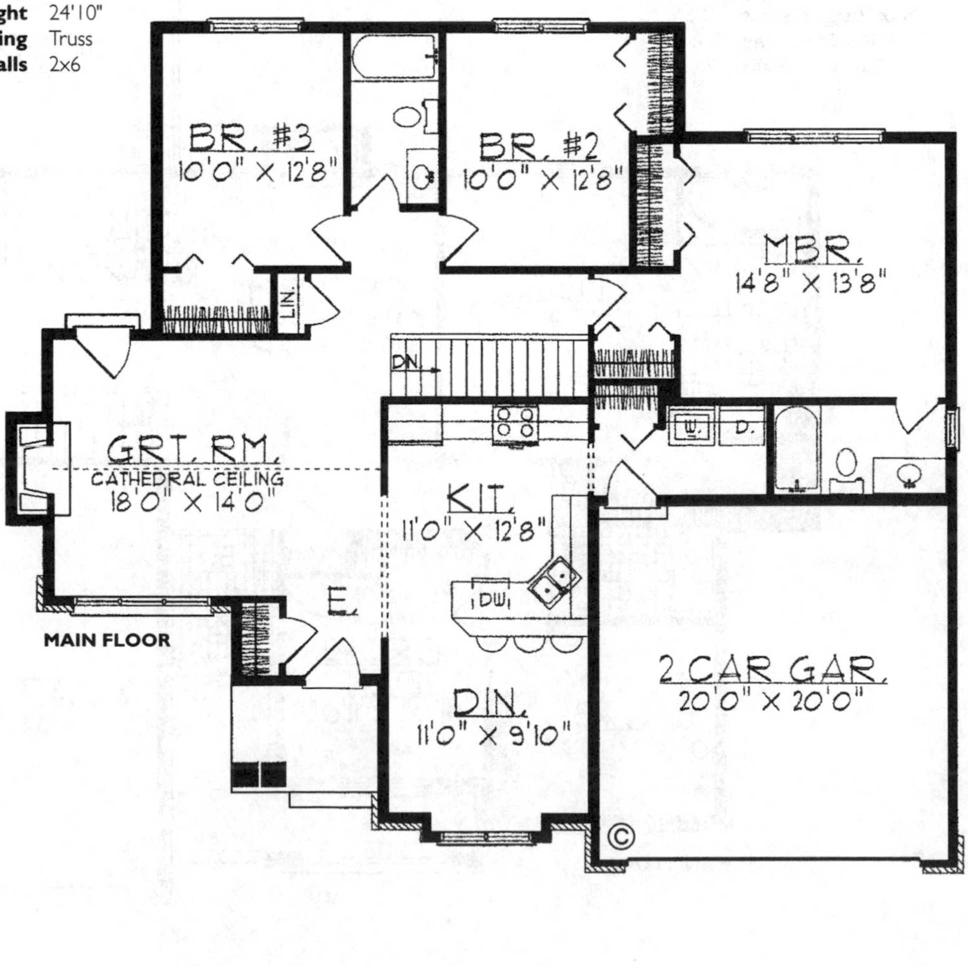

BR. #3
10'0" X 12'8"

BR. #2
10'0" X 12'8"

MBR.
14'8" X 13'8"

LIN.

DN

GRT. RM.
CATHEDRAL CEILING
18'0" X 14'0"

KIT.
11'0" X 12'8"

W. D.

DW

E.

2 CAR GAR.
20'0" X 20'0"

DIN.
11'0" X 9'10"

©

MAIN FLOOR

Design 99926

Units	Single
Price Code	A
Total Finished	1,463 sq. ft.
Main Finished	1,163 sq. ft.
Basement Unfinished	1,446 sq. ft.
Garage Unfinished	390 sq. ft.
Deck Unfinished	100 sq. ft.
Porch Unfinished	40 sq. ft.
Dimensions	40'x60'
Foundation	Basement
Bedrooms	3
Full Baths	2
Main Ceiling	8'
Vaulted Ceiling	11'
Max Ridge Height	18'6"
Roof Framing	Truss
Exterior Walls	2x6

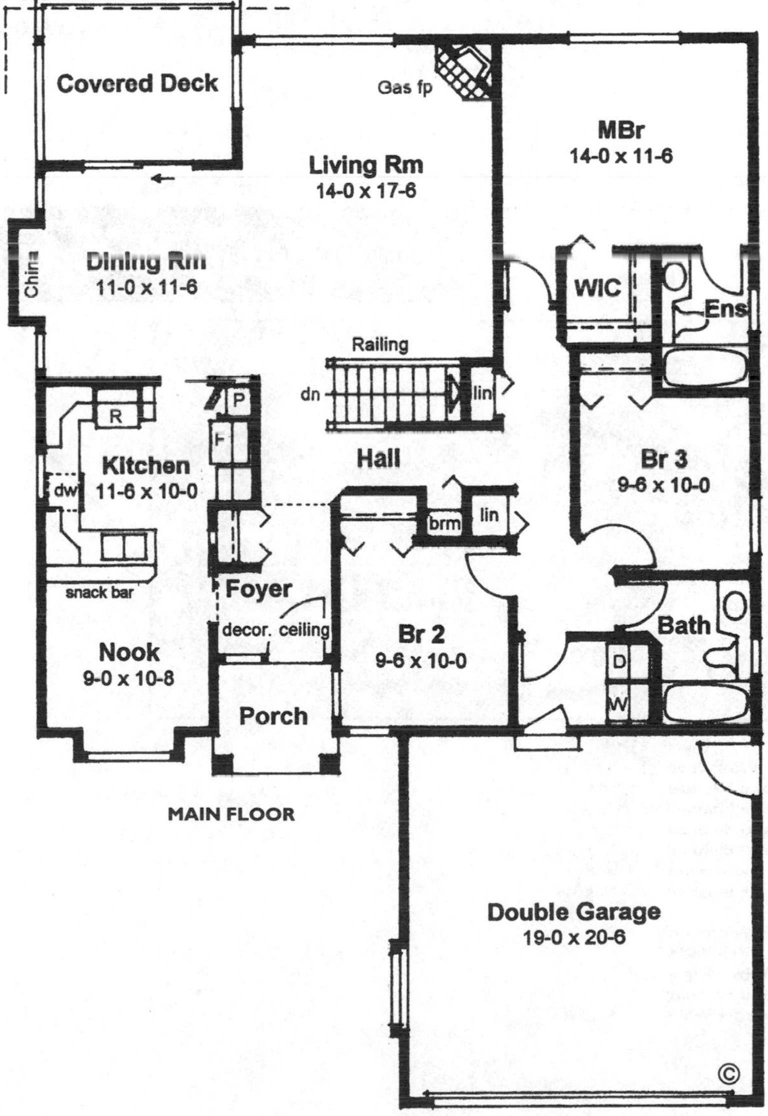

MAIN FLOOR

Design 91554

Units Single
Price Code A
Total Finished 1,467 sq. ft.
Main Finished 1,467 sq. ft.
Garage Unfinished 400 sq. ft.
Dimensions 49'x43'
Foundation Crawlspace
Bedrooms 3
Full Baths 2
Main Ceiling 8'1"
Vaulted Ceiling 13'
Max Ridge Height 20'6"
Roof Framing Truss
Exterior Walls 2x6

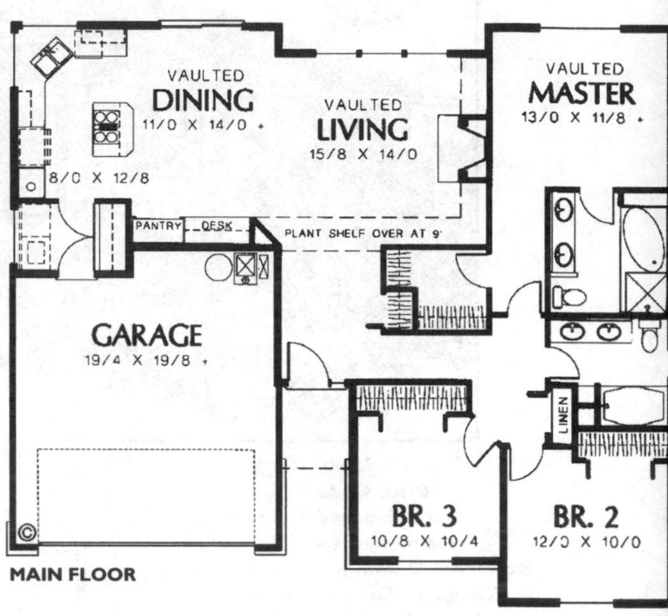

Design 93416

Units Single
Price Code A
Total Finished 1,475 sq. ft.
Main Finished 1,475 sq. ft.
Garage Unfinished 455 sq. ft.
Porch Unfinished 234 sq. ft.
Dimensions 43'x43'
Foundation Crawlspace
Slab
Bedrooms 3
Full Baths 2
Max Ridge Height 24'
Roof Framing Stick
Exterior Walls 2x4

Garage
20x21
Deck
Walk
MASTER BATH
OPTION
Dining
10X11
Bath
Master
16X13
VAULTED CEILING
Kitchen
14X10
Bath
Br 3
10X11
Family Room
21X15
10' CEILING
Br 2
12-6X11
Porch

MAIN FLOOR

Design 60084

Units	Single
Price Code	A
Total Finished	1,477 sq. ft.
Main Finished	1,477 sq. ft.
Bonus Unfinished	283 sq. ft.
Basement Unfinished	1,477 sq. ft.
Garage Unfinished	420 sq. ft.
Dimensions	51'x51'4"
Foundation	Basement Crawlspace
Bedrooms	3
Full Baths	2
Main Ceiling	8'
Second Ceiling	8'
Max Ridge Height	24'
Roof Framing	Stick
Exterior Walls	2x4

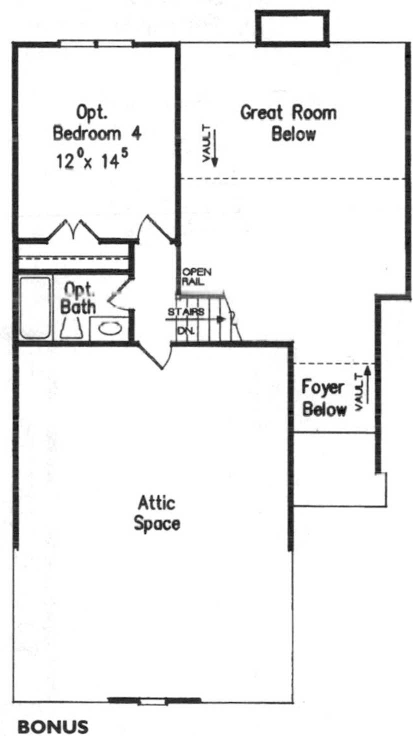

BONUS

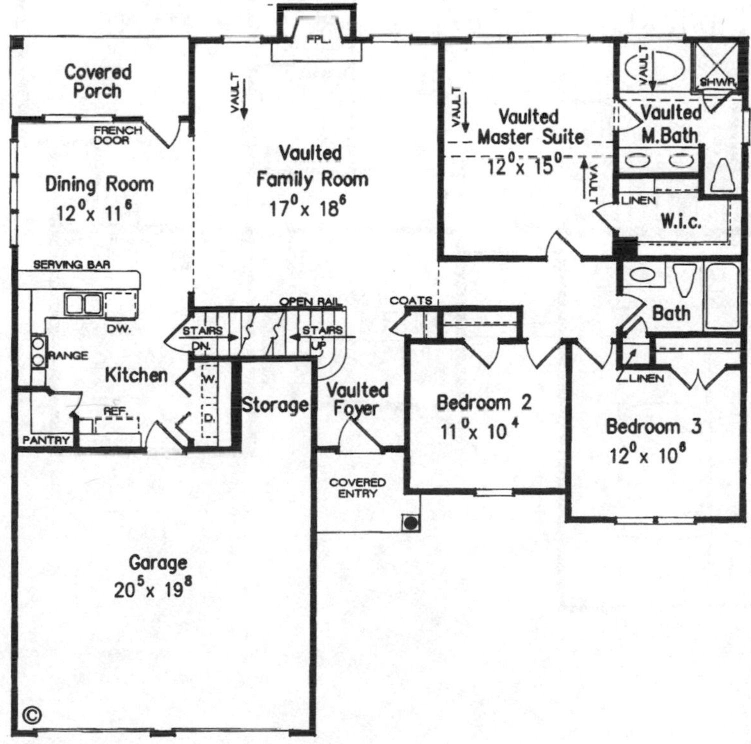

MAIN FLOOR

Design 91847

Units	Single
Price Code	A
Total Finished	1,479 sq. ft.
Main Finished	1,479 sq. ft.
Basement Unfinished	1,430 sq. ft.
Garage Unfinished	528 sq. ft.
Dimensions	56'x46'6"
Foundation	Basement Crawlspace Slab
Bedrooms	3
Full Baths	2
Main Ceiling	8'
Max Ridge Height	19'4"
Roof Framing	Truss
Exterior Walls	2x6

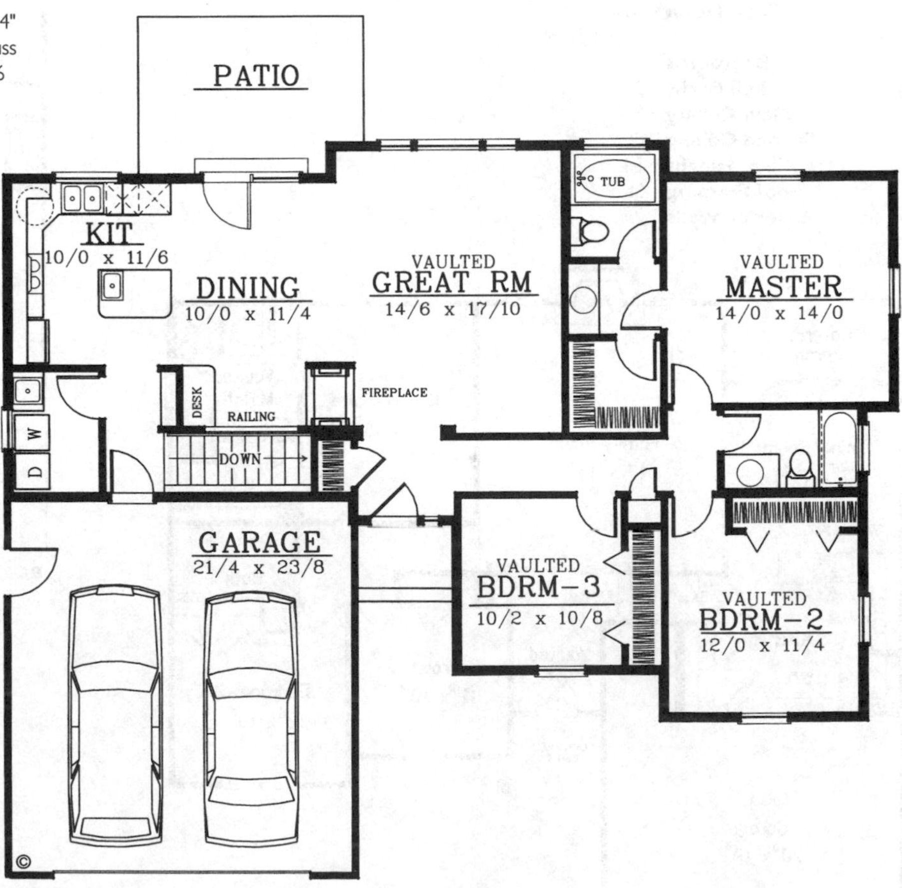

MAIN FLOOR

Design 99490

Units	Single
Price Code	A
Total Finished	1,479 sq. ft.
Main Finished	1,479 sq. ft.
Dimensions	48'x50'
Foundation	Basement Slab
Bedrooms	3
Full Baths	2
Max Ridge Height	21'6"
Roof Framing	Stick
Exterior Walls	2x4

* Alternate foundation options available at an additional charge. Please call 1-800-235-5700 for more information.

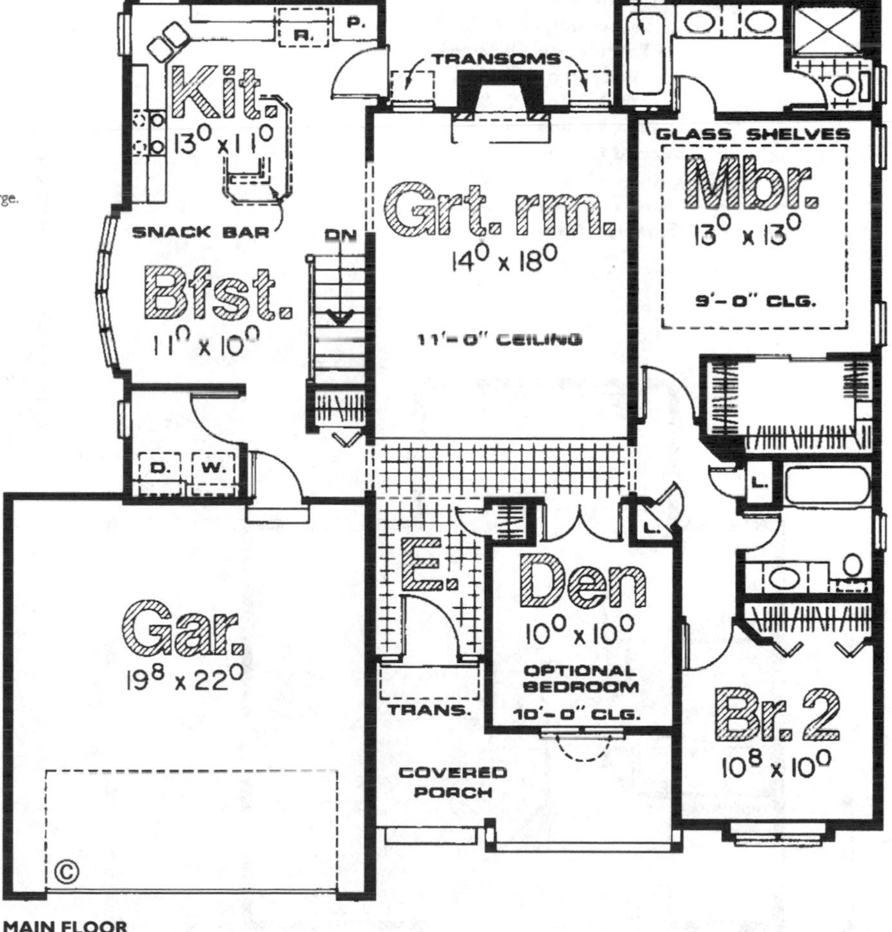

MAIN FLOOR

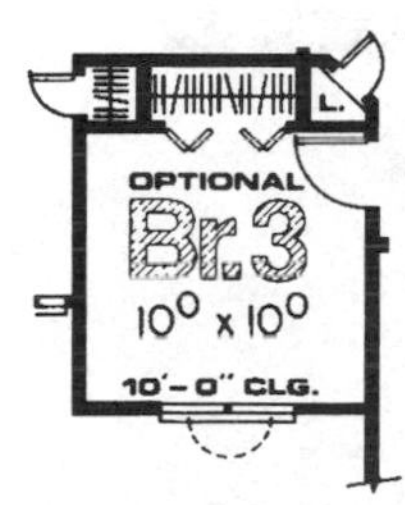

THIRD BEDROOM OPTION

Design 65001

Units Single
Price Code A
Total Finished 1,480 sq. ft.
First Finished 1,024 sq. ft.
Second Finished 456 sq. ft.
Basement Unfinished 1,024 sq. ft.
Dimensions 32'x40'
Foundation Basement
Bedrooms 2
Full Baths 2
First Ceiling 8'
Second Ceiling 8'
Max Ridge Height 23'8"
Roof Framing Truss
Exterior Walls 2x6

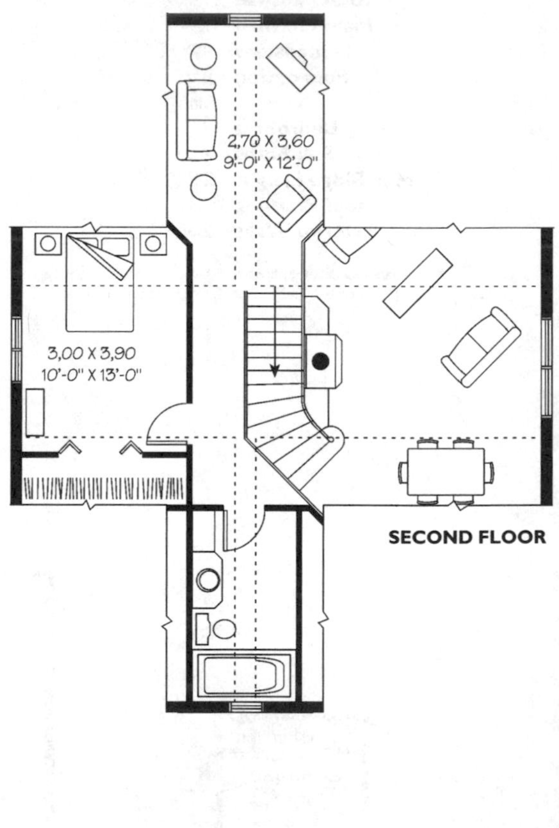

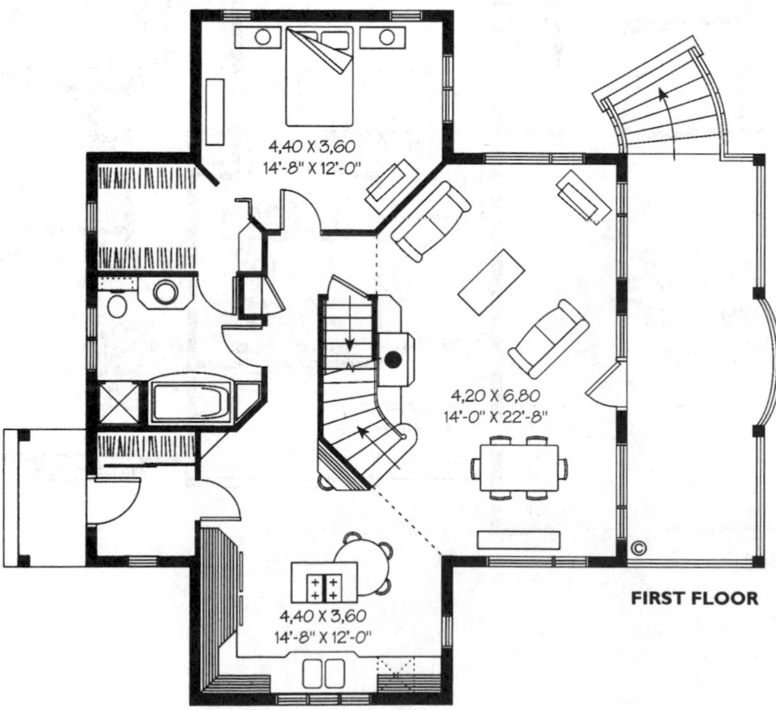

Design 61032

Units	Single
Price Code	A
Total Finished	1,485 sq. ft.
Main Finished	1,485 sq. ft.
Dimensions	51'6"x49'
Foundation	Crawlspace Slab
Bedrooms	3
Full Baths	2

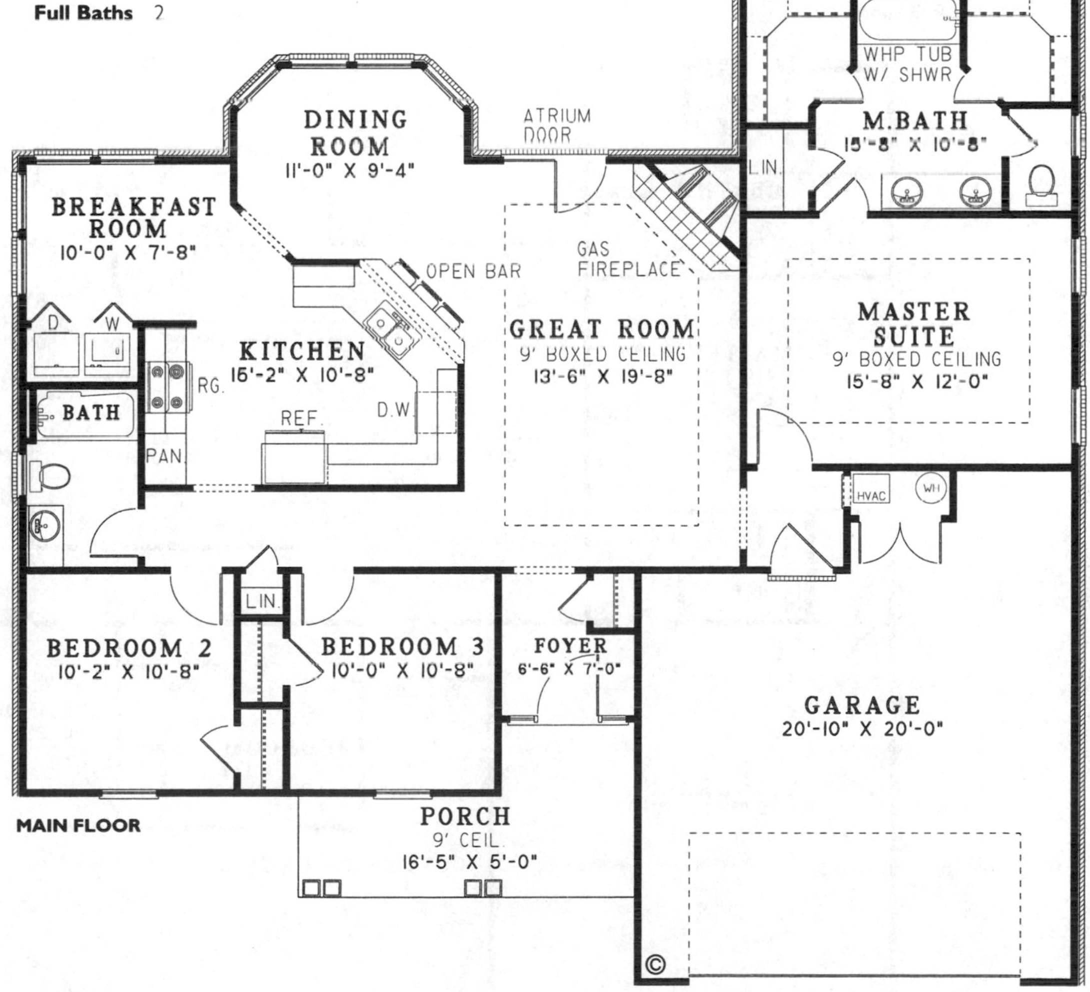

Design 61033

Units	Single
Price Code	A
Total Finished	1,485 sq. ft.
Main Finished	1,485 sq. ft.
Dimensions	51'6"x49'10"
Foundation	Crawlspace Slab
Bedrooms	3
Full Baths	2

MAIN FLOOR

Design 82026

Units Single
Price Code A
Total Finished 1,485 sq. ft.
Main Finished 1,485 sq. ft.
Garage Unfinished 415 sq. ft.
Porch Unfinished 180 sq. ft.
Dimensions 51'6"x49'10"
Foundation Crawlspace
Slab
Bedrooms 3
Full Baths 2
Main Ceiling 9'
Roof Framing Stick
Exterior Walls 2x4

Design 61035

Units Single
Price Code A
Total Finished 1,490 sq. ft.
Main Finished 1,490 sq. ft.
Garage Unfinished 386 sq. ft.
Porch Unfinished 20 sq. ft.
Dimensions 31'6"x72'10"
Foundation Crawlspace
Slab
Bedrooms 3
Full Baths 2
Main Ceiling 9'
Exterior Walls 2x4

©
GARAGE 18'-4" X 20'-0"
PATIO
PANTRY
STRG
WH
LAU
D W
BRKFST ROOM 12'-0" X 8'-6"
REF.
KITCHEN 14'-0" X 11'-0"
RG DW
BEDROOM 3 11'-4" X 10'-6"
LIN
LIN
GREAT ROOM 19'-0" X 15'-2"
OPT. GAS FIREPLACE
BATH
LIN
BEDROOM 2 11'-4" X 10'-6"
MASTER SUITE 14'-2" X 12'-0"
PORCH 16'-6" X 6'-6"
MAIN FLOOR

Design 34150

Units	Single
Price Code	A
Total Finished	1,492 sq. ft.
Main Finished	1,492 sq. ft.
Basement Unfinished	1,486 sq. ft.
Garage Unfinished	462 sq. ft.
Dimensions	56'x48'
Foundation	Basement Crawlspace Slab
Bedrooms	3
Full Baths	2
Main Ceiling	8'
Vaulted Ceiling	13'
Max Ridge Height	19'
Roof Framing	Stick
Exterior Walls	2x4, 2x6

Please note: The photographed home may have been modified to suit homeowner preferences. If you order plans, have a builder or design professional check them against the photograph to confirm actual construction details.

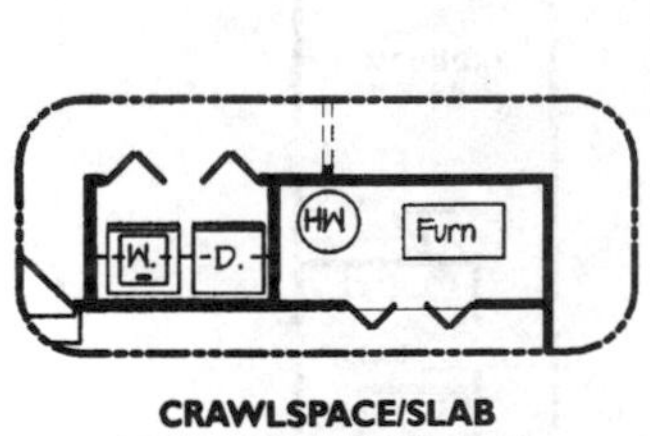

CRAWLSPACE/SLAB FOUNDATION OPTION

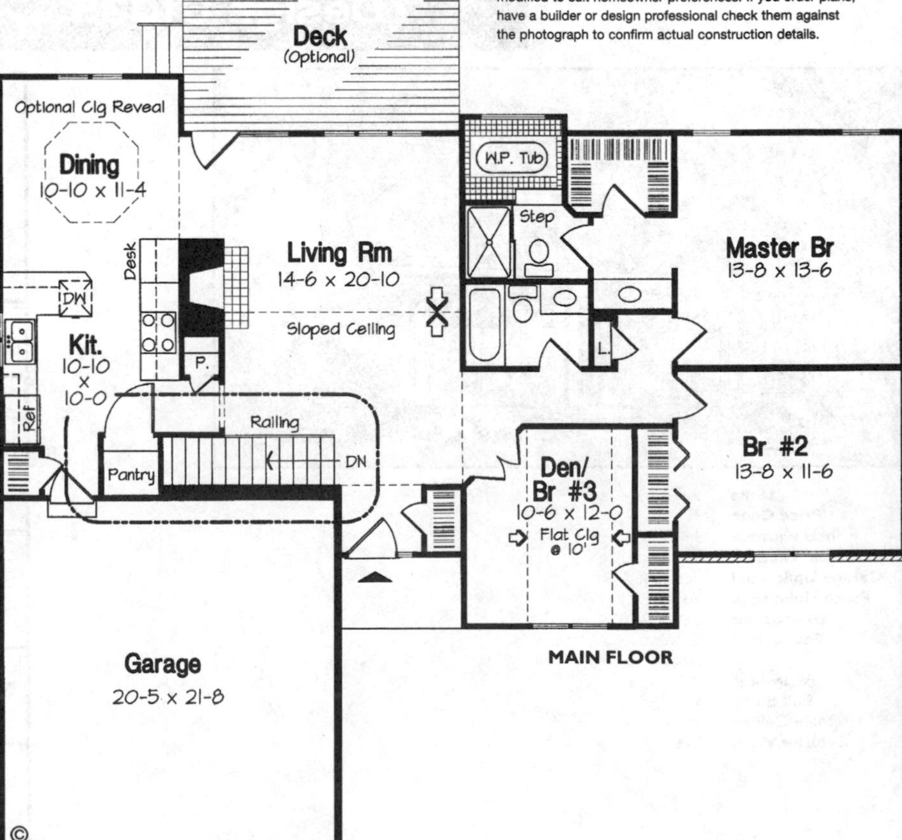

MAIN FLOOR

Design 90692

Units	Single
Price Code	A
Total Finished	1,492 sq. ft.
Main Finished	1,492 sq. ft.
Dimensions	67'10"x28'4"
Foundation	Basement Slab
Bedrooms	3
Full Baths	2

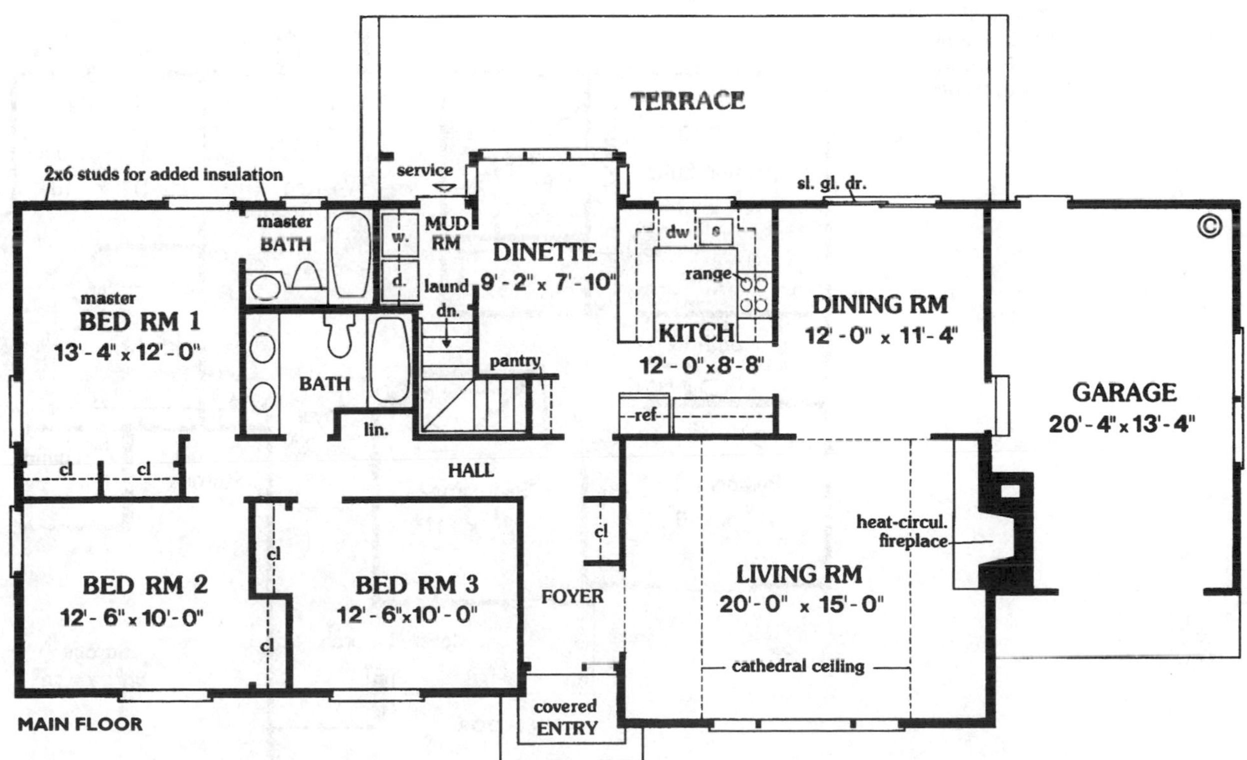

Design 98472

Units	Single
Price Code	A
Total Finished	1,492 sq. ft.
Main Finished	1,492 sq. ft.
Garage Unfinished	465 sq. ft.
Dimensions	56'x49'10"
Foundation	Basement Crawlspace
Bedrooms	3
Full Baths	2
Main Ceiling	9'
Max Ridge Height	27'6"
Roof Framing	Stick
Exterior Walls	2x4

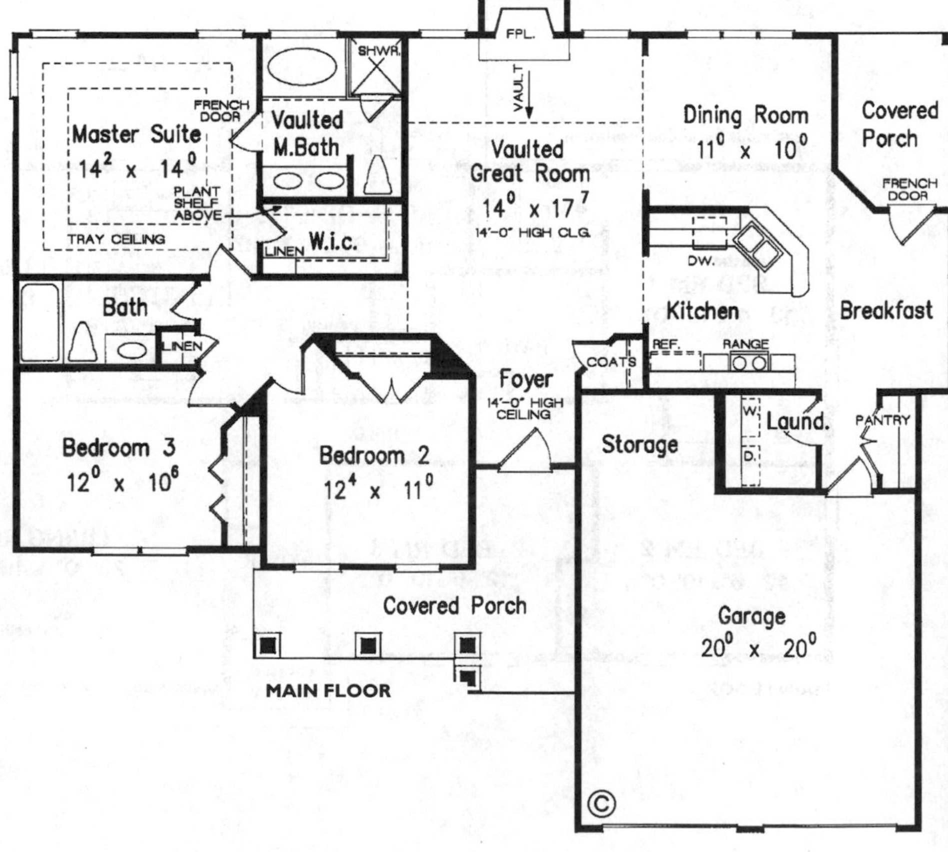

Design 99922

Units	Single
Price Code	A
Total Finished	1,493 sq. ft.
Main Finished	1,493 sq. ft.
Basement Unfinished	1,493 sq. ft.
Garage Unfinished	441 sq. ft.
Deck Unfinished	140 sq. ft.
Porch Unfinished	30 sq. ft.
Dimensions	48'x58'
Foundation	Basement
Bedrooms	3
Full Baths	2
Main Ceiling	8'
Vaulted Ceiling	10'6"
Max Ridge Height	20'
Roof Framing	Truss
Exterior Walls	2x6

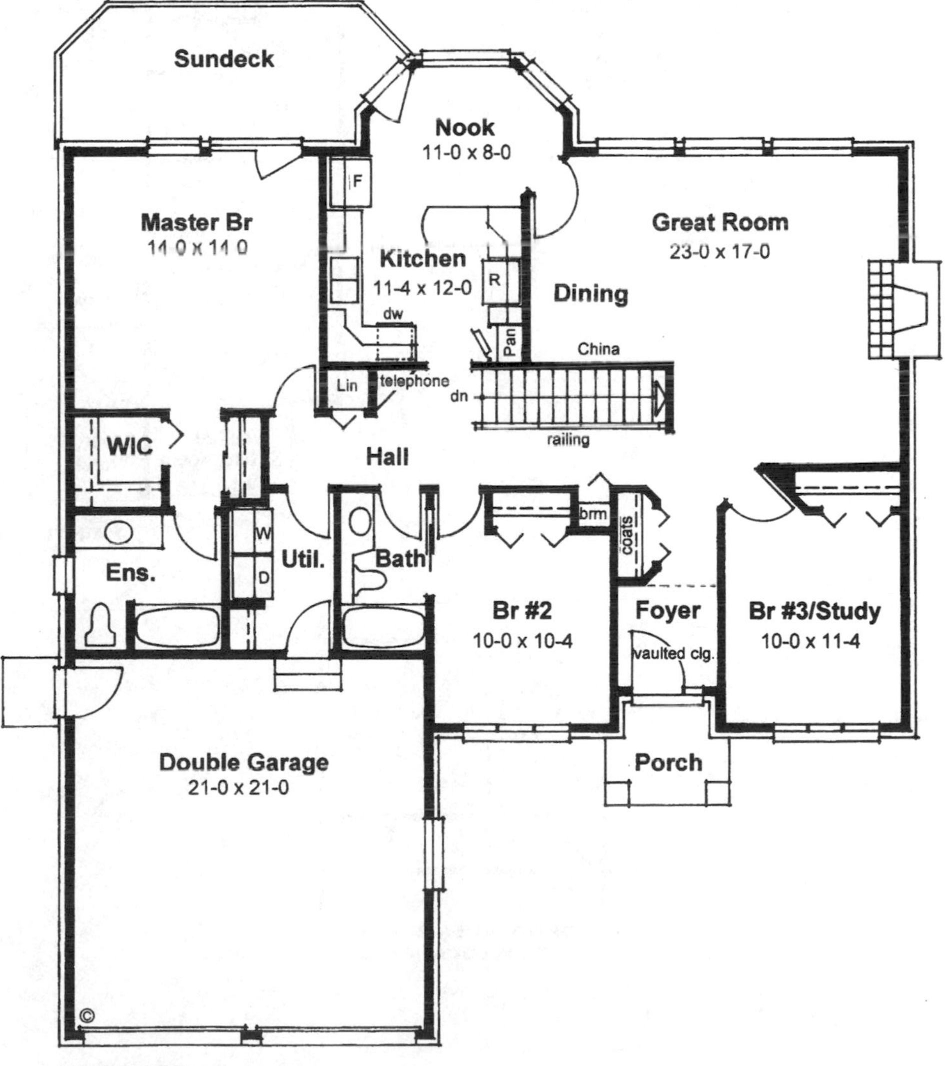

MAIN FLOOR

Design 98441

Units	Single
Price Code	B
Total Finished	1,502 sq. ft.
Main Finished	1,502 sq. ft.
Basement Unfinished	1,555 sq. ft.
Garage Unfinished	448 sq. ft.
Dimensions	51'x50'6"
Foundation	Basement Crawlspace
Bedrooms	3
Full Baths	2
Max Ridge Height	24'9"
Roof Framing	Stick
Exterior Walls	2x4

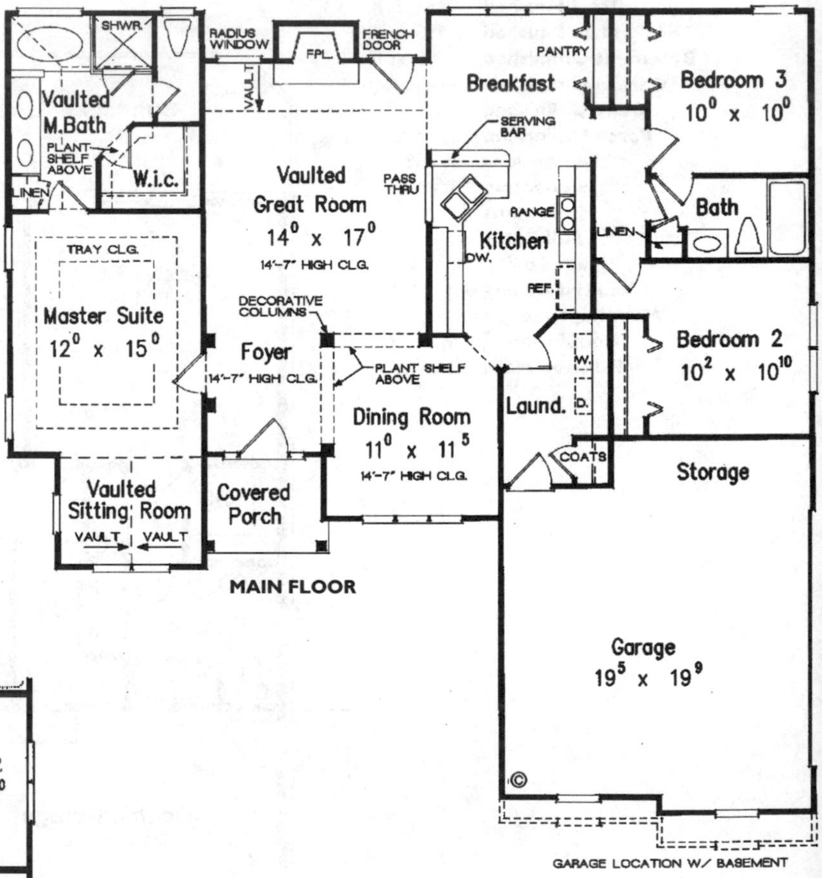

MAIN FLOOR

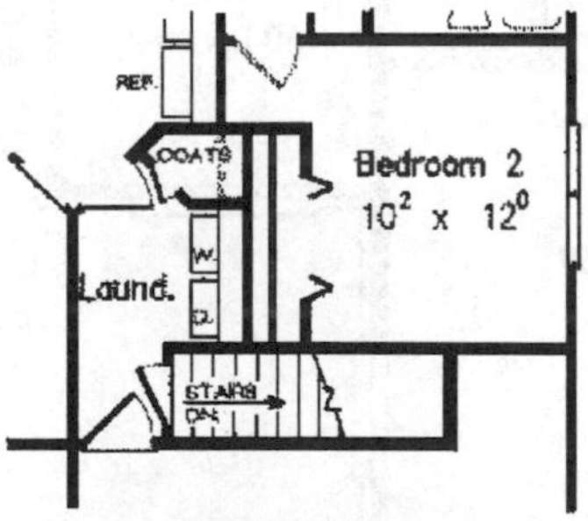

GARAGE LOCATION W/ BASEMENT

OPTIONAL BASEMENT STAIR LOCATION

Design 92649

Units	Single
Price Code	B
Total Finished	1,508 sq. ft.
Main Finished	1,508 sq. ft.
Basement Unfinished	1,439 sq. ft.
Garage Unfinished	440 sq. ft.
Dimensions	60'x47'
Foundation	Basement
Bedrooms	3
Full Baths	2
Main Ceiling	8'
Max Ridge Height	21'9"
Roof Framing	Truss
Exterior Walls	2x4

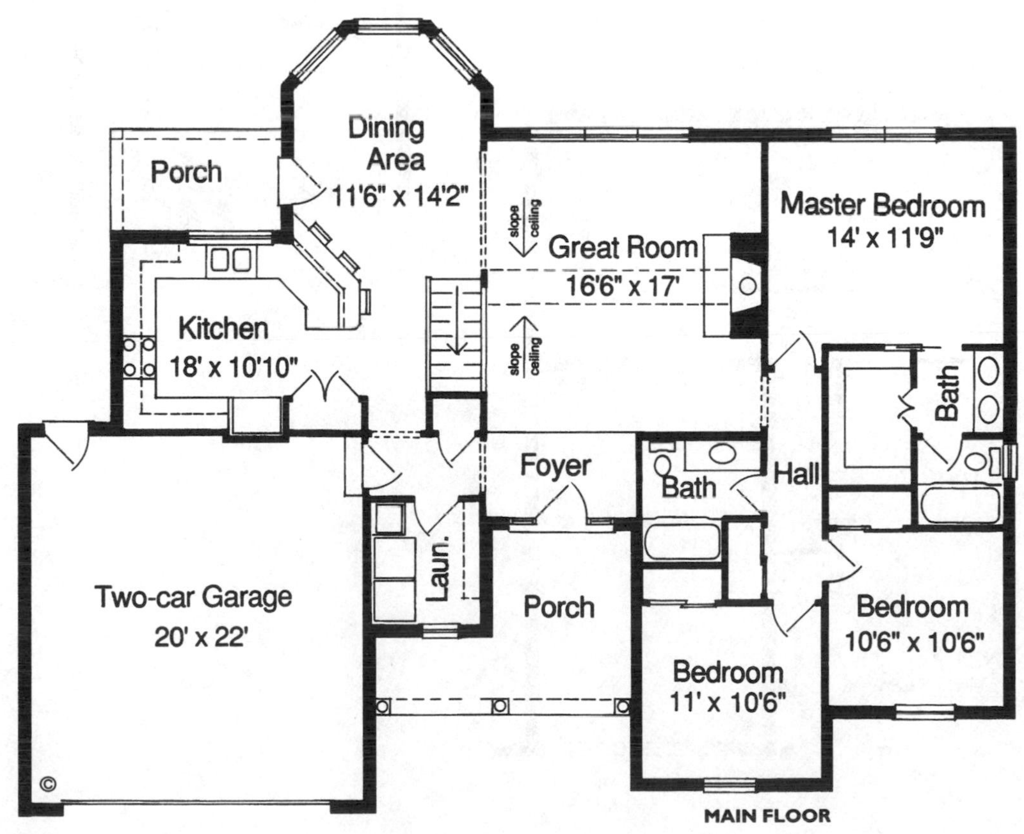

MAIN FLOOR

Design 65198

Units	Single
Price Code	B
Total Finished	1,519 sq. ft.
First Finished	788 sq. ft.
Second Finished	731 sq. ft.
Garage Unfinished	266 sq. ft.
Dimensions	32'x36'
Foundation	Basement
Bedrooms	3
Full Baths	1
3/4 Baths	1

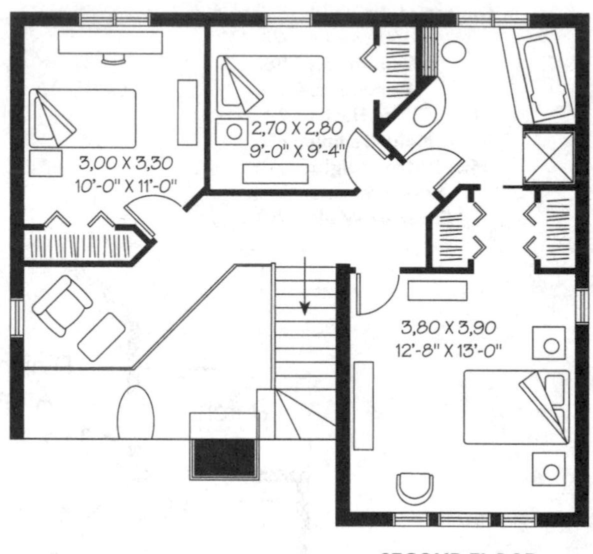

SECOND FLOOR

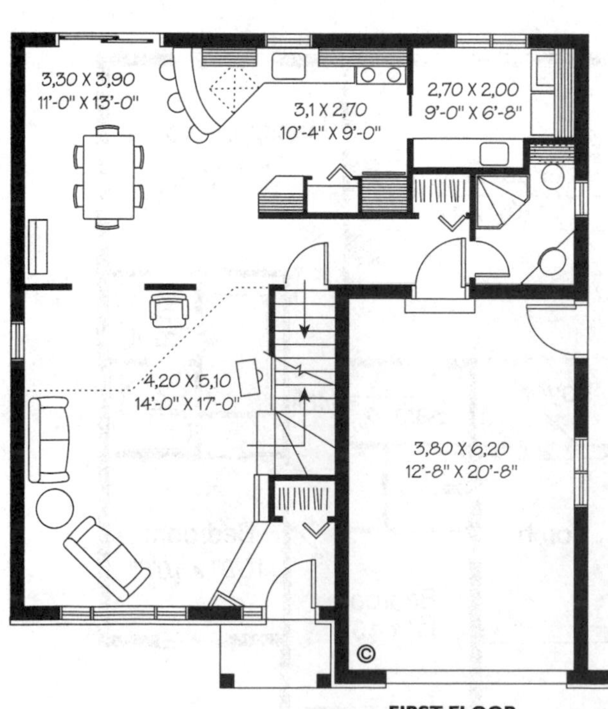

FIRST FLOOR

Units	Single
Price Code	B
Total Finished	1,520 sq. ft.
Main Finished	1,520 sq. ft.
Dimensions	40'x59'
Foundation	Pier/Post
Bedrooms	4
Full Baths	2
Main Ceiling	9'
Max Ridge Height	32'
Roof Framing	Stick
Exterior Walls	2x4

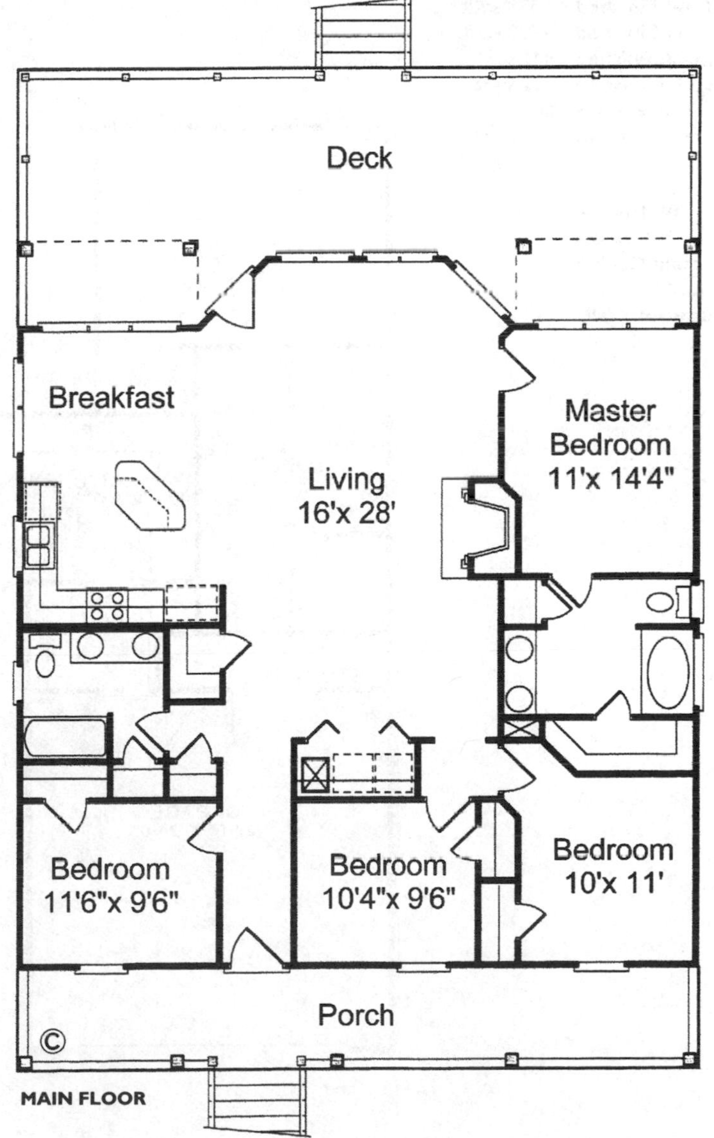

MAIN FLOOR

Design 82033

Units	Single
Price Code	B
Total Finished	1,538 sq. ft.
Main Finished	1,538 sq. ft.
Garage Unfinished	441 sq. ft.
Porch Unfinished	142 sq. ft.
Dimensions	50'x56'
Foundation	Basement Crawlspace Slab
Bedrooms	3
Full Baths	2
Main Ceiling	8'
Roof Framing	Stick
Exterior Walls	2x4

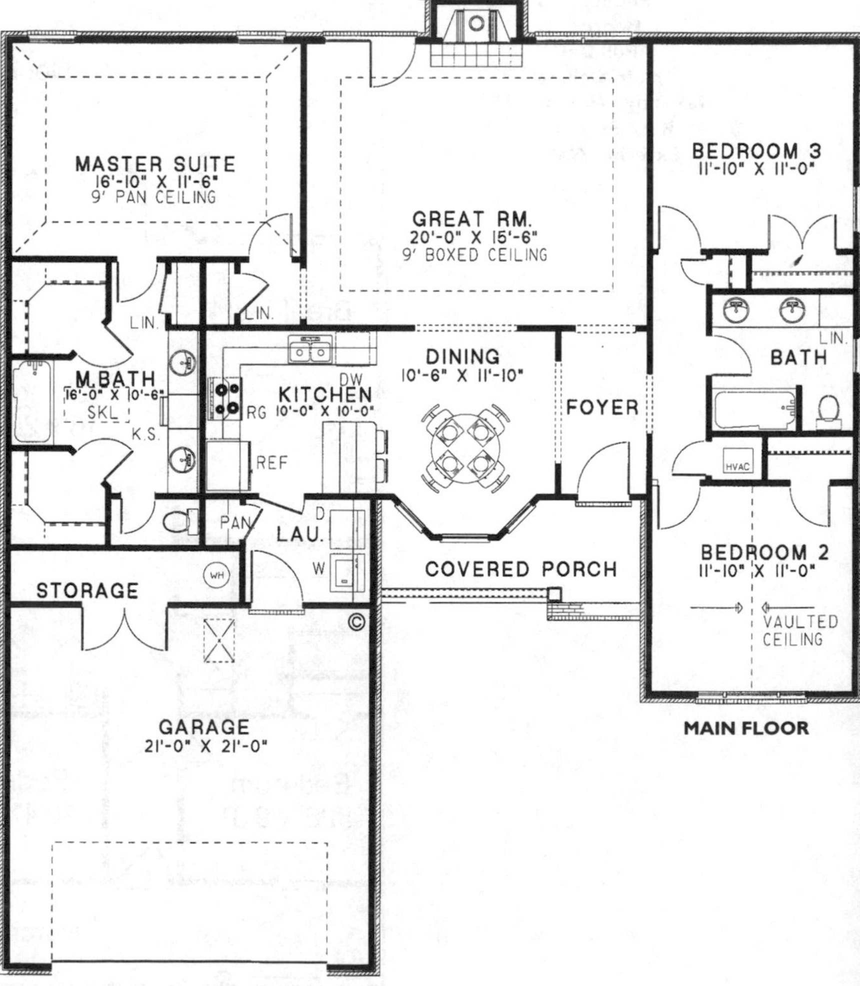

MAIN FLOOR

Design 97261

Units	Single
Price Code	B
Total Finished	1,538 sq. ft.
Main Finished	1,466 sq. ft.
Lower Finished	72 sq. ft.
Basement Unfinished	902 sq. ft.
Garage Unfinished	495 sq. ft.
Dimensions	44'x36'6"
Foundation	Basement
Bedrooms	3
Full Baths	2
Main Ceiling	8'
Max Ridge Height	24'
Roof Framing	Stick
Exterior Walls	2x4

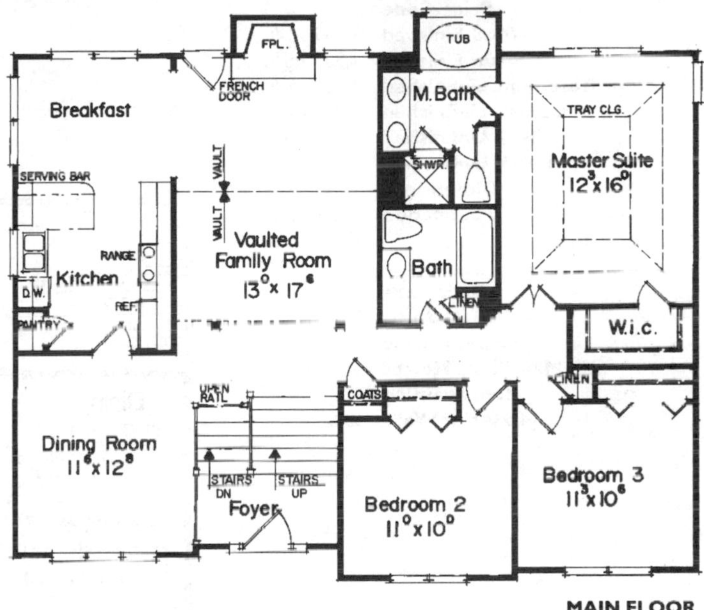

MAIN FLOOR

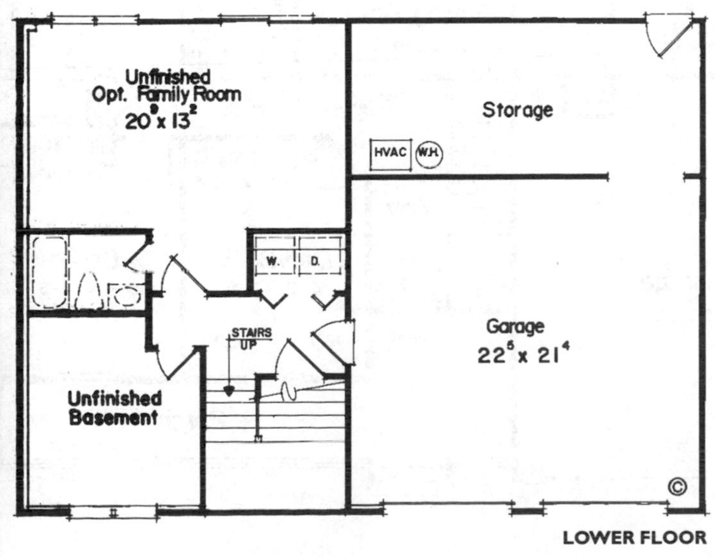

LOWER FLOOR

Units	Single
Price Code	B
Total Finished	1,539 sq. ft.
Main Finished	1,539 sq. ft.
Basement Unfinished	1,530 sq. ft.
Garage Unfinished	460 sq. ft.
Deck Unfinished	160 sq. ft.
Porch Unfinished	182 sq. ft.
Dimensions	50'x45'4"
Foundation	Basement Crawlspace Slab
Bedrooms	3
Full Baths	2
Main Ceiling	8'
Max Ridge Height	21'
Roof Framing	Stick
Exterior Walls	2x6

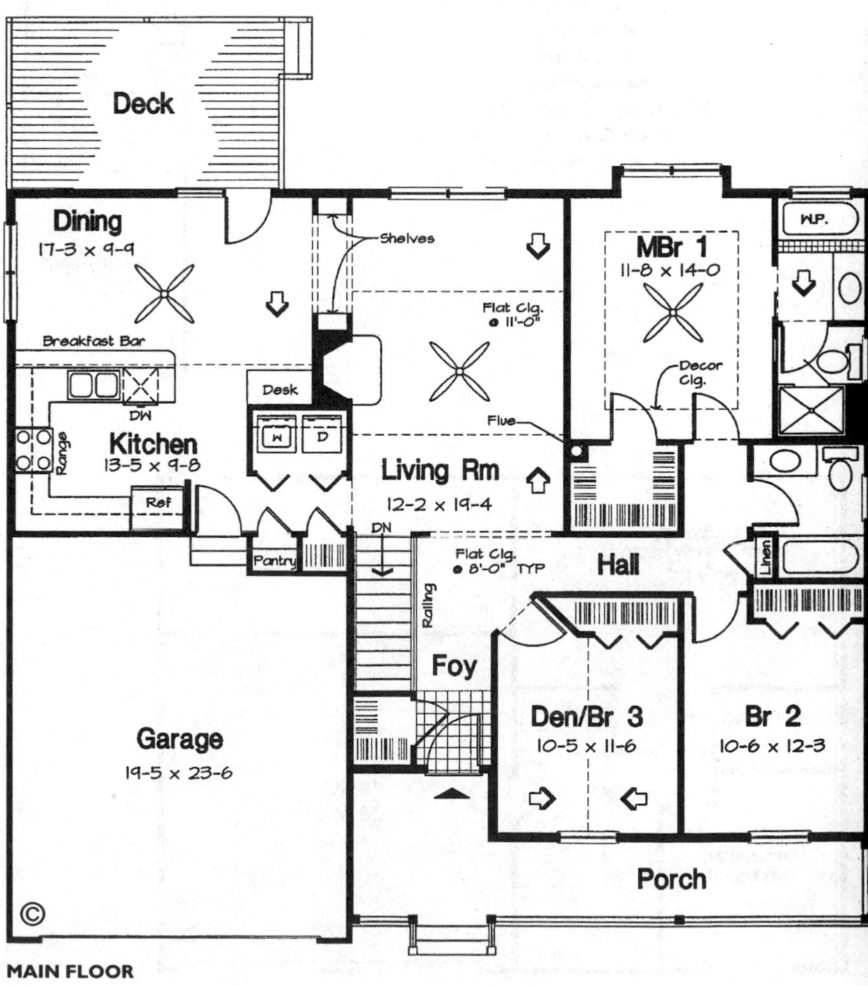

MAIN FLOOR

Design 24654

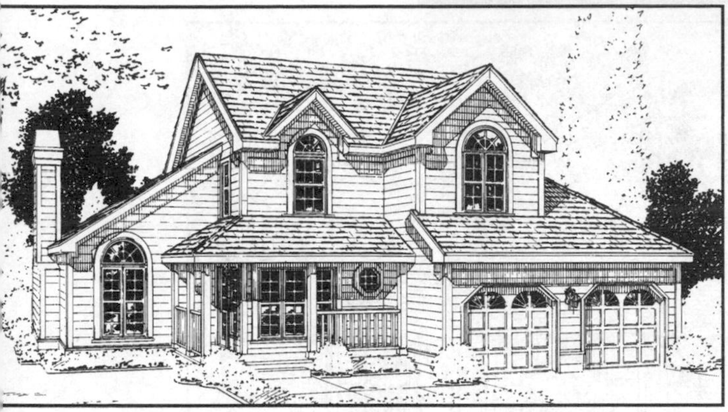

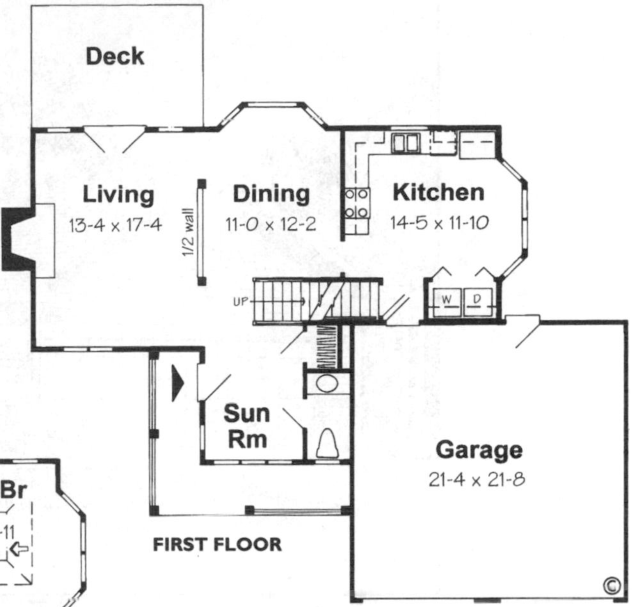

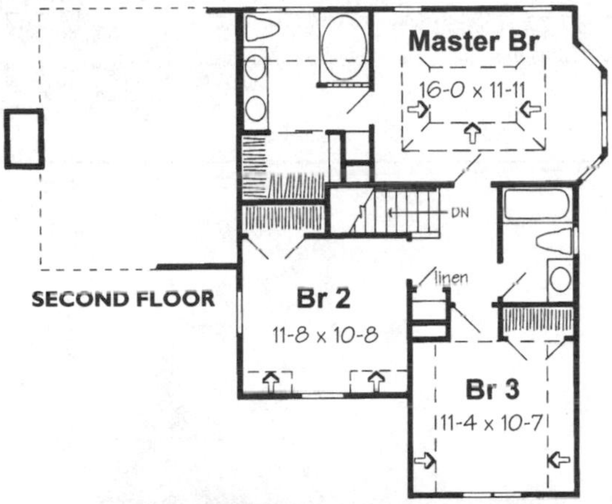

Units	Single
Price Code	B
Total Finished	1,554 sq. ft.
First Finished	806 sq. ft.
Second Finished	748 sq. ft.
Garage Unfinished	467 sq. ft.
Dimensions	50'x40'
Foundation	Basement Crawlspace Slab
Bedrooms	3
Full Baths	2
Half Baths	1
First Ceiling	8'
Second Ceiling	8'
Max Ridge Height	29'
Roof Framing	Stick
Exterior Walls	2x4

FIRST FLOOR

SECOND FLOOR

Design 94920

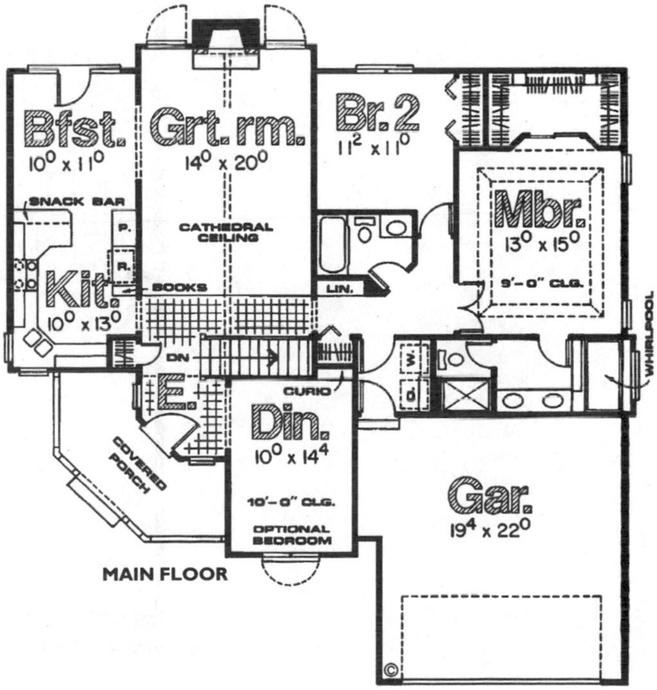

Units	Single
Price Code	B
Total Finished	1,554 sq. ft.
Main Finished	1,554 sq. ft.
Basement Unfinished	1,554 sq. ft.
Garage Unfinished	464 sq. ft.
Dimensions	50'x52'8"
Foundation	Basement
Bedrooms	2
Full Baths	2
Main Ceiling	8'
Max Ridge Height	24'
Roof Framing	Stick
Exterior Walls	2x4

lternate foundation options available at an additional charge. Please call 1-800-235-5700 for more information.

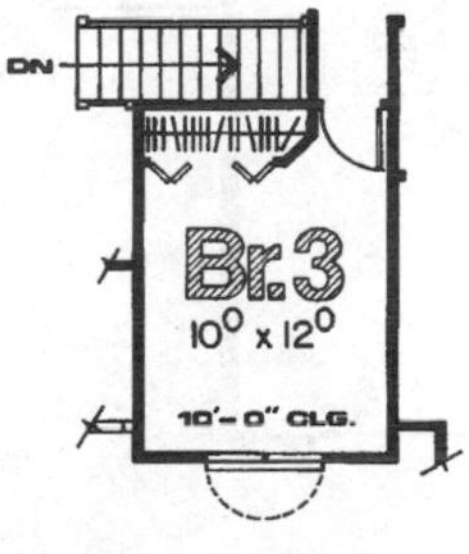

MAIN FLOOR

THIRD BEDROOM OPTION

Design 99152

Units	Single
Price Code	B
Total Finished	1,557 sq. ft.
Main Finished	1,557 sq. ft.
Basement Unfinished	1,557 sq. ft.
Garage Unfinished	440 sq. ft.
Dimensions	53'x49'
Foundation	Basement
Bedrooms	3
Full Baths	2
Max Ridge Height	21'
Roof Framing	Truss
Exterior Walls	2x4

DIN.
13'0" X 10'0"
GREAT RM.
CATHEDRAL CEILING
14'8" X 21'0"
MBR.
TRAY CEILING
15'4" X 15'0"
SHELVES
LIN.
DW.
KIT.
12'8" X 10'10"
D.
W.
DN
E.
BR.#3
11'10" X 10'0"
BR.#2
12'0" X 10'4"
2 CAR GAR.
21'4" X 20'8"
©

MAIN FLOOR

Design 63088

Units	Single
Price Code	B
Total Finished	1,558 sq. ft.
Main Finished	1,558 sq. ft.
Garage Unfinished	413 sq. ft.
Dimensions	50'x45'
Foundation	Slab
Bedrooms	3
Full Baths	2
Main Ceiling	10'-14'6"
Max Ridge Height	21'
Roof Framing	Truss
Exterior Walls	2x4

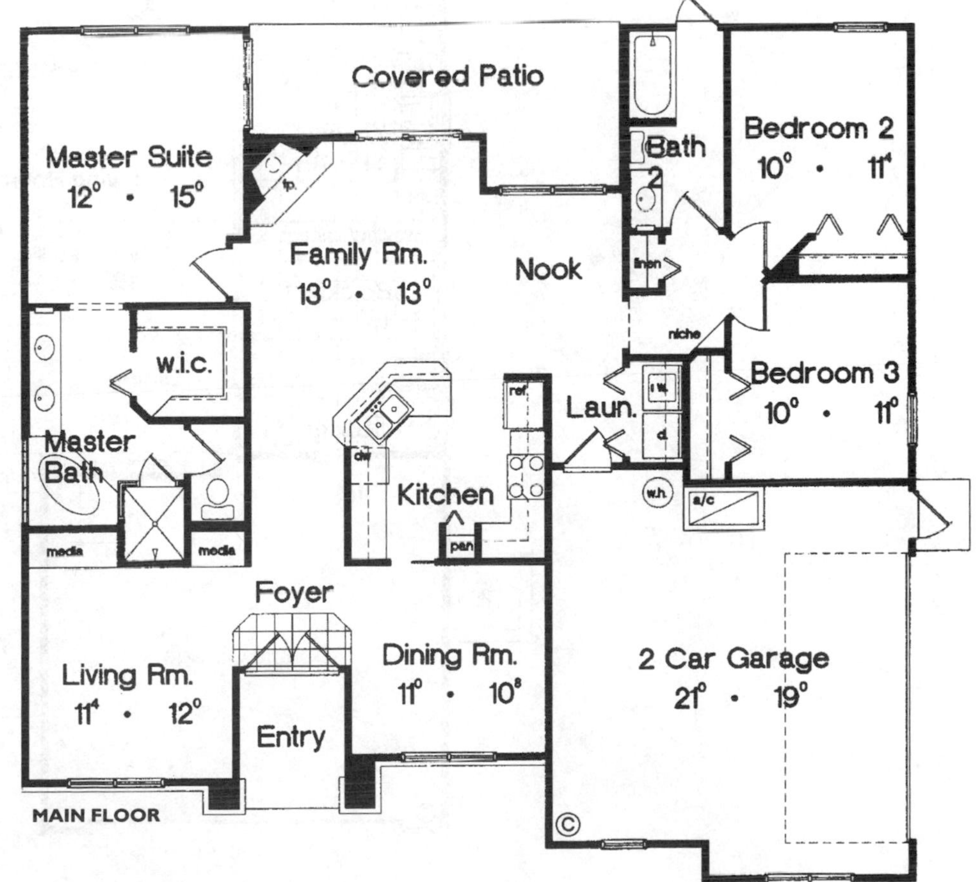

Units	Single
Price Code	B
Total Finished	1,571 sq. ft.
Main Finished	1,571 sq. ft.
Garage Unfinished	381 sq. ft.
Porch Unfinished	123 sq. ft.
Dimensions	40'x55'
Foundation	Slab
Bedrooms	3
Full Baths	2
Max Ridge Height	20'
Roof Framing	Truss
Exterior Walls	2x4

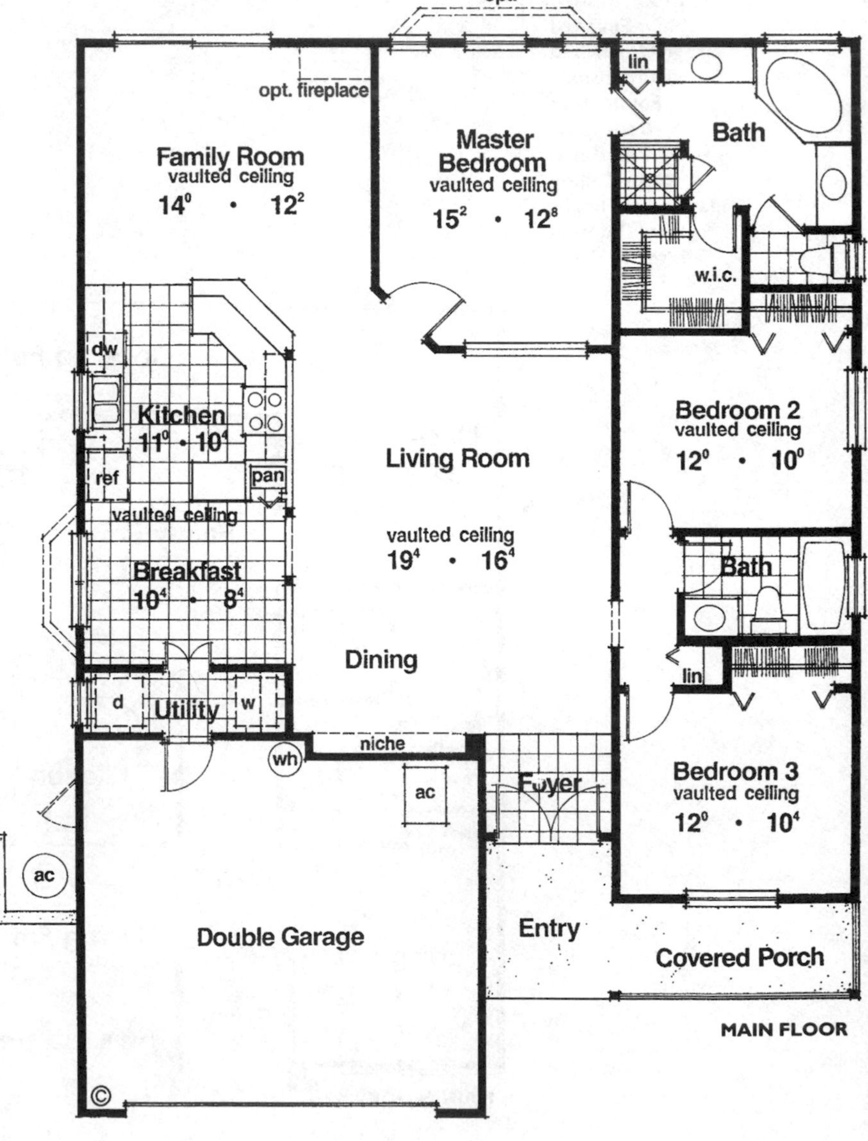

Design 63089

Units	Single
Price Code	B
Total Finished	1,571 sq. ft.
Main Finished	1,571 sq. ft.
Garage Unfinished	381 sq. ft.
Dimensions	40'x55'
Foundation	Slab
Bedrooms	3
Full Baths	2
Max Ridge Height	20'
Roof Framing	Truss
Exterior Walls	2x4

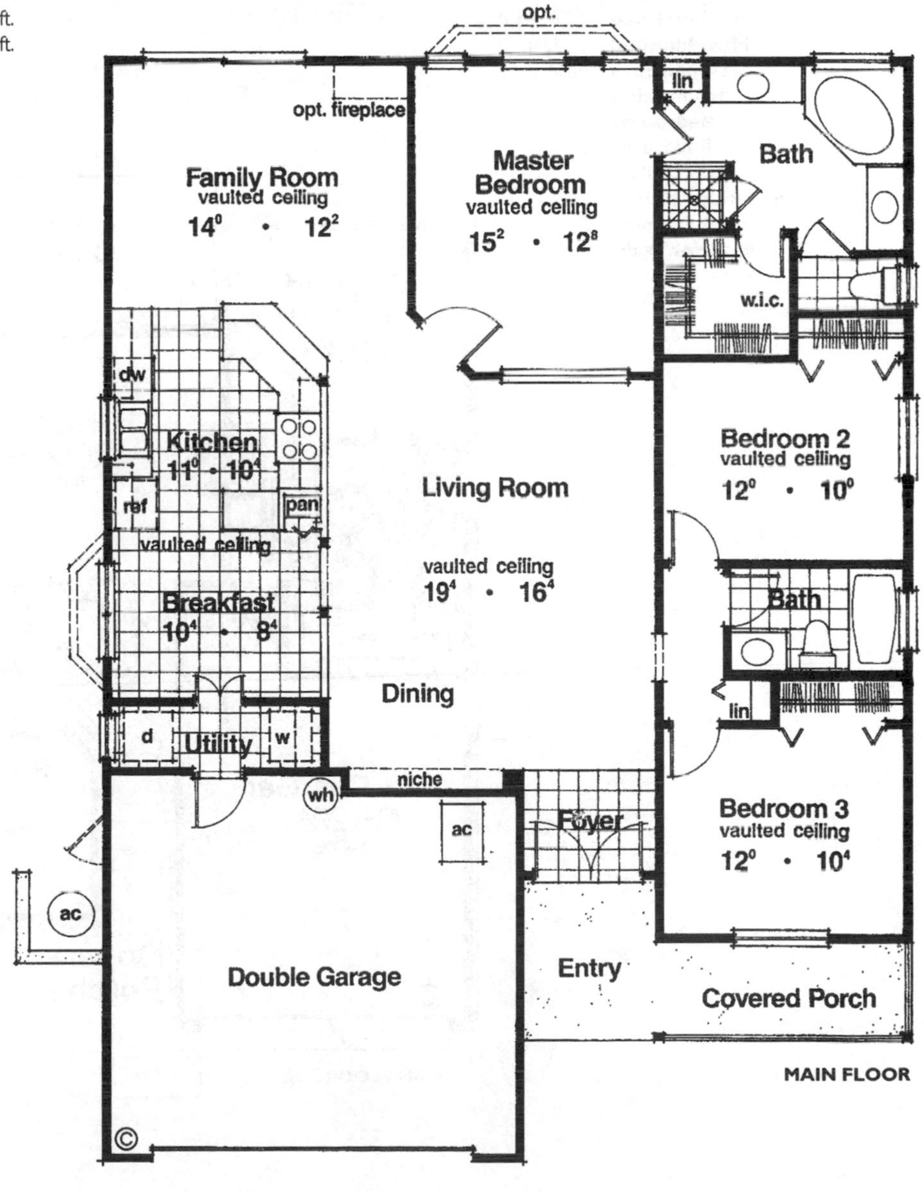

opt.
lin
opt. fireplace
Family Room
vaulted ceiling
14^{0} • 12^{2}
Master Bedroom
vaulted ceiling
15^{2} • 12^{8}
Bath
w.i.c.
dw
Kitchen
11^{0} • 10^{4}
ref
pan
vaulted ceiling
Breakfast
10^{4} • 8^{4}
Living Room
vaulted ceiling
19^{4} • 16^{4}
Bedroom 2
vaulted ceiling
12^{0} • 10^{0}
Bath
lin
Dining
d
Utility
w
wh
niche
ac
Foyer
Bedroom 3
vaulted ceiling
12^{0} • 10^{4}
ac
Double Garage
Entry
Covered Porch
©

MAIN FLOOR

Design 66044

Units	Single
Price Code	B
Total Finished	1,573 sq. ft.
Main Finished	1,573 sq. ft.
Dimensions	48'x51'
Foundation	Slab
Bedrooms	3
Full Baths	2
Main Ceiling	8'-10'
Max Ridge Height	24'
Roof Framing	Stick
Exterior Walls	2x4

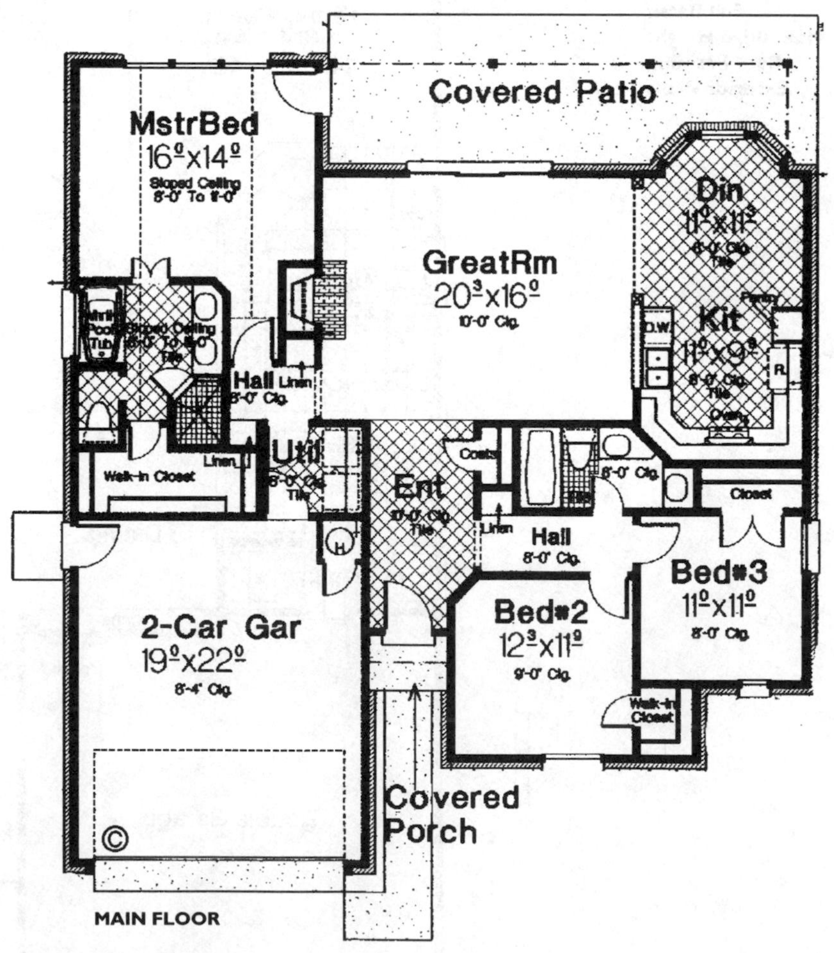

MAIN FLOOR

Design 93062

Units	Single
Price Code	B
Total Finished	1,575 sq. ft.
Main Finished	1,575 sq. ft.
Garage Unfinished	474 sq. ft.
Porch Unfinished	41 sq. ft.
Dimensions	55'6"x52'
Foundation	Crawlspace Slab
Bedrooms	3
Full Baths	2
Main Ceiling	10'
Max Ridge Height	20'
Roof Framing	Truss
Exterior Walls	2x4

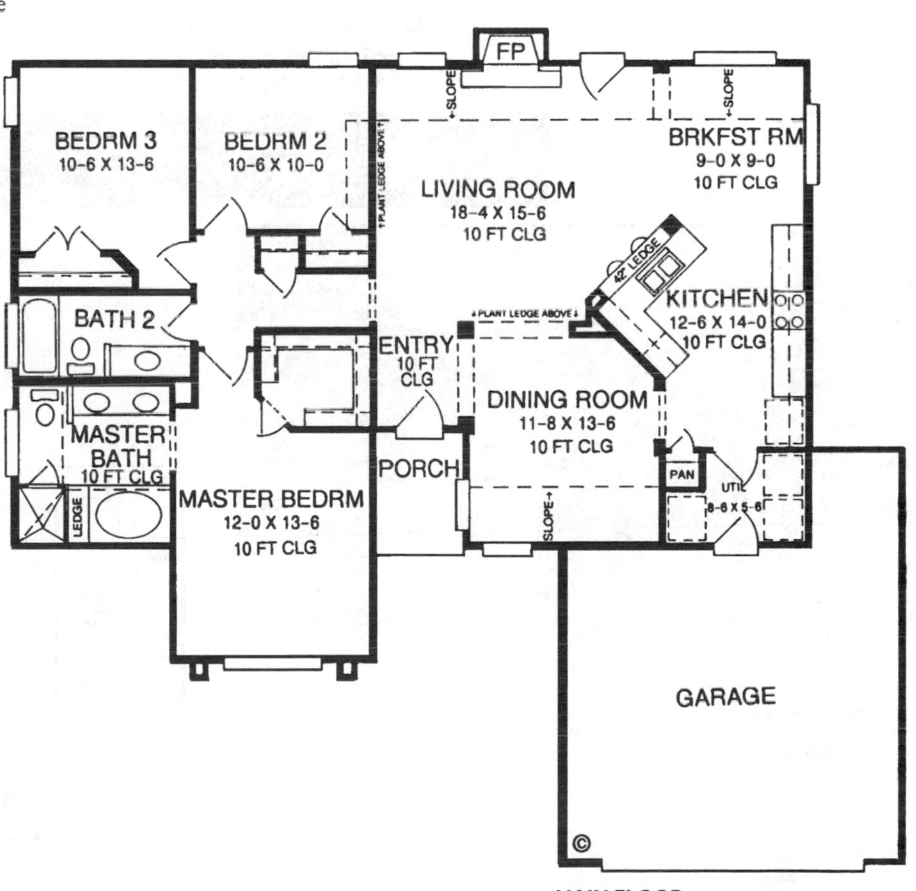

MAIN FLOOR

Design 98414

Units Single
Price Code B
Total Finished 1,575 sq. ft.
Main Finished 1,575 sq. ft.
Basement Unfinished 1,658 sq. ft.
Garage Unfinished 459 sq. ft.
Dimensions 50'x52'6"
Foundation Basement
Crawlspace
Bedrooms 3
Full Baths 2
Main Ceiling 9'
Max Ridge Height 23'6"
Roof Framing Stick
Exterior Walls 2x4

WET BAR
Dining Room
11^3 x 10^7
W. D.
Laund
STORAGE
Storage
STAIRS DN.
Garage
19^5 x 19^8

OPTIONAL BASEMENT STAIR LOCATION

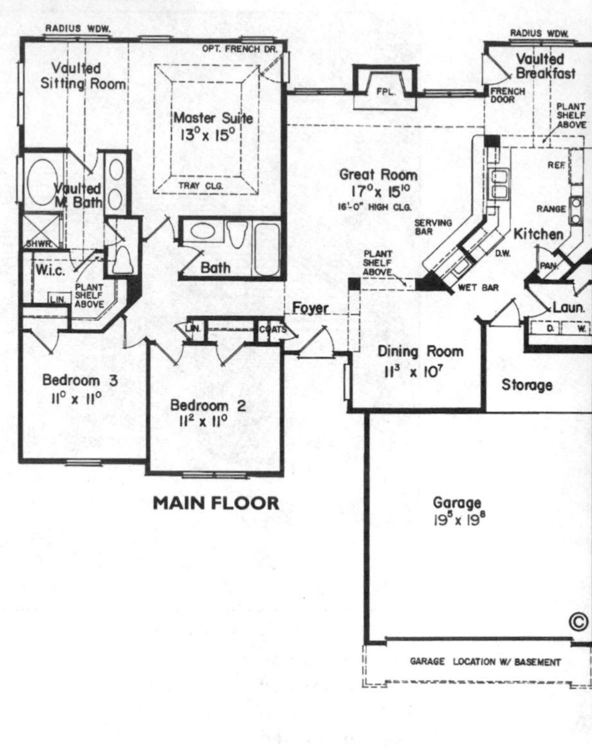

Design 97464

Units Single
Price Code B
Total Finished 1,577 sq. ft.
Main Finished 1,577 sq. ft.
Garage Unfinished 489 sq. ft.
Deck Unfinished 28 sq. ft.
Dimensions 59'4"x49'4"
Foundation Basement
Bedrooms 2
Full Baths 1
3/4 Baths 1
Half Baths 1
Max Ridge Height 22'3"
Roof Framing Stick
Exterior Walls 2x4

* Alternate foundation options available at an additional charge.
Please call 1-800-235-5700 for more information.

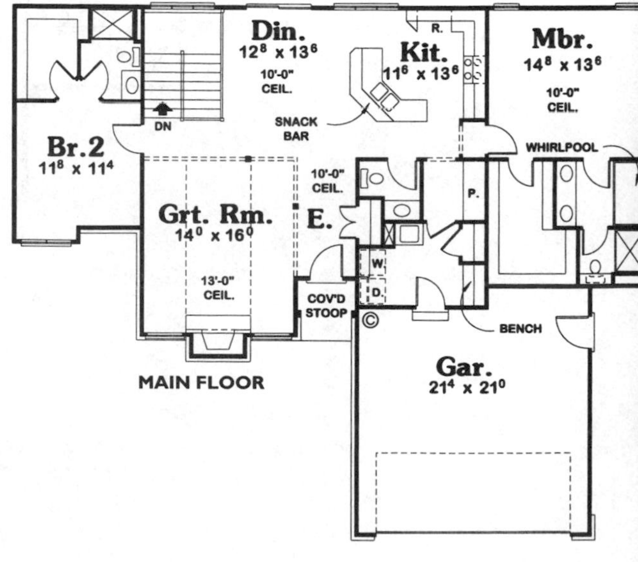

Design 94823

Units	Single
Price Code	B
Total Finished	1,580 sq. ft.
Main Finished	1,580 sq. ft.
Garage Unfinished	479 sq. ft.
Deck Unfinished	180 sq. ft.
Dimensions	62'2"x50'8"
Foundation	Crawlspace Slab
Bedrooms	3
Full Baths	2
Main Ceiling	8'
Max Ridge Height	22'
Roof Framing	Stick
Exterior Walls	2x4

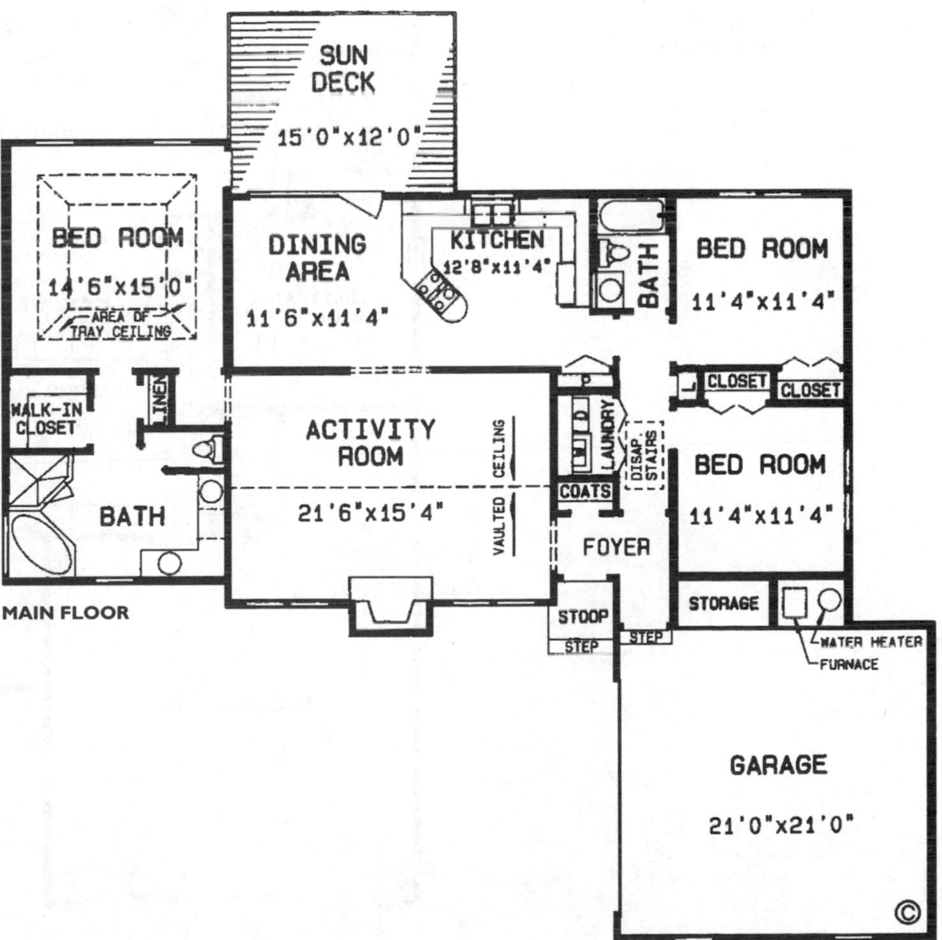

MAIN FLOOR

Design 63083

Units	Single
Price Code	B
Total Finished	1,589 sq. ft.
Main Finished	1,589 sq. ft.
Garage Unfinished	480 sq. ft.
Dimensions	43'x59'
Foundation	Slab
Bedrooms	3
Full Baths	2
Main Ceiling	11'
Vaulted Ceiling	13'
Max Ridge Height	19'
Roof Framing	Truss

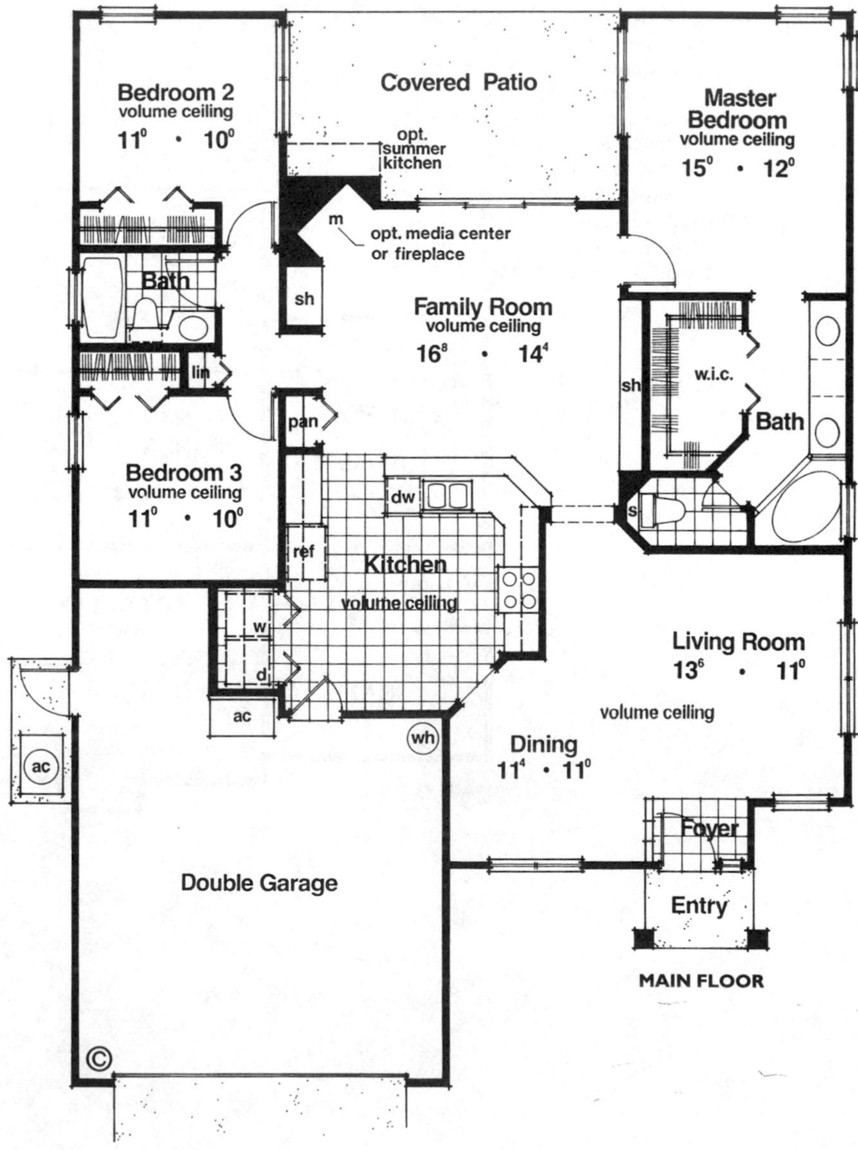

Design 98959

Units	Single
Price Code	B
Total Finished	1,591 sq. ft.
Main Finished	1,591 sq. ft.
Garage Unfinished	480 sq. ft.
Deck Unfinished	280 sq. ft.
Dimensions	46'x64'
Foundation	Basement
Bedrooms	3
Full Baths	2
Main Ceiling	9'
Max Ridge Height	20'
Roof Framing	Stick
Exterior Walls	2x4

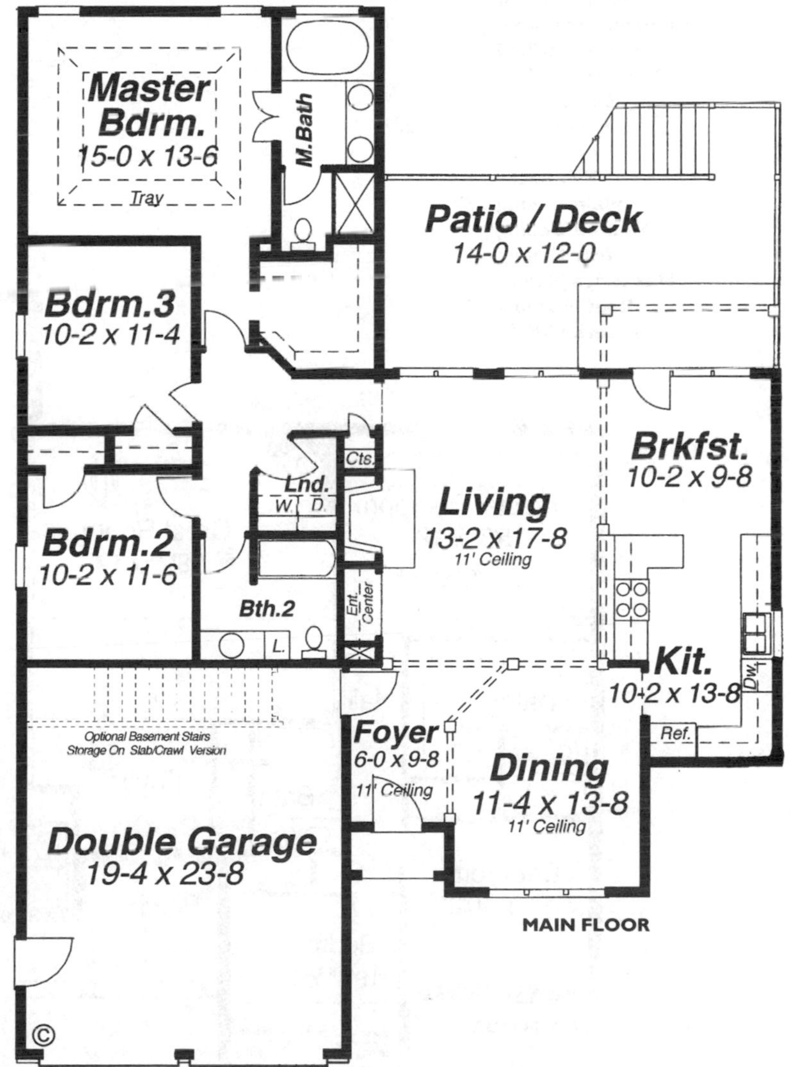

MAIN FLOOR

Design 97740

Units	Single
Price Code	B
Total Finished	1,593 sq. ft.
Main Finished	1,593 sq. ft.
Basement Unfinished	1,593 sq. ft.
Garage Unfinished	550 sq. ft.
Porch Unfinished	104 sq. ft.
Dimensions	60'x48'10"
Foundation	Basement
Bedrooms	3
Full Baths	2
Main Ceiling	8'
Vaulted Ceiling	11'6"
Tray Ceiling	9'
Max Ridge Height	21'6"
Roof Framing	Truss
Exterior Walls	2x4

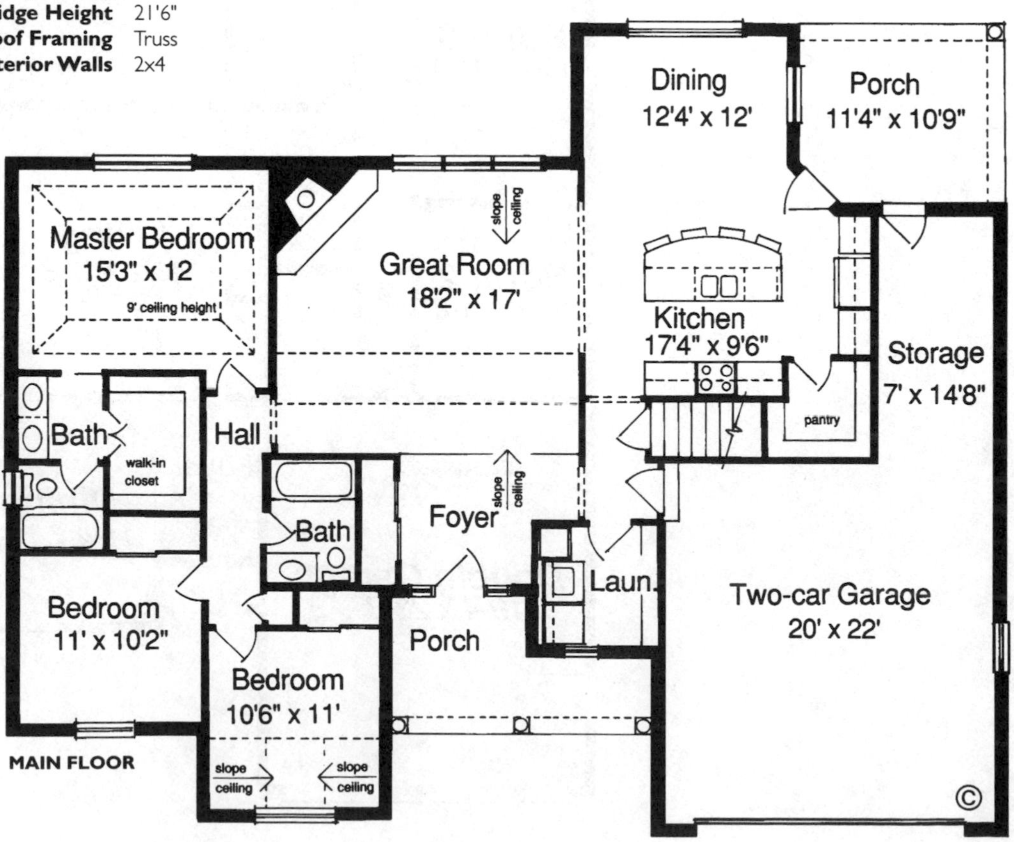

Dining
12'4' x 12'
Porch
11'4" x 10'9"
Master Bedroom
15'3" x 12
9' ceiling height
slope ceiling
Great Room
18'2" x 17'
Kitchen
17'4" x 9'6"
Storage
7' x 14'8"
pantry
Bath
Hall
walk-in closet
Bath
Foyer
slope ceiling
Laun.
Two-car Garage
20' x 22'
Bedroom
11' x 10'2"
Porch
Bedroom
10'6" x 11'
slope ceiling
slope ceiling
©

MAIN FLOOR

Design 93419

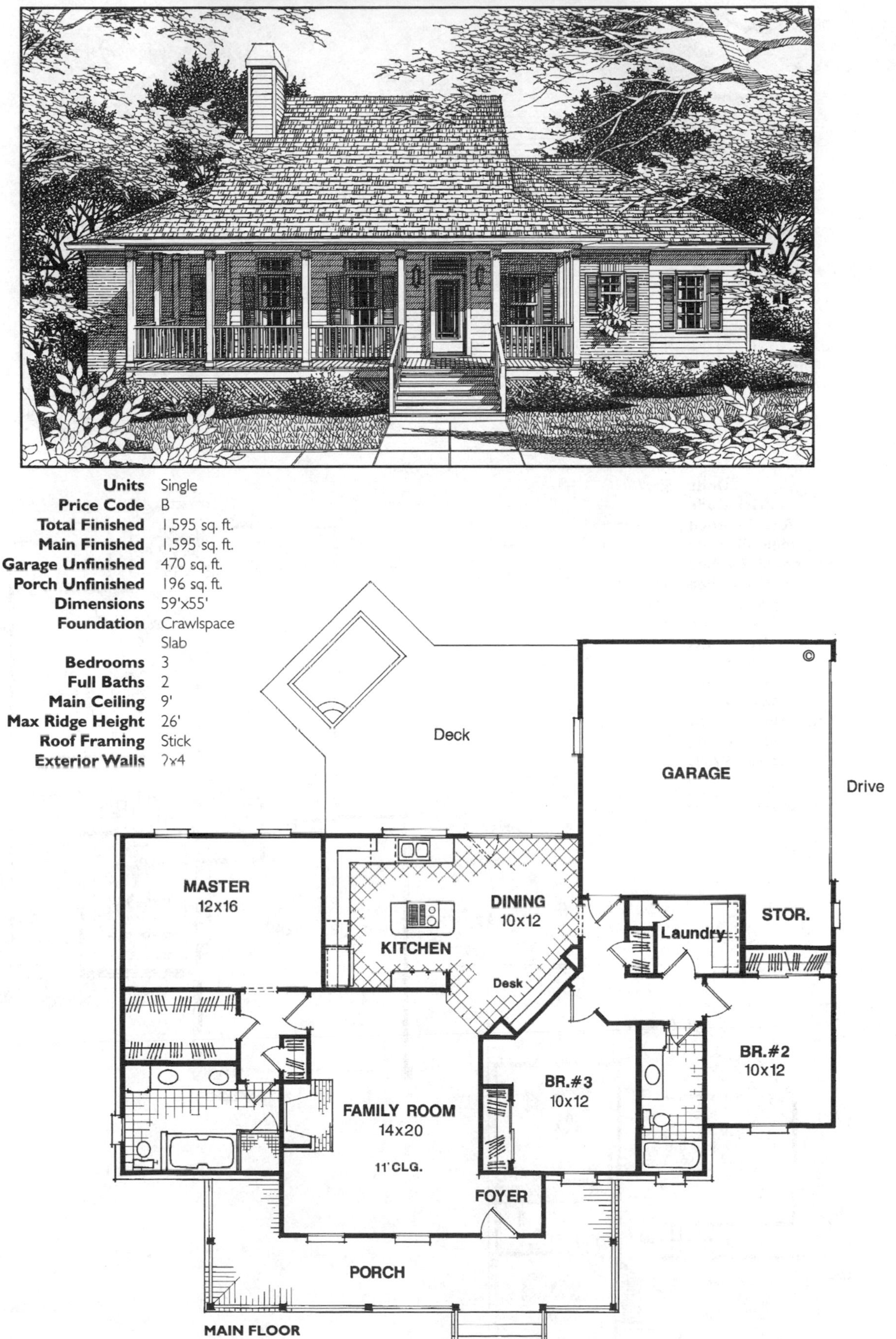

Units	Single
Price Code	B
Total Finished	1,595 sq. ft.
Main Finished	1,595 sq. ft.
Garage Unfinished	470 sq. ft.
Porch Unfinished	196 sq. ft.
Dimensions	59'x55'
Foundation	Crawlspace Slab
Bedrooms	3
Full Baths	2
Main Ceiling	9'
Max Ridge Height	26'
Roof Framing	Stick
Exterior Walls	2x4

Design 97489

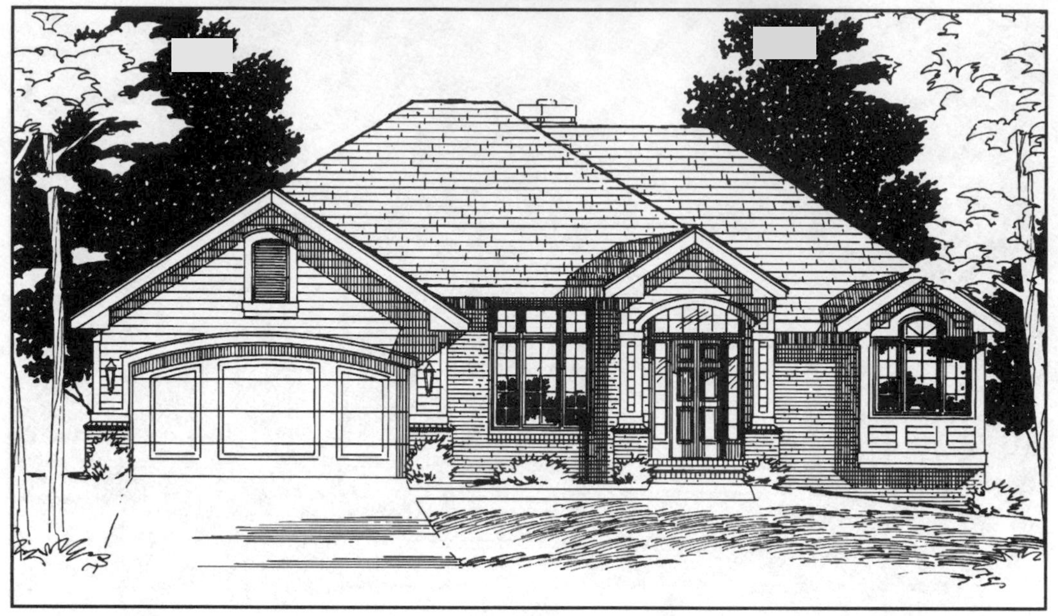

Units	Single
Price Code	B
Total Finished	1,595 sq. ft.
Main Finished	1,595 sq. ft.
Basement Unfinished	790 sq. ft.
Garage Unfinished	476 sq. ft.
Dimensions	52'x56'
Foundation	Basement
Bedrooms	3
Full Baths	2
Half Baths	1
Main Ceiling	8'
Max Ridge Height	20'9"
Roof Framing	Stick
Exterior Walls	2x4

* Alternate foundation options available at an additional charge. Please call 1-800-235-5700 for more information.

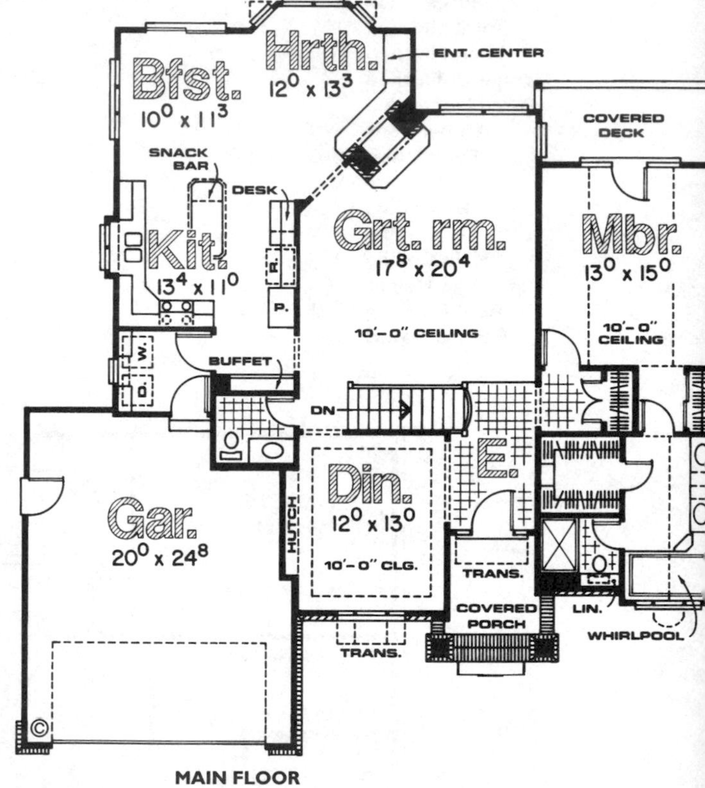

MAIN FLOOR

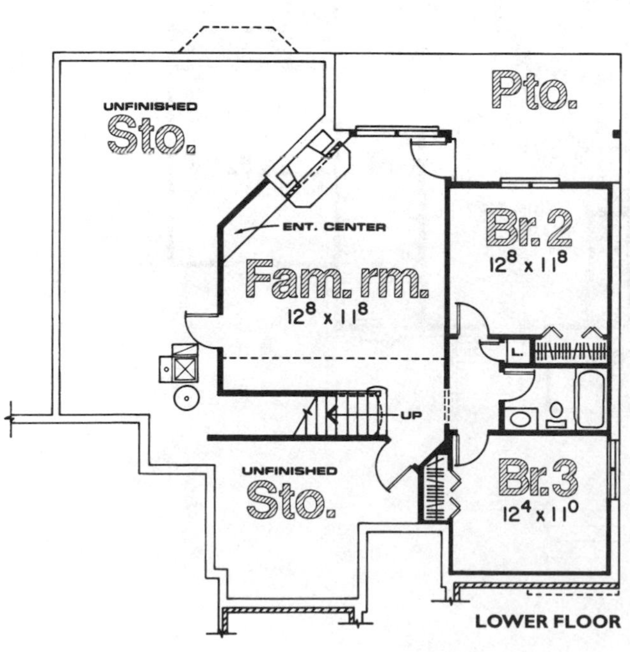

LOWER FLOOR

Design 97763

Units	Single
Price Code	B
Total Finished	1,595 sq. ft.
Main Finished	1,595 sq. ft.
Basement Unfinished	1,589 sq. ft.
Garage Unfinished	409 sq. ft.
Deck Unfinished	279 sq. ft.
Dimensions	48'x51'4"
Foundation	Basement
Bedrooms	3
Full Baths	2
Main Ceiling	8'
Vaulted Ceiling	14'
Max Ridge Height	24'6"
Roof Framing	Truss
Exterior Walls	2x4

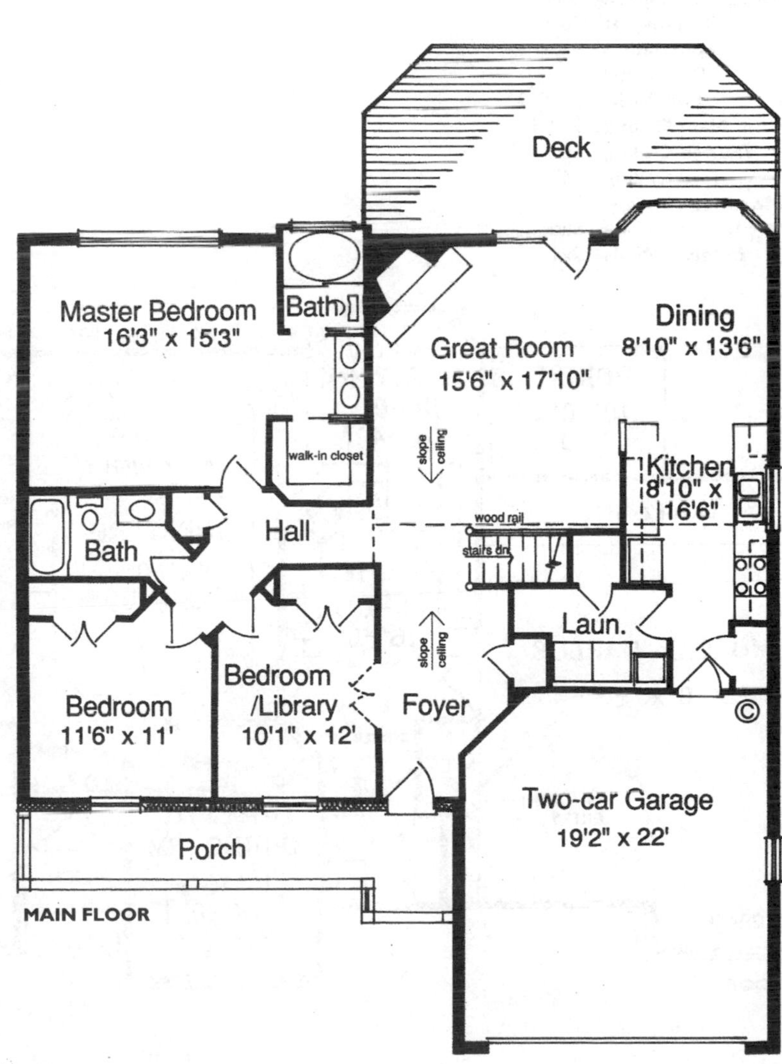

MAIN FLOOR

Units	Single
Price Code	B
Total Finished	1,595 sq. ft.
Main Finished	1,595 sq. ft.
Basement Unfinished	1,595 sq. ft.
Garage Unfinished	548 sq. ft.
Dimensions	70'x37'4"
Foundation	Basement
Bedrooms	3
Full Baths	2
Main Ceiling	9'1"
Vaulted Ceiling	10'9"
Tray Ceiling	14'
Max Ridge Height	22'
Roof Framing	Stick
Exterior Walls	2x4

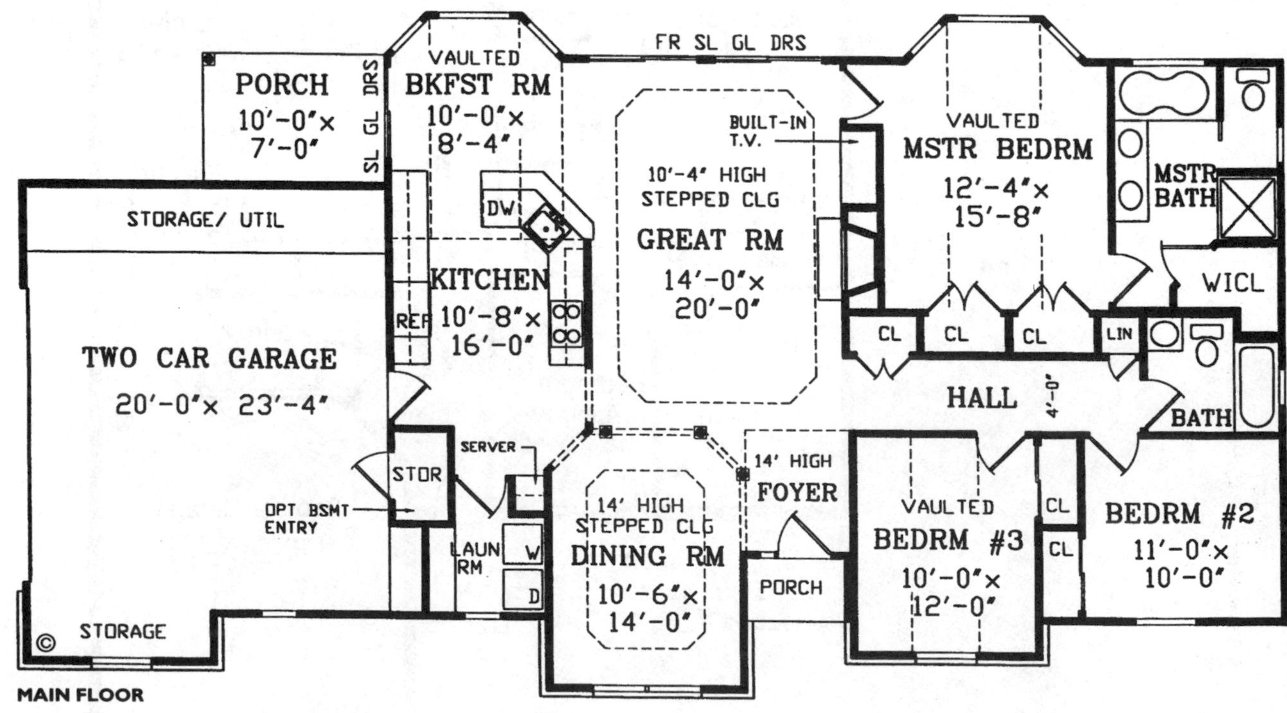

MAIN FLOOR

Design 98560

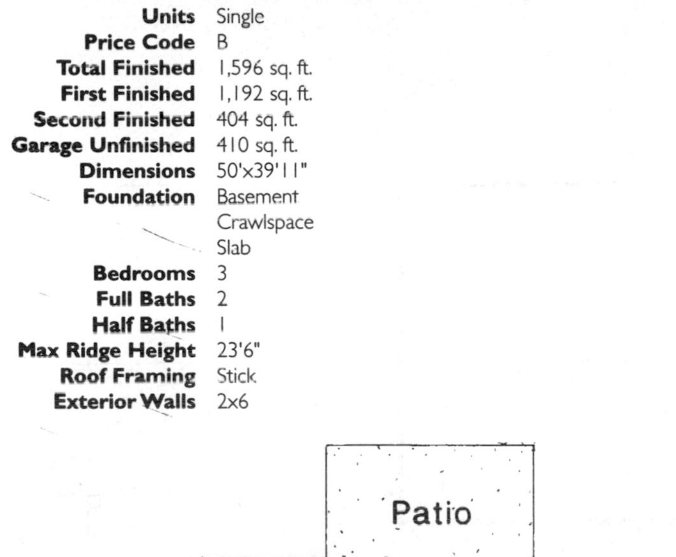

Units	Single
Price Code	B
Total Finished	1,596 sq. ft.
First Finished	1,192 sq. ft.
Second Finished	404 sq. ft.
Garage Unfinished	410 sq. ft.
Dimensions	50'x39'11"
Foundation	Basement Crawlspace Slab
Bedrooms	3
Full Baths	2
Half Baths	1
Max Ridge Height	23'6"
Roof Framing	Stick
Exterior Walls	2x6

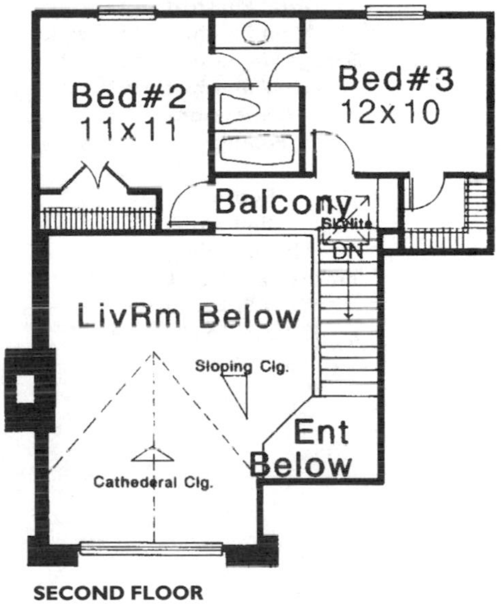

SECOND FLOOR

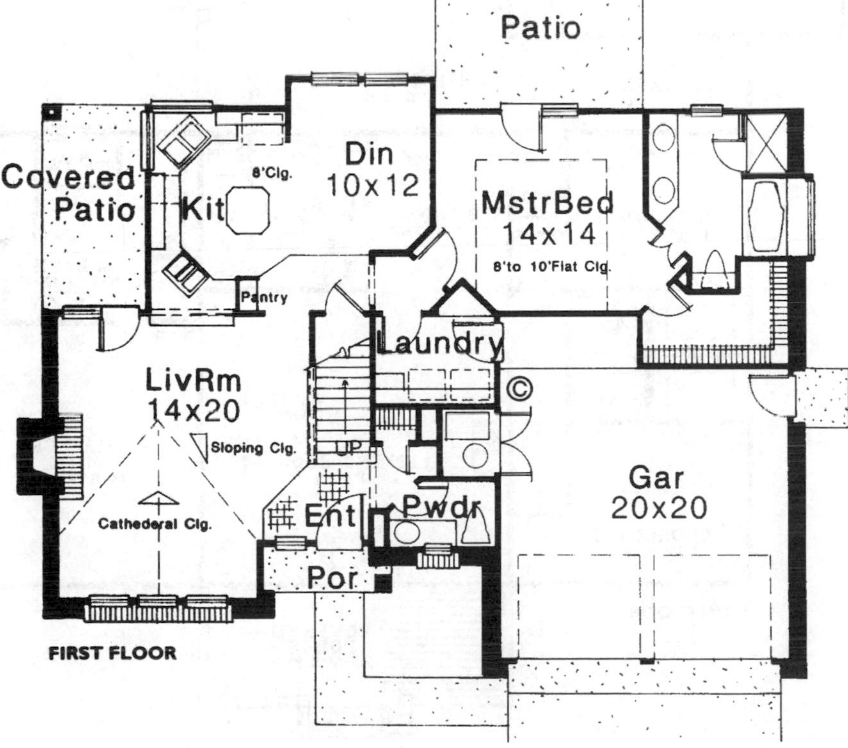

FIRST FLOOR

Design 62086

Units	Single
Price Code	B
Total Finished	1,597 sq. ft.
Main Finished	1,597 sq. ft.
Garage Unfinished	585 sq. ft.
Porch Unfinished	354 sq. ft.
Dimensions	59'x67'
Foundation	Crawlspace Slab
Bedrooms	3
Full Baths	2
Main Ceiling	9'
Max Ridge Height	19'10"
Roof Framing	Stick
Exterior Walls	2x4

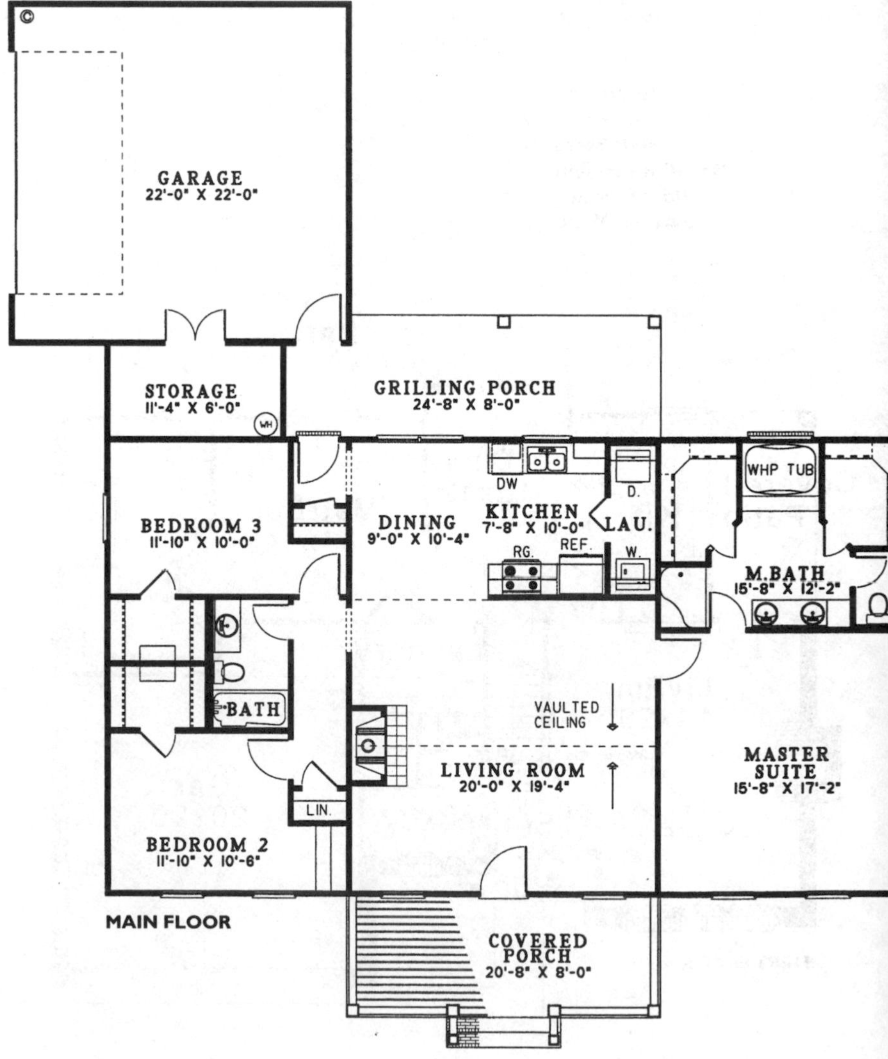

MAIN FLOOR

Design 50007

Units	Single
Price Code	B
Total Finished	1,598 sq. ft.
Main Finished	1,598 sq. ft.
Basement Unfinished	1,598 sq. ft.
Garage Unfinished	478 sq. ft.
Porch Unfinished	161 sq. ft.
Dimensions	59'4"x45'6"
Foundation	Basement
Bedrooms	3
Full Baths	1
3/4 Baths	1
Main Ceiling	8'
Max Ridge Height	18'8"
Roof Framing	Truss
Exterior Walls	2x4

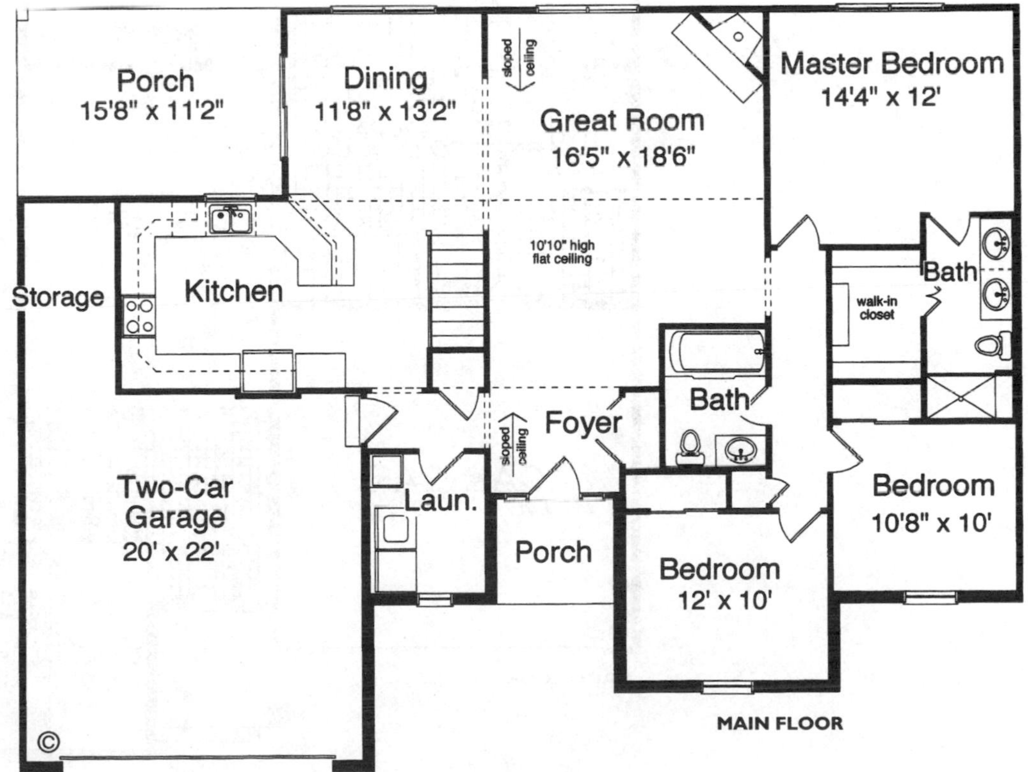

Design 99163

Units	Single
Price Code	B
Total Finished	1,600 sq. ft.
Main Finished	1,600 sq. ft.
Basement Unfinished	1,600 sq. ft.
Garage Unfinished	406 sq. ft.
Deck Unfinished	118 sq. ft.
Dimensions	54'8"x45'
Foundation	Basement
Bedrooms	3
Full Baths	2
Max Ridge Height	25'
Roof Framing	Truss
Exterior Walls	2x4

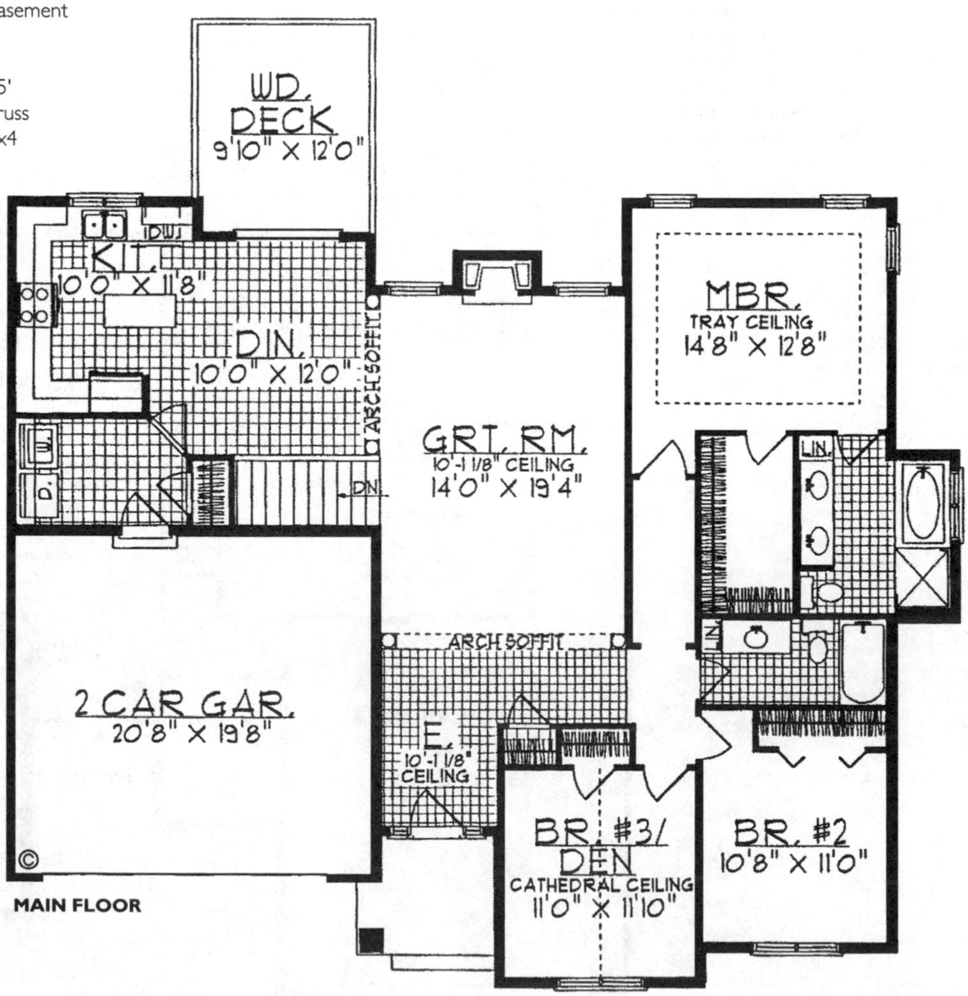

WD. DECK 9'10" X 12'0"
KIT. 10'0" X 11'8"
DIN. 10'0" X 12'0"
GRT. RM. 10'-1 1/8" CEILING 14'0" X 19'4"
MBR. TRAY CEILING 14'8" X 12'8"
2 CAR GAR. 20'8" X 19'8"
E. 10'-1 1/8" CEILING
BR. #3/ DEN CATHEDRAL CEILING 11'0" X 11'10"
BR. #2 10'8" X 11'0"

MAIN FLOOR

Design 62058

Units	Single
Price Code	C
Total Finished	1,601 sq. ft.
Main Finished	1,601 sq. ft.
Garage Unfinished	771 sq. ft.
Porch Unfinished	279 sq. ft.
Dimensions	39'x77'2"
Foundation	Crawlspace Slab
Bedrooms	3
Full Baths	2
Main Ceiling	9'
Max Ridge Height	22'
Roof Framing	Stick
Exterior Walls	2x4

GARAGE
21'-0" X 20'-0"
GRILLING PORCH
LAU.
STOR.
PATIO
KITCHEN
12'-4" X 10'-10"
WHP TUB
M.BATH
7'-10" X 19'-8"
MASTER SUITE
12'-0" X 16'-8"
10' BOXED CEILING
DINING
17'-8" X 10'-0"
COMP CENTER
W.I.C.
8" COLUMNS
BATH
GREAT ROOM
14'-10" X 19'-9"
10' BOXED CEILING
BEDROOM 3
11'-0" X 12'-6"
FOYER
COVERED PORCH
20'-8" X 8'-0"
OPT BOOK SHELVES
BEDROOM 2 / STUDY
12'-0" X 13'-8"

MAIN FLOOR

Design 91115

Units	Single
Price Code	B
Total Finished	1,611 sq. ft.
Main Finished	1,611 sq. ft.
Garage Unfinished	501 sq. ft.
Dimensions	53'10"x50'4"
Foundation	Slab
Bedrooms	3
Full Baths	2
Max Ridge Height	21'
Roof Framing	Stick
Exterior Walls	2x4

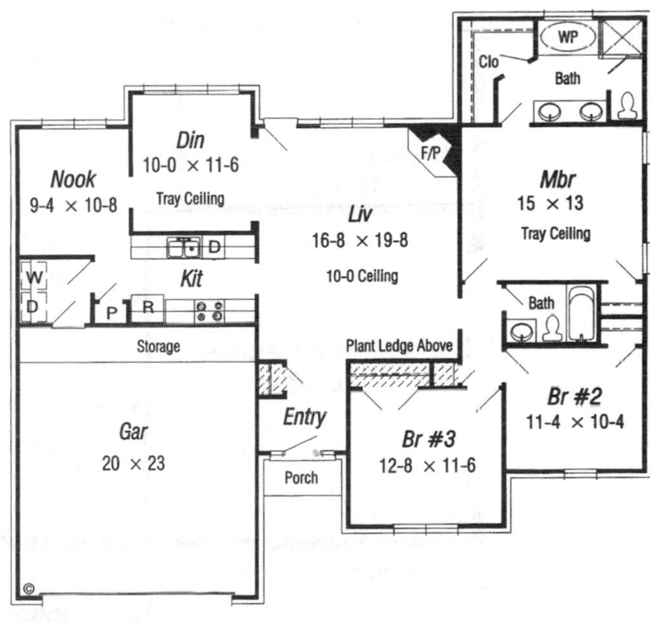

MAIN FLOOR

Design 97759

Units	Single
Price Code	B
Total Finished	1,611 sq. ft.
Main Finished	1,611 sq. ft.
Basement Unfinished	1,611 sq. ft.
Garage Unfinished	430 sq. ft.
Deck Unfinished	228 sq. ft.
Porch Unfinished	163 sq. ft.
Dimensions	67'x44'4"
Foundation	Basement
Bedrooms	3
Full Baths	2
Main Ceiling	8'
Vaulted Ceiling	10'
Tray Ceiling	10'
Max Ridge Height	22'6"
Roof Framing	Truss
Exterior Walls	2x4

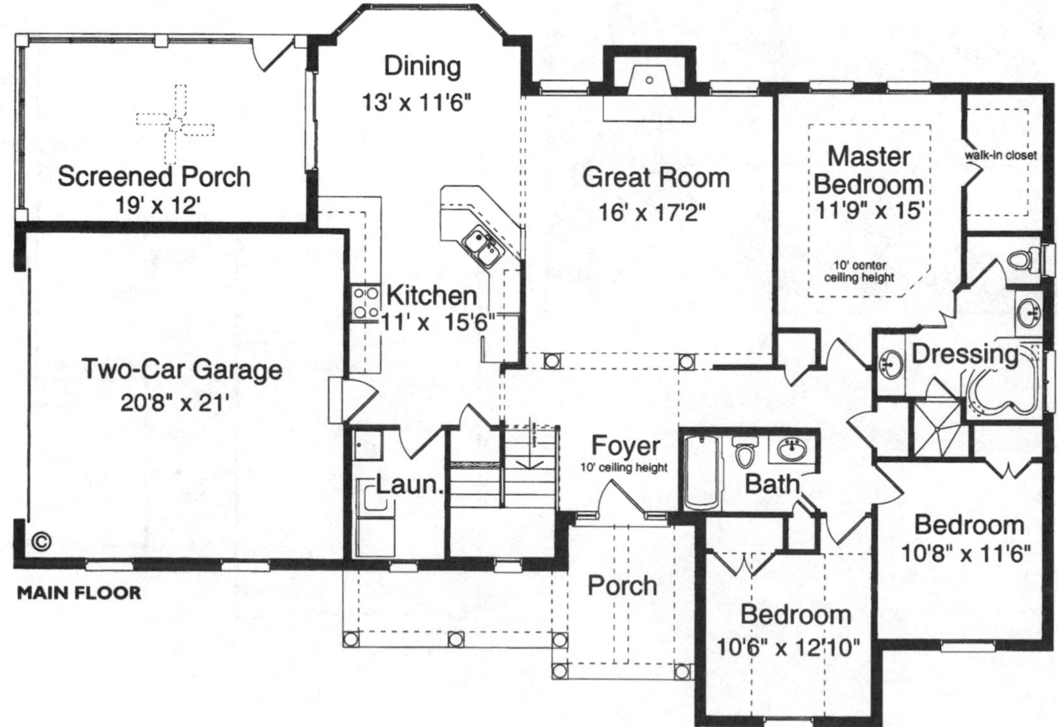

MAIN FLOOR

Design 97760

Units	Single
Price Code	B
Total Finished	1,611 sq. ft.
Main Finished	1,611 sq. ft.
Garage Unfinished	430 sq. ft.
Deck Unfinished	228 sq. ft.
Porch Unfinished	163 sq. ft.
Dimensions	66'4"x43'10"
Foundation	Basement
Bedrooms	3
Full Baths	2
Main Ceiling	8'
Vaulted Ceiling	10'
Tray Ceiling	10'
Max Ridge Height	22'6"
Roof Framing	Truss
Exterior Walls	2x4

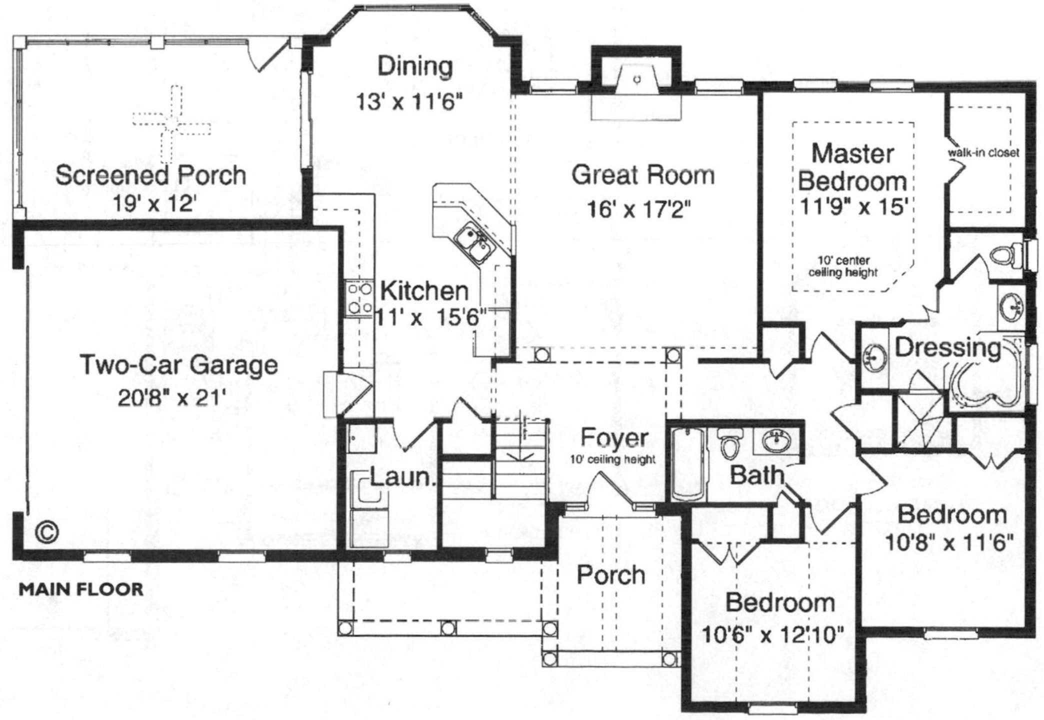

Design 97495

Units	Single
Price Code	B
Total Finished	1,622 sq. ft.
Main Finished	1,622 sq. ft.
Garage Unfinished	469 sq. ft.
Dimensions	51'x52'
Foundation	Basement
Bedrooms	3
Full Baths	2
Main Ceiling	8'
Max Ridge Height	20'6"
Roof Framing	Stick
Exterior Walls	2x4

* Alternate foundation options available at an additional charge. Please call 1-800-235-5700 for more information.

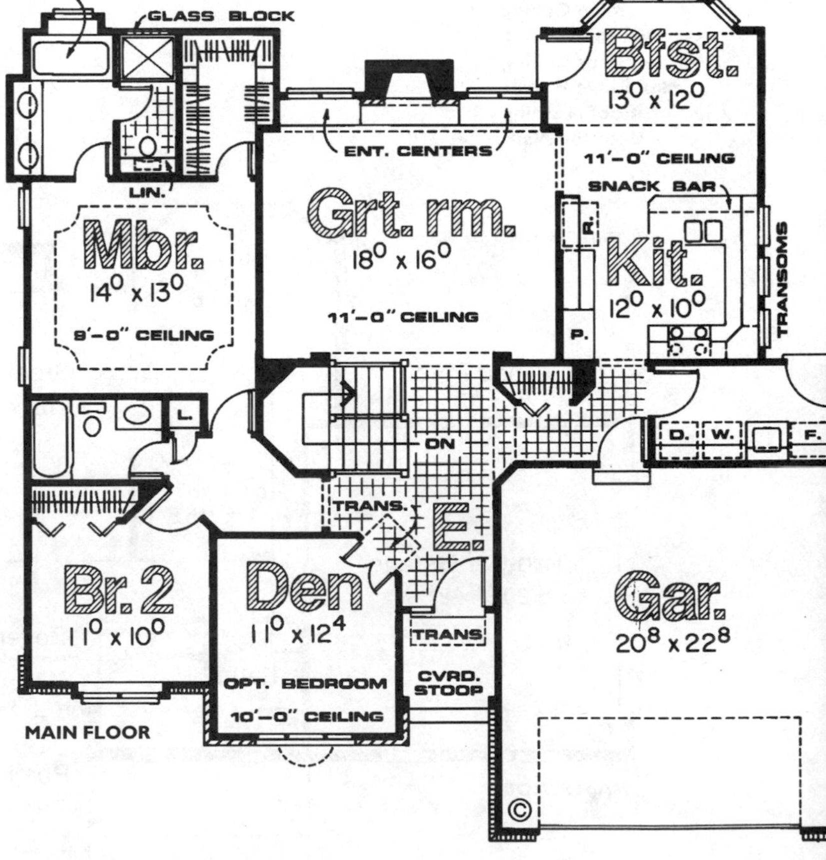

MAIN FLOOR

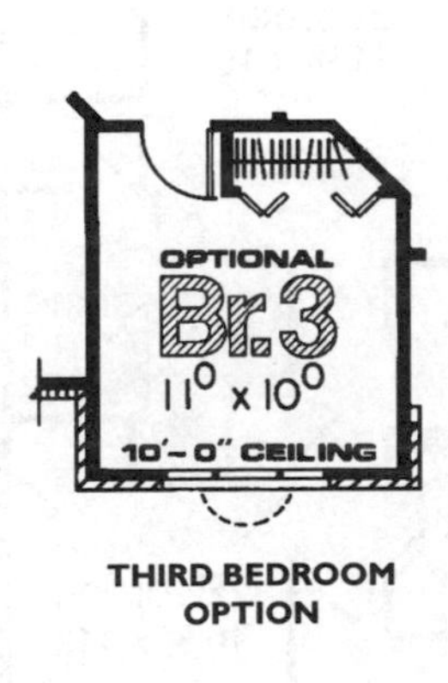

THIRD BEDROOM OPTION

Design 64017

Units	Single
Price Code	B
Total Finished	1,624 sq. ft.
Main Finished	1,624 sq. ft.
Bonus Unfinished	142 sq. ft.
Garage Unfinished	462 sq. ft.
Dimensions	60'x48'
Foundation	Crawlspace Slab
Bedrooms	3
Full Baths	2
Main Ceiling	8'
Roof Framing	Stick
Exterior Walls	2x4

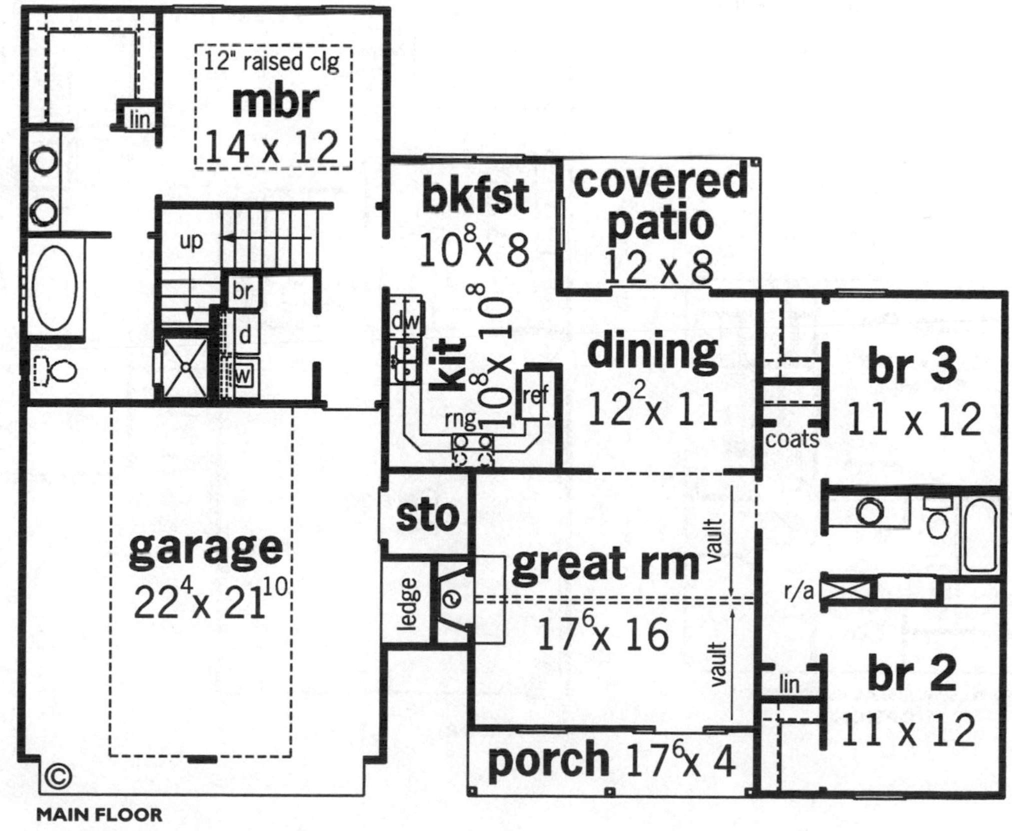

MAIN FLOOR

Design 24701

Units	Single
Price Code	B
Total Finished	1,625 sq. ft.
Main Finished	1,625 sq. ft.
Basement Unfinished	1,625 sq. ft.
Garage Unfinished	455 sq. ft.
Dimensions	54'x48'4"
Foundation	Basement Crawlspace Slab
Bedrooms	3
Full Baths	2
Main Ceiling	8'-9'
Max Ridge Height	22'
Roof Framing	Stick
Exterior Walls	2x4, 2x6

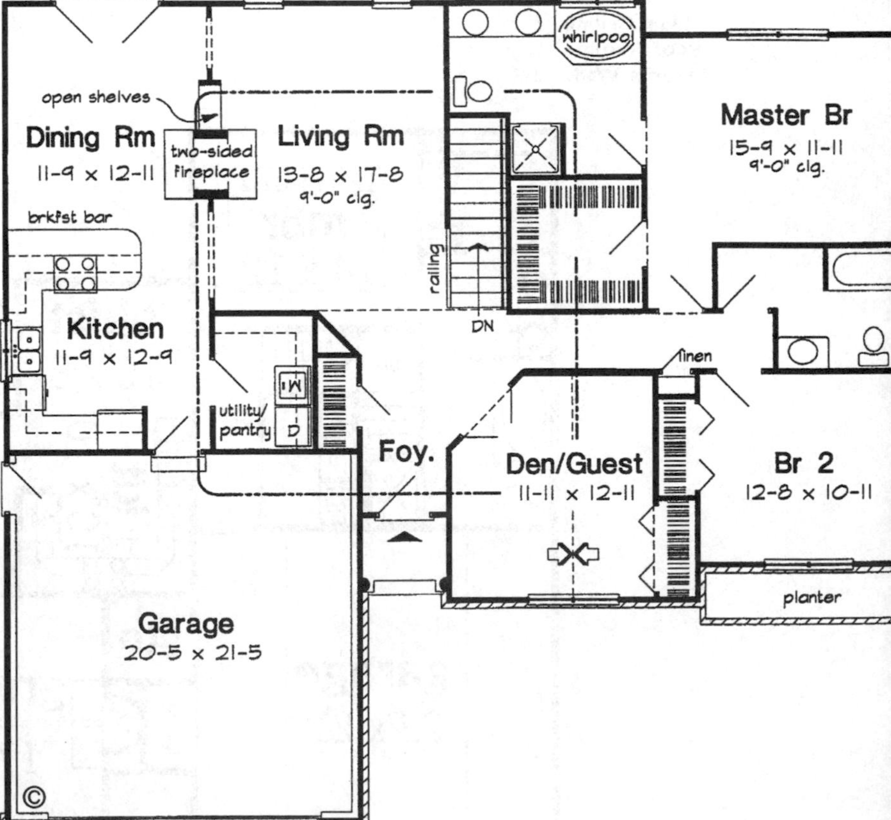

MAIN FLOOR

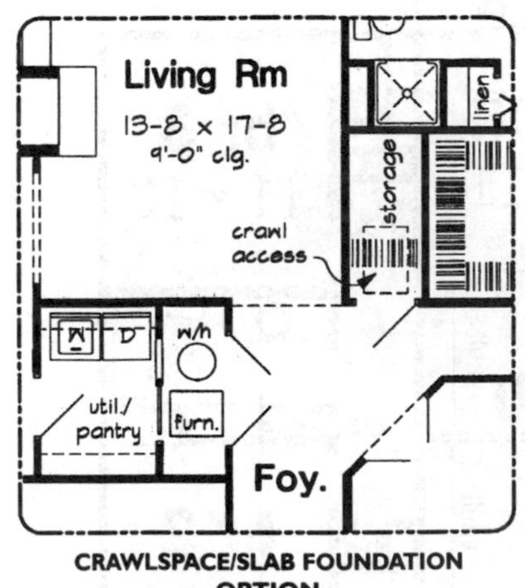

CRAWLSPACE/SLAB FOUNDATION OPTION

Design 63091

Units	Single
Price Code	B
Total Finished	1,627 sq. ft.
Main Finished	1,627 sq. ft.
Garage Unfinished	420 sq. ft.
Dimensions	46'x70'
Foundation	Slab
Bedrooms	3
Full Baths	2
Main Ceiling	10'
Max Ridge Height	25'8"
Exterior Walls	2x4

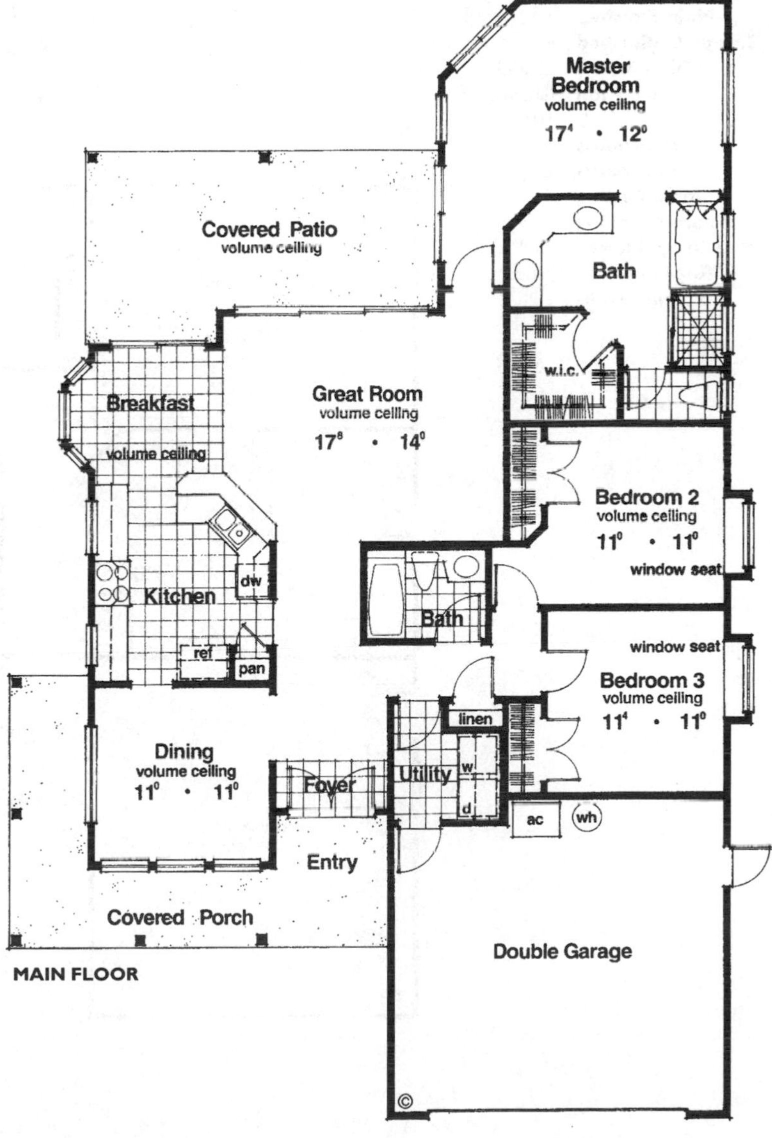

MAIN FLOOR

Design 96805

Units	Single
Price Code	B
Total Finished	1,627 sq. ft.
Main Finished	1,627 sq. ft.
Garage Unfinished	480 sq. ft.
Dimensions	52'x53'
Foundation	Crawlspace Slab
Bedrooms	3
Full Baths	2
Main Ceiling	8'2"
Vaulted Ceiling	13'9"
Max Ridge Height	20'8"
Roof Framing	Truss
Exterior Walls	2x4

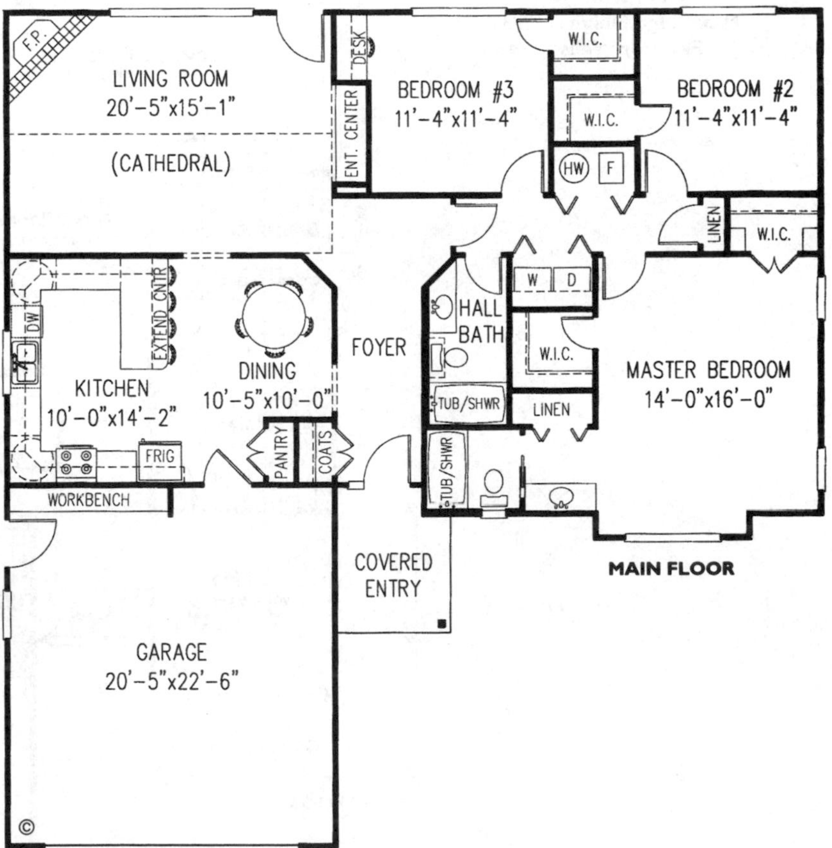

MAIN FLOOR

Design 93418

Units	Single
Price Code	B
Total Finished	1,631 sq. ft.
Main Finished	1,631 sq. ft.
Basement Unfinished	1,015 sq. ft.
Garage Unfinished	616 sq. ft.
Porch Unfinished	115 sq. ft.
Dimensions	48'x44'
Foundation	Basement
Bedrooms	3
Full Baths	2
Max Ridge Height	26'
Roof Framing	Stick
Exterior Walls	2x4

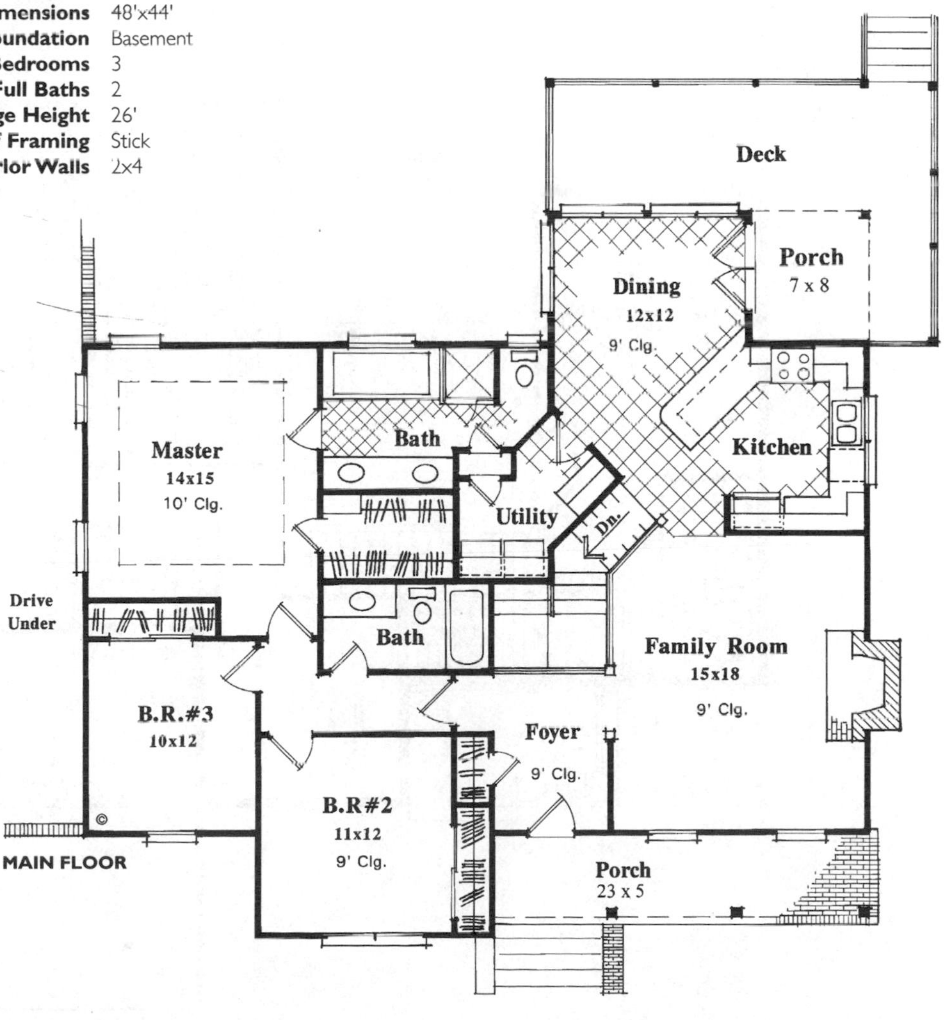

Deck

Porch
7 x 8

Dining
12x12
9' Clg.

Kitchen

Master
14x15
10' Clg.

Bath

Utility

Dn.

Drive
Under

Bath

Family Room
15x18
9' Clg.

B.R.#3
10x12

Foyer
9' Clg.

B.R#2
11x12
9' Clg.

Porch
23 x 5

MAIN FLOOR

Design 97115

Units	Single
Price Code	B
Total Finished	1,633 sq. ft.
Main Finished	1,633 sq. ft.
Basement Unfinished	1,633 sq. ft.
Dimensions	53'x52'
Foundation	Basement
Bedrooms	3
Full Baths	2
Max Ridge Height	20'
Roof Framing	Truss
Exterior Walls	2x6

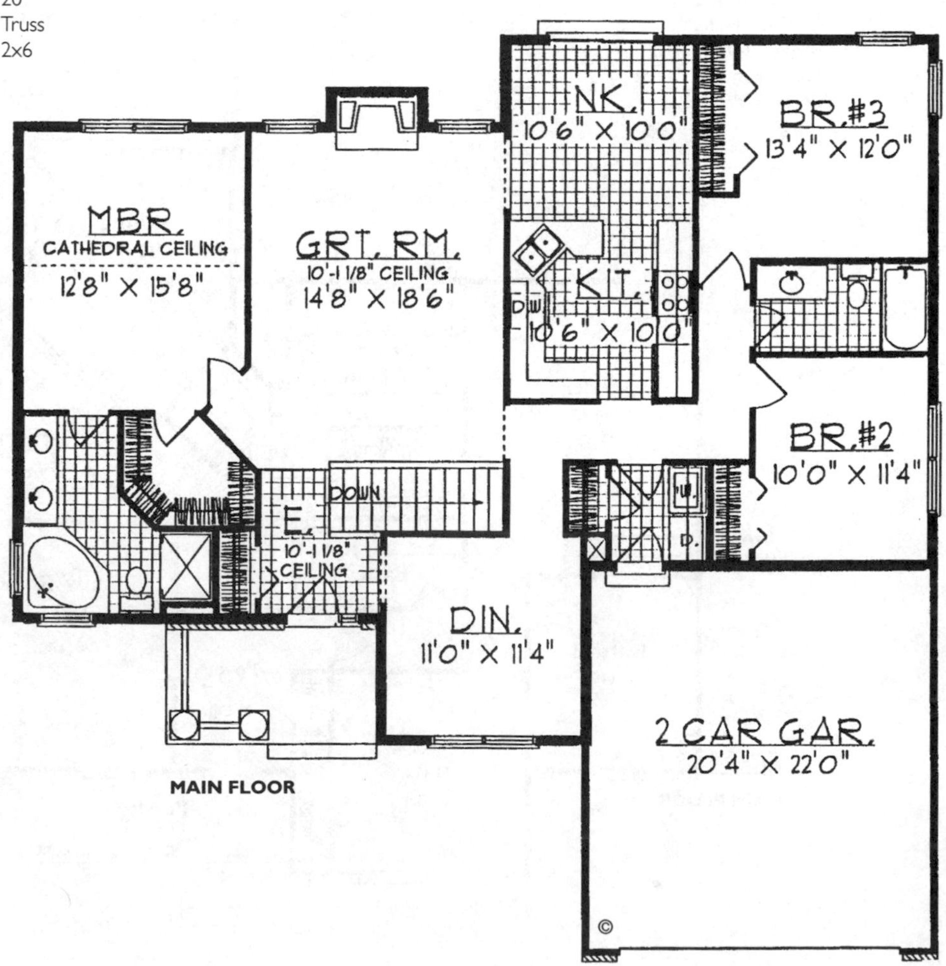

MAIN FLOOR

Design 68079

Units	Single
Price Code	B
Total Finished	1,636 sq. ft.
Main Finished	1,636 sq. ft.
Basement Unfinished	1,636 sq. ft.
Garage Unfinished	508 sq. ft.
Deck Unfinished	158 sq. ft.
Dimensions	53'4"x49'4"
Foundation	Basement Crawlspace Slab
Bedrooms	2
Full Baths	2
Main Ceiling	9'
Max Ridge Height	24'3"
Roof Framing	Stick
Exterior Walls	2x4

* Alternate foundation options available at an additional charge. Please call 1-800-235-5700 for more information.

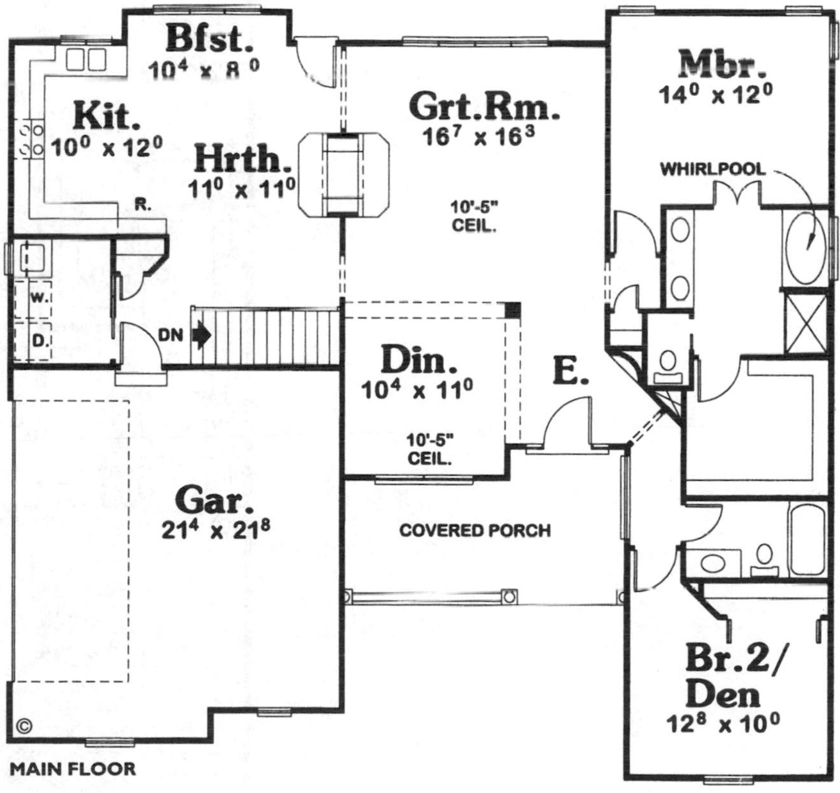

Design 97455

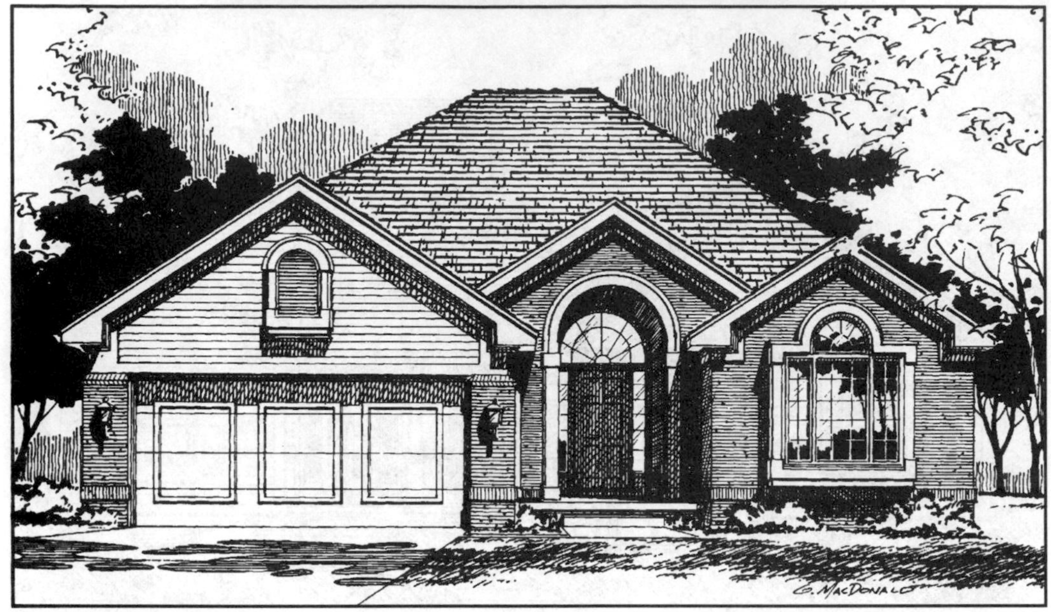

Units	Single
Price Code	B
Total Finished	1,636 sq. ft.
Main Finished	1,636 sq. ft.
Garage Unfinished	448 sq. ft.
Dimensions	42'x59'8"
Foundation	Basement
Bedrooms	3
Full Baths	2
Main Ceiling	8'
Max Ridge Height	21'
Roof Framing	Stick
Exterior Walls	2x4, 2x6

* Alternate foundation options available at an additional charge. Please call 1-800-235-5700 for more information.

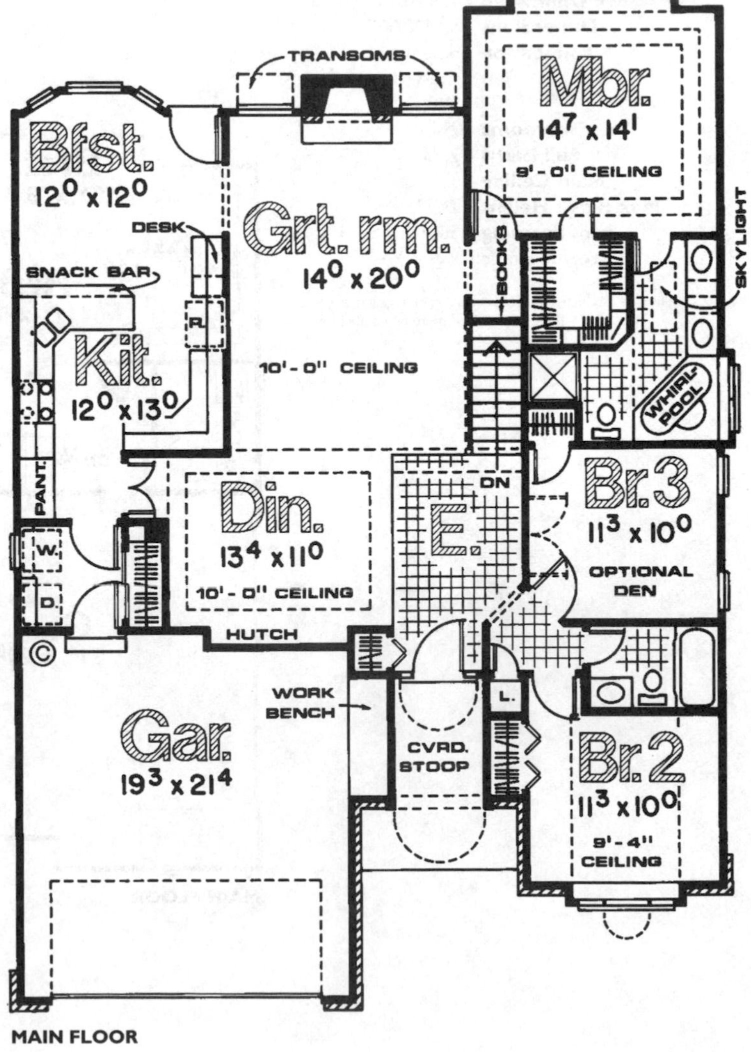

MAIN FLOOR

Design 92242

Units	Single
Price Code	B
Total Finished	1,639 sq. ft.
Main Finished	1,639 sq. ft.
Garage Unfinished	442 sq. ft.
Deck Unfinished	145 sq. ft.
Porch Unfinished	52 sq. ft.
Dimensions	49'10"x57'1"
Foundation	Slab
Bedrooms	3
Full Baths	2
Main Ceiling	8'
Second Ceiling	10'
Vaulted Ceiling	10'
Max Ridge Height	24'6"
Roof Framing	Stick
Exterior Walls	2x4

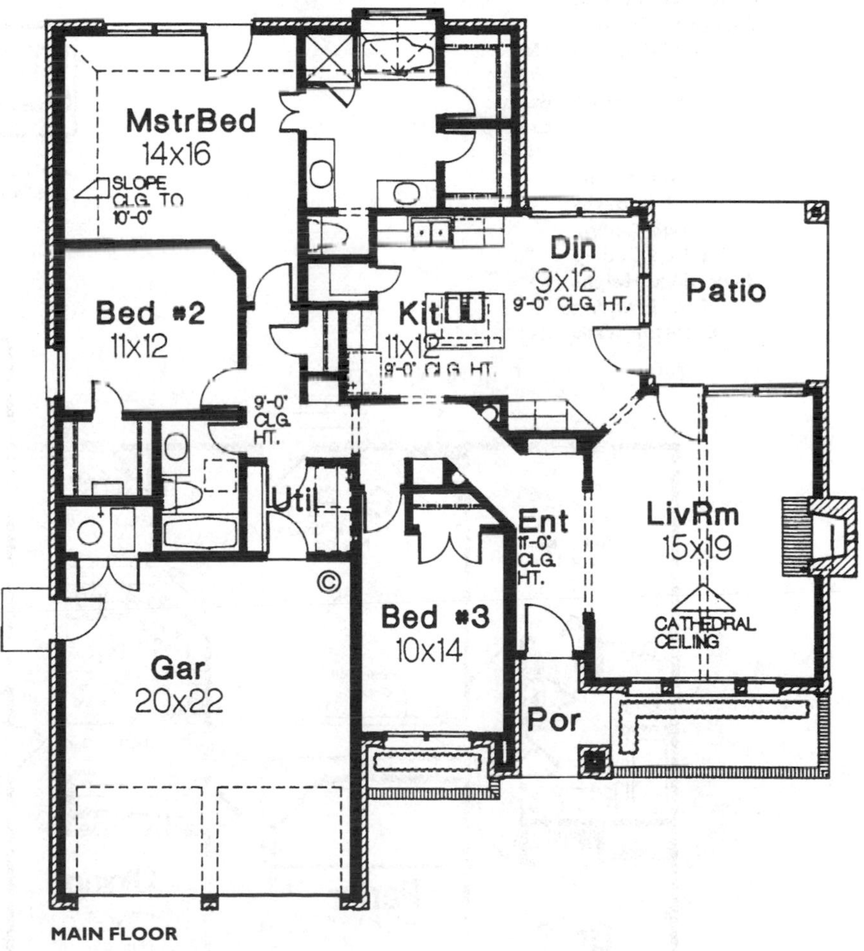

MAIN FLOOR

Design 24717

Units	Single
Price Code	B
Total Finished	1,642 sq. ft.
Main Finished	1,642 sq. ft.
Basement Unfinished	1,642 sq. ft.
Garage Unfinished	430 sq. ft.
Porch Unfinished	156 sq. ft.
Dimensions	59'x44'
Foundation	Basement Crawlspace Slab
Bedrooms	3
Full Baths	2
Main Ceiling	9'
Vaulted Ceiling	13'6"
Max Ridge Height	24'
Roof Framing	Stick
Exterior Walls	2x4

DN 14R

OPTIONAL BASEMENT STAIR LOCATION

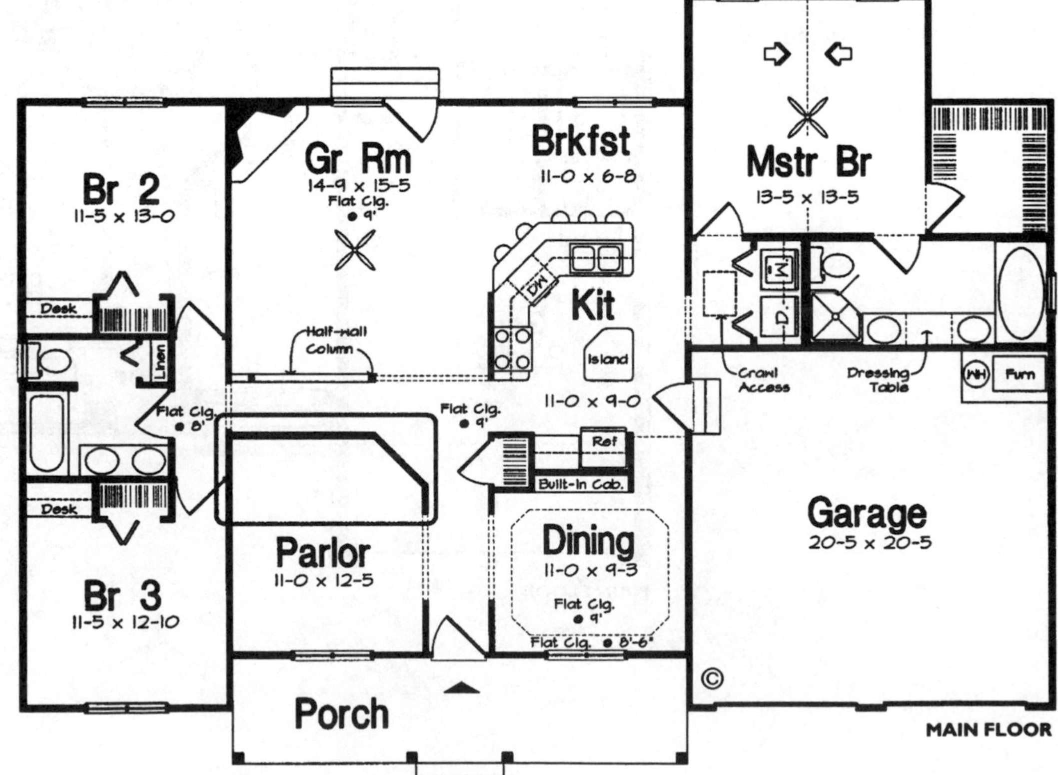

MAIN FLOOR

Design 96507

Units	Single
Price Code	B
Total Finished	1,647 sq. ft.
Main Finished	1,647 sq. ft.
Garage Unfinished	528 sq. ft.
Porch Unfinished	187 sq. ft.
Dimensions	51'x70'
Foundation	Crawlspace Slab
Bedrooms	3
Full Baths	2
Main Ceiling	9'
Max Ridge Height	23'
Roof Framing	Stick
Exterior Walls	2x4

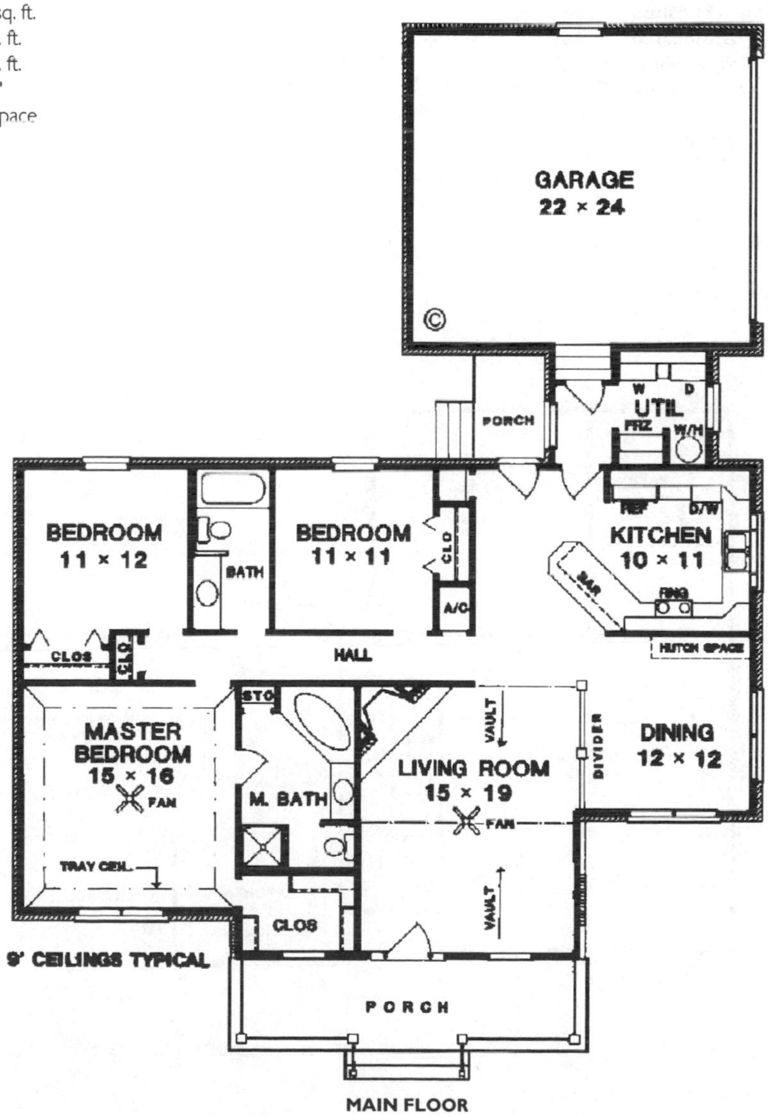

GARAGE
22 × 24

PORCH

UTIL

KITCHEN
10 × 11

BEDROOM
11 × 12

BATH

BEDROOM
11 × 11

HALL

MASTER BEDROOM
15 × 16

M. BATH

LIVING ROOM
15 × 19

DINING
12 × 12

9' CEILINGS TYPICAL

PORCH

MAIN FLOOR

Design 96513

Units	Single
Price Code	B
Total Finished	1,648 sq. ft.
Main Finished	1,648 sq. ft.
Garage Unfinished	479 sq. ft.
Dimensions	68'x50'
Foundation	Crawlspace Slab
Bedrooms	3
Full Baths	2
Half Baths	1
Main Ceiling	9'
Max Ridge Height	20'
Roof Framing	Stick
Exterior Walls	2x4

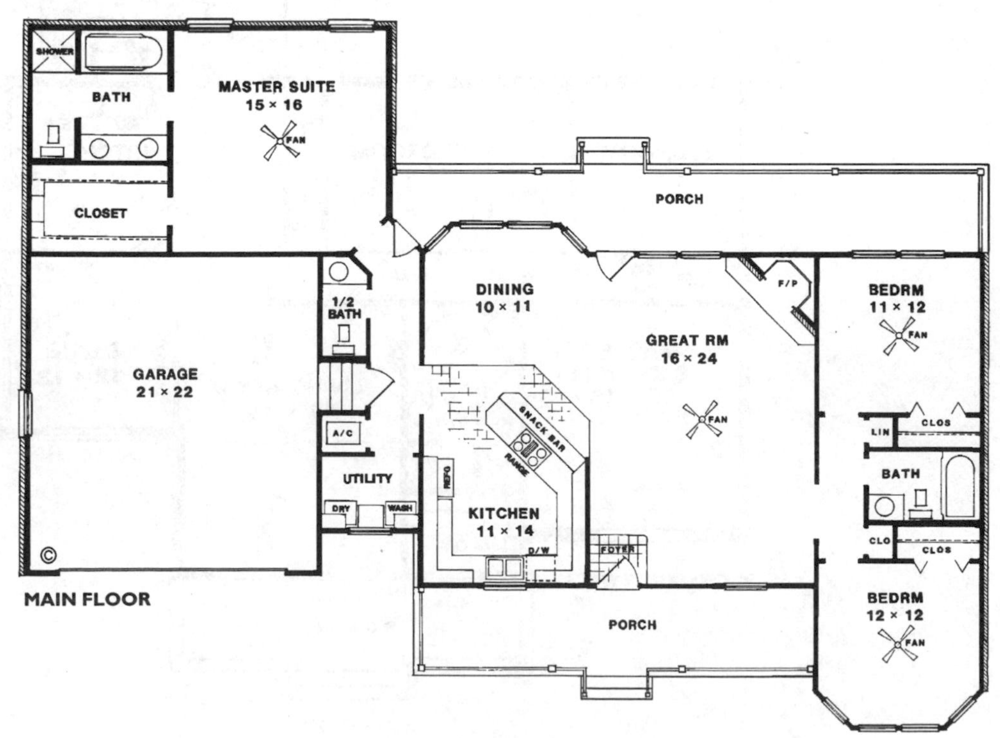

Design 94651

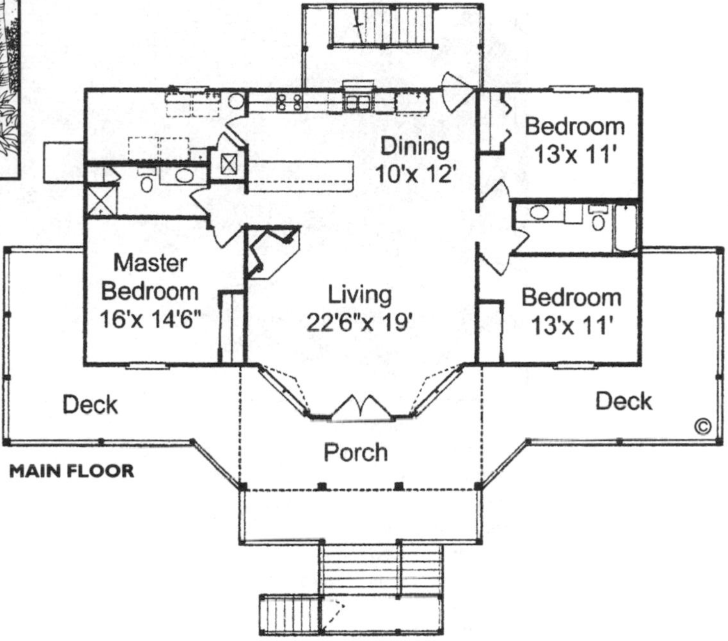

Units	Single
Price Code	B
Total Finished	1,649 sq. ft.
Main Finished	1,649 sq. ft.
Dimensions	72'x55'
Foundation	Pier/Post
Bedrooms	3
Full Baths	1
3/4 Baths	1
Main Ceiling	8'
Max Ridge Height	28'
Roof Framing	Stick
Exterior Walls	2x4

Dining 10'x 12'
Bedroom 13'x 11'
Master Bedroom 16'x 14'6"
Living 22'6"x 19'
Bedroom 13'x 11'
Deck
Deck
Porch
©
MAIN FLOOR

Design 94938

PHOTOGRAPHY: COURTESY OF THE DESIGNER

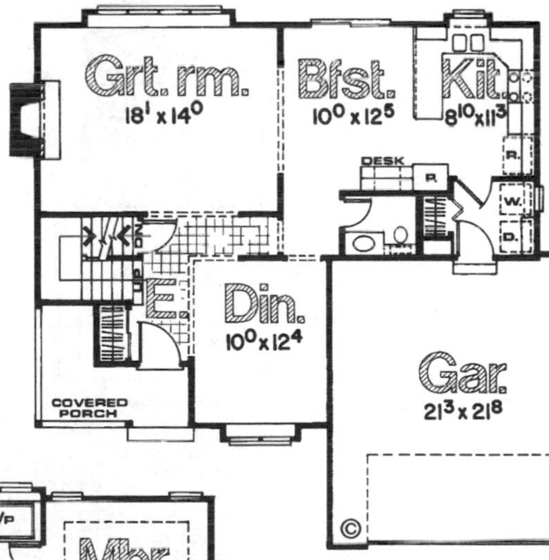

Units	Single
Price Code	B
Total Finished	1,650 sq. ft.
First Finished	891 sq. ft.
Second Finished	759 sq. ft.
Basement Unfinished	891 sq. ft.
Garage Unfinished	484 sq. ft.
Dimensions	44'x40'
Foundation	Basement
Bedrooms	3
Full Baths	2
Half Baths	1
Max Ridge Height	25'6"
Roof Framing	Stick
Exterior Walls	2x4

Please note: The photographed home may have been modified to suit homeowner preferences. If you order plans, have a builder or design professional check them against the photograph to confirm actual construction details.

[Al]ternate foundation options available at an additional charge. Please call 1-800-235-5700 for more information.

Grt. rm. 18' x 14'
Bfst. 10' x 12'5
Kit. 8'10 x 11'3
DESK
R.
W.
D.
E.
Din. 10' x 12'4
Gar. 21'3 x 21'8
COVERED PORCH
©
FIRST FLOOR

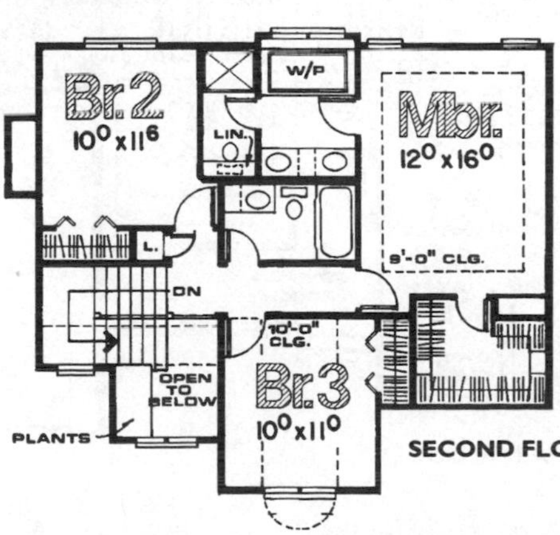

Br. 2 10' x 11'6
W/P
LIN.
Mbr. 12' x 16'
L.
9'-0" CLG.
DN
10'-0" CLG.
OPEN TO BELOW
Br. 3 10' x 11'
PLANTS
SECOND FLOOR

Design 94921

Units	Single
Price Code	B
Total Finished	1,651 sq. ft.
Main Finished	1,651 sq. ft.
Basement Unfinished	1,651 sq. ft.
Garage Unfinished	480 sq. ft.
Dimensions	62'x56'
Foundation	Basement
Bedrooms	3
Full Baths	2
Max Ridge Height	24'
Roof Framing	Stick
Exterior Walls	2x4

* Alternate foundation options available at an additional charge. Please call 1-800-235-5700 for more information.

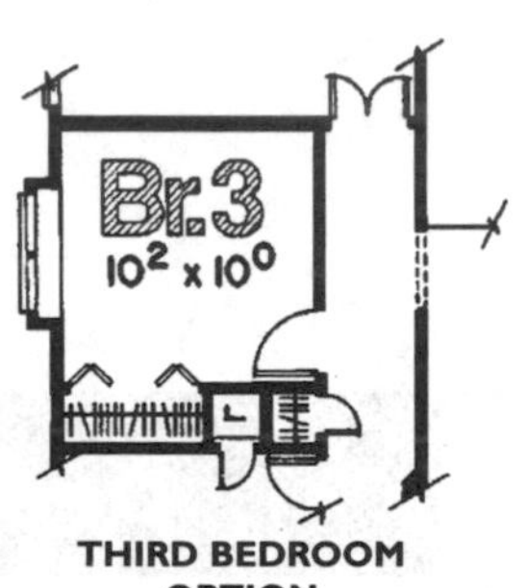

THIRD BEDROOM OPTION

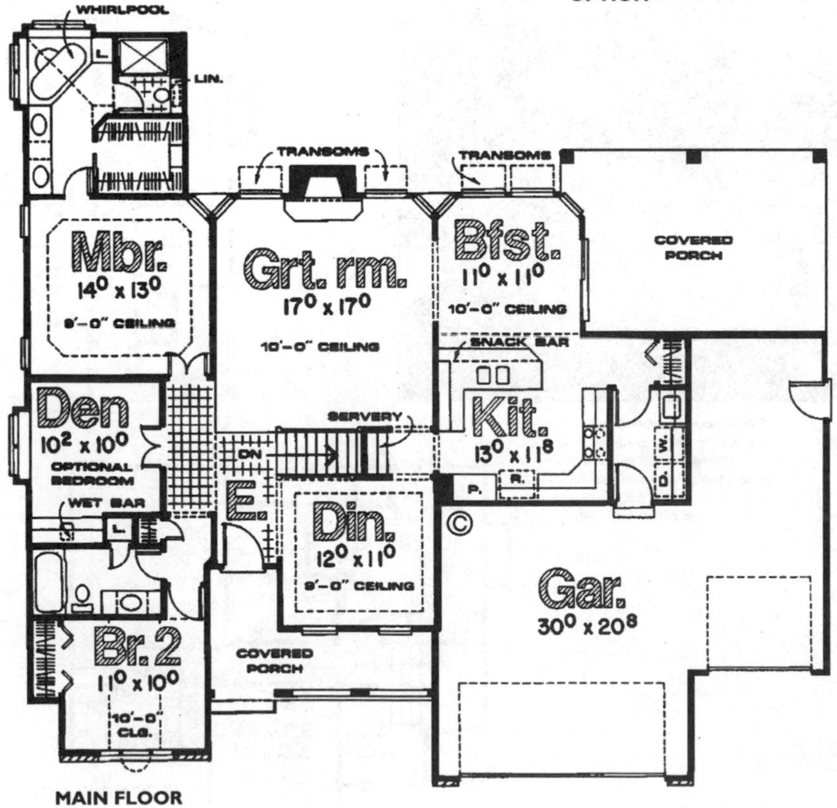

MAIN FLOOR

Design 96506

Units	Single
Price Code	B
Total Finished	1,654 sq. ft.
Main Finished	1,654 sq. ft.
Garage Unfinished	480 sq. ft.
Porch Unfinished	401 sq. ft.
Dimensions	68'x46'
Foundation	Crawlspace Slab
Bedrooms	3
Full Baths	2
Half Baths	1
Main Ceiling	9'
Max Ridge Height	21'
Roof Framing	Stick
Exterior Walls	2x4

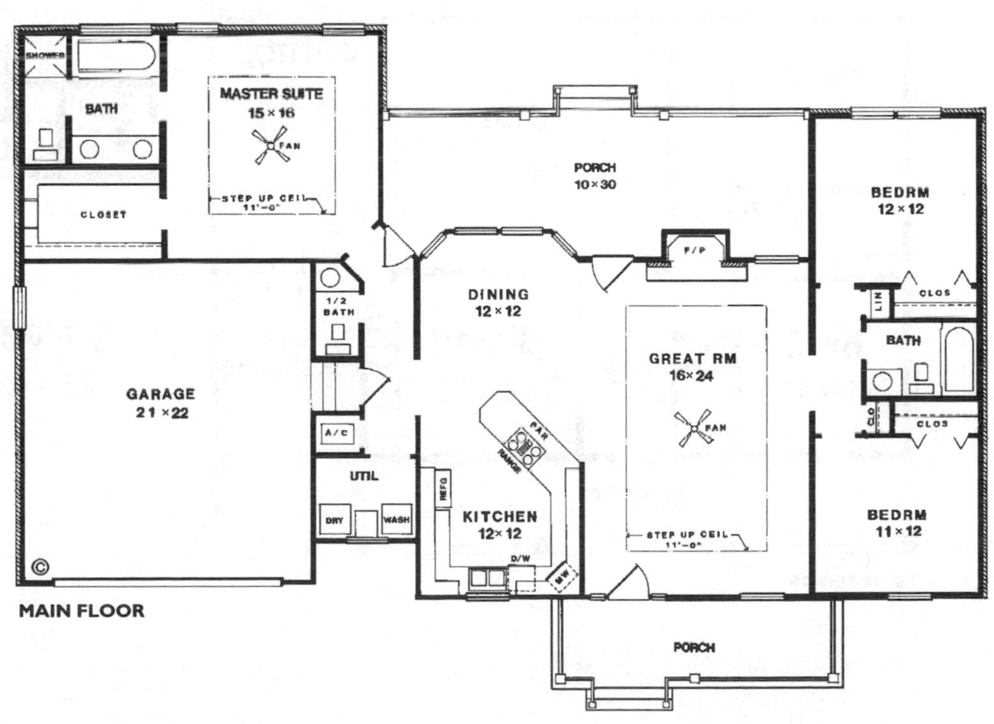

MAIN FLOOR

Design 92560

Units	Single
Price Code	B
Total Finished	1,660 sq. ft.
Main Finished	1,660 sq. ft.
Garage Unfinished	484 sq. ft.
Porch Unfinished	447 sq. ft.
Dimensions	66'10"x46'5"
Foundation	Crawlspace Slab
Bedrooms	3
Full Baths	2
Main Ceiling	9'
Max Ridge Height	20'6"
Roof Framing	Stick
Exterior Walls	2x4

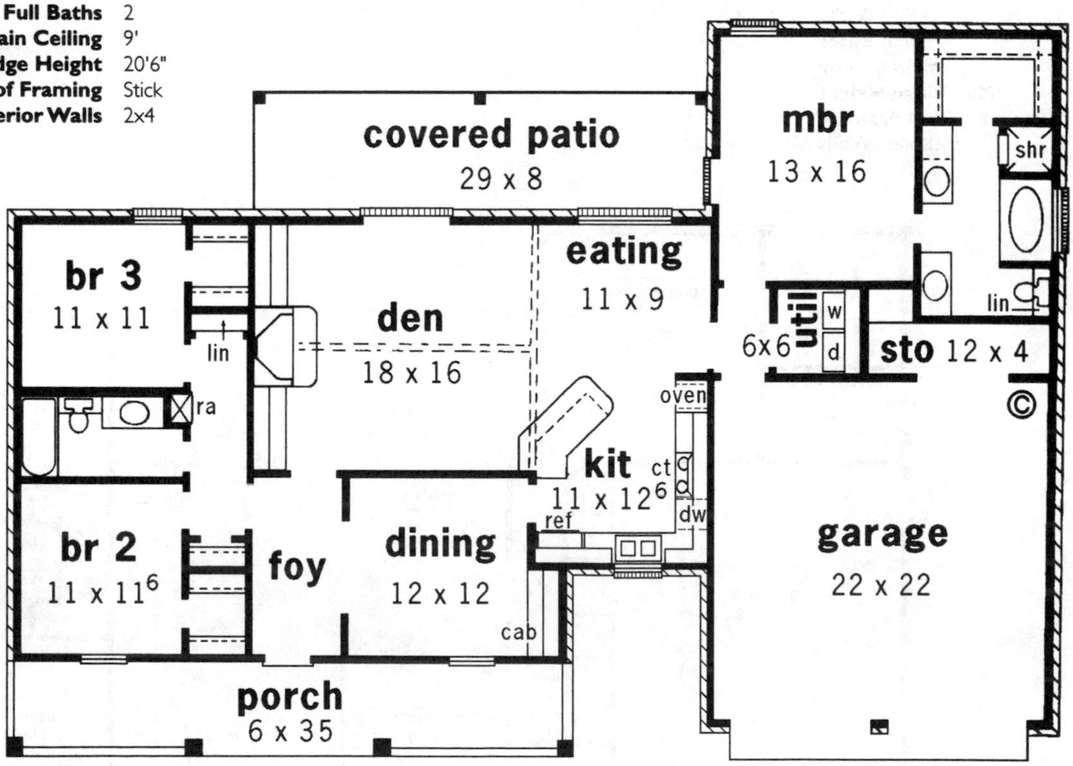

covered patio 29 x 8
mbr 13 x 16
shr
lin
br 3 11 x 11
lin
den 18 x 16
eating 11 x 9
util 6x6
w
d
sto 12 x 4
ra
oven
kit 11 x 12[6]
ct
dw
ref
©
br 2 11 x 11[6]
foy
dining 12 x 12
garage 22 x 22
cab
porch 6 x 35

MAIN FLOOR

Design 67007

Units	Single
Price Code	B
Total Finished	1,670 sq. ft.
Main Finished	1,670 sq. ft.
Bonus Unfinished	350 sq. ft.
Garage Unfinished	474 sq. ft.
Porch Unfinished	10 sq. ft.
Dimensions	53'x55'9"
Foundation	Slab
Bedrooms	3
Full Baths	2
Main Ceiling	8'
Vaulted Ceiling	11'
Tray Ceiling	13'
Max Ridge Height	24'9"
Roof Framing	Truss

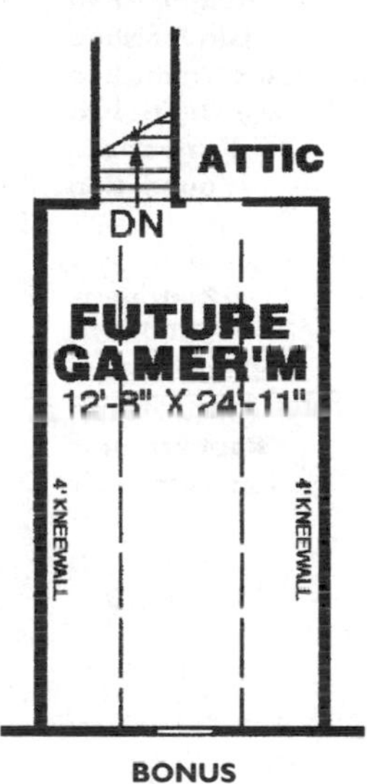

BONUS

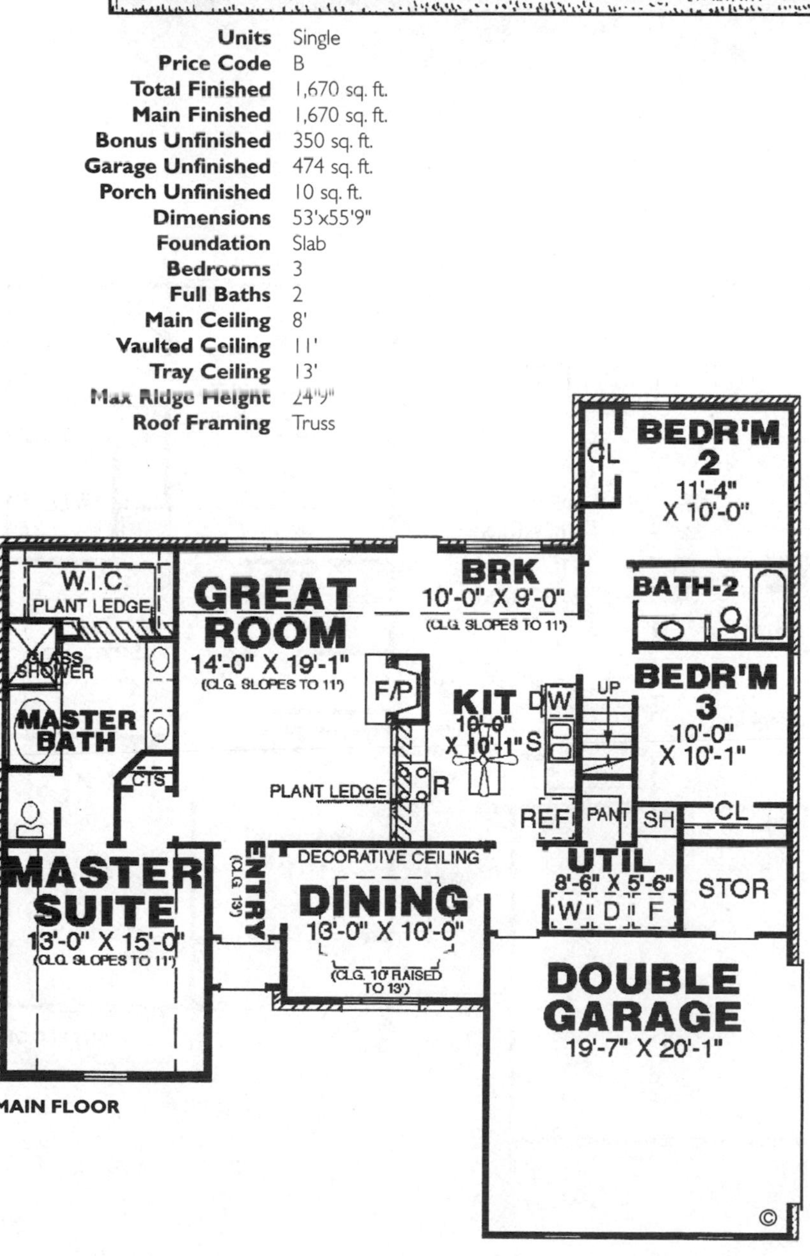

MAIN FLOOR

Design 98423

Units	Single
Price Code	B
Total Finished	1,671 sq. ft.
Main Finished	1,671 sq. ft.
Basement Unfinished	1,685 sq. ft.
Garage Unfinished	400 sq. ft.
Dimensions	50'x51'
Foundation	Basement Crawlspace Slab
Bedrooms	3
Full Baths	2
Main Ceiling	9'
Max Ridge Height	22'6"
Roof Framing	Stick
Exterior Walls	2x4

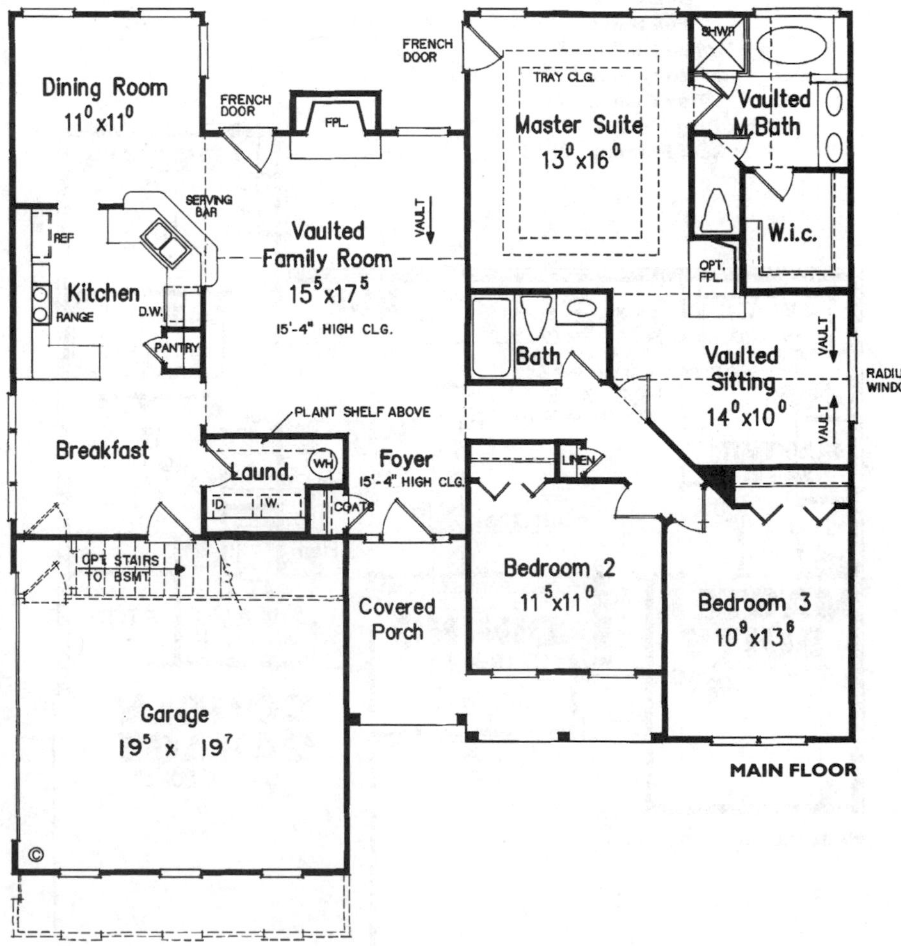

Design 62028

Units	Single
Price Code	B
Total Finished	1,672 sq. ft.
First Finished	1,140 sq. ft.
Second Finished	532 sq. ft.
Porch Unfinished	328 sq. ft.
Dimensions	27'x54'
Foundation	Crawlspace Slab
Bedrooms	3
Full Baths	2
Half Baths	1
First Ceiling	9'
Second Ceiling	8'
Exterior Walls	2x4

ATTIC
STORAGE
DN.
COMP.
DESK
LIN.
BATH
LIN
BEDROOM 2
11'-8" X 12'-0"
BEDROOM 3
12'-0" X 13'-5"
PORCH
14'-8" X 8'-0"

SECOND FLOOR

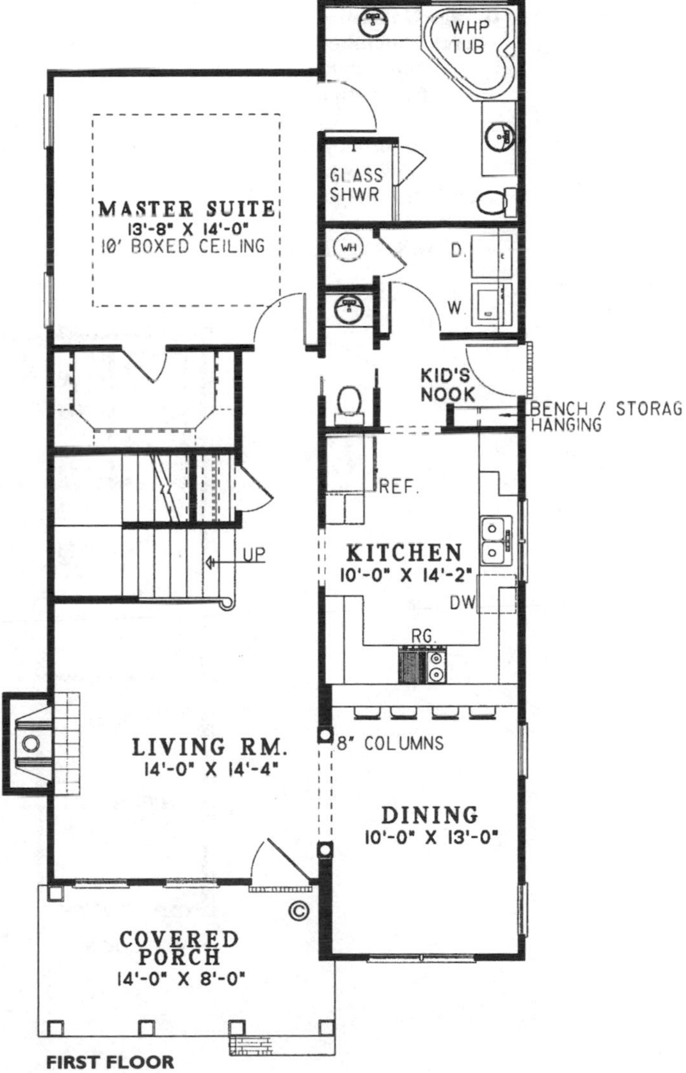

FIRST FLOOR

Design 90486

Units	Single
Price Code	B
Total Finished	1,672 sq. ft.
Main Finished	1,672 sq. ft.
Garage Unfinished	650 sq. ft.
Porch Unfinished	320 sq. ft.
Dimensions	52'10"x66'9"
Foundation	Crawlspace Slab
Bedrooms	3
Full Baths	2
Max Ridge Height	22'10"
Roof Framing	Stick
Exterior Walls	2x4

STORAGE
21-4 x 6-0

©

GARAGE
21-4 x 21-8

W.I. CLOS.
SPA TUB
BATH
SHWR

COVERED PATIO
14-0 x 10-0

FURN
WTR HTR

REFG
DW
KITCHEN
11-0 x 12-0
OVEN
COOK TOP
BAR

MASTER BEDROOM
14-8 x 13-0
TRAY CEILING

BATH

VENT-FREE FIREPLACE

GREAT ROOM
20-0 x 15-0
CATHEDRAL CEILING

PANTRY

BREAKFAST
11-0 x 9-0

CLOSET
LINEN
CLOSET
COATS

BEDROOM
11-0 x 12-4

BEDROOM
11-0 x 12-0

FOYER
17'-8" CLG.

DINING
11-0 x 12-0

SINK
W
D
LAUNDRY
11-0 x 7-0
FRZR

MAIN FLOOR

PORCH
30-0 x 6-0

Design 97263

Units	Single
Price Code	B
Total Finished	1,674 sq. ft.
Main Finished	1,674 sq. ft.
Basement Unfinished	1,703 sq. ft.
Garage Unfinished	410 sq. ft.
Dimensions	45'6"x58'
Foundation	Basement Crawlspace
Bedrooms	3
Full Baths	2
Max Ridge Height	25'
Roof Framing	Stick
Exterior Walls	2x4

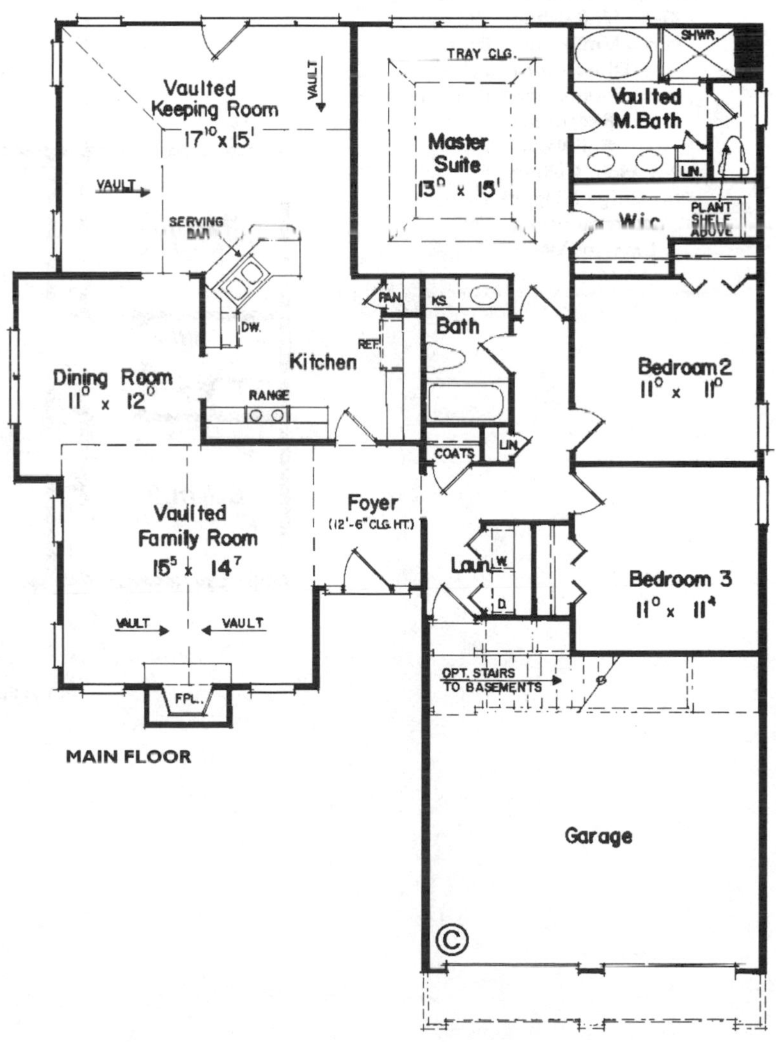

MAIN FLOOR

Units	Single
Price Code	B
Total Finished	1,676 sq. ft.
Main Finished	1,676 sq. ft.
Garage Unfinished	552 sq. ft.
Deck Unfinished	192 sq. ft.
Porch Unfinished	89 sq. ft.
Dimensions	56'x62'
Foundation	Basement
Bedrooms	3
Full Baths	2
Main Ceiling	9'
Max Ridge Height	23'
Roof Framing	Stick
Exterior Walls	2x4

*Alternate foundation and exterior options available. See plan 98968 (page 209) for more information.

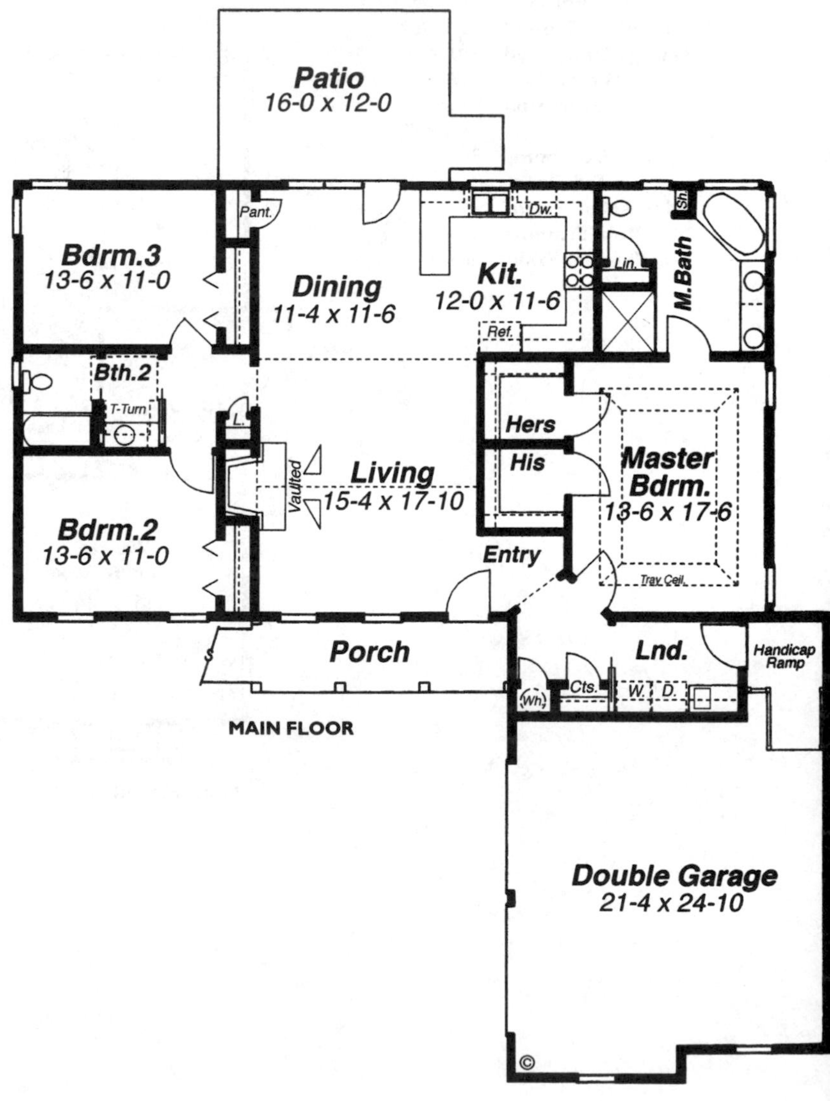

MAIN FLOOR

Design 98968

Units	Single
Price Code	B
Total Finished	1,676 sq. ft.
Main Finished	1,676 sq. ft.
Garage Unfinished	522 sq. ft.
Deck Unfinished	192 sq. ft.
Porch Unfinished	89 sq. ft.
Dimensions	56'x62'
Foundation	Crawlspace Slab
Bedrooms	3
Full Baths	2
Main Ceiling	9'
Max Ridge Height	23'
Roof Framing	Stick
Exterior Walls	2x4

*Alternate foundation and exterior options available. See plan 98960 (page 208) for more information.

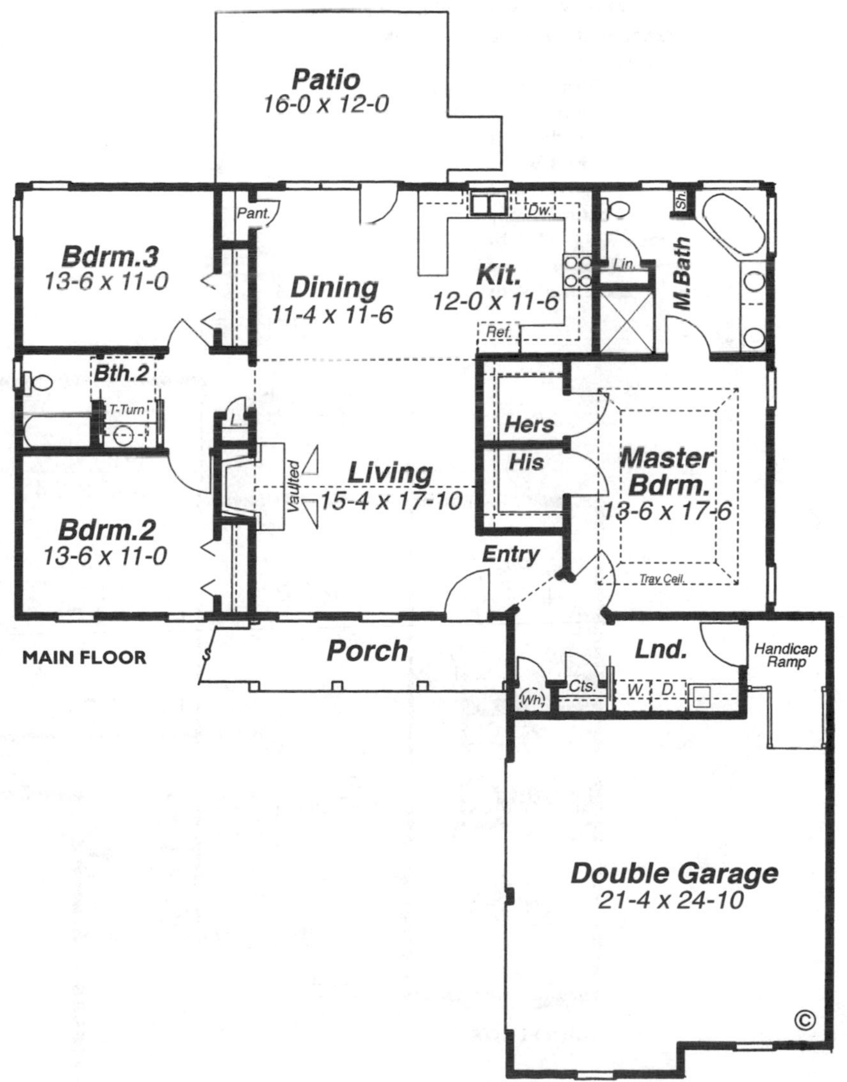

Design 99191

Units	Single
Price Code	B
Total Finished	1,676 sq. ft.
Main Finished	1,676 sq. ft.
Garage Unfinished	757 sq. ft.
Deck Unfinished	163 sq. ft.
Dimensions	70'8"x50'4"
Foundation	Basement
Bedrooms	3
Full Baths	1
3/4 Baths	1
Main Ceiling	8'
Max Ridge Height	22'
Roof Framing	Truss
Exterior Walls	2x6

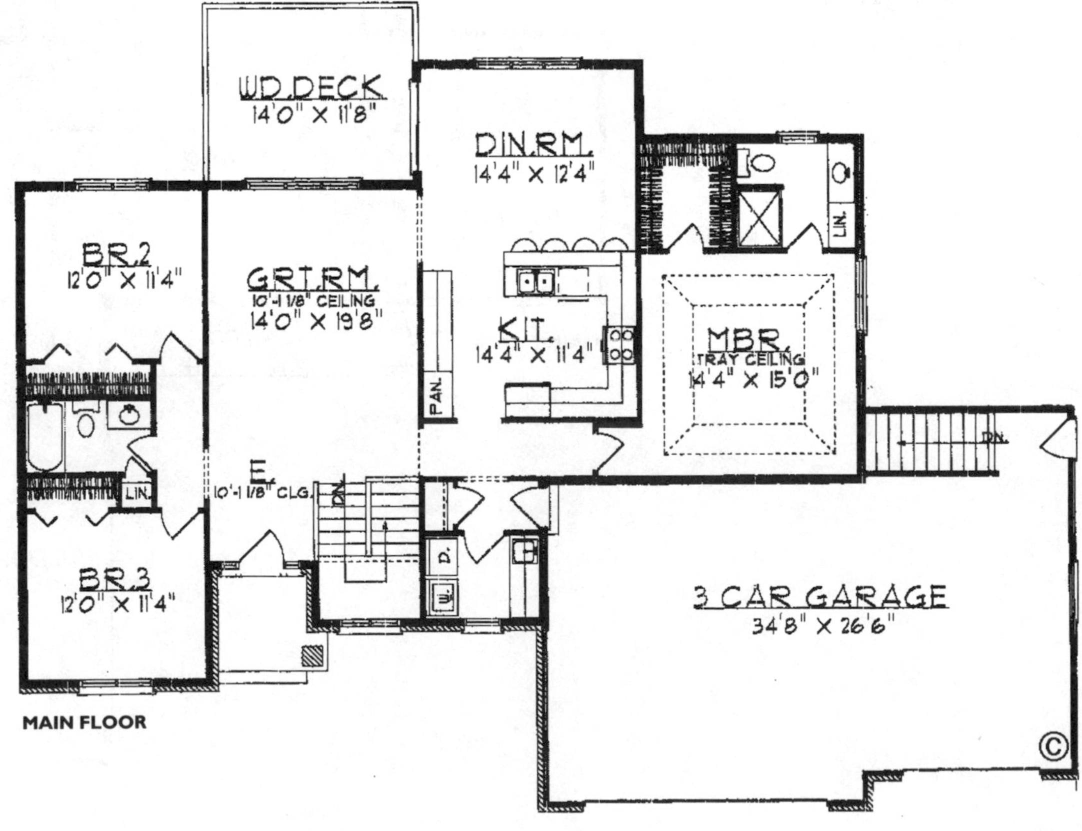

MAIN FLOOR

Design 92563

Units	Single
Price Code	B
Total Finished	1,680 sq. ft.
Main Finished	1,680 sq. ft.
Garage Unfinished	538 sq. ft.
Porch Unfinished	24 sq. ft.
Dimensions	66'10"x44'10"
Foundation	Crawlspace Slab
Bedrooms	3
Full Baths	2
Main Ceiling	9'
Max Ridge Height	20'6"
Roof Framing	Stick
Exterior Walls	2x4

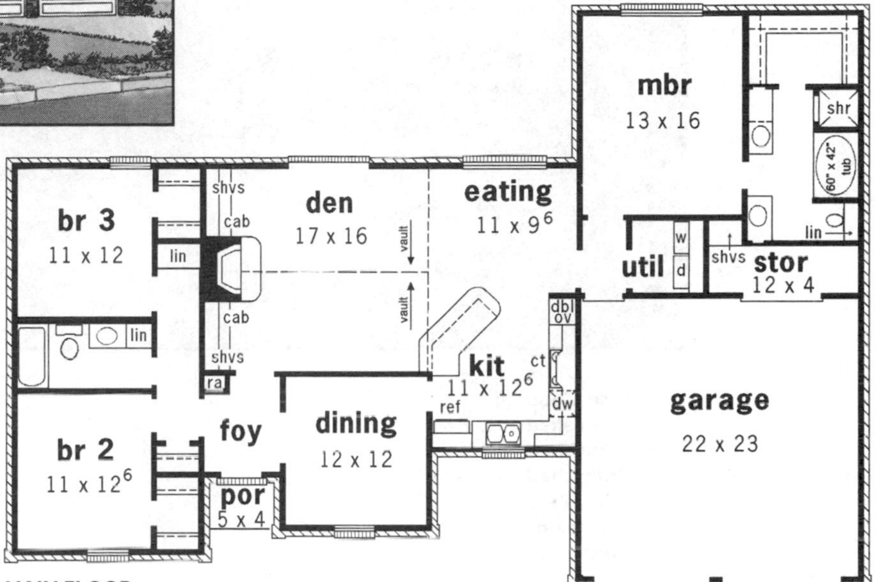

MAIN FLOOR

Design 92434

Units	Single
Price Code	B
Total Finished	1,681 sq. ft.
Main Finished	1,681 sq. ft.
Garage Unfinished	427 sq. ft.
Dimensions	55'8"x53'2"
Foundation	Slab
Bedrooms	3
Full Baths	2
Main Ceiling	9'
Vaulted Ceiling	11'
Tray Ceiling	11'
Max Ridge Height	21'8"
Roof Framing	Stick

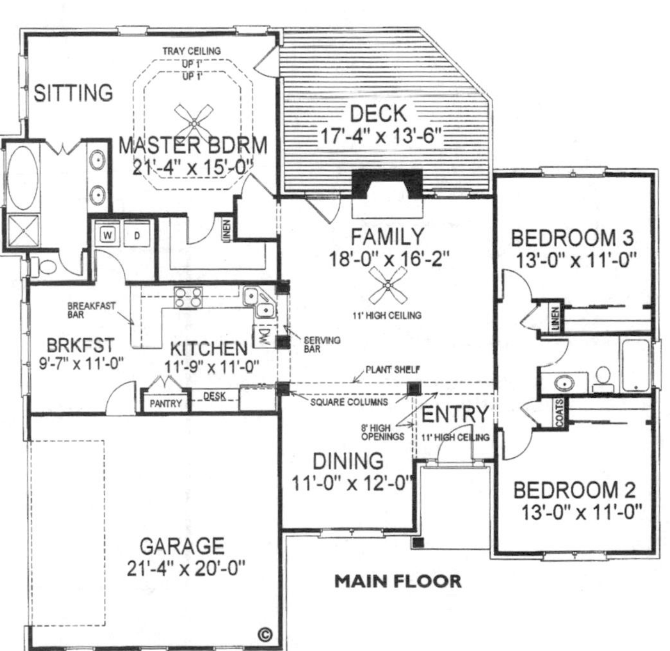

MAIN FLOOR

Design 34029

Units	Single
Price Code	B
Total Finished	1,686 sq. ft.
Main Finished	1,686 sq. ft.
Basement Unfinished	1,676 sq. ft.
Garage Unfinished	484 sq. ft.
Dimensions	61'x54'
Foundation	Basement Crawlspace Slab
Bedrooms	3
Full Baths	1
3/4 Baths	1
Main Ceiling	8'
Max Ridge Height	23'
Roof Framing	Stick
Exterior Walls	2x4, 2x6

Please note: The photographed home may have been modified to suit homeowner preferences. If you order plans, have a builder or design professional check them against the photograph to confirm actual construction details.

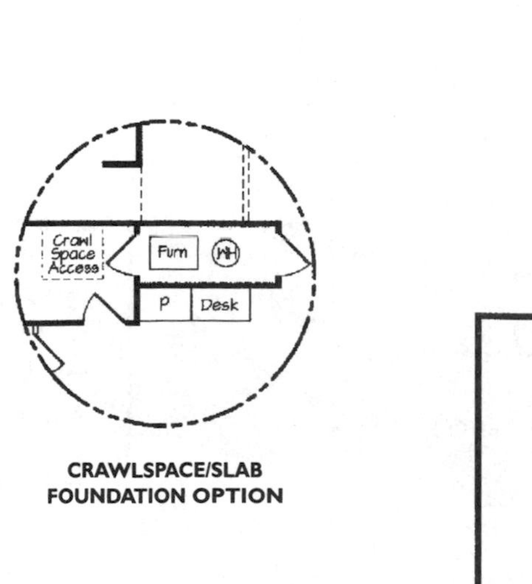

CRAWLSPACE/SLAB FOUNDATION OPTION

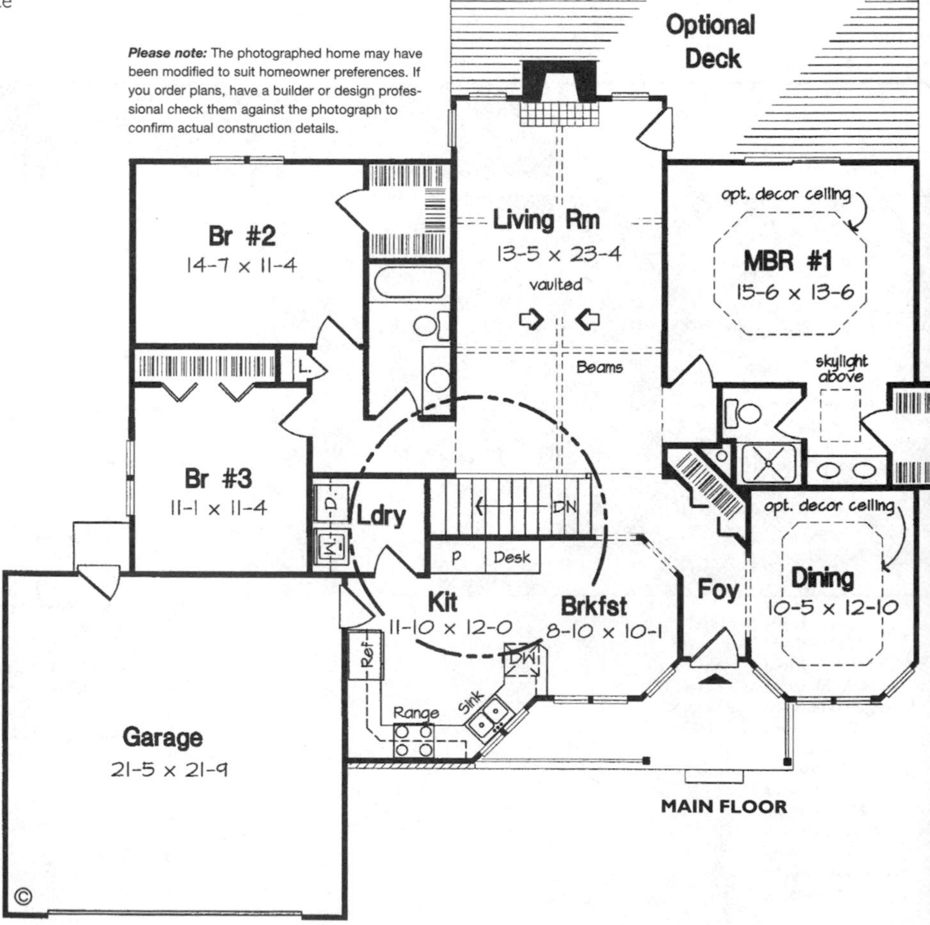

MAIN FLOOR

Design 97617

Units	Single
Price Code	B
Total Finished	1,688 sq. ft.
Main Finished	1,688 sq. ft.
Basement Unfinished	1,702 sq. ft.
Garage Unfinished	402 sq. ft.
Dimensions	50'x51'
Foundation	Basement Crawlspace Slab
Bedrooms	4
Full Baths	2
Max Ridge Height	24'6"
Roof Framing	Stick
Exterior Walls	2x4

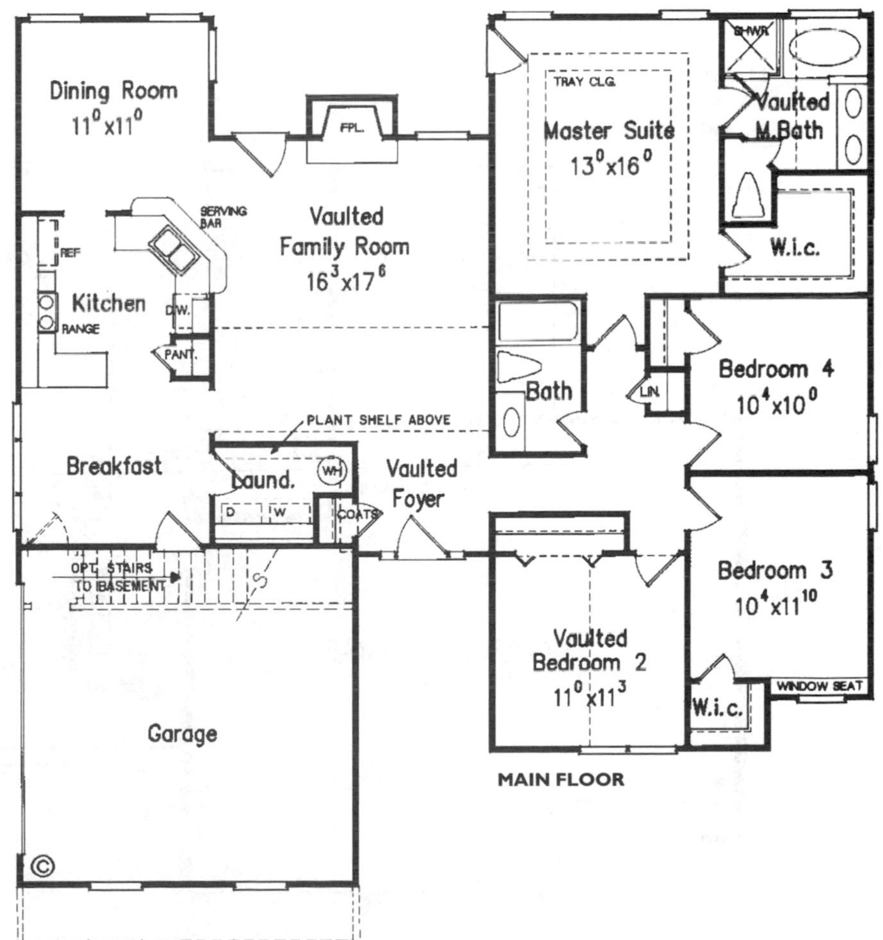

Design 99180

Units	Single
Price Code	B
Total Finished	1,690 sq. ft.
Main Finished	1,690 sq. ft.
Basement Unfinished	1,690 sq. ft.
Garage Unfinished	959 sq. ft.
Deck Unfinished	231 sq. ft.
Dimensions	74'4"x48'
Foundation	Basement
Bedrooms	3
Full Baths	1
3/4 Baths	1
Max Ridge Height	23'8"
Roof Framing	Truss
Exterior Walls	2x6

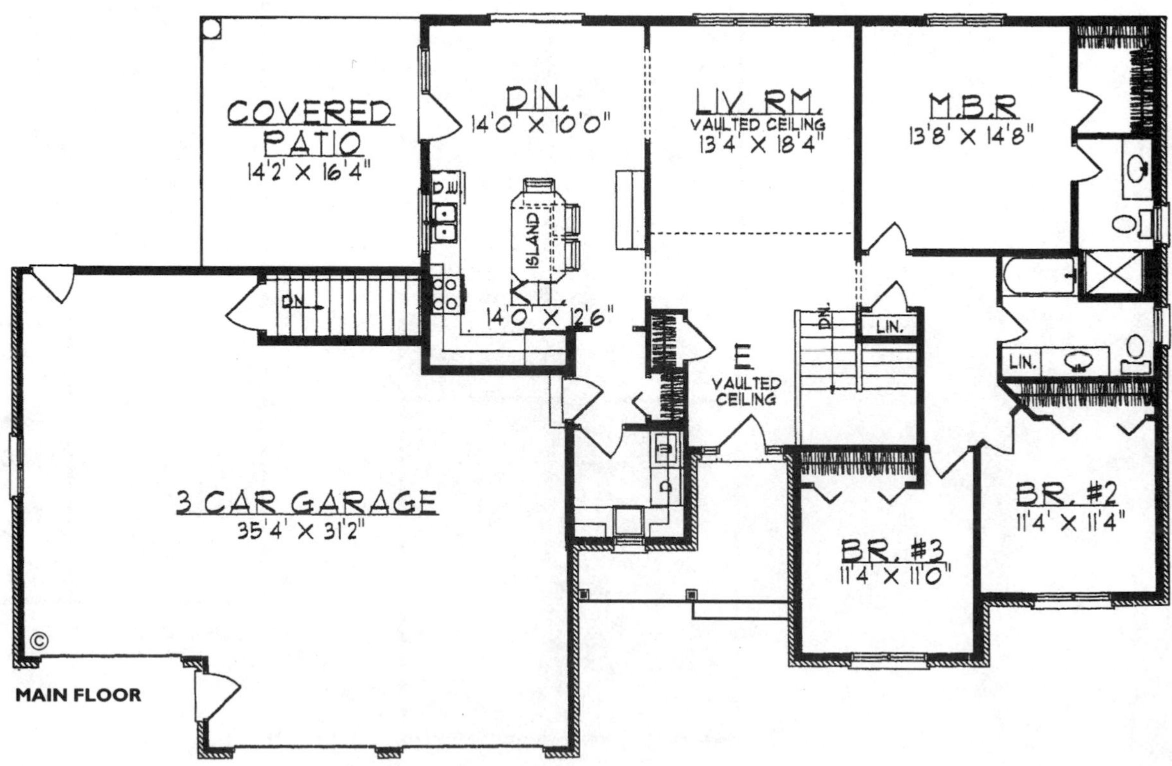

MAIN FLOOR

Design 97254

Units	Single
Price Code	B
Total Finished	1,692 sq. ft.
Main Finished	1,692 sq. ft.
Bonus Unfinished	358 sq. ft.
Basement Unfinished	1,705 sq. ft.
Garage Unfinished	472 sq. ft.
Dimensions	54'x56'6"
Foundation	Basement Crawlspace
Bedrooms	3
Full Baths	2
Max Ridge Height	27'
Roof Framing	Stick
Exterior Walls	2x4

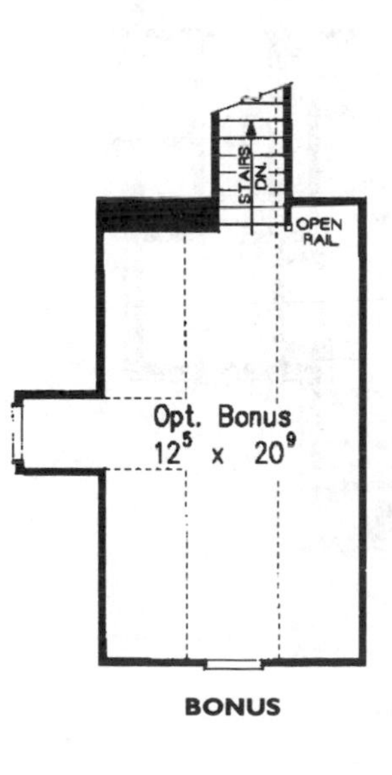

BONUS

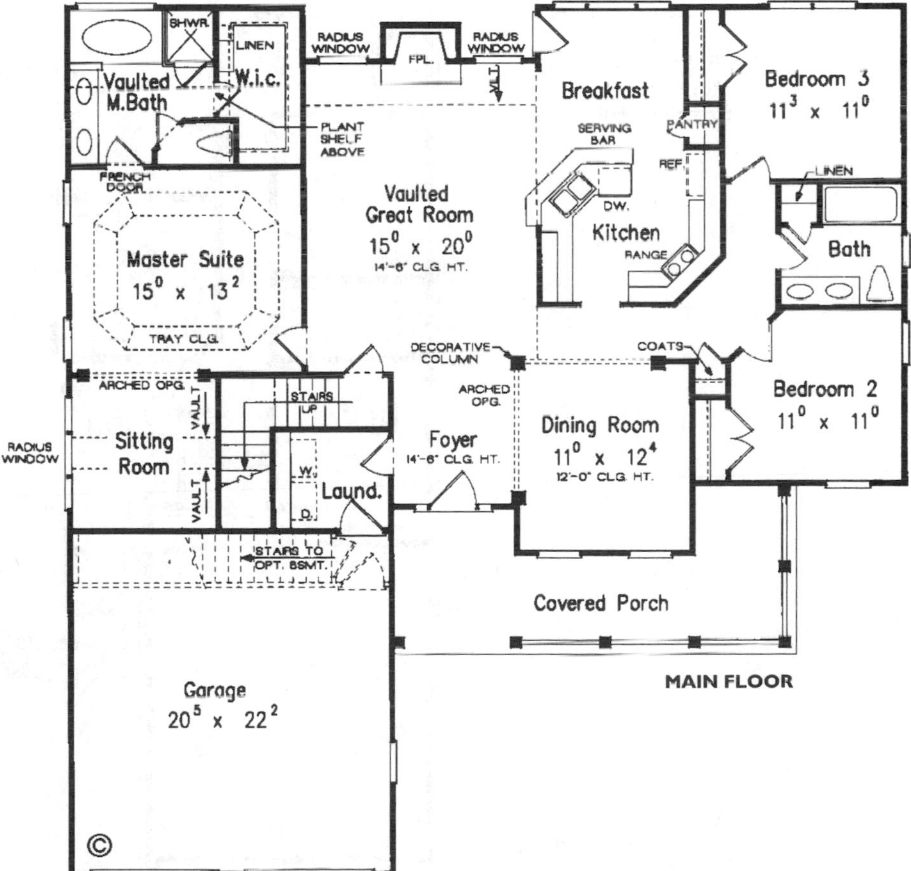

MAIN FLOOR

Design 92290

Units	Single
Price Code	B
Total Finished	1,696 sq. ft.
Main Finished	1,696 sq. ft.
Garage Unfinished	389 sq. ft.
Deck Unfinished	200 sq. ft.
Porch Unfinished	30 sq. ft.
Dimensions	50'x62'2"
Foundation	Slab
Bedrooms	4
Full Baths	2
Max Ridge Height	22'
Roof Framing	Stick
Exterior Walls	2x4

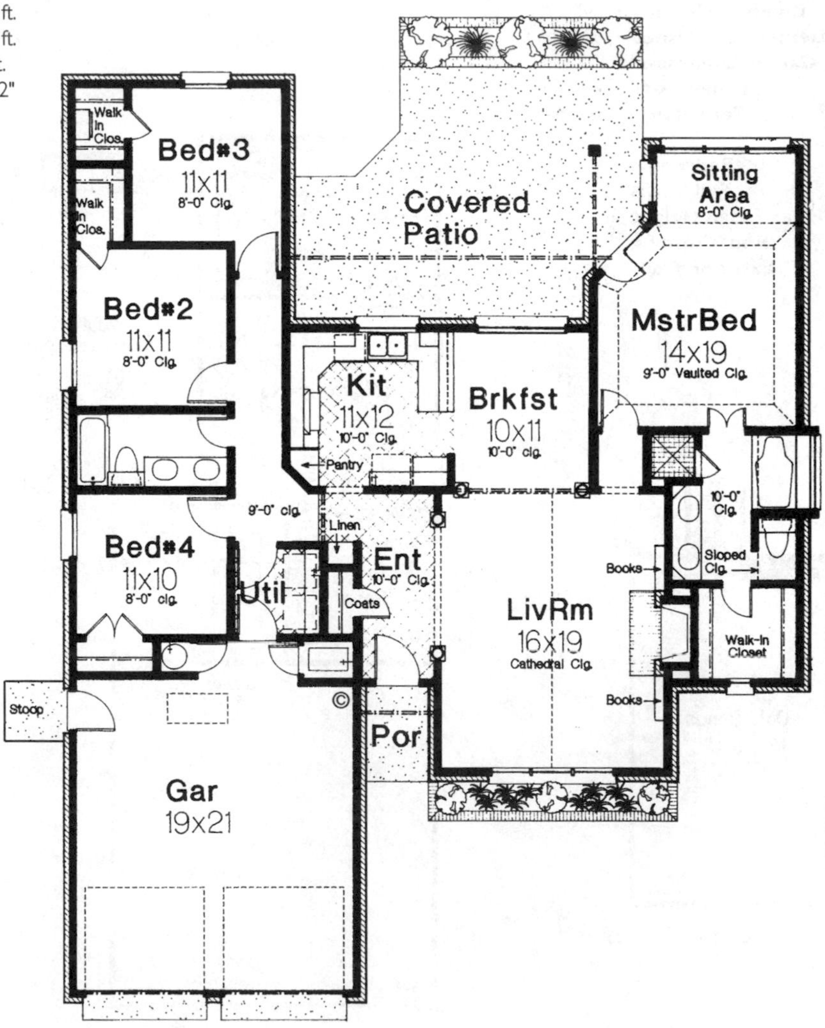

MAIN FLOOR

Design 94925

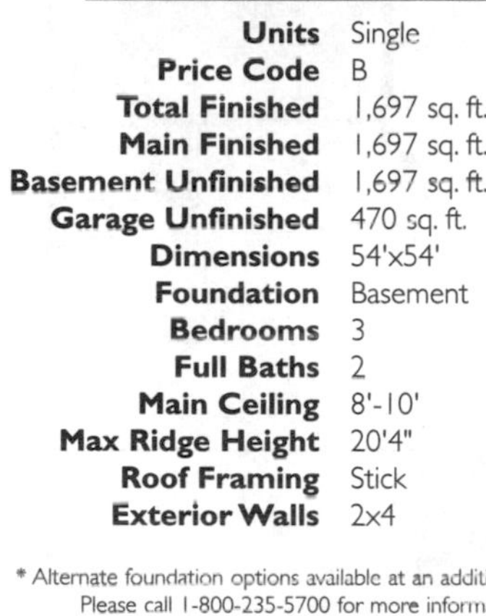

Units	Single
Price Code	B
Total Finished	1,697 sq. ft.
Main Finished	1,697 sq. ft.
Basement Unfinished	1,697 sq. ft.
Garage Unfinished	470 sq. ft.
Dimensions	54'x54'
Foundation	Basement
Bedrooms	3
Full Baths	2
Main Ceiling	8'-10'
Max Ridge Height	20'4"
Roof Framing	Stick
Exterior Walls	2x4

* Alternate foundation options available at an additional charge. Please call 1-800-235-5700 for more information.

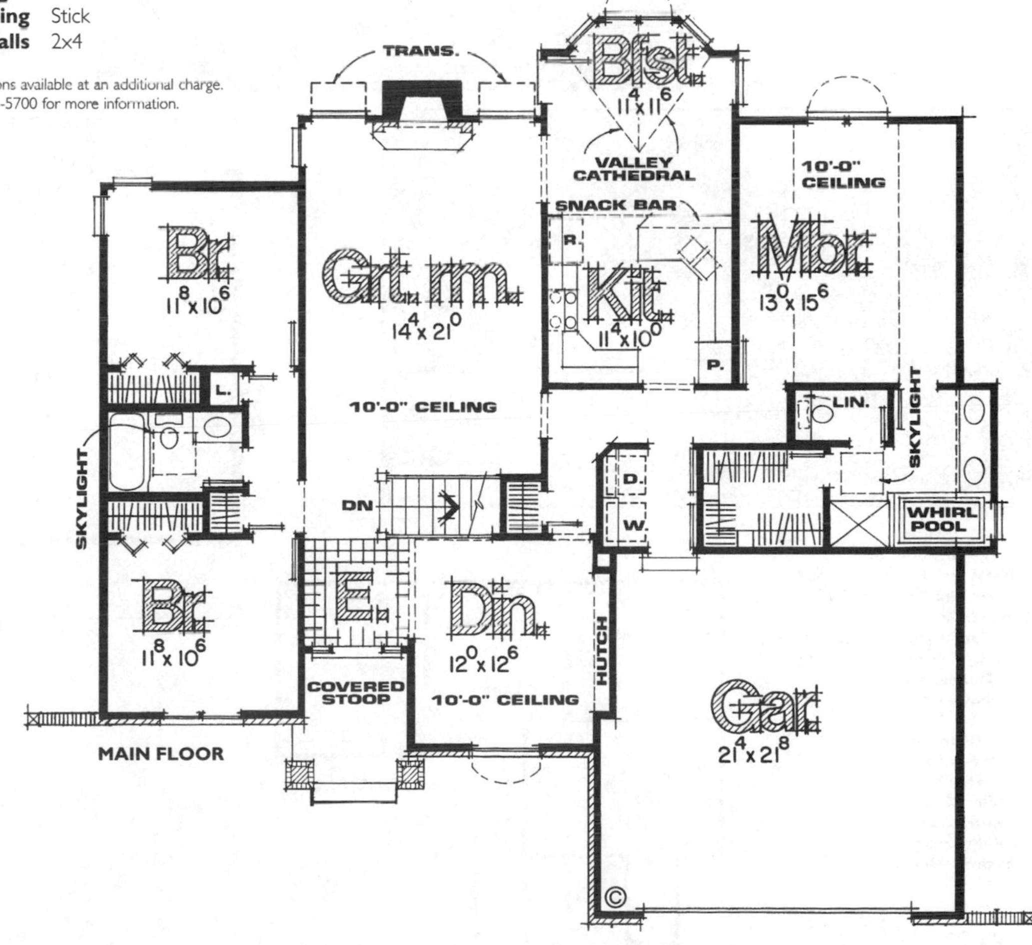

Design 81010

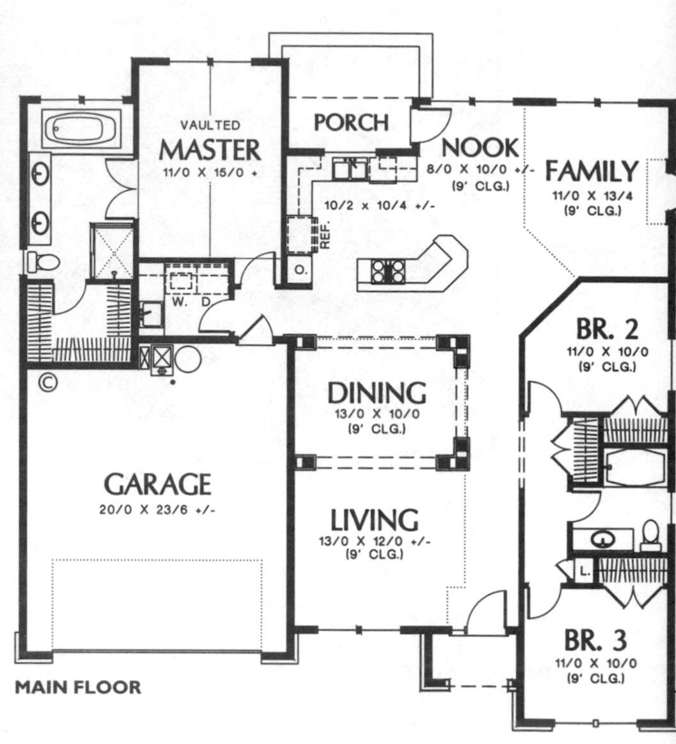

Units	Single
Price Code	B
Total Finished	1,699 sq. ft.
Main Finished	1,699 sq. ft.
Dimensions	50'x51'
Foundation	Crawlspace
Bedrooms	3
Full Baths	2
Main Ceiling	9'
Max Ridge Height	23'
Roof Framing	Truss
Exterior Walls	2x6

Design 96524

Units	Single
Price Code	B
Total Finished	1,705 sq. ft.
First Finished	1,056 sq. ft.
Second Finished	649 sq. ft.
Garage Unfinished	562 sq. ft.
Porch Unfinished	162 sq. ft.
Dimensions	45'x45'
Foundation	Crawlspace Slab
Bedrooms	4
Full Baths	2
Half Baths	1
First Ceiling	8'
Second Ceiling	8'
Max Ridge Height	25'
Exterior Walls	2x4

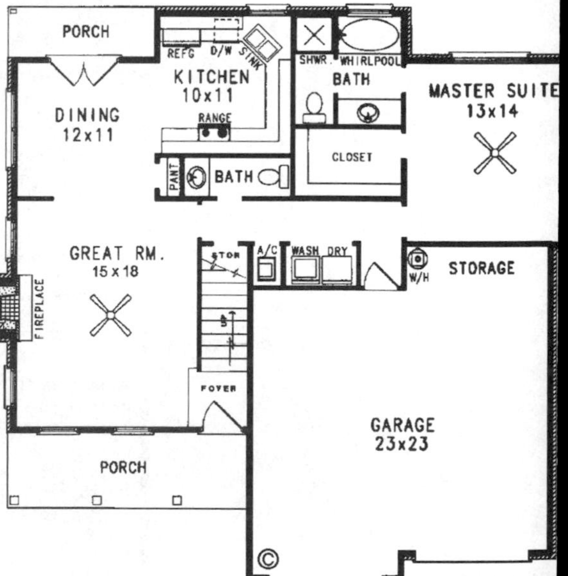

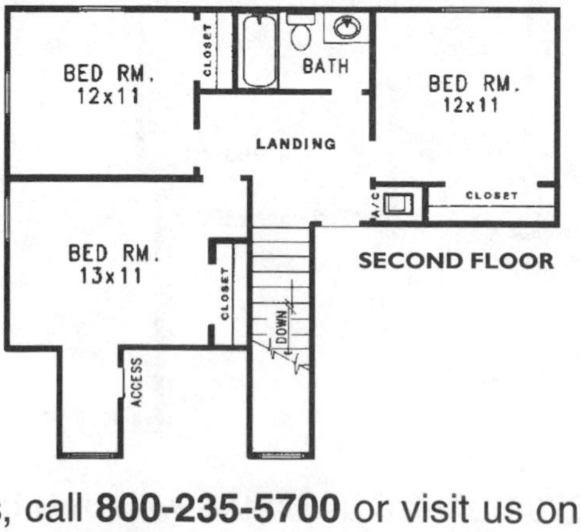

SECOND FLOOR

FIRST FLOOR

Design 94922

Units	Single
Price Code	B
Total Finished	1,710 sq. ft.
Main Finished	1,710 sq. ft.
Basement Unfinished	1,710 sq. ft.
Garage Unfinished	480 sq. ft.
Dimensions	53'4"x54'10"
Foundation	Basement
Bedrooms	3
Full Baths	2
Max Ridge Height	20'3"
Roof Framing	Stick
Exterior Walls	2x4

* Alternate foundation options available at an additional charge. Please call 1-800-235-5700 for more information.

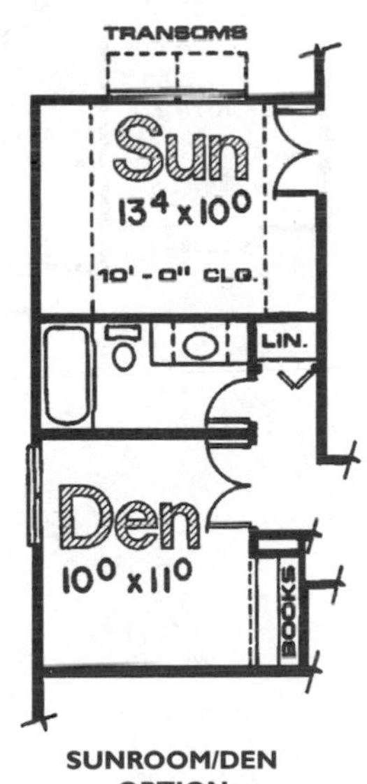

SUNROOM/DEN OPTION

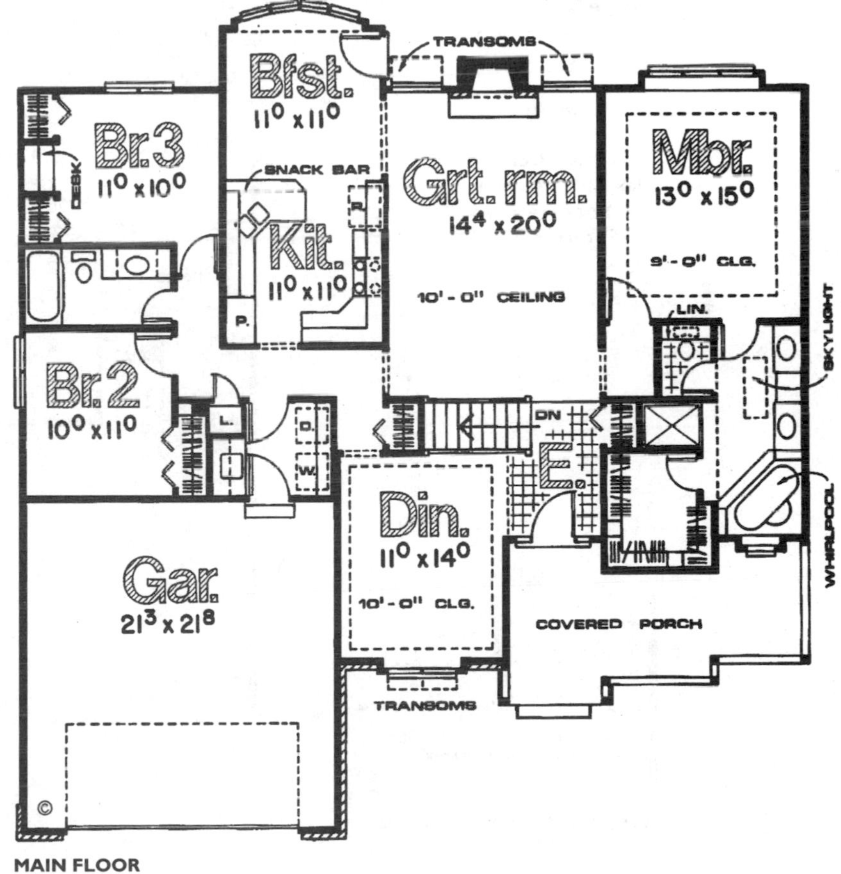

MAIN FLOOR

Design 97222

Units	Single
Price Code	B
Total Finished	1,712 sq. ft.
Main Finished	1,712 sq. ft.
Basement Unfinished	1,760 sq. ft.
Garage Unfinished	400 sq. ft.
Dimensions	55'x55'
Foundation	Basement Crawlspace
Bedrooms	3
Full Baths	2
Main Ceiling	9'
Max Ridge Height	21'6"
Roof Framing	Stick
Exterior Walls	2x4

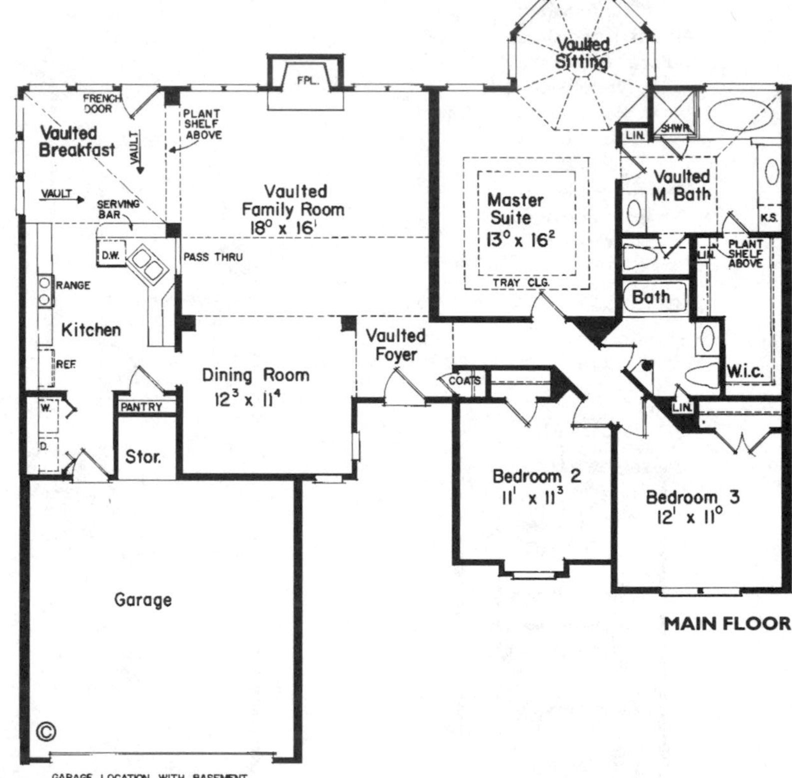

MAIN FLOOR

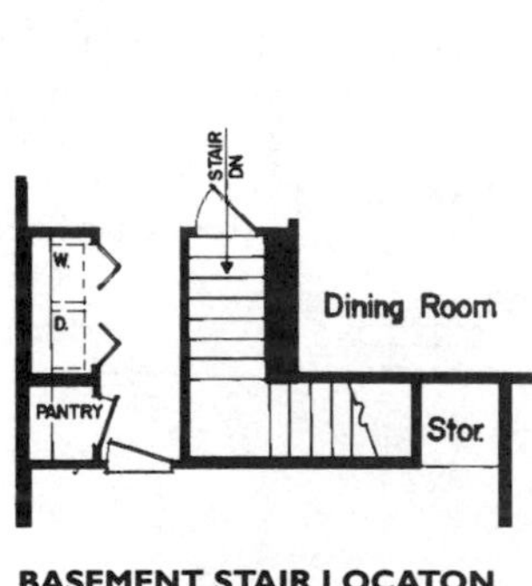

BASEMENT STAIR LOCATON OPTION

Design 98456

Units	Single
Price Code	B
Total Finished	1,715 sq. ft.
Main Finished	1,715 sq. ft.
Basement Unfinished	1,715 sq. ft.
Garage Unfinished	450 sq. ft.
Dimensions	55'x51'6"
Foundation	Basement Crawlspace Slab
Bedrooms	3
Full Baths	2
Main Ceiling	9'1"
Max Ridge Height	25'
Roof Framing	Stick
Exterior Walls	2x4

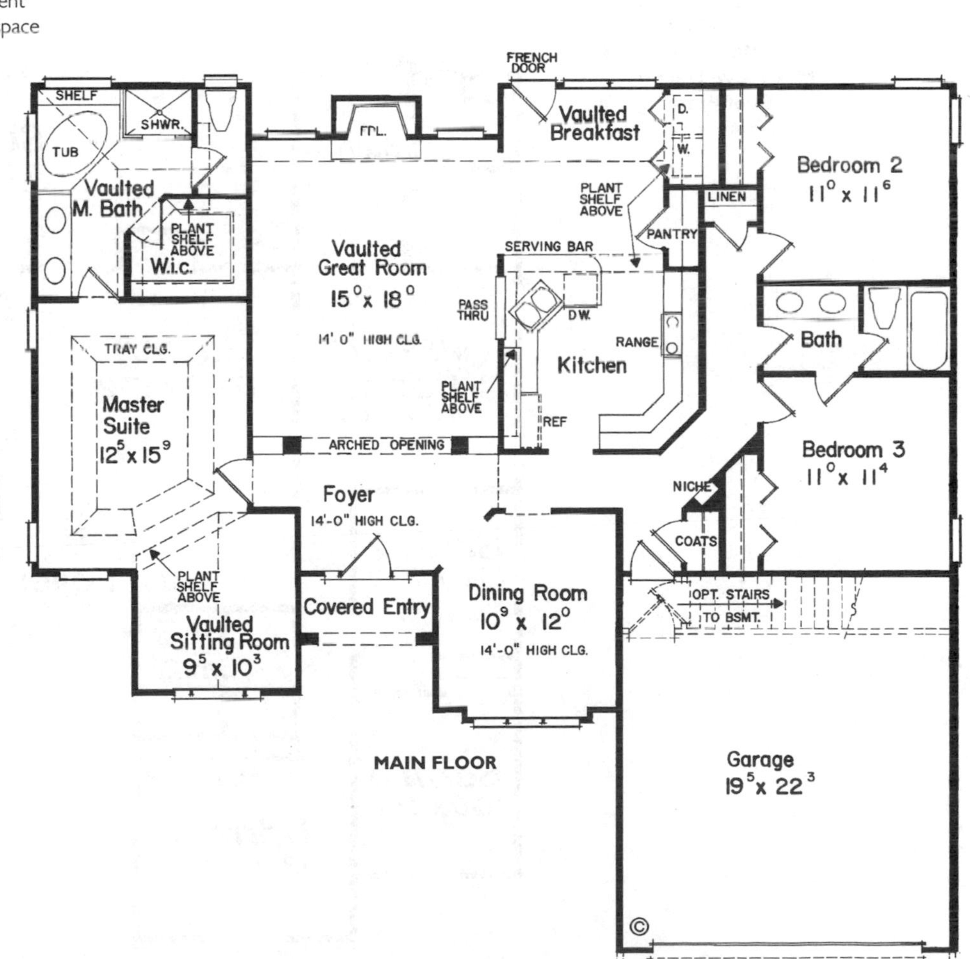

Design 98981

Units	Single
Price Code	B
Total Finished	1,716 sq. ft.
Main Finished	1,716 sq. ft.
Dimensions	56'x55'
Foundation	Crawlspace Slab
Bedrooms	4
Full Baths	2
Main Ceiling	8'
Max Ridge Height	20'
Roof Framing	Stick
Exterior Walls	2x4

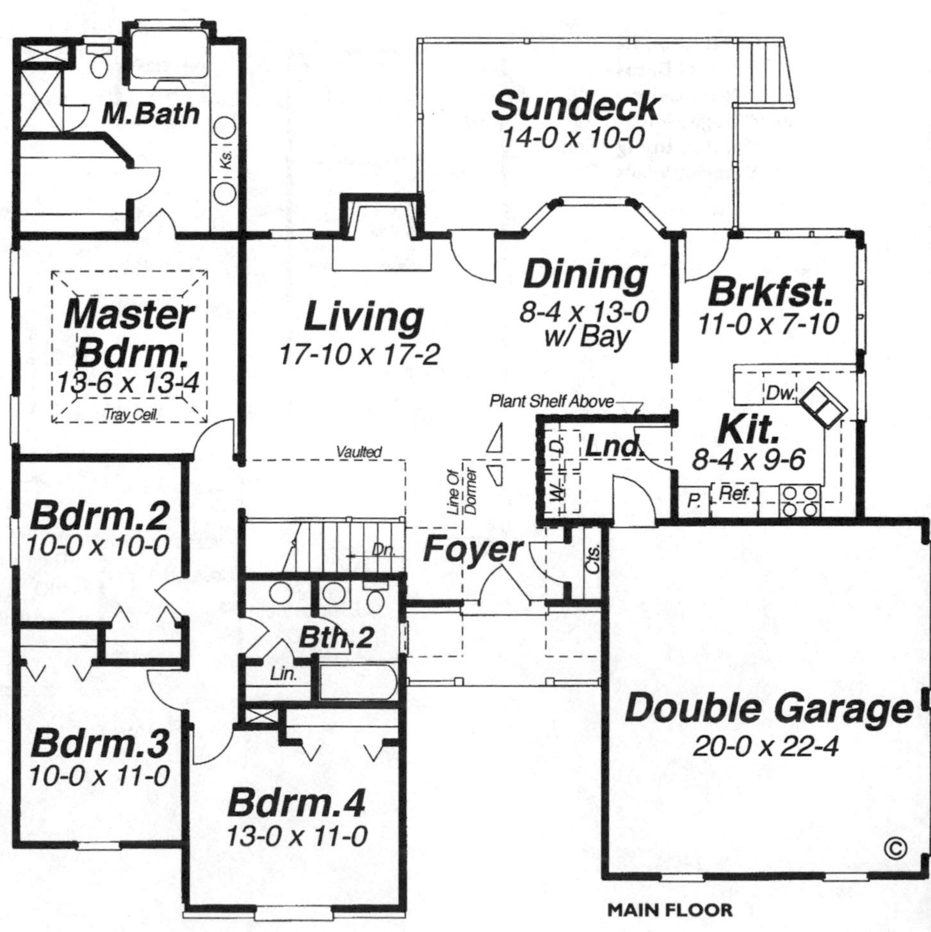

MAIN FLOOR

 To order blueprints, call **800-235-5700** or visit us on the web, **familyhomeplans.com**

Design 97933

Units	Single
Price Code	B
Total Finished	1,724 sq. ft.
Main Finished	1,724 sq. ft.
Garage Unfinished	460 sq. ft.
Dimensions	50'x50'
Foundation	Basement
Bedrooms	3
Full Baths	2
Main Ceiling	9'
Max Ridge Height	24'4"
Roof Framing	Stick
Exterior Walls	2x4

* Alternate foundation options available at an additional charge. Please call 1-800-235-5700 for more information.

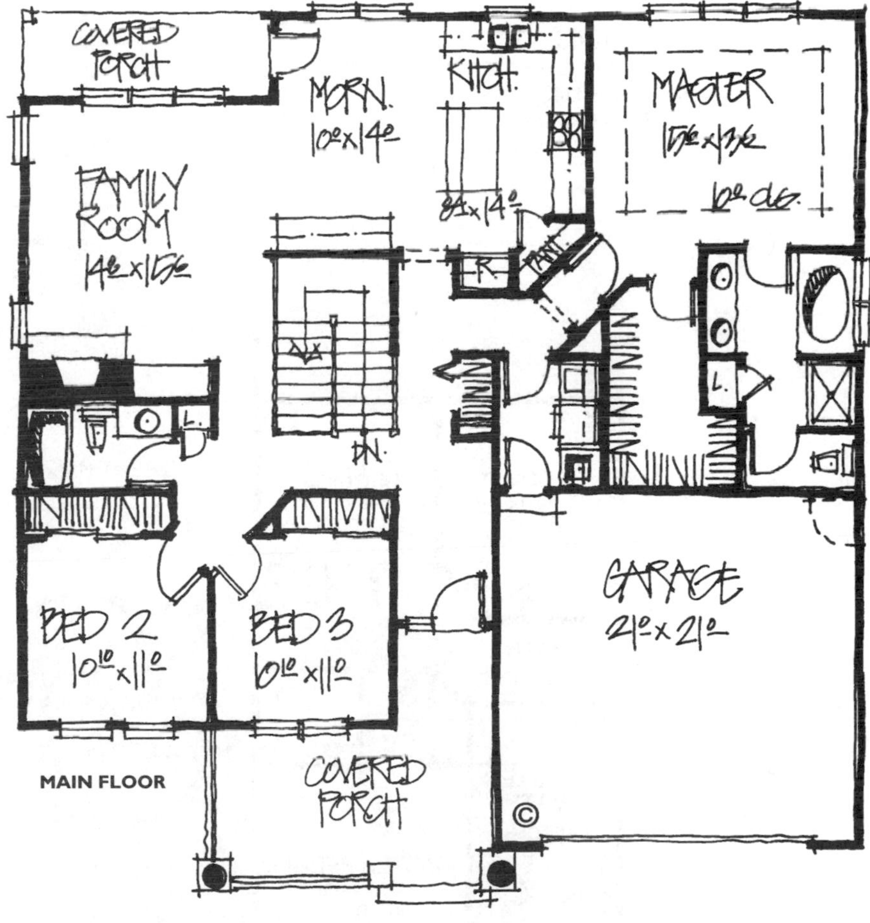

MAIN FLOOR

Design 93079

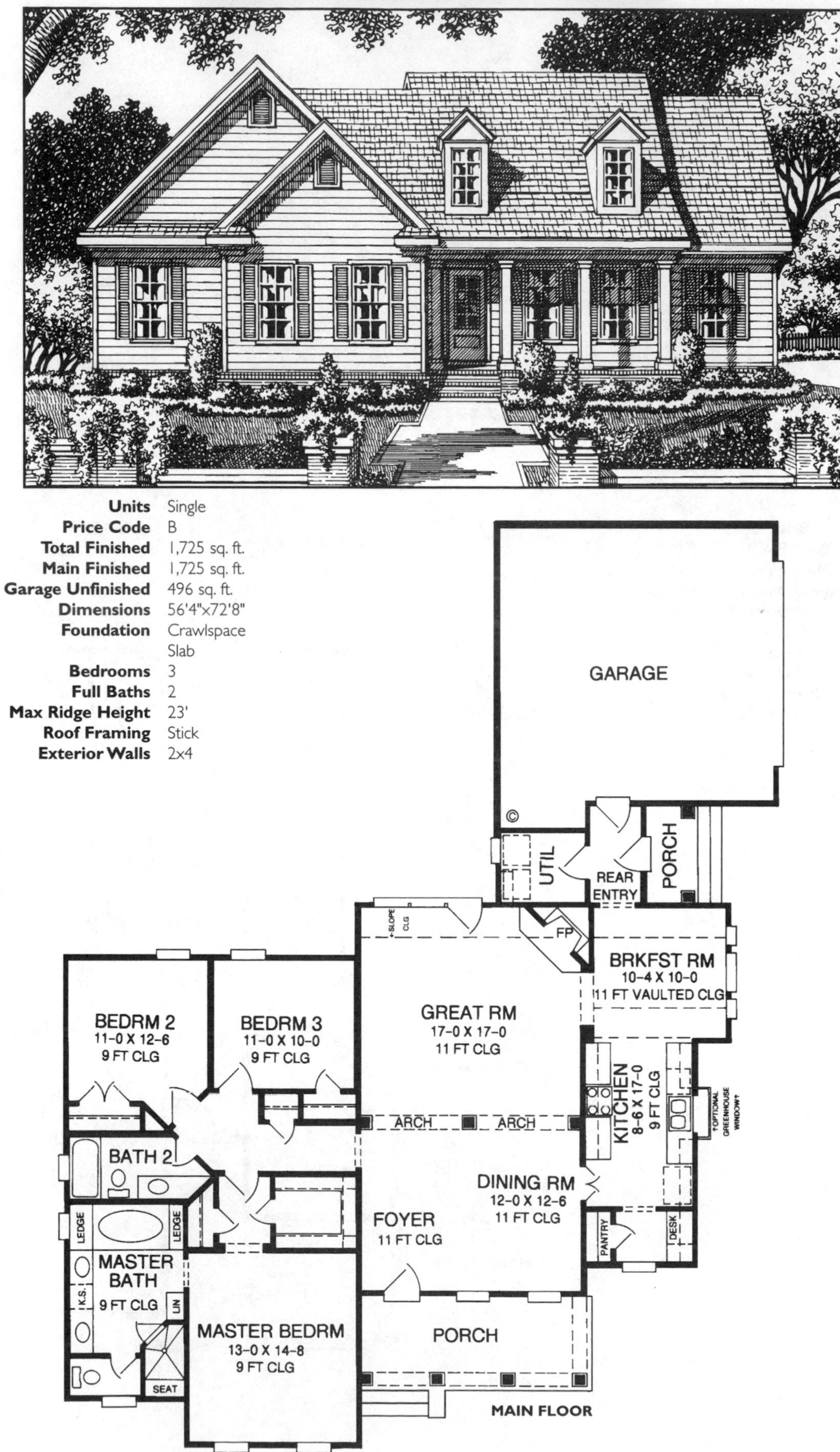

Units	Single
Price Code	B
Total Finished	1,725 sq. ft.
Main Finished	1,725 sq. ft.
Garage Unfinished	496 sq. ft.
Dimensions	56'4"x72'8"
Foundation	Crawlspace Slab
Bedrooms	3
Full Baths	2
Max Ridge Height	23'
Roof Framing	Stick
Exterior Walls	2x4

Design 99923

Units	Single
Price Code	B
Total Finished	1,734 sq. ft.
Main Finished	1,734 sq. ft.
Basement Unfinished	1,842 sq. ft.
Garage Unfinished	528 sq. ft.
Deck Unfinished	252 sq. ft.
Porch Unfinished	132 sq. ft.
Dimensions	66'x48'
Foundation	Basement
Bedrooms	3
Full Baths	2
Half Baths	1
Main Ceiling	8'
Vaulted Ceiling	10'
Max Ridge Height	22'
Roof Framing	Truss
Exterior Walls	2x6

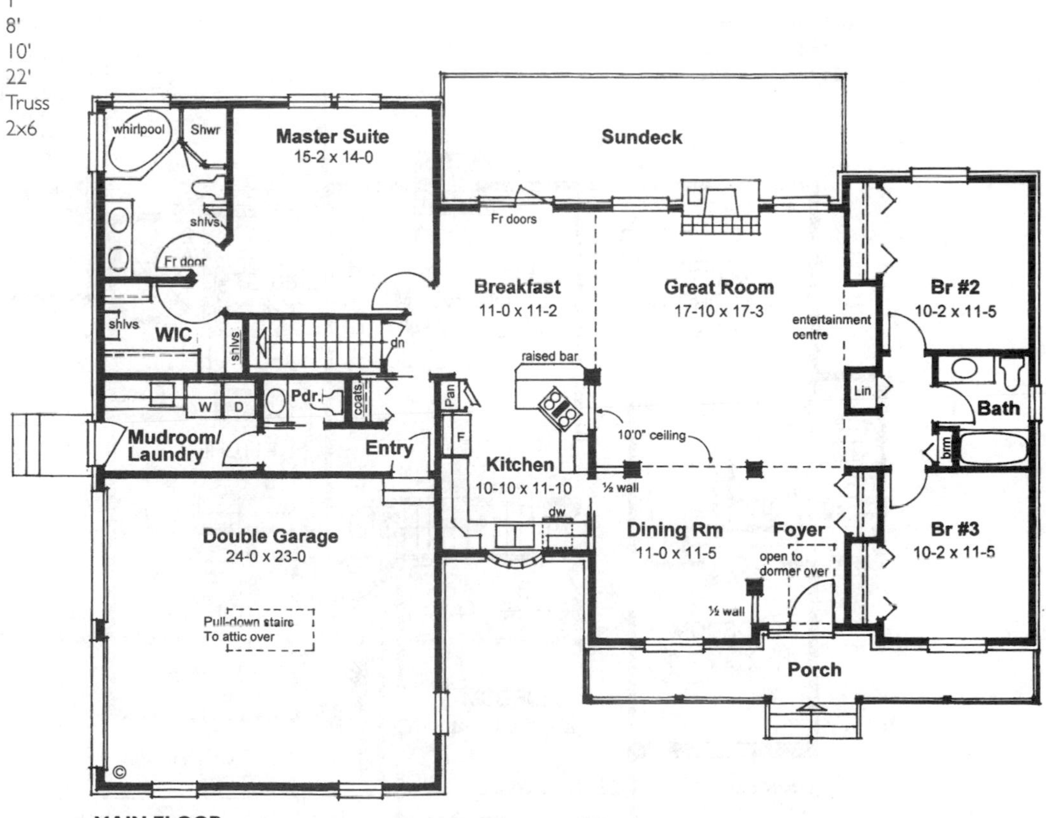

Design 20100

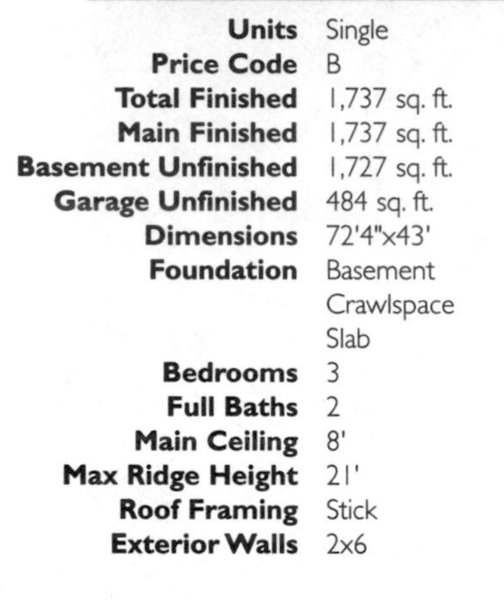

Units	Single
Price Code	B
Total Finished	1,737 sq. ft.
Main Finished	1,737 sq. ft.
Basement Unfinished	1,727 sq. ft.
Garage Unfinished	484 sq. ft.
Dimensions	72'4"x43'
Foundation	Basement Crawlspace Slab
Bedrooms	3
Full Baths	2
Main Ceiling	8'
Max Ridge Height	21'
Roof Framing	Stick
Exterior Walls	2x6

Please note: The photographed home may have been modified to suit homeowner preferences. If you order plans, have a builder or design professional check them against the photograph to confirm actual construction details.

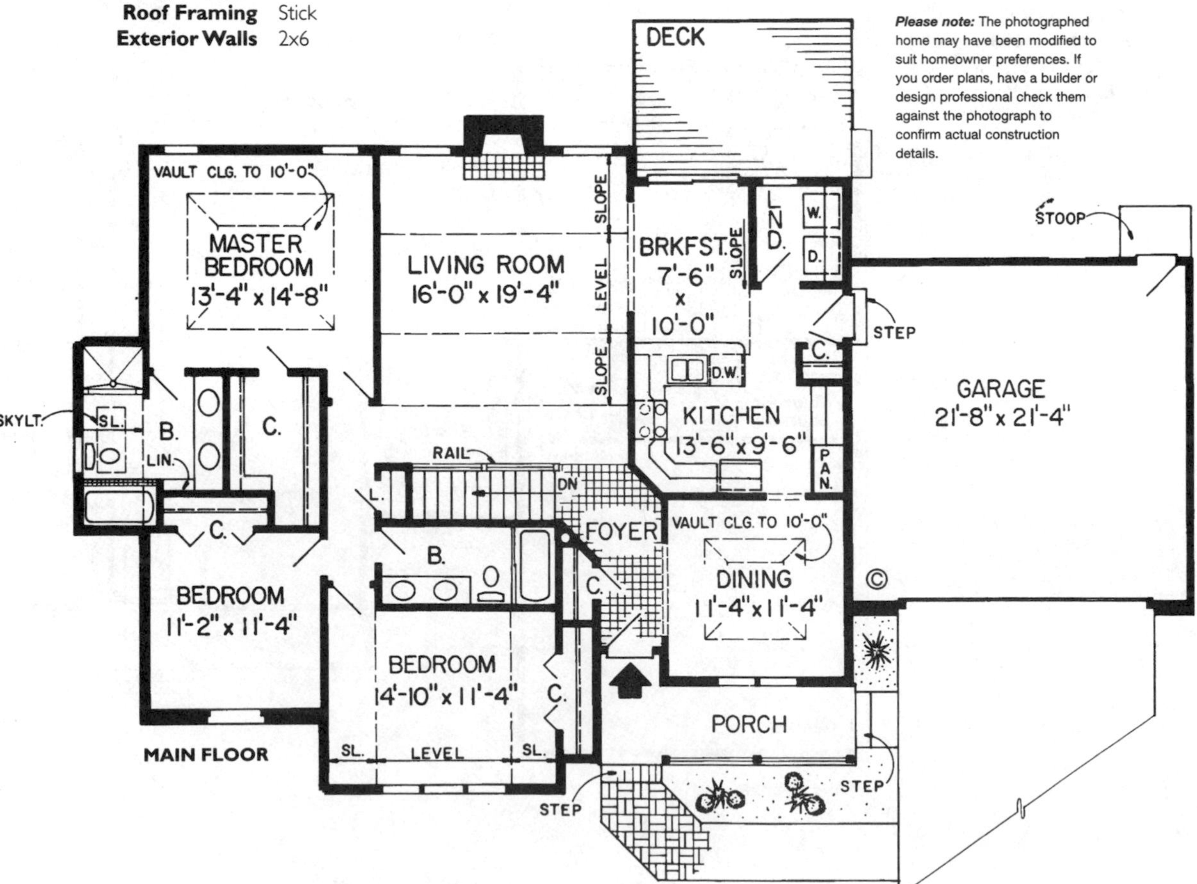

MAIN FLOOR

Design 10839

PHOTOGRAPHY: JOHN EHRENCLOU

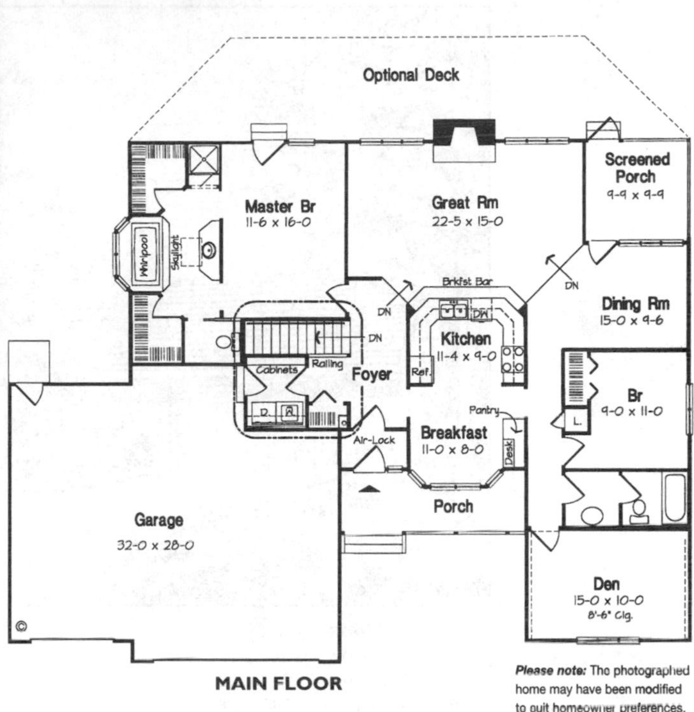

MAIN FLOOR

Units	Single
Price Code	B
Total Finished	1,738 sq. ft.
Main Finished	1,738 sq. ft.
Basement Unfinished	1,083 sq. ft.
Garage Unfinished	796 sq. ft.
Porch Unfinished	100 sq. ft.
Dimensions	66'x52'
Foundation	Basement Crawlspace Slab
Bedrooms	2
Full Baths	2
Main Ceiling	8'
Max Ridge Height	24'6"
Roof Framing	Stick
Exterior Walls	2x4, 2x6

Furn.
Crawl Space Access

CRAWLSPACE/SLAB FOUNDATION OPTION

Please note: The photographed home may have been modified to suit homeowner preferences. If you order plans, have a builder or design professional check them against the photograph to confirm actual construction details.

Design 93149

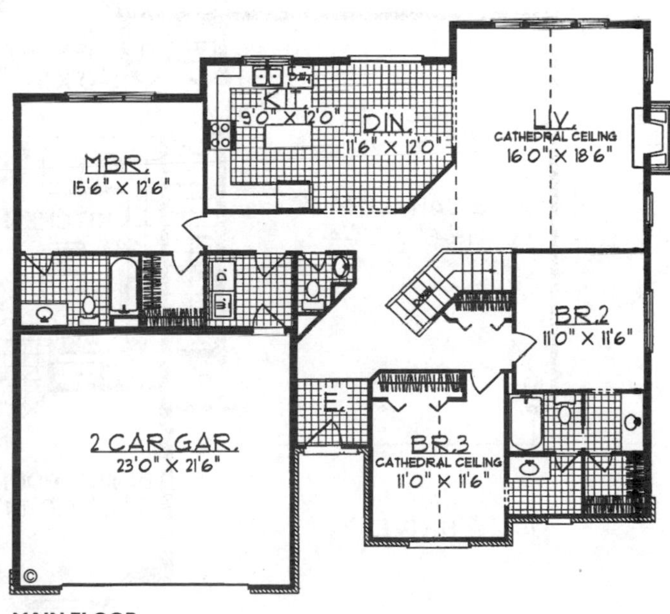

MAIN FLOOR

Units	Single
Price Code	B
Total Finished	1,739 sq. ft.
Main Finished	1,739 sq. ft.
Basement Unfinished	1,739 sq. ft.
Dimensions	54'x48'
Foundation	Basement
Bedrooms	3
Full Baths	2
Half Baths	1
Max Ridge Height	22'6"
Roof Framing	Stick
Exterior Walls	2x6

Design 10596

Units	Single
Price Code	B
Total Finished	1,740 sq. ft.
Main Finished	1,740 sq. ft.
Basement Unfinished	1,377 sq. ft.
Garage Unfinished	480 sq. ft.
Dimensions	74'x36'8"
Foundation	Basement
Bedrooms	3
Full Baths	2
Max Ridge Height	19'
Roof Framing	Stick
Exterior Walls	2x6

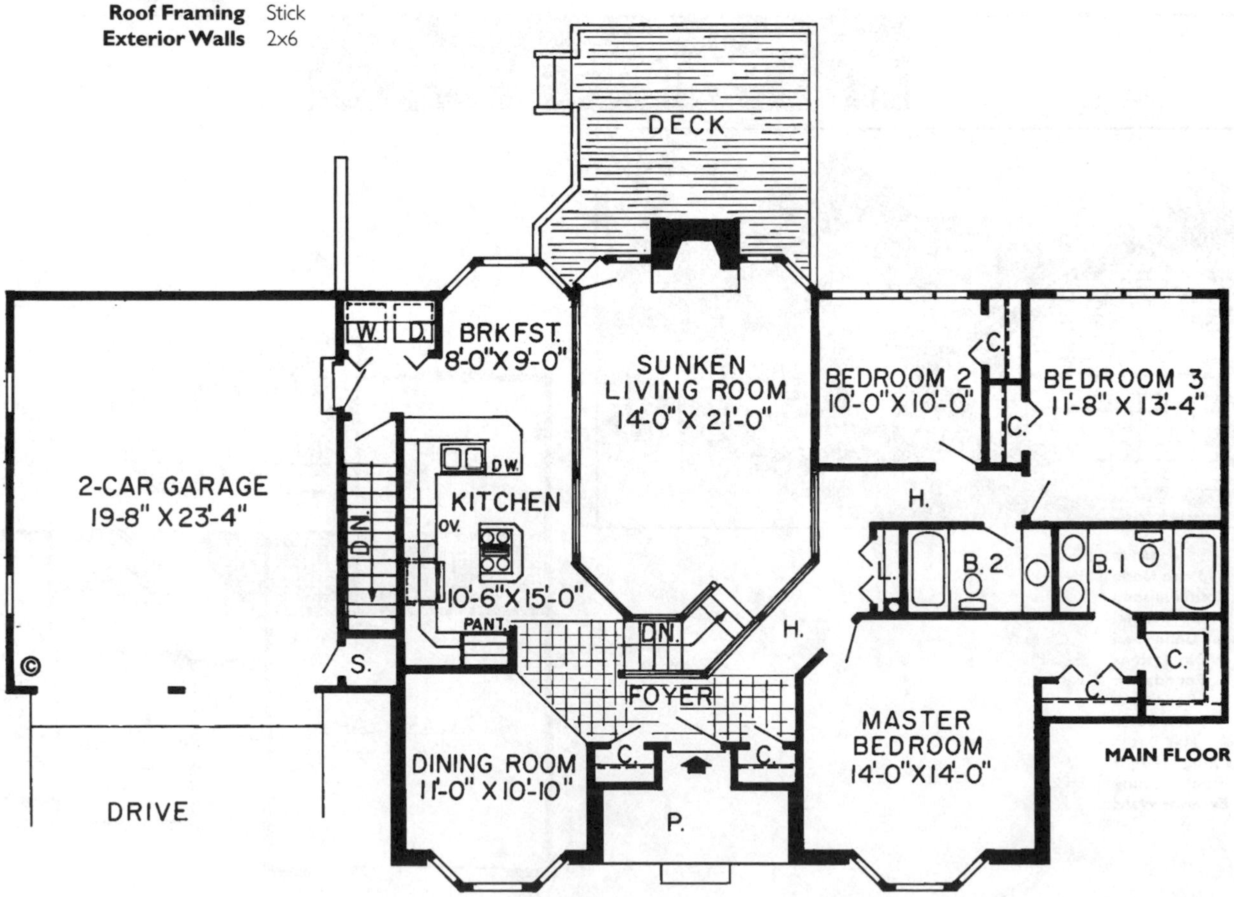

DECK
W.
D.
BRKFST.
8'-0"X9'-0"
SUNKEN
LIVING ROOM
14'-0" X 21'-0"
BEDROOM 2
10'-0"X10'-0"
C.
BEDROOM 3
11'-8" X 13'-4"
C.
2-CAR GARAGE
19-8" X23'-4"
DW.
KITCHEN
OV.
DN.
10'-6"X15'-0"
PANT.
H.
B. 2
B. 1
L.
DN.
H.
S.
C.
FOYER
C.
C.
MASTER
BEDROOM
14'-0"X14'-0"
DINING ROOM
11'-0" X10'-10"
C.
C.
DRIVE
P.
MAIN FLOOR

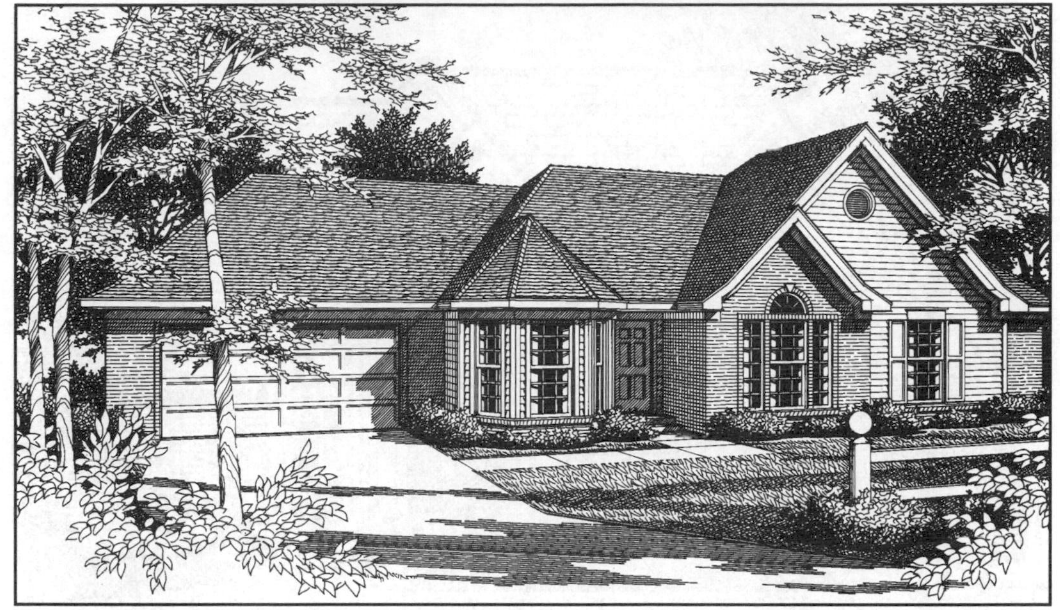

Units	Single
Price Code	B
Total Finished	1,742 sq. ft.
Main Finished	1,742 sq. ft.
Garage Unfinished	566 sq. ft.
Porch Unfinished	14 sq. ft.
Dimensions	78'10"x40'10"
Foundation	Crawlspace Slab
Bedrooms	3
Full Baths	2
Max Ridge Height	22'
Roof Framing	Truss
Exterior Walls	2x4

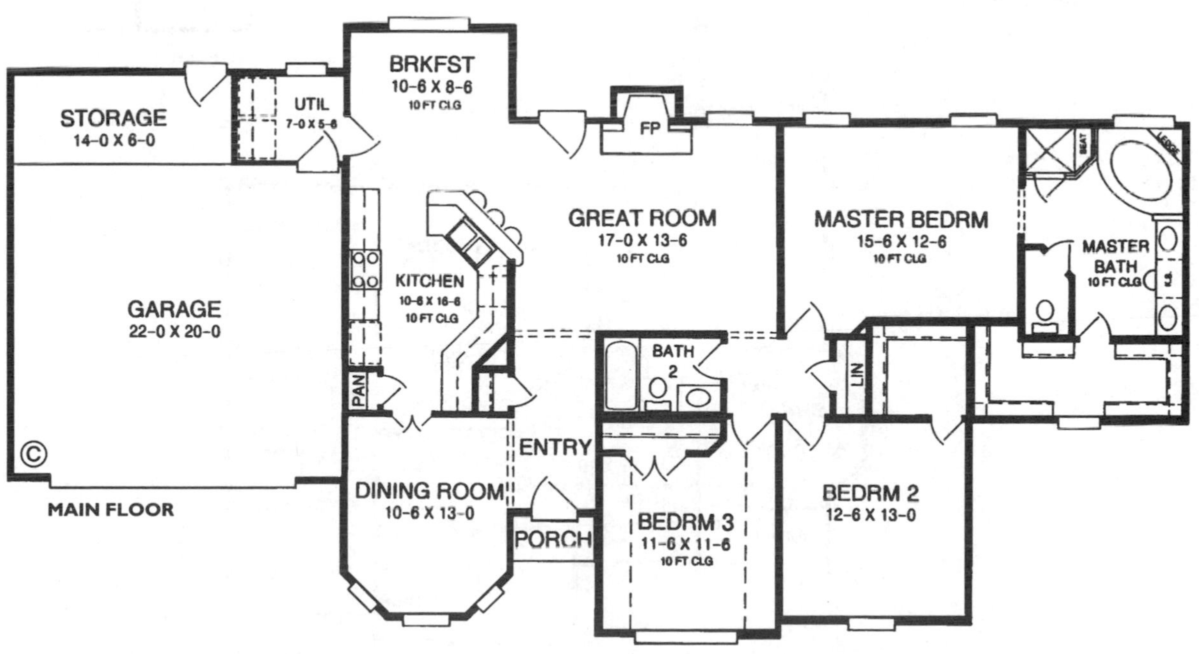

Design 67006

Units	Single
Price Code	B
Total Finished	1,744 sq. ft.
Main Finished	1,744 sq. ft.
Bonus Unfinished	264 sq. ft.
Garage Unfinished	487 sq. ft.
Porch Unfinished	24 sq. ft.
Dimensions	51'x63'
Foundation	Slab
Bedrooms	3
Full Baths	2
Main Ceiling	8'
Vaulted Ceiling	13'6"
Max Ridge Height	23'
Roof Framing	Stick
Exterior Walls	2x4

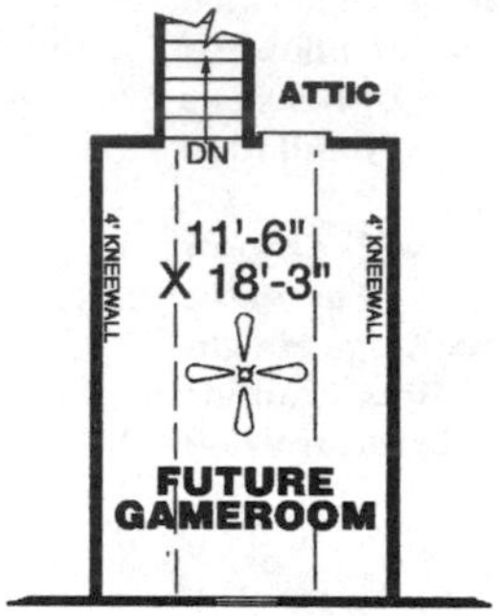

ATTIC
DN
4' KNEEWALL
11'-6" X 18'-3"
4' KNEEWALL
FUTURE GAMEROOM

BONUS

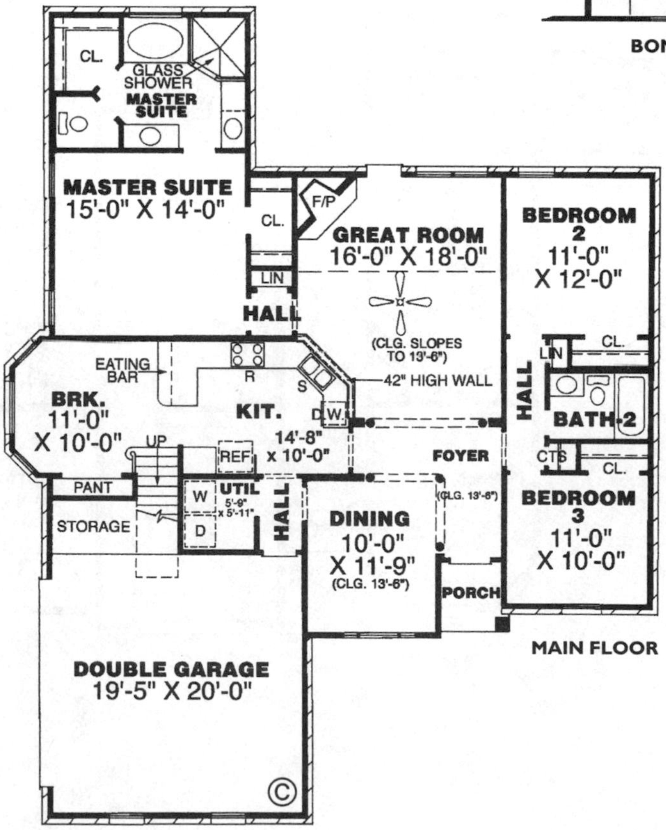

CL.
GLASS SHOWER
MASTER SUITE
MASTER SUITE 15'-0" X 14'-0"
CL.
LIN
HALL
F/P
GREAT ROOM 16'-0" X 18'-0"
(CLG. SLOPES TO 13'-6")
42" HIGH WALL
BEDROOM 2 11'-0" X 12'-0"
CL.
LIN
HALL
BATH-2
CTS
CL.
BEDROOM 3 11'-0" X 10'-0"
EATING BAR
R
S
BRK. 11'-0" X 10'-0"
KIT. 14'-8" x 10'-0"
D.W.
UP
REF
FOYER
PANT
W
UTIL 5'-9" x 5'-11"
D
HALL
DINING 10'-0" X 11'-9" (CLG. 13'-6")
(CLG. 13'-6")
STORAGE
PORCH
DOUBLE GARAGE 19'-5" X 20'-0"
©

MAIN FLOOR

Design 82050

Units	Single
Price Code	B
Total Finished	1,746 sq. ft.
Main Finished	1,746 sq. ft.
Garage Unfinished	491 sq. ft.
Porch Unfinished	596 sq. ft.
Dimensions	67'x54'10"
Foundation	Basement Crawlspace Slab
Bedrooms	3
Full Baths	2
Main Ceiling	9'
Roof Framing	Stick
Exterior Walls	2x4

MASTER SUITE
10' BOXED CEILING
12'-8" X 18'-0"

M.BATH
9'-4" X 11'-8"
FRENCH DOORS
LIN
WHP TUB
GLASS BLOCKS

BED RM. 2
13'-0" X 11'-0"

SCREENED PORCH
17'-0" X 10'-0"

BRKFAST RM.
13'-0" X 8'-8"

ISLAND
PAN
DW
RG
KITCHEN
13'-0" X 10'-10"
REF

LAU.
8'-0" X 5'-6"
D
W
WH

STORAGE
9'-4" X 5'-6"

GREAT RM.
11' BOXED CEILING
17'-0" X 16'-4"
10' CEILING

GARAGE
22'-4" X 22'-0"

OPTIONAL SIDE LOAD GARAGE

DINING RM.
10' BOXED CEILING
13'-0" X 11'-6"

BED RM. 3
13'-0" X 11'-0"

FOYER
10' CEILING
17'-0" X 4'-0"

©

COVERED PORCH
44'-10" X 8'-0"

MAIN FLOOR

Design 92655

Units	Single
Price Code	B
Total Finished	1,746 sq. ft.
Main Finished	1,746 sq. ft.
Basement Unfinished	1,697 sq. ft.
Garage Unfinished	480 sq. ft.
Porch Unfinished	111 sq. ft.
Dimensions	65'10"x56'
Foundation	Basement
Bedrooms	3
Full Baths	2
Max Ridge Height	21'6"
Roof Framing	Truss
Exterior Walls	2x4

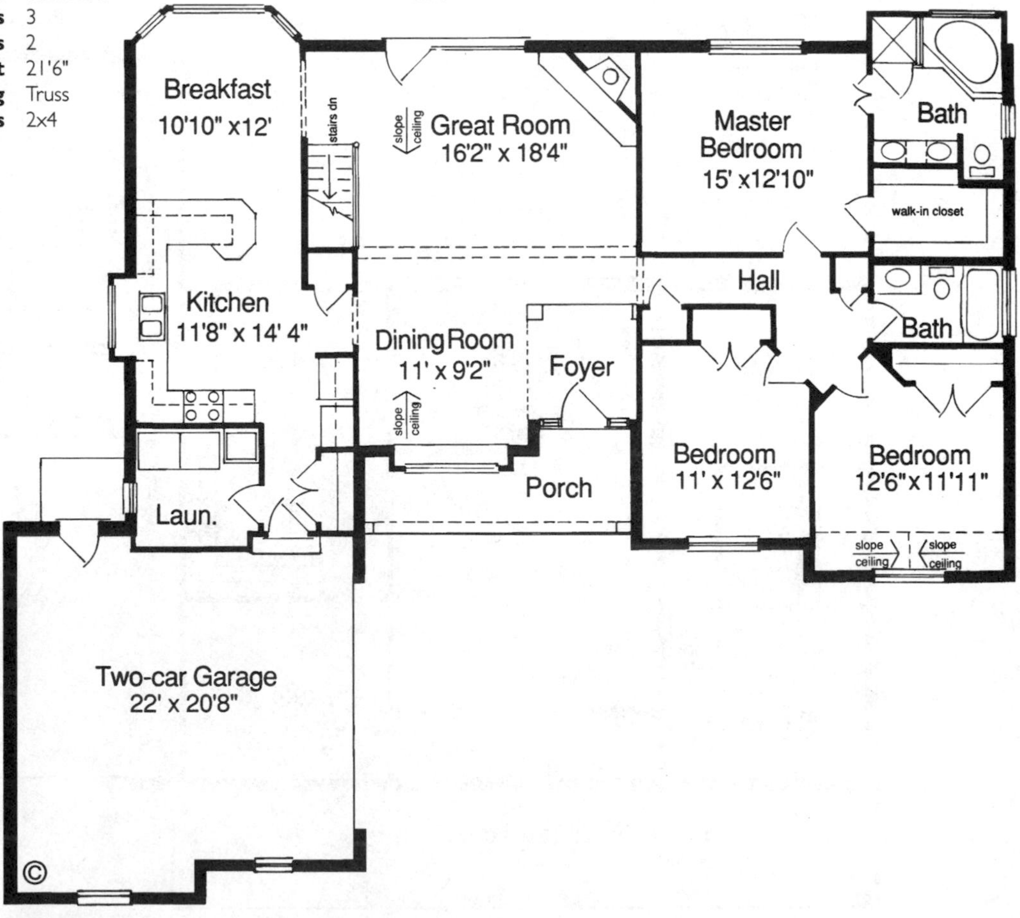

Patio

Breakfast
10'10" x12'

stairs dn

slope ceiling

Great Room
16'2" x 18'4"

Master
Bedroom
15' x12'10"

Bath

walk-in closet

Kitchen
11'8" x 14' 4"

Hall

Bath

Dining Room
11' x 9'2"

Foyer

slope ceiling

Bedroom
11' x 12'6"

Bedroom
12'6"x11'11"

Porch

Laun.

slope ceiling

slope ceiling

Two-car Garage
22' x 20'8"

©

MAIN FLOOR

Design 98224

Units	Single
Price Code	C
Total Finished	1,751 sq. ft.
Main Finished	1,751 sq. ft.
Dimensions	64'x40'6"
Foundation	Basement Crawlspace
Bedrooms	3
Full Baths	2
Half Baths	1
Main Ceiling	9'
Vaulted Ceiling	12'
Tray Ceiling	12'
Max Ridge Height	16'
Roof Framing	Stick
Exterior Walls	2x4

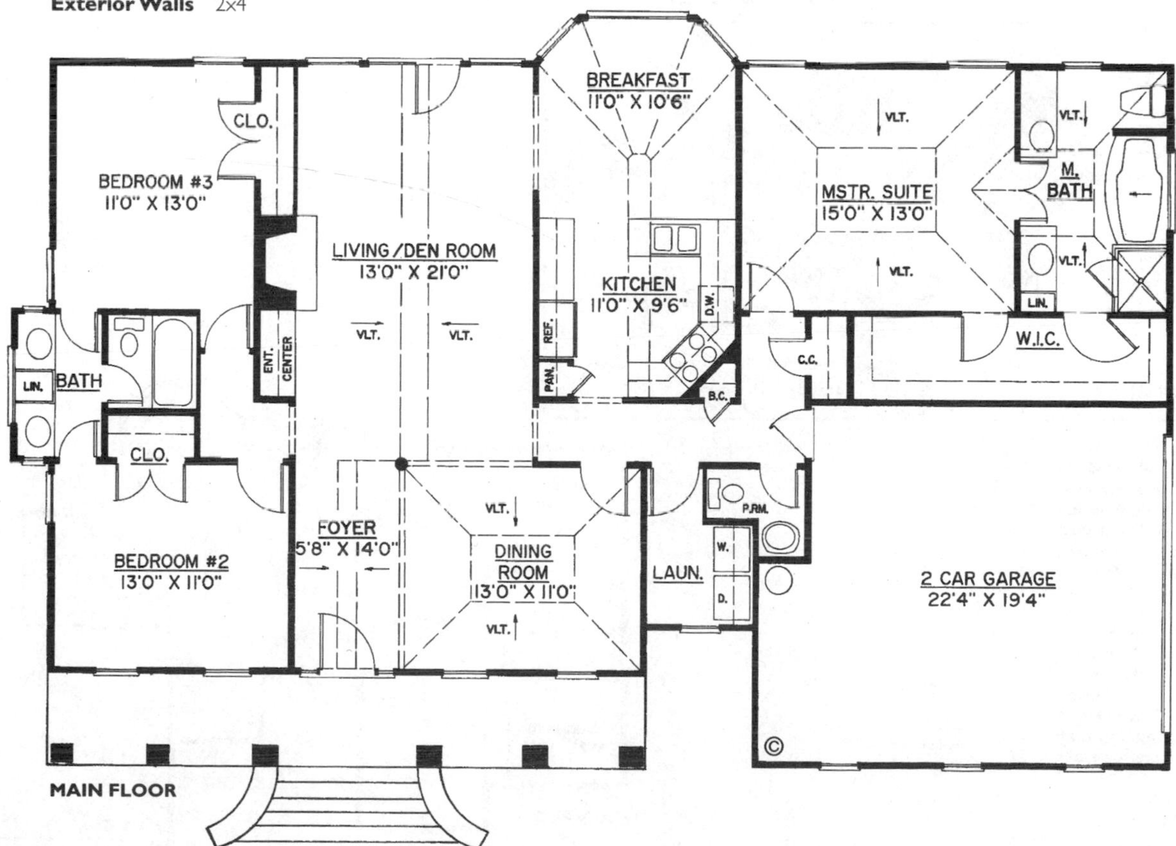

Design 92531

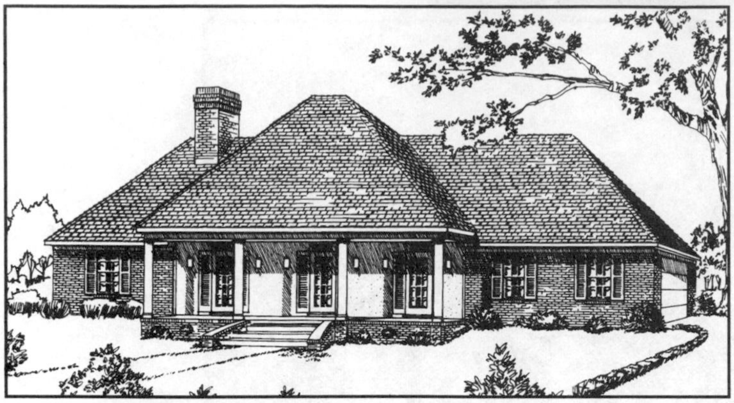

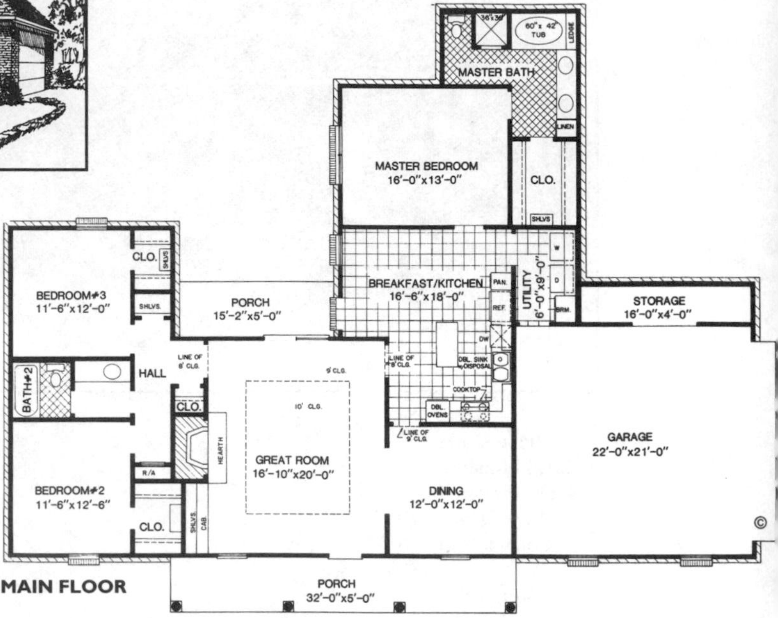

36"x36"
60" x 42" TUB
LEDGE
MASTER BATH
LINEN
MASTER BEDROOM
16'-0"x13'-0"
CLO.
SHLVS
BEDROOM#3
11'-6"x12'-0"
CLO.
SHLVS
SHLVS.
PORCH
15'-2"x5'-0"
BREAKFAST/KITCHEN
16'-6"x18'-0"
PAN
REF
UTILITY
6'-0"x9'-0"
W
D
BRM
STORAGE
16'-0"x4'-0"
BATH#2
HALL
LINE OF 8' CLG.
9' CLG.
LINE OF 8' CLG.
DW
DBL. SINK DISPOSAL
CLO.
10' CLG.
COOKTOP
DBL. OVENS
HEARTH
GREAT ROOM
16'-10"x20'-0"
LINE OF 9' CLG.
GARAGE
22'-0"x21'-0"
R/A
BEDROOM#2
11'-6"x12'-6"
CLO.
SHLVS
CAB
DINING
12'-0"x12'-0"
PORCH
32'-0"x5'-0"
MAIN FLOOR

Units	Single
Price Code	C
Total Finished	1,754 sq. ft.
Main Finished	1,754 sq. ft.
Garage Unfinished	552 sq. ft.
Porch Unfinished	236 sq. ft.
Dimensions	69'10"x53'5"
Foundation	Crawlspace Slab
Bedrooms	3
Full Baths	2
Max Ridge Height	22'
Roof Framing	Stick
Exterior Walls	2x4

Design 97757

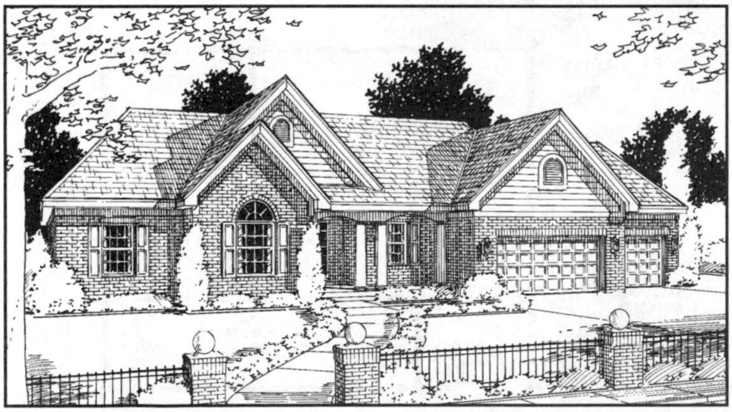

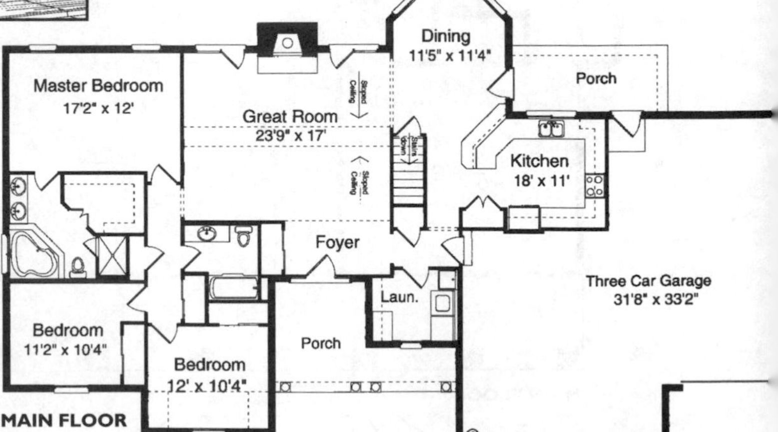

Dining
11'5" x 11'4"
Porch
Master Bedroom
17'2" x 12'
Great Room
23'9" x 17'
Sloped Ceiling
Kitchen
18' x 11'
Foyer
Laun.
Three Car Garage
31'8" x 33'2"
Bedroom
11'2" x 10'4"
Porch
Bedroom
12' x 10'4"
MAIN FLOOR

Units	Single
Price Code	B
Total Finished	1,755 sq. ft.
Main Finished	1,755 sq. ft.
Basement Unfinished	1,725 sq. ft.
Garage Unfinished	796 sq. ft.
Deck Unfinished	44 sq. ft.
Porch Unfinished	138 sq. ft.
Dimensions	78'6"x47'7"
Foundation	Basement
Bedrooms	3
Full Baths	2
Main Ceiling	8'
Max Ridge Height	22'
Roof Framing	Truss
Exterior Walls	2x4

Design 99185

Units	Single
Price Code	C
Total Finished	1,755 sq. ft.
Main Finished	1,755 sq. ft.
Basement Unfinished	1,755 sq. ft.
Porch Unfinished	164 sq. ft.
Dimensions	70'x64'
Foundation	Basement
Bedrooms	3
Full Baths	1
3/4 Baths	1
Half Baths	1
Main Ceiling	9'-10'
Max Ridge Height	24'8"
Roof Framing	Truss
Exterior Walls	2x6

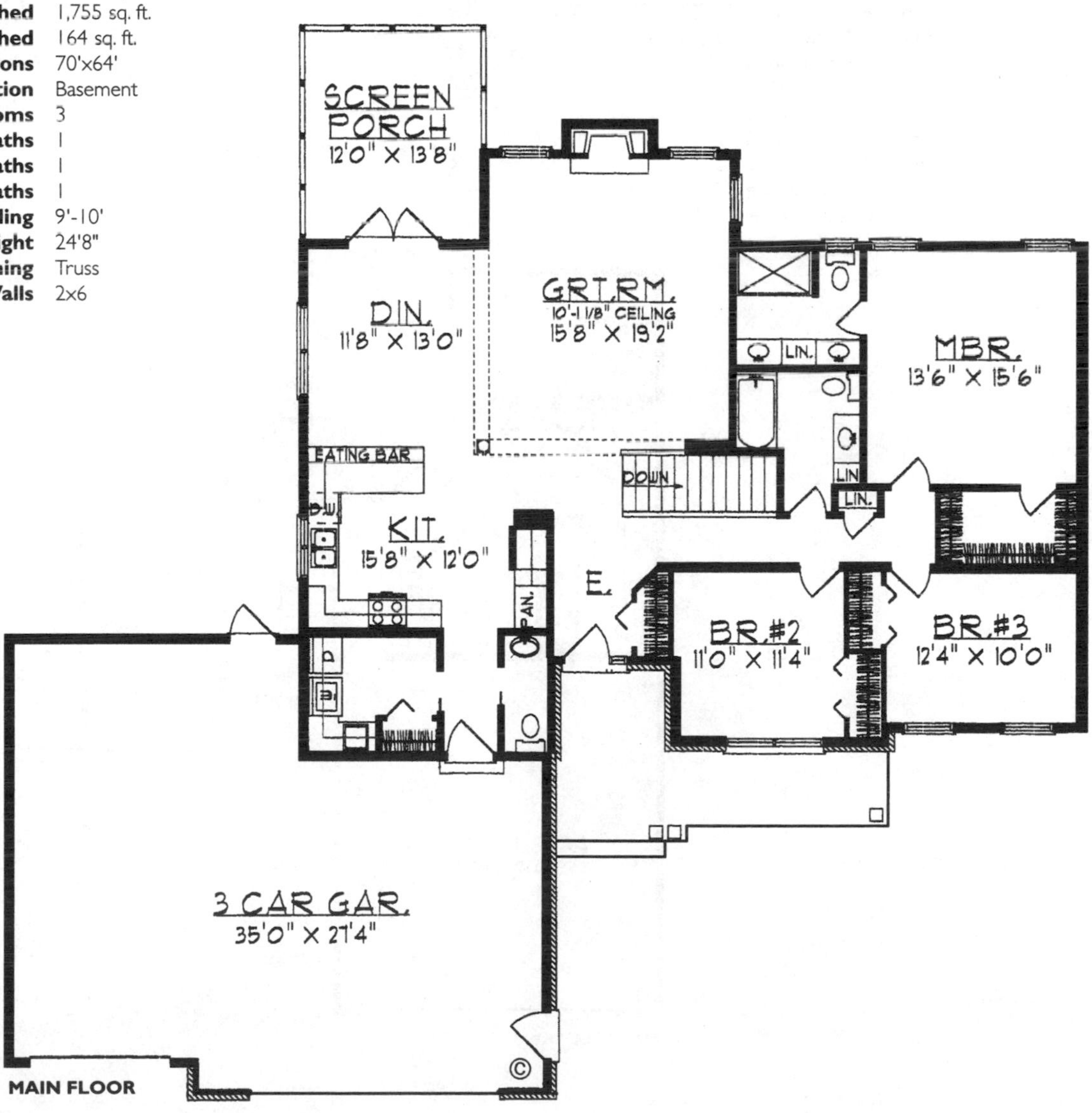

SCREEN PORCH
12'0" X 13'8"
GRT.RM.
10'-1 1/8" CEILING
15'8" X 19'2"
DIN.
11'8" X 13'0"
MBR.
13'6" X 15'6"
EATING BAR
DOWN
KIT.
15'8" X 12'0"
E.
BR.#2
11'0" X 11'4"
BR.#3
12'4" X 10'0"
3 CAR GAR.
35'0" X 27'4"

MAIN FLOOR

Design 93104

Units	Single
Price Code	C
Total Finished	1,756 sq. ft.
Main Finished	1,756 sq. ft.
Basement Unfinished	1,756 sq. ft.
Garage Unfinished	536 sq. ft.
Dimensions	58'x55'
Foundation	Basement
Bedrooms	3
Full Baths	2
Max Ridge Height	23'
Roof Framing	Truss
Exterior Walls	2x6

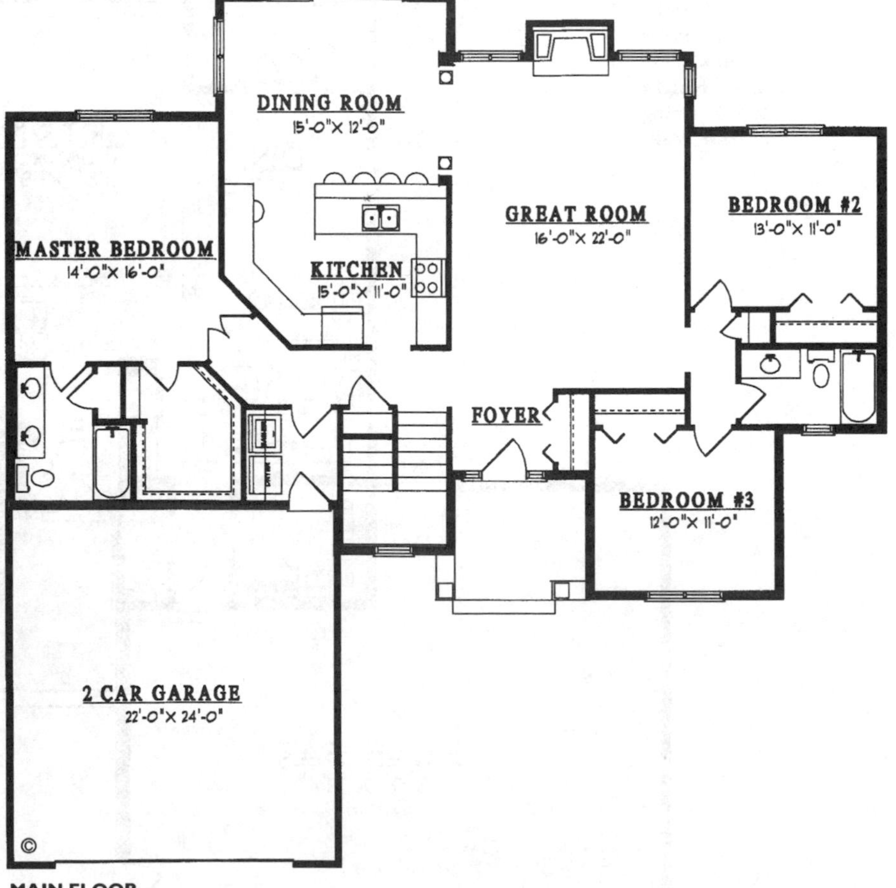

MAIN FLOOR

Design 63090

Units	Single
Price Code	C
Total Finished	1,758 sq. ft.
Main Finished	1,758 sq. ft.
Garage Unfinished	409 sq. ft.
Dimensions	60'x45'
Foundation	Slab
Bedrooms	3
Full Baths	2
Main Ceiling	10'
Max Ridge Height	20'8"
Roof Framing	Truss
Exterior Walls	2x4

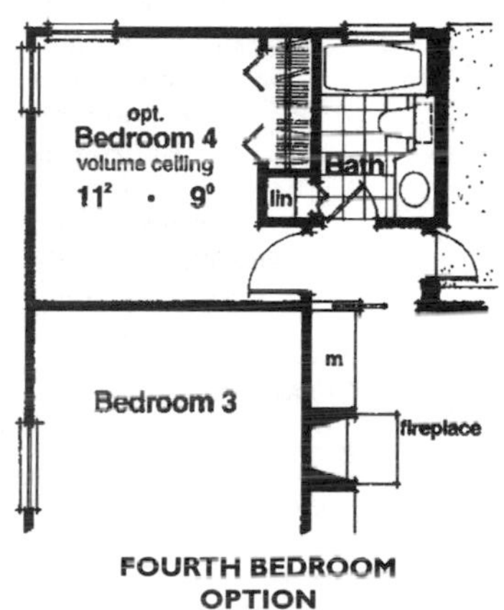

FOURTH BEDROOM OPTION

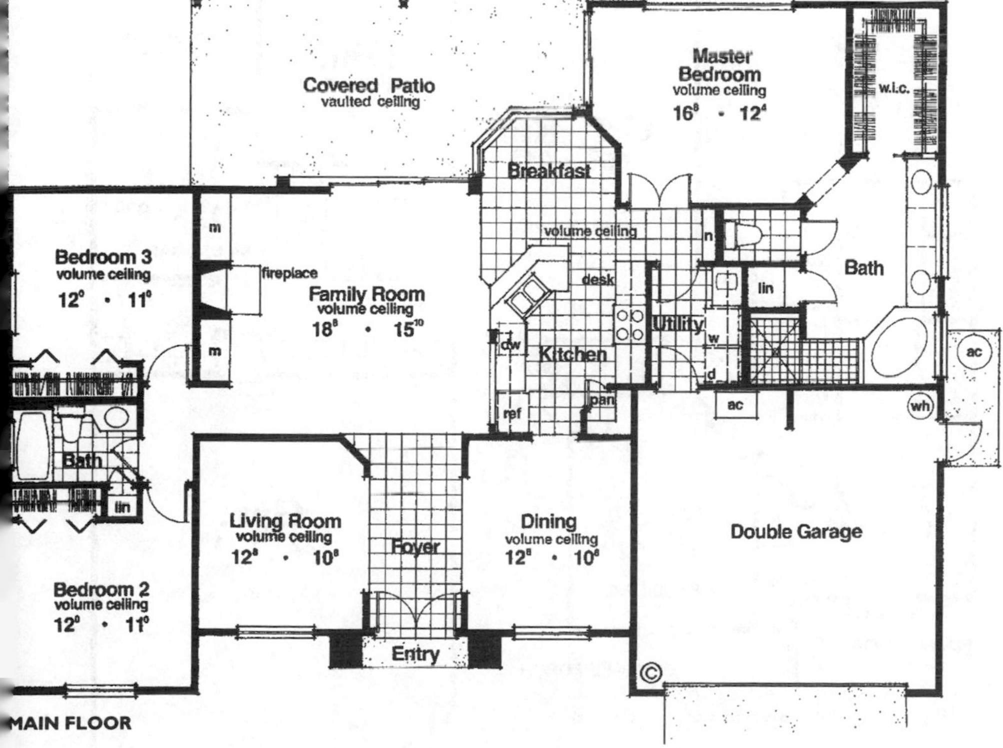

MAIN FLOOR

Design 97456

Units	Single
Price Code	C
Total Finished	1,758 sq. ft.
Main Finished	1,758 sq. ft.
Garage Unfinished	494 sq. ft.
Dimensions	55'4"x49'8"
Foundation	Basement
Bedrooms	3
Full Baths	2
Main Ceiling	9'
Max Ridge Height	26'
Roof Framing	Stick
Exterior Walls	2x4

* Alternate foundation options available at an additional charge.
Please call 1-800-235-5700 for more information.

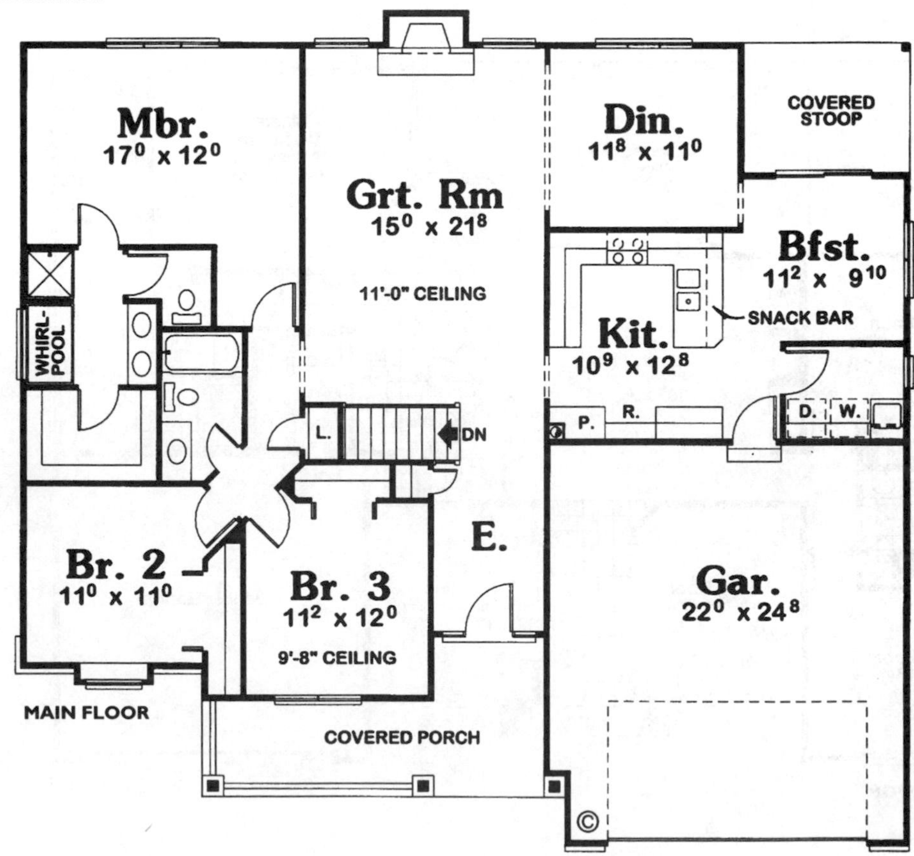

Design 97755

Units	Single
Price Code	C
Total Finished	1,759 sq. ft.
Main Finished	1,759 sq. ft.
Basement Unfinished	1,759 sq. ft.
Garage Unfinished	440 sq. ft.
Porch Unfinished	214 sq. ft.
Dimensions	82'10"x47'5"
Foundation	Basement
Bedrooms	3
Full Baths	2
Main Ceiling	8'
Max Ridge Height	20'
Roof Framing	Truss
Exterior Walls	2x4

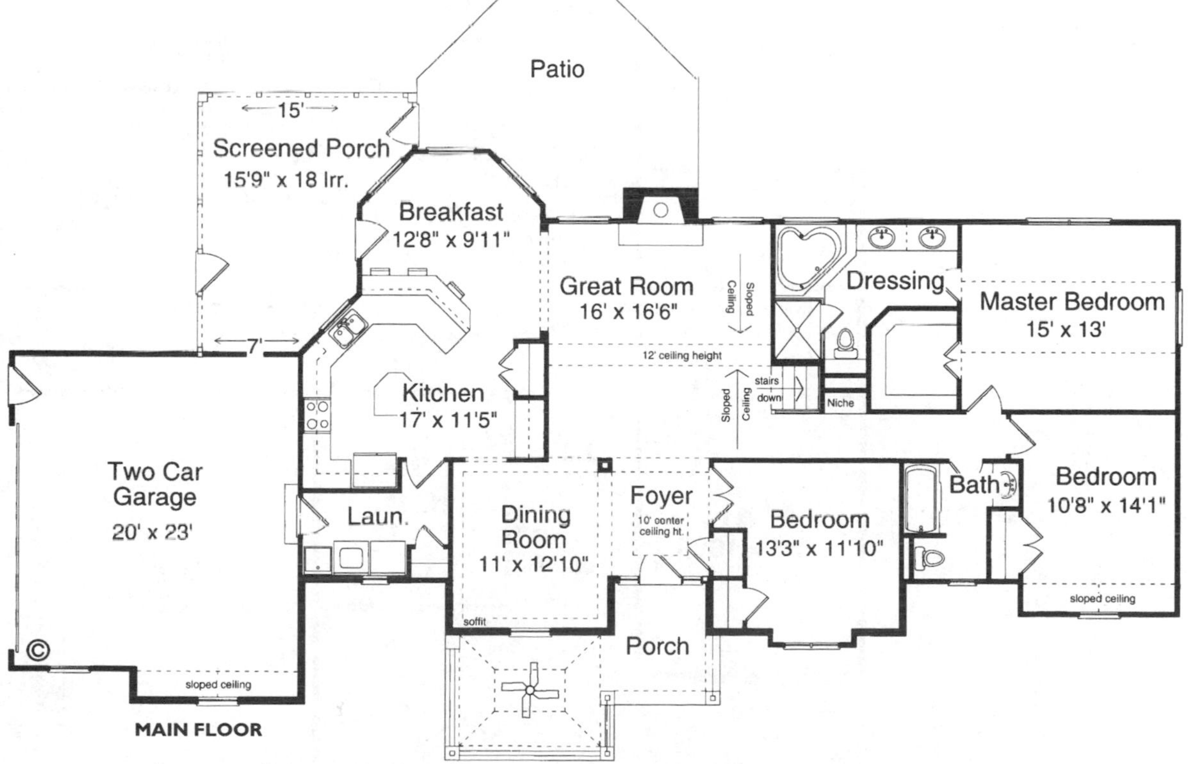

Design 99498

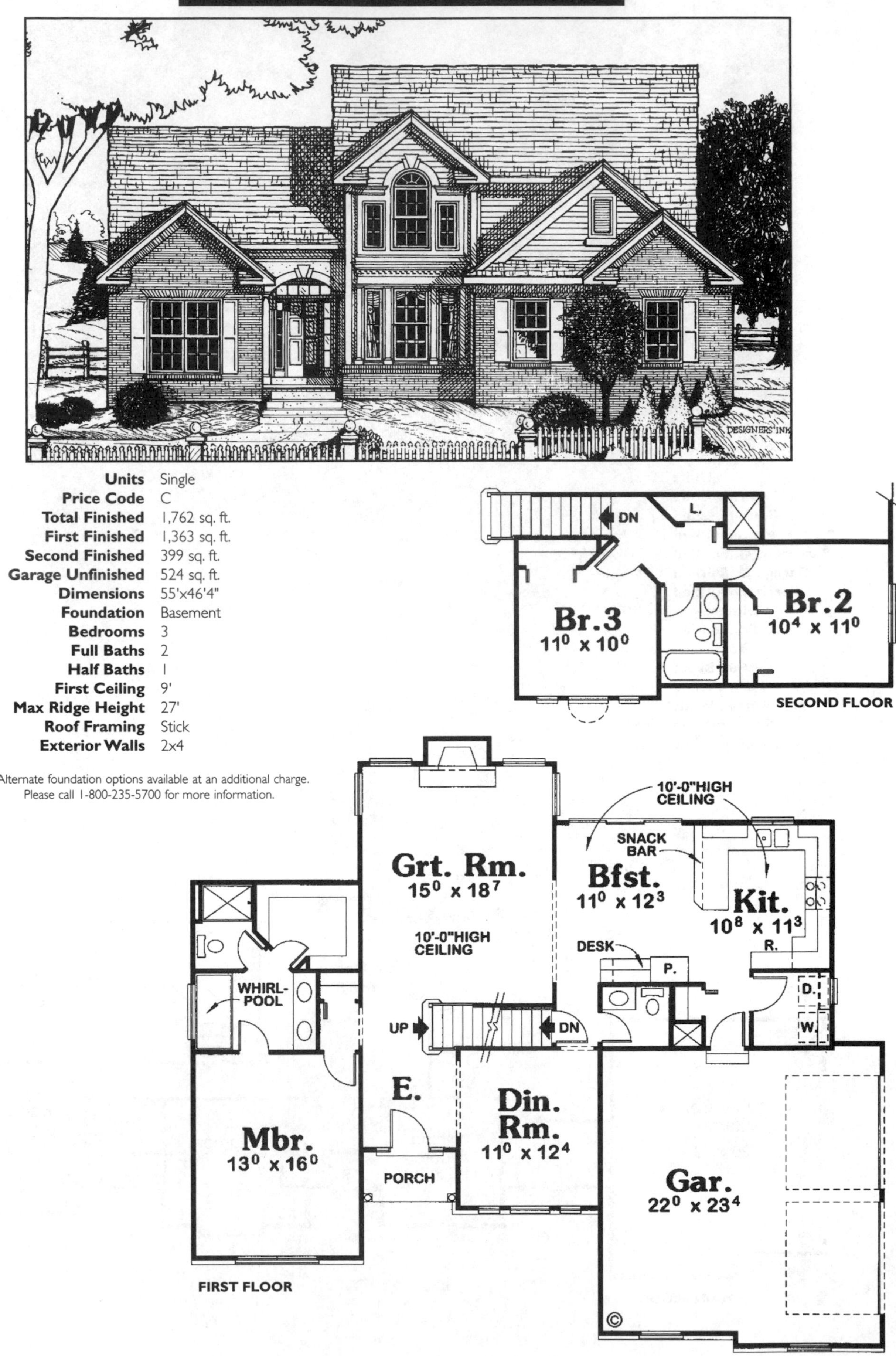

Units	Single
Price Code	C
Total Finished	1,762 sq. ft.
First Finished	1,363 sq. ft.
Second Finished	399 sq. ft.
Garage Unfinished	524 sq. ft.
Dimensions	55'x46'4"
Foundation	Basement
Bedrooms	3
Full Baths	2
Half Baths	1
First Ceiling	9'
Max Ridge Height	27'
Roof Framing	Stick
Exterior Walls	2x4

* Alternate foundation options available at an additional charge. Please call 1-800-235-5700 for more information.

Design 93133

Units Single
Price Code C
Total Finished 1,763 sq. ft.
Main Finished 1,763 sq. ft.
Basement Unfinished 1,763 sq. ft.
Garage Unfinished 658 sq. ft.
Dimensions 67'8"x42'8"
Foundation Basement
Bedrooms 3
Full Baths 2
Main Ceiling 8'
Vaulted Ceiling 14'
Max Ridge Height 22'
Roof Framing Truss
Exterior Walls 2x6

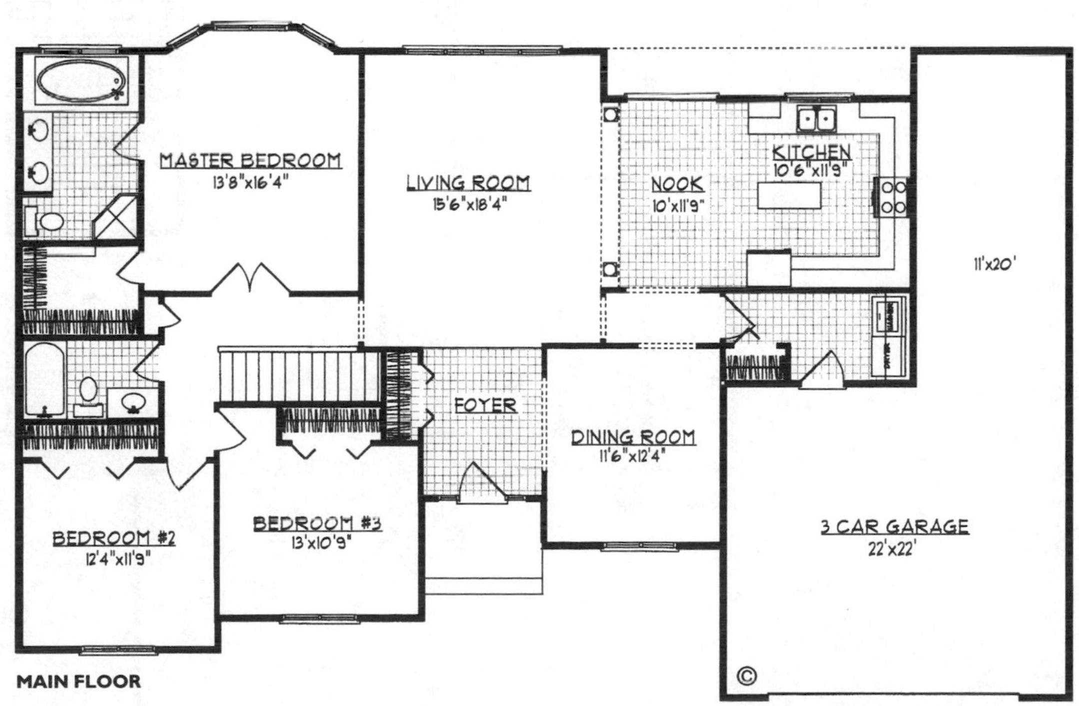

MAIN FLOOR

Design 63048

Units Single
Price Code B
Total Finished 1,765 sq. ft.
Main Finished 1,765 sq. ft.
Deck Unfinished 90 sq. ft.
Porch Unfinished 130 sq. ft.
Dimensions 58'x54'
Foundation Slab
Bedrooms 4
Full Baths 1
3/4 Baths 1
Main Ceiling 8'
Max Ridge Height 20'
Roof Framing Truss

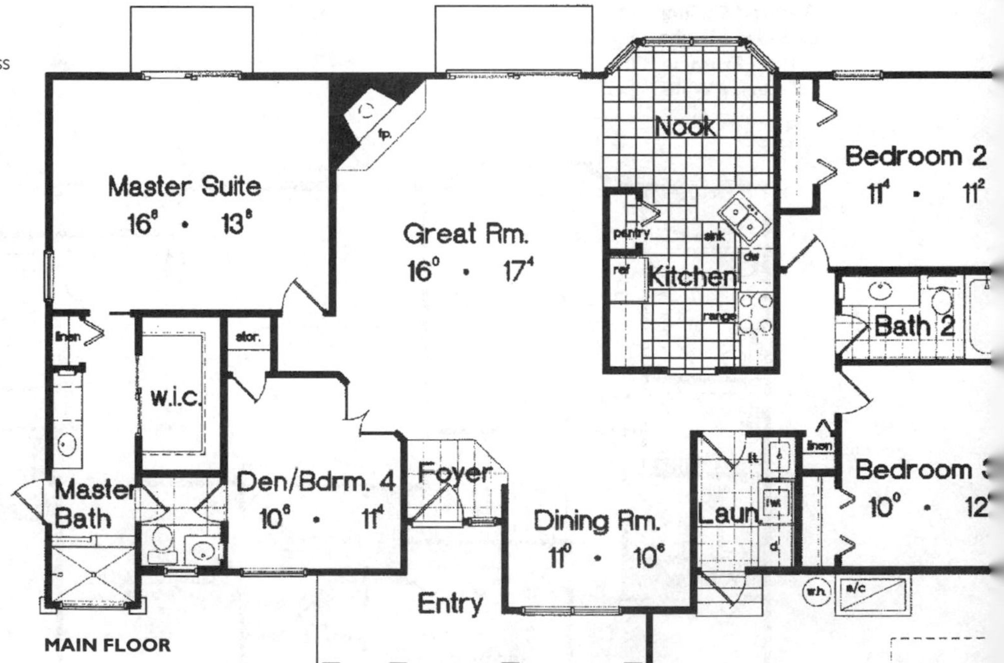

Master Suite $16^{6} \cdot 13^{6}$
Great Rm. $16^{0} \cdot 17^{4}$
Nook
Bedroom 2 $11^{4} \cdot 11^{2}$
Kitchen
Bath 2
W.i.c.
Den/Bdrm. 4 $10^{6} \cdot 11^{4}$
Foyer
Master Bath
Dining Rm. $11^{0} \cdot 10^{6}$
Laun.
Bedroom 3 $10^{0} \cdot 12$
Entry
2 Car Garage $21^{4} \cdot 22^{0}$

MAIN FLOOR

Design 98931

Units	Single
Price Code	C
Total Finished	1,765 sq. ft.
First Finished	1,210 sq. ft.
Second Finished	555 sq. ft.
Garage Unfinished	612 sq. ft.
Deck Unfinished	184 sq. ft.
Porch Unfinished	144 sq. ft.
Dimensions	43'4"x37'
Foundation	Basement
Bedrooms	3
Full Baths	2
Half Baths	1
Max Ridge Height	27'
Roof Framing	Stick
Exterior Walls	2x6

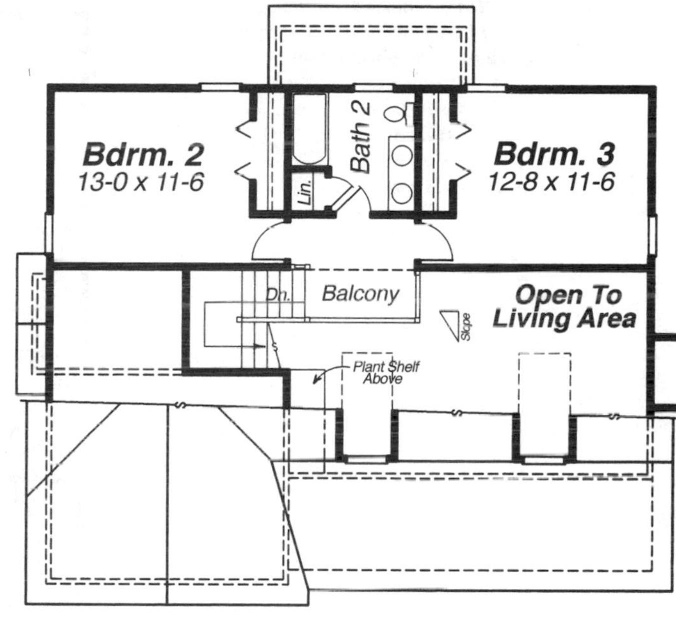

SECOND FLOOR

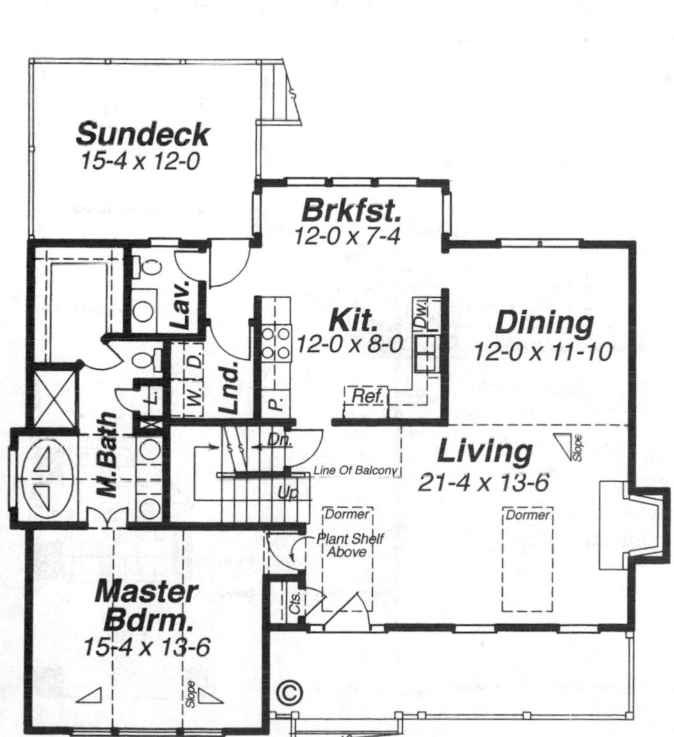

FIRST FLOOR

Design 63086

Units	Single
Price Code	C
Total Finished	1,768 sq. ft.
Main Finished	1,768 sq. ft.
Garage Unfinished	338 sq. ft.
Dimensions	40'x60'
Foundation	Slab
Bedrooms	3
Full Baths	2
Max Ridge Height	21'4"
Roof Framing	Truss
Exterior Walls	2x4

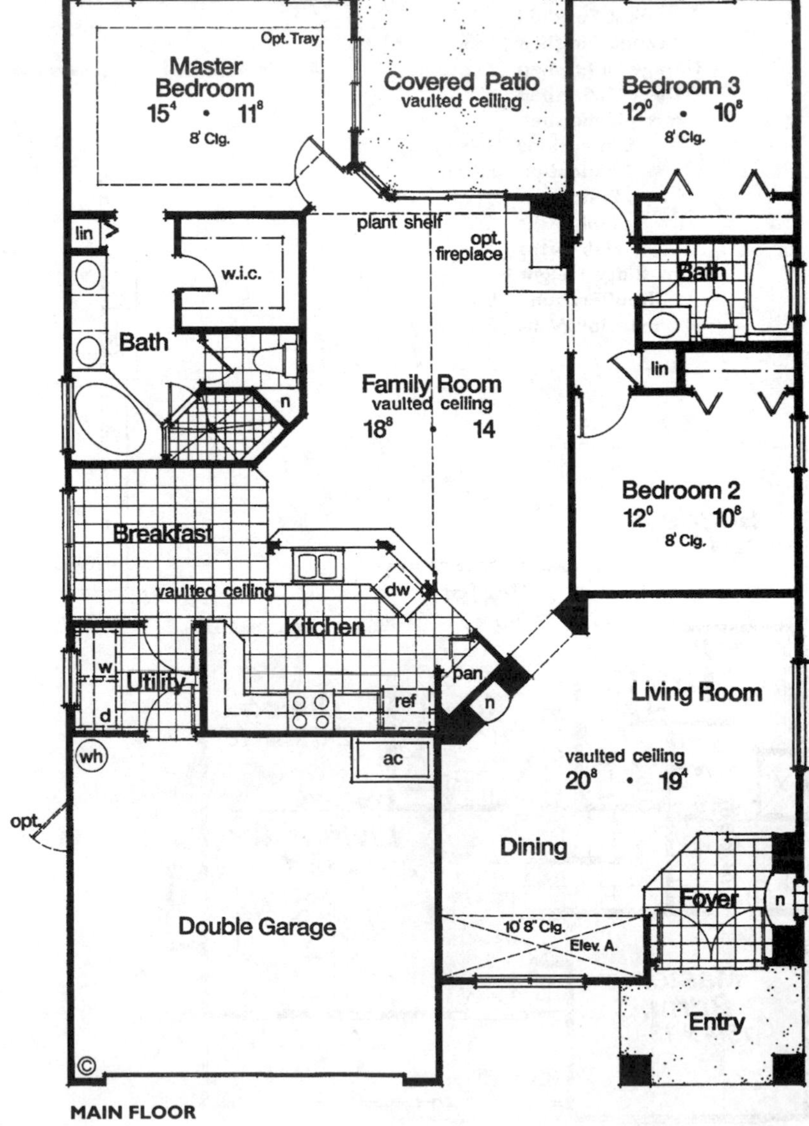

MAIN FLOOR

Design 65664

Units	Single
Price Code	C
Total Finished	1,770 sq. ft.
Main Finished	1,770 sq. ft.
Dimensions	64'x48'
Foundation	Crawlspace Slab
Bedrooms	3
Full Baths	2
Main Ceiling	8'-12'
Max Ridge Height	29'
Roof Framing	Stick
Exterior Walls	2x6

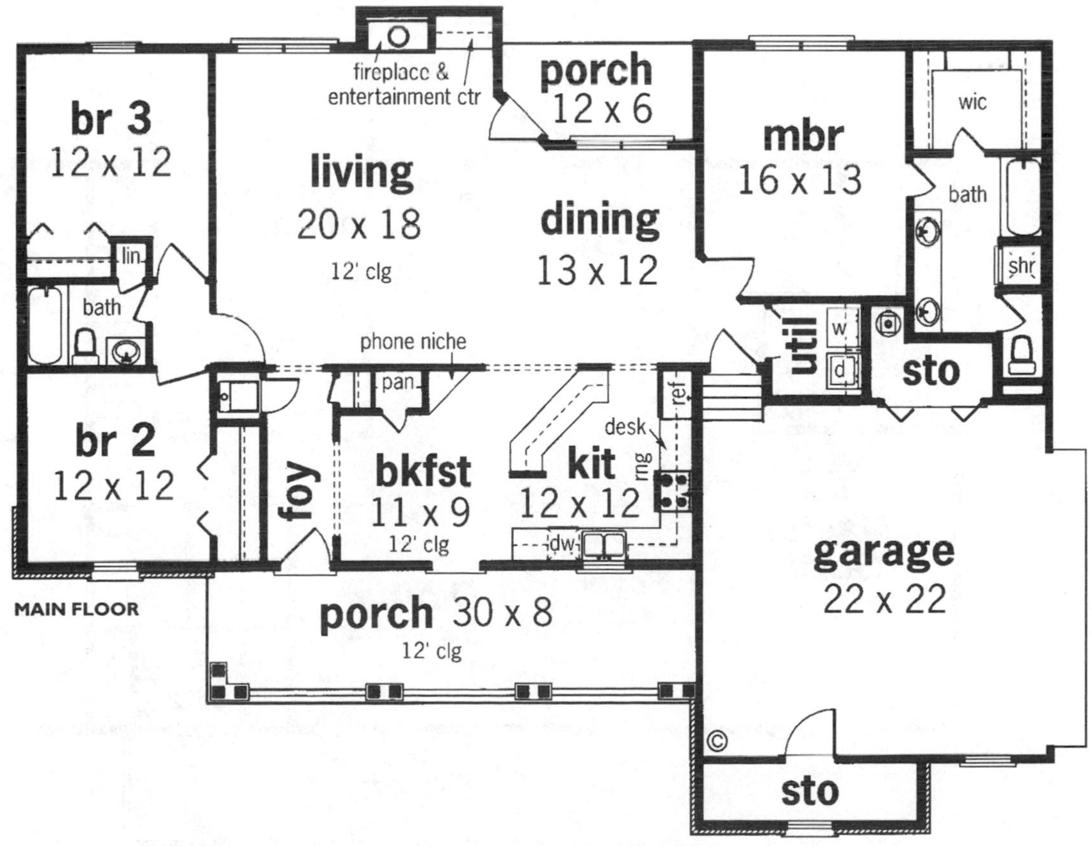

Design 98958

Units	Single
Price Code	C
Total Finished	1,770 sq. ft.
Main Finished	1,770 sq. ft.
Garage Unfinished	645 sq. ft.
Porch Unfinished	182 sq. ft.
Dimensions	59'x48'
Foundation	Basement
Bedrooms	3
Full Baths	2
Main Ceiling	9'
Max Ridge Height	22'
Roof Framing	Stick
Exterior Walls	2x4

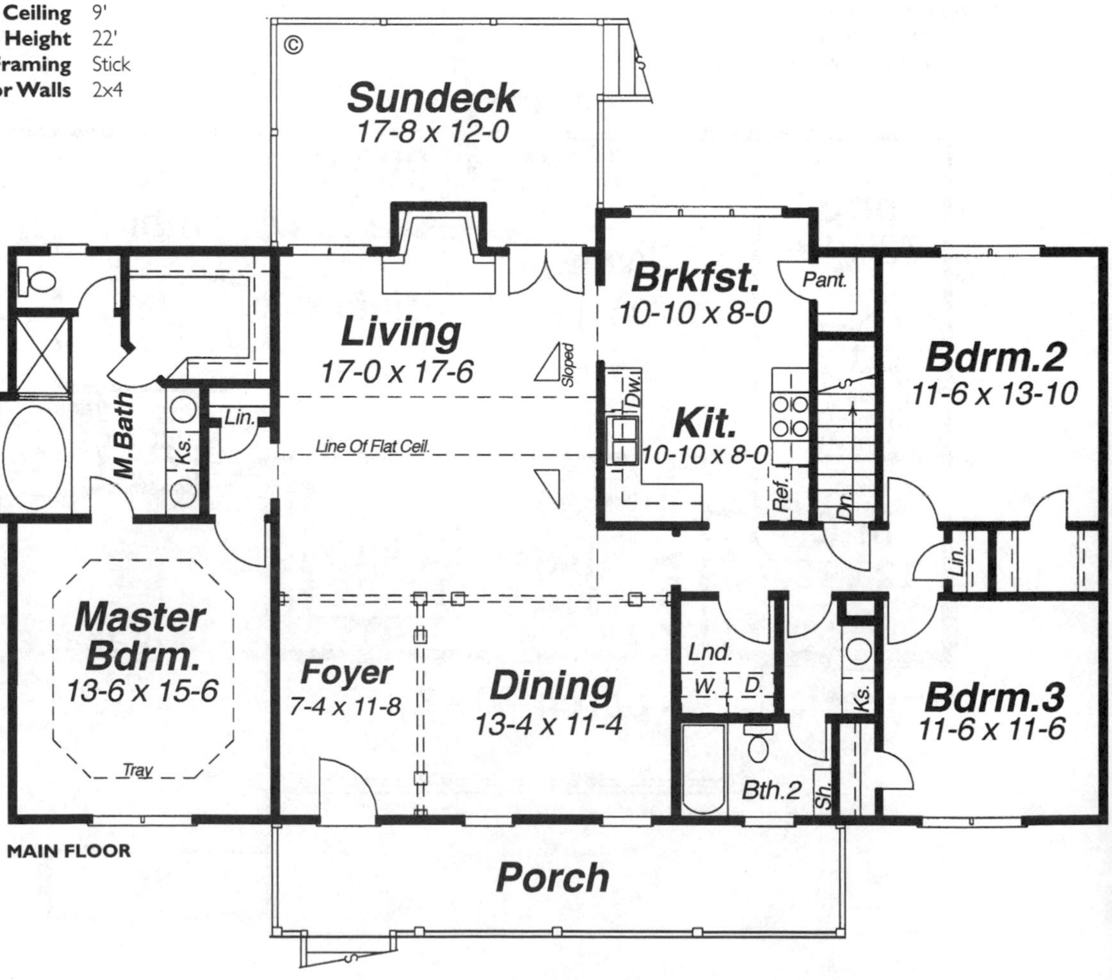

©

Sundeck
17-8 x 12-0

Living
17-0 x 17-6

Sloped

Line Of Flat Ceil.

Brkfst.
10-10 x 8-0

Pant.

Kit.
10-10 x 8-0

Dw.

Ref.

Dn.

Bdrm.2
11-6 x 13-10

Lin.

M.Bath

Ks.

Lin.

Master Bdrm.
13-6 x 15-6

Tray

Foyer
7-4 x 11-8

Dining
13-4 x 11-4

Lnd.

W. D.

Ks.

Bth.2

Sh.

Bdrm.3
11-6 x 11-6

MAIN FLOOR

Porch

Design 63087

Units	Single
Price Code	C
Total Finished	1,771 sq. ft.
Main Finished	1,771 sq. ft.
Garage Unfinished	394 sq. ft.
Dimensions	60'x54'4"
Foundation	Slab
Bedrooms	4
Full Baths	2
Max Ridge Height	18'2"
Roof Framing	Truss

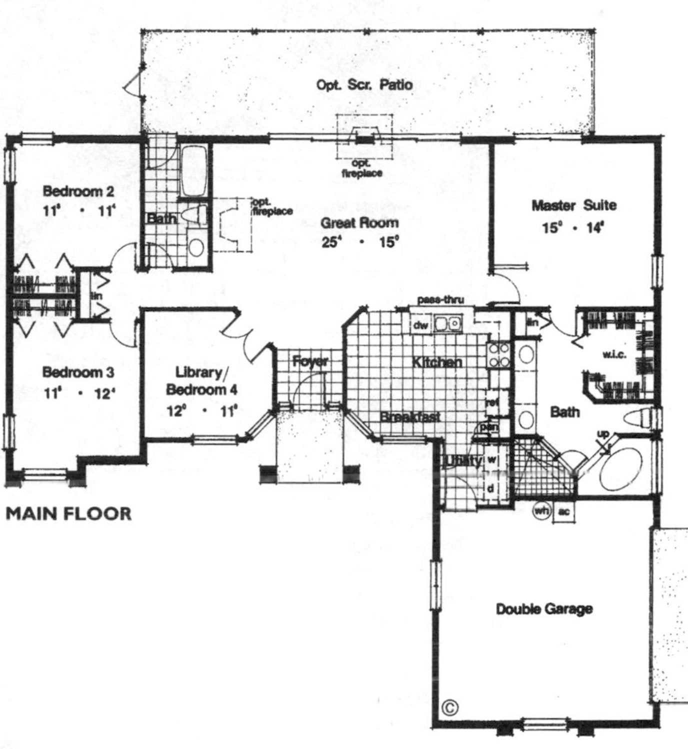

MAIN FLOOR

Design 98464

Units	Single
Price Code	C
Total Finished	1,779 sq. ft.
Main Finished	1,779 sq. ft.
Basement Unfinished	1,818 sq. ft.
Garage Unfinished	499 sq. ft.
Dimensions	57'x56'4"
Foundation	Basement Crawlspace
Bedrooms	3
Full Baths	2
Main Ceiling	9'
Max Ridge Height	24'6"
Roof Framing	Stick
Exterior Walls	2x4

OPTIONAL BASEMENT STAIR LOCATION

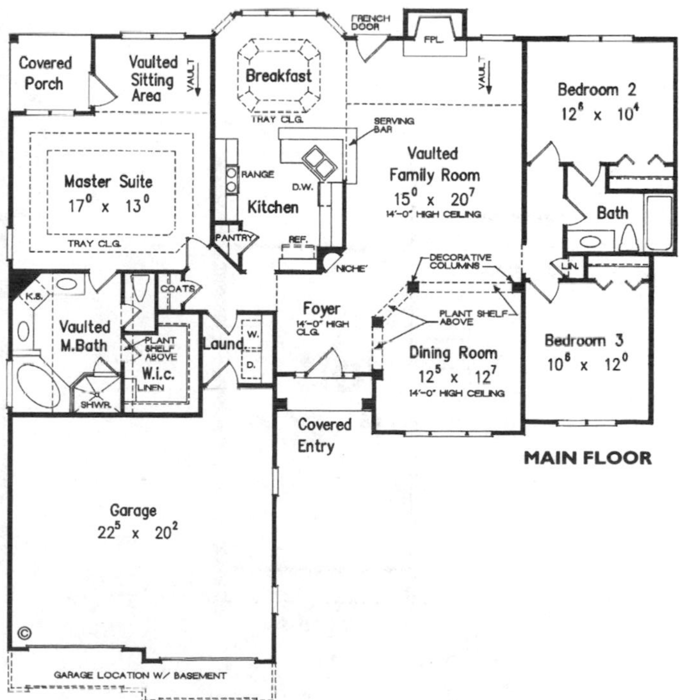

MAIN FLOOR

Design 63111

Units	Single
Price Code	C
Total Finished	1,782 sq. ft.
Main Finished	1,782 sq. ft.
Bonus Unfinished	262 sq. ft.
Garage Unfinished	394 sq. ft.
Dimensions	40'x61'
Foundation	Slab
Bedrooms	3
Full Baths	2
Main Ceiling	8'
Max Ridge Height	20'4"
Roof Framing	Truss

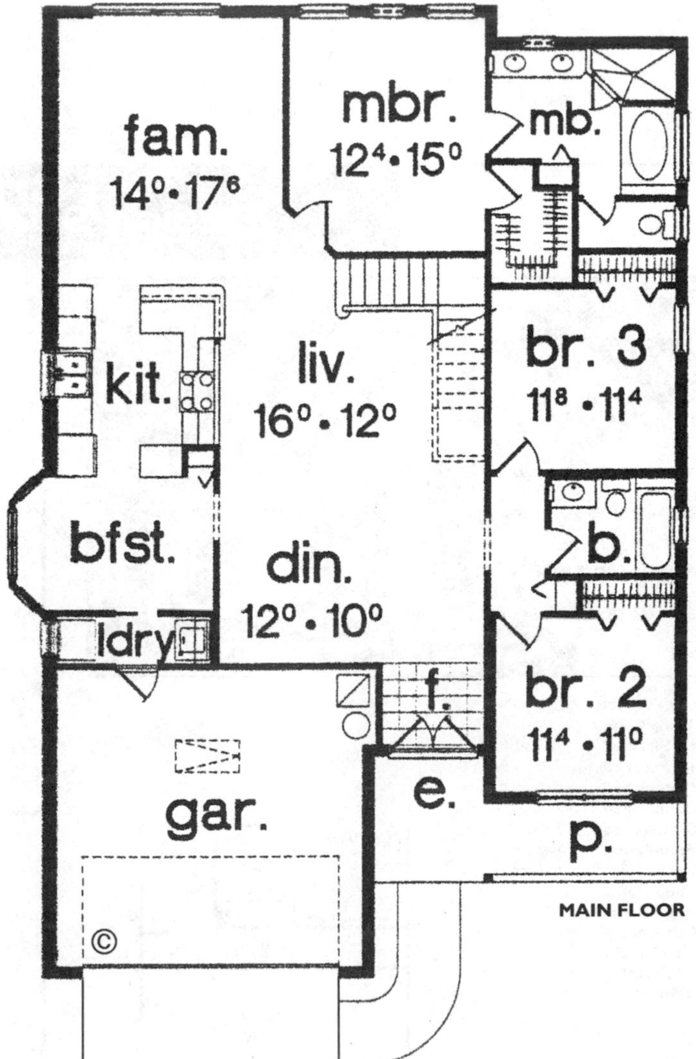

MAIN FLOOR

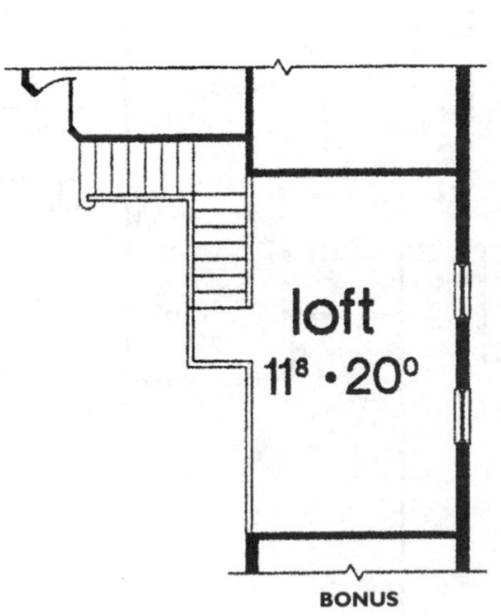

BONUS

Design 92630

PHOTOGRAPHY: DONNA AND RON KOLB, EXPOSURES UNLIMITED

Units	Single
Price Code	C
Total Finished	1,782 sq. ft.
Main Finished	1,782 sq. ft.
Basement Unfinished	1,735 sq. ft.
Garage Unfinished	407 sq. ft.
Dimensions	67'2"x47'
Foundation	Basement
Bedrooms	3
Full Baths	2
Max Ridge Height	20'
Roof Framing	Truss
Exterior Walls	2x4

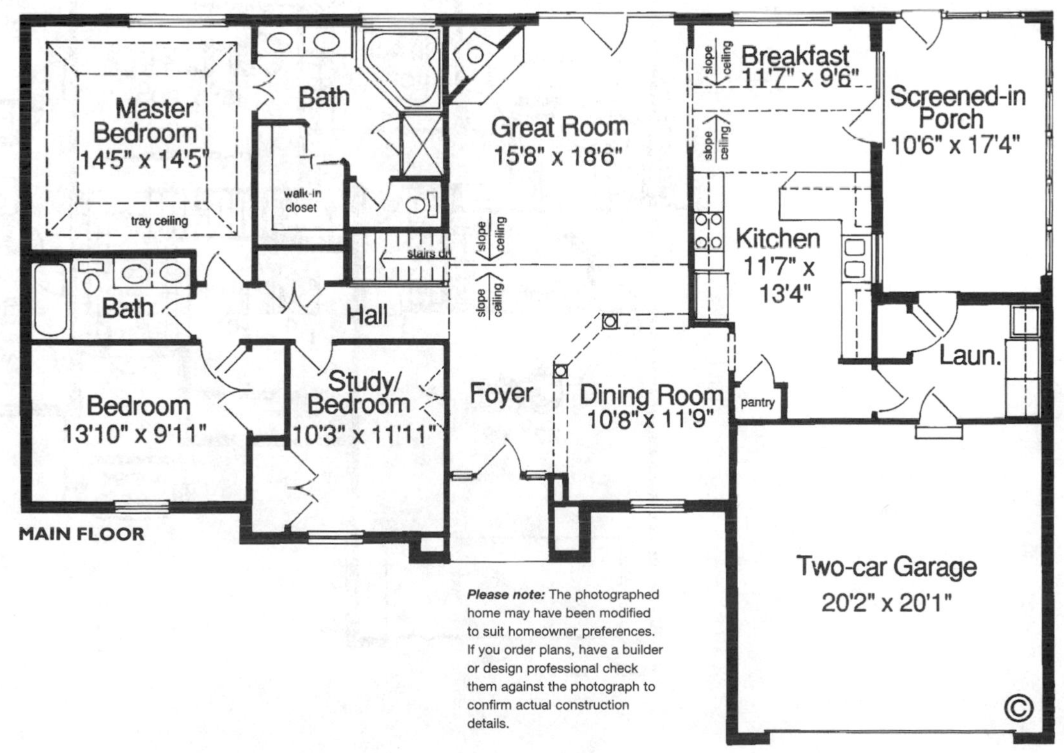

Please note: The photographed home may have been modified to suit homeowner preferences. If you order plans, have a builder or design professional check them against the photograph to confirm actual construction details.

Design 94917

Units Single
Price Code C
Total Finished 1,782 sq. ft.
Main Finished 1,782 sq. ft.
Basement Unfinished 1,782 sq. ft.
Garage Unfinished 466 sq. ft.
Dimensions 52'x59'4"
Foundation Basement
Slab
Bedrooms 3
Full Baths 2
Max Ridge Height 21'
Roof Framing Stick
Exterior Walls 2x4

* Alternate foundation options available at an additional charge. Please call 1-800-235-5700 for more information.

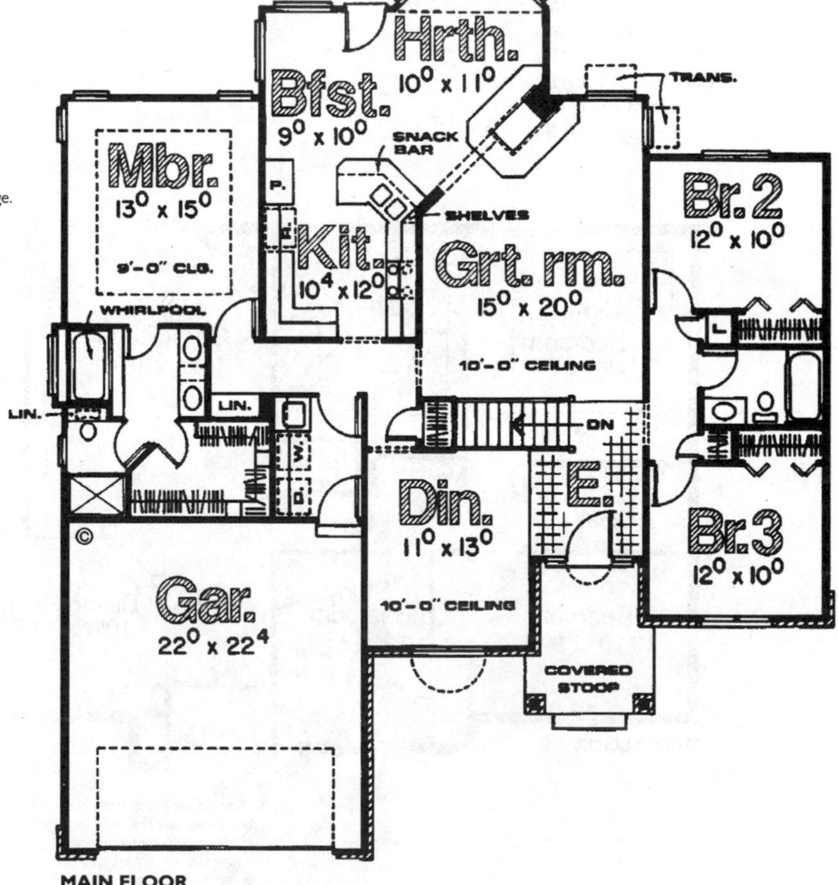

MAIN FLOOR

Design 93166

Units	Single
Price Code	C
Total Finished	1,785 sq. ft.
Main Finished	1,785 sq. ft.
Basement Unfinished	1,785 sq. ft.
Dimensions	63'x46'
Foundation	Basement
Bedrooms	3
Full Baths	2
Half Baths	1
Max Ridge Height	23'
Roof Framing	Stick
Exterior Walls	2x6

MAIN FLOOR

Design 97466

Units	Single
Price Code	C
Total Finished	1,790 sq. ft.
Main Finished	1,790 sq. ft.
Garage Unfinished	546 sq. ft.
Deck Unfinished	170 sq. ft.
Dimensions	55'x57'
Foundation	Basement
Bedrooms	3
Full Baths	2
Main Ceiling	9'
Max Ridge Height	27'9"
Roof Framing	Stick
Exterior Walls	2x4

* Alternate foundation options available at an additional charge. Please call 1-800-235-5700 for more information.

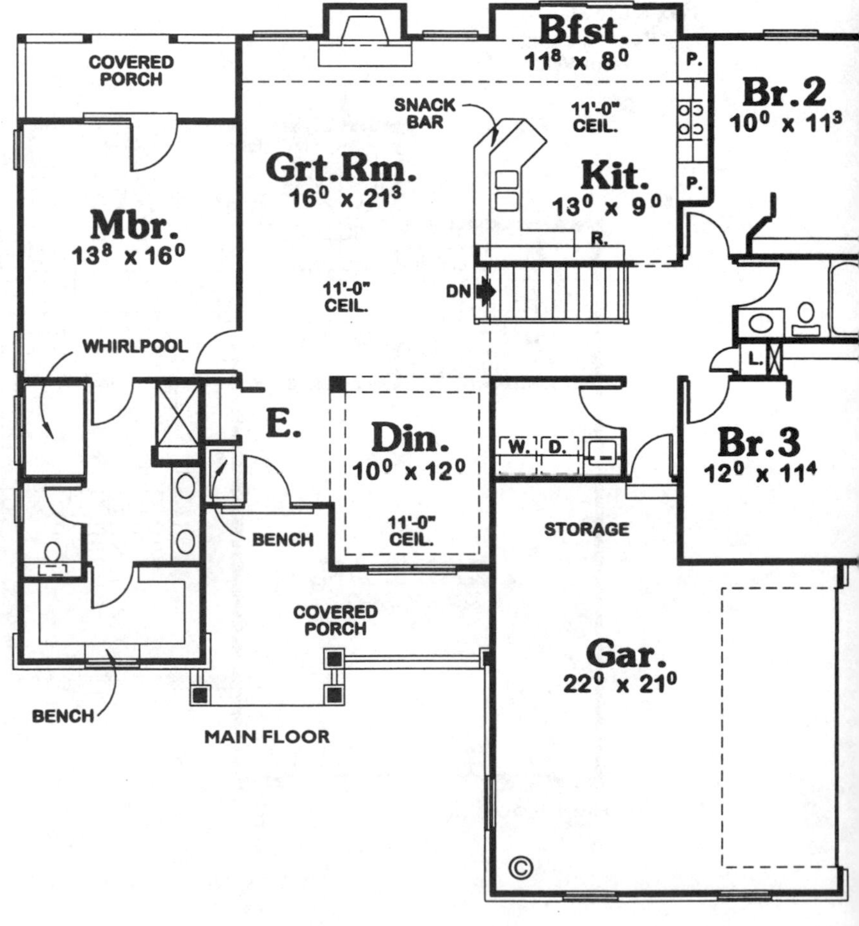

Design 20198

Units	Single
Price Code	C
Total Finished	1,792 sq. ft.
Main Finished	1,792 sq. ft.
Basement Unfinished	818 sq. ft.
Garage Unfinished	857 sq. ft.
Dimensions	56'x32'
Foundation	Basement
Bedrooms	3
Full Baths	2
Main Ceiling	8'
Max Ridge Height	25'
Roof Framing	Stick
Exterior Walls	2x4, 2x6

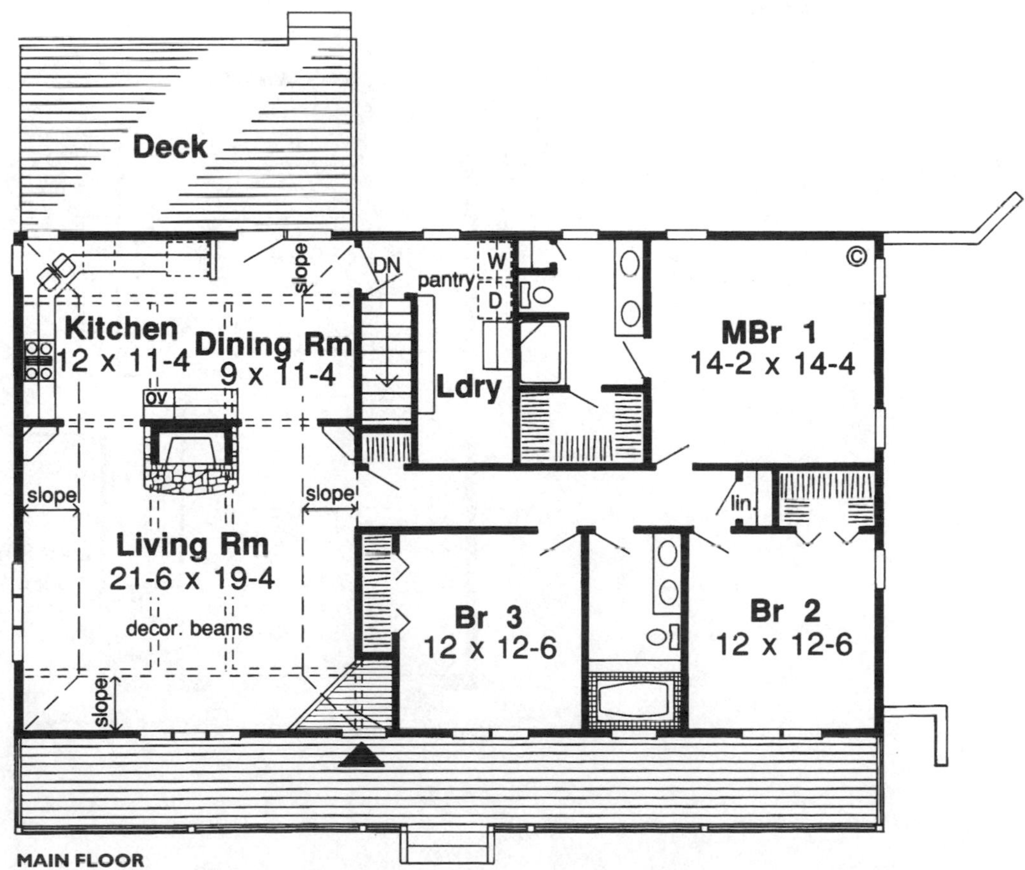

MAIN FLOOR

Design 98561

Units	Single
Price Code	C
Total Finished	1,794 sq. ft.
Main Finished	1,794 sq. ft.
Garage Unfinished	460 sq. ft.
Deck Unfinished	102 sq. ft.
Dimensions	60'x45'4"
Foundation	Crawlspace Slab
Bedrooms	3
Full Baths	2
Main Ceiling	8'-10'
Max Ridge Height	30'6"
Roof Framing	Stick
Exterior Walls	2x4

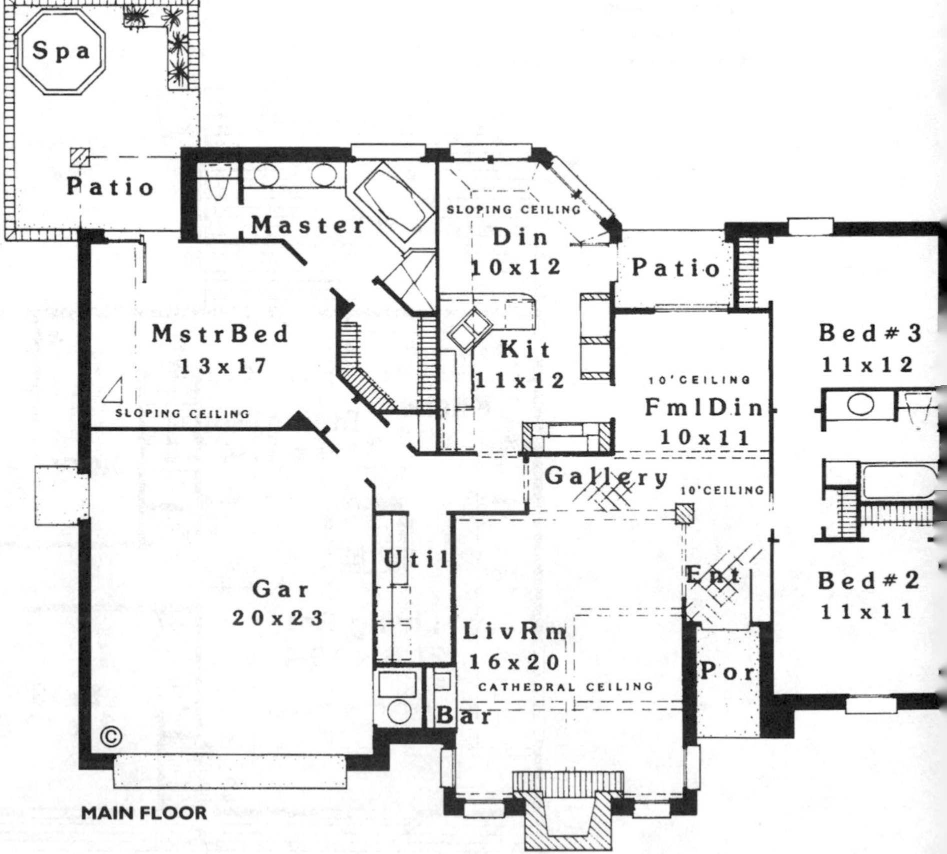

MAIN FLOOR

Design 93176

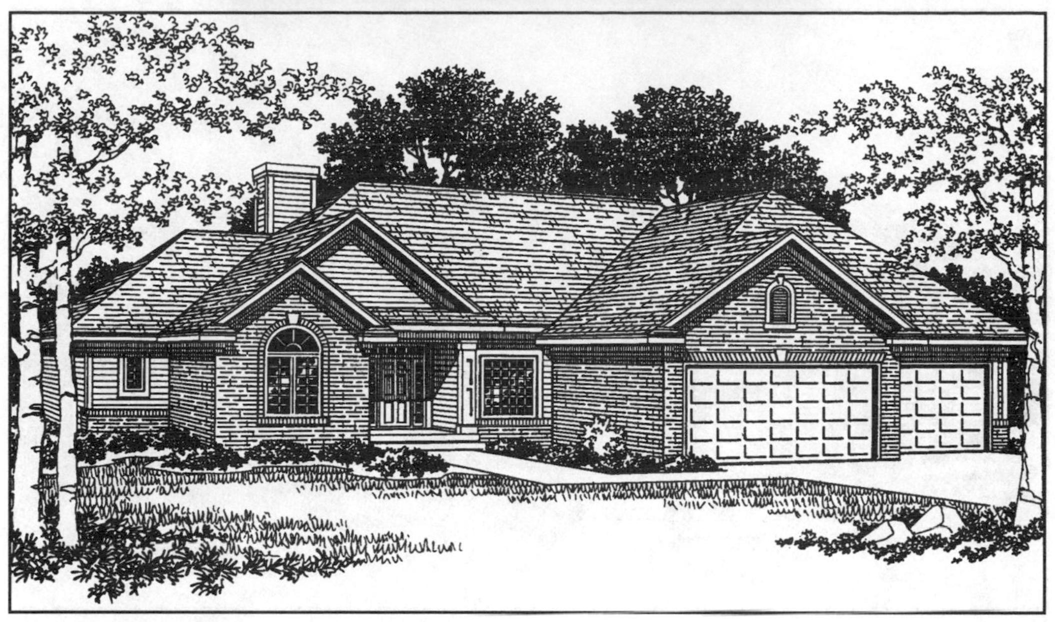

Units	Single
Price Code	C
Total Finished	1,795 sq. ft.
Main Finished	1,795 sq. ft.
Basement Unfinished	1,795 sq. ft.
Porch Unfinished	160 sq. ft.
Dimensions	68'x59'
Foundation	Basement
Bedrooms	3
Full Baths	2
Max Ridge Height	22'
Roof Framing	Stick
Exterior Walls	2x6

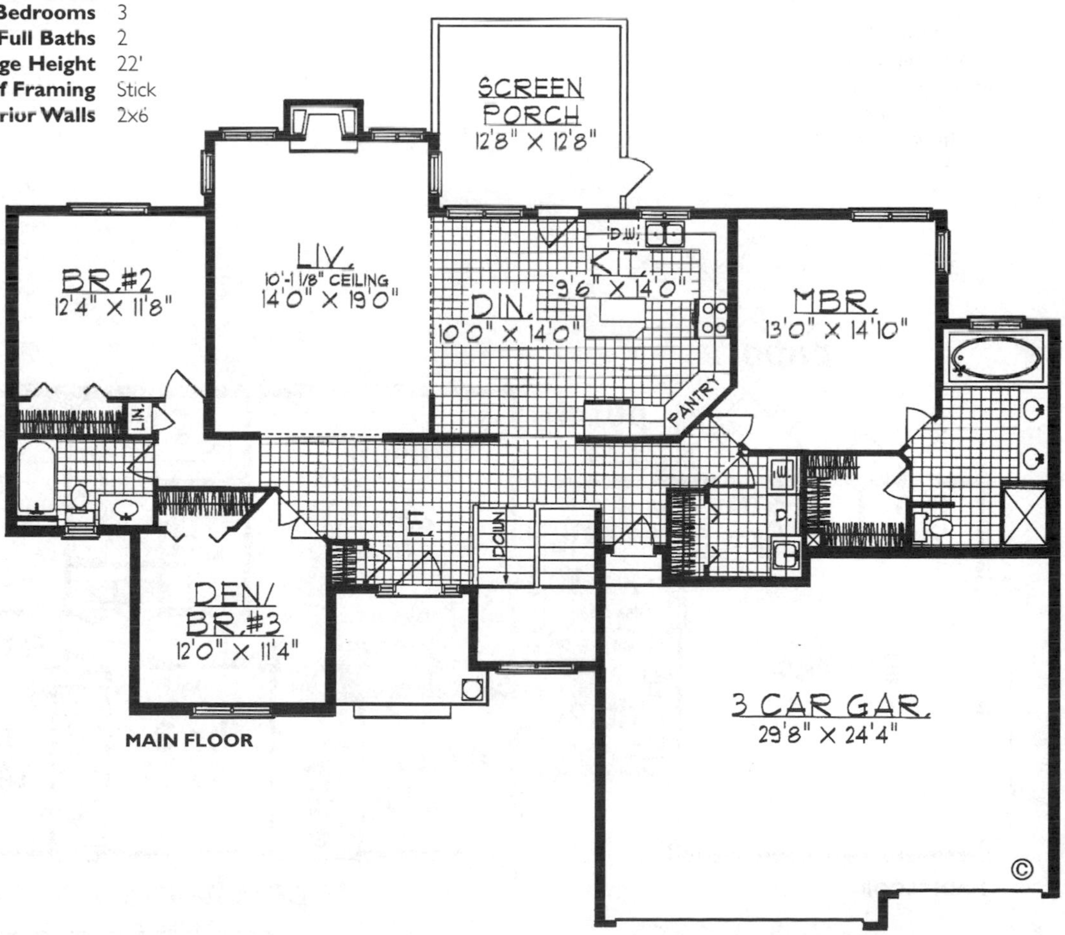

SCREEN PORCH
12'8" X 12'8"

BR.#2
12'4" X 11'8"

LIV.
10'-1 1/8" CEILING
14'0" X 19'0"

DIN.
10'0" X 14'0"

KIT.
9'6" X 14'0"

DW

PANTRY

MBR.
13'0" X 14'10"

LIN.

E.

DOWN

DEN/
BR.#3
12'0" X 11'4"

3 CAR GAR.
29'8" X 24'4"

©

MAIN FLOOR

This plan is not to be built within a 20 mile radius of Iowa City, IA.

Design 65621

Units	Single
Price Code	C
Total Finished	1,800 sq. ft.
Main Finished	1,800 sq. ft.
Dimensions	80'x40'
Foundation	Crawlspace Slab
Bedrooms	3
Full Baths	2
Main Ceiling	8'
Vaulted Ceiling	12'
Max Ridge Height	25'
Roof Framing	Stick
Exterior Walls	2x4

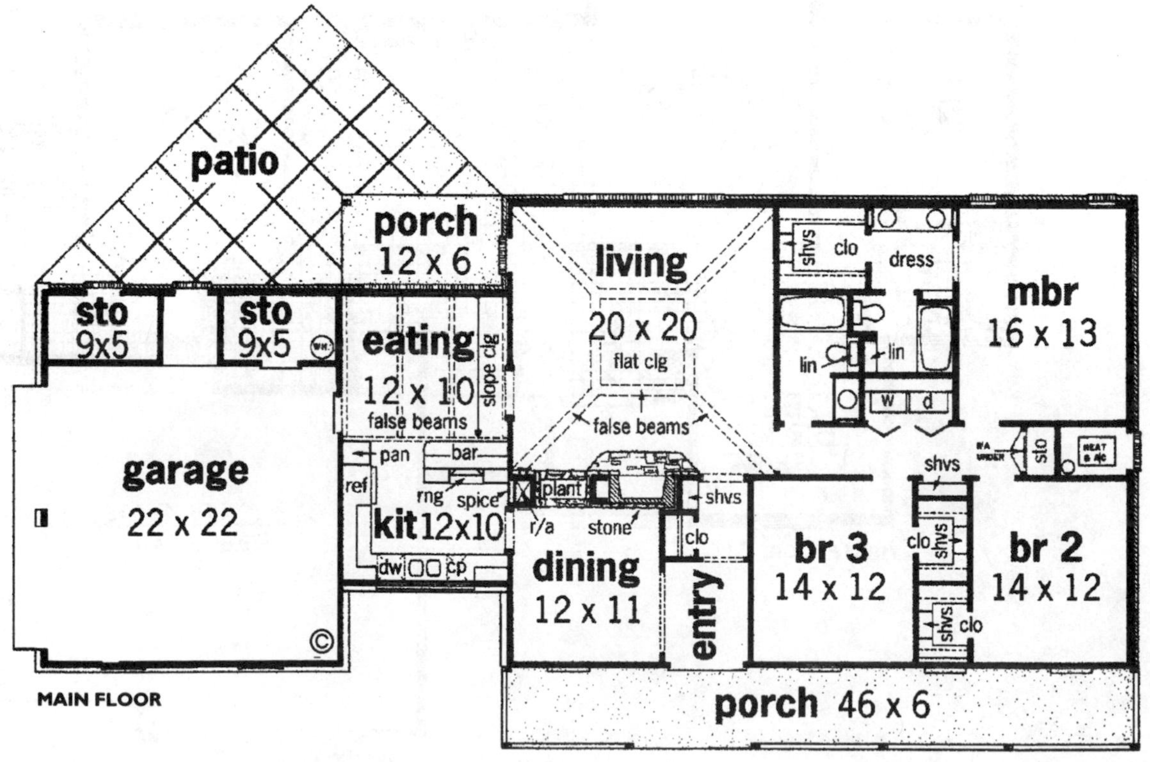

MAIN FLOOR

Design 65622

Units	Single
Price Code	C
Total Finished	1,800 sq. ft.
Main Finished	1,800 sq. ft.
Dimensions	66'x60'
Foundation	Basement Crawlspace Slab
Bedrooms	3
Full Baths	2
Main Ceiling	8'
Max Ridge Height	29'
Roof Framing	Stick
Exterior Walls	2x6

shvs
lin
clo
mbr
15 x 14
shr
frz
brm
clo
sto
10x6
util 9x6
sto
6 x 4
WH
w
d
pan
line of 12' clg
eating
10 x 8
porch
15 x 12
slope of clg
br 3
12 x 11
clo
clo
desk
ref
ct
kit
13 x 11
bar
dw
skylight
lin
lin
garage
25 x 22
cp
ovs
pan
living
18 x 16
br 2
14 x 11
clo
dining
14 x 12
shvs
entry 11x4
clo
clo
porch 44 x 6
©

MAIN FLOOR

Design 65623

Units	Single
Price Code	C
Total Finished	1,800 sq. ft.
Main Finished	1,800 sq. ft.
Dimensions	66'x60'
Foundation	Crawlspace Slab
Bedrooms	3
Full Baths	2
Main Ceiling	8'
Max Ridge Height	26'
Roof Framing	Stick
Exterior Walls	2x6

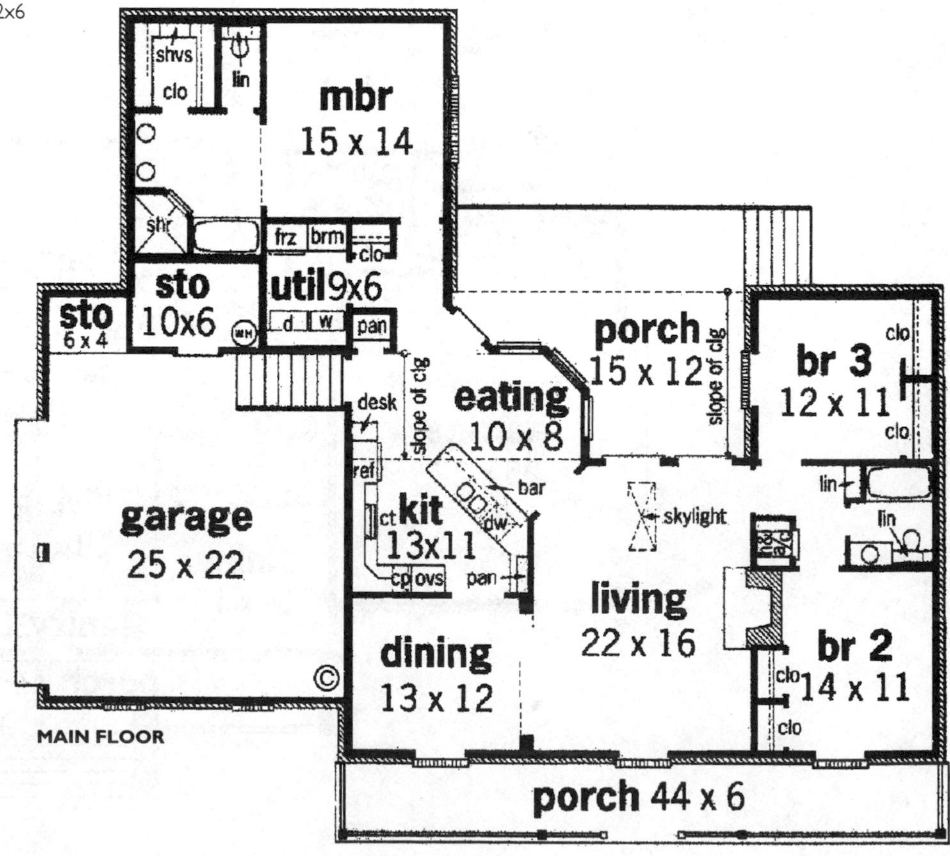

MAIN FLOOR

Design 65625

Units	Single
Price Code	C
Total Finished	1,800 sq. ft.
Main Finished	1,800 sq. ft.
Dimensions	66'x60'
Foundation	Crawlspace Slab
Bedrooms	3
Full Baths	2
Main Ceiling	8'
Max Ridge Height	26'
Roof Framing	Stick
Exterior Walls	2x6

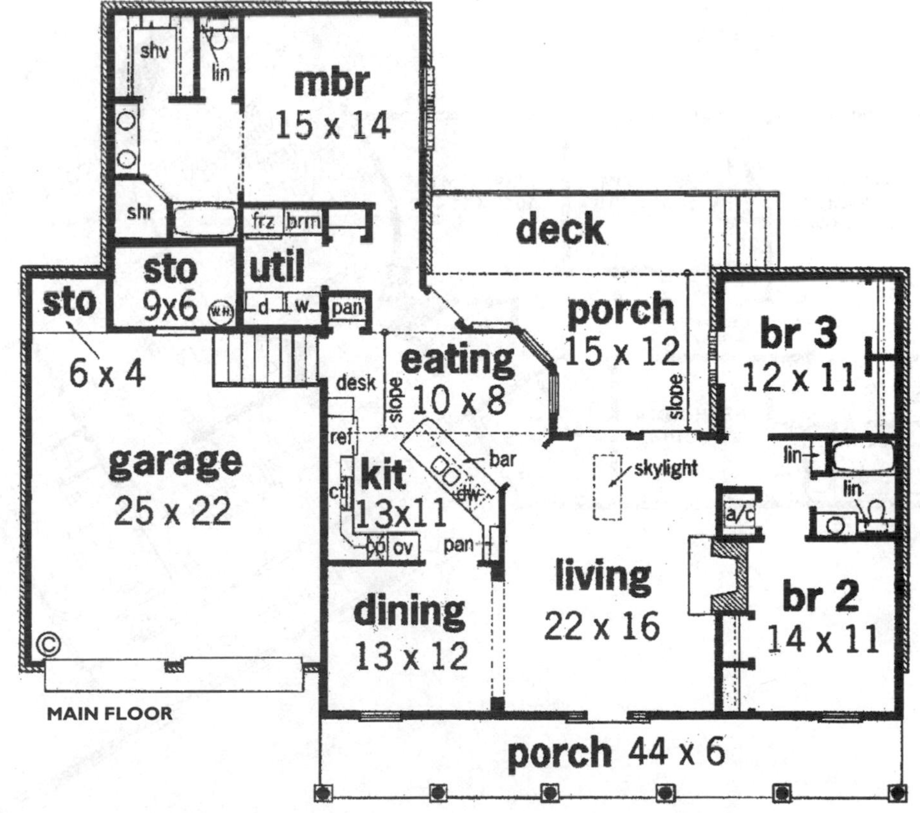

MAIN FLOOR

Design 99055

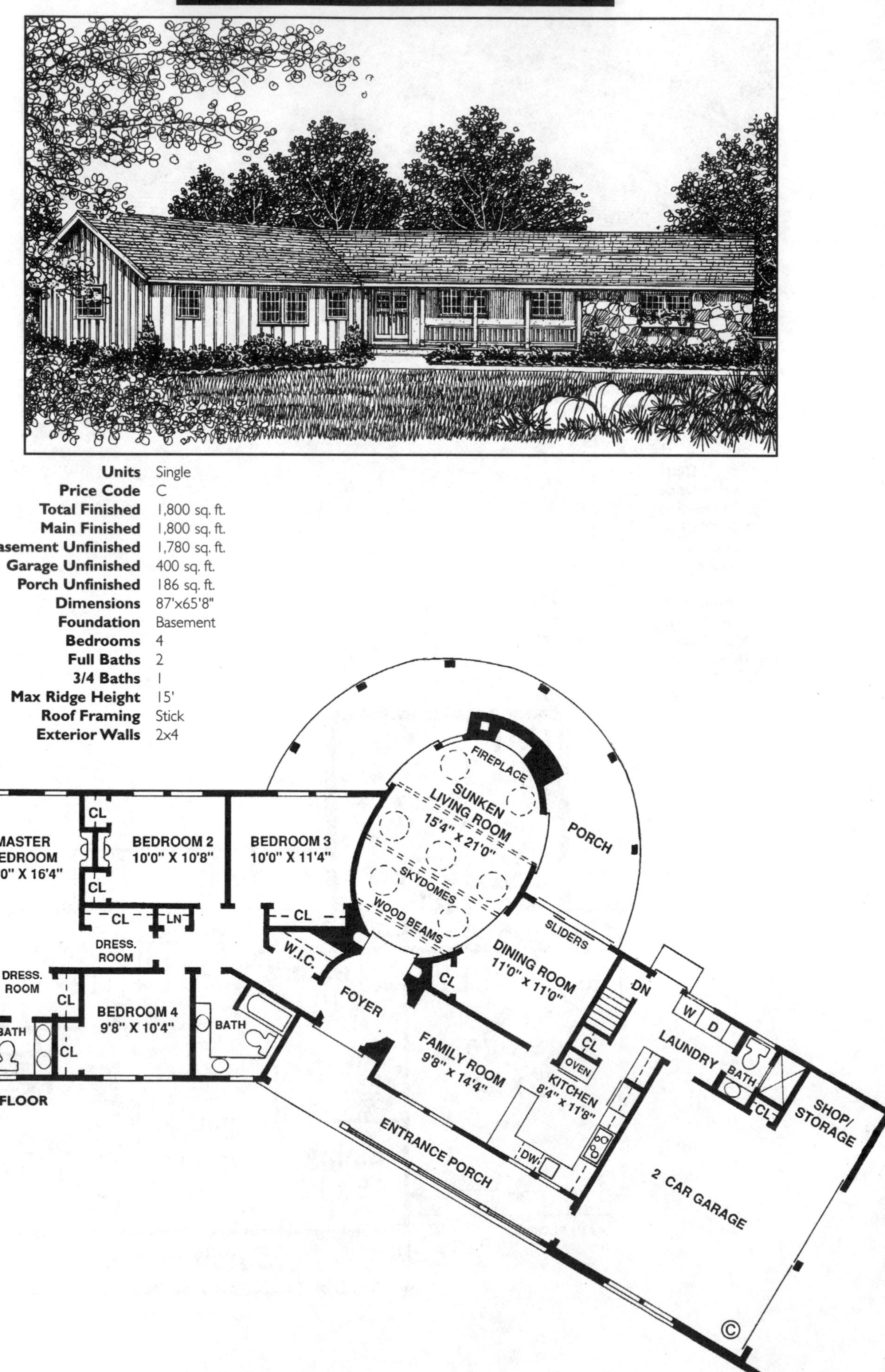

Units	Single
Price Code	C
Total Finished	1,800 sq. ft.
Main Finished	1,800 sq. ft.
Basement Unfinished	1,780 sq. ft.
Garage Unfinished	400 sq. ft.
Porch Unfinished	186 sq. ft.
Dimensions	87'x65'8"
Foundation	Basement
Bedrooms	4
Full Baths	2
3/4 Baths	1
Max Ridge Height	15'
Roof Framing	Stick
Exterior Walls	2x4

Design 63054

Units	Single
Price Code	C
Total Finished	1,806 sq. ft.
Main Finished	1,806 sq. ft.
Garage Unfinished	491 sq. ft.
Porch Unfinished	216 sq. ft.
Dimensions	54'x58'8"
Foundation	Slab
Bedrooms	3
Full Baths	2
Main Ceiling	8'
Vaulted Ceiling	13'6"
Max Ridge Height	18'
Roof Framing	Truss

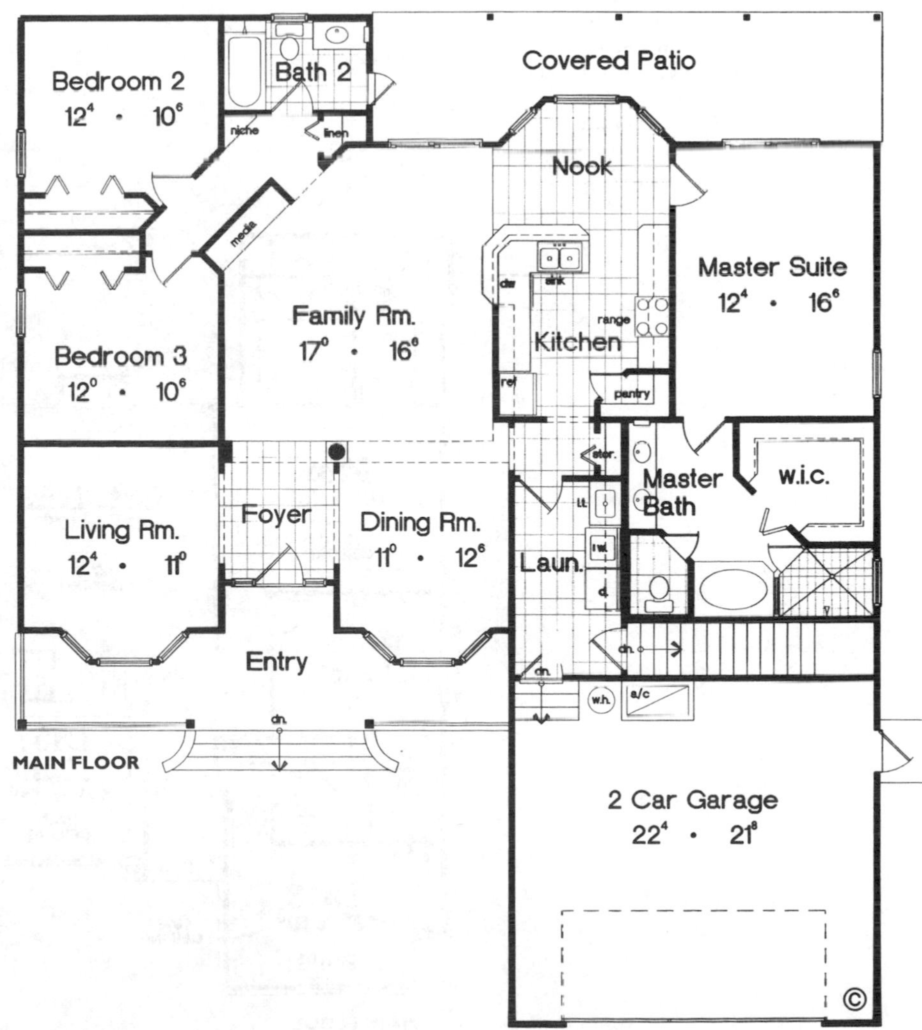

MAIN FLOOR

Design 97462

Units	Single
Price Code	B
Total Finished	1,806 sq. ft.
Main Finished	1,806 sq. ft.
Garage Unfinished	655 sq. ft.
Dimensions	65'4"x56'
Foundation	Basement
Bedrooms	3
Full Baths	2
Main Ceiling	9'
Max Ridge Height	21'
Roof Framing	Stick
Exterior Walls	2x4

* Alternate foundation options available at an additional charge.
Please call 1-800-235-5700 for more information.

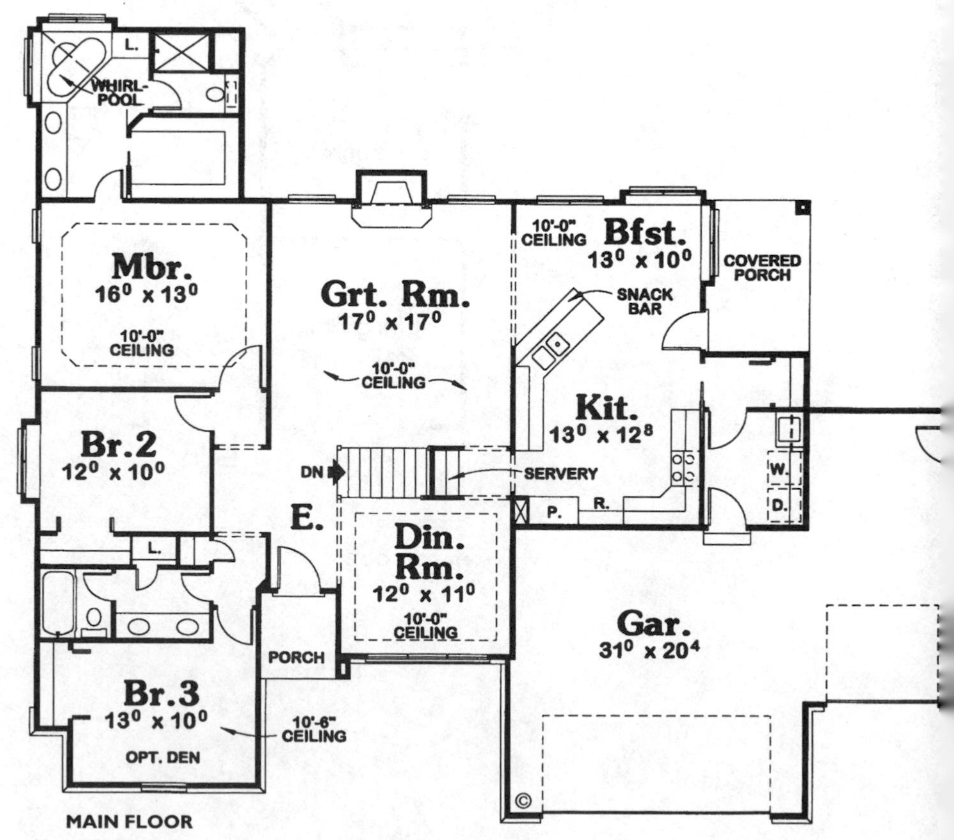

Design 94928

Units	Single
Price Code	C
Total Finished	1,808 sq. ft.
Main Finished	1,808 sq. ft.
Basement Unfinished	1,808 sq. ft.
Garage Unfinished	551 sq. ft.
Dimensions	64'x44'
Foundation	Basement
Bedrooms	3
Full Baths	2
Half Baths	1
Main Ceiling	8'
Max Ridge Height	22'5"
Roof Framing	Stick
Exterior Walls	2x4

Alternate foundation options available at an additional charge.
Please call 1-800-235-5700 for more information.

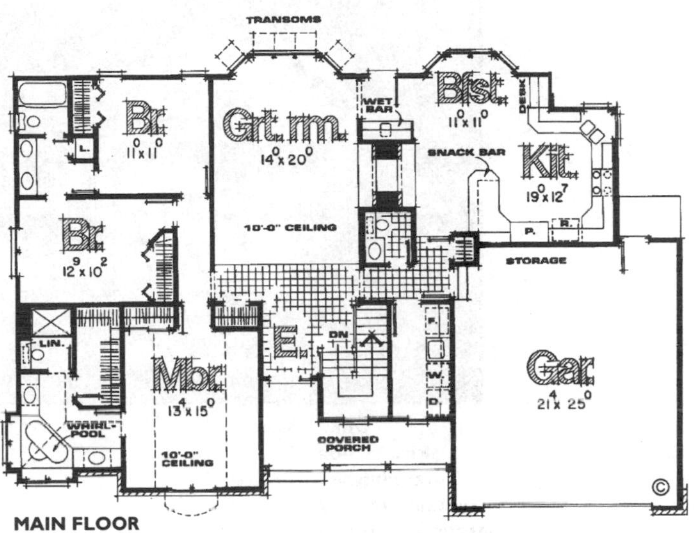

Design 90441

Units	Single
Price Code	C
Total Finished	1,811 sq. ft.
Main Finished	1,811 sq. ft.
Basement Unfinished	1,811 sq. ft.
Garage Unfinished	484 sq. ft.
Deck Unfinished	336 sq. ft.
Porch Unfinished	390 sq. ft.
Dimensions	89'6"x44'4"
Foundation	Basement Crawlspace Slab
Bedrooms	3
Full Baths	2
Main Ceiling	8'
Max Ridge Height	16'4"
Roof Framing	Stick
Exterior Walls	2x4

DECK 28-0 x 12-0
BATH
BEDROOM 2 11-0 x 13-6
DINING 12-0 x 13-6
KITCHEN 10-0 x 13-8
SCR. PORCH 12-0 x 20-0
GARAGE 22-0 x 22-0
UTILITY
HALL
MASTER BEDROOM 12-0 x 18-0
BEDROOM 3 12-0 x 11-4
GREAT ROOM 19-0 x 17-6
PORCH 25-0 x 8-0
MAIN FLOOR

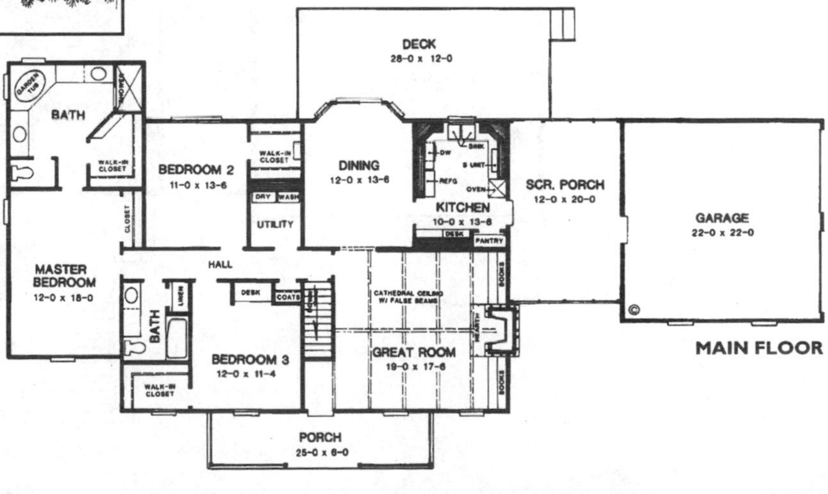

Design 62084

Units	Single
Price Code	C
Total Finished	1,813 sq. ft.
Main Finished	1,813 sq. ft.
Garage Unfinished	426 sq. ft.
Dimensions	65'8"x57'
Foundation	Crawlspace Slab
Bedrooms	3
Full Baths	2
Main Ceiling	9'
Max Ridge Height	23'10"
Roof Framing	Stick
Exterior Walls	2x4

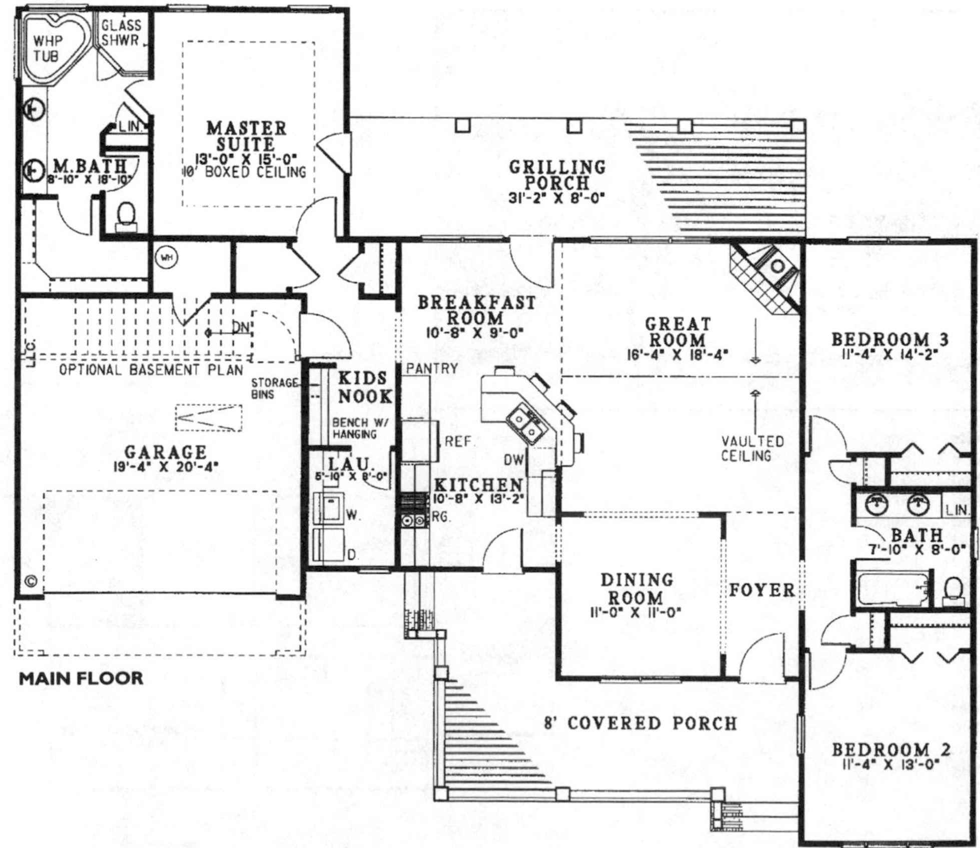

MAIN FLOOR

Design 97300

Units	Single
Price Code	C
Total Finished	1,814 sq. ft.
Main Finished	1,814 sq. ft.
Basement Unfinished	1,814 sq. ft.
Dimensions	58'x56'
Foundation	Basement
Bedrooms	3
Full Baths	2
Main Ceiling	9'1/8"
Max Ridge Height	27'8"
Roof Framing	Truss
Exterior Walls	2x6

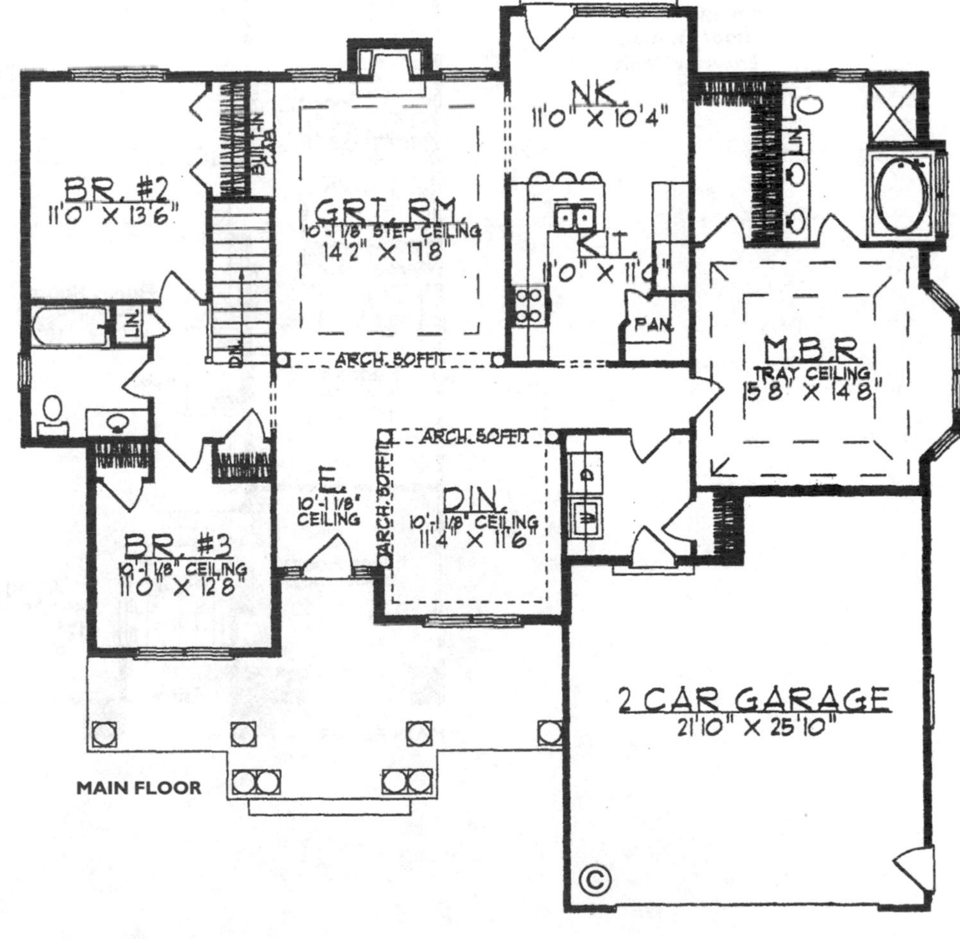

Design 63112

Units	Single
Price Code	C
Total Finished	1,817 sq. ft.
Main Finished	1,817 sq. ft.
Garage Unfinished	420 sq. ft.
Dimensions	50'x63'
Foundation	Slab
Bedrooms	3
Full Baths	2
Main Ceiling	10'
Max Ridge Height	26'5"
Roof Framing	Truss
Exterior Walls	2x4

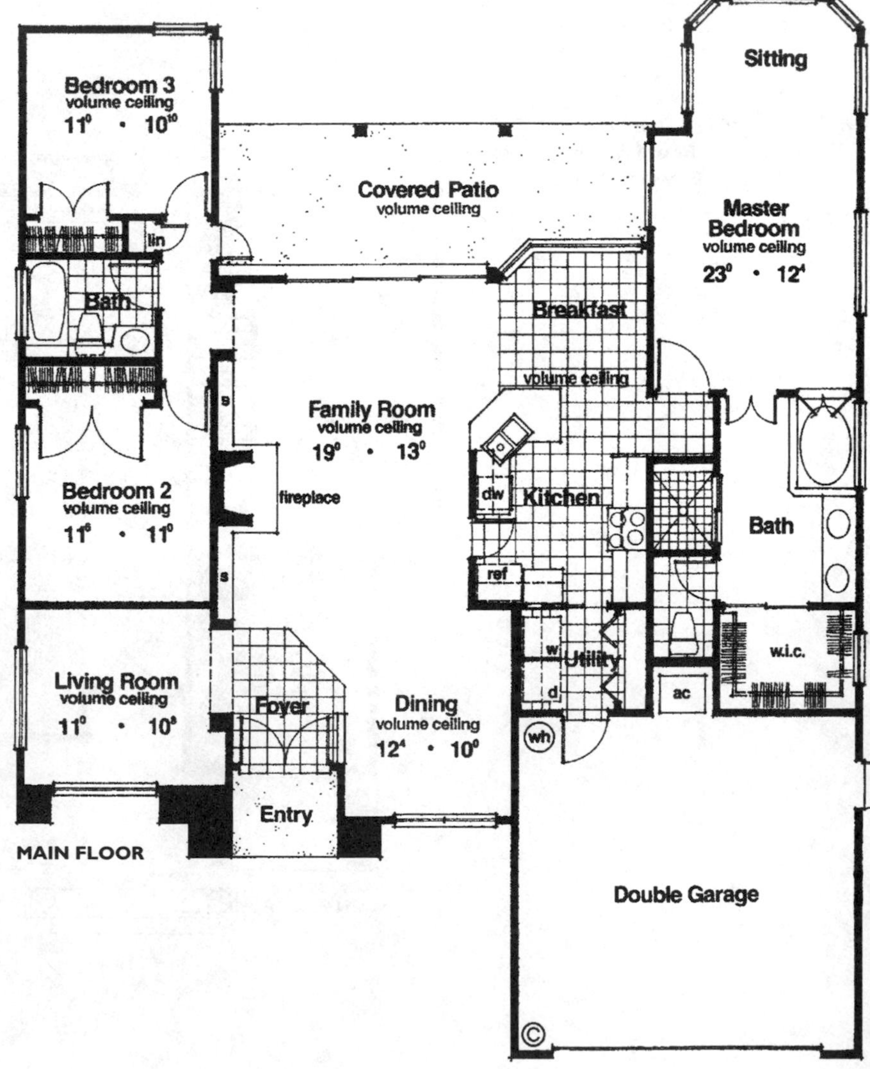

Design 93155

Units	Single
Price Code	C
Total Finished	1,817 sq. ft.
Main Finished	1,817 sq. ft.
Basement Unfinished	1,817 sq. ft.
Dimensions	57'x56'
Foundation	Basement
Bedrooms	3
Full Baths	2
Max Ridge Height	22'
Roof Framing	Stick
Exterior Walls	2x6

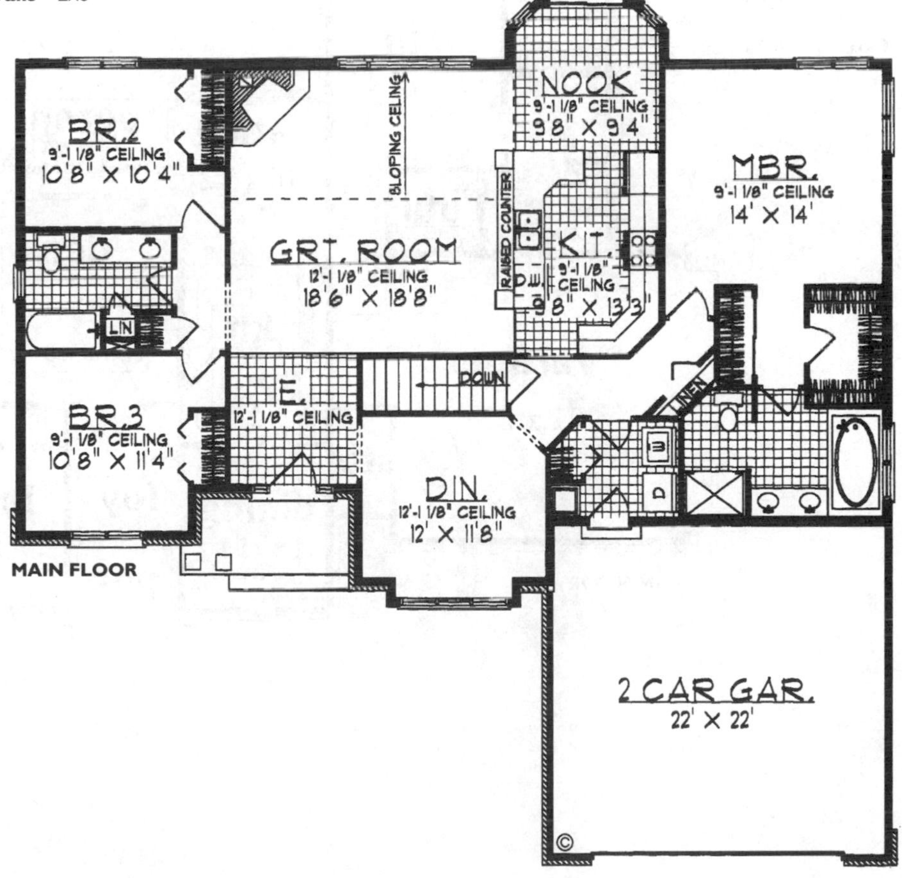

Design 92551

Units	Single
Price Code	C
Total Finished	1,818 sq. ft.
Main Finished	1,818 sq. ft.
Garage Unfinished	522 sq. ft.
Dimensions	67'10"x48'5"
Foundation	Crawlspace Slab
Bedrooms	4
Full Baths	2
Main Ceiling	9'
Max Ridge Height	22'
Roof Framing	Stick
Exterior Walls	2x4

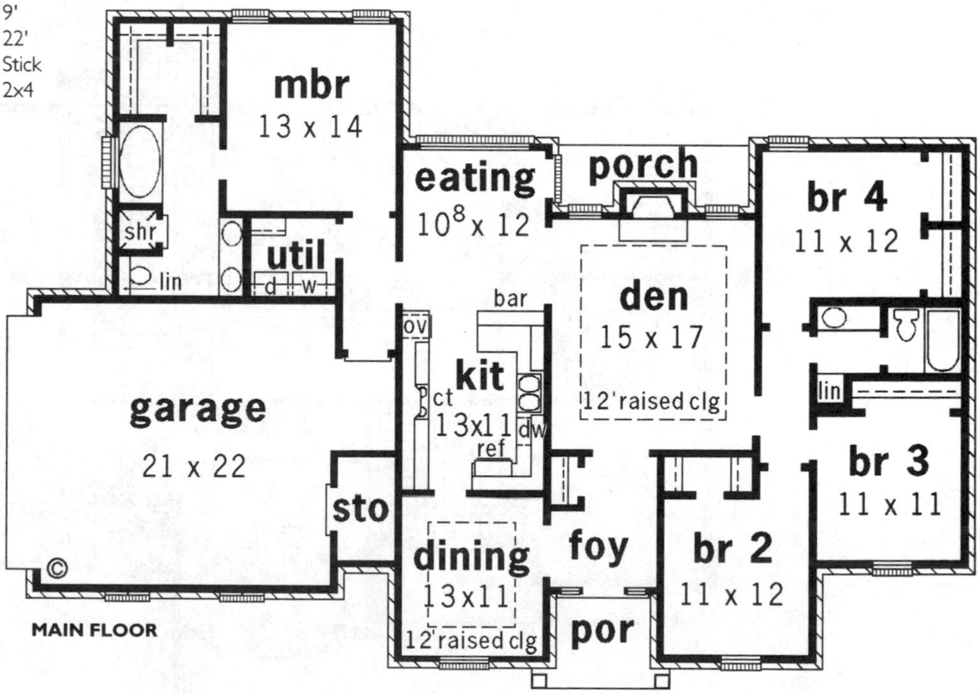

mbr 13 x 14
eating 10^8 x 12
porch
br 4 11 x 12
shr
lin
util
d w
bar
ov
den 15 x 17
12' raised clg
kit 13x11
ct
dw
ref
lin
garage 21 x 22
br 3 11 x 11
sto
dining 13x11
12' raised clg
foy
br 2 11 x 12
por
©

MAIN FLOOR

Design 93423

Units	Single
Price Code	C
Total Finished	1,829 sq. ft.
First Finished	1,339 sq. ft.
Second Finished	490 sq. ft.
Bonus Unfinished	145 sq. ft.
Garage Unfinished	491 sq. ft.
Porch Unfinished	173 sq. ft.
Dimensions	57'x60'
Foundation	Basement
Bedrooms	3
Full Baths	2
Half Baths	1
First Ceiling	9'
Second Ceiling	8'
Max Ridge Height	29'
Roof Framing	Stick
Exterior Walls	2x4

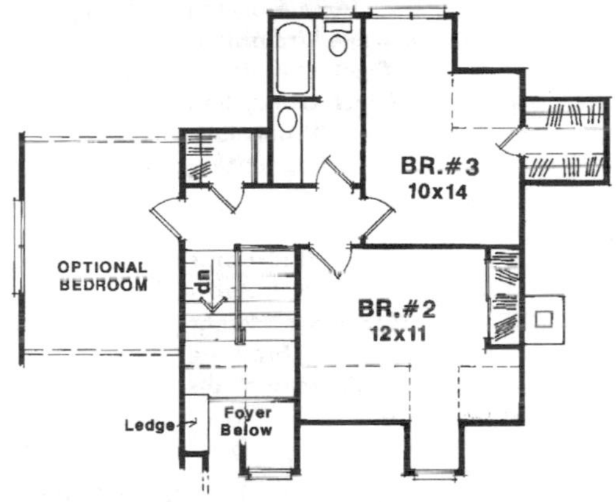

OPTIONAL BEDROOM
BR. #3 10x14
BR. #2 12x11
dn
Ledge
Foyer Below

SECOND FLOOR

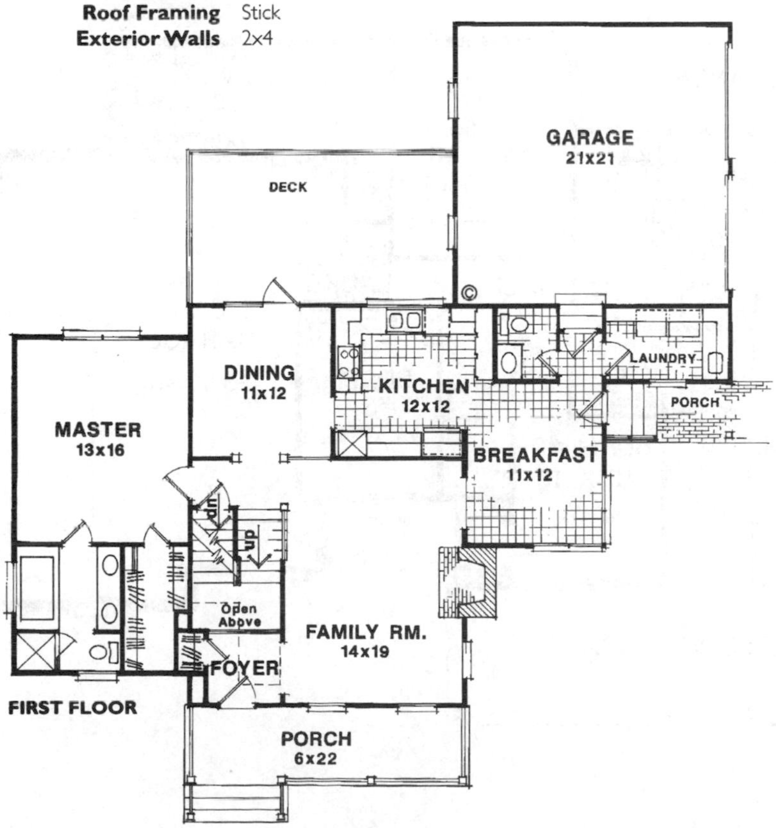

GARAGE 21x21
DECK
DINING 11x12
KITCHEN 12x12
LAUNDRY
PORCH
BREAKFAST 11x12
MASTER 13x16
up
up
Open Above
FAMILY RM. 14x19
FOYER
PORCH 6x22

FIRST FLOOR

Design 92220

Units	Single
Price Code	C
Total Finished	1,830 sq. ft.
Main Finished	1,830 sq. ft.
Garage Unfinished	759 sq. ft.
Deck Unfinished	315 sq. ft.
Porch Unfinished	390 sq. ft.
Dimensions	75'x52'3"
Foundation	Basement Crawlspace Slab
Bedrooms	3
Full Baths	2
Max Ridge Height	27'3"
Roof Framing	Stick
Exterior Walls	2x4

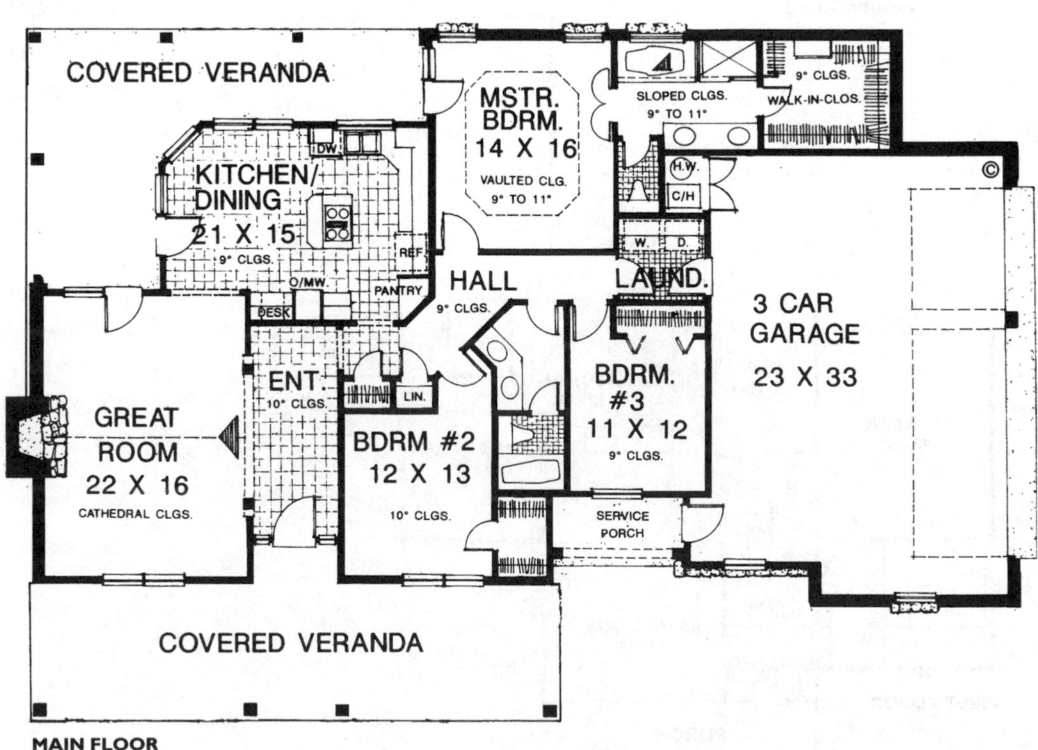

Design 98957

Units	Single
Price Code	C
Total Finished	1,830 sq. ft.
Main Finished	1,830 sq. ft.
Garage Unfinished	390 sq. ft.
Dimensions	49'x64'
Foundation	Basement Crawlspace Slab
Bedrooms	3
Full Baths	2
Main Ceiling	8'
Max Ridge Height	21'
Roof Framing	Stick
Exterior Walls	2x4

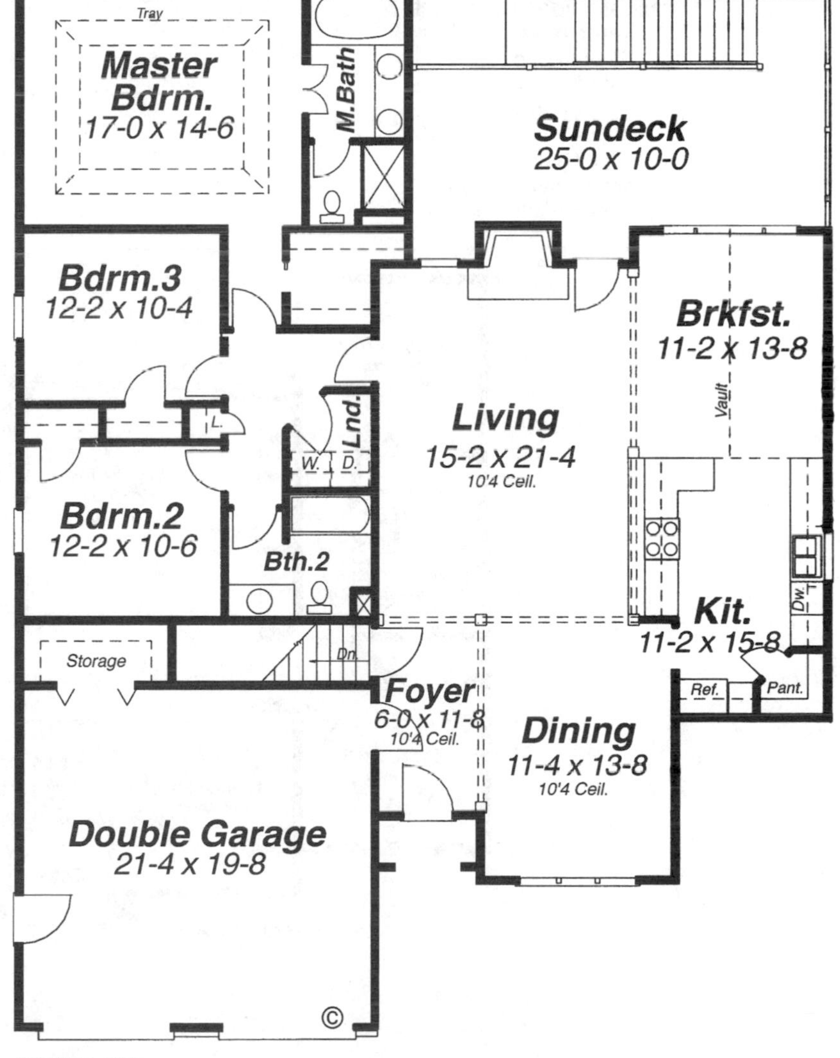

MAIN FLOOR

Design 63027

Units	Single
Price Code	C
Total Finished	1,833 sq. ft.
Main Finished	1,833 sq. ft.
Garage Unfinished	392 sq. ft.
Dimensions	59'4"x48'8"
Foundation	Slab
Bedrooms	3
Full Baths	2
Main Ceiling	10'
Max Ridge Height	19'6"
Roof Framing	Truss
Exterior Walls	2x4

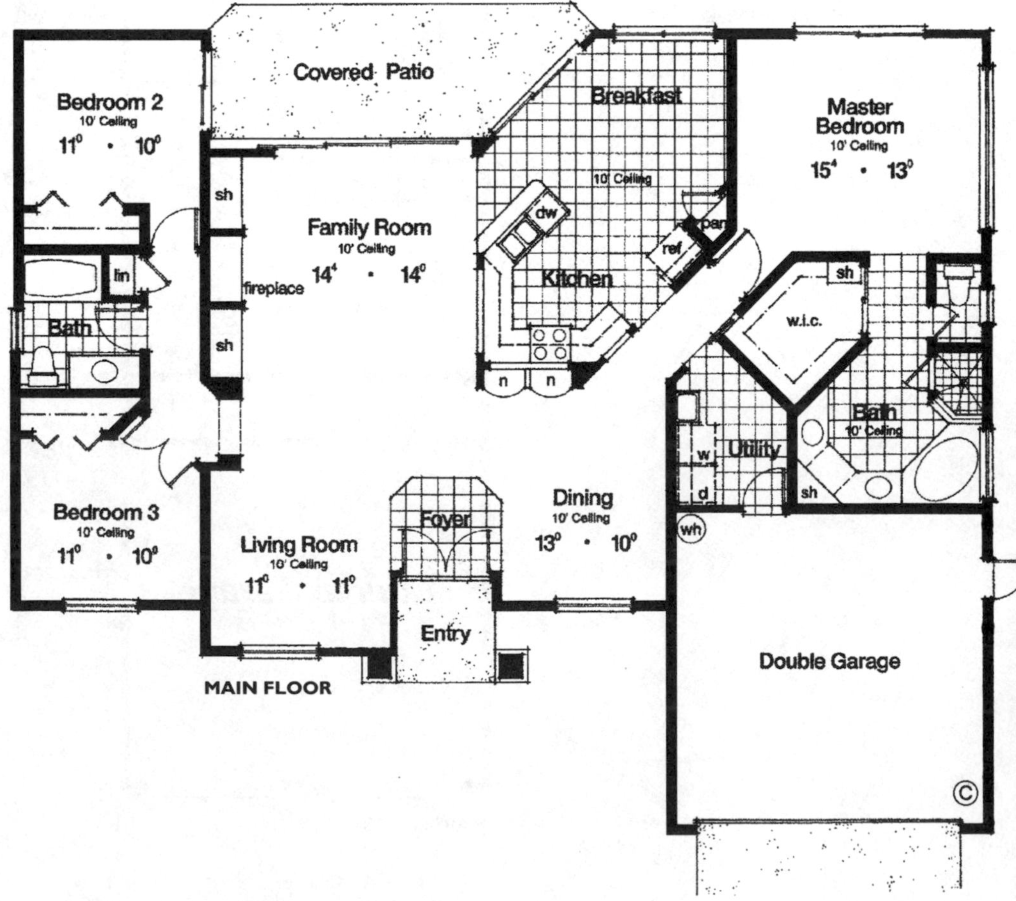

Design 99918

Units	Single
Price Code	C
Total Finished	1,833 sq. ft.
Main Finished	1,833 sq. ft.
Basement Unfinished	1,815 sq. ft.
Garage Unfinished	506 sq. ft.
Porch Unfinished	39 sq. ft.
Dimensions	48'x59'
Foundation	Basement
Bedrooms	3
Full Baths	2
Main Ceiling	8'
Vaulted Ceiling	11'
Max Ridge Height	20'
Roof Framing	Truss
Exterior Walls	2x6

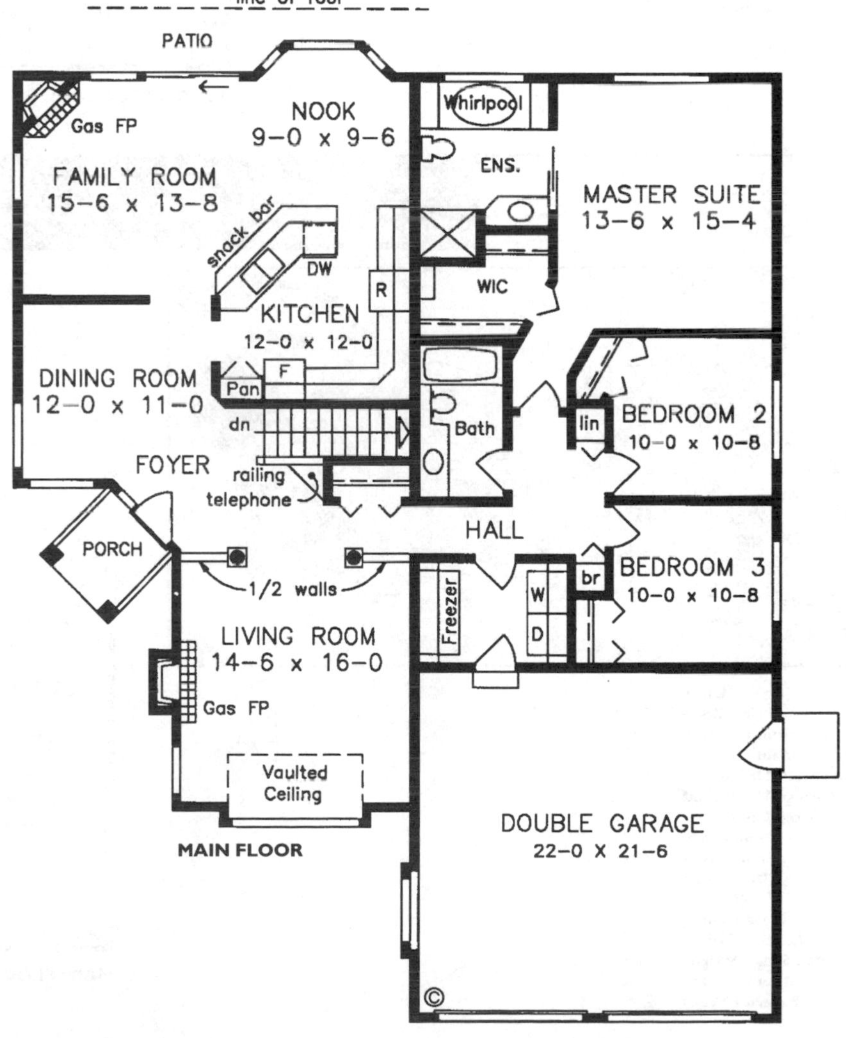

Design 32228

PHOTOGRAPHY: JOHN KANE

Units	Single
Price Code	C
Total Finished	1,834 sq. ft.
First Finished	1,154 sq. ft.
Second Finished	680 sq. ft.
Basement Unfinished	1,154 sq. ft.
Deck Unfinished	45 sq. ft.
Porch Unfinished	640 sq. ft.
Dimensions	36'x50'
Foundation	Basement
Bedrooms	3
Full Baths	2
First Ceiling	9'
Second Ceiling	8'
Vaulted Ceiling	19'
Max Ridge Height	36'8"
Roof Framing	Stick
Exterior Walls	2x4

Please note: The photographed home may have been modified to suit homeowner preferences. If you order plans, have a builder or design professional check them against the photograph to confirm actual construction details.

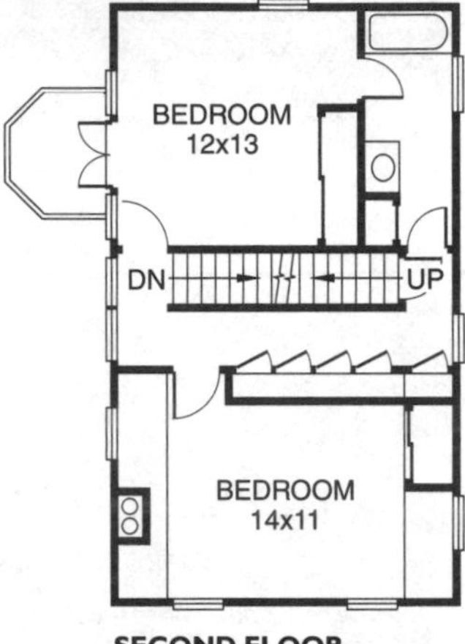

SECOND FLOOR

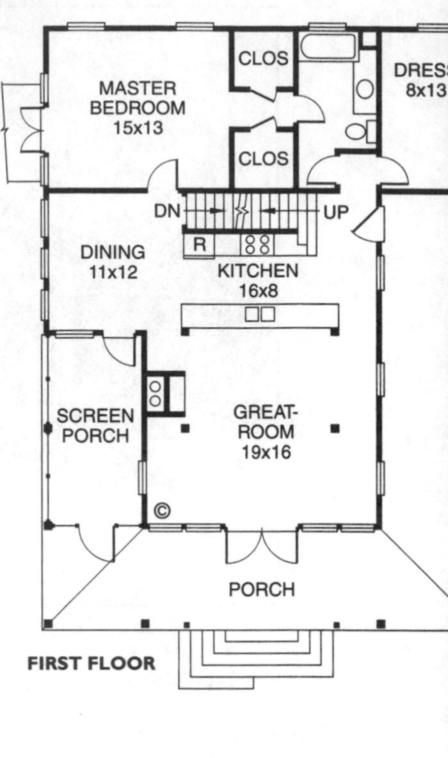

FIRST FLOOR

Design 97764

Units	Single
Price Code	C
Total Finished	1,834 sq. ft.
Main Finished	1,834 sq. ft.
Basement Unfinished	1,834 sq. ft.
Garage Unfinished	485 sq. ft.
Porch Unfinished	140 sq. ft.
Dimensions	66'9"x50'7"
Foundation	Basement
Bedrooms	3
Full Baths	2
Main Ceiling	8'
Vaulted Ceiling	10'
Max Ridge Height	22'3"
Roof Framing	Truss
Exterior Walls	2x4

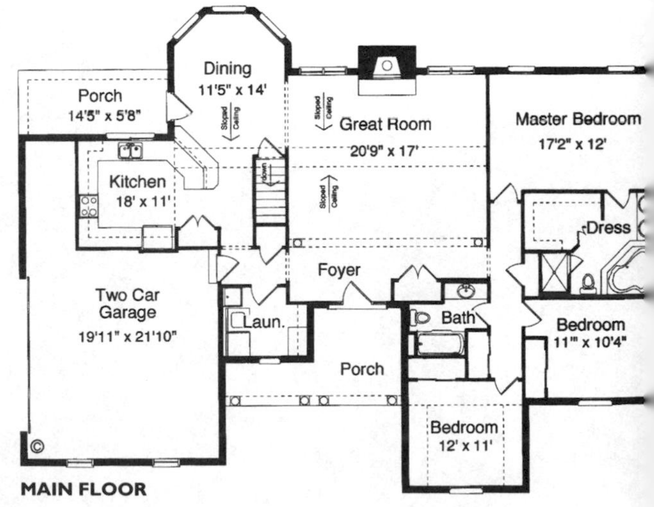

MAIN FLOOR

Design 91122

Units	Single
Price Code	C
Total Finished	1,838 sq. ft.
Main Finished	1,838 sq. ft.
Garage Unfinished	452 sq. ft.
Dimensions	48'6"x59'10"
Foundation	Slab
Bedrooms	3
Full Baths	2
Max Ridge Height	35'
Roof Framing	Stick
Exterior Walls	2x4

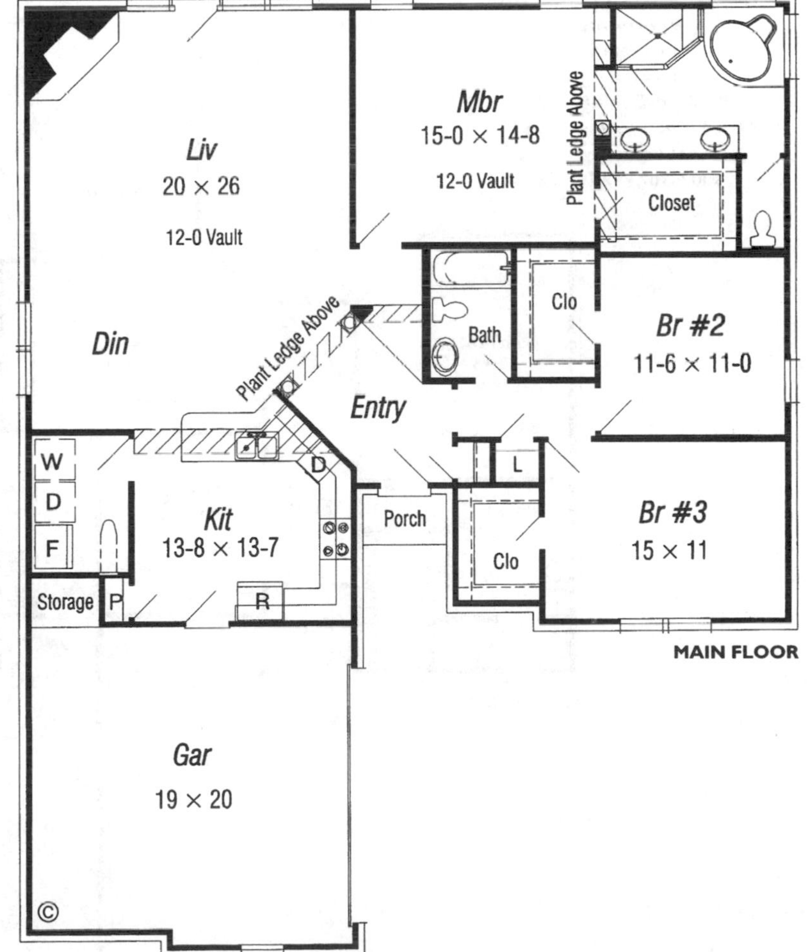

MAIN FLOOR

Design 93425

Units	Single
Price Code	C
Total Finished	1,842 sq. ft.
Main Finished	1,842 sq. ft.
Garage Unfinished	507 sq. ft.
Dimensions	56'4"x68'6"
Foundation	Crawlspace Slab
Bedrooms	3
Full Baths	2
Main Ceiling	9'
Vaulted Ceiling	12'
Max Ridge Height	20'6"
Roof Framing	Stick
Exterior Walls	2x4

Porch
11 x 6/10

Family Room
14 x 17/1
12' Vaulted Clg.
Bookcase

Breakfast
10/9 x 11/6
9' Ceiling

Master
14 x 16
9' Ceiling

Skylight

Kitchen
17/5 x 9

P

L

Br. #2
11 x 12/10
9' Ceiling

Skylight

Foyer
6 x 8

Dining
11 x12
10' Ceiling

Utility
W D

Br. #3
11 x12
9' Ceiling

L

Porch

MAIN FLOOR

Garage
22 x 22

©

Design 97416

Units	Single
Price Code	C
Total Finished	1,842 sq. ft.
Main Finished	1,842 sq. ft.
Garage Unfinished	498 sq. ft.
Dimensions	62'x48'
Foundation	Basement
Bedrooms	3
Full Baths	2
Half Baths	1
Max Ridge Height	20'9"
Roof Framing	Stick

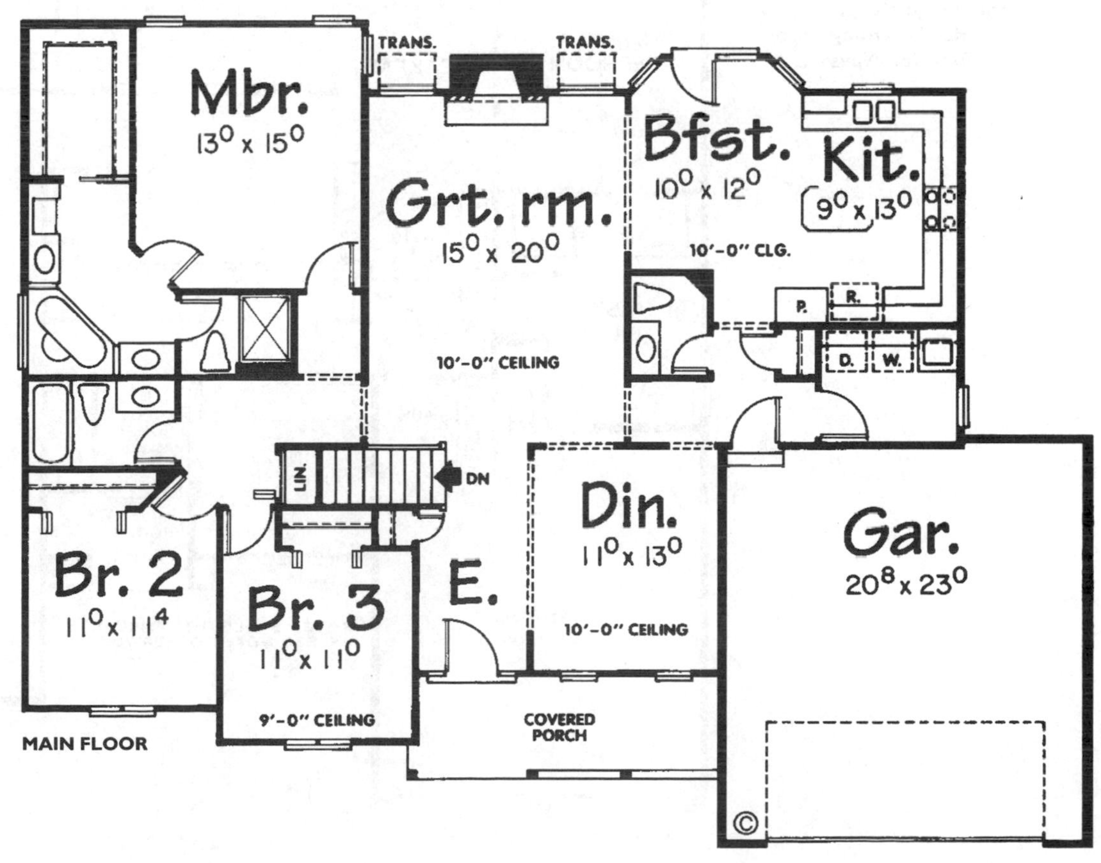

Design 90466

Units	Single
Price Code	C
Total Finished	1,845 sq. ft.
Main Finished	1,845 sq. ft.
Garage Unfinished	512 sq. ft.
Deck Unfinished	216 sq. ft.
Porch Unfinished	38 sq. ft.
Dimensions	57'2"x54'10"
Foundation	Crawlspace Slab
Bedrooms	3
Full Baths	2
Half Baths	1
Main Ceiling	8'
Max Ridge Height	23'10"
Roof Framing	Stick
Exterior Walls	2x4

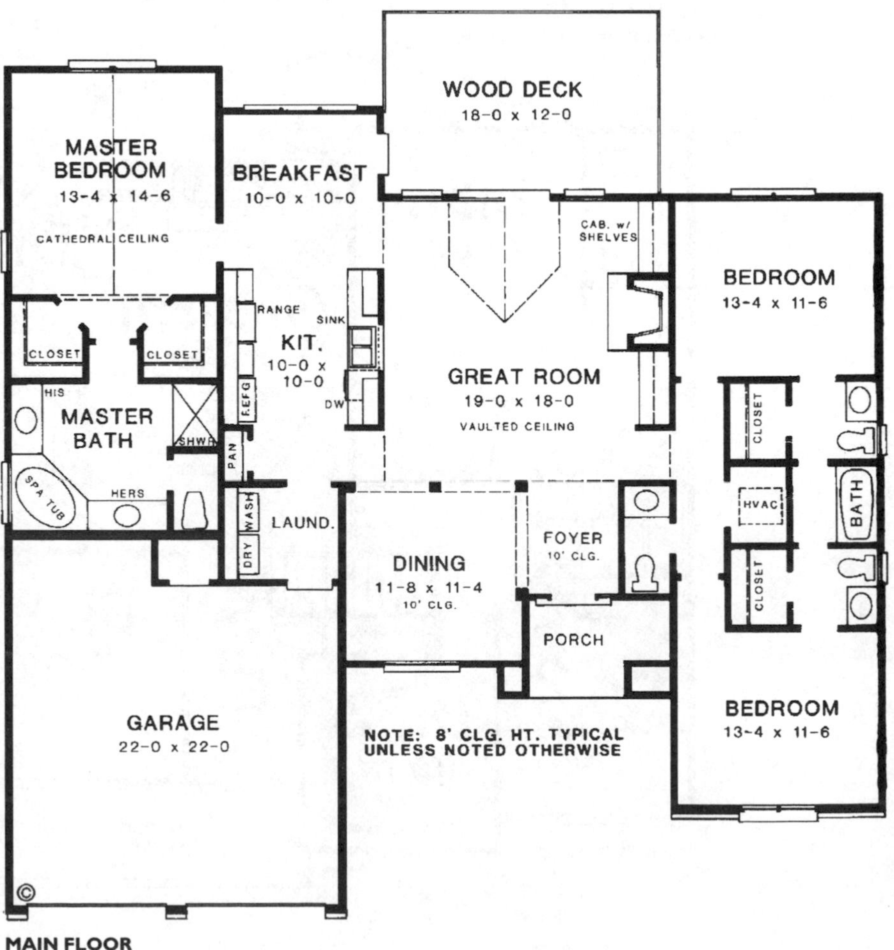

MAIN FLOOR

Design 98425

Units	Single
Price Code	C
Total Finished	1,845 sq. ft.
Main Finished	1,845 sq. ft.
Bonus Unfinished	409 sq. ft.
Basement Unfinished	1,845 sq. ft.
Garage Unfinished	529 sq. ft.
Dimensions	56'x60'
Foundation	Basement Crawlspace
Bedrooms	3
Full Baths	2
Half Baths	1
Main Ceiling	9'
Max Ridge Height	26'6"
Roof Framing	Stick
Exterior Walls	2x4

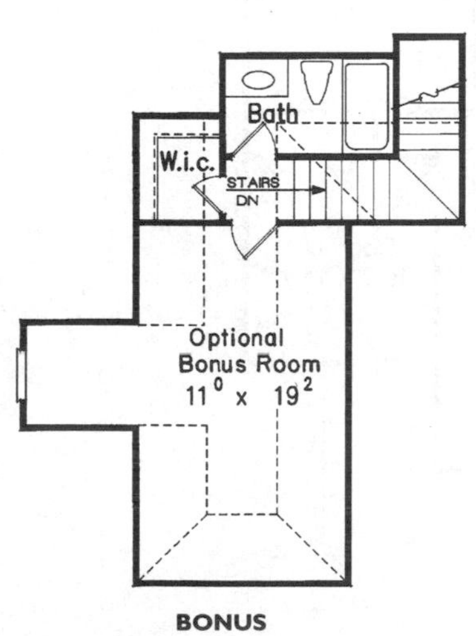

BONUS

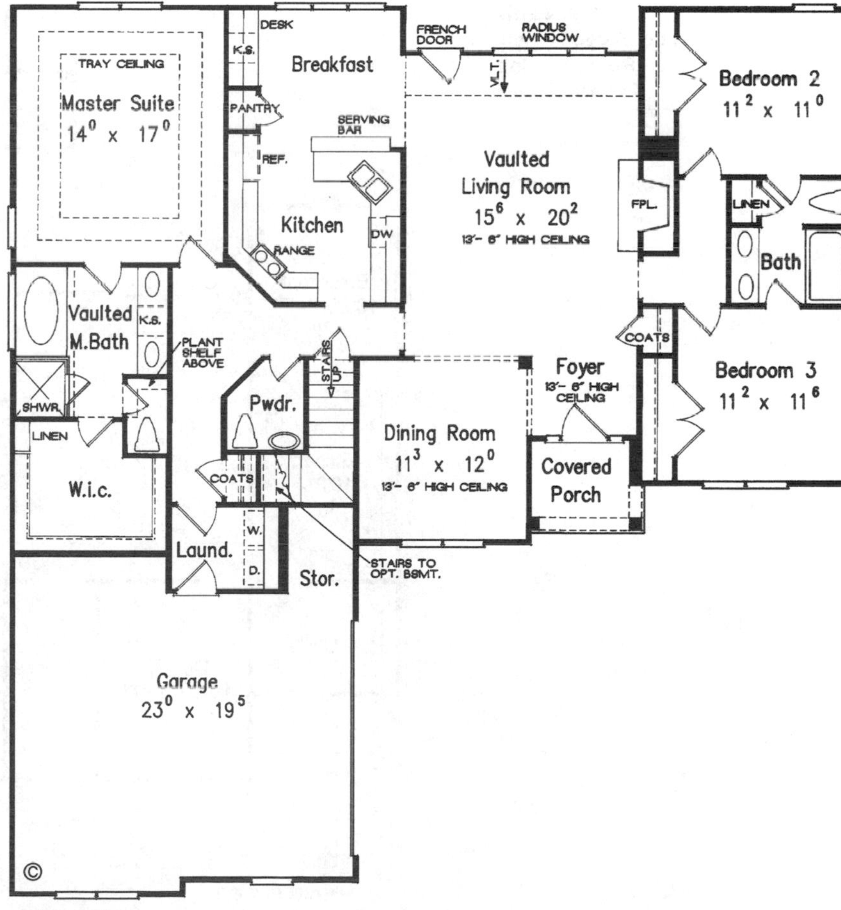

MAIN FLOOR

Design 94692

Units	Single
Price Code	C
Total Finished	1,847 sq. ft.
Main Finished	1,847 sq. ft.
Garage Unfinished	593 sq. ft.
Porch Unfinished	528 sq. ft.
Dimensions	49'6"x72'5"
Foundation	Slab
Bedrooms	3
Full Baths	2
Max Ridge Height	24'8"
Roof Framing	Stick
Exterior Walls	2x4

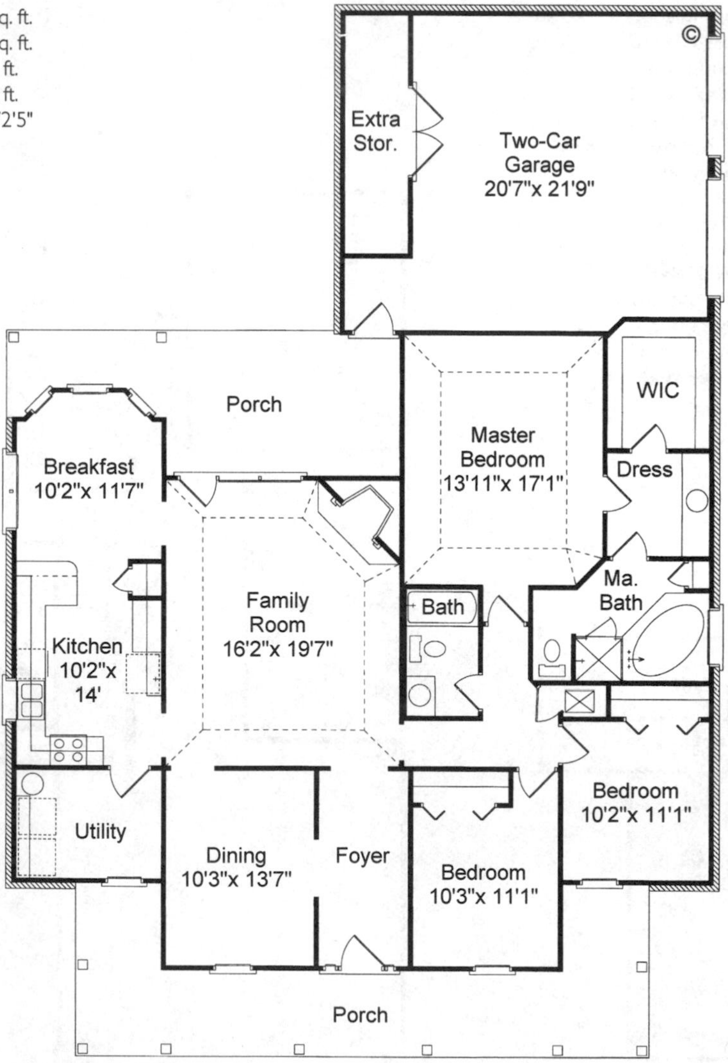

Extra Stor.
Two-Car Garage 20'7"x 21'9"
©
Porch
WIC
Master Bedroom 13'11"x 17'1"
Dress
Breakfast 10'2"x 11'7"
Family Room 16'2"x 19'7"
Ma. Bath
Bath
Kitchen 10'2"x 14'
Bedroom 10'2"x 11'1"
Utility
Dining 10'3"x 13'7"
Foyer
Bedroom 10'3"x 11'1"
Porch

MAIN FLOOR

Design 99434

Units	Single
Price Code	C
Total Finished	1,850 sq. ft.
Main Finished	1,850 sq. ft.
Garage Unfinished	487 sq. ft.
Dimensions	62'x48'
Foundation	Basement
Bedrooms	3
Full Baths	2
Main Ceiling	8'
Max Ridge Height	20'
Roof Framing	Stick
Exterior Walls	2x4

* Alternate foundation options available at an additional charge.
Please call 1-800-235-5700 for more information.

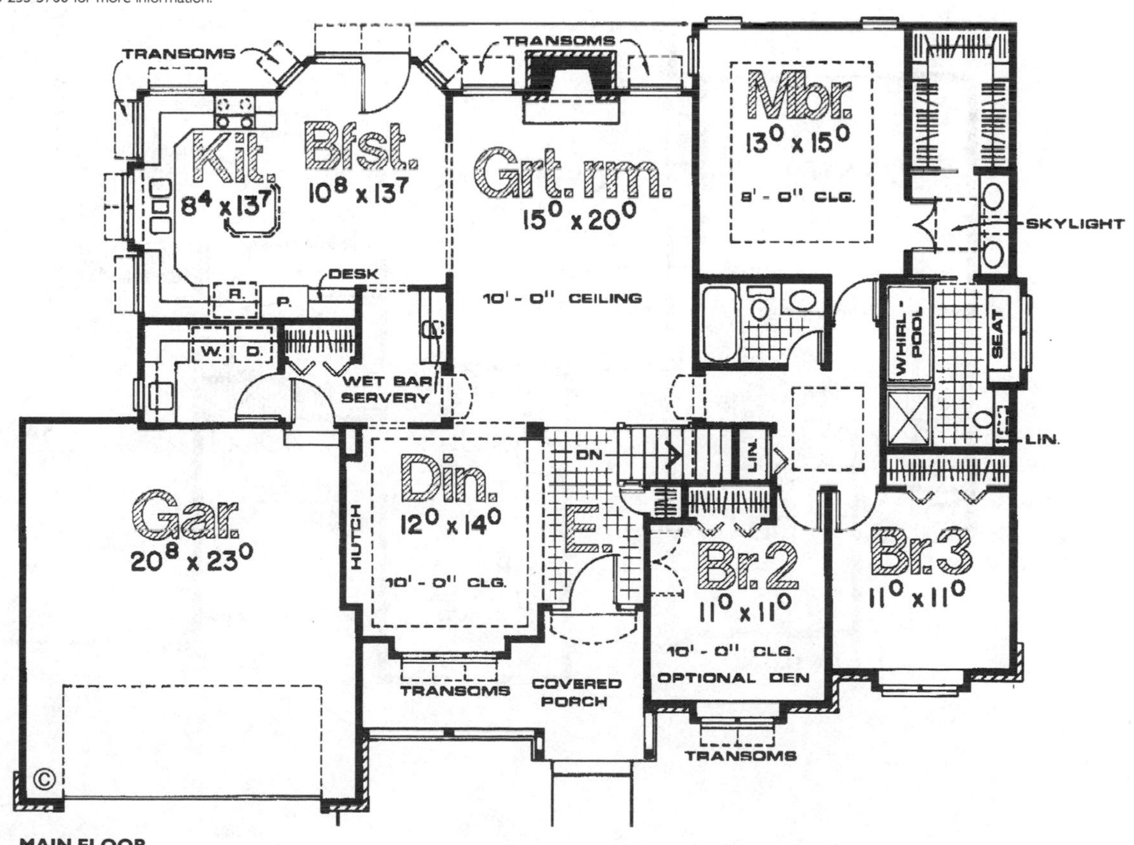

Design 81008

Units	Single
Price Code	C
Total Finished	1,852 sq. ft.
Main Finished	1,852 sq. ft.
Garage Unfinished	757 sq. ft.
Dimensions	70'x45'
Foundation	Crawlspace
Bedrooms	3
Full Baths	2

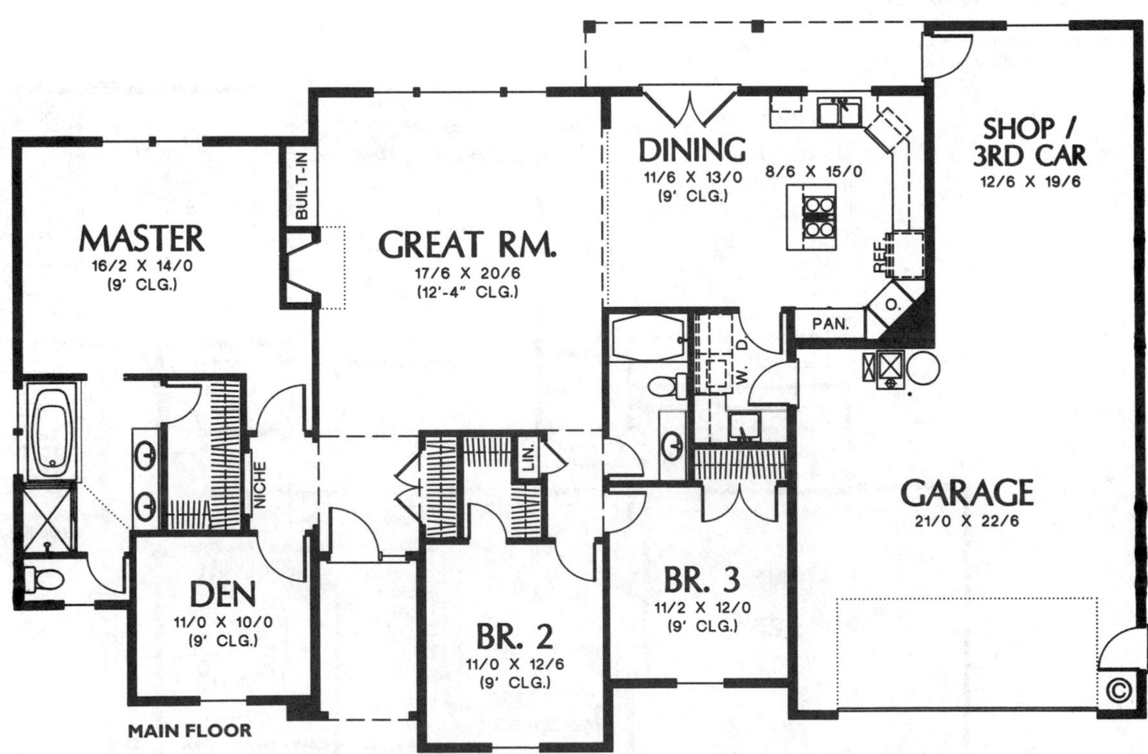

Design 97719

Units	Single
Price Code	C
Total Finished	1,855 sq. ft.
Main Finished	1,855 sq. ft.
Dimensions	66'3"x48'2"
Foundation	Basement
Bedrooms	3
Full Baths	2
Max Ridge Height	22'
Roof Framing	Stick
Exterior Walls	2x4

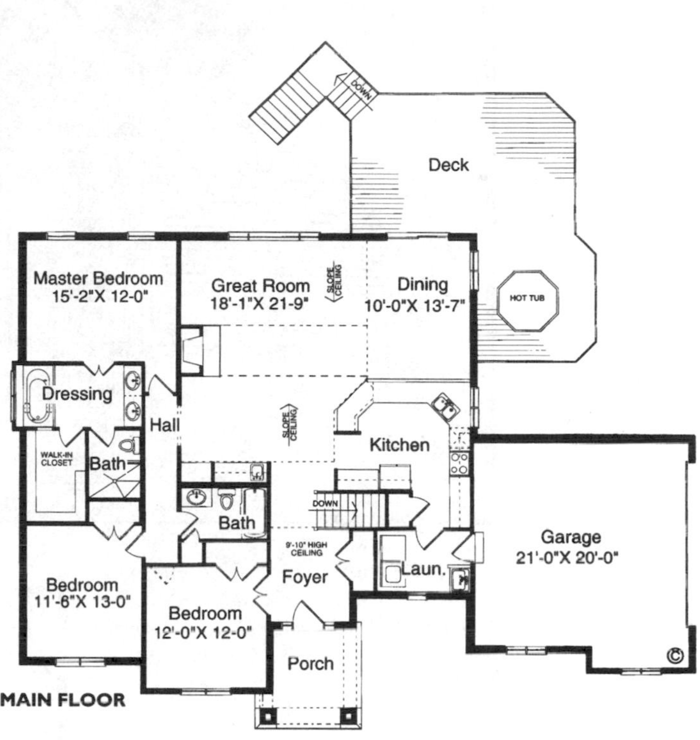

Design 94656

PHOTOGRAPHY: COURTESY OF THE DESIGNER

Units	Single
Price Code	C
Total Finished	1,856 sq. ft.
First Finished	1,046 sq. ft.
Second Finished	810 sq. ft.
Dimensions	28'x55'
Foundation	Crawlspace Pier/Post
Bedrooms	3
Full Baths	3
First Ceiling	9'
Second Ceiling	9'
Max Ridge Height	34'6"
Roof Framing	Stick
Exterior Walls	2x4

Please note: The photographed home may have been modified to suit homeowner preferences. If you order plans, have a builder or design professional check them against the photograph to confirm actual construction details.

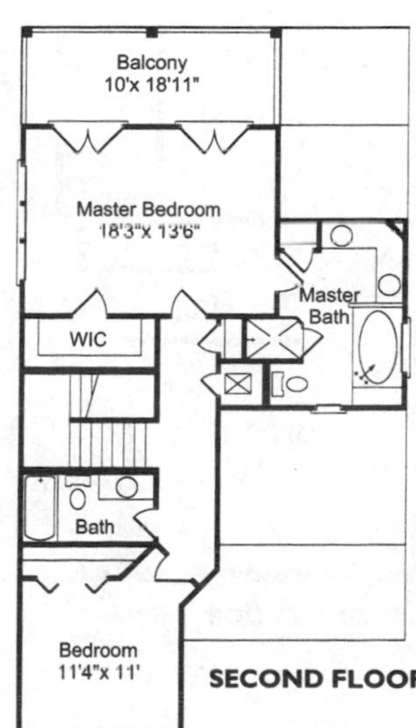

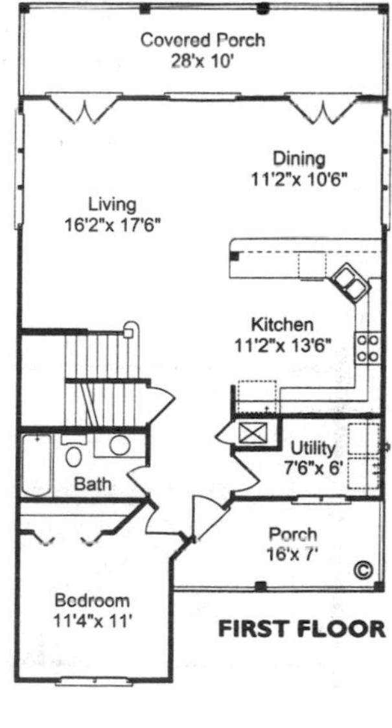

Design 97707

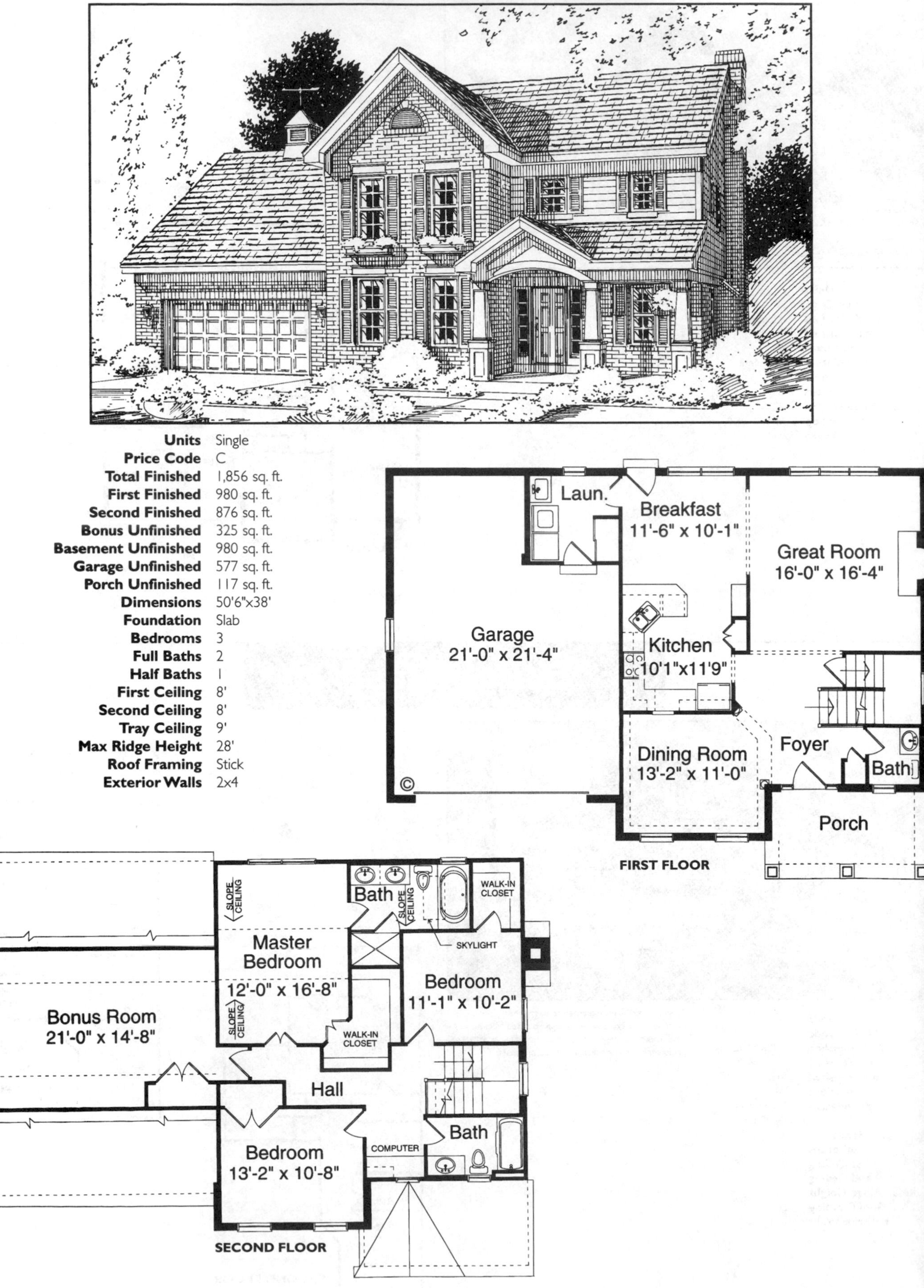

Units	Single
Price Code	C
Total Finished	1,856 sq. ft.
First Finished	980 sq. ft.
Second Finished	876 sq. ft.
Bonus Unfinished	325 sq. ft.
Basement Unfinished	980 sq. ft.
Garage Unfinished	577 sq. ft.
Porch Unfinished	117 sq. ft.
Dimensions	50'6"x38'
Foundation	Slab
Bedrooms	3
Full Baths	2
Half Baths	1
First Ceiling	8'
Second Ceiling	8'
Tray Ceiling	9'
Max Ridge Height	28'
Roof Framing	Stick
Exterior Walls	2x4

Design 98408

Units	Single
Price Code	C
Total Finished	1,856 sq. ft.
Main Finished	1,856 sq. ft.
Basement Unfinished	1,856 sq. ft.
Garage Unfinished	429 sq. ft.
Dimensions	59'x54'6"
Foundation	Basement Crawlspace Slab
Bedrooms	3
Full Baths	2
Main Ceiling	9'
Max Ridge Height	25'6"
Roof Framing	Stick
Exterior Walls	2x4

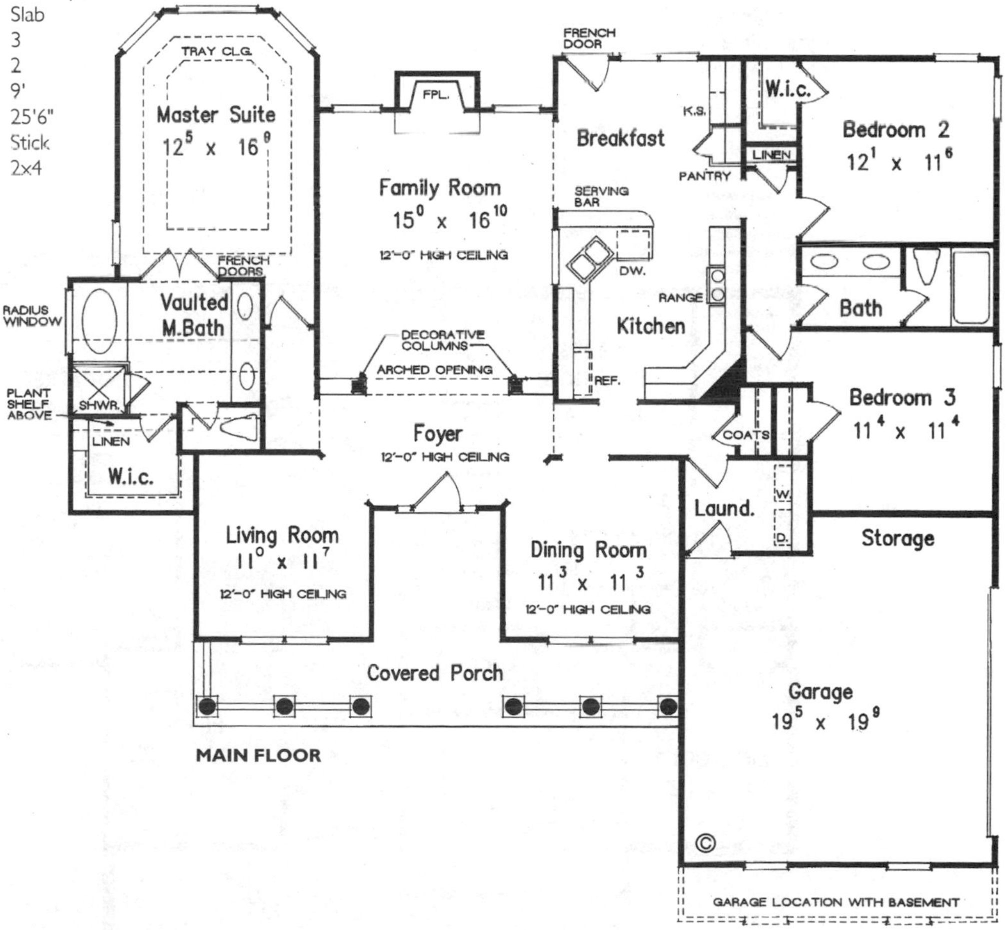

TRAY CLG.
Master Suite
12^5 x 16^9
FRENCH DOORS
RADIUS WINDOW
Vaulted M.Bath
PLANT SHELF ABOVE
SHWR.
LINEN
W.i.c.
FPL.
Family Room
15^0 x 16^{10}
12'-0" HIGH CEILING
DECORATIVE COLUMNS
ARCHED OPENING
Foyer
12'-0" HIGH CEILING
Living Room
11^0 x 11^7
12'-0" HIGH CEILING
Dining Room
11^3 x 11^3
12'-0" HIGH CEILING
Covered Porch
FRENCH DOOR
Breakfast
K.S.
PANTRY
SERVING BAR
DW.
RANGE
Kitchen
REF.
COATS
Laund.
W.
D.
W.i.c.
LINEN
Bedroom 2
12^1 x 11^6
Bath
Bedroom 3
11^4 x 11^4
Storage
Garage
19^5 x 19^9
©
GARAGE LOCATION WITH BASEMENT

MAIN FLOOR

Design 50034

PHOTOGRAPHY: COURTESY OF THE DESIGNER

Units	Single
Price Code	C
Total Finished	1,860 sq. ft.
Main Finished	1,860 sq. ft.
Basement Unfinished	1,860 sq. ft.
Dimensions	64'2"x44'2"
Foundation	Basement
Bedrooms	3
Full Baths	2
Main Ceiling	9'
Max Ridge Height	23'
Roof Framing	Truss
Exterior Walls	2x4

Please note: The photographed home may have been modified to suit homeowner preferences. If you order plans, have a builder or design professional check them against the photograph to confirm actual construction details.

Deck

WALK-IN CLOSET

Master Bedroom
12' x 14'6"
10'10" CEILING

ALCOVE 3'6" X 6'6"

TV ALCOVE

SLOPED CEILING

Great Room
16'6" x 21'2"
11'1" CEILING HT

Breakfast
12'9" x 13'

Porch
11'8" x 11'

Kitchen
12'6" x 10'11"

Laun.

HANGING SPACE

Dressing

STAIRS DOWN

Hall

Bath

PANTRY

Foyer

Dining Room
10'10" x 12'2"

Garage
19'8" x 23'2"

Bedroom
10' x 12'

Bedroom
11'3" x 11'1"

Porch

MAIN FLOOR

©

Design 99679

Units	Single
Price Code	C
Total Finished	1,860 sq. ft.
Main Finished	1,860 sq. ft.
Basement Unfinished	1,860 sq. ft.
Garage Unfinished	434 sq. ft.
Dimensions	57'4"x49'8"
Foundation	Basement Crawlspace Slab
Bedrooms	3
Full Baths	2
Main Ceiling	8'
Vaulted Ceiling	13'8"
Tray Ceiling	11'6"
Max Ridge Height	18'
Roof Framing	Stick
Exterior Walls	2x4

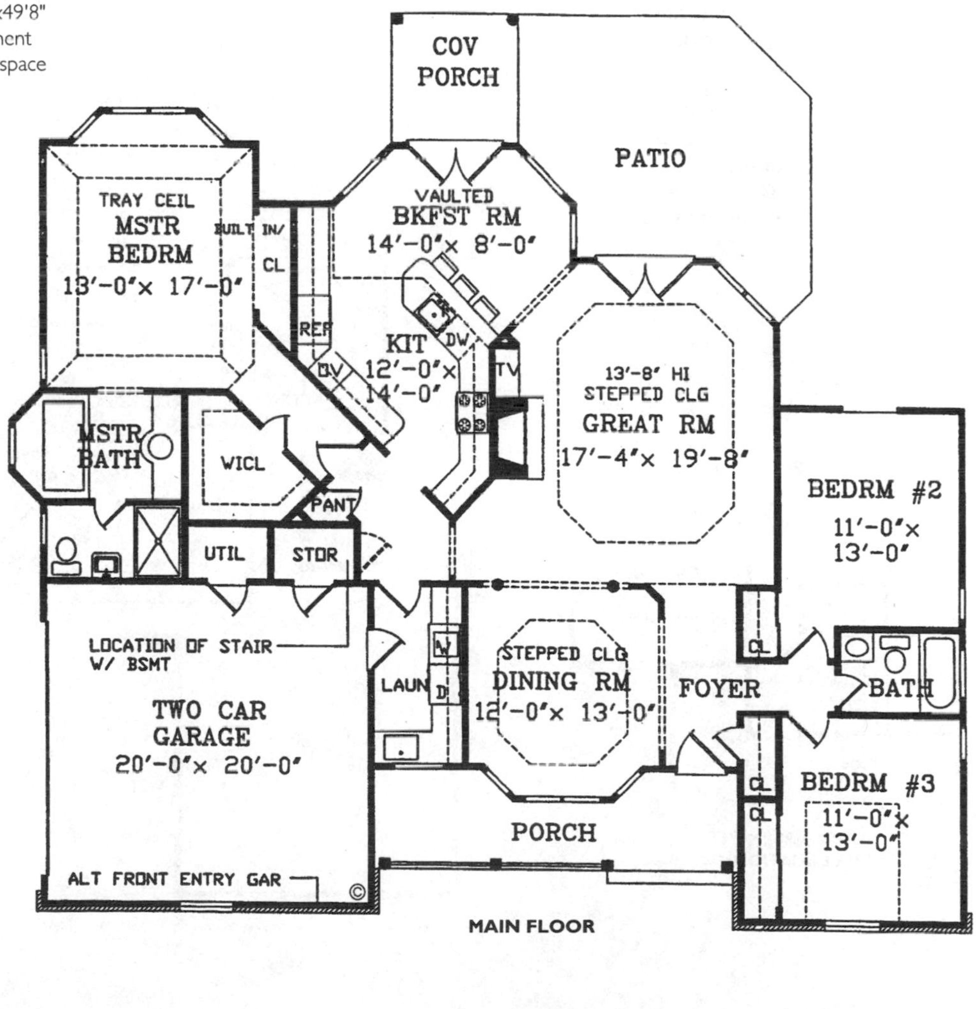

COV PORCH
PATIO
TRAY CEIL MSTR BEDRM 13'-0"× 17'-0"
BUILT IN/
CL
VAULTED BKFST RM 14'-0"× 8'-0"
REF
DW
OV
KIT 12'-0"× 14'-0"
TV
13'-8" HI STEPPED CLG GREAT RM 17'-4"× 19'-8"
MSTR BATH
WICL
PANT
UTIL
STOR
BEDRM #2 11'-0"× 13'-0"
CL
BATH
LOCATION OF STAIR W/ BSMT
LAUN
D
STEPPED CLG DINING RM 12'-0"× 13'-0"
FOYER
TWO CAR GARAGE 20'-0"× 20'-0"
CL
CL
BEDRM #3 11'-0"× 13'-0"
PORCH
ALT FRONT ENTRY GAR
©

MAIN FLOOR

Design 97616

Units	Single
Price Code	C
Total Finished	1,861 sq. ft.
Main Finished	1,861 sq. ft.
Basement Unfinished	1,898 sq. ft.
Garage Unfinished	450 sq. ft.
Dimensions	58'6"x56'
Foundation	Basement Crawlspace
Bedrooms	3
Full Baths	2
Half Baths	1
Max Ridge Height	24'6"
Roof Framing	Stick
Exterior Walls	2x4

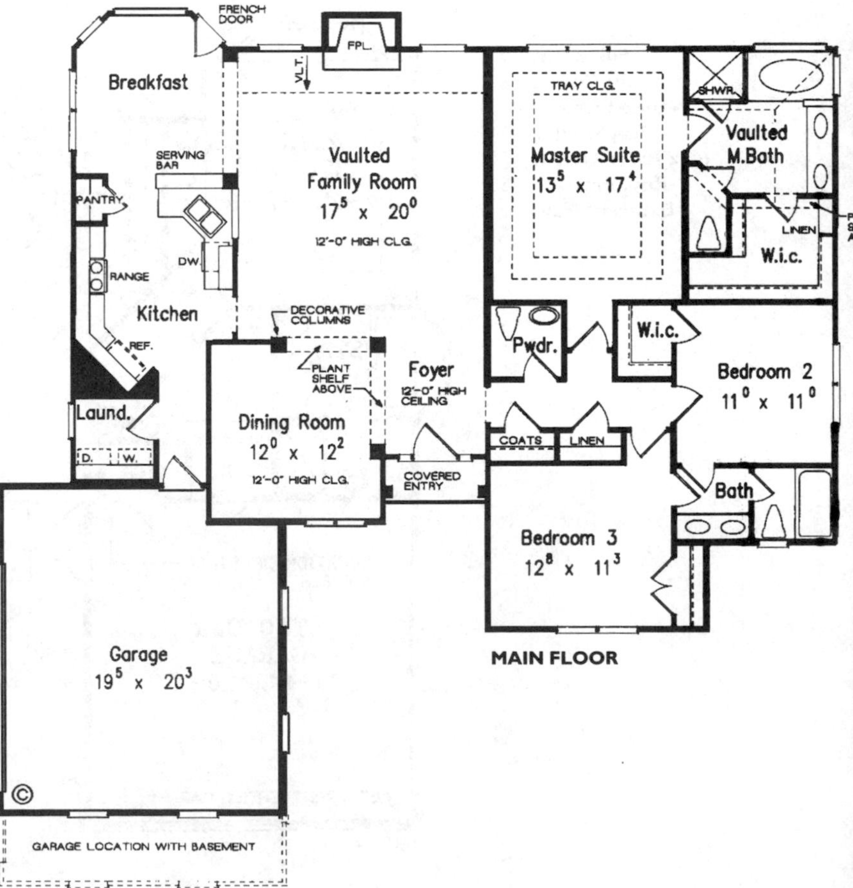

MAIN FLOOR

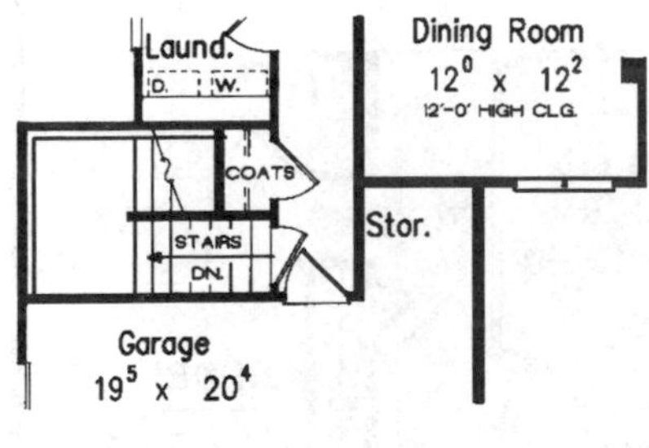

OPTIONAL BASEMENT STAIR LOCATION

Design 97777

Units	Single
Price Code	C
Total Finished	1,861 sq. ft.
Main Finished	1,861 sq. ft.
Basement Unfinished	1,861 sq. ft.
Garage Unfinished	433 sq. ft.
Deck Unfinished	120 sq. ft.
Porch Unfinished	21 sq. ft.
Dimensions	50'8"x59'10"
Foundation	Basement
Bedrooms	3
Full Baths	2
Main Ceiling	9'
Tray Ceiling	10'
Max Ridge Height	23'
Roof Framing	Truss
Exterior Walls	2x4

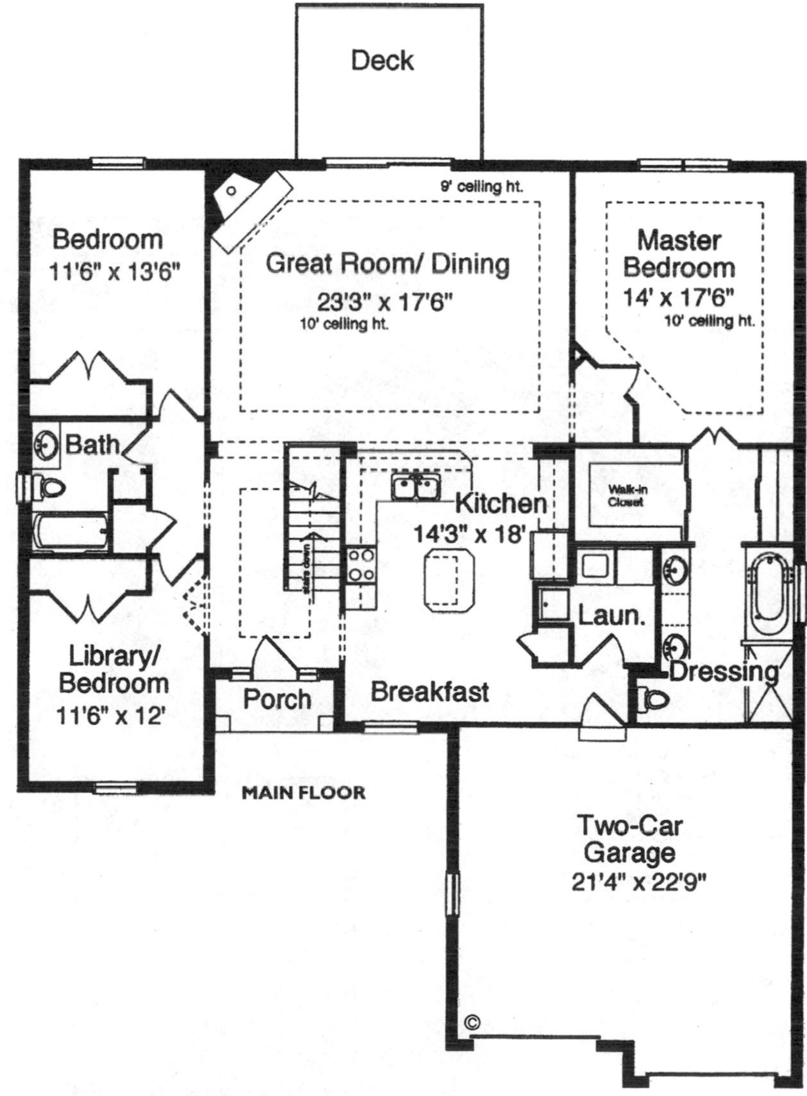

Design 91157

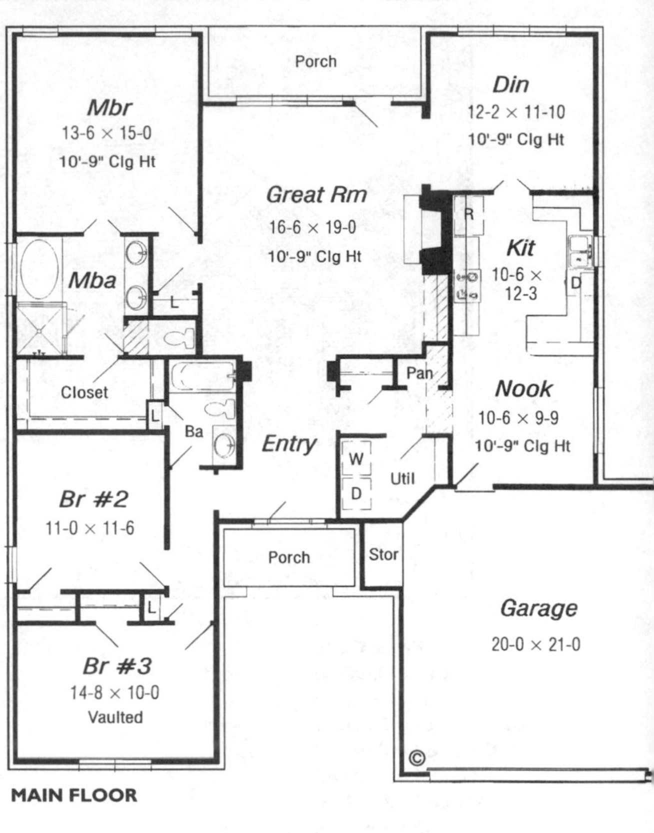

Units	Single
Price Code	C
Total Finished	1,862 sq. ft.
Main Finished	1,862 sq. ft.
Garage Unfinished	481 sq. ft.
Porch Unfinished	135 sq. ft.
Dimensions	50'4½"x56'11½"
Foundation	Crawlspace
Bedrooms	3
Full Baths	2

Design 65207

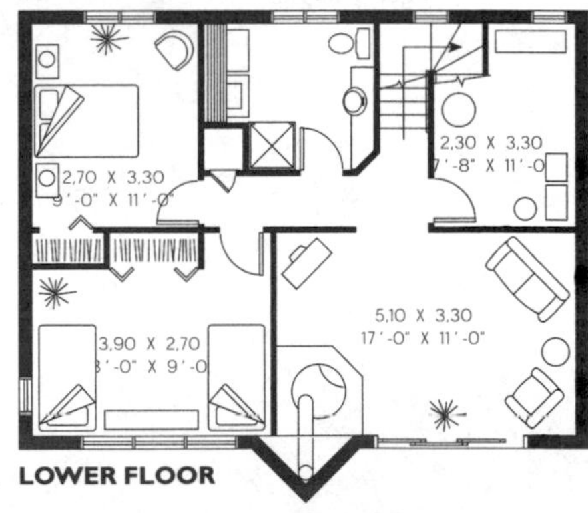

Units	Single
Price Code	C
Total Finished	1,864 sq. ft.
First Finished	790 sq. ft.
Second Finished	287 sq. ft.
Lower Finished	787 sq. ft.
Dimensions	32'4"x24'4"
Foundation	Basement
Bedrooms	3
Full Baths	1
3/4 Baths	1
Max Ridge Height	29'6"
Roof Framing	Truss

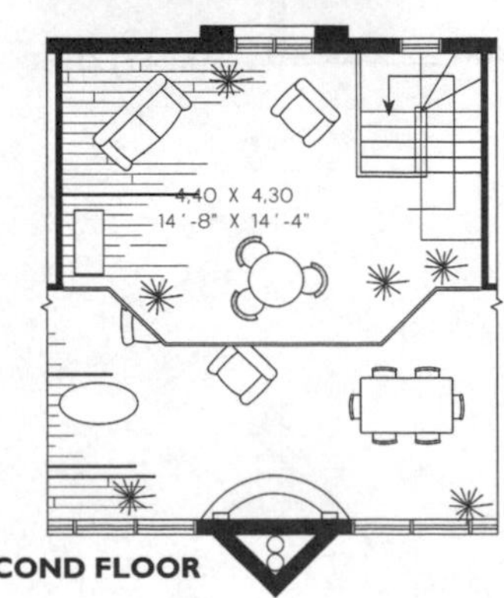

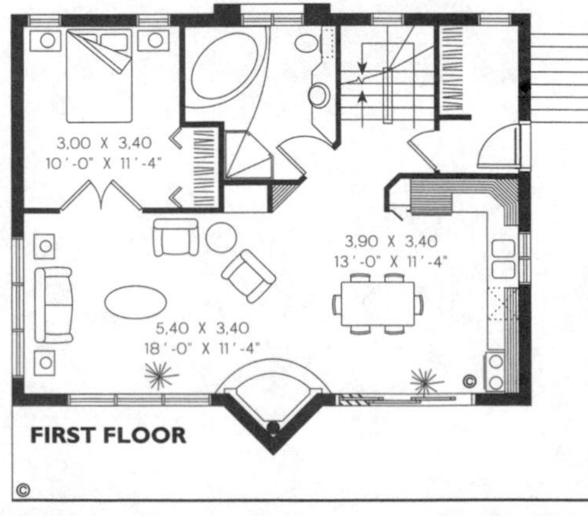

Design 65645

PHOTOGRAPHY: COURTESY OF THE DESIGNER

Please note: The photographed home may have been modified to suite homeowner preferences. If you order plans, have a builder or design professional check them against the photograph to confirm actual construction details.

Units	Single
Price Code	C
Total Finished	1,865 sq. ft.
Main Finished	1,865 sq. ft.
Dimensions	62'x64'
Foundation	Crawlspace Slab
Bedrooms	3
Full Baths	2
Main Ceiling	8'
Max Ridge Height	27'
Roof Framing	Stick
Exterior Walls	2x6

Design 93192

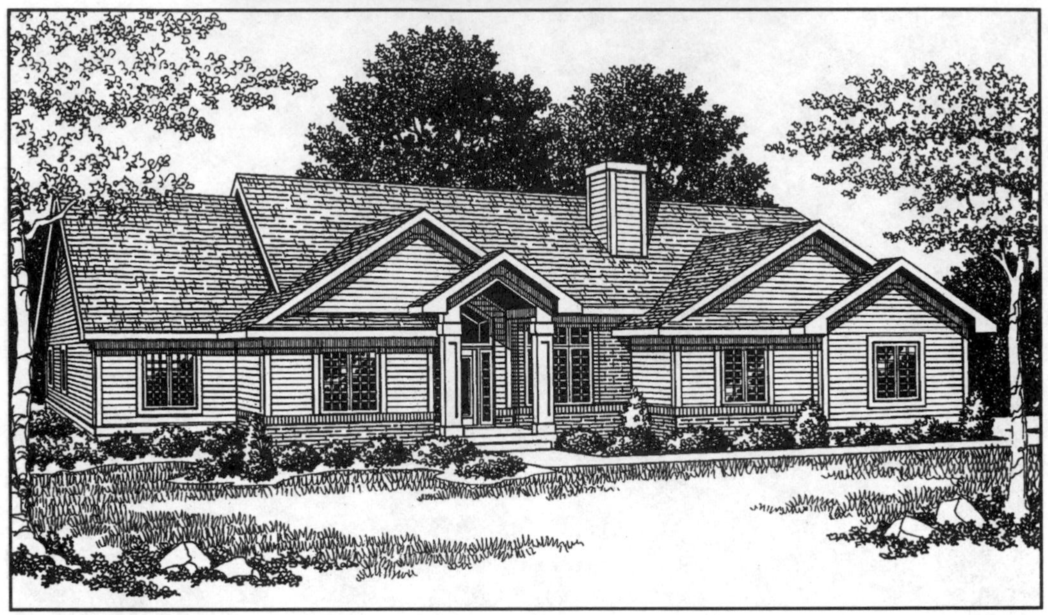

Units	Single
Price Code	C
Total Finished	1,868 sq. ft.
Main Finished	1,868 sq. ft.
Basement Unfinished	1,868 sq. ft.
Dimensions	72'x41'8"
Foundation	Basement
Bedrooms	3
Full Baths	2
Half Baths	1
Max Ridge Height	21'8"
Roof Framing	Truss
Exterior Walls	2x6

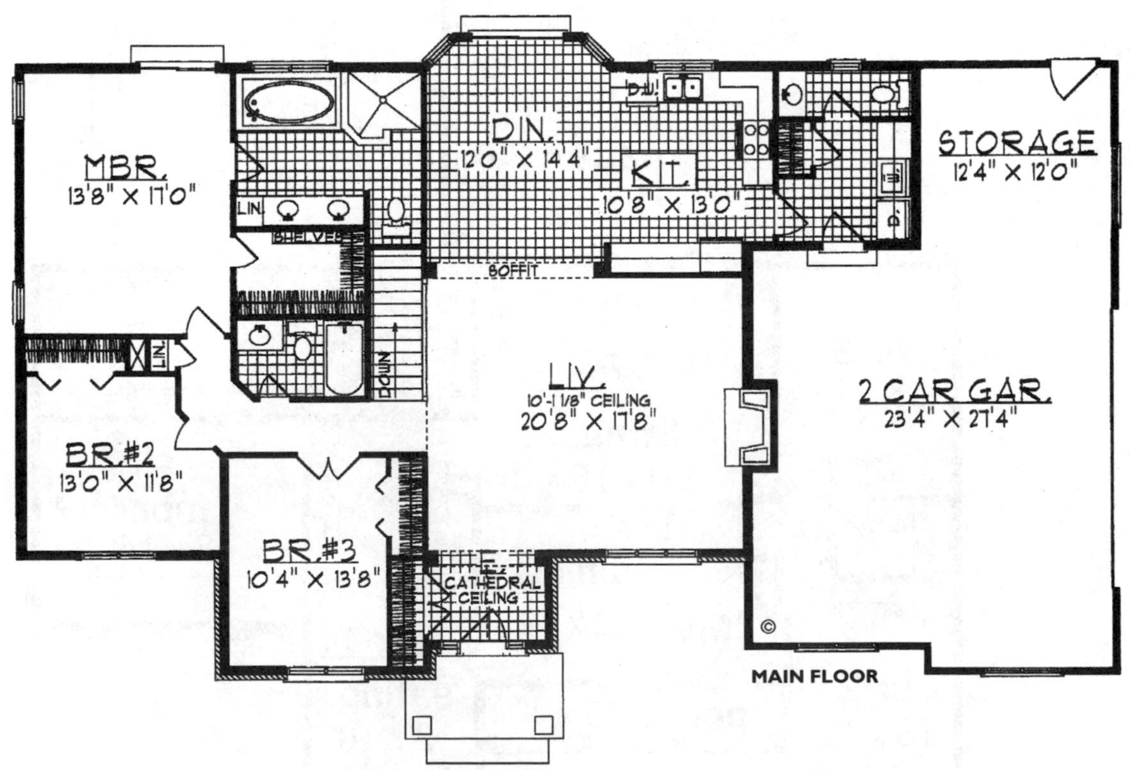

MAIN FLOOR

Design 63115

Units	Single
Price Code	C
Total Finished	1,869 sq. ft.
Main Finished	1,869 sq. ft.
Garage Unfinished	470 sq. ft.
Dimensions	61'8"x53'
Foundation	Slab
Bedrooms	3
Full Baths	2
Main Ceiling	10'
Max Ridge Height	20'
Roof Framing	Truss
Exterior Walls	2x4

MAIN FLOOR

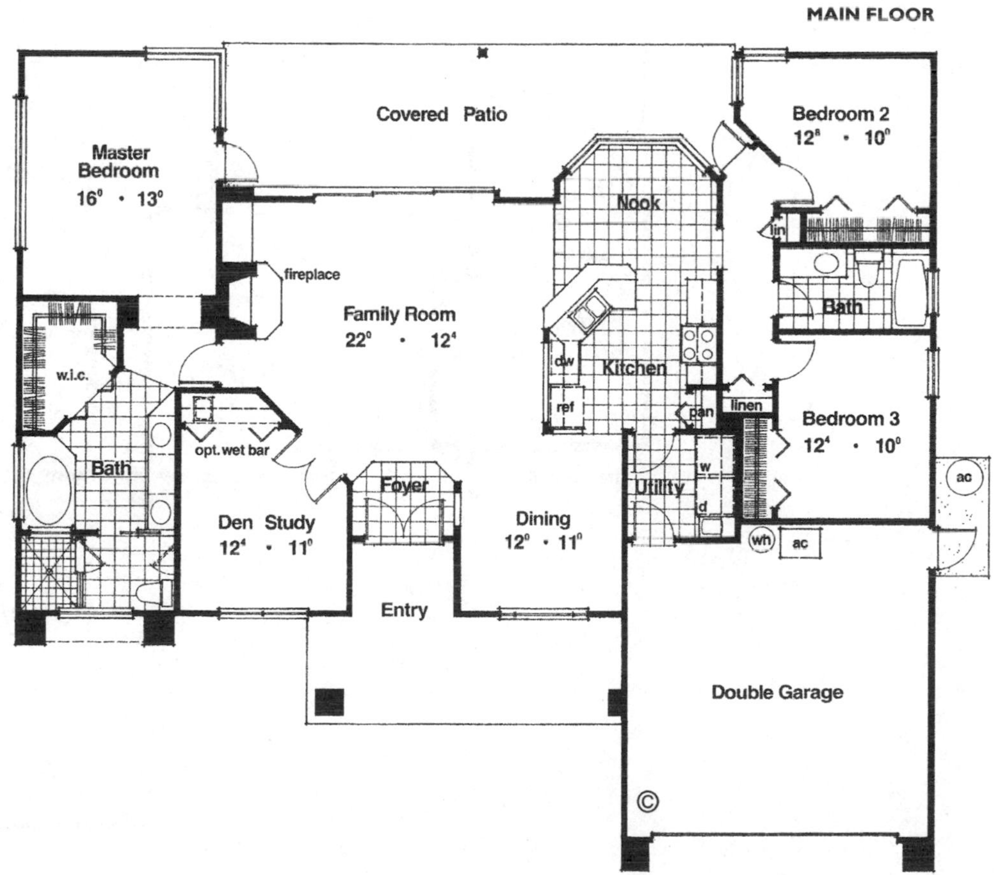

Design 98956

Units	Single
Price Code	C
Total Finished	1,869 sq. ft.
Main Finished	1,869 sq. ft.
Garage Unfinished	505 sq. ft.
Dimensions	54'x60'
Foundation	Basement Crawlspace Slab
Bedrooms	3
Full Baths	2
Main Ceiling	8'
Max Ridge Height	24'
Roof Framing	Stick
Exterior Walls	2x4

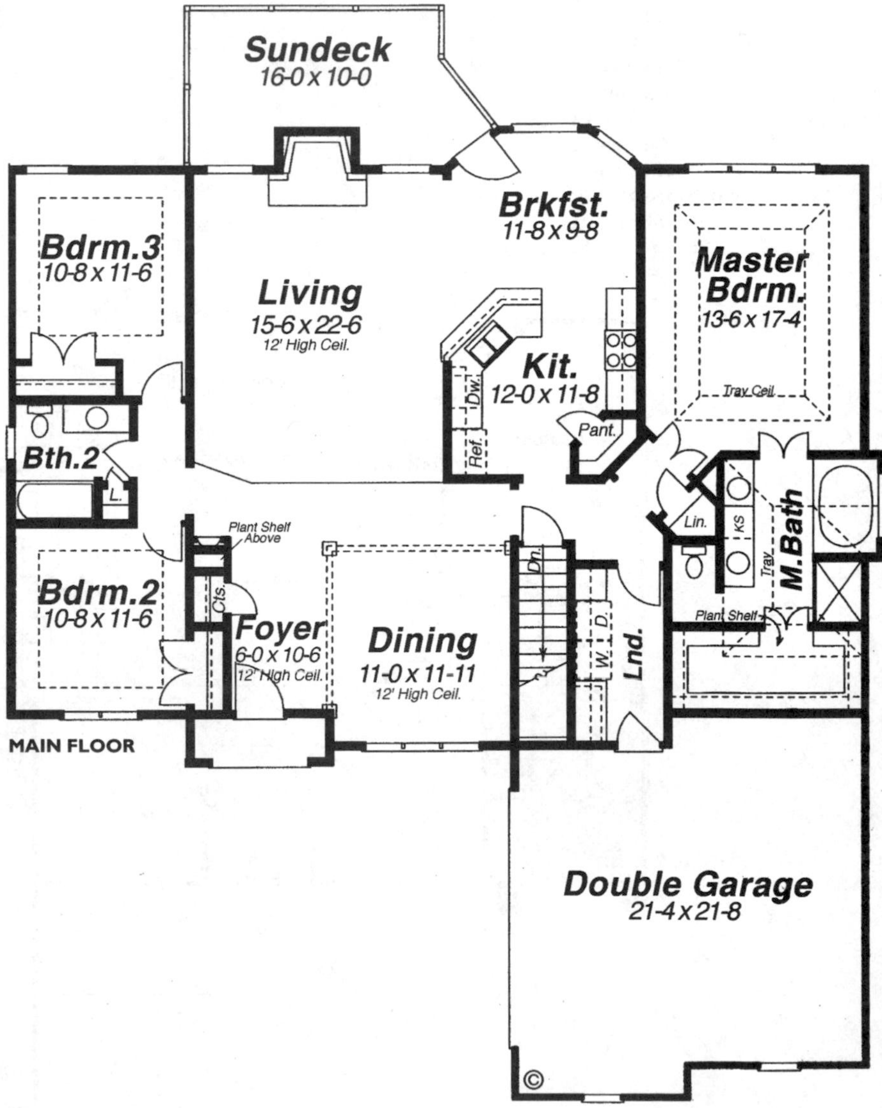

Design 63116

Units	Single
Price Code	C
Total Finished	1,872 sq. ft.
Main Finished	1,872 sq. ft.
Garage Unfinished	398 sq. ft.
Dimensions	40'x66'8"
Foundation	Slab
Bedrooms	3
Full Baths	1
3/4 Baths	1
Max Ridge Height	18'3"
Roof Framing	Truss

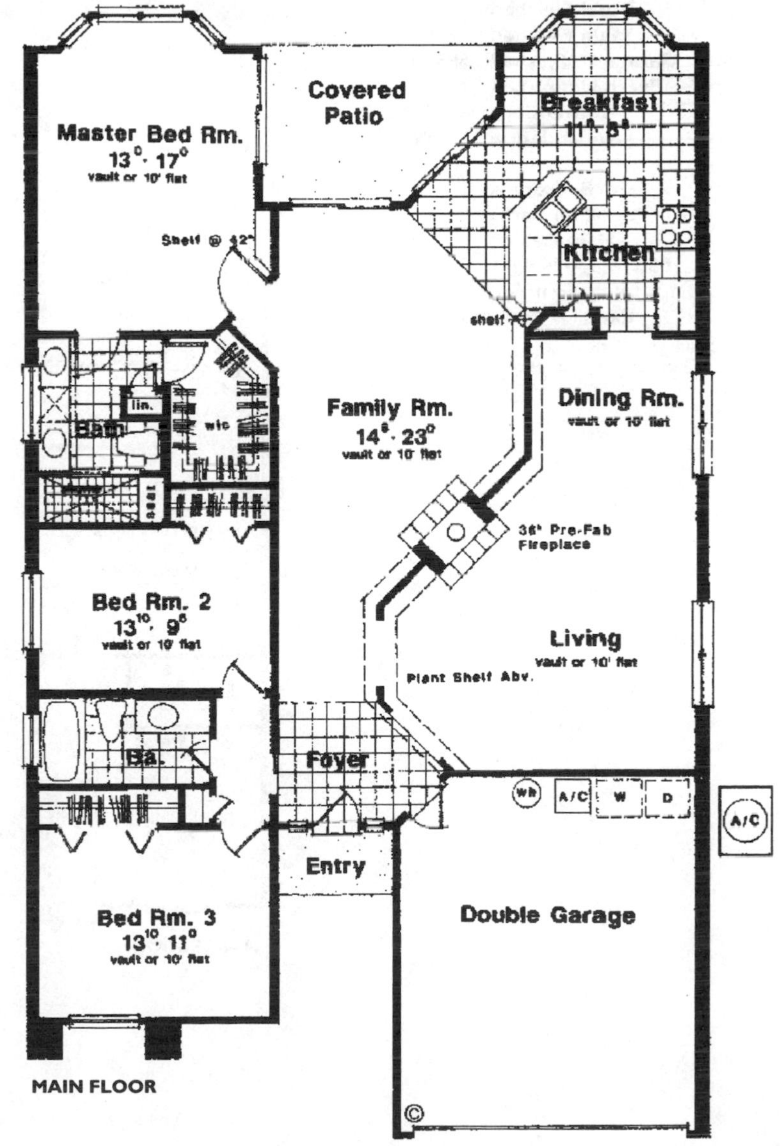

MAIN FLOOR

Design 93080

Units	Single
Price Code	C
Total Finished	1,890 sq. ft.
Main Finished	1,890 sq. ft.
Garage Unfinished	565 sq. ft.
Porch Unfinished	241 sq. ft.
Dimensions	65'10"x53'5"
Foundation	Crawlspace Slab
Bedrooms	3
Full Baths	2
Main Ceiling	10'
Max Ridge Height	21'6"
Roof Framing	Stick
Exterior Walls	2x4

* Alternate front porch and maximum ridge height available. See plan 96601 (page 297) for more information.

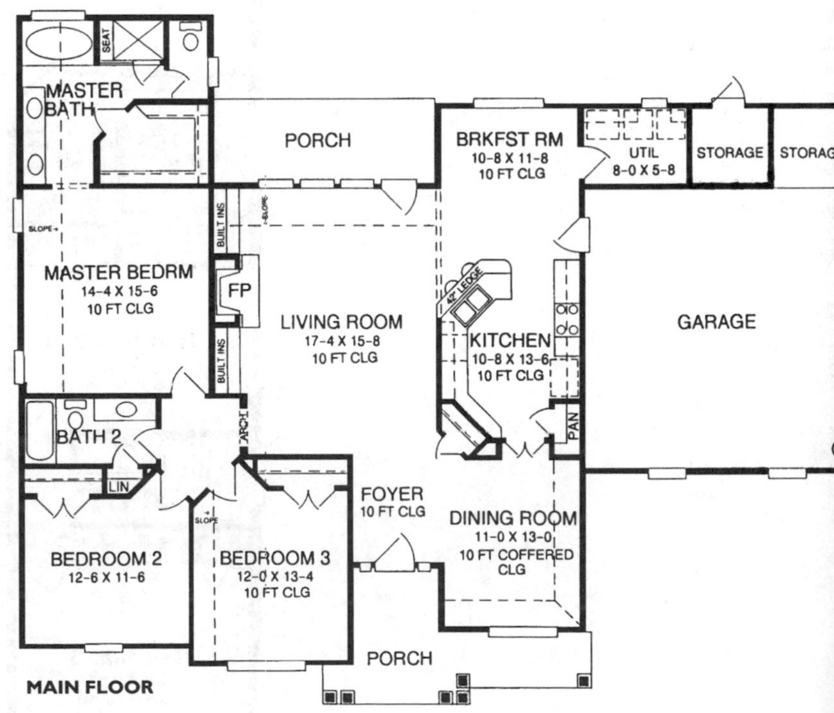

Design 96601

Units	Single
Price Code	C
Total Finished	1,890 sq. ft.
Main Finished	1,890 sq. ft.
Garage Unfinished	565 sq. ft.
Porch Unfinished	241 sq. ft.
Dimensions	65'10"x53'5"
Foundation	Crawlspace Slab
Bedrooms	3
Full Baths	2
Max Ridge Height	21'4"
Roof Framing	Stick
Exterior Walls	2x4

* Alternate front porch and maximum ridge height available. See plan 93080 (page 296) for more information.

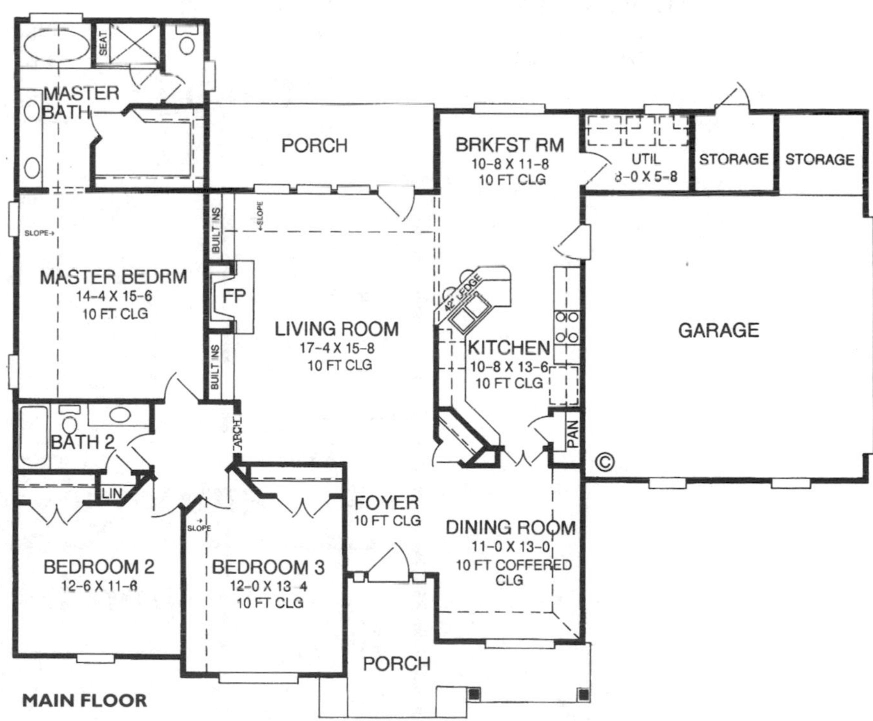

Design 65624

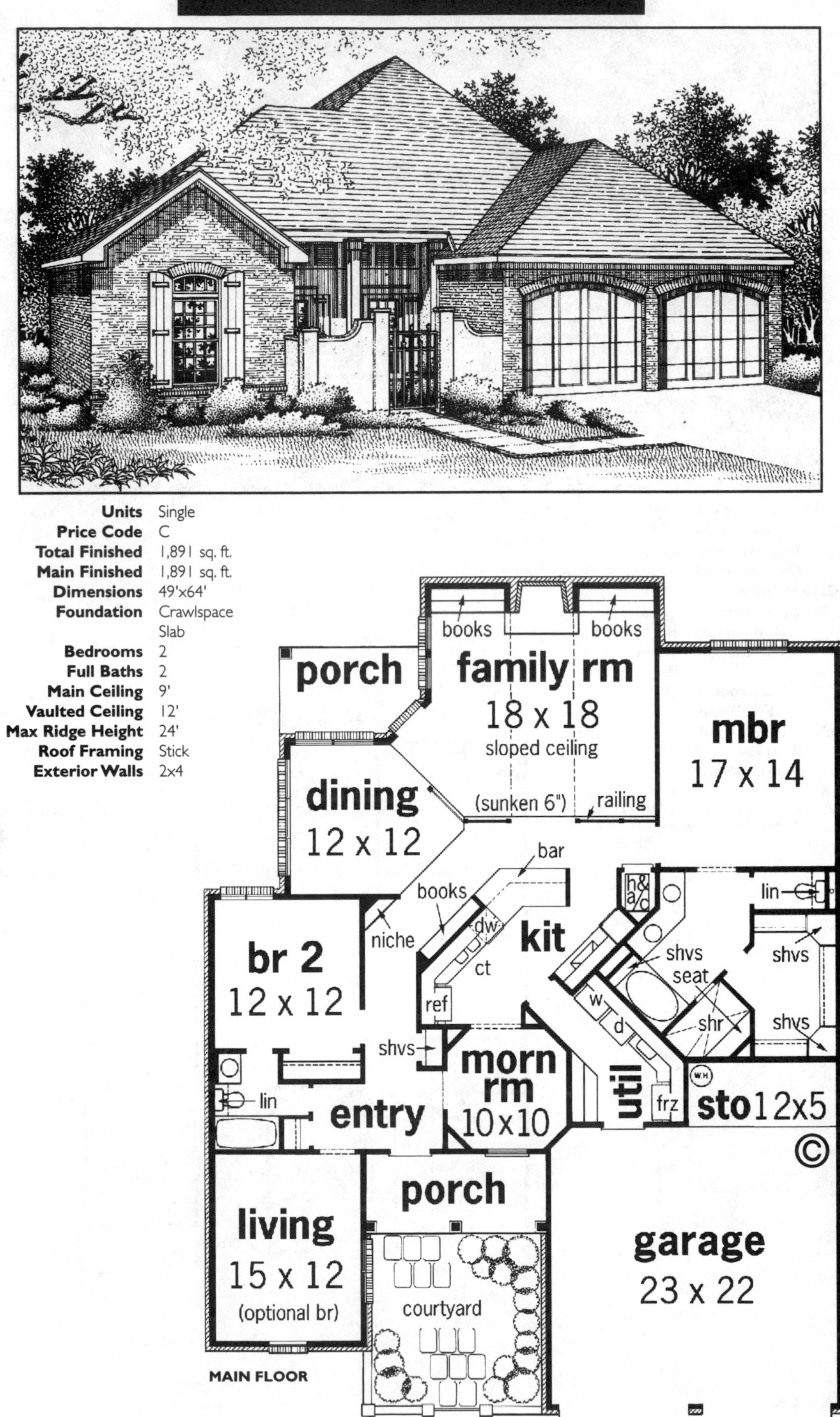

Units	Single
Price Code	C
Total Finished	1,891 sq. ft.
Main Finished	1,891 sq. ft.
Dimensions	49'x64'
Foundation	Crawlspace Slab
Bedrooms	2
Full Baths	2
Main Ceiling	9'
Vaulted Ceiling	12'
Max Ridge Height	24'
Roof Framing	Stick
Exterior Walls	2x4

Design 63045

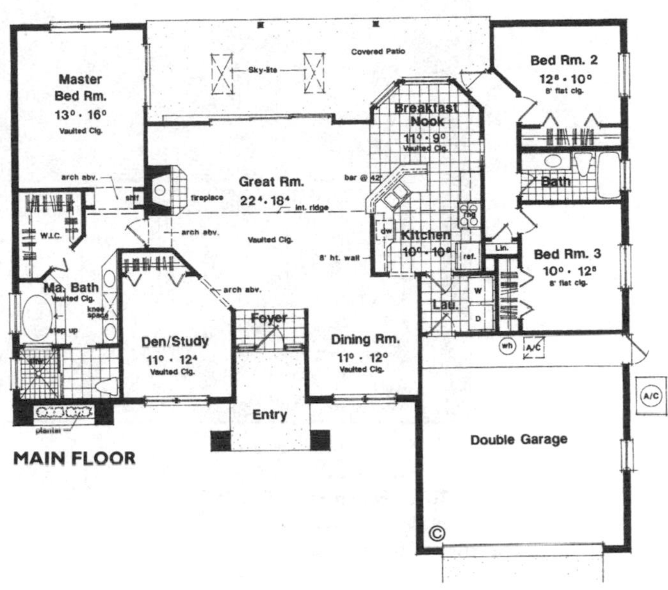

Units	Single
Price Code	C
Total Finished	1,901 sq. ft.
Main Finished	1,901 sq. ft.
Garage Unfinished	484 sq. ft.
Porch Unfinished	383 sq. ft.
Dimensions	62'x53'8"
Foundation	Slab
Bedrooms	3
Full Baths	2
Main Ceiling	8'
Max Ridge Height	20'
Roof Framing	Truss

Design 98589

Units	Single
Price Code	C
Total Finished	1,902 sq. ft.
Main Finished	1,902 sq. ft.
Garage Unfinished	636 sq. ft.
Deck Unfinished	210 sq. ft.
Porch Unfinished	185 sq. ft.
Dimensions	84'7"x34'5"
Foundation	Slab
Bedrooms	3
Full Baths	2
Half Baths	1
Roof Framing	Stick
Exterior Walls	2x4

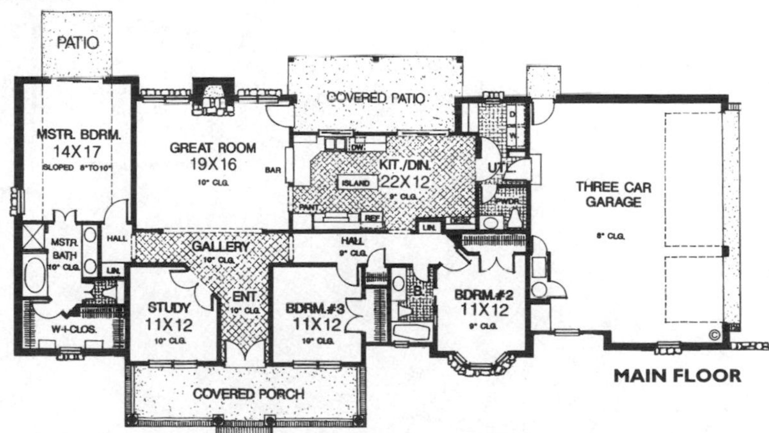

Units	Single
Price Code	C
Total Finished	1,904 sq. ft.
Main Finished	1,904 sq. ft.
Basement Unfinished	1,904 sq. ft.
Garage Unfinished	612 sq. ft.
Dimensions	98'x42'
Foundation	Basement
Bedrooms	2
Full Baths	2
Main Ceiling	11'
Max Ridge Height	24'8"
Roof Framing	Stick
Exterior Walls	2x6

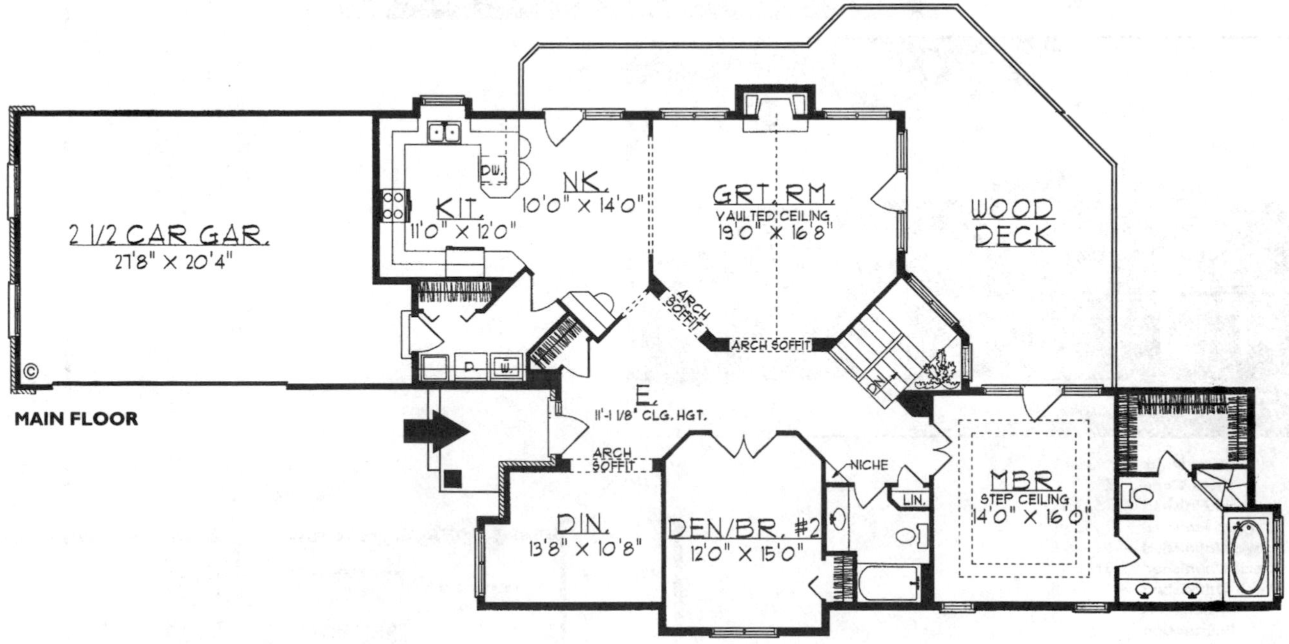

MAIN FLOOR

Design 63141

Units	Single
Price Code	C
Total Finished	1,906 sq. ft.
Main Finished	1,906 sq. ft.
Garage Unfinished	441 sq. ft.
Dimensions	58'2"x59'10"
Foundation	Slab
Bedrooms	4
Full Baths	2
Main Ceiling	8'
Max Ridge Height	18'5"
Roof Framing	Truss

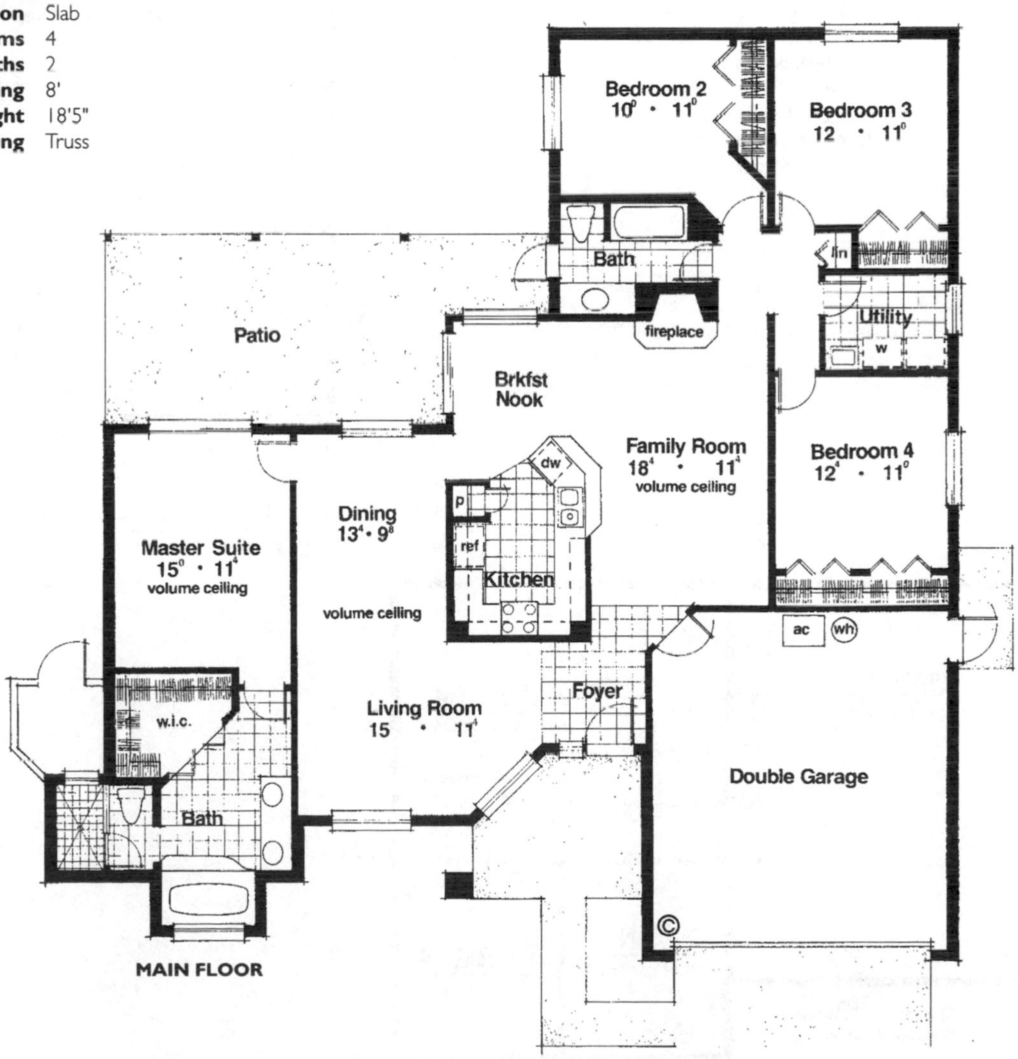

Bedroom 2
$10^{0} \cdot 11^{0}$

Bedroom 3
$12 \cdot 11^{0}$

Bath

lin

Utility

w

Patio

fireplace

Brkfst
Nook

Family Room
$18^{4} \cdot 11^{4}$
volume ceiling

Bedroom 4
$12^{4} \cdot 11^{0}$

dw

p

ref

Kitchen

Dining
$13^{4} \cdot 9^{8}$

volume ceiling

Master Suite
$15^{0} \cdot 11^{4}$
volume ceiling

ac

wh

w.i.c.

Foyer

Living Room
$15 \cdot 11^{4}$

Double Garage

Bath

©

MAIN FLOOR

Design 91839

Units	Single
Price Code	C
Total Finished	1,906 sq. ft.
Main Finished	1,224 sq. ft.
Lower Finished	682 sq. ft.
Basement Unfinished	520 sq. ft.
Dimensions	42'x32'
Foundation	Basement
Bedrooms	4
Full Baths	3
Max Ridge Height	21'4"
Roof Framing	Truss
Exterior Walls	2x6

MAIN FLOOR

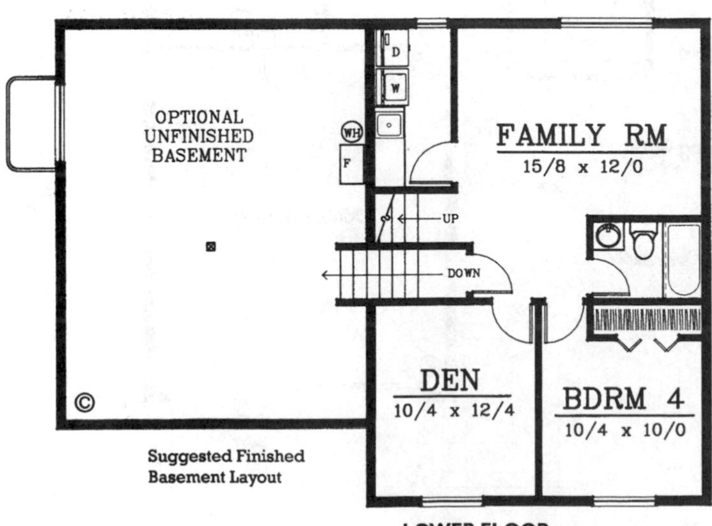

LOWER FLOOR

Design 99113

Units	Single
Price Code	C
Total Finished	1,906 sq. ft.
Main Finished	1,906 sq. ft.
Basement Unfinished	1,906 sq. ft.
Dimensions	72'x44'8"
Foundation	Basement
Bedrooms	3
Full Baths	2
Half Baths	1
Max Ridge Height	12'4"
Roof Framing	Truss
Exterior Walls	2x6

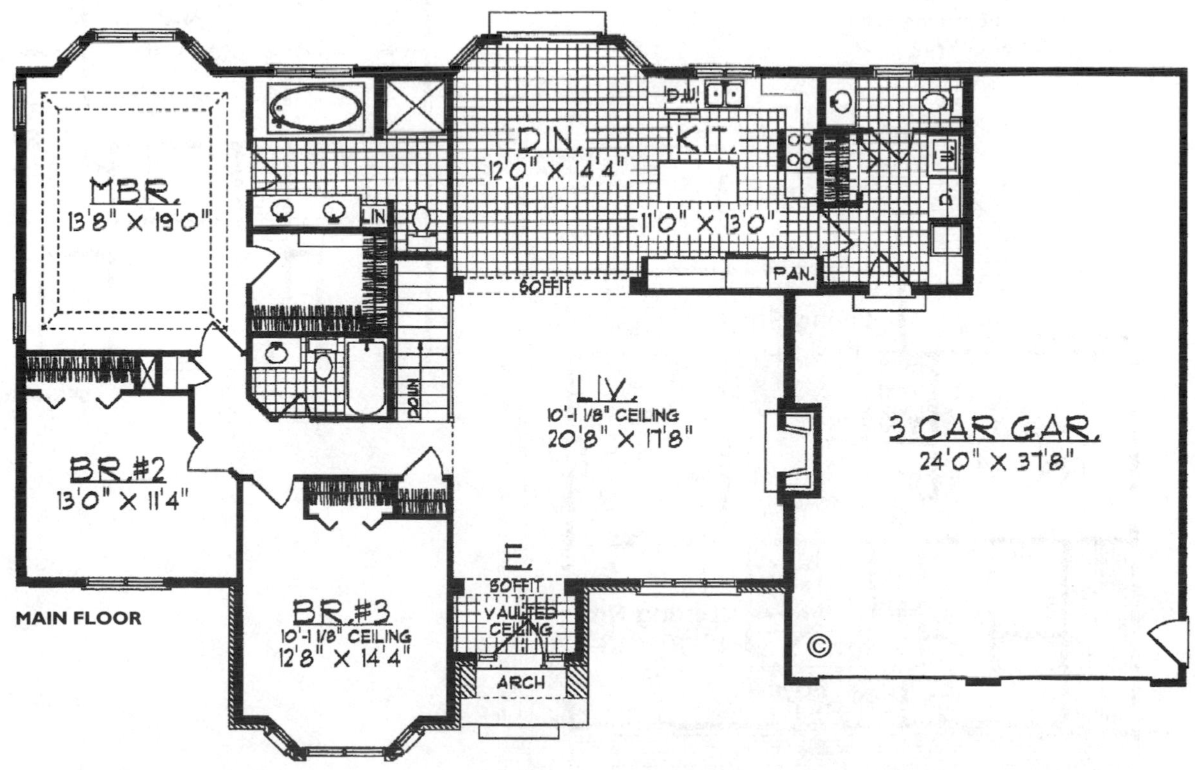

MAIN FLOOR

Design 10785

Units	Single
Price Code	C
Total Finished	1,907 sq. ft.
First Finished	1,269 sq. ft.
Second Finished	638 sq. ft.
Basement Unfinished	1,269 sq. ft.
Dimensions	47'x39'
Foundation	Basement Crawlspace Slab
Bedrooms	3
Full Baths	2
Half Baths	1
First Ceiling	8'
Second Ceiling	8'
Max Ridge Height	24'
Roof Framing	Stick
Exterior Walls	2x6

CRAWLSPACE/SLAB FOUNDATION OPTION

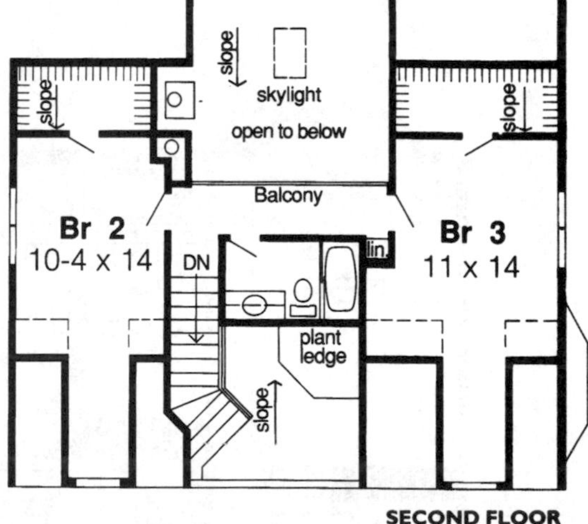

SECOND FLOOR

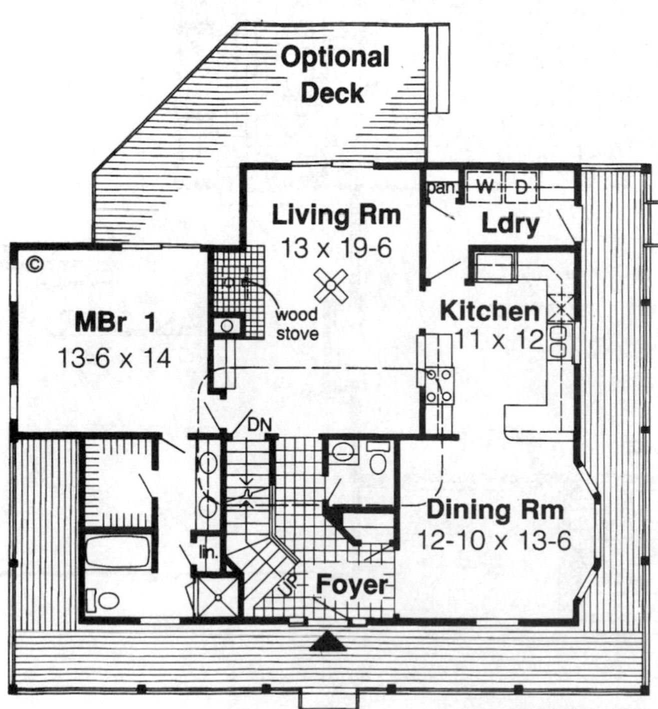

FIRST FLOOR

Design 66084

Units	Single
Price Code	C
Total Finished	1,907 sq. ft.
Main Finished	1,907 sq. ft.
Bonus Unfinished	369 sq. ft.
Garage Unfinished	430 sq. ft.
Deck Unfinished	160 sq. ft.
Porch Unfinished	85 sq. ft.
Dimensions	52'x59'9"
Foundation	Slab
Bedrooms	3
Full Baths	2
Max Ridge Height	26'
Roof Framing	Stick
Exterior Walls	2x4

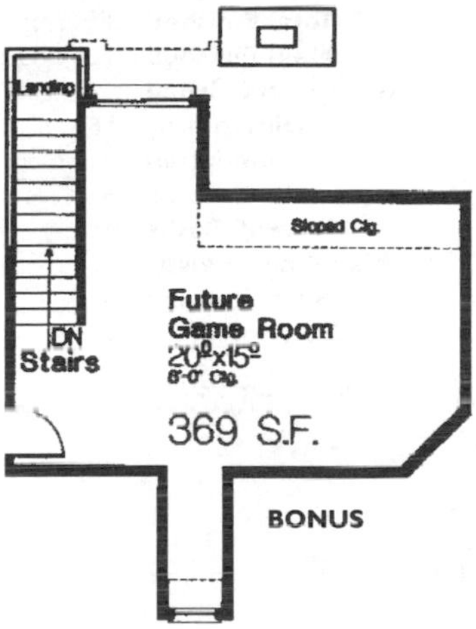

Landing
Sloped Clg.
DN Stairs
Future Game Room 20⁰x15⁰ 8'-0" Clg.
369 S.F.

BONUS

Sitting
Oval Window
Stairs
UP
42" brick F.P.
Line of Floor Above
Covered Patio 7⁰x18⁰
Dining 12⁰x10⁰
MstrBed 15²x17⁹ Vaulted Clg. 8'-0" to 10'-0"
T.V. Space
GreatRm 20⁰x19⁶ 9'-0" Clg.
Kitchen 12⁰x11¹
Pantry
Coats
Hall
Mstr. Bath
Util
Ent
Line of Floor Above
Bed#3 10⁰x11⁰ 9'-0" Clg.
Hall
Linen
Bath two
Walk-in Closet
Covered Porch
Walk-in Closet
Bed#2 13⁰x13⁶ 9'-0" Clg.
Walk-in Closet
Double Garage

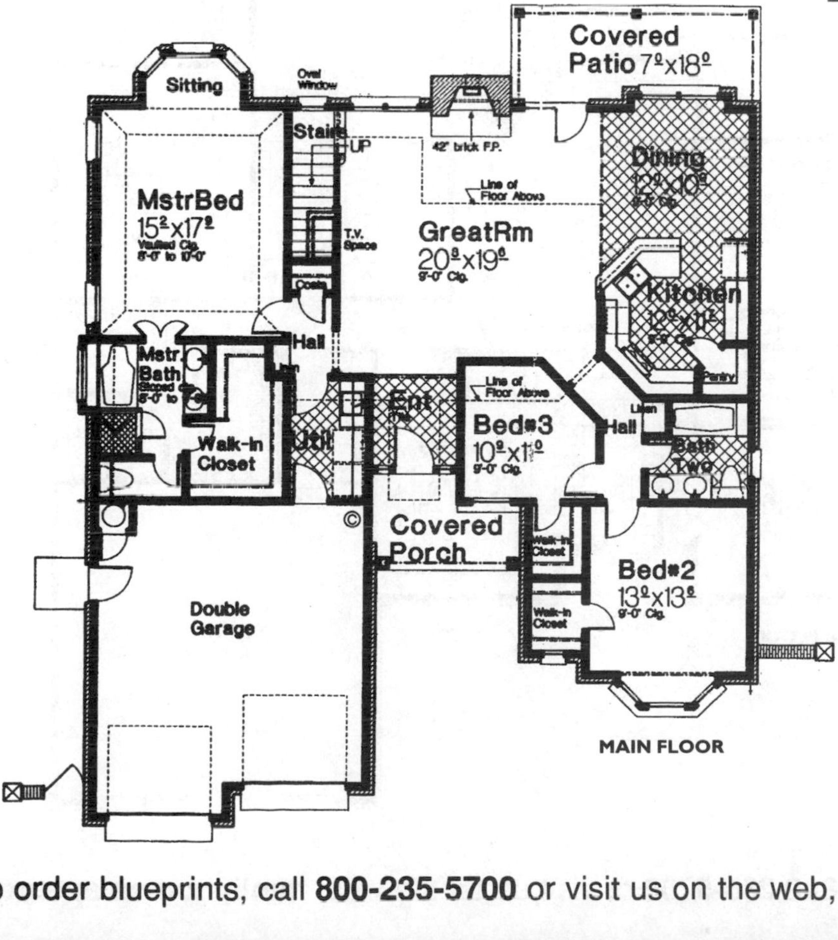

MAIN FLOOR

Design 94966

Units	Single
Price Code	C
Total Finished	1,911 sq. ft.
Main Finished	1,911 sq. ft.
Garage Unfinished	481 sq. ft.
Dimensions	56'x58'
Foundation	Basement
Bedrooms	3
Full Baths	2
Max Ridge Height	22'7"
Roof Framing	Stick
Exterior Walls	2x4

* Alternate foundation options available at an additional charge. Please call 1-800-235-5700 for more information.

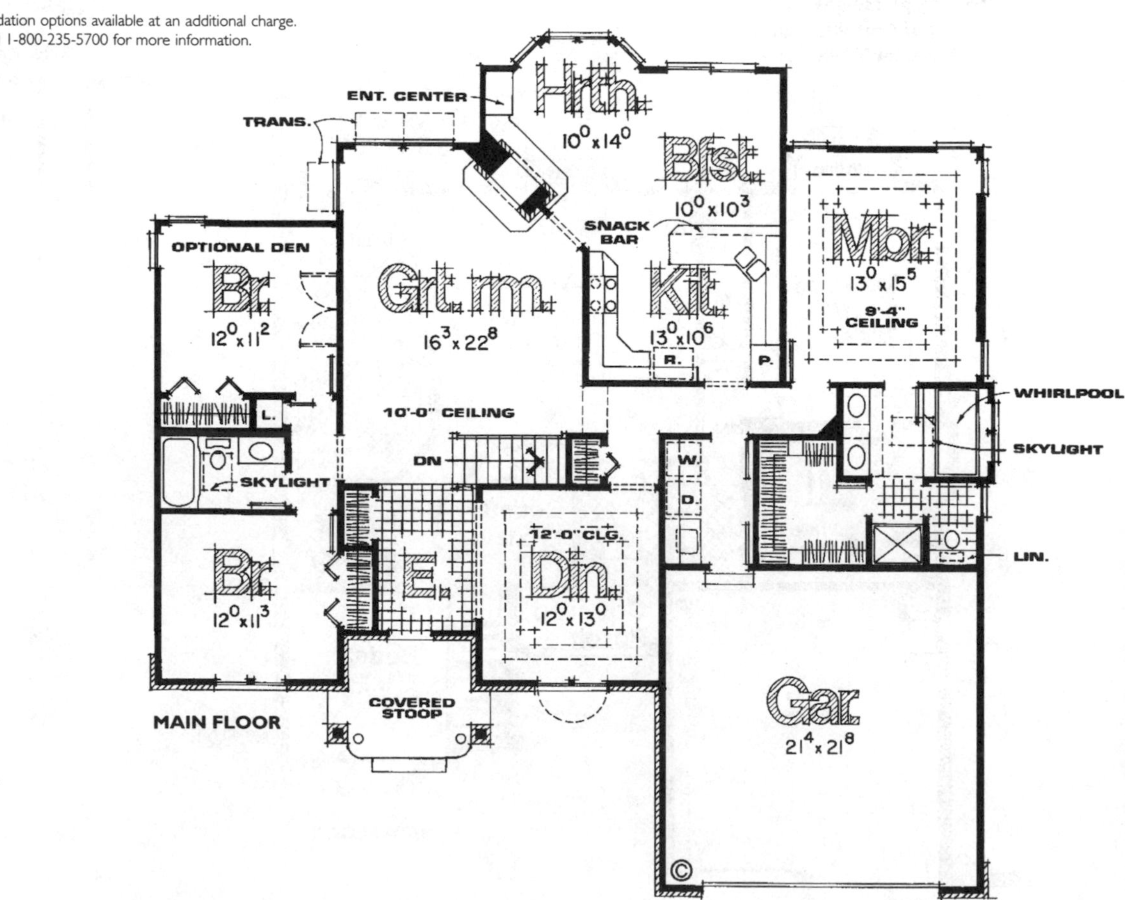

Design 97618

Units	Single
Price Code	C
Total Finished	1,915 sq. ft.
Main Finished	1,915 sq. ft.
Basement Unfinished	1,932 sq. ft.
Garage Unfinished	489 sq. ft.
Dimensions	56'6"x57'6"
Foundation	Basement Crawlspace
Bedrooms	4
Full Baths	3
Max Ridge Height	22'6"
Roof Framing	Stick
Exterior Walls	2x4

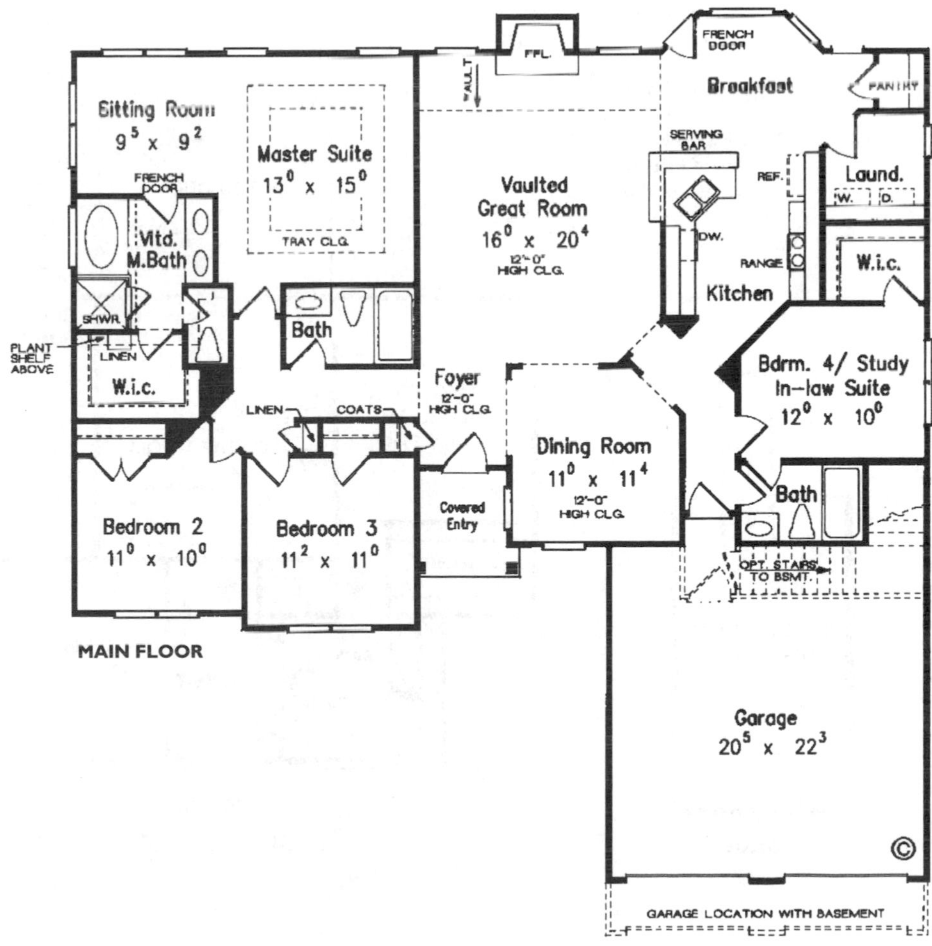

Design 90480

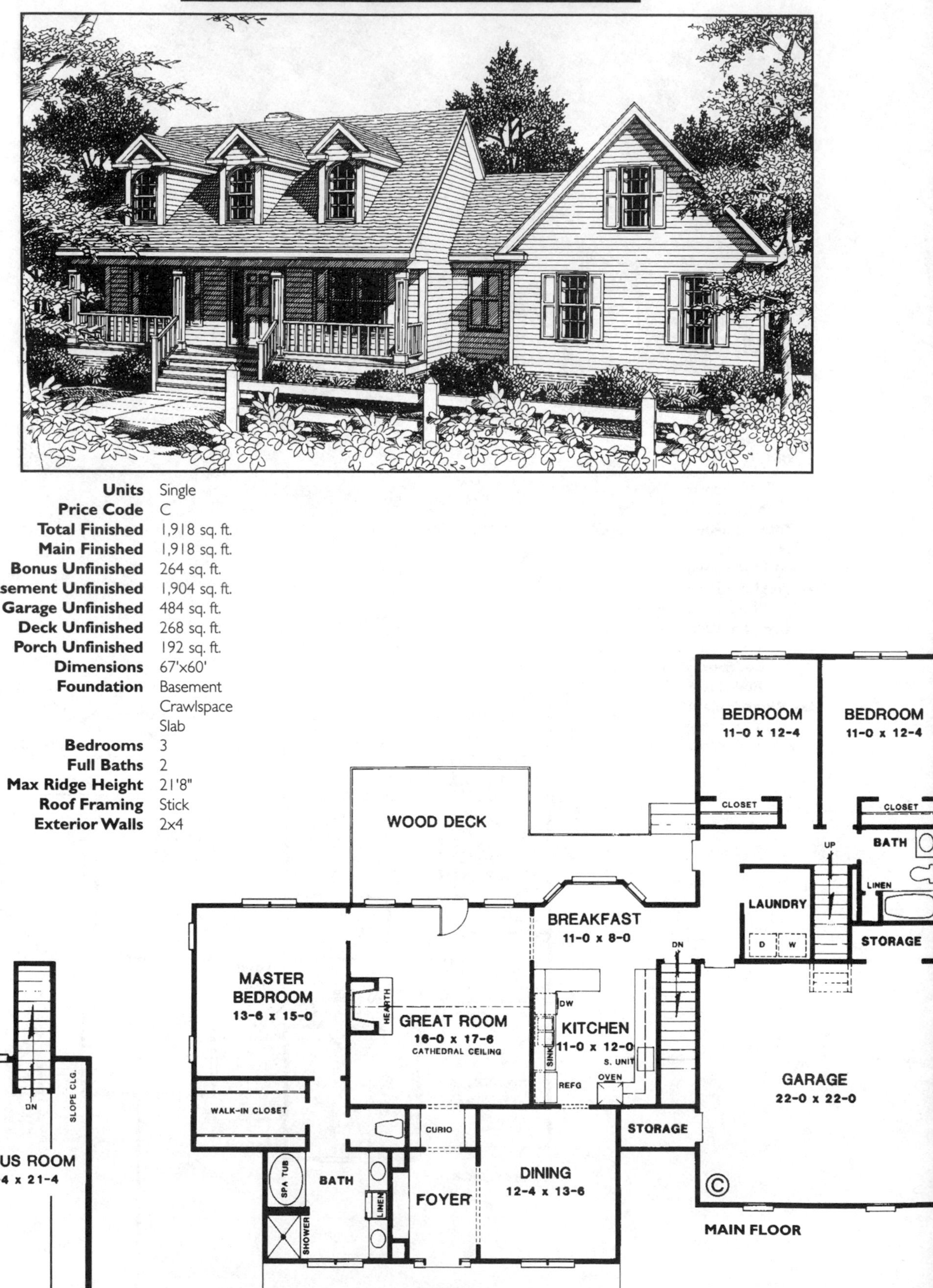

Units	Single
Price Code	C
Total Finished	1,918 sq. ft.
Main Finished	1,918 sq. ft.
Bonus Unfinished	264 sq. ft.
Basement Unfinished	1,904 sq. ft.
Garage Unfinished	484 sq. ft.
Deck Unfinished	268 sq. ft.
Porch Unfinished	192 sq. ft.
Dimensions	67'x60'
Foundation	Basement Crawlspace Slab
Bedrooms	3
Full Baths	2
Max Ridge Height	21'8"
Roof Framing	Stick
Exterior Walls	2x4

Design 63001

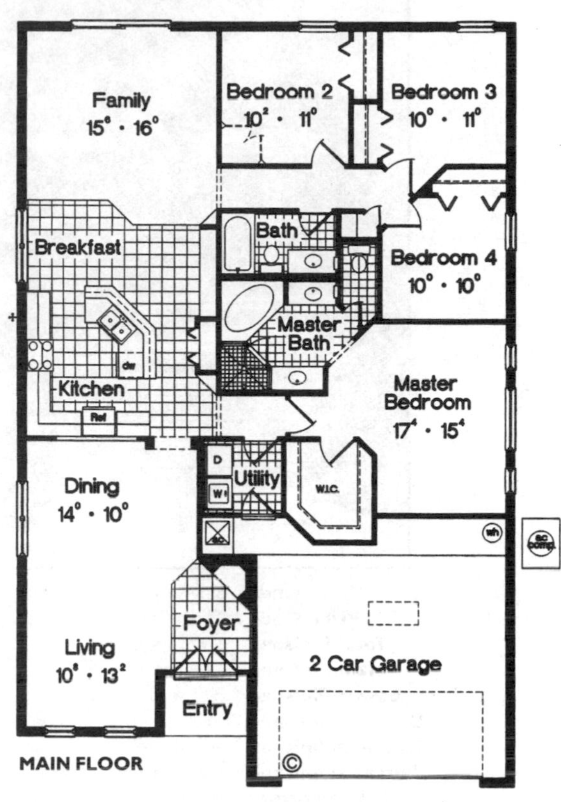

Units	Single
Price Code	C
Total Finished	1,919 sq. ft.
Main Finished	1,919 sq. ft.
Garage Unfinished	454 sq. ft.
Dimensions	40'x62'
Foundation	Slab
Bedrooms	4
Full Baths	2
Main Ceiling	8'
Max Ridge Height	18'6"
Roof Framing	Stick

Design 97870

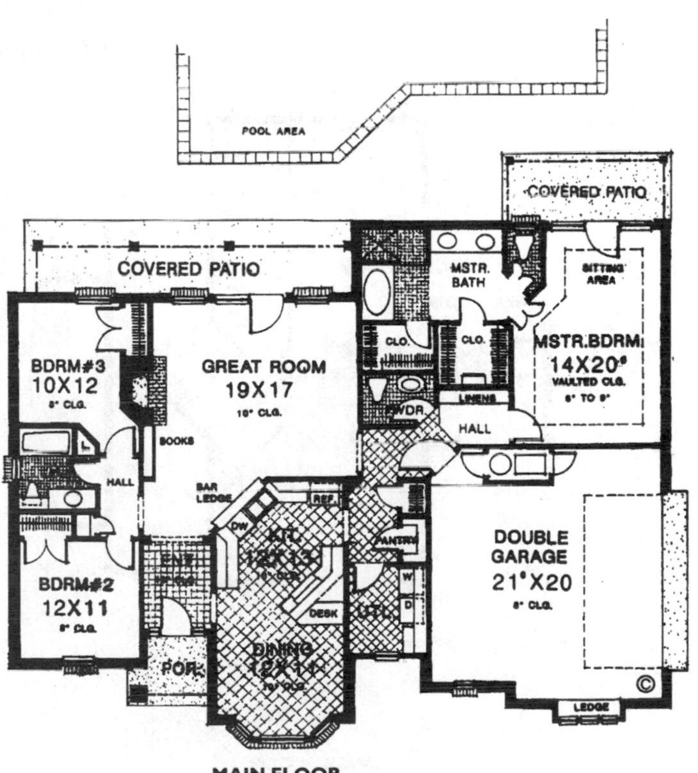

Units	Single
Price Code	C
Total Finished	1,920 sq. ft.
Main Finished	1,920 sq. ft.
Garage Unfinished	483 sq. ft.
Deck Unfinished	150 sq. ft.
Porch Unfinished	42 sq. ft.
Dimensions	61'x48'7"
Foundation	Slab
Bedrooms	3
Full Baths	2
Half Baths	1
Main Ceiling	8'-10'
Max Ridge Height	30'
Roof Framing	Stick
Exterior Walls	2x4

Design 65157

Units	Single
Price Code	C
Total Finished	1,921 sq. ft.
Main Finished	1,099 sq. ft.
Lower Finished	822 sq. ft.
Bonus Unfinished	310 sq. ft.
Garage Unfinished	447 sq. ft.
Porch Unfinished	1,032 sq. ft.
Dimensions	60'x41'
Foundation	Basement
Bedrooms	3
Full Baths	1
3/4 Baths	3
Main Ceiling	9'
Max Ridge Height	30'10"
Roof Framing	Truss
Exterior Walls	2x6

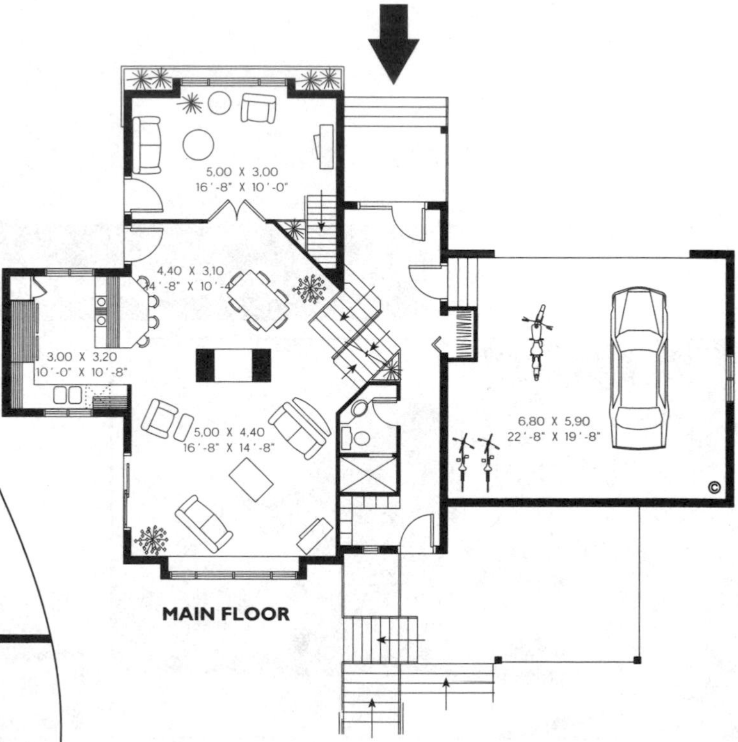

5,00 X 3,00
16'-8" X 10'-0"

4,40 X 3,10
14'-8" X 10'-4"

3,00 X 3,20
10'-0" X 10'-8"

5,00 X 4,40
16'-8" X 14'-8"

6,80 X 5,90
22'-8" X 19'-8"

MAIN FLOOR

3,10 X 3,00
10'-4" X 10'-0"

3,10 X 3,00
10'-4" X 10'-0"

4,30 X 3,50
14'-4" X 11'-8"

LOWER FLOOR

Design 99192

Units	Single
Price Code	C
Total Finished	1,921 sq. ft.
Main Finished	1,921 sq. ft.
Basement Unfinished	1,921 sq. ft.
Garage Unfinished	486 sq. ft.
Dimensions	53'8"x59'
Foundation	Basement
Bedrooms	3
Full Baths	2
Main Ceiling	9'
Tray Ceiling	11'
Max Ridge Height	25'3"
Roof Framing	Truss
Exterior Walls	2x4

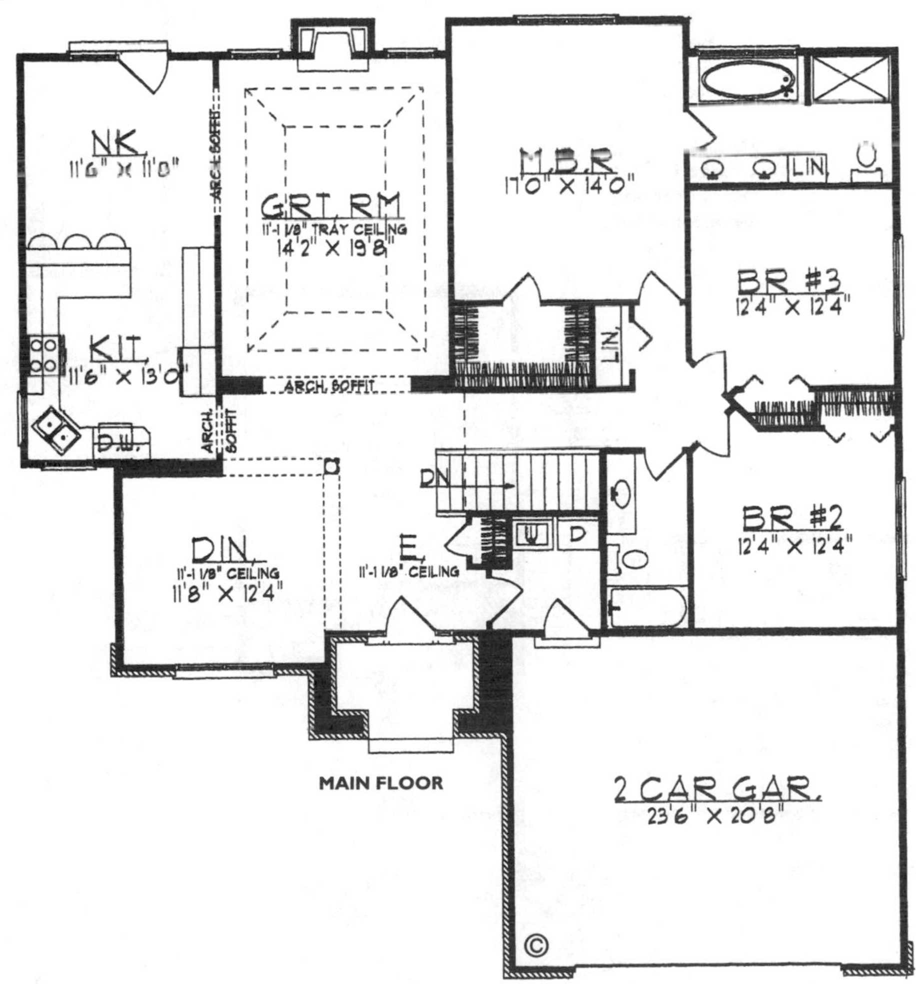

Design 65012

Units	Single
Price Code	C
Total Finished	1,922 sq. ft.
First Finished	1,293 sq. ft.
Second Finished	629 sq. ft.
Basement Unfinished	1,293 sq. ft.
Garage Unfinished	606 sq. ft.
Dimensions	58'x55'
Foundation	Basement
Bedrooms	3
Full Baths	2
Half Baths	1
First Ceiling	9'2"
Second Ceiling	8'2"
Max Ridge Height	26'8"
Roof Framing	Truss
Exterior Walls	2x6

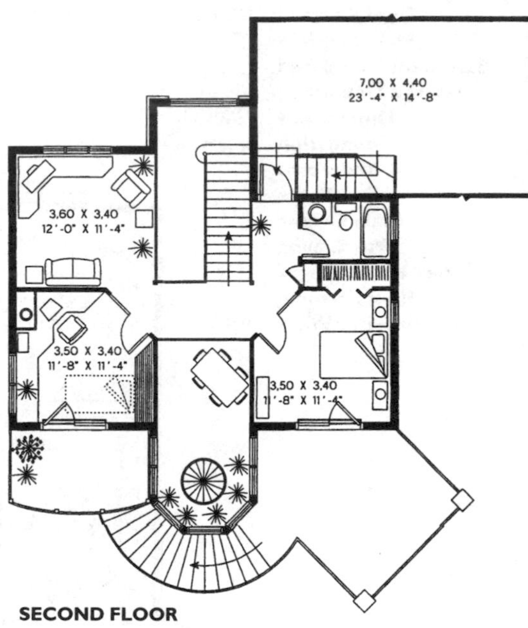

SECOND FLOOR

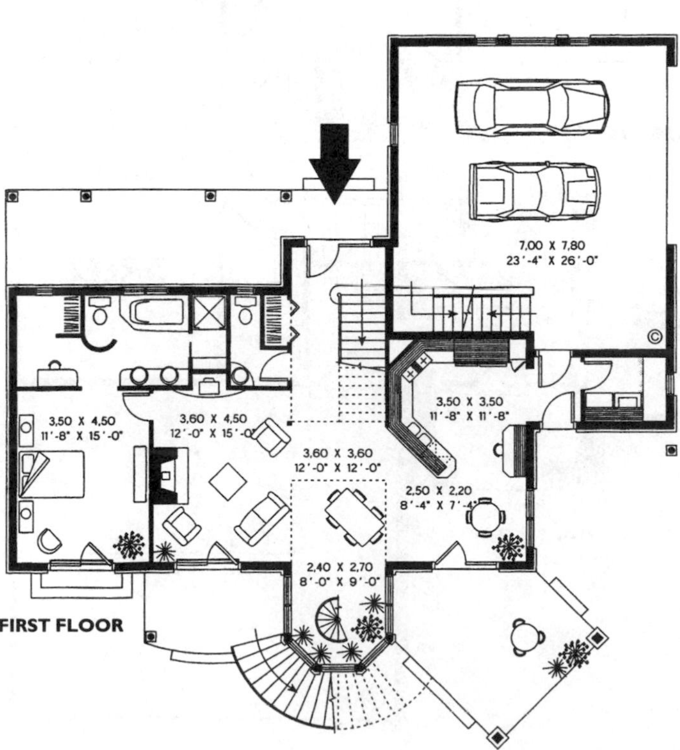

FIRST FLOOR

Design 97330

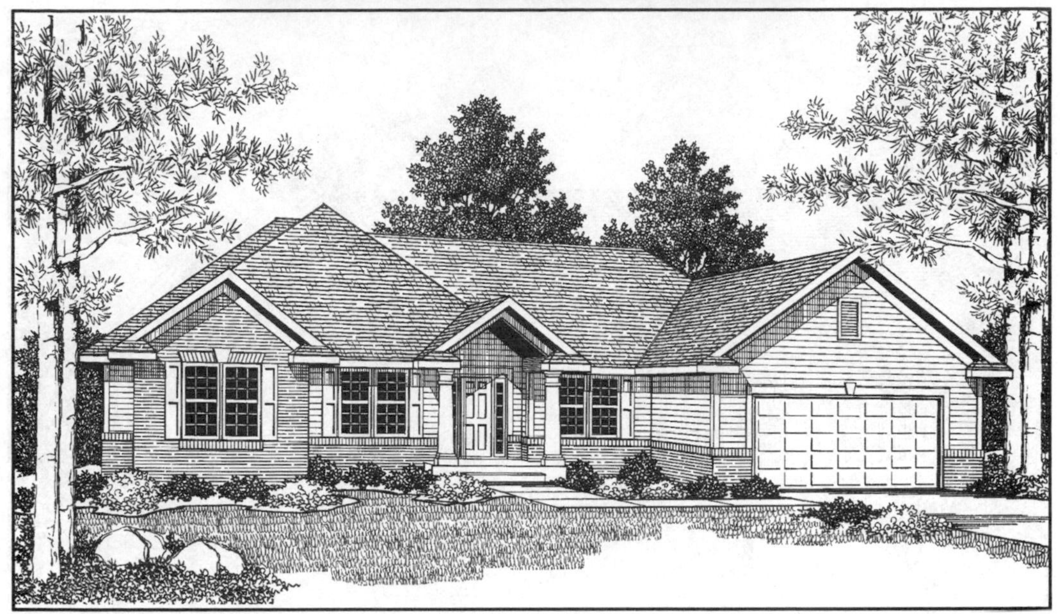

Units	Single
Price Code	C
Total Finished	1,923 sq. ft.
Main Finished	1,923 sq. ft.
Basement Unfinished	1,923 sq. ft.
Garage Unfinished	668 sq. ft.
Dimensions	70'8"x45'
Foundation	Basement
Bedrooms	4
Full Baths	2
Main Ceiling	9'
Max Ridge Height	21'4"
Roof Framing	Truss
Exterior Walls	2x6

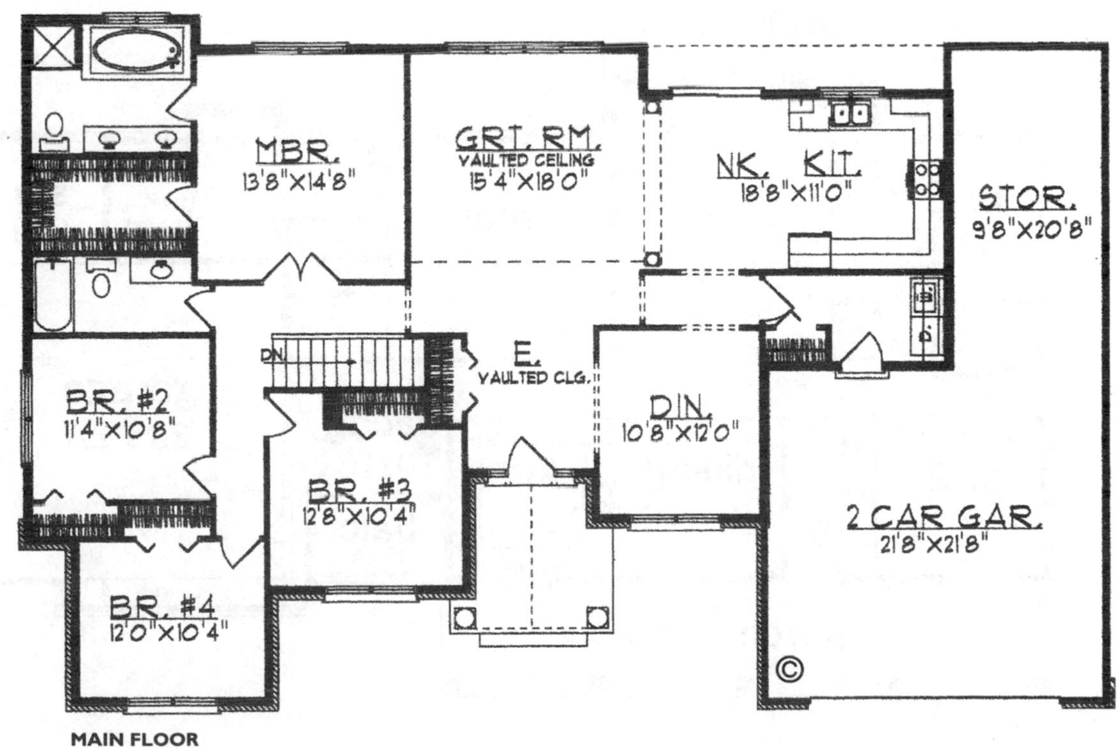

MAIN FLOOR

Design 65672

Units	Single
Price Code	C
Total Finished	1,925 sq. ft.
Main Finished	1,925 sq. ft.
Dimensions	78'x52'
Foundation	Crawlspace Slab
Bedrooms	3
Full Baths	2
Main Ceiling	9'
Max Ridge Height	30'
Roof Framing	Stick
Exterior Walls	2x6

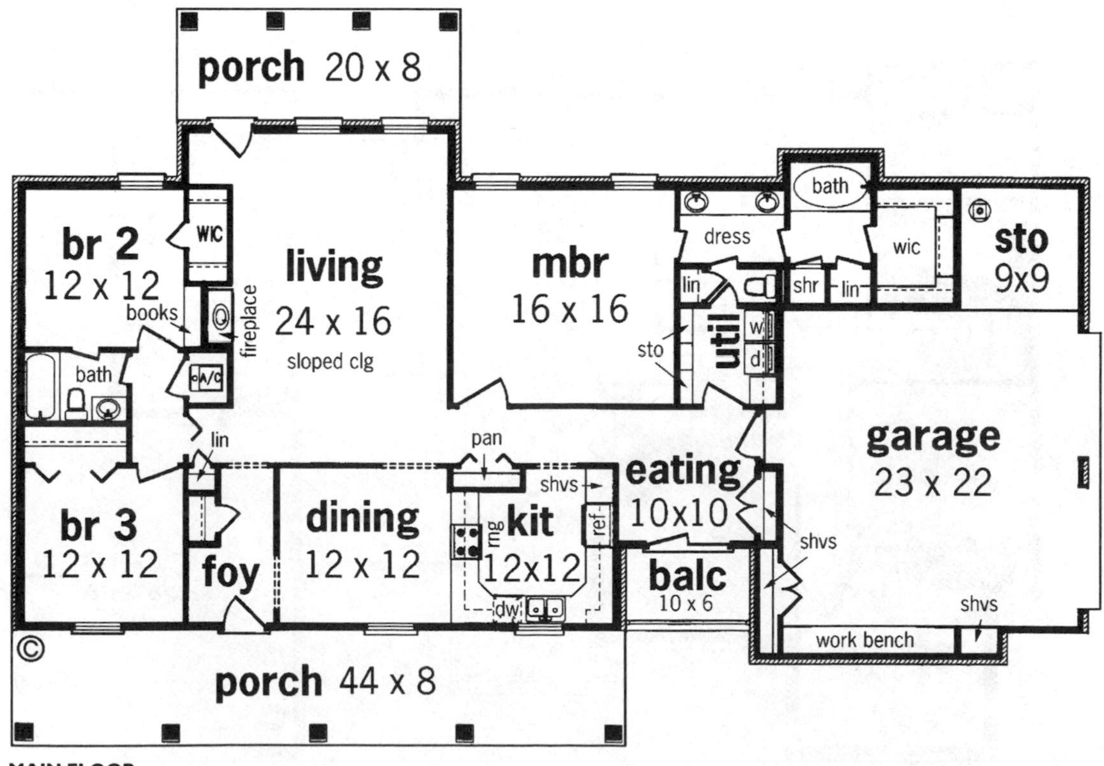

MAIN FLOOR

Design 97277

Units	Single
Price Code	C
Total Finished	1,927 sq. ft.
Main Finished	1,927 sq. ft.
Bonus Unfinished	424 sq. ft.
Basement Unfinished	1,927 sq. ft.
Garage Unfinished	494 sq. ft.
Dimensions	55'6"x64'
Foundation	Basement Crawlspace
Bedrooms	3
Full Baths	2
Main Ceiling	9'
Second Ceiling	8'
Max Ridge Height	28'2"
Roof Framing	Stick
Exterior Walls	2x4

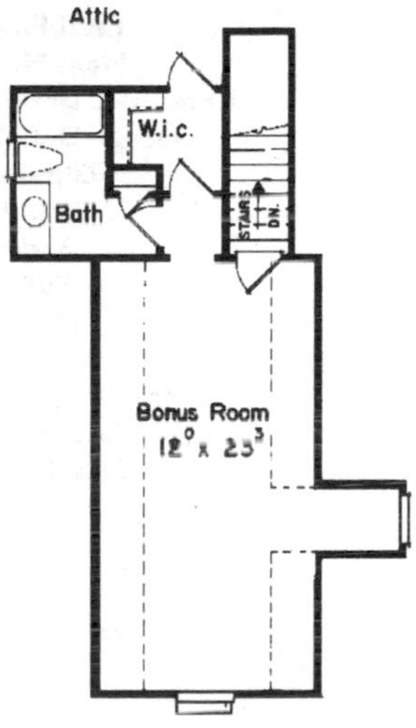

BONUS

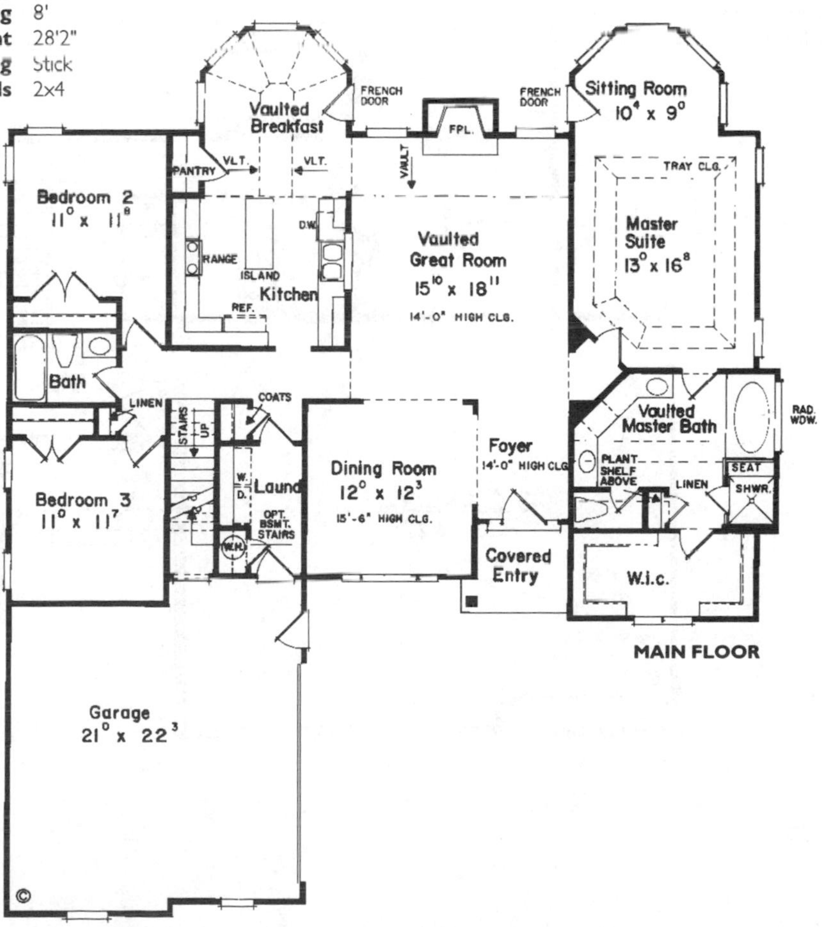

MAIN FLOOR

Design 97335

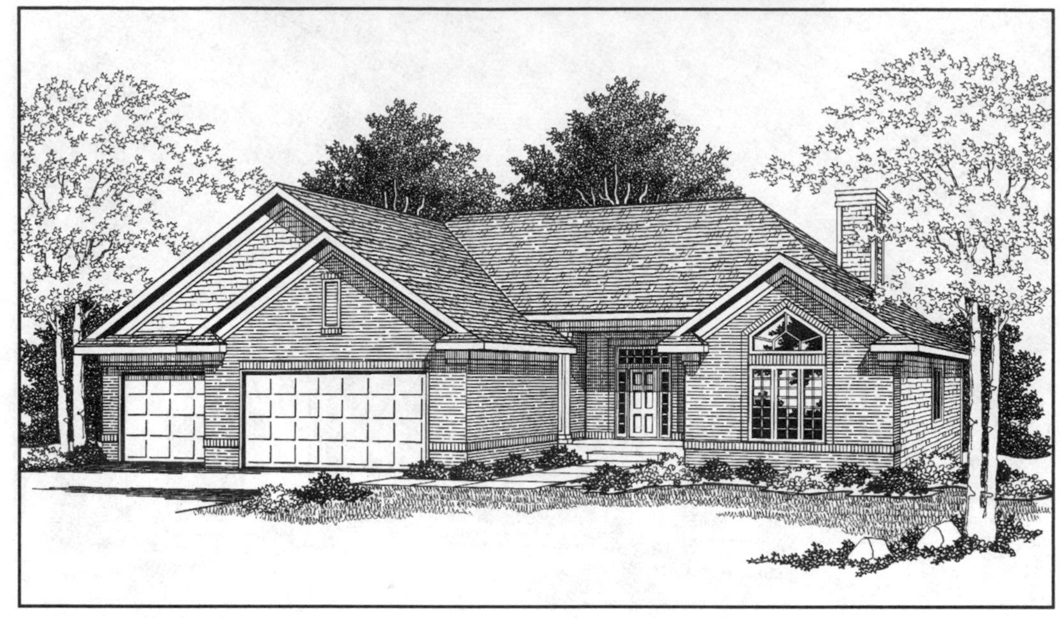

Units	Single
Price Code	C
Total Finished	1,927 sq. ft.
Main Finished	1,927 sq. ft.
Basement Unfinished	1,927 sq. ft.
Garage Unfinished	911 sq. ft.
Dimensions	62'x56'
Foundation	Basement
Bedrooms	3
Full Baths	2
Half Baths	1
Main Ceiling	9'
Max Ridge Height	22'11"
Roof Framing	Truss
Exterior Walls	2x6

BR. #2
11'10"X13'4"

MBR.
TRAY CEILING
14'8"X15'0"

KIT.
15'0"X15'4"

PAN.

ARCH

BR. #3
10'8"X11'0"

DIN.
15'0"X11'8"

ARCH

DN

E.
12'-1 1/8" CLG.

GRT. RM.
CATHEDRAL CEILING
15'0"X19'8"

3 CAR GAR.
33'4"X27'4"

©

MAIN FLOOR

Design 98238

Units	Single
Price Code	C
Total Finished	1,928 sq. ft.
Main Finished	1,928 sq. ft.
Bonus Unfinished	160 sq. ft.
Garage Unfinished	400 sq. ft.
Porch Unfinished	315 sq. ft.
Dimensions	58'x47'
Foundation	Basement
Bedrooms	4
Full Baths	2
Main Ceiling	9'
Max Ridge Height	24'
Roof Framing	Stick
Exterior Walls	2x4

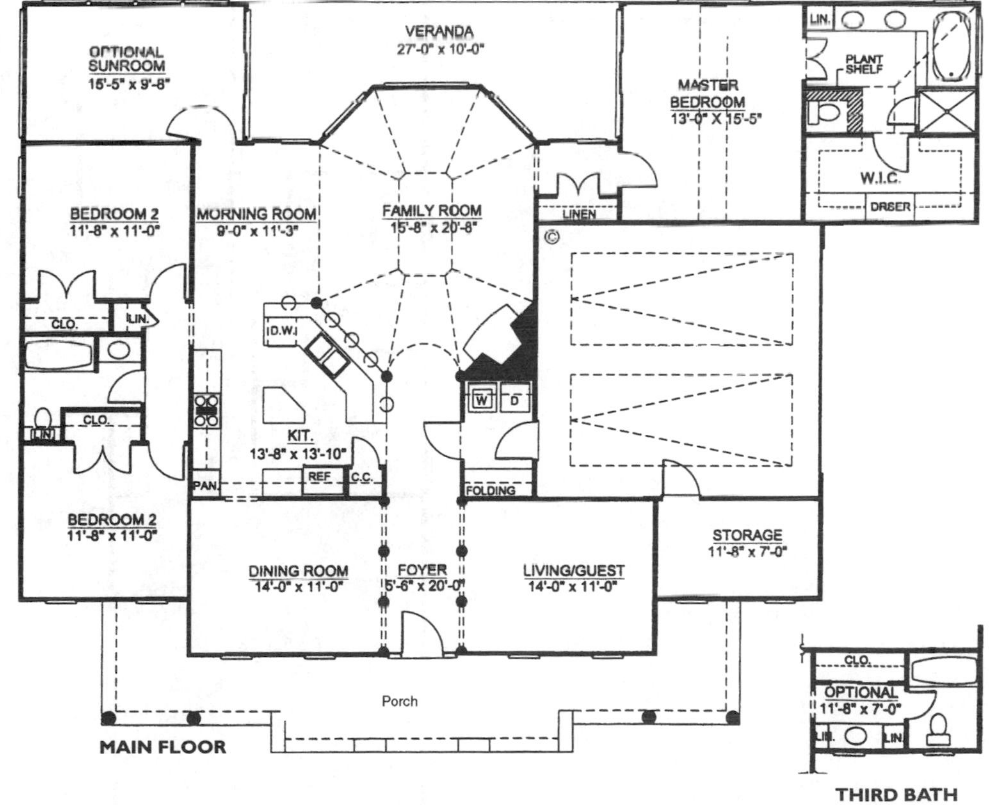

Design 62053

Units	Single
Price Code	C
Total Finished	1,930 sq. ft.
Main Finished	1,930 sq. ft.
Garage Unfinished	509 sq. ft.
Porch Unfinished	357 sq. ft.
Dimensions	52'x71'6"
Foundation	Slab
Bedrooms	4
Full Baths	2
Main Ceiling	8'
Max Ridge Height	26'8"
Roof Framing	Truss
Exterior Walls	2x4, 2x6

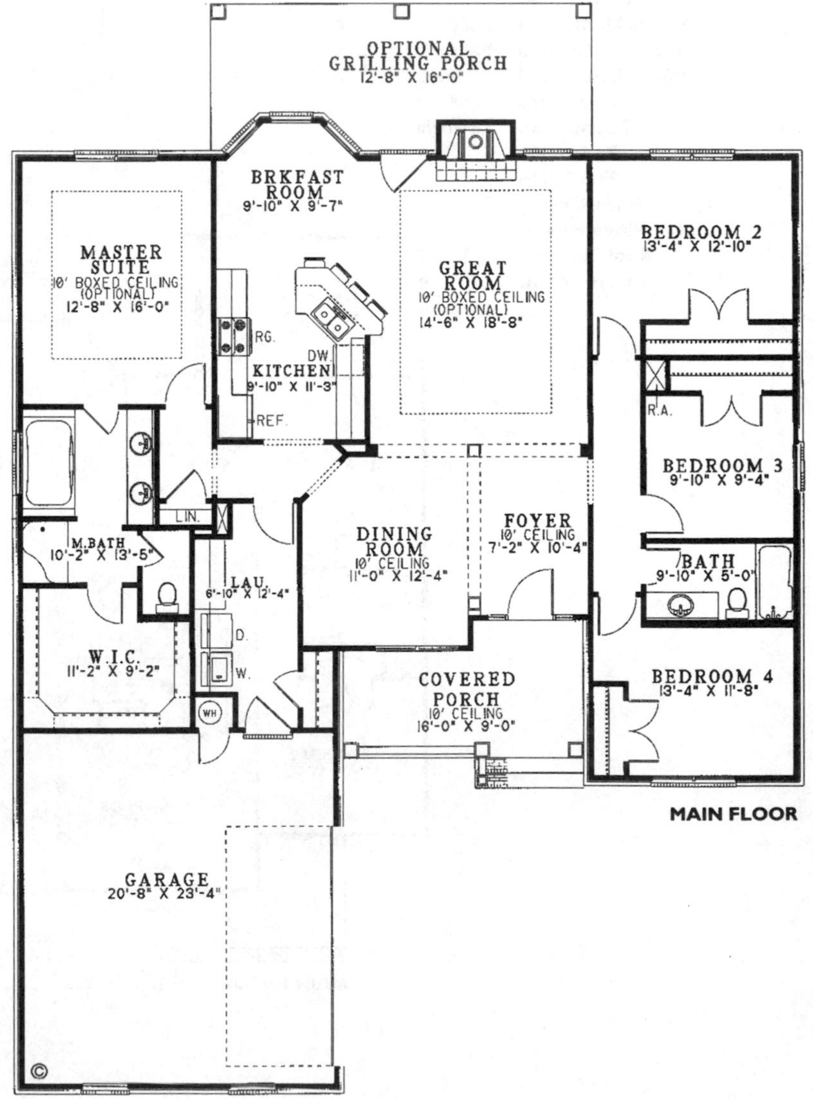

MAIN FLOOR

Design 65647

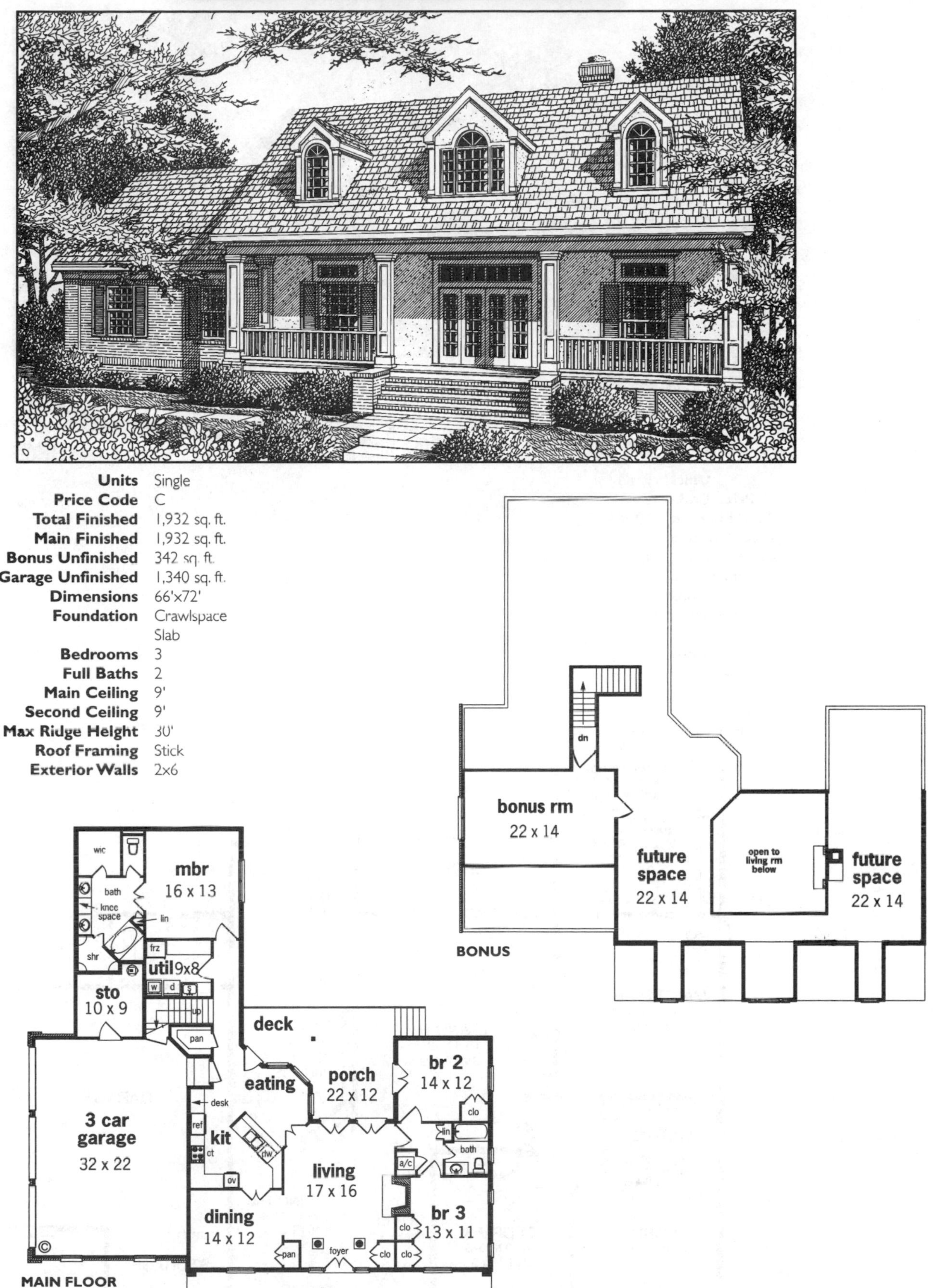

Units	Single
Price Code	C
Total Finished	1,932 sq. ft.
Main Finished	1,932 sq. ft.
Bonus Unfinished	342 sq. ft.
Garage Unfinished	1,340 sq. ft.
Dimensions	66'x72'
Foundation	Crawlspace Slab
Bedrooms	3
Full Baths	2
Main Ceiling	9'
Second Ceiling	9'
Max Ridge Height	30'
Roof Framing	Stick
Exterior Walls	2x6

Design 93098

Units	Single
Price Code	C
Total Finished	1,932 sq. ft.
Main Finished	1,932 sq. ft.
Garage Unfinished	552 sq. ft.
Deck Unfinished	225 sq. ft.
Dimensions	65'10"x53'5"
Foundation	Crawlspace Slab
Bedrooms	3
Full Baths	2
Max Ridge Height	22'4"
Roof Framing	Stick
Exterior Walls	2x4

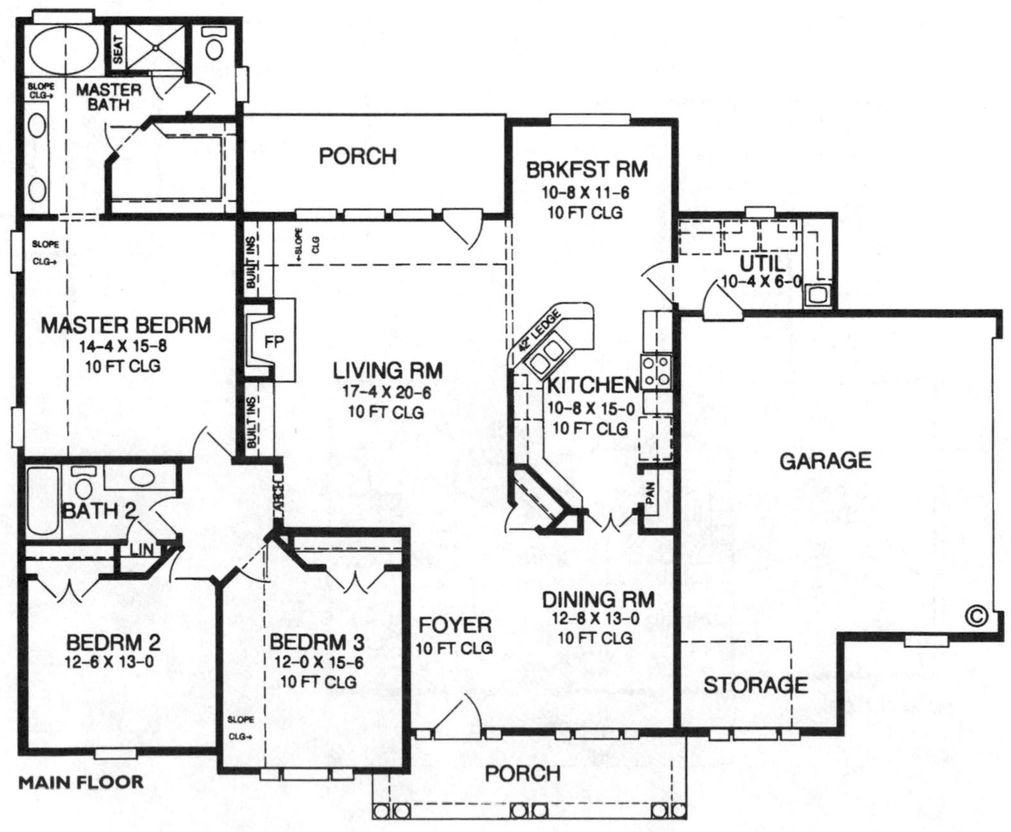

Design 65670

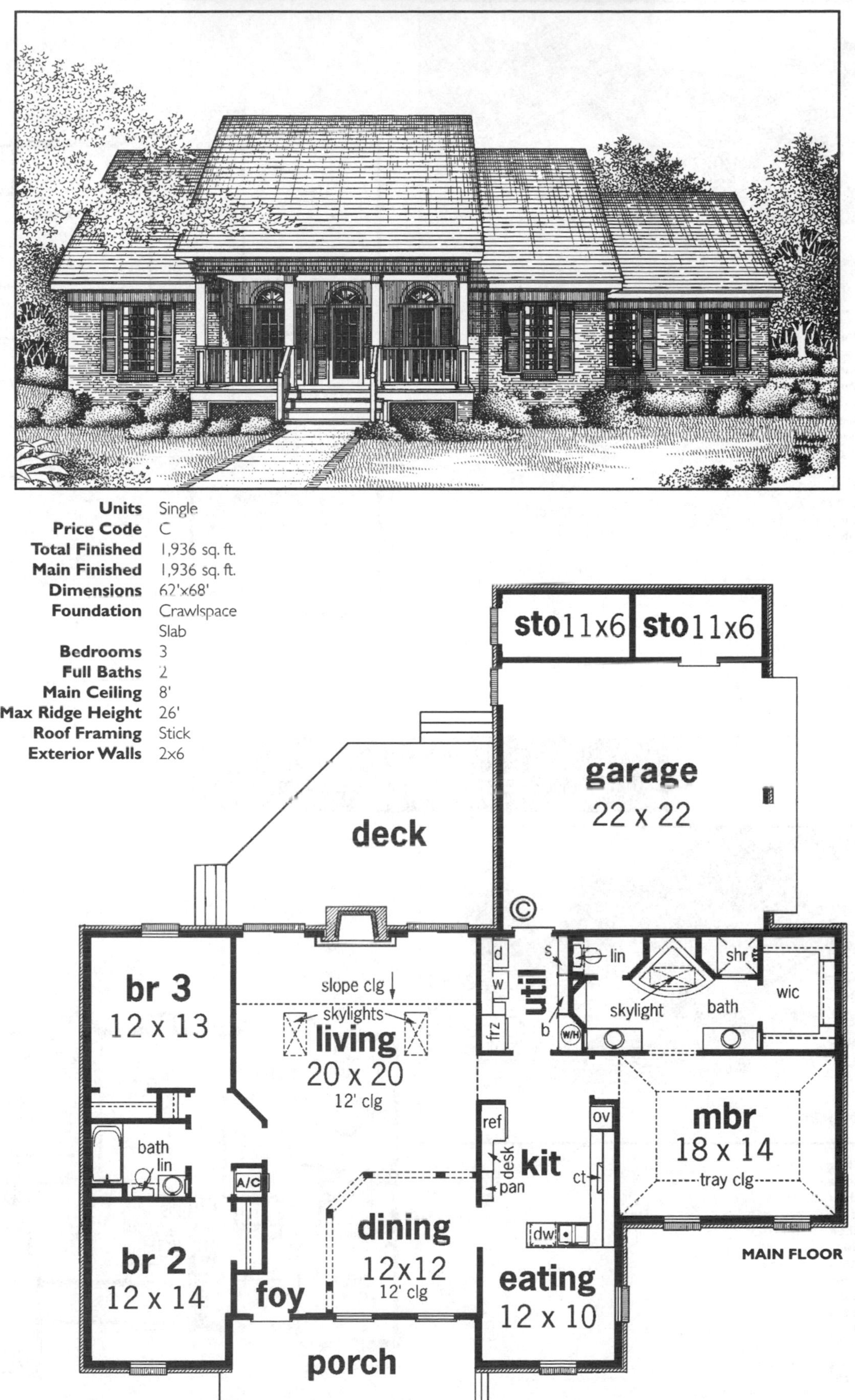

Units	Single
Price Code	C
Total Finished	1,936 sq. ft.
Main Finished	1,936 sq. ft.
Dimensions	62'x68'
Foundation	Crawlspace Slab
Bedrooms	3
Full Baths	2
Main Ceiling	8'
Max Ridge Height	26'
Roof Framing	Stick
Exterior Walls	2x6

Design 82034

Units	Single
Price Code	C
Total Finished	1,940 sq. ft.
Main Finished	1,940 sq. ft.
Garage Unfinished	417 sq. ft.
Porch Unfinished	188 sq. ft.
Dimensions	58'x54'10"
Foundation	Crawlspace Slab
Bedrooms	4
Full Baths	2
Main Ceiling	8'
Roof Framing	Stick
Exterior Walls	2x4

COVERED PORCH
18'-5" X 4'-0"
BREAKFAST ROOM
9'-4" X 10'-11"
BEDROOM 4
13'-6" X 14'-6"
MASTER SUITE
15'-0" X 15'-0"
9' PAN CEILING
GREAT ROOM
9' BOX CEILING
15'-0" X 19'-6"
BATH
BUILT-INS
KITCHEN
9'-11" X 12'-7"
REF.
PAN
RG.
DW
KNEE SPACE
M.BATH
15'-0" X 11'-8"
WHP TUB
BEDROOM 3
10'-0" X 10'-4"
DINING ROOM
11'-6" X 9'-8"
FOYER
7'-0" X 7'-0"
LIN.
LAU.
STORAGE
WH
BEDROOM 2
12'-4" X 10'-6"
10" RND COL W/ BASE
4' PORCH
GARAGE
20'-10" X 20'-0"

MAIN FLOOR

Design 99115

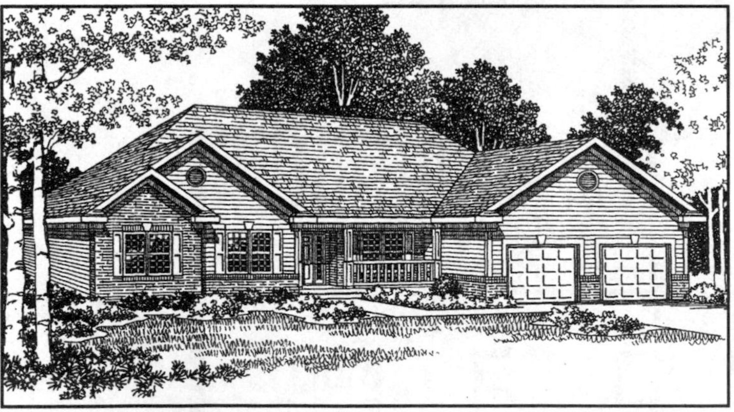

Units	Single
Price Code	C
Total Finished	1,947 sq. ft.
Main Finished	1,947 sq. ft.
Basement Unfinished	1,947 sq. ft.
Dimensions	69'8"x46'
Foundation	Basement
Bedrooms	3
Full Baths	2
Half Baths	1
Main Ceiling	8'
Max Ridge Height	22'4"
Roof Framing	Truss
Exterior Walls	2x6

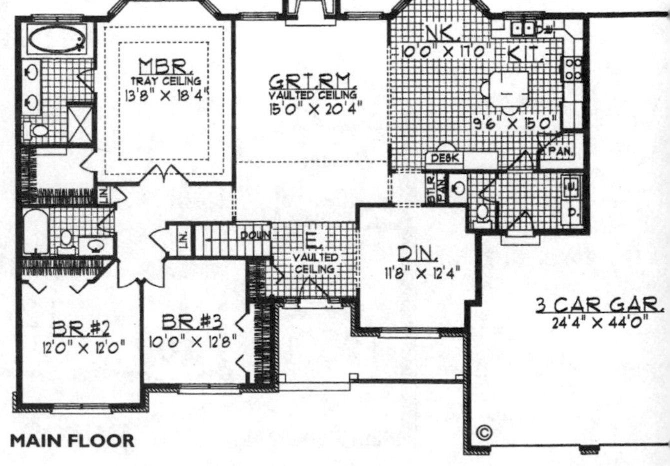

MAIN FLOOR

Design 97993

Units	Single
Price Code	C
Total Finished	1,948 sq. ft.
Main Finished	1,948 sq. ft.
Basement Unfinished	1,948 sq. ft.
Garage Unfinished	517 sq. ft.
Dimensions	64'x52'
Foundation	Basement Crawlspace Slab
Bedrooms	3
Full Baths	2
Half Baths	1
Main Ceiling	8'
Max Ridge Height	20'
Roof Framing	Stick
Exterior Walls	2x4

* Alternate foundation options available at an additional charge. Please call 1-800-235-5700 for more information.

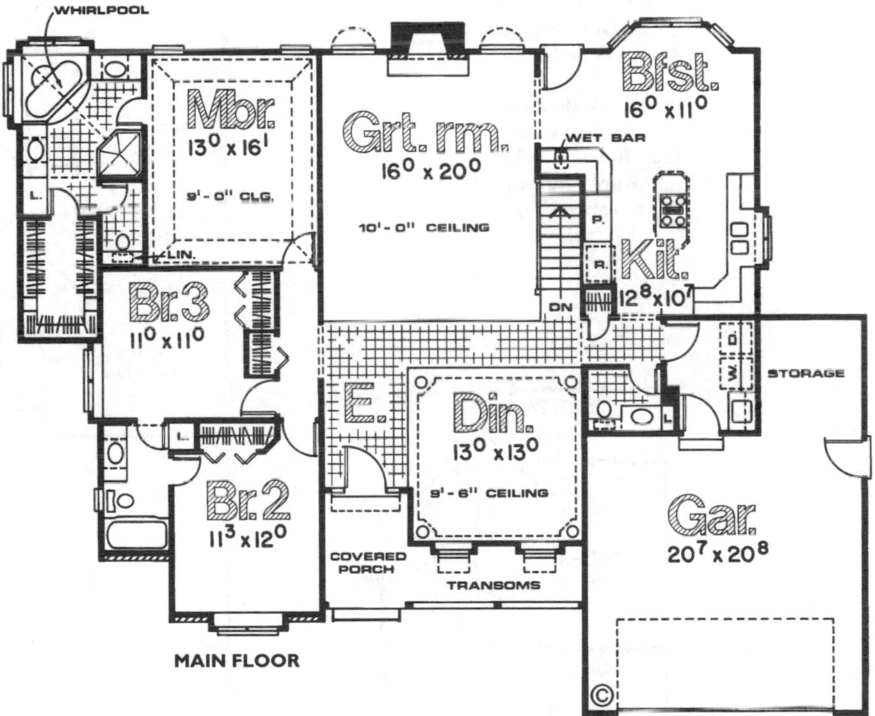

Design 93031

Units	Single
Price Code	C
Total Finished	1,955 sq. ft.
Main Finished	1,955 sq. ft.
Bonus Unfinished	240 sq. ft.
Garage Unfinished	561 sq. ft.
Porch Unfinished	215 sq. ft.
Dimensions	60'10"x65'
Foundation	Crawlspace Slab
Bedrooms	3
Full Baths	2
Max Ridge Height	24'
Roof Framing	Stick
Exterior Walls	2x4

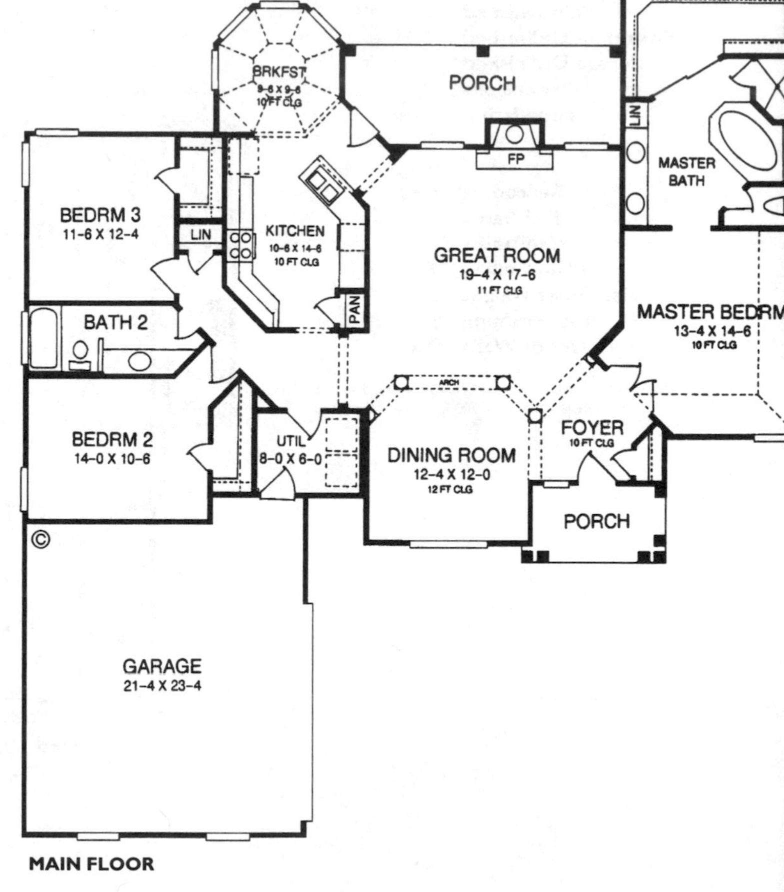

MAIN FLOOR

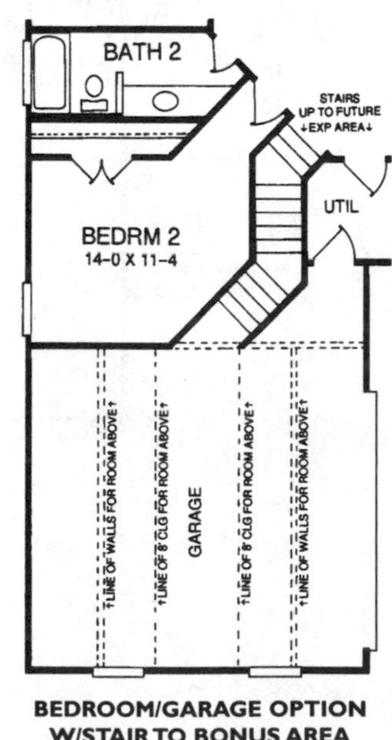

BEDROOM/GARAGE OPTION W/STAIR TO BONUS AREA

Design 93085

Units	Single
Price Code	C
Total Finished	1,955 sq. ft.
Main Finished	1,955 sq. ft.
Garage Unfinished	517 sq. ft.
Porch Unfinished	204 sq. ft.
Dimensions	65'x58'8"
Foundation	Crawlspace Slab
Bedrooms	3
Full Baths	2
Max Ridge Height	22'
Roof Framing	Stick
Exterior Walls	2x4

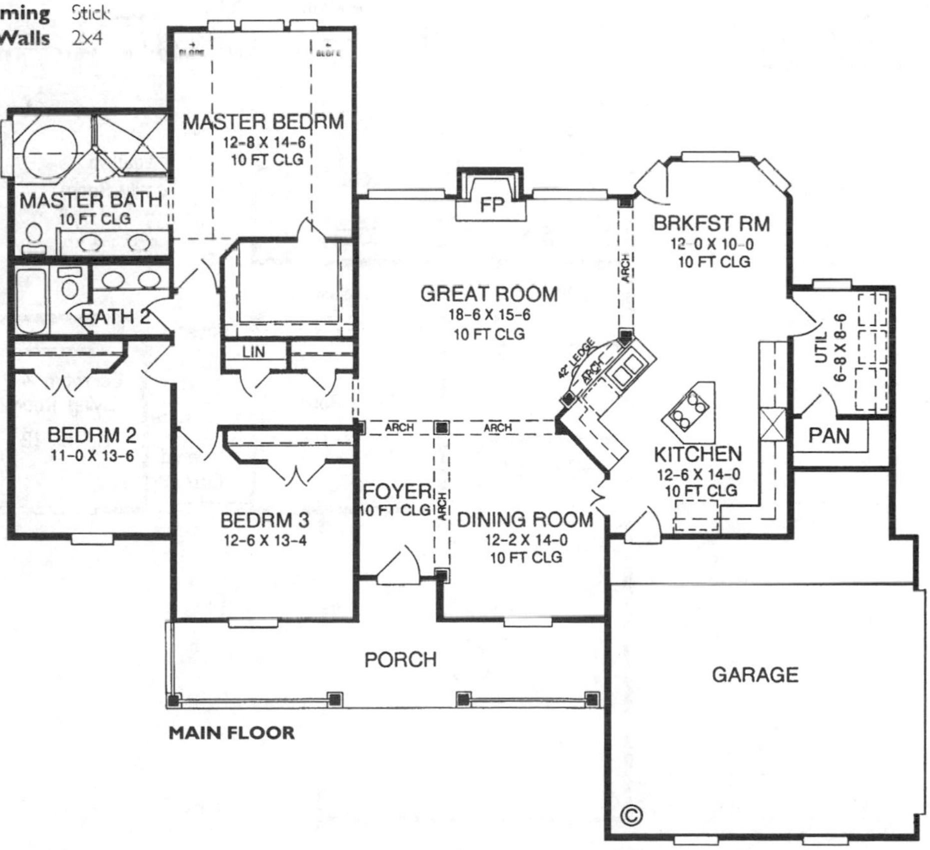

MASTER BEDRM
12-8 X 14-6
10 FT CLG

MASTER BATH
10 FT CLG

BATH 2

LIN

FP

GREAT ROOM
18-6 X 15-6
10 FT CLG

ARCH

42" LEDGE

BRKFST RM
12-0 X 10-0
10 FT CLG

UTIL
6-8 X 8-6

PAN

KITCHEN
12-6 X 14-0
10 FT CLG

BEDRM 2
11-0 X 13-6

BEDRM 3
12-6 X 13-4

FOYER
10 FT CLG

DINING ROOM
12-2 X 14-0
10 FT CLG

PORCH

GARAGE

©

MAIN FLOOR

Design 97227

Units	Single
Price Code	C
Total Finished	1,960 sq. ft.
Main Finished	1,960 sq. ft.
Basement Unfinished	1,993 sq. ft.
Garage Unfinished	476 sq. ft.
Dimensions	59'x62'
Foundation	Basement Crawlspace
Bedrooms	4
Full Baths	3
Main Ceiling	9'1⅛"
Max Ridge Height	24'
Roof Framing	Stick
Exterior Walls	2x4

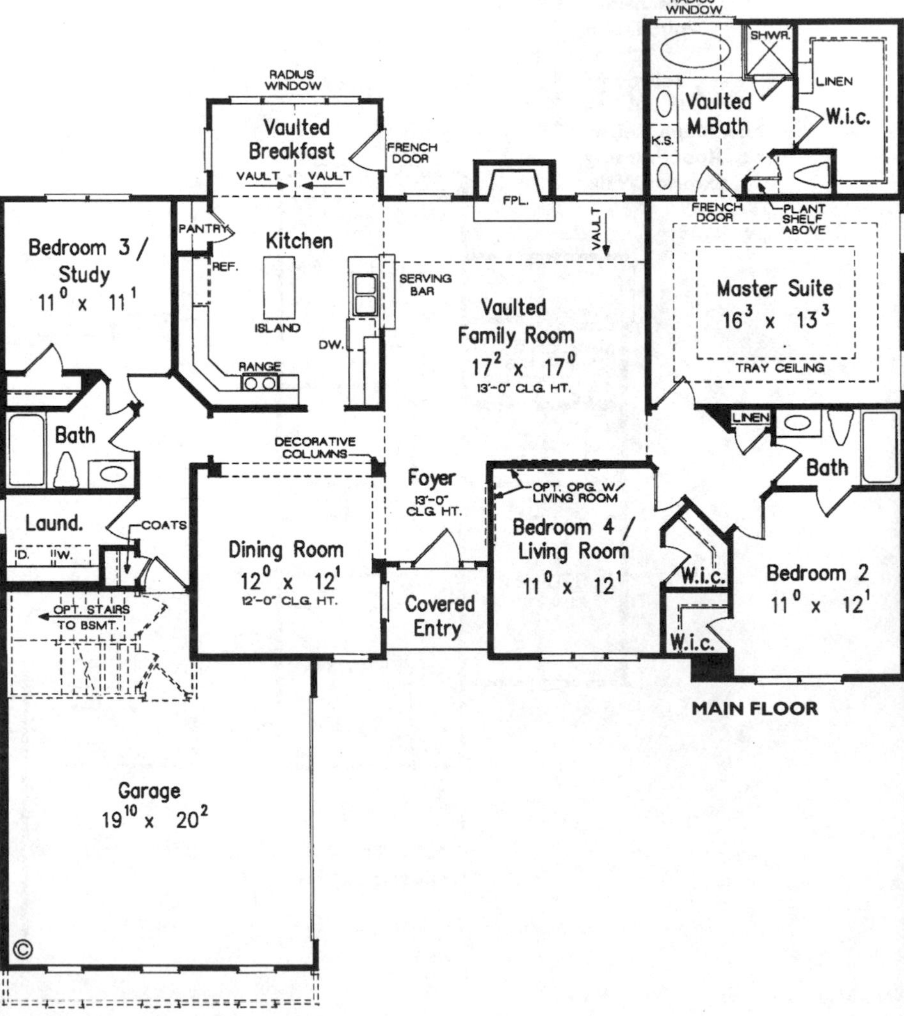

MAIN FLOOR

Design 69103

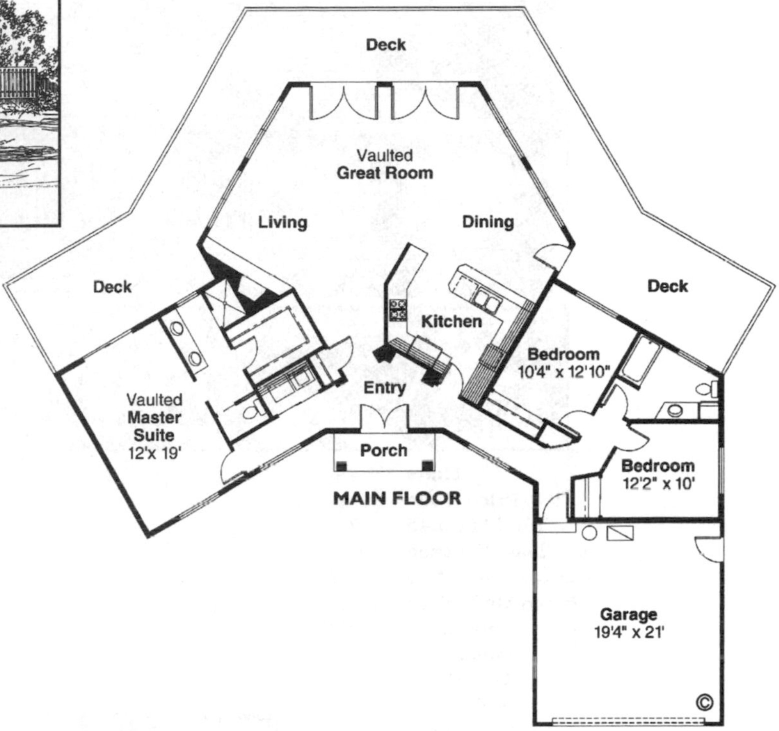

Units	Single
Price Code	C
Total Finished	1,965 sq. ft.
Main Finished	1,965 sq. ft.
Garage Unfinished	440 sq. ft.
Dimensions	71'x68'1"
Foundation	Crawlspace
Bedrooms	3
Full Baths	1
3/4 Baths	1
Main Ceiling	10'
Vaulted Ceiling	14'2"
Max Ridge Height	21'
Roof Framing	Truss
Exterior Walls	2x6

Deck
Vaulted Great Room
Living
Dining
Deck
Deck
Kitchen
Bedroom 10'4" x 12'10"
Entry
Vaulted Master Suite 12'x 19'
Porch
Bedroom 12'2" x 10'
MAIN FLOOR
Garage 19'4" x 21'

Design 92668

Please note: The photographed home may have been modified to suit homeowner preferences. If you order plans, have a builder or design professional check them against the photograph to confirm actual construction details.

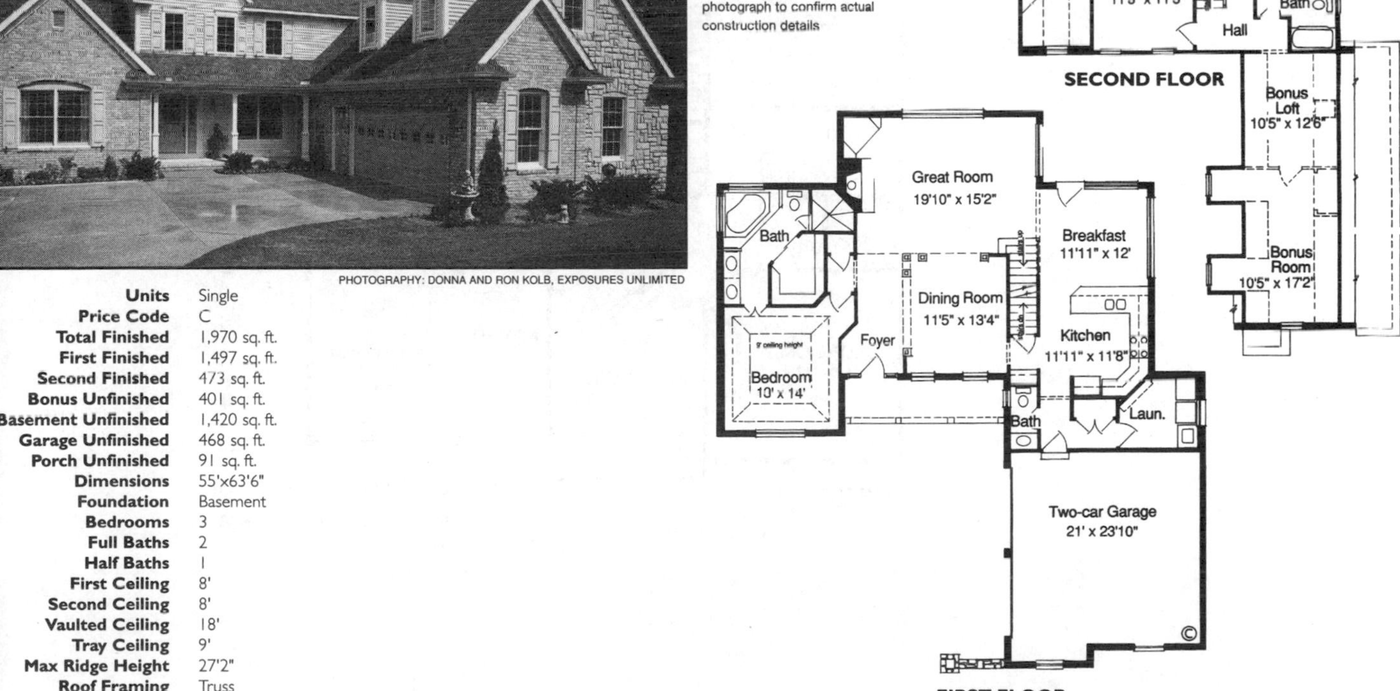

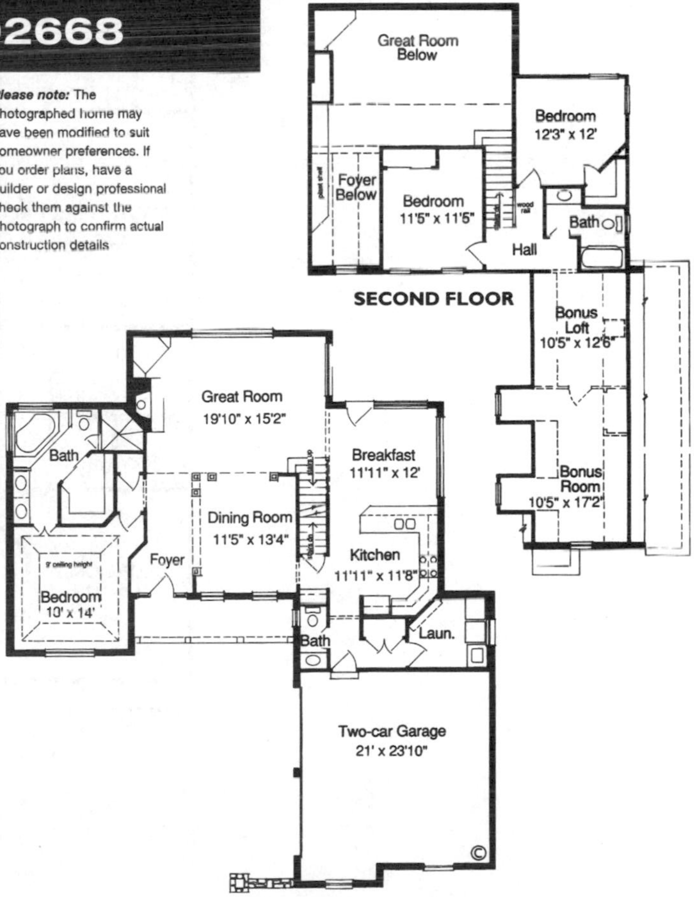

PHOTOGRAPHY: DONNA AND RON KOLB, EXPOSURES UNLIMITED

Units	Single
Price Code	C
Total Finished	1,970 sq. ft.
First Finished	1,497 sq. ft.
Second Finished	473 sq. ft.
Bonus Unfinished	401 sq. ft.
Basement Unfinished	1,420 sq. ft.
Garage Unfinished	468 sq. ft.
Porch Unfinished	91 sq. ft.
Dimensions	55'x63'6"
Foundation	Basement
Bedrooms	3
Full Baths	2
Half Baths	1
First Ceiling	8'
Second Ceiling	8'
Vaulted Ceiling	18'
Tray Ceiling	9'
Max Ridge Height	27'2"
Roof Framing	Truss
Exterior Walls	2x4

Design 93077

Units	Single
Price Code	C
Total Finished	1,971 sq. ft.
Main Finished	1,971 sq. ft.
Garage Unfinished	498 sq. ft.
Porch Unfinished	373 sq. ft.
Dimensions	66'2"x62'4"
Foundation	Crawlspace
Bedrooms	3
Full Baths	2
Max Ridge Height	20'
Roof Framing	Stick
Exterior Walls	2x4

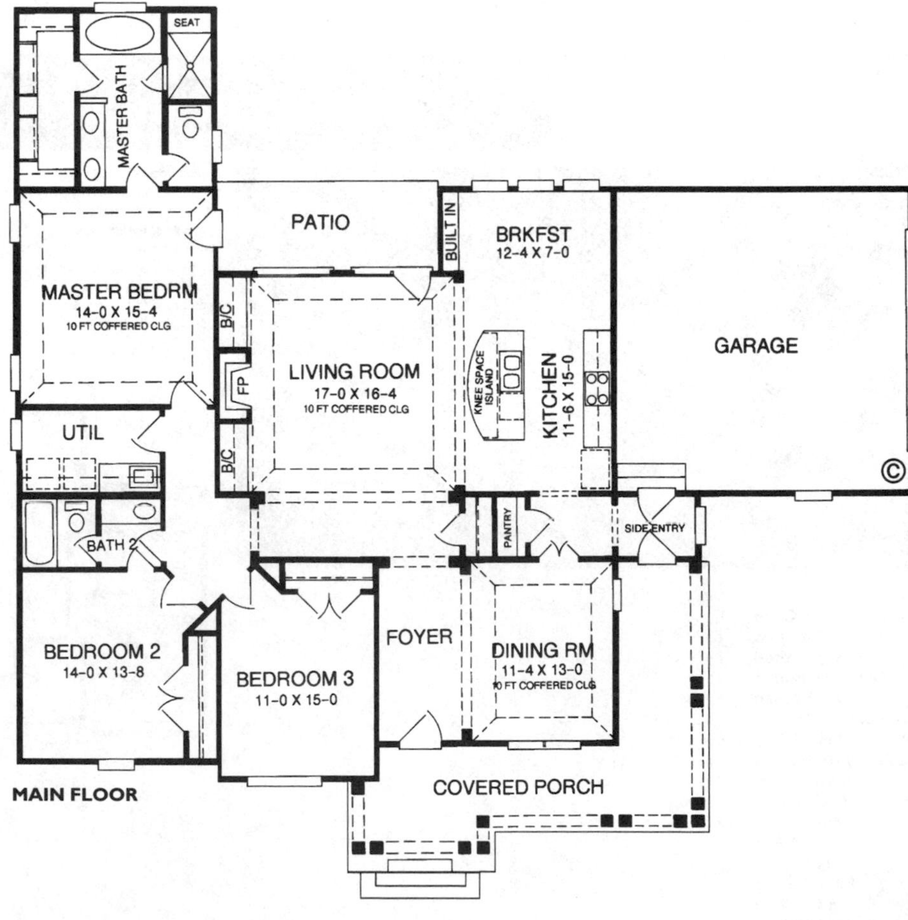

Design 24400

PHOTOGRAPHY: VICTORIA PALAGI

Units	Single
Price Code	C
Total Finished	1,978 sq. ft.
First Finished	1,034 sq. ft.
Second Finished	944 sq. ft.
Basement Unfinished	984 sq. ft.
Garage Unfinished	675 sq. ft.
Dimensions	67'6"x39'6"
Foundation	Basement Crawlspace Slab
Bedrooms	4
Full Baths	2
Half Baths	1
First Ceiling	9'
Second Ceiling	8'
Max Ridge Height	29'
Roof Framing	Stick
Exterior Walls	2x4, 2x6

CRAWLSPACE/SLAB FOUNDATION OPTION

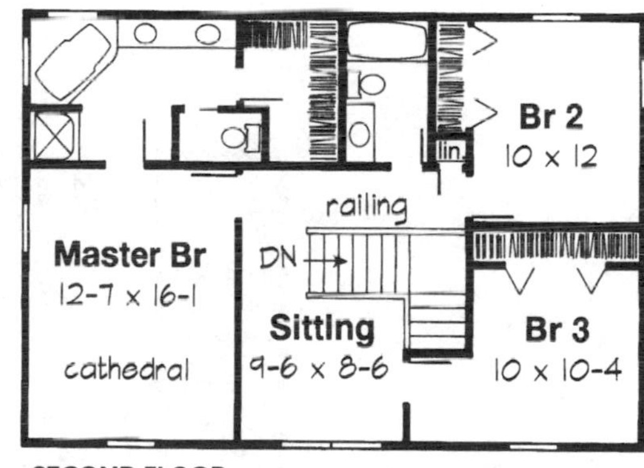

SECOND FLOOR

Please note: The photographed home may have been modified to suit homeowner preferences. If you order plans, have a builder or design professional check them against the photograph to confirm actual construction details.

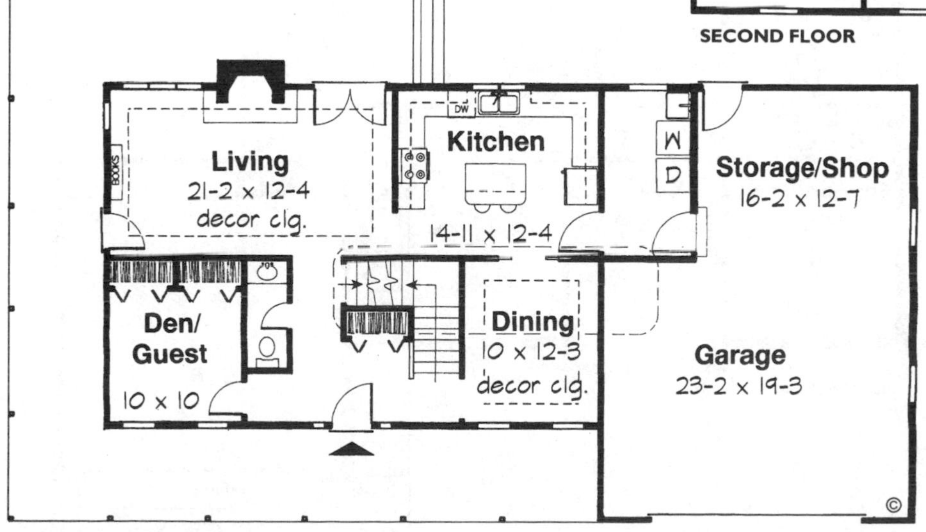

FIRST FLOOR

Design 10514

Units Single
Price Code C
Total Finished 1,980 sq. ft.
Main Finished 1,980 sq. ft.
Garage Unfinished 434 sq. ft.
Dimensions 60'x51'
Foundation Crawlspace
Bedrooms 3
Full Baths 2
Max Ridge Height 20'
Roof Framing Stick
Exterior Walls 2x6

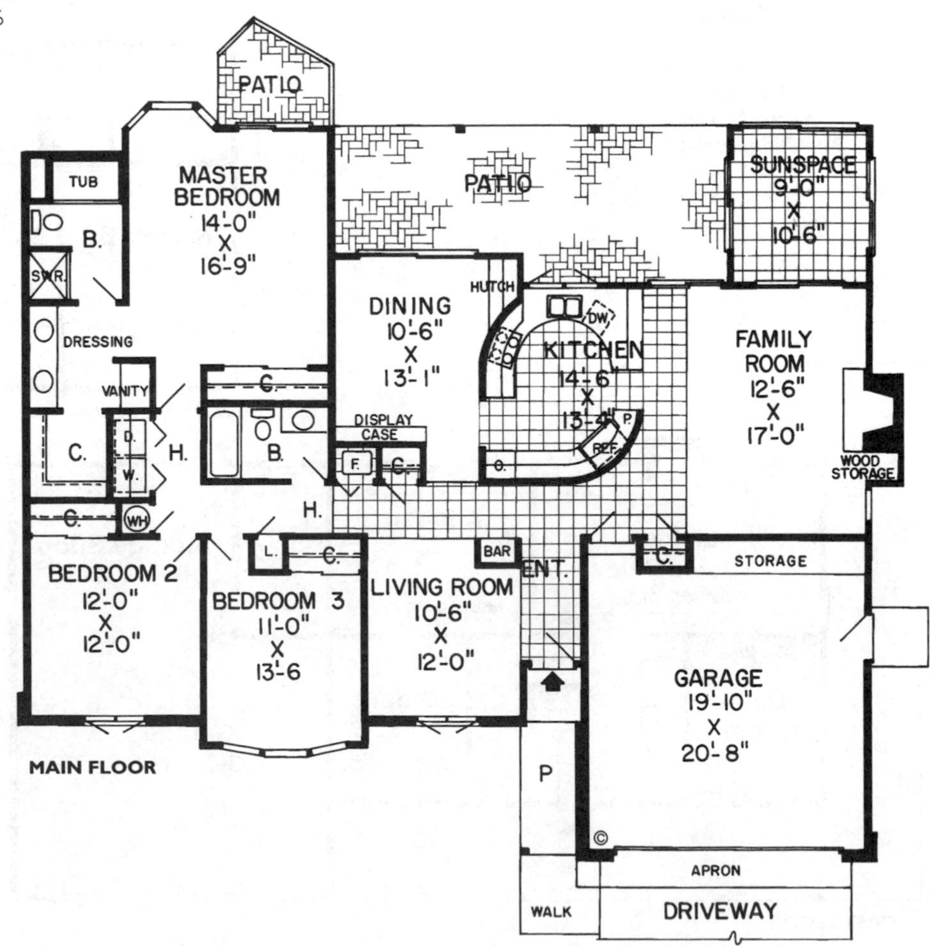

MAIN FLOOR

Design 19299

PHOTOGRAPHY: STEVE GRAHAM

Units	Single
Price Code	C
Total Finished	1,980 sq. ft.
Main Finished	1,980 sq. ft.
Garage Unfinished	484 sq. ft.
Dimensions	64'8"x55'
Foundation	Combo Basement/Crawlspace
Bedrooms	3
Full Baths	2
Half Baths	1
Main Ceiling	8'
Max Ridge Height	21'
Roof Framing	Stick
Exterior Walls	2x4

Please note: The photographed home may have been modified to suit homeowner preferences. If you order plans, have a builder or design professional check them against the photograph to confirm actual construction details.

DECK
DECK
BRKFST 10½x9½
FAMILY 15x19½
BATH
MASTER BEDRM 13½x17½
KIT 12½x10
CLOS
W D
BATH
DINING 13x12
ENTRY
LAV
BEDRM 10½x13½
BEDRM 11x11
PORCH
GARAGE 21x21
©

MAIN FLOOR

Design 92544

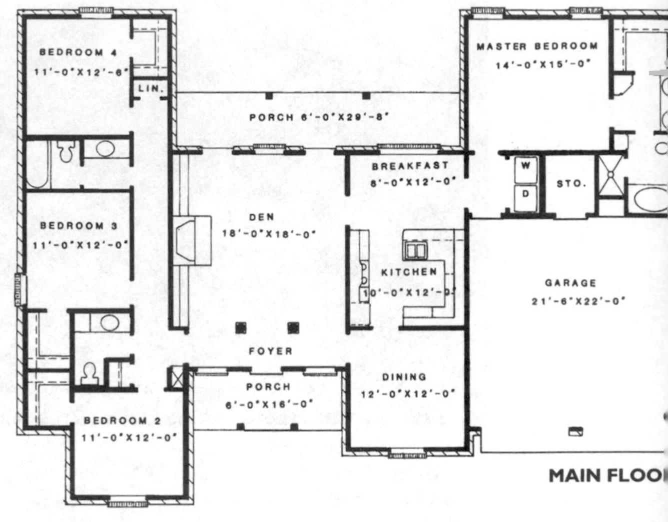

MAIN FLOOR

Units	Single
Price Code	C
Total Finished	1,987 sq. ft.
Main Finished	1,987 sq. ft.
Garage Unfinished	515 sq. ft.
Porch Unfinished	274 sq. ft.
Dimensions	67'x49'
Foundation	Crawlspace Slab
Bedrooms	4
Full Baths	2
Half Baths	1
Main Ceiling	9'
Max Ridge Height	22'
Roof Framing	Truss
Exterior Walls	2x4

Design 82028

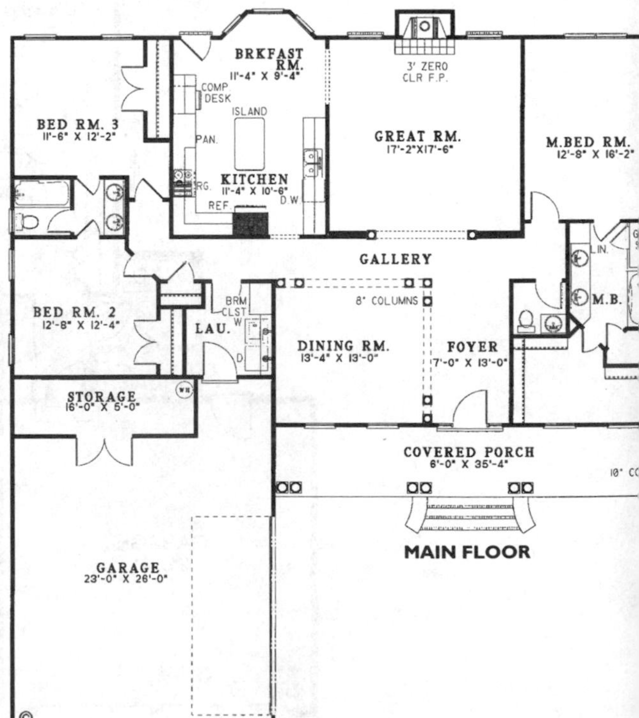

MAIN FLOOR

Units	Single
Price Code	C
Total Finished	1,988 sq. ft.
Main Finished	1,988 sq. ft.
Garage Unfinished	598 sq. ft.
Porch Unfinished	385 sq. ft.
Dimensions	59'x65'4"
Foundation	Crawlspace Slab
Bedrooms	3
Full Baths	2
Half Baths	1
Main Ceiling	9'
Roof Framing	Stick
Exterior Walls	2x4

Design 64173

Units	Single
Price Code	H
Total Finished	1,989 sq. ft.
Main Finished	1,989 sq. ft.
Bonus Unfinished	274 sq. ft.
Garage Unfinished	525 sq. ft.
Dimensions	81'x50'
Foundation	Crawlspace
Bedrooms	3
Full Baths	2
Max Ridge Height	27'
Roof Framing	Stick/Truss
Exterior Walls	2x6

* Alternate foundation options available at an additional charge. Please call 1-800-235-5700 for more information.

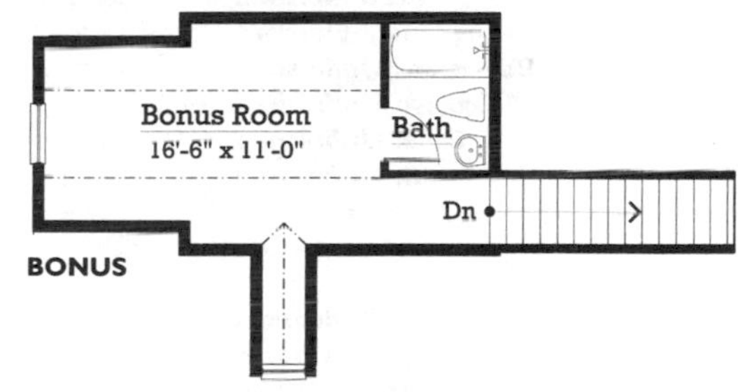

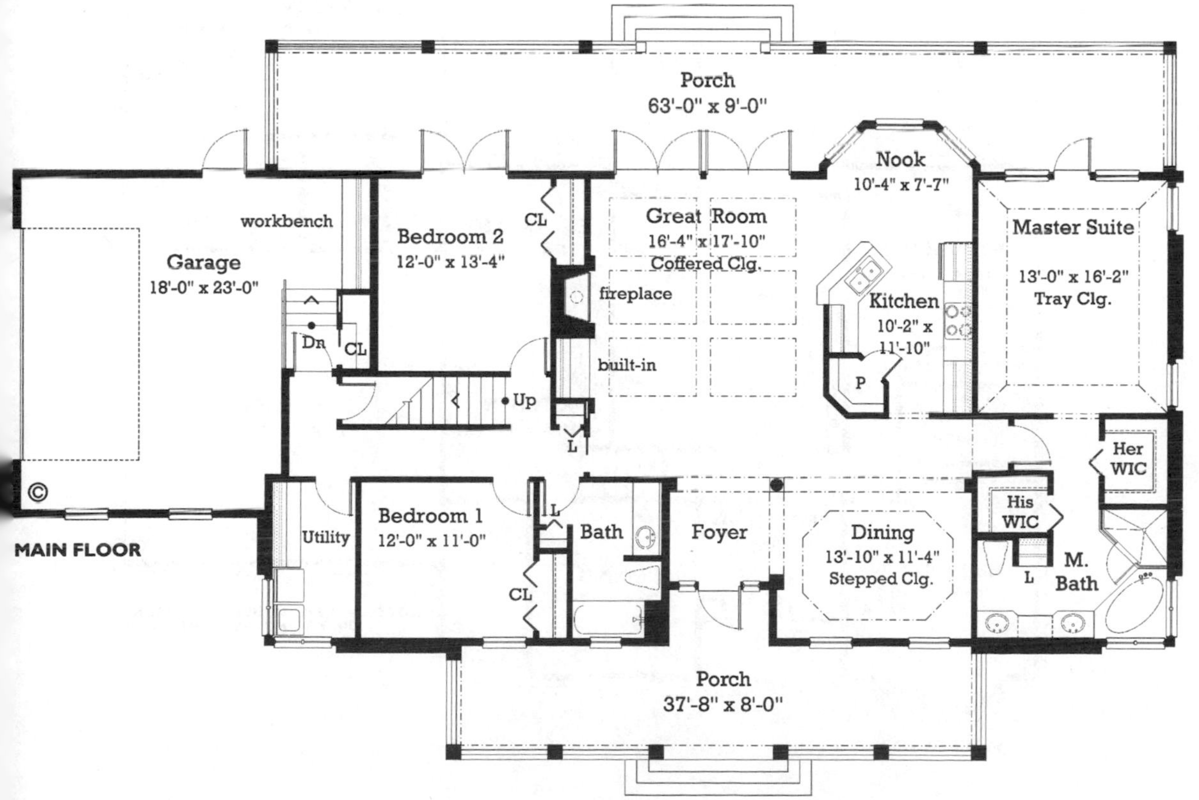

Design 90465

Units	Single
Price Code	C
Total Finished	1,990 sq. ft.
Main Finished	1,990 sq. ft.
Basement Unfinished	1,415 sq. ft.
Garage Unfinished	484 sq. ft.
Deck Unfinished	416 sq. ft.
Porch Unfinished	36 sq. ft.
Dimensions	64'10"x57'4"
Foundation	Basement Crawlspace
Bedrooms	3
Full Baths	2
Main Ceiling	9'
Max Ridge Height	27'6"
Roof Framing	Stick
Exterior Walls	2x4

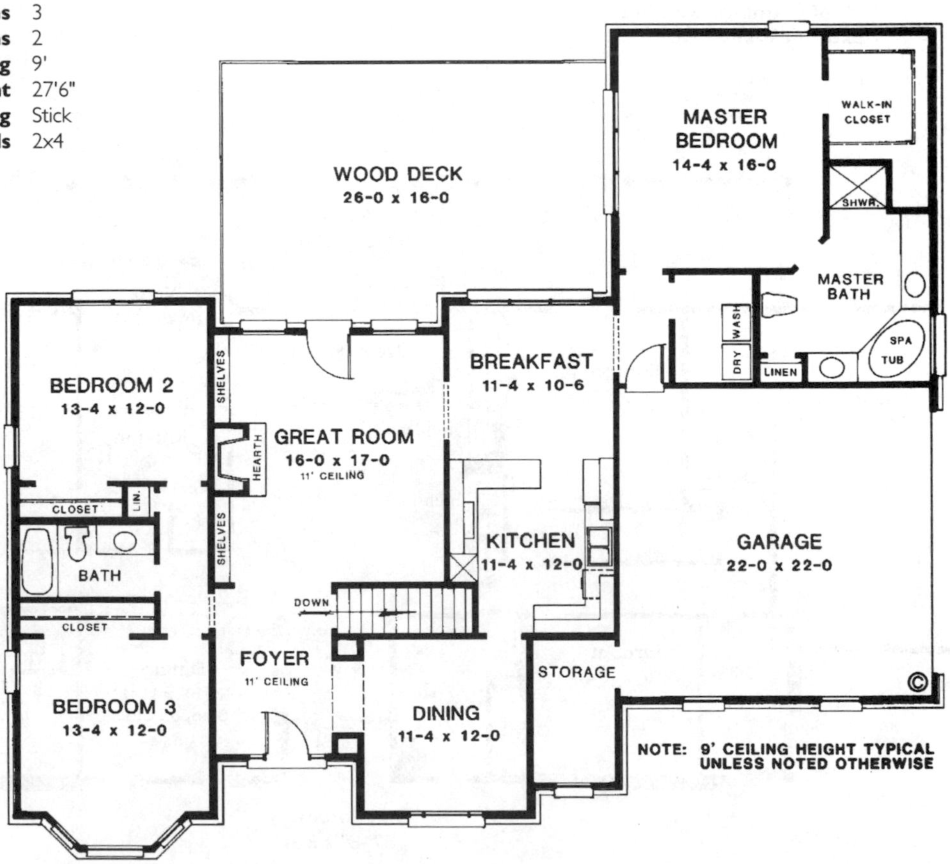

WOOD DECK 26-0 x 16-0

MASTER BEDROOM 14-4 x 16-0

WALK-IN CLOSET

SHWR.

MASTER BATH

SPA TUB

WASH

DRY

LINEN

BEDROOM 2 13-4 x 12-0

SHELVES

HEARTH

GREAT ROOM 16-0 x 17-0 11' CEILING

BREAKFAST 11-4 x 10-6

CLOSET

LIN.

BATH

KITCHEN 11-4 x 12-0

GARAGE 22-0 x 22-0

DOWN

CLOSET

FOYER 11' CEILING

STORAGE

BEDROOM 3 13-4 x 12-0

DINING 11-4 x 12-0

©

NOTE: 9' CEILING HEIGHT TYPICAL UNLESS NOTED OTHERWISE

MAIN FLOOR

Design 65234

Units	Single
Price Code	E
Total Finished	1,995 sq. ft.
First Finished	1,525 sq. ft.
Second Finished	470 sq. ft.
Basement Unfinished	1,525 sq. ft.
Garage Unfinished	596 sq. ft.
Dimensions	56'x53'2"
Foundation	Basement
Bedrooms	3
Full Baths	2
Half Baths	1
First Ceiling	9'
Second Ceiling	8'
Max Ridge Height	29'9"
Roof Framing	Truss
Exterior Walls	2x6

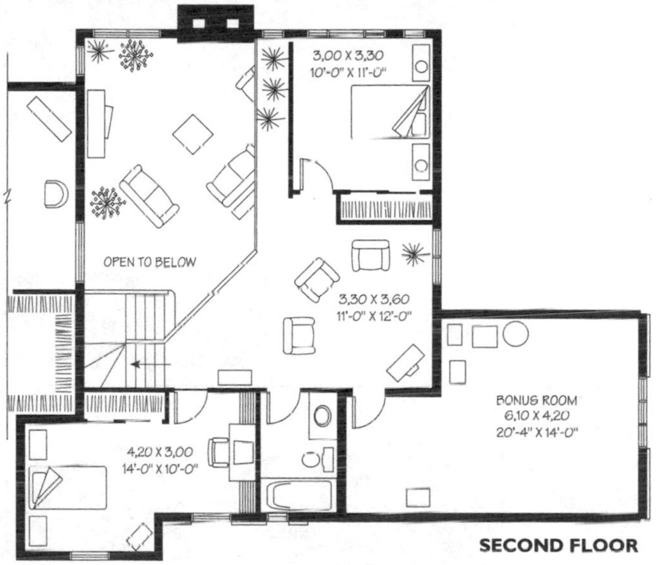

3,00 X 3,30
10'-0" X 11'-0"

OPEN TO BELOW

3,30 X 3,60
11'-0" X 12'-0"

BONUS ROOM
6,10 X 4,20
20'-4" X 14'-0"

4,20 X 3,00
14'-0" X 10'-0"

SECOND FLOOR

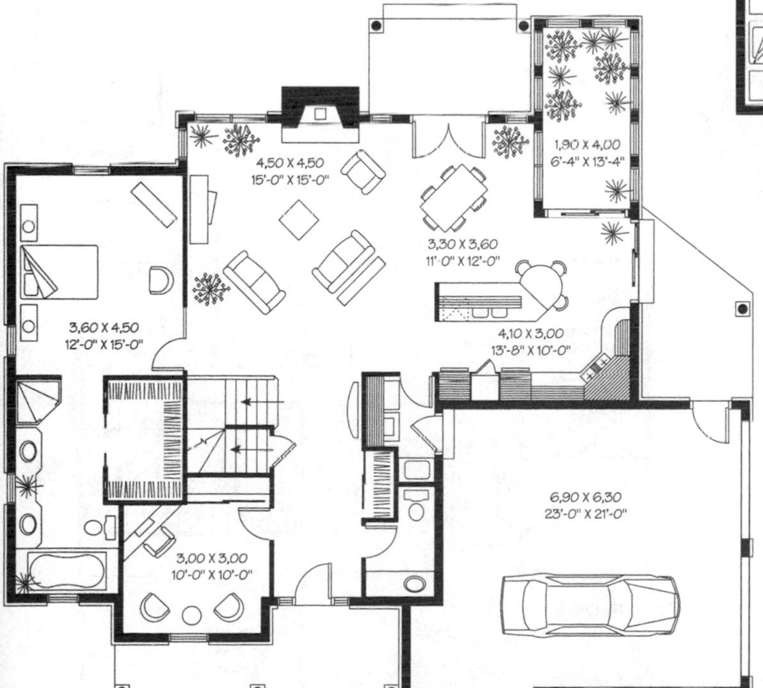

1,90 X 4,00
6'-4" X 13'-4"

4,50 X 4,50
15'-0" X 15'-0"

3,30 X 3,60
11'-0" X 12'-0"

3,60 X 4,50
12'-0" X 15'-0"

4,10 X 3,00
13'-8" X 10'-0"

6,90 X 6,30
23'-0" X 21'-0"

3,00 X 3,00
10'-0" X 10'-0"

©

FIRST FLOOR

Design 91125

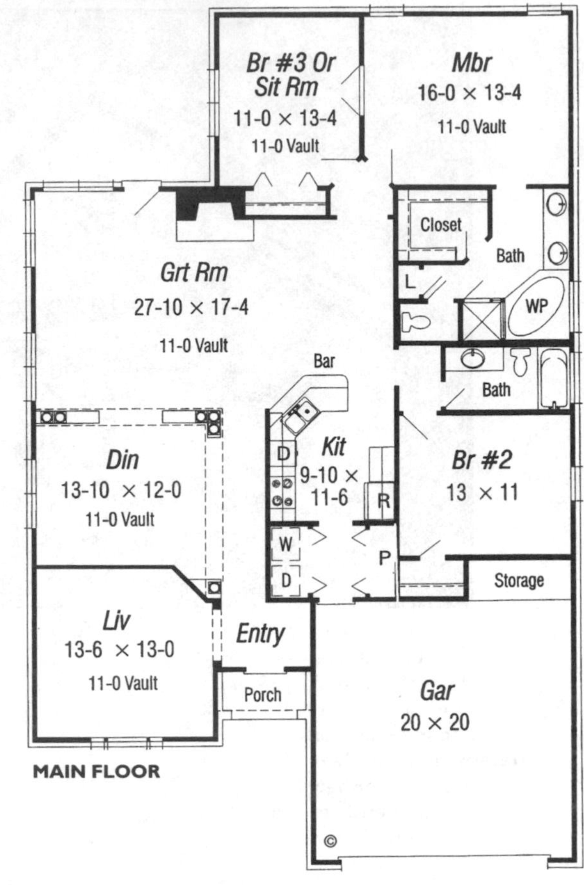

Units	Single
Price Code	C
Total Finished	1,995 sq. ft.
Main Finished	1,995 sq. ft.
Garage Unfinished	469 sq. ft.
Porch Unfinished	24 sq. ft.
Dimensions	43'x67'8"
Foundation	Slab
Bedrooms	3
Full Baths	2
Max Ridge Height	20'9"
Roof Framing	Stick
Exterior Walls	2x4

Design 97912

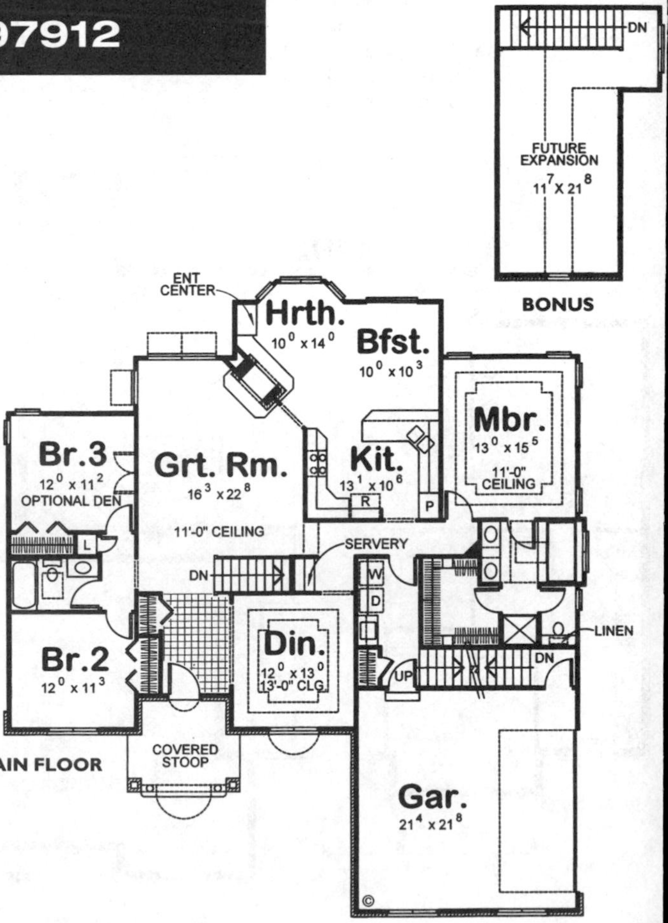

Units	Single
Price Code	C
Total Finished	1,995 sq. ft.
Main Finished	1,995 sq. ft.
Bonus Unfinished	308 sq. ft.
Basement Unfinished	1,995 sq. ft.
Dimensions	56'x62'
Foundation	Basement
Bedrooms	3
Full Baths	2
Main Ceiling	9'
Max Ridge Height	26'
Exterior Walls	2x4

* Alternate foundation options available at an additional charge. Please call 1-800-235-5700 for more information.

MAIN FLOOR

BONUS

Design 94926

Units	Single
Price Code	C
Total Finished	1,996 sq. ft.
Main Finished	1,996 sq. ft.
Garage Unfinished	683 sq. ft.
Dimensions	64'x50'
Foundation	Basement
Bedrooms	3
Full Baths	2
Main Ceiling	10'
Max Ridge Height	21'9"
Roof Framing	Stick
Exterior Walls	2x4

* Alternate foundation options available at an additional charge. Please call 1-800-235-5700 for more information.

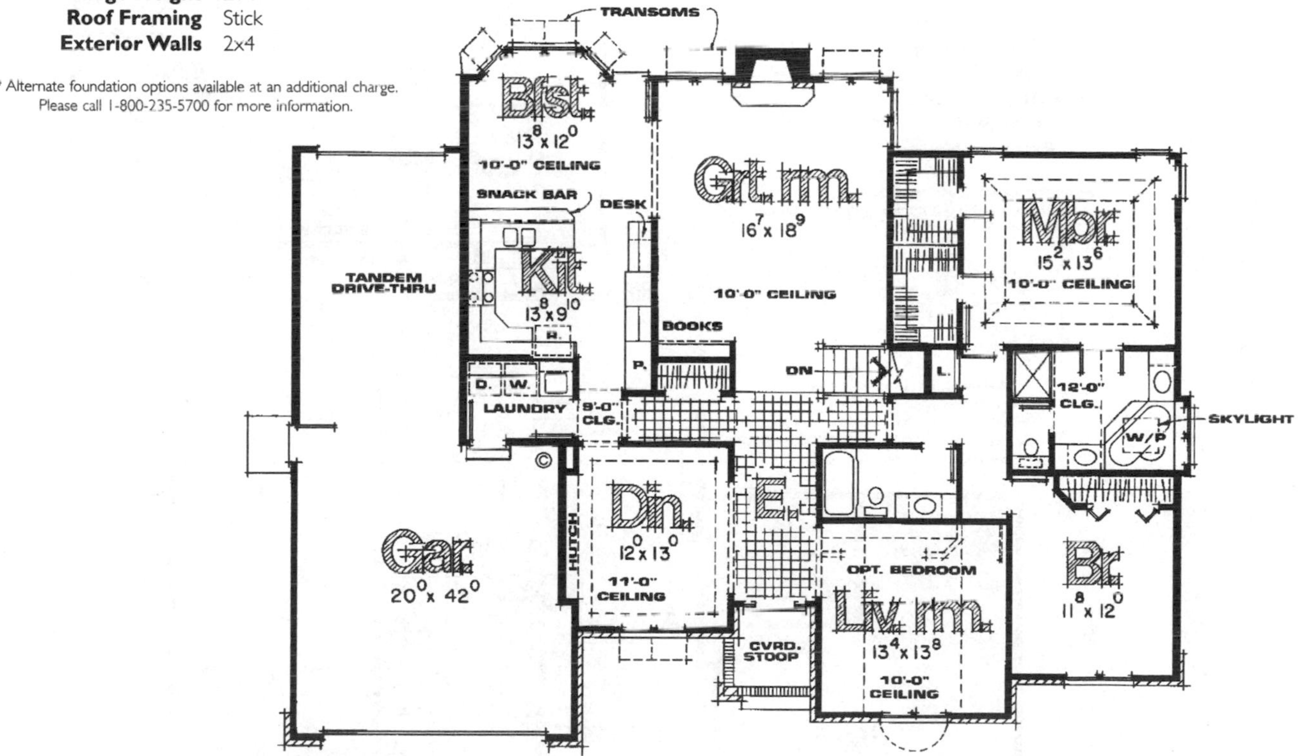

MAIN FLOOR

Design 94904

Units	Single
Price Code	C
Total Finished	1,998 sq. ft.
First Finished	1,093 sq. ft.
Second Finished	905 sq. ft.
Basement Unfinished	1,093 sq. ft.
Garage Unfinished	527 sq. ft.
Dimensions	55'4"x37'8"
Foundation	Basement
Bedrooms	3
Full Baths	2
Half Baths	1
First Ceiling	8'
Second Ceiling	8'
Max Ridge Height	29'
Roof Framing	Stick
Exterior Walls	2x4

* Alternate foundation options available at an additional charge. Please call 1-800-235-5700 for more information.

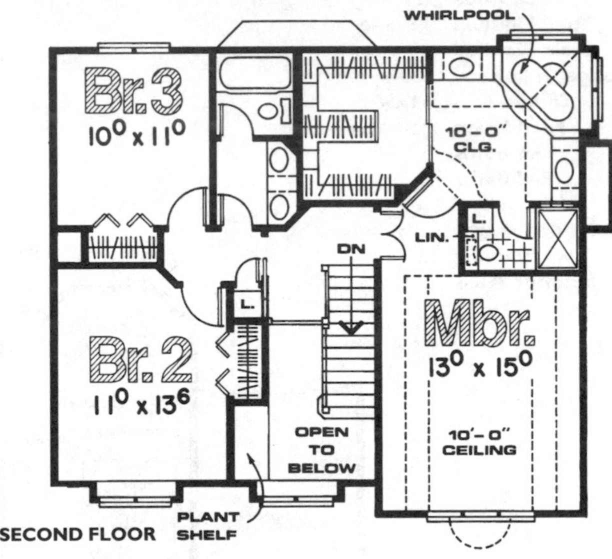

Please note: The photographed home may have been modified to suit homeowner preferences. If you order plans, have a builder or design professional check them against the photograph to confirm actual construction details.

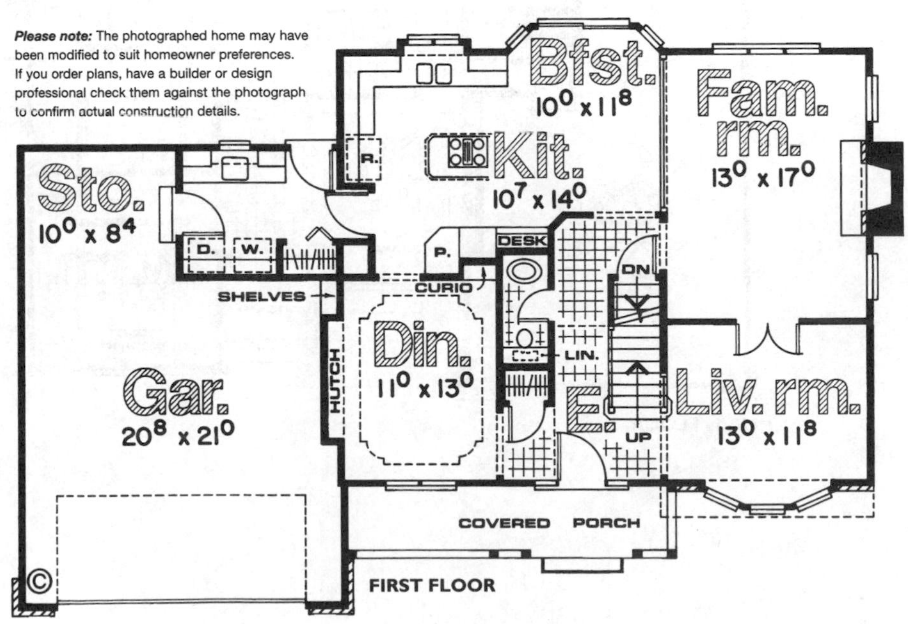

Design 65630

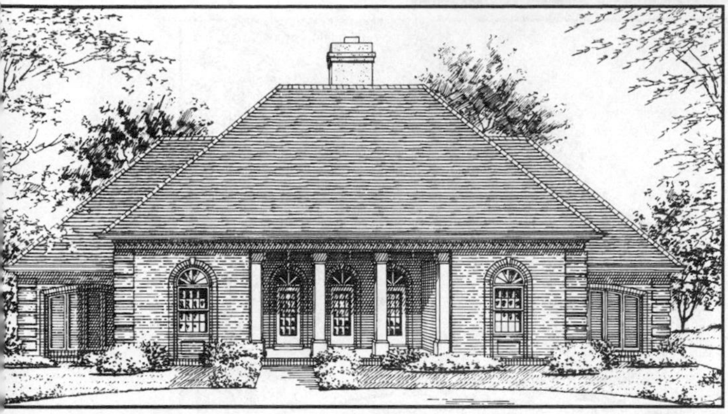

Units	Single
Price Code	C
Total Finished	2,000 sq. ft.
Main Finished	2,000 sq. ft.
Dimensions	68'x64'
Foundation	Crawlspace Slab
Bedrooms	3
Full Baths	2
Max Ridge Height	28'
Roof Framing	Stick
Exterior Walls	2x4

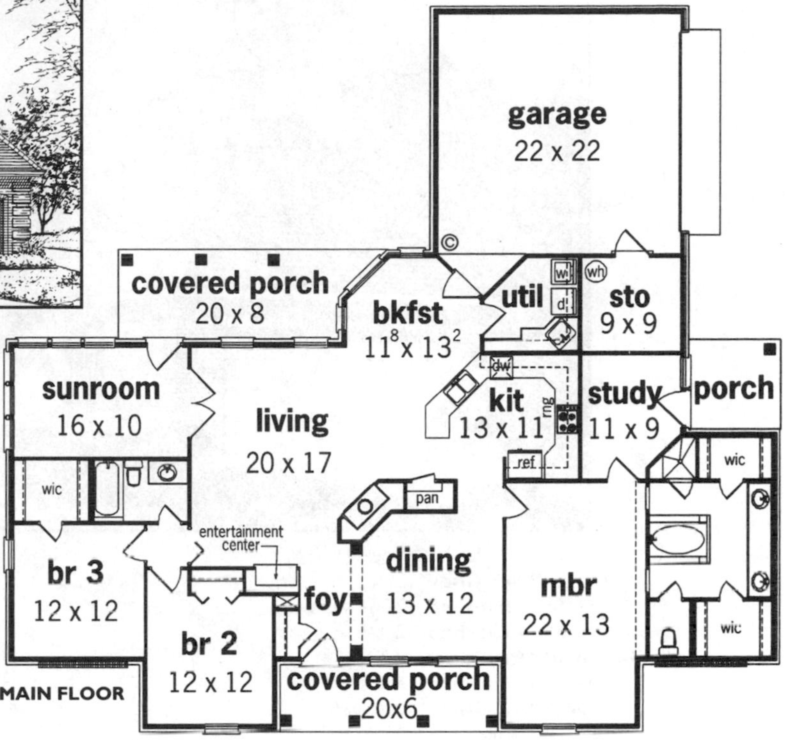

MAIN FLOOR

Design 63055

Units	Single
Price Code	C
Total Finished	2,000 sq. ft.
First Finished	1,667 sq. ft.
Second Finished	333 sq. ft.
Garage Unfinished	777 sq. ft.
Dimensions	60'8"x70'4"
Foundation	Slab
Bedrooms	3
Full Baths	2
3/4 Baths	1
First Ceiling	8'
Max Ridge Height	26'6"
Roof Framing	Truss

SECOND FLOOR

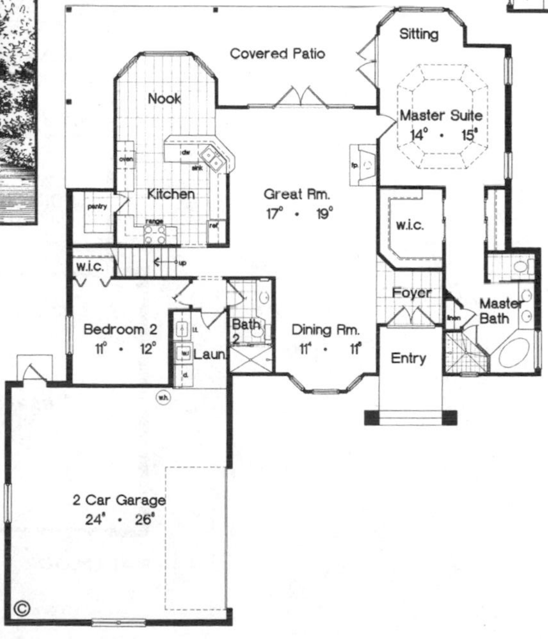

FIRST FLOOR

Design 86019

Units	Single
Price Code	D
Total Finished	2,001 sq. ft.
Main Finished	2,001 sq. ft.
Basement Unfinished	979 sq. ft.
Garage Unfinished	455 sq. ft.
Deck Unfinished	220 sq. ft.
Porch Unfinished	21 sq. ft.
Dimensions	39'6"x84'10"
Foundation	Combo Basement/ Crawlspace
Bedrooms	3
Full Baths	2
Main Ceiling	8'
Max Ridge Height	27'7"
Roof Framing	Stick
Exterior Walls	2x4

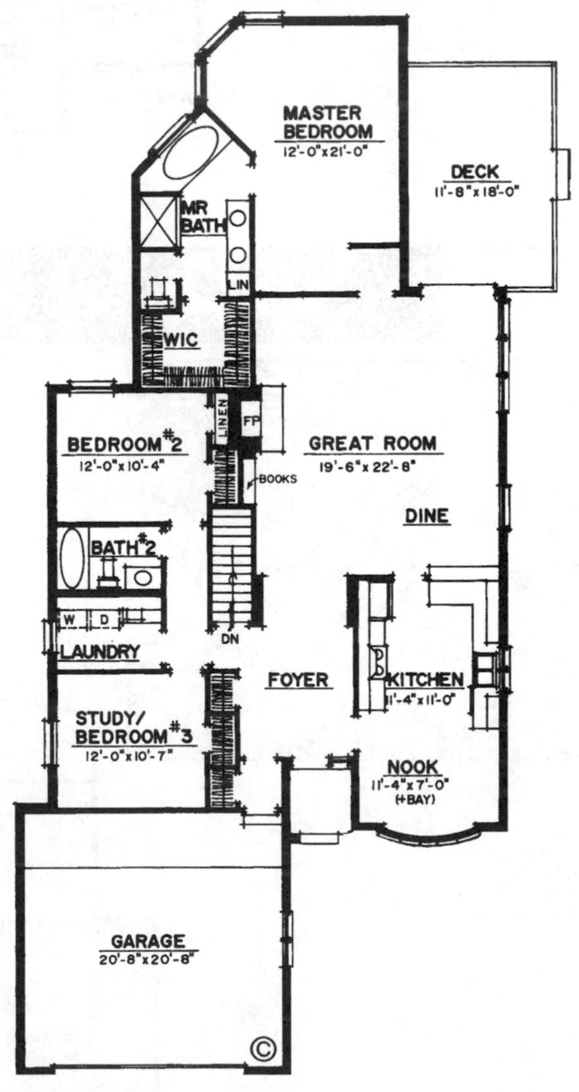

MAIN FLOOR

Design 65626

Units Single
Price Code D
Total Finished 2,002 sq. ft.
Main Finished 2,002 sq. ft.
Dimensions 66'x60'
Foundation Crawlspace
Slab
Bedrooms 3
Full Baths 2
Main Ceiling 8'
Max Ridge Height 29'
Roof Framing Stick
Exterior Walls 2x6

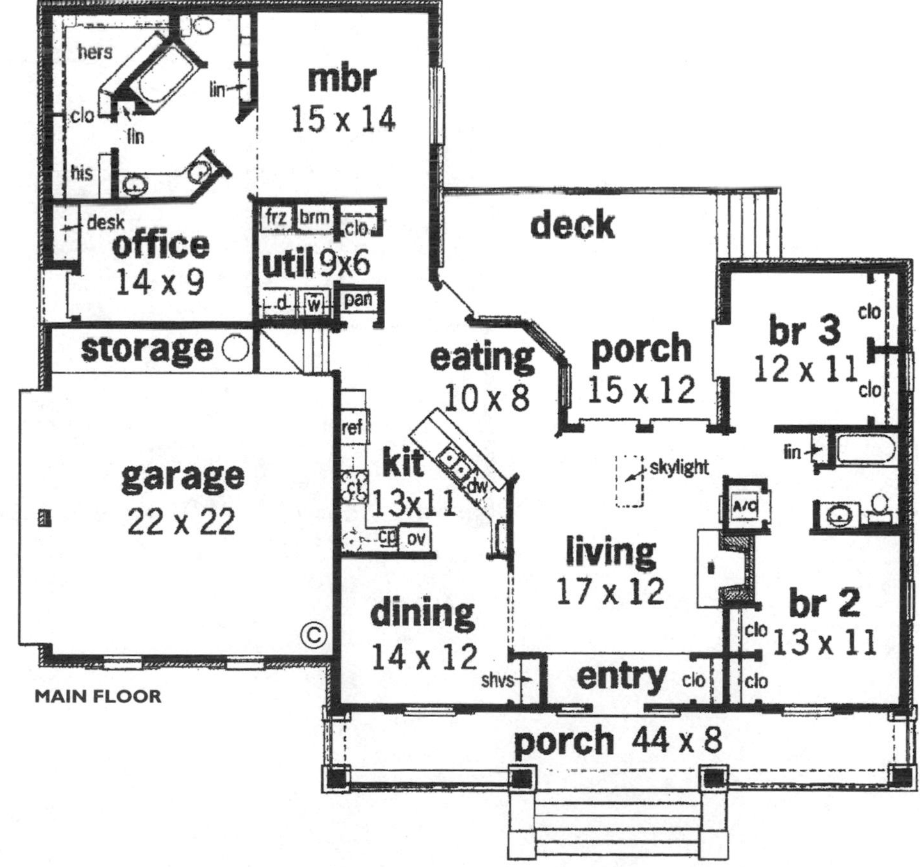

MAIN FLOOR

Design 63125

Units	Single
Price Code	D
Total Finished	2,005 sq. ft.
Main Finished	2,005 sq. ft.
Garage Unfinished	466 sq. ft.
Dimensions	58'x60'
Foundation	Slab
Bedrooms	3
Full Baths	2
Main Ceiling	10'
Max Ridge Height	20'10"
Roof Framing	Truss

Covered Patio

Master Bedroom
volume ceiling
16^{0} · 12^{0}

Bedroom 2
volume ceiling
13^{10} · 12^{0}

lin

Breakfast

Great Room
vaulted ceiling
20^{0} · 18^{0}

vaulted ceiling

lin

Bath

Bath

w.i.c.

lin

dw

Kitchen

p

Bedroom 3
volume ceiling
12^{0} · 11^{6}

opt. fireplace

Foyer

Living Room
volume ceiling
15^{0} · 12^{0}

Dining
vaulted ceiling
12^{4} · 12^{0}

ref

w

Utility

d

ac

Entry

wh

MAIN FLOOR

Double Garage

©

Design 97151

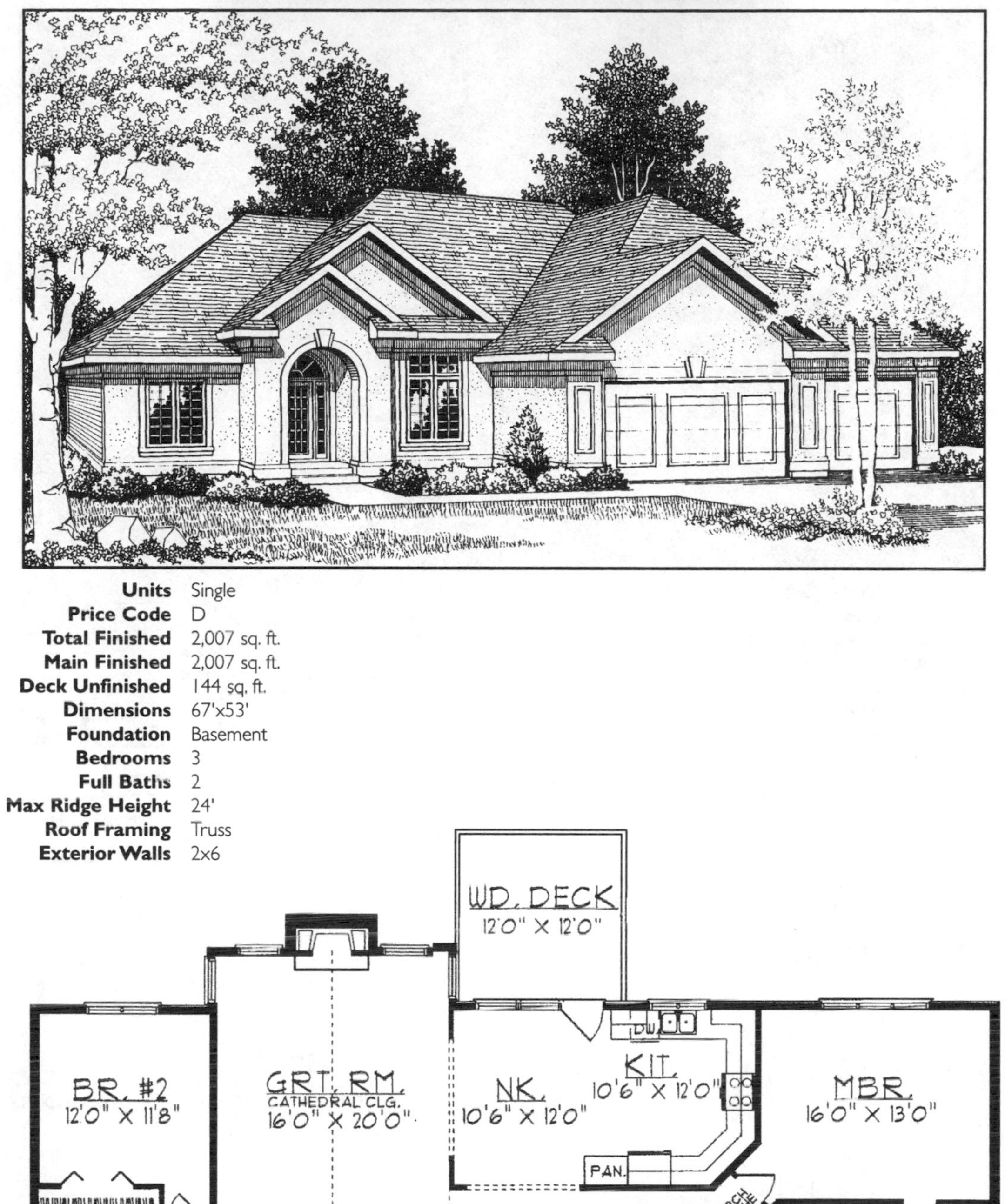

Units	Single
Price Code	D
Total Finished	2,007 sq. ft.
Main Finished	2,007 sq. ft.
Deck Unfinished	144 sq. ft.
Dimensions	67'x53'
Foundation	Basement
Bedrooms	3
Full Baths	2
Max Ridge Height	24'
Roof Framing	Truss
Exterior Walls	2x6

MAIN FLOOR

Design 65125

Units	Single
Price Code	D
Total Finished	2,012 sq. ft.
First Finished	1,324 sq. ft.
Second Finished	688 sq. ft.
Basement Unfinished	1,324 sq. ft.
Garage Unfinished	425 sq. ft.
Dimensions	56'x41'
Foundation	Basement
Bedrooms	4
Full Baths	2
First Ceiling	8'
Second Ceiling	8'
Max Ridge Height	25'
Roof Framing	Truss
Exterior Walls	2x6

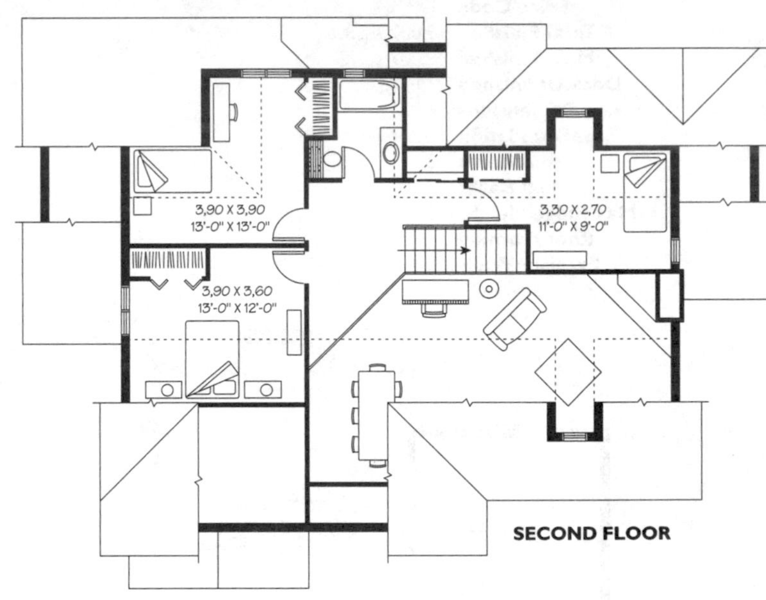

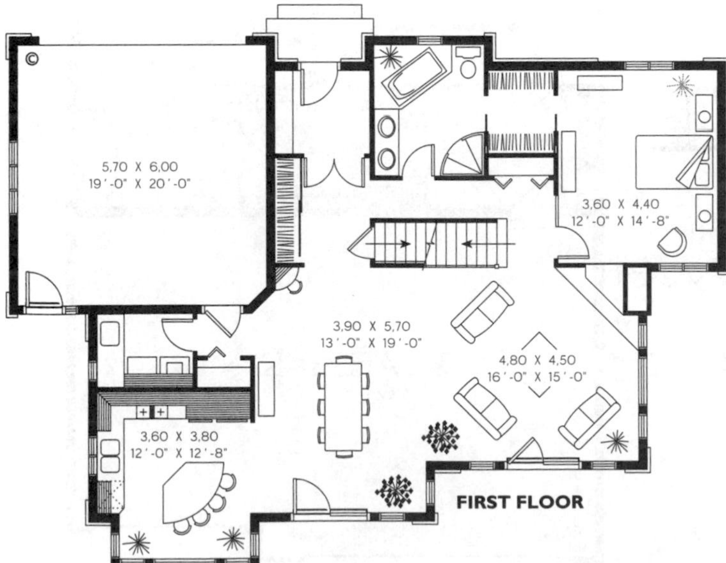

Design 69148

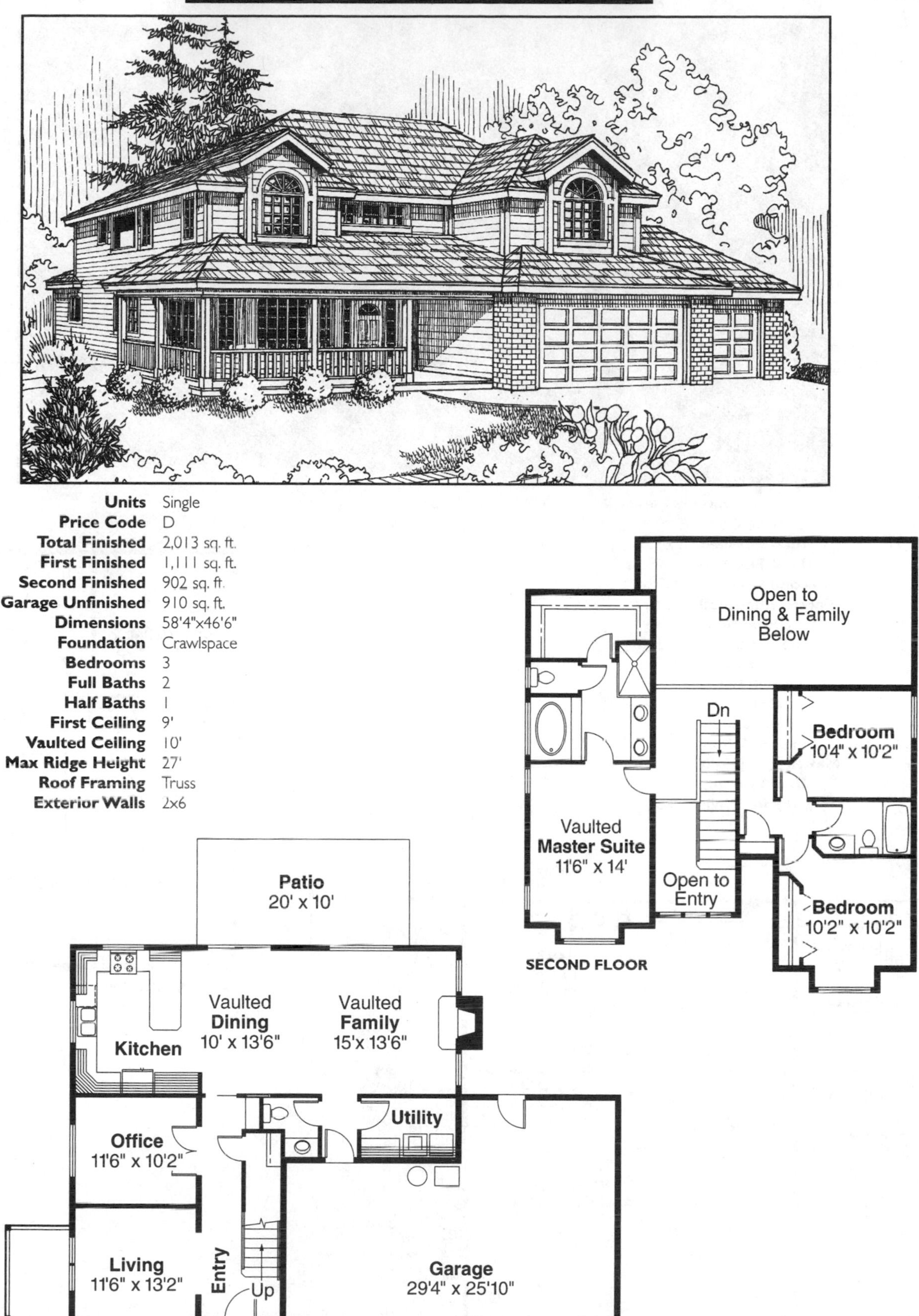

Units	Single
Price Code	D
Total Finished	2,013 sq. ft.
First Finished	1,111 sq. ft.
Second Finished	902 sq. ft.
Garage Unfinished	910 sq. ft.
Dimensions	58'4"x46'6"
Foundation	Crawlspace
Bedrooms	3
Full Baths	2
Half Baths	1
First Ceiling	9'
Vaulted Ceiling	10'
Max Ridge Height	27'
Roof Framing	Truss
Exterior Walls	2x6

Design 10515

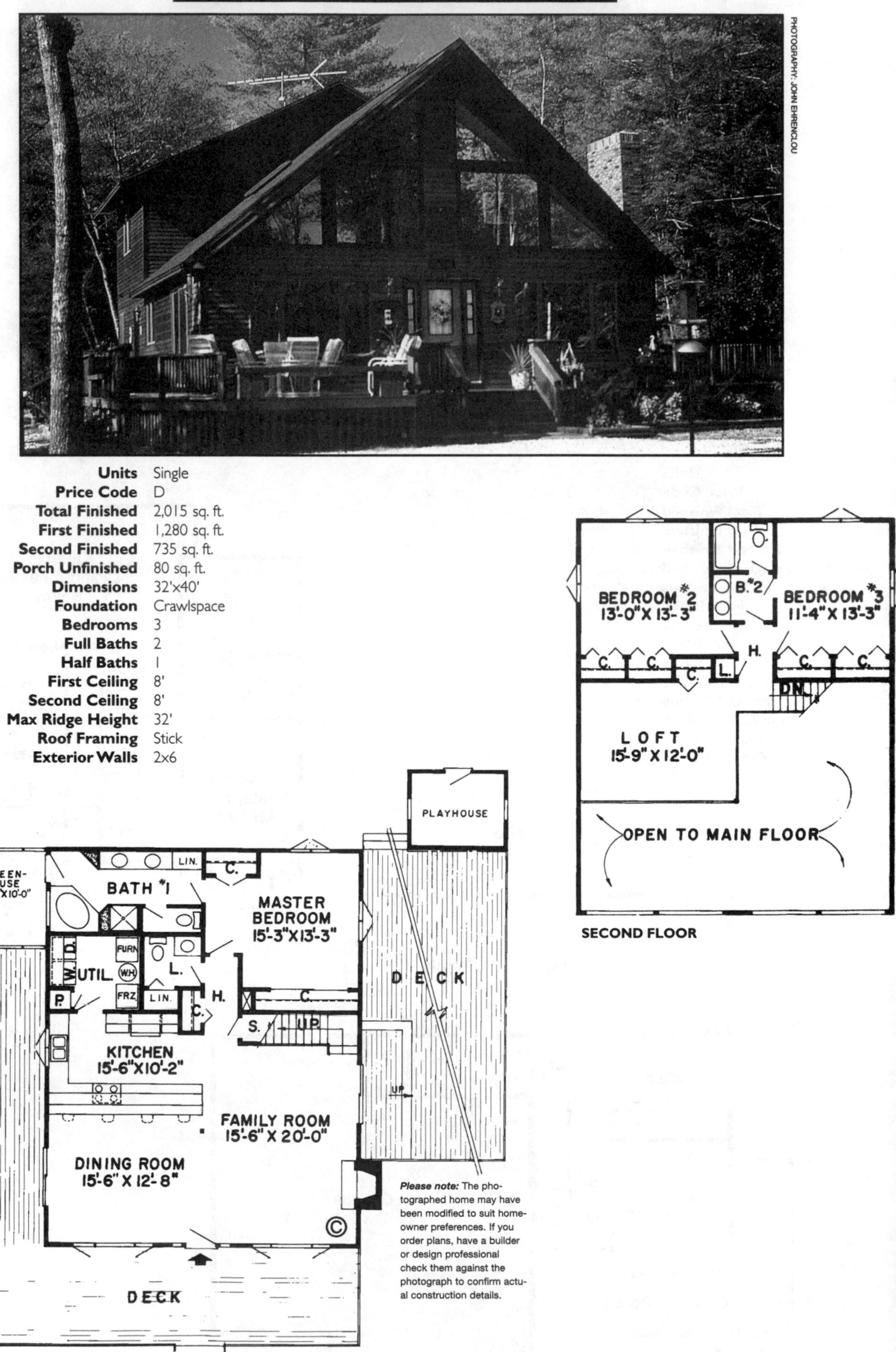

Units	Single
Price Code	D
Total Finished	2,015 sq. ft.
First Finished	1,280 sq. ft.
Second Finished	735 sq. ft.
Porch Unfinished	80 sq. ft.
Dimensions	32'x40'
Foundation	Crawlspace
Bedrooms	3
Full Baths	2
Half Baths	1
First Ceiling	8'
Second Ceiling	8'
Max Ridge Height	32'
Roof Framing	Stick
Exterior Walls	2x6

Please note: The photographed home may have been modified to suit homeowner preferences. If you order plans, have a builder or design professional check them against the photograph to confirm actual construction details.

Design 97308

Units	Single
Price Code	D
Total Finished	2,017 sq. ft.
Main Finished	2,017 sq. ft.
Garage Unfinished	912 sq. ft.
Dimensions	81'x51'4"
Foundation	Basement
Bedrooms	3
Full Baths	2
Half Baths	1
Main Ceiling	9'1⅛"
Max Ridge Height	24'8"
Roof Framing	Truss
Exterior Walls	2x6

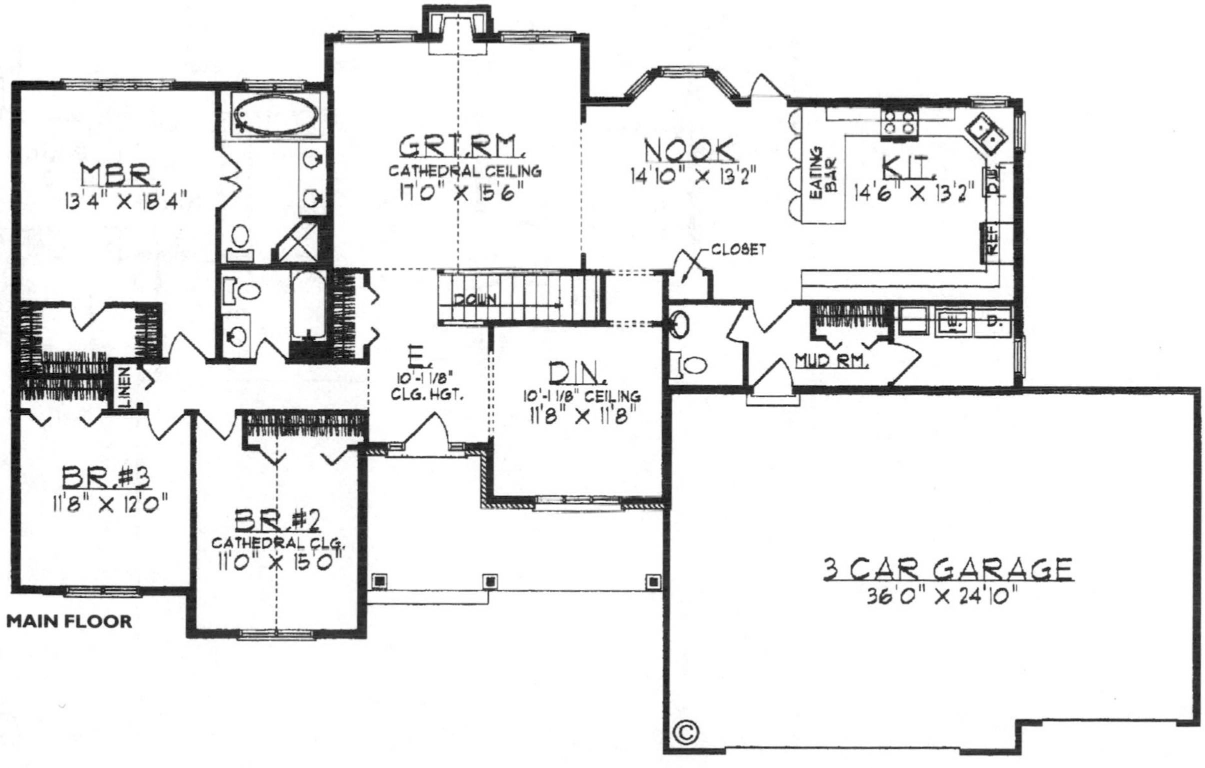

Design 98361

Units	Single
Price Code	D
Total Finished	2,029 sq. ft.
Main Finished	2,029 sq. ft.
Basement Unfinished	2,029 sq. ft.
Garage Unfinished	704 sq. ft.
Dimensions	76'x71'4"
Foundation	Basement
Bedrooms	2
Full Baths	2
Half Baths	1
Max Ridge Height	24'
Roof Framing	Truss
Exterior Walls	2x6

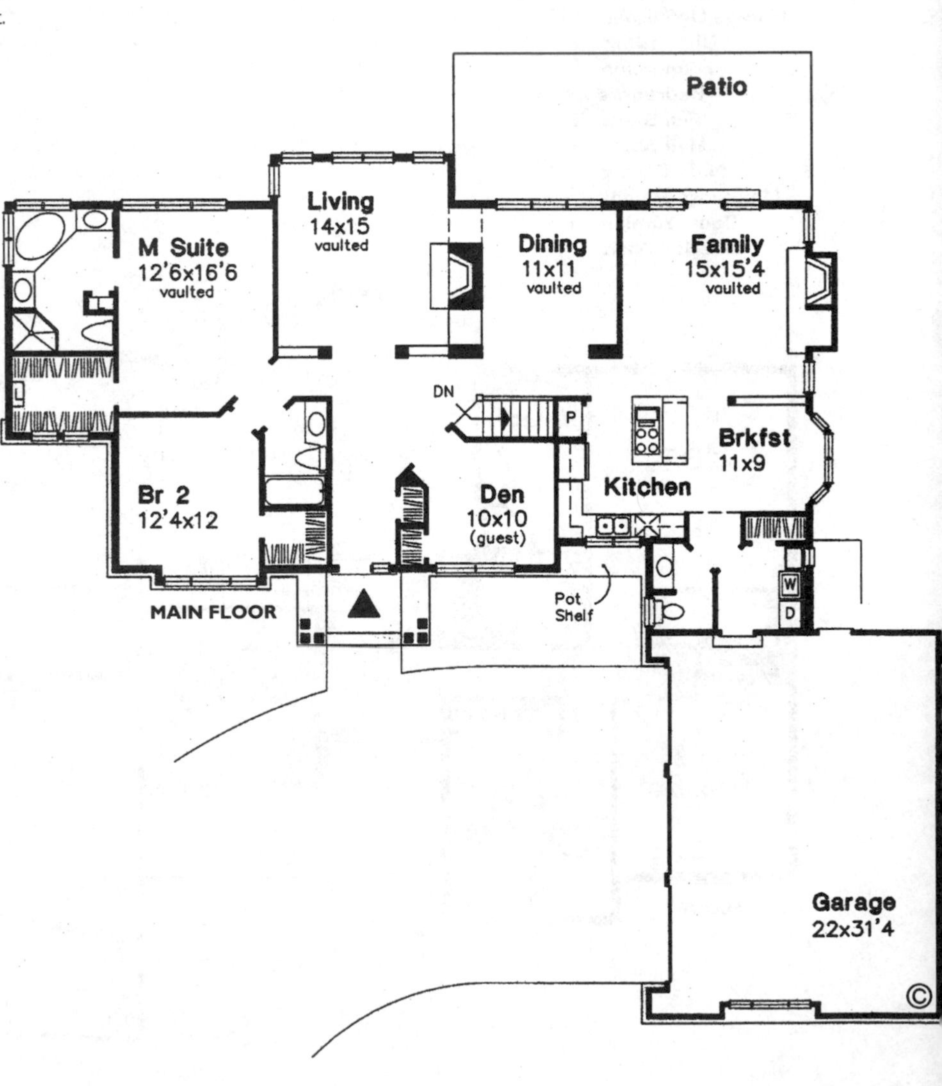

Design 69105

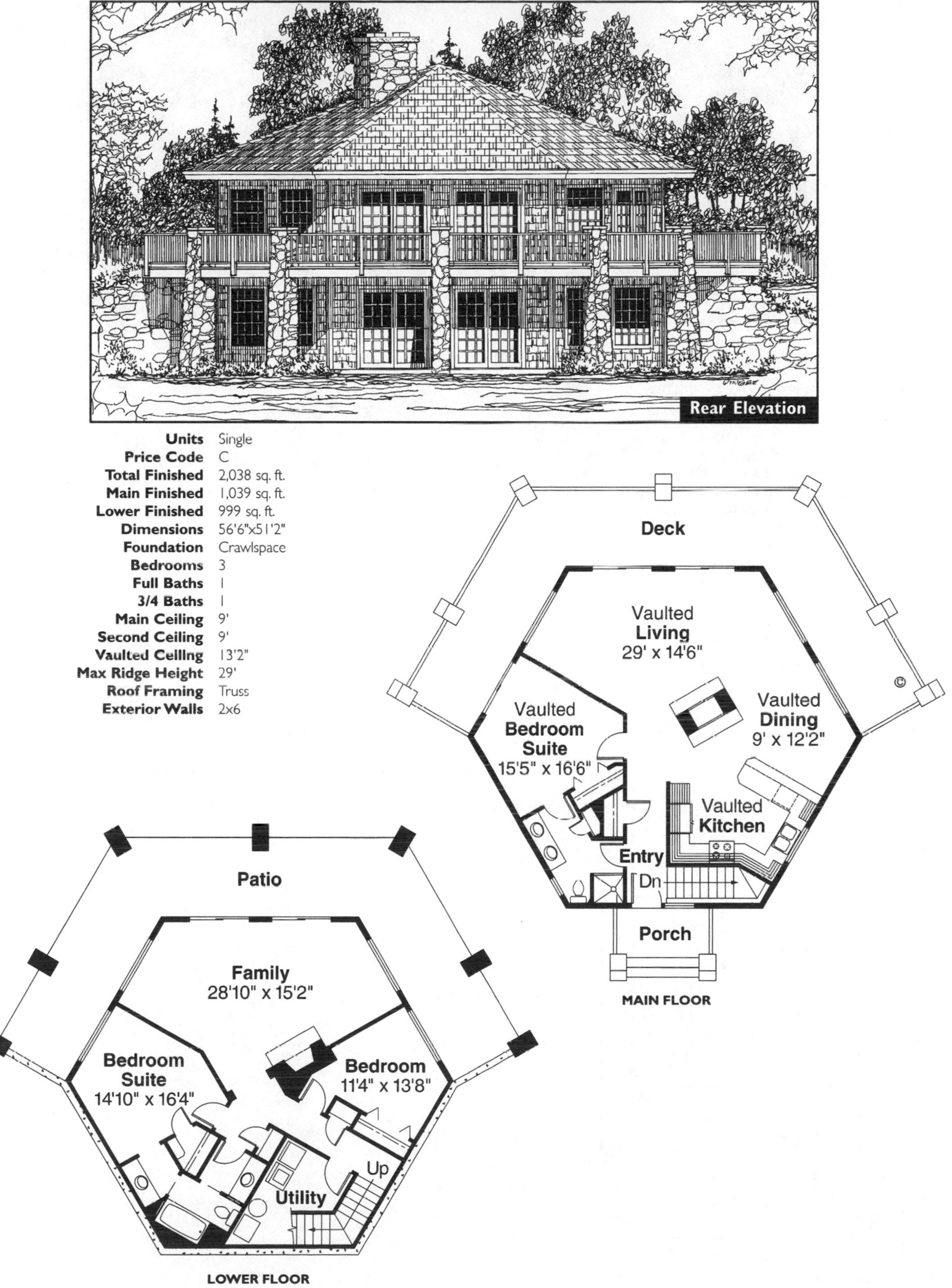

Design 97406

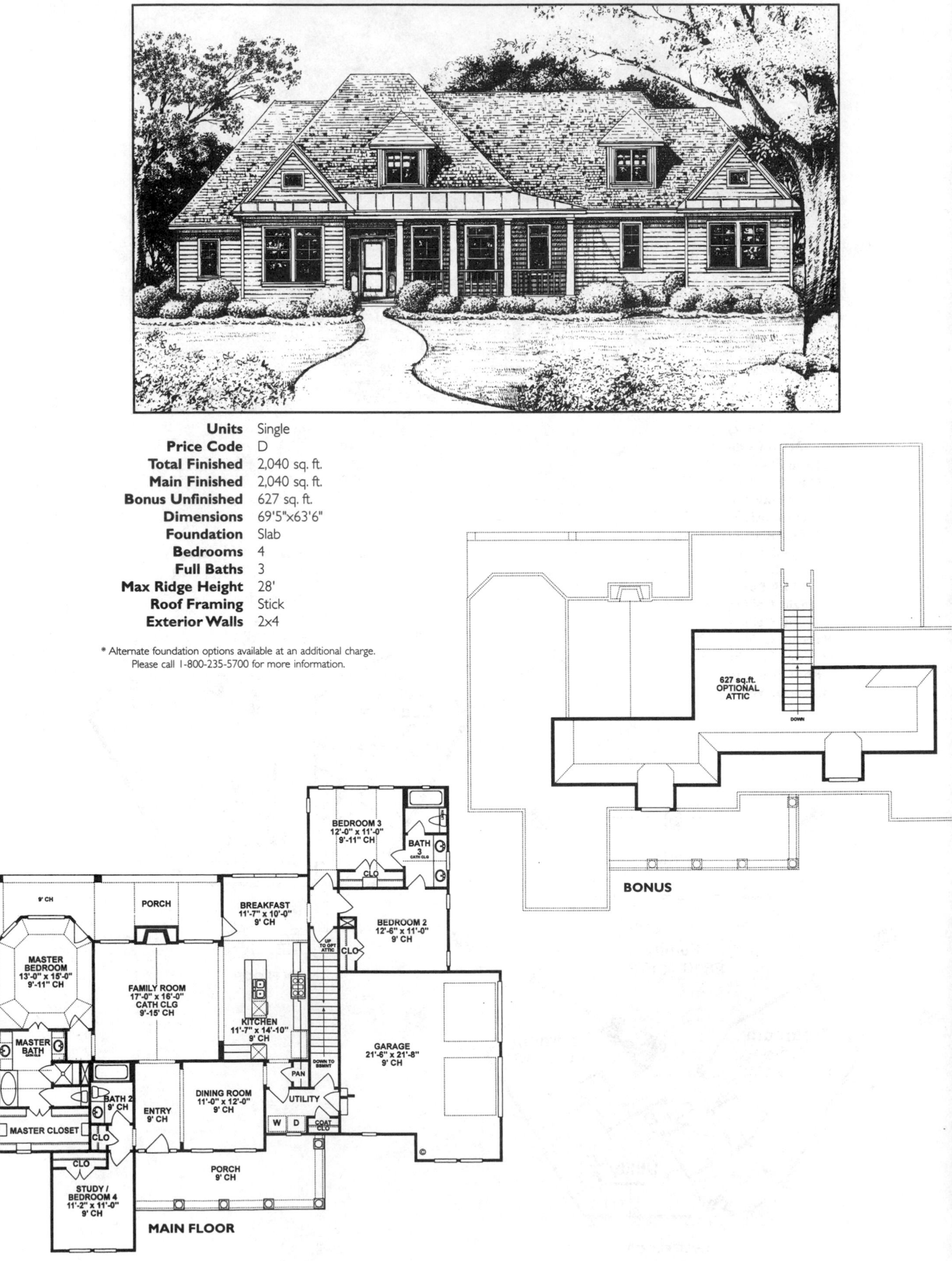

Units	Single
Price Code	D
Total Finished	2,040 sq. ft.
Main Finished	2,040 sq. ft.
Bonus Unfinished	627 sq. ft.
Dimensions	69'5"x63'6"
Foundation	Slab
Bedrooms	4
Full Baths	3
Max Ridge Height	28'
Roof Framing	Stick
Exterior Walls	2x4

* Alternate foundation options available at an additional charge.
Please call 1-800-235-5700 for more information.

Design 63050

Units	Single
Price Code	D
Total Finished	2,041 sq. ft.
Main Finished	2,041 sq. ft.
Garage Unfinished	452 sq. ft.
Porch Unfinished	340 sq. ft.
Dimensions	60'4"x56'
Foundation	Slab
Bedrooms	4
Full Baths	2
Max Ridge Height	19'
Roof Framing	Truss
Exterior Walls	2x4

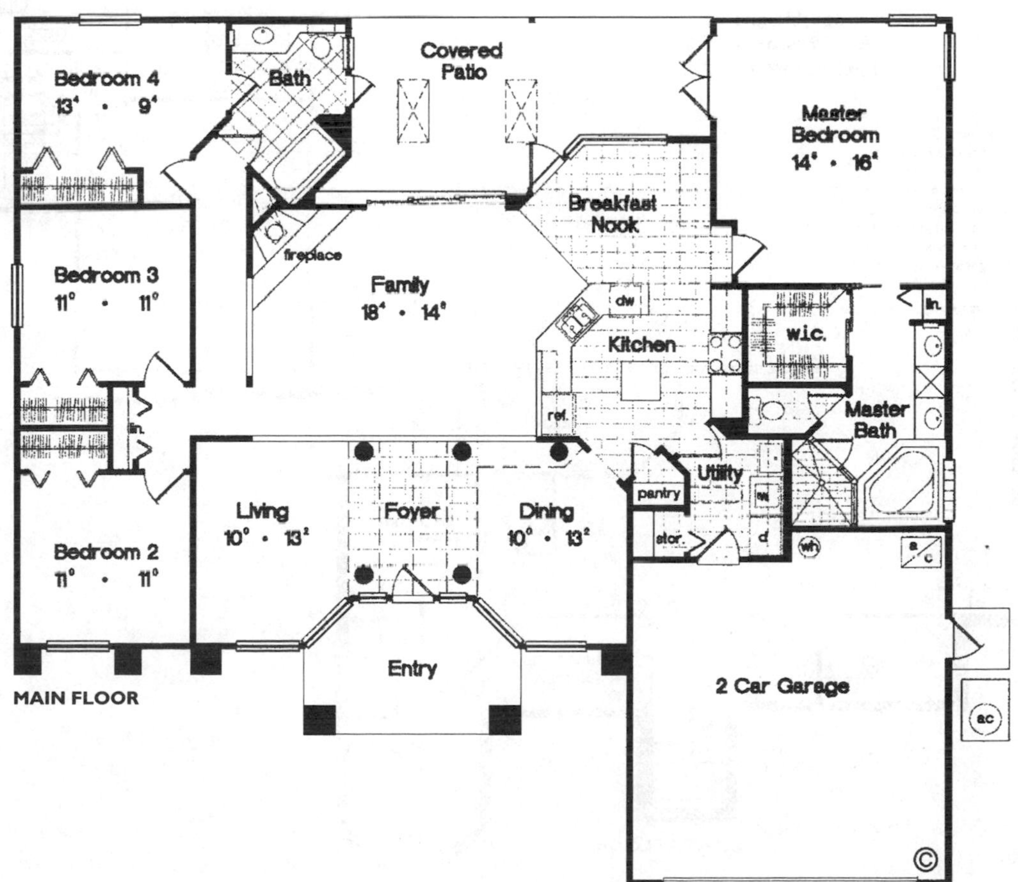

Design 92688

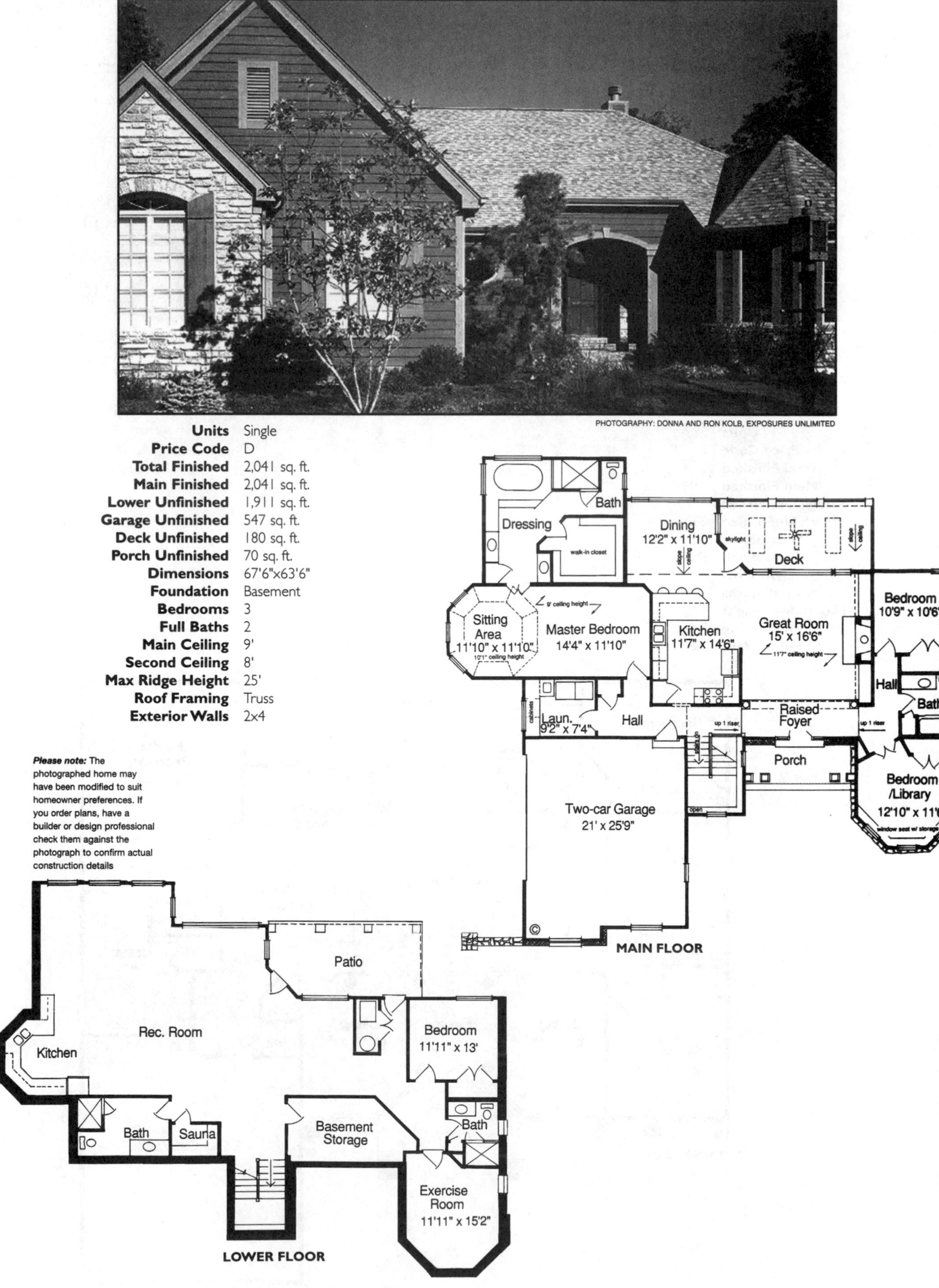

Units	Single
Price Code	D
Total Finished	2,041 sq. ft.
Main Finished	2,041 sq. ft.
Lower Unfinished	1,911 sq. ft.
Garage Unfinished	547 sq. ft.
Deck Unfinished	180 sq. ft.
Porch Unfinished	70 sq. ft.
Dimensions	67'6"x63'6"
Foundation	Basement
Bedrooms	3
Full Baths	2
Main Ceiling	9'
Second Ceiling	8'
Max Ridge Height	25'
Roof Framing	Truss
Exterior Walls	2x4

Please note: The photographed home may have been modified to suit homeowner preferences. If you order plans, have a builder or design professional check them against the photograph to confirm actual construction details

Design 94984

Units	Single
Price Code	D
Total Finished	2,042 sq. ft.
Main Finished	2,042 sq. ft.
Garage Unfinished	506 sq. ft.
Dimensions	65'4"x42'
Foundation	Basement
Bedrooms	3
Full Baths	2
Half Baths	1
Main Ceiling	8'
Max Ridge Height	19'
Roof Framing	Stick
Exterior Walls	2x4

* Alternate foundation options available at an additional charge. Please call 1-800-235-5700 for more information.

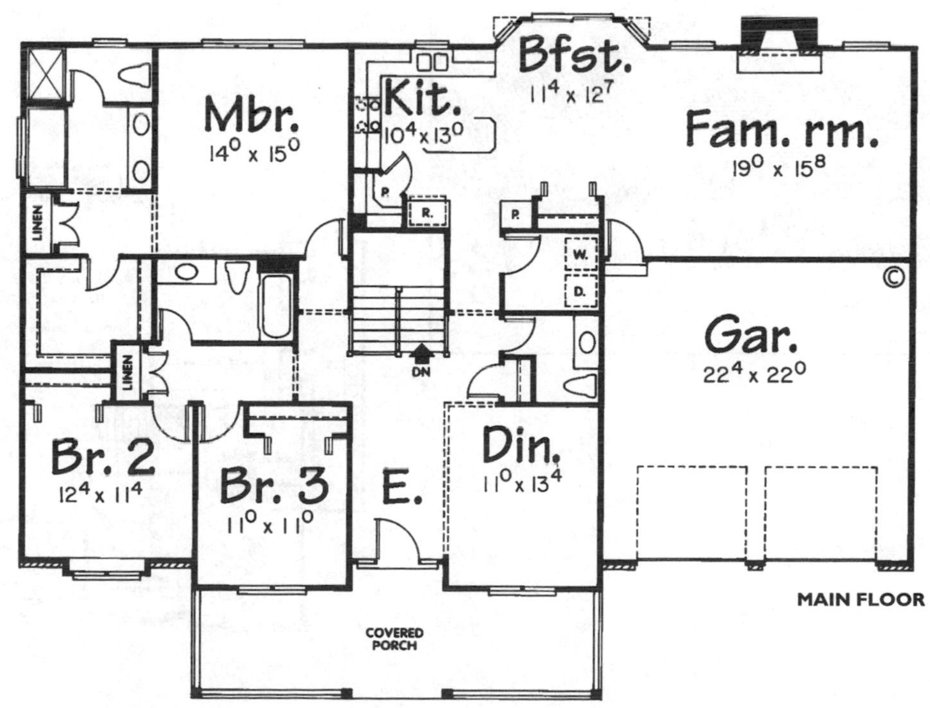

MAIN FLOOR

Design 24736

Units	Single
Price Code	D
Total Finished	2,044 sq. ft.
First Finished	1,403 sq. ft.
Second Finished	641 sq. ft.
Basement Unfinished	1,394 sq. ft.
Garage Unfinished	680 sq. ft.
Deck Unfinished	156 sq. ft.
Porch Unfinished	231 sq. ft.
Dimensions	68'x47'
Foundation	Basement Crawlspace Slab
Bedrooms	3
Full Baths	2
Half Baths	1
First Ceiling	9'
Second Ceiling	8'
Vaulted Ceiling	12'9"
Roof Framing	Truss
Exterior Walls	2x4

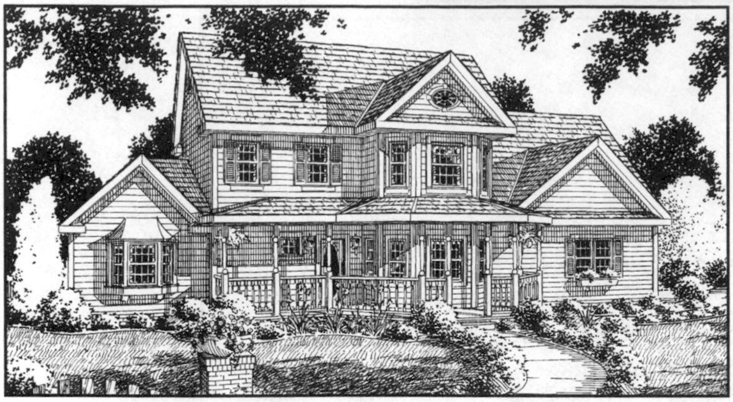

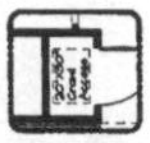

CRAWLSPACE/SLAB FOUNDATION OPTION

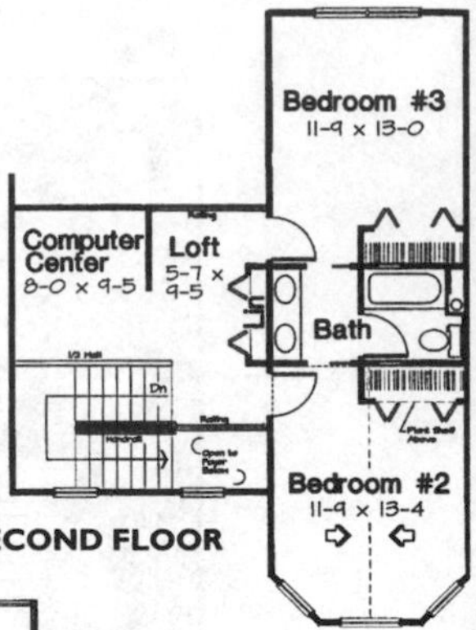

Bedroom #3
11-9 x 13-0
Computer Center
8-0 x 9-5
Loft
5-7 x 9-5
Bath
Bedroom #2
11-9 x 13-4

SECOND FLOOR

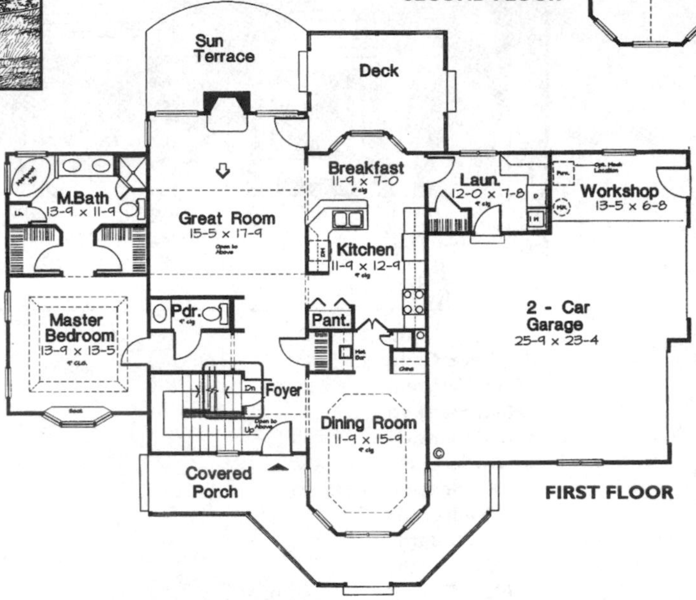

Sun Terrace
Deck
Breakfast
11-9 x 7-0
Laun.
12-0 x 7-8
Workshop
13-5 x 6-8
M.Bath
13-9 x 11-9
Great Room
15-5 x 17-9
Kitchen
11-9 x 12-9
2 - Car Garage
25-9 x 23-4
Master Bedroom
13-9 x 13-5
Pdr.
Pant.
Foyer
Dining Room
11-9 x 15-9
Covered Porch

FIRST FLOOR

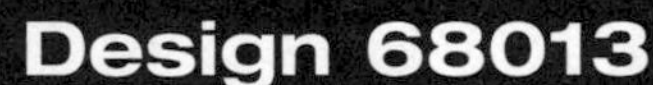

Design 68013

Units	Single
Price Code	D
Total Finished	2,047 sq. ft.
Main Finished	2,047 sq. ft.
Basement Unfinished	2,047 sq. ft.
Garage Unfinished	573 sq. ft.
Dimensions	66'x53'4"
Foundation	Basement Crawlspace Slab
Bedrooms	3
Full Baths	2
Half Baths	1
Main Ceiling	8'
Max Ridge Height	21'6"
Roof Framing	Stick
Exterior Walls	2x4

* Alternate foundation options available at an additional charge. Please call 1-800-235-5700 for more information.

Br. 3
11⁰ x 12⁰

THIRD BEDROOM OPTION

TRANSOMS
WHIRLPOOL
SEAT
Mbr.
13⁰ x 15⁸
9'-0" CEILING
Grt. rm.
16⁰ x 21⁰
10'-0" CEILING
Bfst.
13⁰ x 13⁵
SNACK BAR
Kit.
14⁰ x 13⁵
LIN.
DN
E.
Din.
15⁰ x 13⁶
10'-0" CLG.
WORK BENCH
Br. 2
11⁰ x 12⁰
10'-0" CLG.
9'-0" CLG.
Den
11⁰ x 14³
OPTIONAL BEDROOM
COVERED PORCH
TRANSOMS
Gar.
21⁴ x 26⁰

MAIN FLOOR

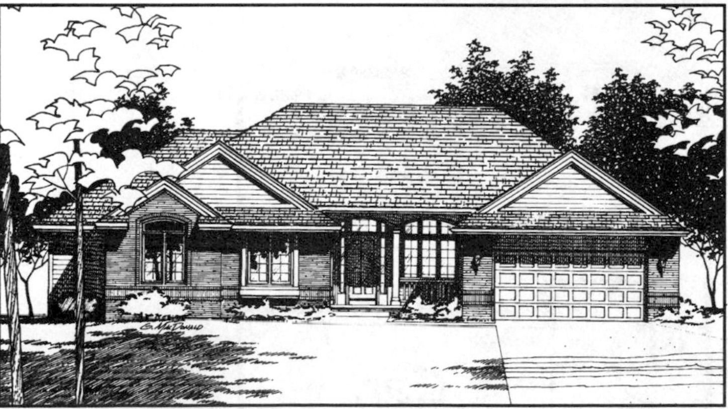

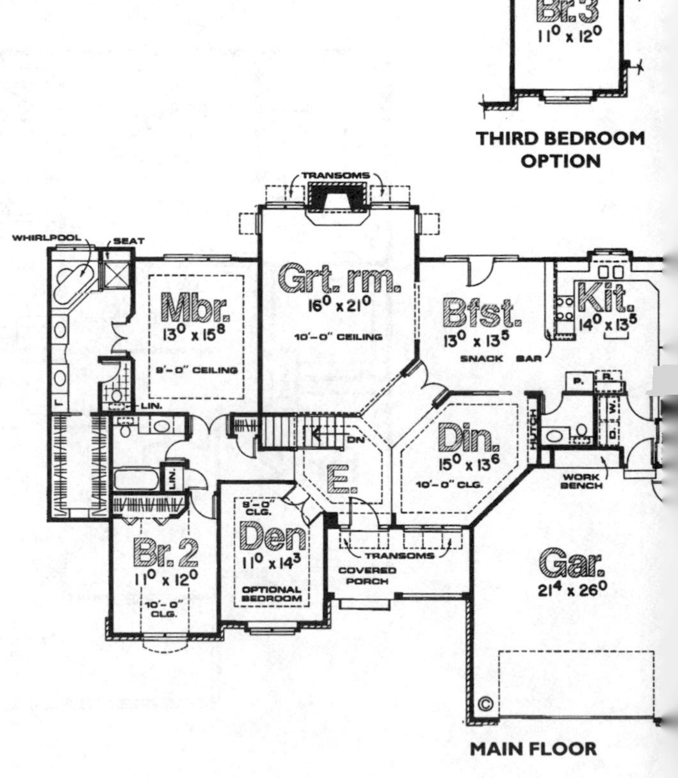

Design 69154

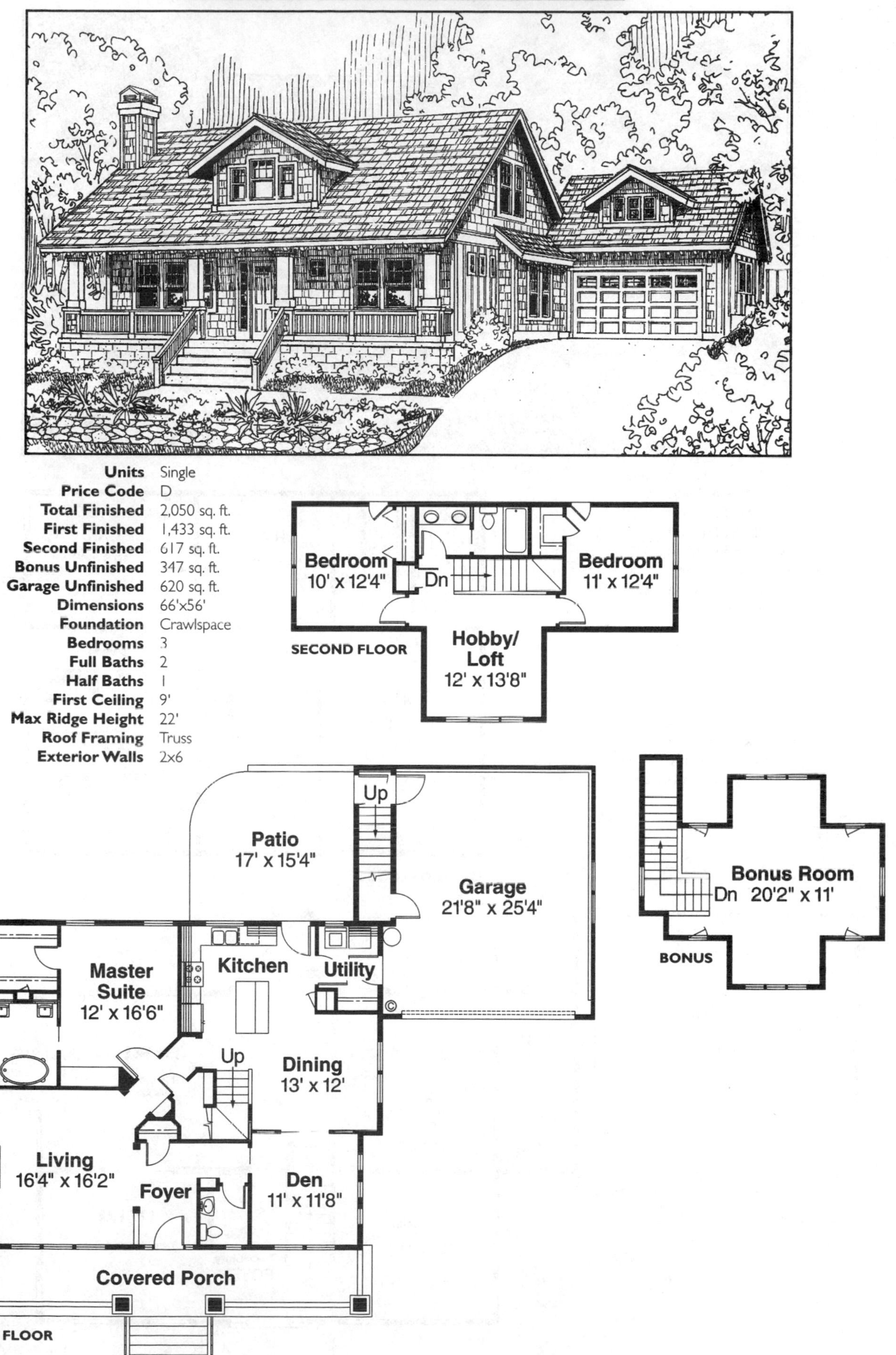

Units	Single
Price Code	D
Total Finished	2,050 sq. ft.
First Finished	1,433 sq. ft.
Second Finished	617 sq. ft.
Bonus Unfinished	347 sq. ft.
Garage Unfinished	620 sq. ft.
Dimensions	66'x56'
Foundation	Crawlspace
Bedrooms	3
Full Baths	2
Half Baths	1
First Ceiling	9'
Max Ridge Height	22'
Roof Framing	Truss
Exterior Walls	2x6

Design 94141

Units	Single
Price Code	D
Total Finished	2,050 sq. ft.
First Finished	1,108 sq. ft.
Second Finished	942 sq. ft.
Basement Unfinished	1,108 sq. ft.
Garage Unfinished	455 sq. ft.
Dimensions	66'x32'
Foundation	Basement
Bedrooms	4
Full Baths	2
Half Baths	1
First Ceiling	8'1⅛"
Second Ceiling	8'1⅛"
Max Ridge Height	28'
Roof Framing	Truss
Exterior Walls	2x4

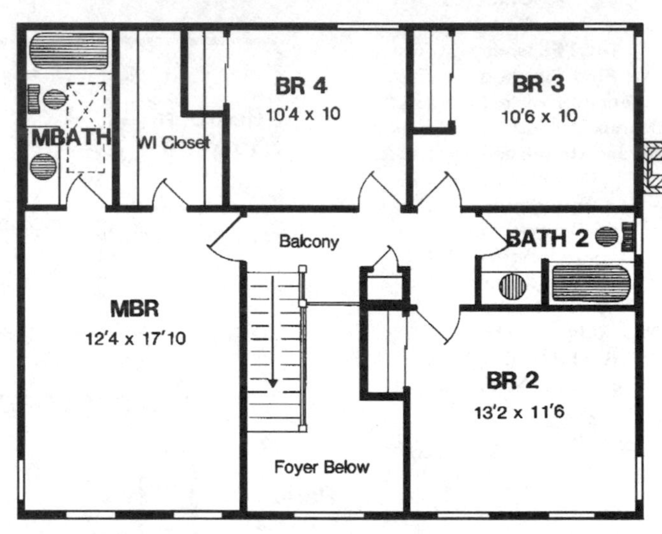

SECOND FLOOR

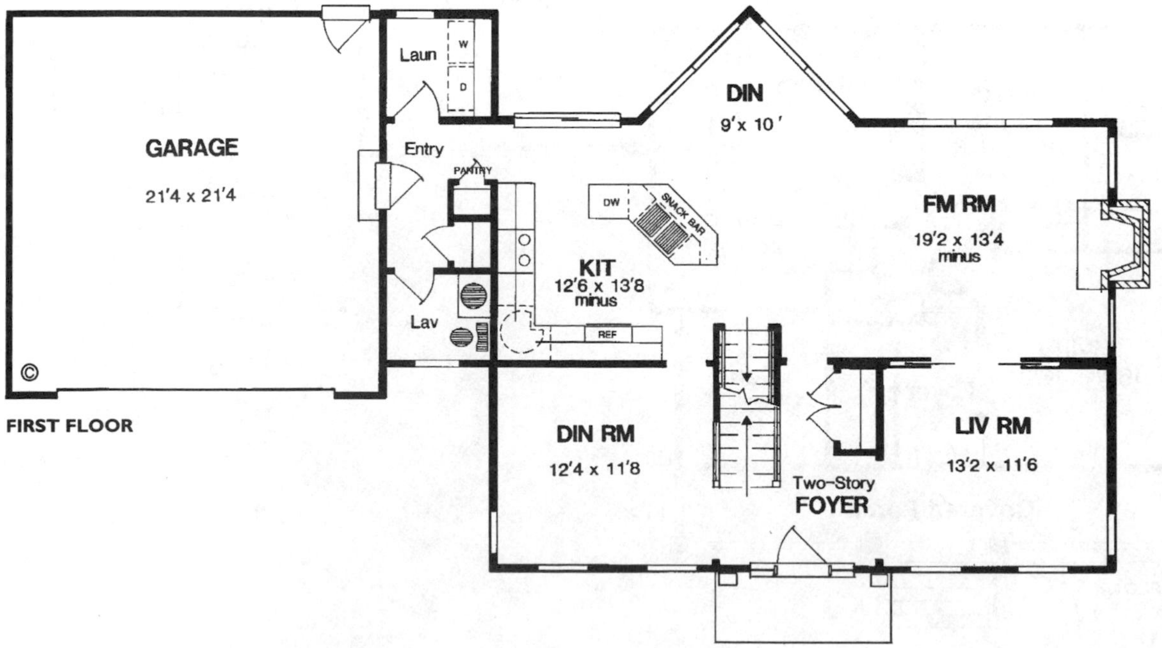

FIRST FLOOR

Design 63120

Units	Single
Price Code	D
Total Finished	2,060 sq. ft.
Main Finished	2,060 sq. ft.
Garage Unfinished	478 sq. ft.
Dimensions	60'4"x56'
Foundation	Slab
Bedrooms	4
Full Baths	2
Main Ceiling	10'
Max Ridge Height	24'
Roof Framing	Truss
Exterior Walls	2x4

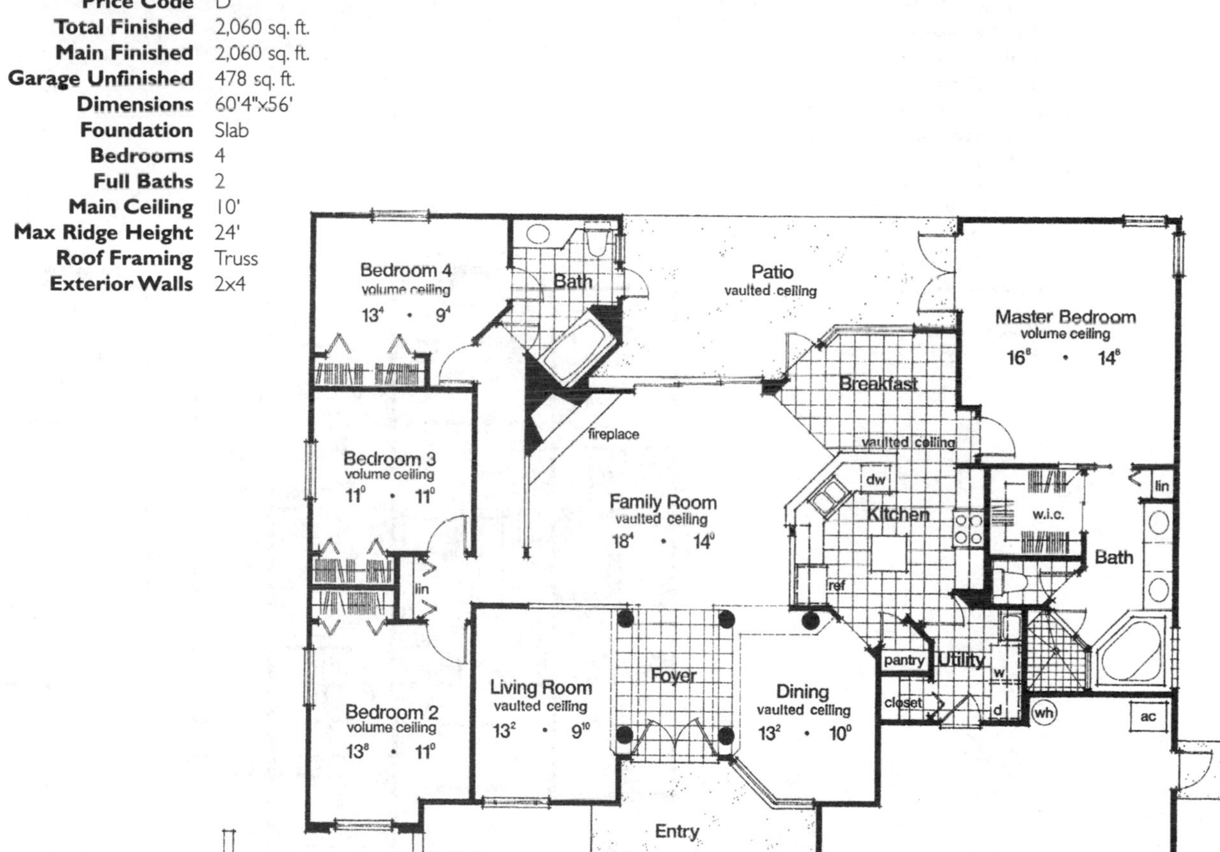

Design 99427

Units Duplex
Price Code G
Total Finished 2,060 sq. ft.
Main Finished 2,060 sq. ft.
Basement Unfinished 2,060 sq. ft.
Garage Unfinished 530 sq. ft.
Dimensions 82'8"x96'
Foundation Basement
Bedrooms 2 or 3
Full Baths 2
Half Baths 1
Roof Framing Stick
Exterior Walls 2x4

* Alternate foundation options available at an additional charge. Please call 1-800-235-5700 for more information.

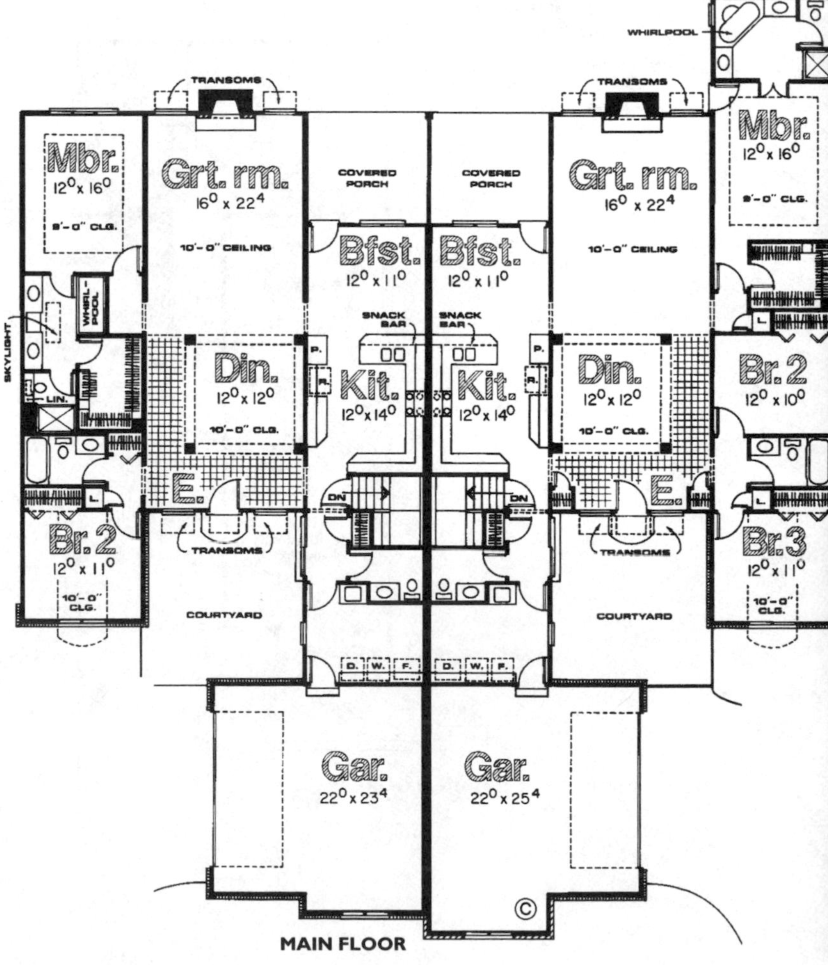

Design 63085

Units	Single
Price Code	D
Total Finished	2,062 sq. ft.
Main Finished	2,062 sq. ft.
Garage Unfinished	514 sq. ft.
Porch Unfinished	647 sq. ft.
Dimensions	63'x56'8"
Foundation	Slab
Bedrooms	3
Full Baths	2
Max Ridge Height	25'4"
Roof Framing	Truss

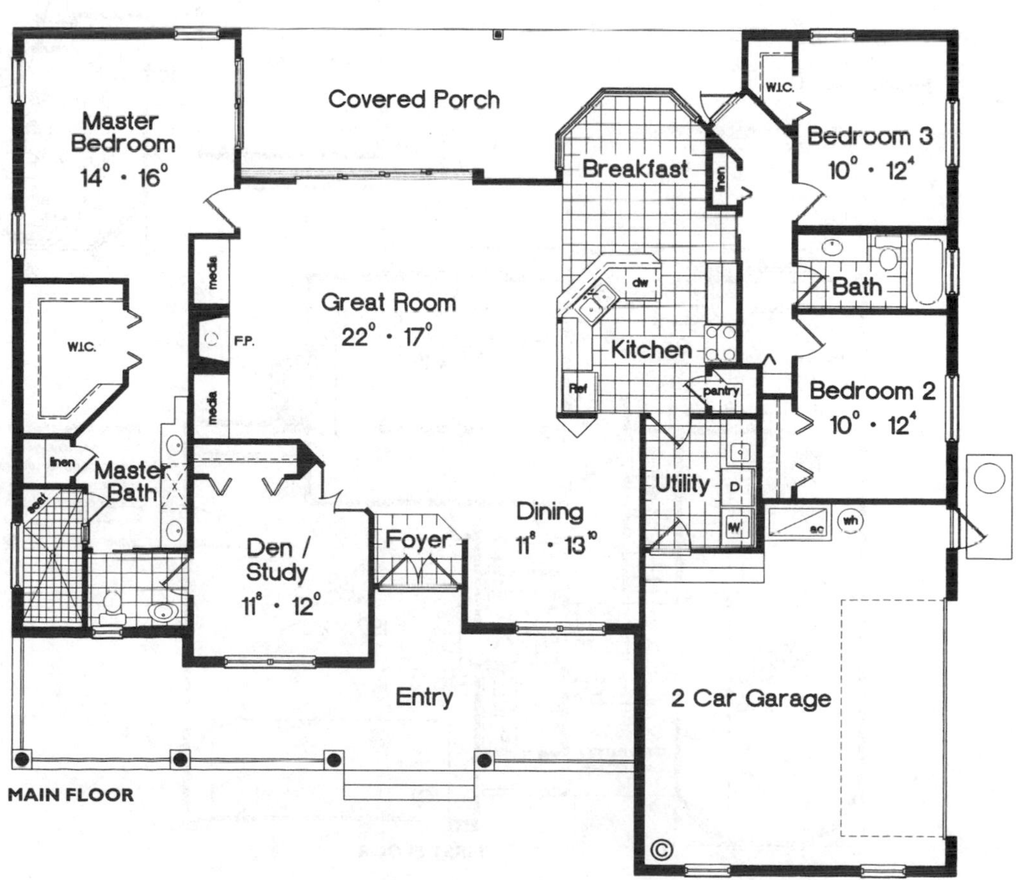

MAIN FLOOR

Design 94936

PHOTOGRAPHY: COURTESY OF THE DESIGNER

Units	Single
Price Code	D
Total Finished	2,078 sq. ft.
First Finished	1,113 sq. ft.
Second Finished	965 sq. ft.
Basement Unfinished	1,113 sq. ft.
Garage Unfinished	486 sq. ft.
Dimensions	46'x41'5"
Foundation	Basement
Bedrooms	4
Full Baths	2
Half Baths	1
First Ceiling	8'
Second Ceiling	8'
Max Ridge Height	25'5"
Roof Framing	Stick
Exterior Walls	2x4

* Alternate foundation options available at an additional charge. Please call 1-800-235-5700 for more information.

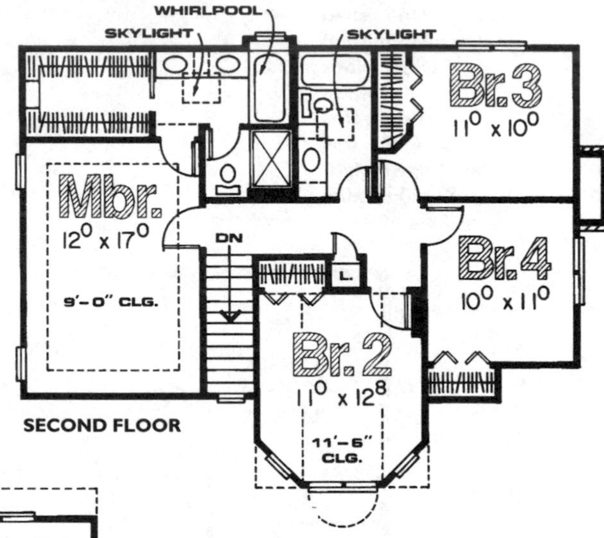

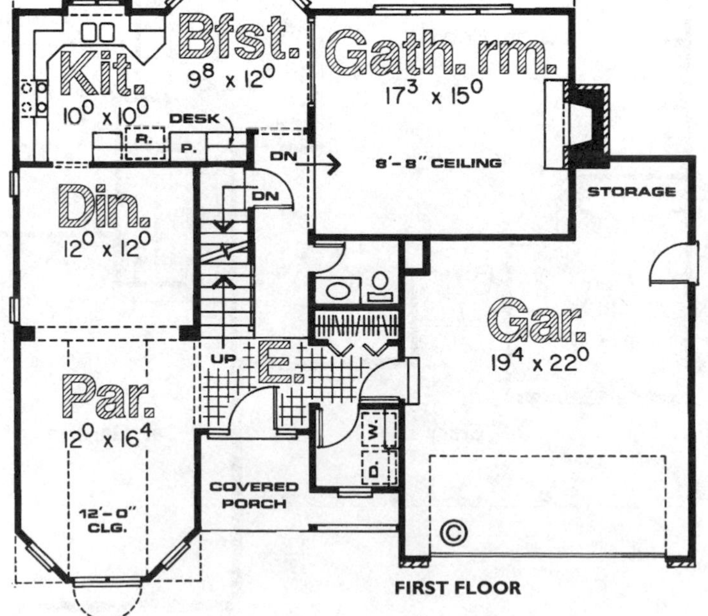

Please note: **The photographed home may have been modified to suit homeowner preferences. If you order plans, have a builder or design professional check them against the photograph to confirm actual construction details.**

Design 98583

Units	Single
Price Code	D
Total Finished	2,078 sq. ft.
Main Finished	2,078 sq. ft.
Garage Unfinished	734 sq. ft.
Deck Unfinished	140 sq. ft.
Porch Unfinished	240 sq. ft.
Dimensions	75'x47'10"
Foundation	Crawlspace Slab
Bedrooms	4
Full Baths	2
Max Ridge Height	27'
Roof Framing	Stick
Exterior Walls	2x4

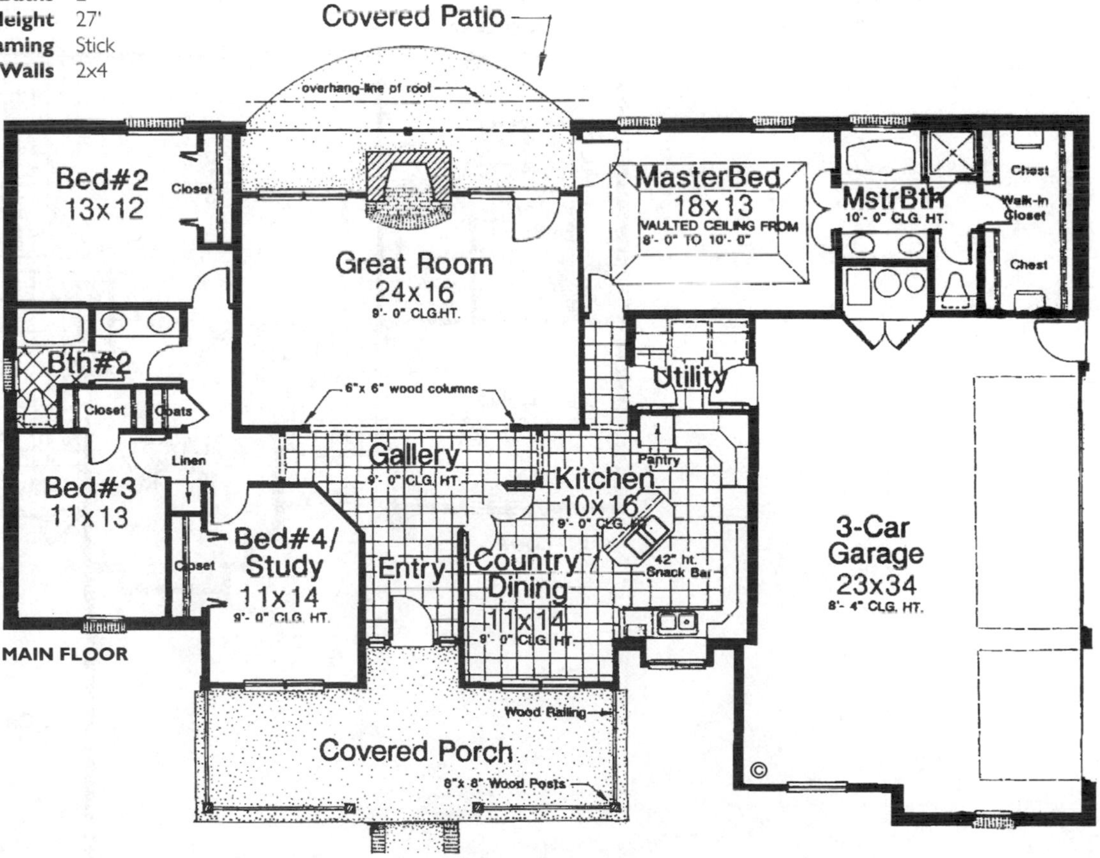

Covered Patio
overhang line of roof
Bed#2
13x12
Closet
Great Room
24x16
9'- 0" CLG.HT.
MasterBed
18x13
VAULTED CEILING FROM
8'- 0" TO 10'- 0"
MstrBth
10'- 0" CLG. HT.
Chest
Walk-in Closet
Chest
Bth#2
Closet
Coats
6"x 6" wood columns
Utility
Linen
Gallery
9'- 0" CLG. HT.
Pantry
Kitchen
10x16
9'- 0" CLG. HT.
Bed#3
11x13
Closet
Bed#4/
Study
11x14
9'- 0" CLG. HT.
Entry
Country
Dining
11x14
9'- 0" CLG. HT.
42" ht. Snack Bar
3-Car
Garage
23x34
8'- 4" CLG. HT.
MAIN FLOOR
Wood Railing
Covered Porch
8"x 8" Wood Posts
©

Design 63052

Units	Single
Price Code	E
Total Finished	2,081 sq. ft.
Main Finished	2,081 sq. ft.
Garage Unfinished	559 sq. ft.
Porch Unfinished	219 sq. ft.
Dimensions	58'x66'8"
Foundation	Slab
Bedrooms	3
Full Baths	2
Main Ceiling	10'-12'
Max Ridge Height	24'
Roof Framing	Truss

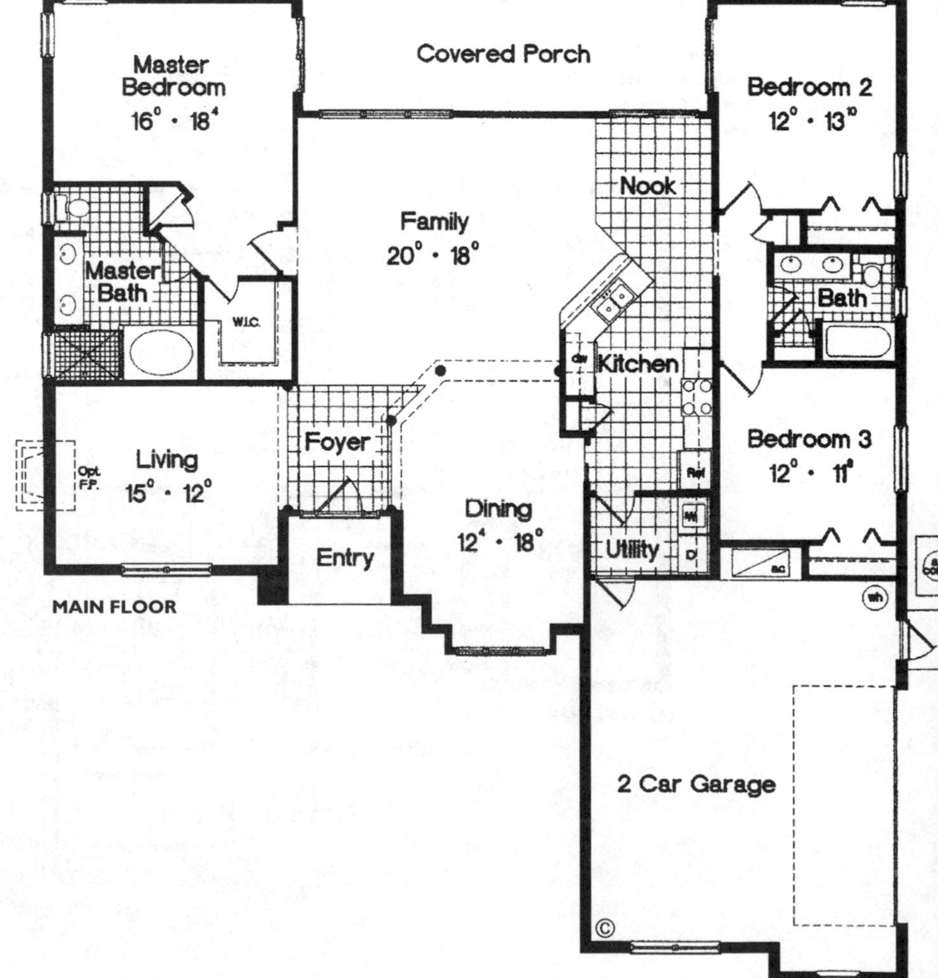

Design 98559

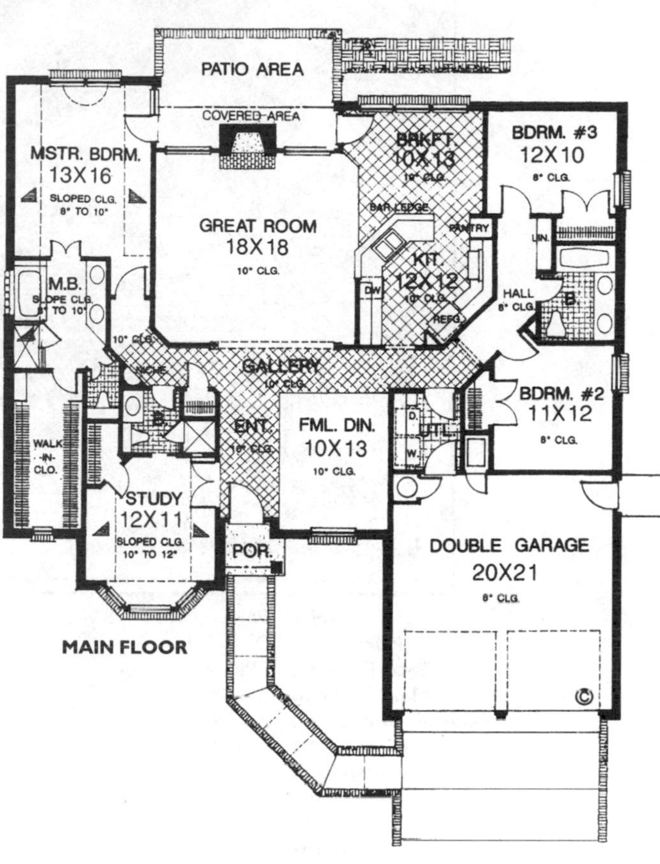

Units	Single
Price Code	D
Total Finished	2,081 sq. ft.
Main Finished	2,081 sq. ft.
Garage Unfinished	422 sq. ft.
Porch Unfinished	240 sq. ft.
Dimensions	55'x57'10"
Foundation	Slab
Bedrooms	3
Full Baths	2
3/4 Baths	1
Max Ridge Height	24'6"
Roof Framing	Stick
Exterior Walls	2x4

Design 24245

PHOTOGRAPHY: MAGGIE COLE

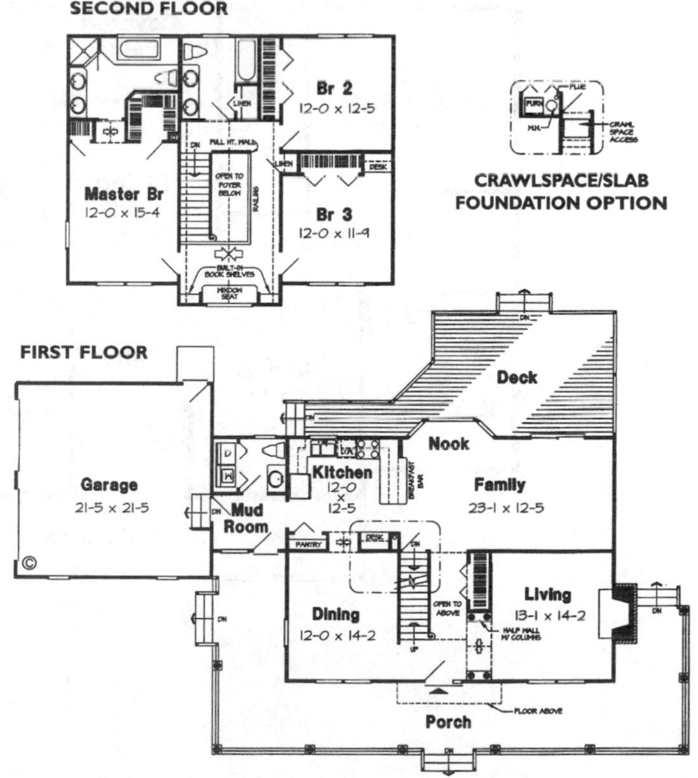

Units	Single
Price Code	D
Total Finished	2,083 sq. ft.
First Finished	1,113 sq. ft.
Second Finished	970 sq. ft.
Basement Unfinished	1,113 sq. ft.
Garage Unfinished	480 sq. ft.
Deck Unfinished	330 sq. ft.
Porch Unfinished	581 sq. ft.
Dimensions	74'x41'6"
Foundation	Basement Crawlspace Slab
Bedrooms	3
Full Baths	2
Half Baths	1
First Ceiling	8'
Second Ceiling	8'
Max Ridge Height	28'6"
Roof Framing	Stick
Exterior Walls	2x4, 2x6

Please note: The photographed home may have been modified to suite homeowner preferences. If you order plans, have a builder or design professional check them against the photograph to confirm actual construction details.

Design 69115

Units	Single
Price Code	D
Total Finished	2,083 sq. ft.
Main Finished	2,083 sq. ft.
Garage Unfinished	533 sq. ft.
Dimensions	84'x43'9"
Foundation	Crawlspace
Bedrooms	3
Full Baths	1
3/4 Baths	1
Main Ceiling	9'
Max Ridge Height	20'10"
Roof Framing	Truss
Exterior Walls	2x6

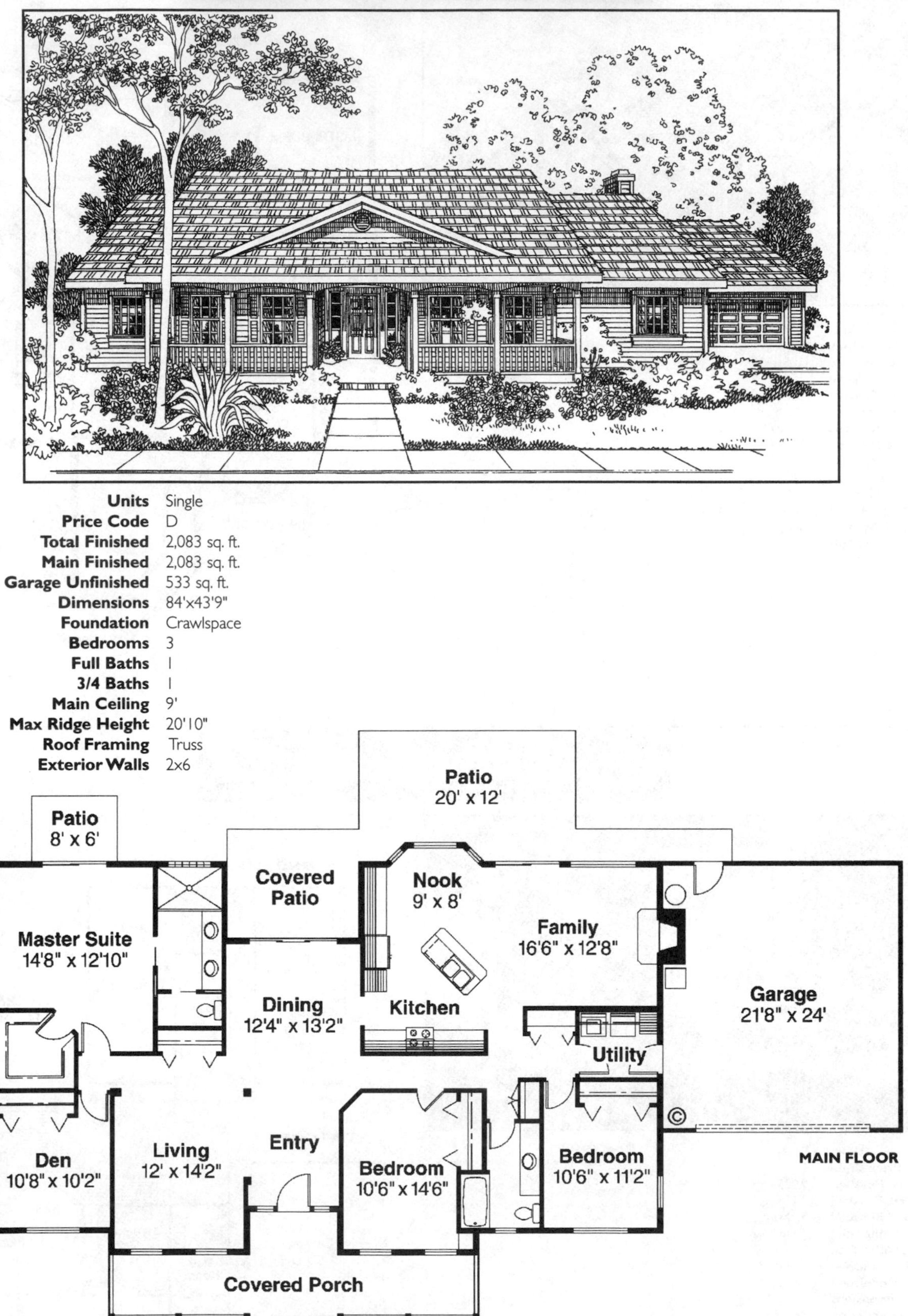

Design 65135

Units	Single
Price Code	D
Total Finished	2,089 sq. ft.
First Finished	1,146 sq. ft.
Second Finished	943 sq. ft.
Bonus Unfinished	313 sq. ft.
Basement Unfinished	483 sq. ft.
Porch Unfinished	168 sq. ft.
Dimensions	56'x38'
Foundation	Basement
Bedrooms	3
Full Baths	2
Half Baths	1
First Ceiling	9'
Second Ceiling	8'
Max Ridge Height	31'3"
Roof Framing	Truss
Exterior Walls	2x6

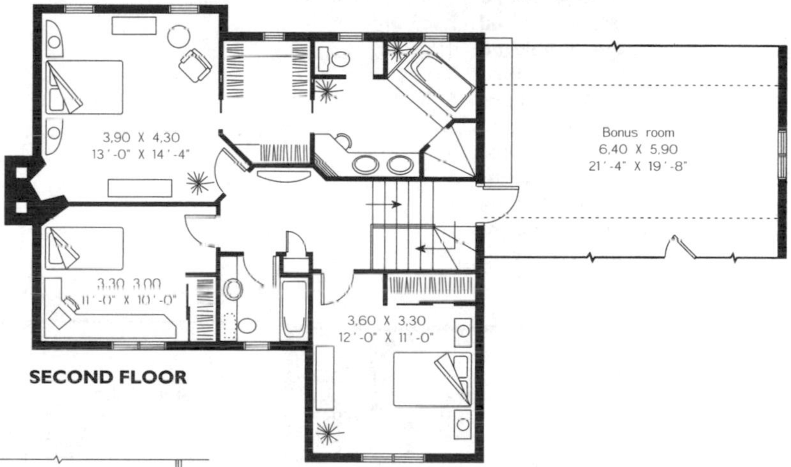

3,90 X 4,30
13'-0" X 14'-4"

Bonus room
6,40 X 5,90
21'-4" X 19'-8"

3,30 3,00
11'-0" X 10'-0"

3,60 X 3,30
12'-0" X 11'-0"

SECOND FLOOR

5,60 X 3,90
18'-8" X 13'-0"

4,00 X 3,30
13'-4" X 11'-0"

6,40 X 6,80
21'-4" X 22'-8"

4,00 X 4,20
13'-4" X 14'-0"

3,60 X 4,00
12'-0" X 13'-4"

©

FIRST FLOOR

Design 63056

Units	Single
Price Code	C
Total Finished	2,089 sq. ft.
Main Finished	2,089 sq. ft.
Garage Unfinished	415 sq. ft.
Deck Unfinished	359 sq. ft.
Dimensions	61'8"x49'11"
Foundation	Slab
Bedrooms	4
Full Baths	3
Main Ceiling	10'
Max Ridge Height	20'10"
Exterior Walls	2x4

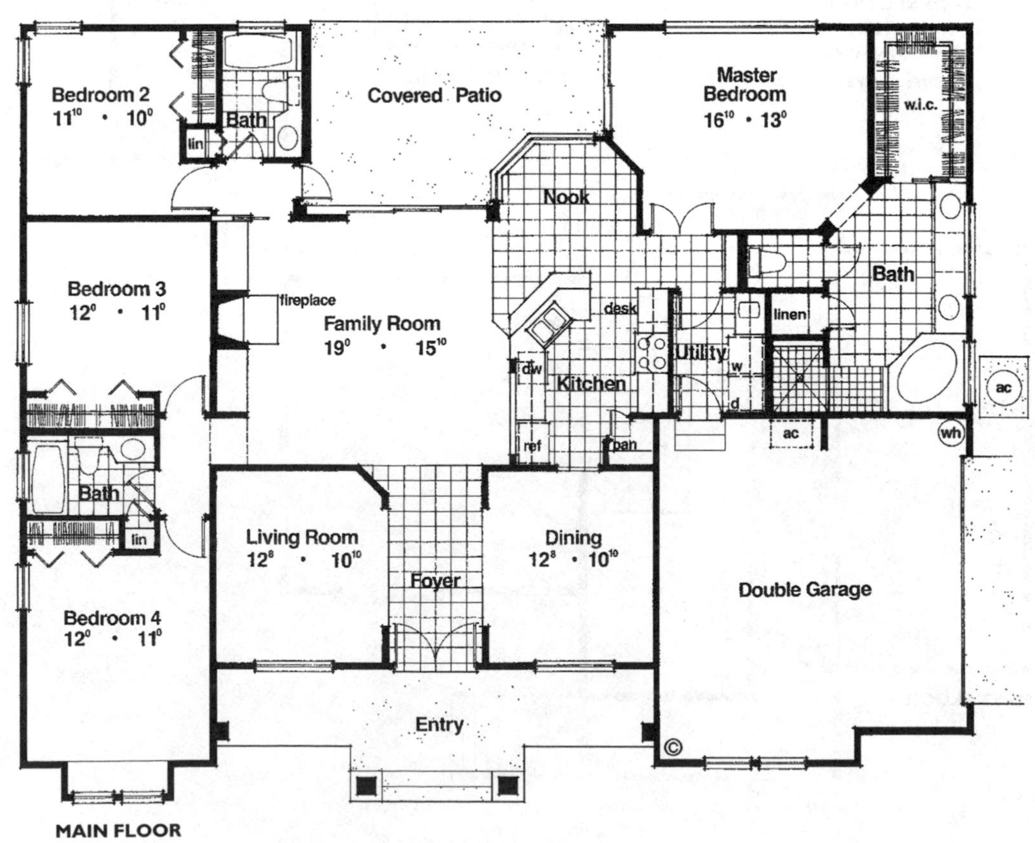

MAIN FLOOR

Design 96529

Units	Single
Price Code	D
Total Finished	2,089 sq. ft.
Main Finished	2,089 sq. ft.
Bonus Unfinished	497 sq. ft.
Garage Unfinished	541 sq. ft.
Dimensions	79'x52'
Foundation	Crawlspace Slab
Bedrooms	3
Full Baths	2
Half Baths	1
Main Ceiling	9'
Max Ridge Height	22'
Roof Framing	Stick
Exterior Walls	2x4

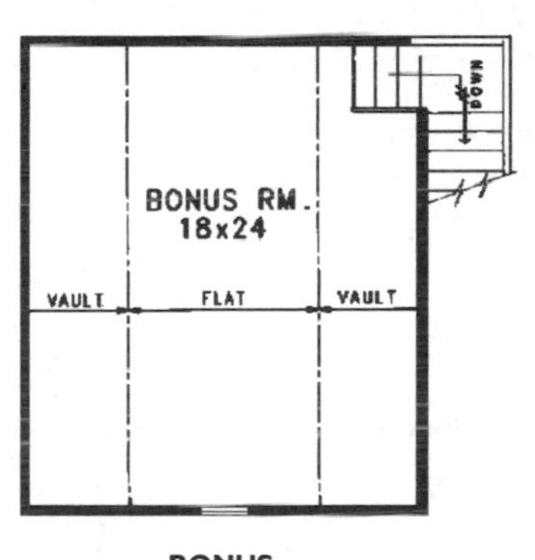

BONUS

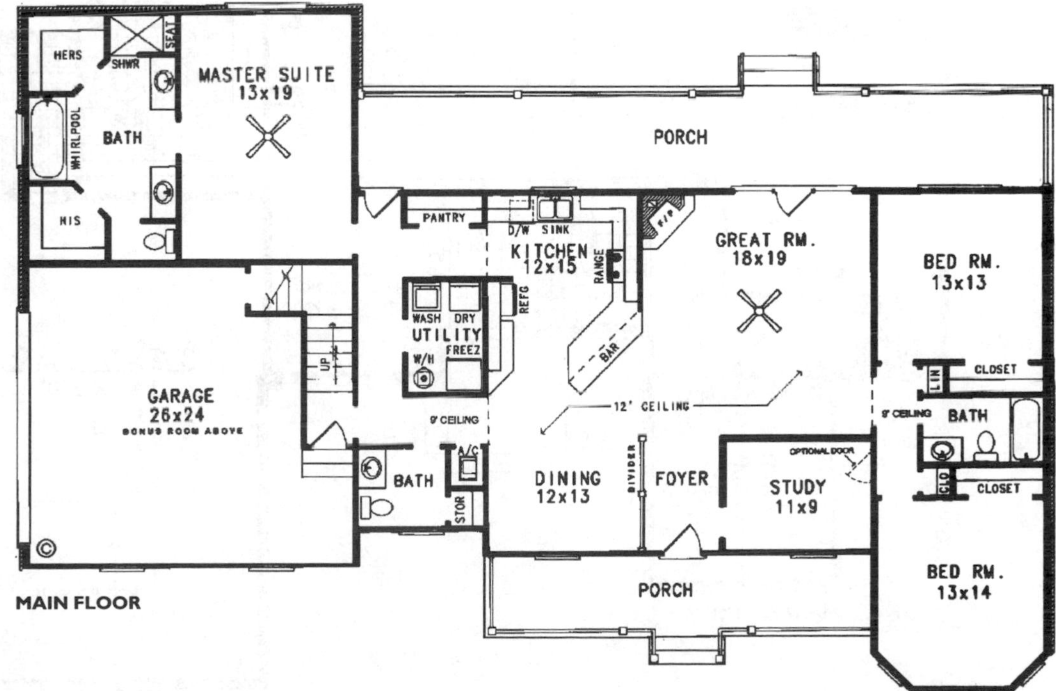

MAIN FLOOR

Design 93158

Units	Single
Price Code	D
Total Finished	2,095 sq. ft.
Main Finished	2,095 sq. ft.
Basement Unfinished	2,095 sq. ft.
Dimensions	67'x58'
Foundation	Basement
Bedrooms	3
Full Baths	2
Max Ridge Height	24'9"
Roof Framing	Stick
Exterior Walls	2x6

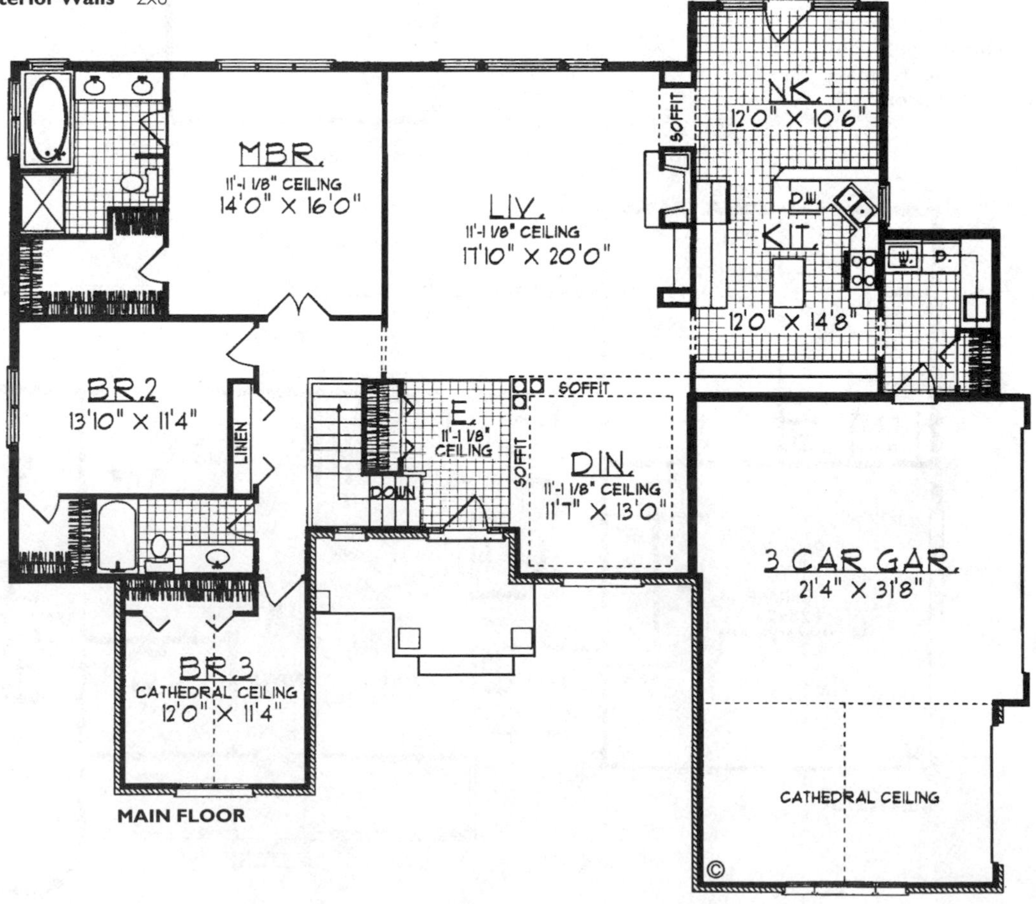

MAIN FLOOR

Design 92444

Units	Single
Price Code	D
Total Finished	2,097 sq. ft.
Main Finished	2,097 sq. ft.
Bonus Unfinished	452 sq. ft.
Garage Unfinished	721 sq. ft.
Dimensions	70'2"x59'
Foundation	Slab
Bedrooms	3
Full Baths	3
Main Ceiling	9'
Max Ridge Height	24'
Roof Framing	Stick
Exterior Walls	2x4

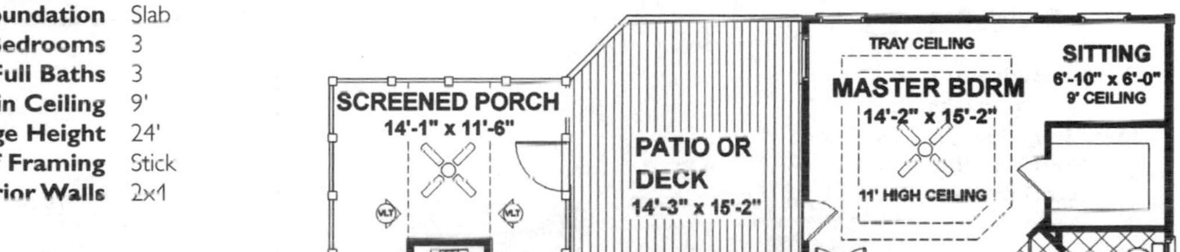

SCREENED PORCH
14'-1" x 11'-6"

PATIO OR DECK
14'-3" x 15'-2"

TRAY CEILING
MASTER BDRM
14'-2" x 15'-2"
11' HIGH CEILING

SITTING
6'-10" x 6'-0"
9' CEILING

BEDROOM 3
11'-0" x 13'-6"
9' CEILING

OPTIONAL TV NICHE ABOVE FIREPLACE

COUNTRY KITCHEN
14'-3" x 22'-6"
9' CEILING

DW

COATS

TO BONUS

LIN.

FAMILY ROOM
14'-0" x 22'-6"
12' HIGH CEILING

10'-6"

LINE OF BONUS ROOM

10'-6"

32'-0"

DESK

BEDROOM 2
11'-0" x 13'-6"
9' CEILING

TRAY CEILING

PANTRY
7'-6" x 4'-6"

LIVING
11'-0" x 12'-0"
9' CEILING

DINING
11'-0" x 12'-0"
10' HIGH CEILING

PORCH
29'-4" x 6'-0"

3 CAR GARAGE
21'-4" x 33'-2"

©

MAIN FLOOR

Design 96539

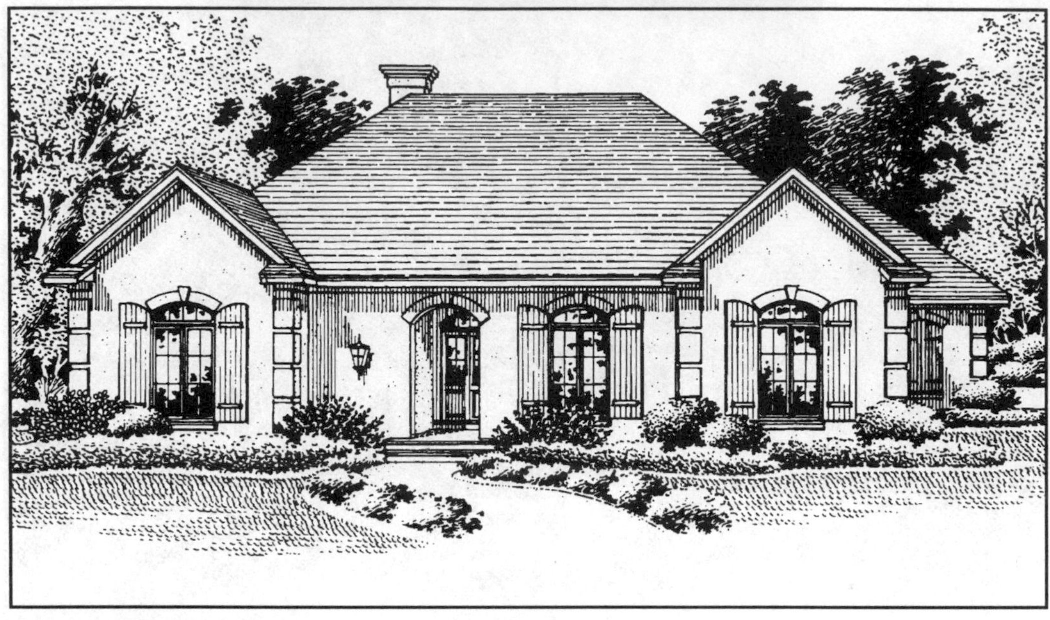

Units	Single
Price Code	D
Total Finished	2,098 sq. ft.
Main Finished	2,098 sq. ft.
Garage Unfinished	590 sq. ft.
Porch Unfinished	292 sq. ft.
Dimensions	69'x64'
Foundation	Crawlspace Slab
Bedrooms	4
Full Baths	3
Max Ridge Height	26'
Roof Framing	Stick
Exterior Walls	2x4

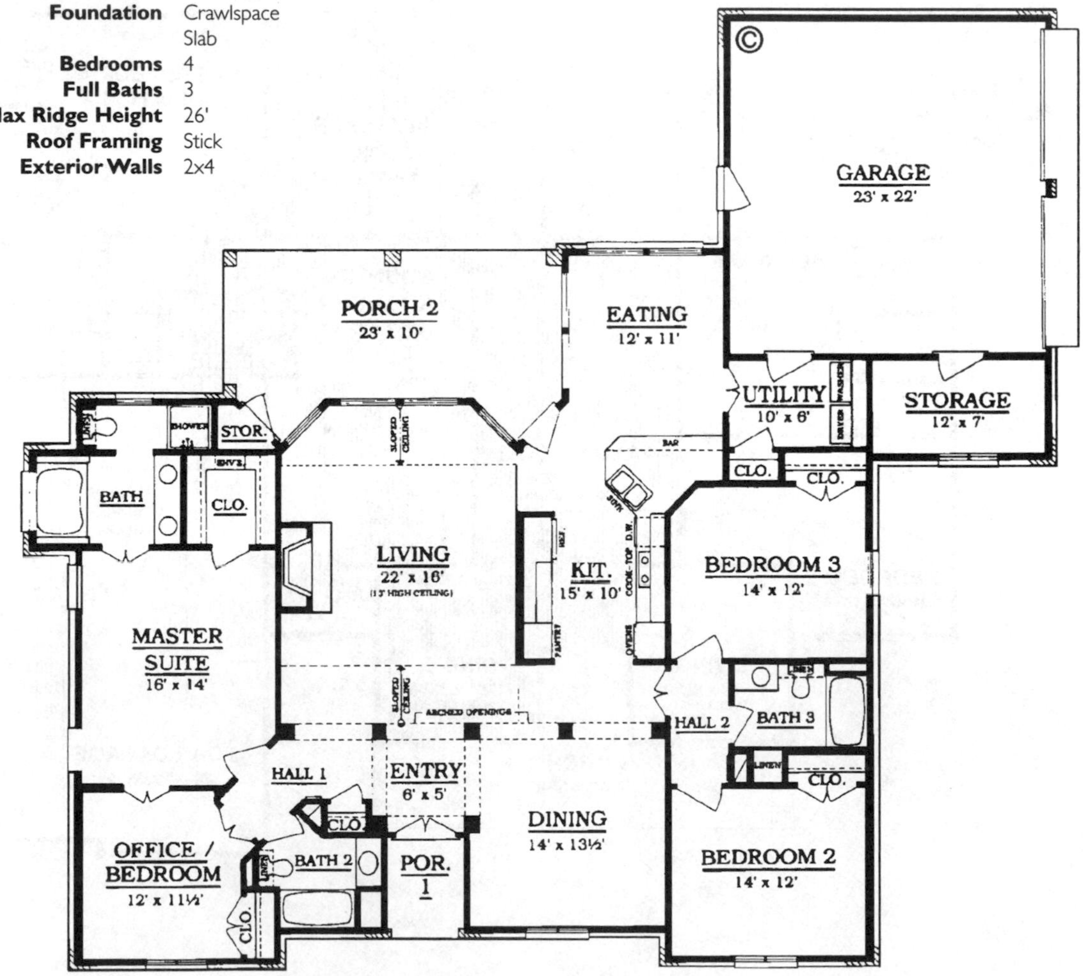

©
GARAGE
23' x 22'
PORCH 2
23' x 10'
EATING
12' x 11'
UTILITY
10' x 6'
WASHER
DRYER
STORAGE
12' x 7'
STOR.
SHOWER
BATH
CLO.
SLOPED CEILING
BAR
LIVING
22' x 16'
(13' HIGH CEILING)
KIT.
15' x 10'
PANTRY
COOK-TOP
D.W.
OVENS
CLO.
CLO.
BEDROOM 3
14' x 12'
MASTER
SUITE
16' x 14'
SLOPED CEILING
ARCHED OPENINGS
HALL 2
BATH 3
LINEN
CLO.
HALL 1
ENTRY
6' x 5'
CLO.
DINING
14' x 13½'
BEDROOM 2
14' x 12'
OFFICE /
BEDROOM
12' x 11½'
LINEN
BATH 2
POR.
1
CLO.

MAIN FLOOR

Design 92610

PHOTOGRAPHY: DONNA AND RON KOLB, EXPOSURES UNLIMITED

Units	Single
Price Code	D
Total Finished	2,101 sq. ft.
First Finished	1,626 sq. ft.
Second Finished	475 sq. ft.
Basement Unfinished	1,512 sq. ft.
Garage Unfinished	438 sq. ft.
Dimensions	59'x60'8"
Foundation	Basement
Bedrooms	3
Full Baths	2
Half Baths	1
First Ceiling	8'
Second Ceiling	8'
Max Ridge Height	31'
Roof Framing	Truss
Exterior Walls	2x4

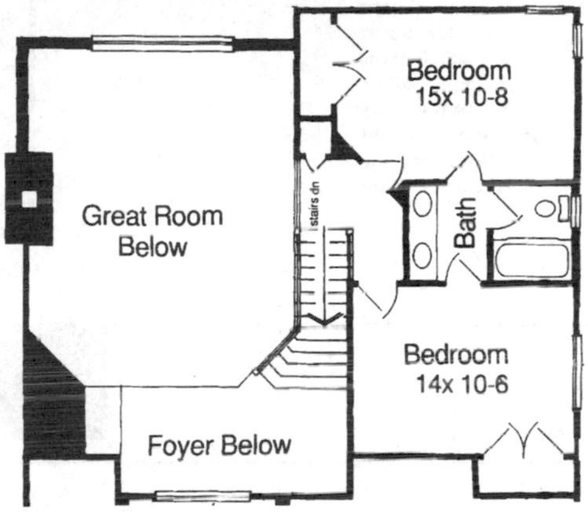

Bedroom 15x 10-8
Great Room Below
stairs dn
Bath
Bedroom 14x 10-6
Foyer Below

SECOND FLOOR

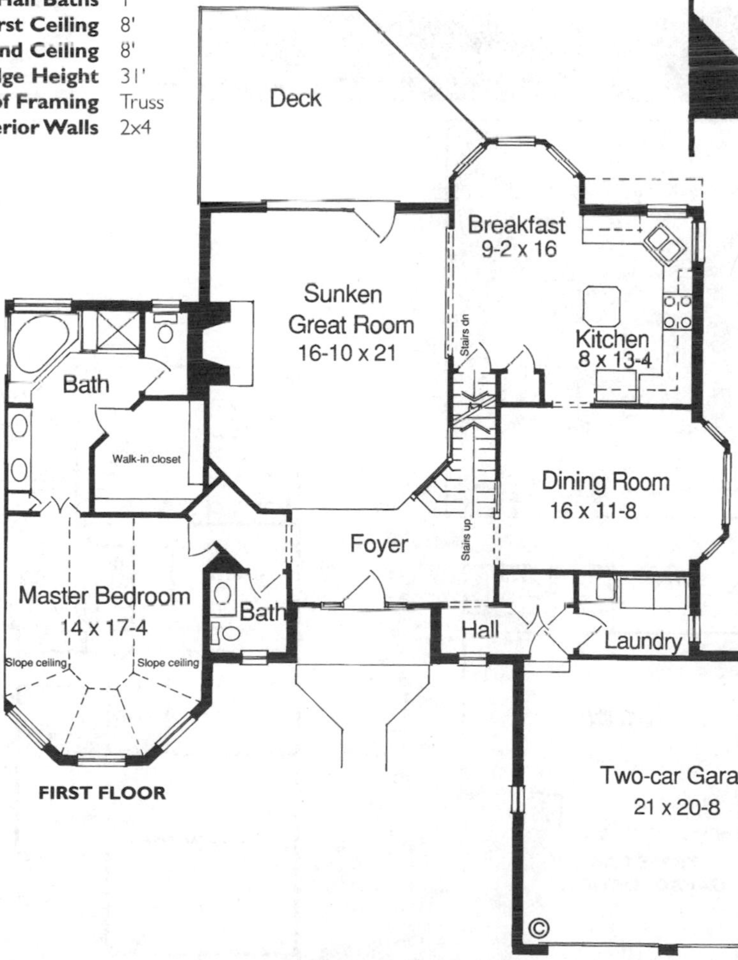

Deck
Breakfast 9-2 x 16
Sunken Great Room 16-10 x 21
Kitchen 8 x 13-4
stairs dn
Bath
Walk-in closet
Dining Room 16 x 11-8
Foyer
Stairs up
Master Bedroom 14 x 17-4
Bath
Hall
Laundry
Slope ceiling
Slope ceiling
Two-car Garage 21 x 20-8
©

FIRST FLOOR

Please note: The photographed home may have been modified to suit homeowner preferences. If you order plans, have a builder or design professional check them against the photograph to confirm actual construction details

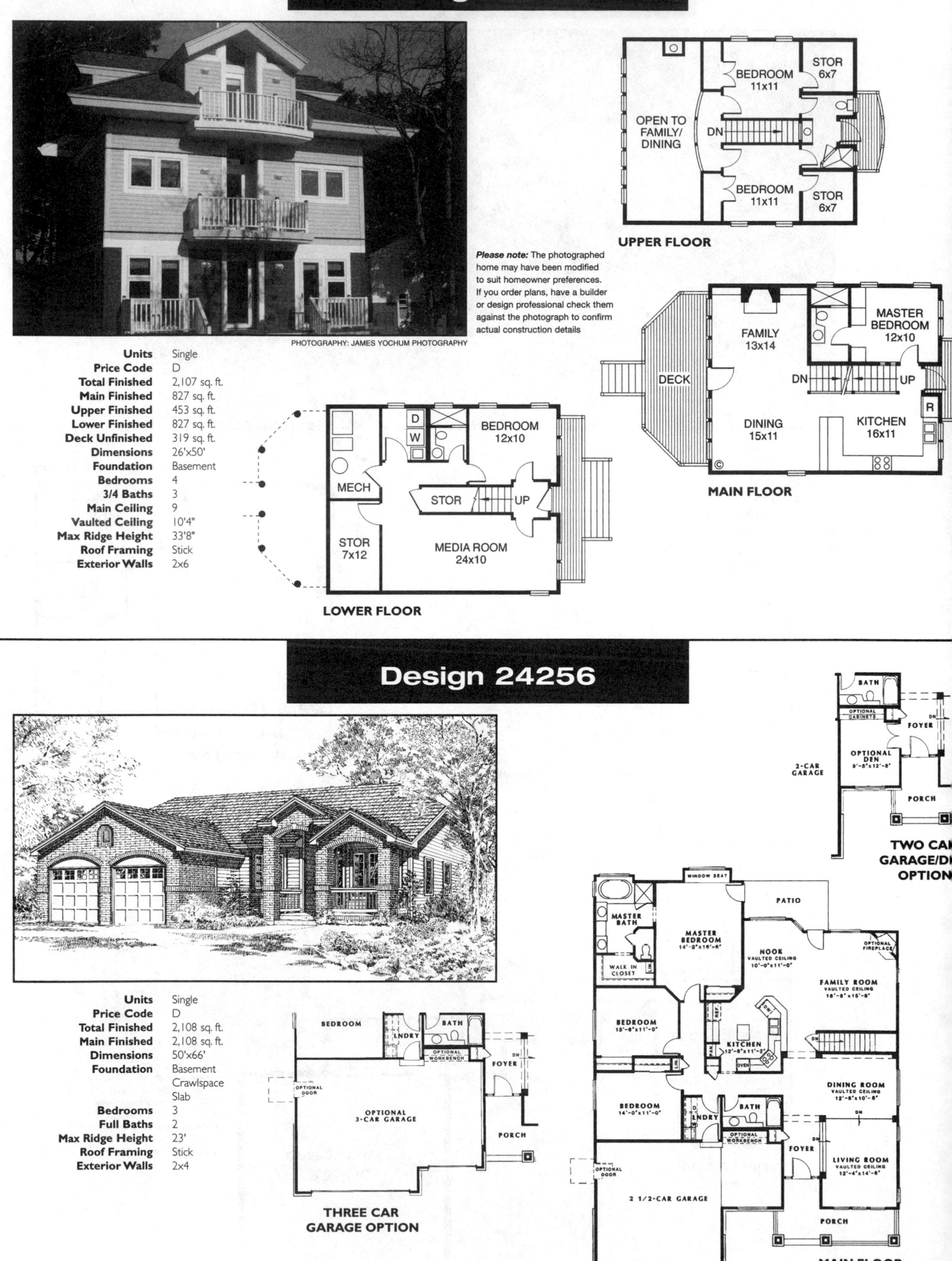
Design 32162
UPPER FLOOR
OPEN TO FAMILY/ DINING
DN
BEDROOM 11x11
BEDROOM 11x11
STOR 6x7
STOR 6x7
Please note: The photographed home may have been modified to suit homeowner preferences. If you order plans, have a builder or design professional check them against the photograph to confirm actual construction details
PHOTOGRAPHY: JAMES YOCHUM PHOTOGRAPHY
MAIN FLOOR
DECK
FAMILY 13x14
MASTER BEDROOM 12x10
DN
UP
DINING 15x11
KITCHEN 16x11
R
LOWER FLOOR
D
W
BEDROOM 12x10
MECH
STOR
UP
STOR 7x12
MEDIA ROOM 24x10
Units Single
Price Code D
Total Finished 2,107 sq. ft.
Main Finished 827 sq. ft.
Upper Finished 453 sq. ft.
Lower Finished 827 sq. ft.
Deck Unfinished 319 sq. ft.
Dimensions 26'x50'
Foundation Basement
Bedrooms 4
3/4 Baths 3
Main Ceiling 9
Vaulted Ceiling 10'4"
Max Ridge Height 33'8"
Roof Framing Stick
Exterior Walls 2x6
Design 24256
Units Single
Price Code D
Total Finished 2,108 sq. ft.
Main Finished 2,108 sq. ft.
Dimensions 50'x66'
Foundation Basement
Crawlspace
Slab
Bedrooms 3
Full Baths 2
Max Ridge Height 23'
Roof Framing Stick
Exterior Walls 2x4
BEDROOM
LNDRY
BATH
OPTIONAL WORKBENCH
FOYER
OPTIONAL DOOR
OPTIONAL 3-CAR GARAGE
PORCH
THREE CAR GARAGE OPTION
BATH
OPTIONAL CABINETS
FOYER
2-CAR GARAGE
OPTIONAL DEN 9'-8"x12'-8"
PORCH
TWO CA
GARAGE/D
OPTION
WINDOW SEAT
PATIO
MASTER BATH
MASTER BEDROOM 14'-8"x16'-6"
WALK IN CLOSET
NOOK VAULTED CEILING 10'-0"x11'-0"
OPTIONAL FIREPLACE
FAMILY ROOM VAULTED CEILING 18'-8"x15'-8"
BEDROOM 13'-8"x11'-0"
KITCHEN 12'-8"x11'-2"
OVEN
DINING ROOM VAULTED CEILING 12'-8"x10'-8"
BEDROOM 14'-0"x11'-0"
LNDRY
BATH
OPTIONAL WORKBENCH
FOYER
LIVING ROOM VAULTED CEILING 12'-4"x14'-8"
OPTIONAL DOOR
2 1/2-CAR GARAGE
PORCH
MAIN FLOOR

Design 24557

Units	Single
Price Code	D
Total Finished	2,110 sq. ft.
Main Finished	2,110 sq. ft.
Basement Unfinished	2,096 sq. ft.
Garage Unfinished	724 sq. ft.
Dimensions	70'x56'
Foundation	Basement Crawlspace Slab
Bedrooms	3
Full Baths	2
Half Baths	1
Max Ridge Height	24'
Roof Framing	Stick
Exterior Walls	2x6

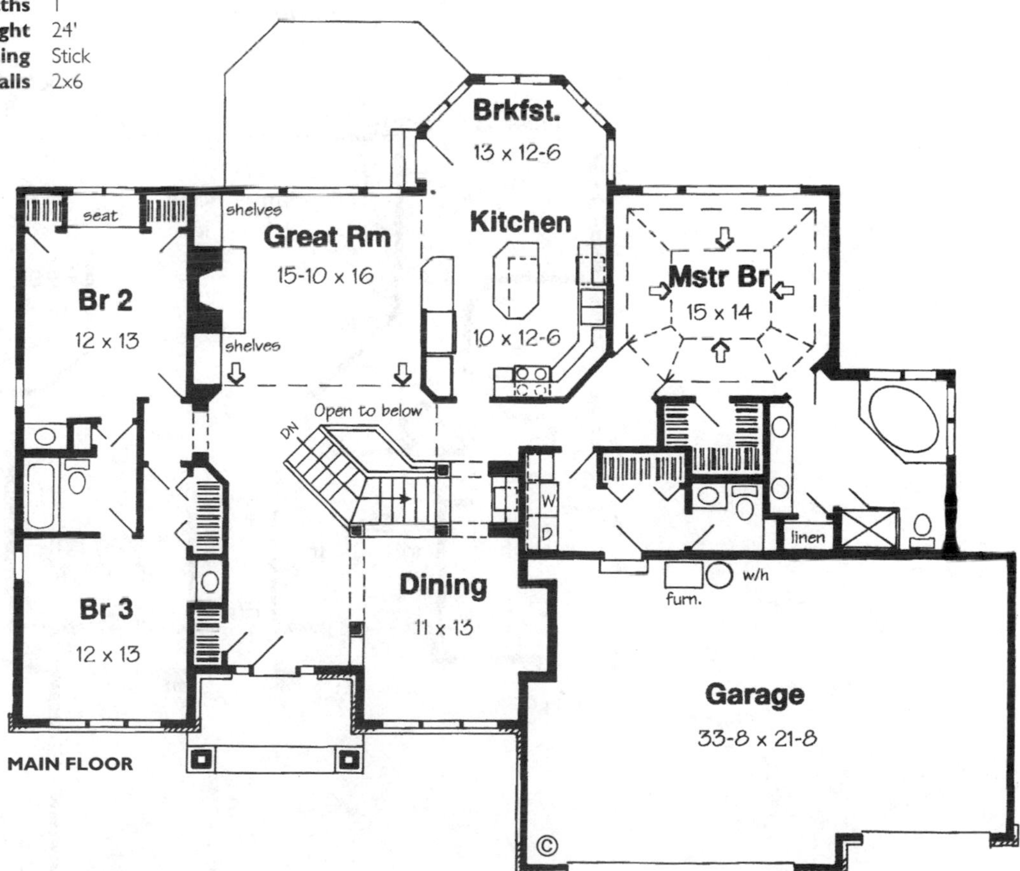

MAIN FLOOR

Units	Single
Price Code	D
Total Finished	2,118 sq. ft.
Main Finished	2,118 sq. ft.
Garage Unfinished	483 sq. ft.
Dimensions	58'x62'
Foundation	Slab
Bedrooms	3
Full Baths	2
Main Ceiling	9'4"
Max Ridge Height	20'9"
Roof Framing	Truss

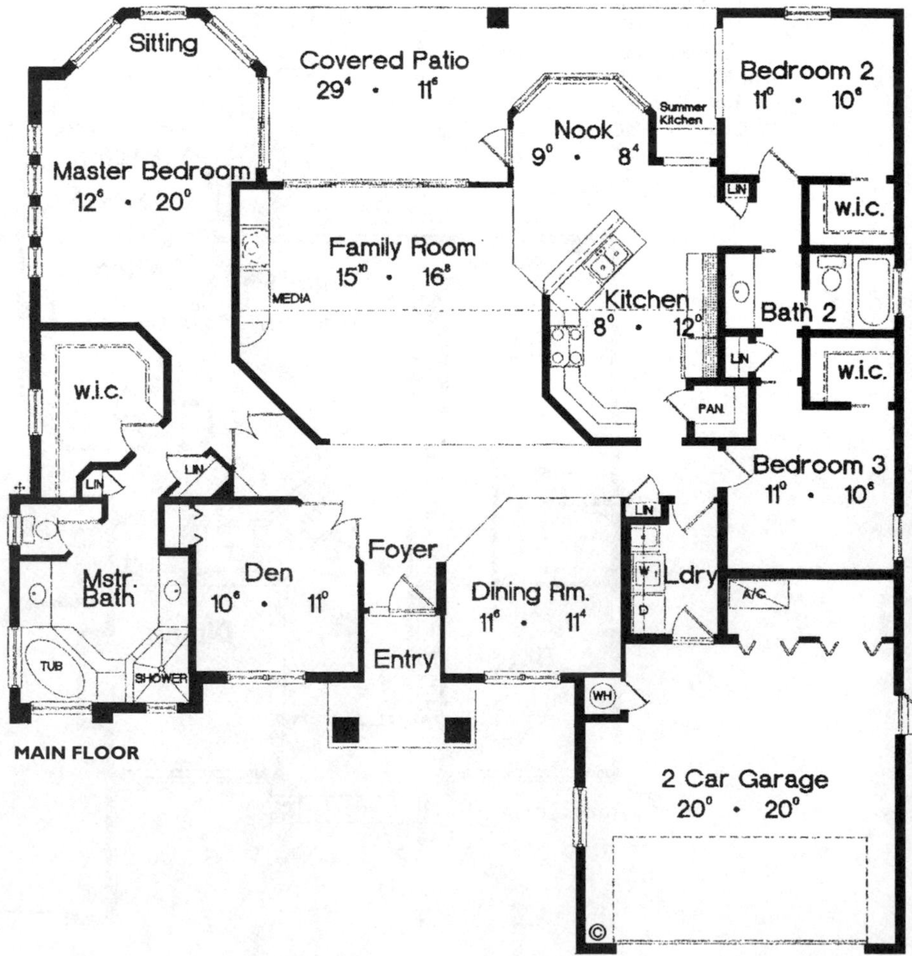

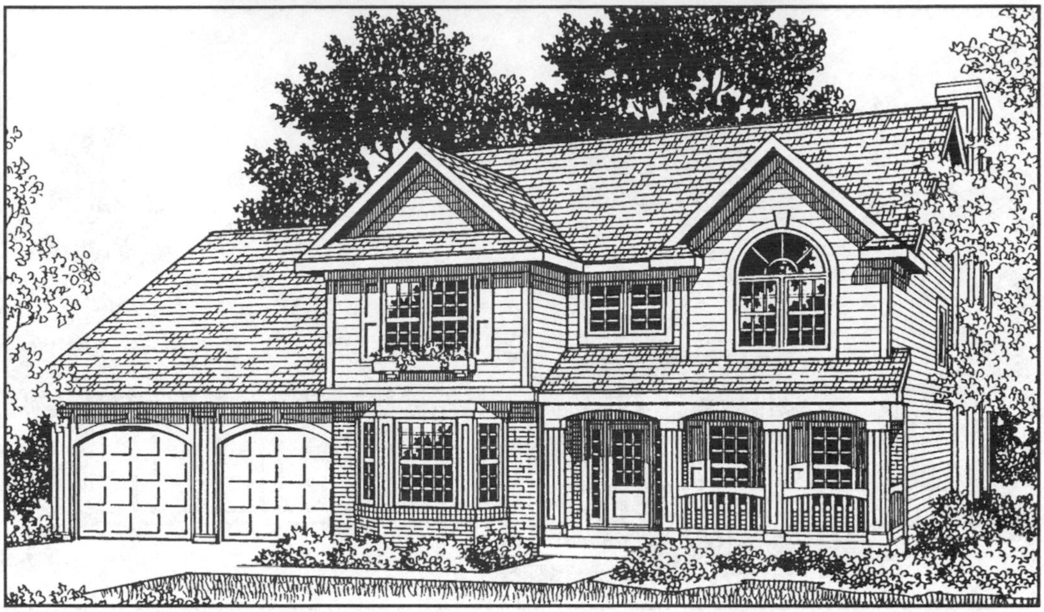

Design 97100

Units	Single
Price Code	D
Total Finished	2,120 sq. ft.
First Finished	995 sq. ft.
Second Finished	1,125 sq. ft.
Basement Unfinished	995 sq. ft.
Dimensions	56'4"x35'8"
Foundation	Basement
Bedrooms	4
Full Baths	1
3/4 Baths	1
Half Baths	1
Max Ridge Height	28'4"
Roof Framing	Truss
Exterior Walls	2x6

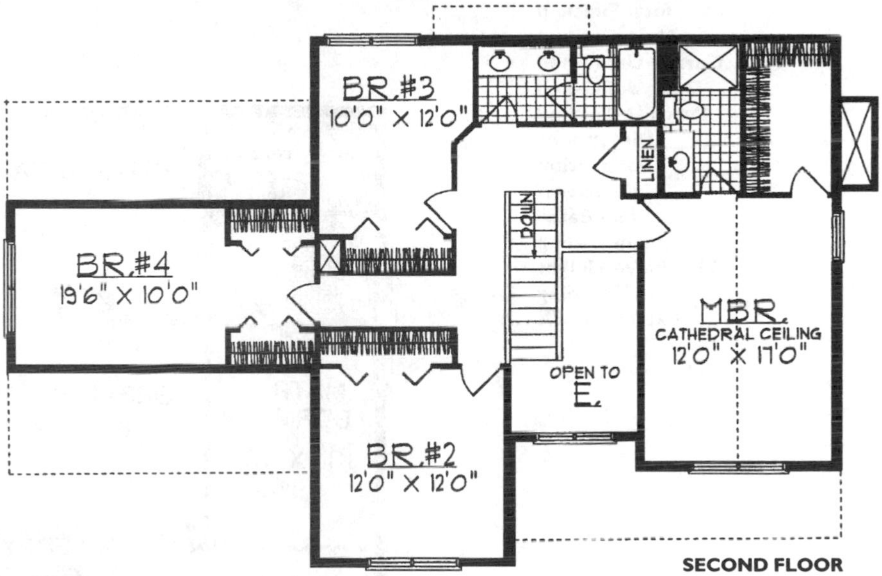

BR.#3
10'0" X 12'0"
LINEN
DOWN
BR.#4
19'6" X 10'0"
MBR.
CATHEDRAL CEILING
12'0" X 17'0"
OPEN TO
E.
BR.#2
12'0" X 12'0"

SECOND FLOOR

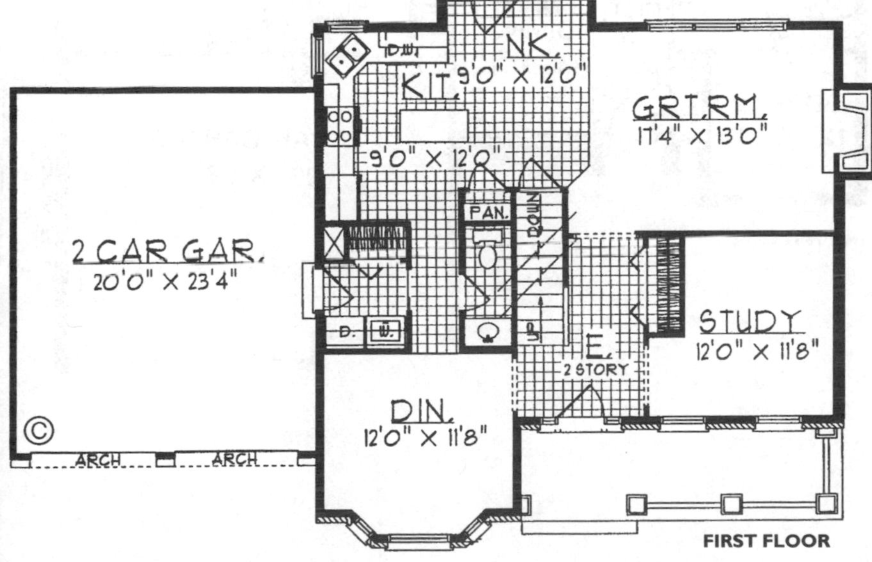

FIRST FLOOR

Design 92280

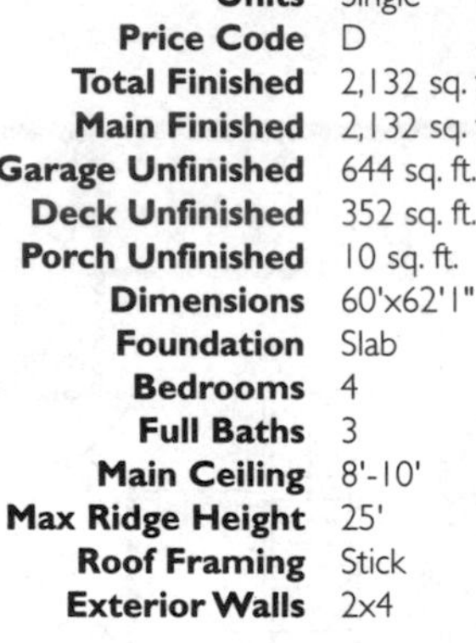

Units	Single
Price Code	D
Total Finished	2,132 sq. ft.
Main Finished	2,132 sq. ft.
Garage Unfinished	644 sq. ft.
Deck Unfinished	352 sq. ft.
Porch Unfinished	10 sq. ft.
Dimensions	60'x62'1"
Foundation	Slab
Bedrooms	4
Full Baths	3
Main Ceiling	8'-10'
Max Ridge Height	25'
Roof Framing	Stick
Exterior Walls	2x4

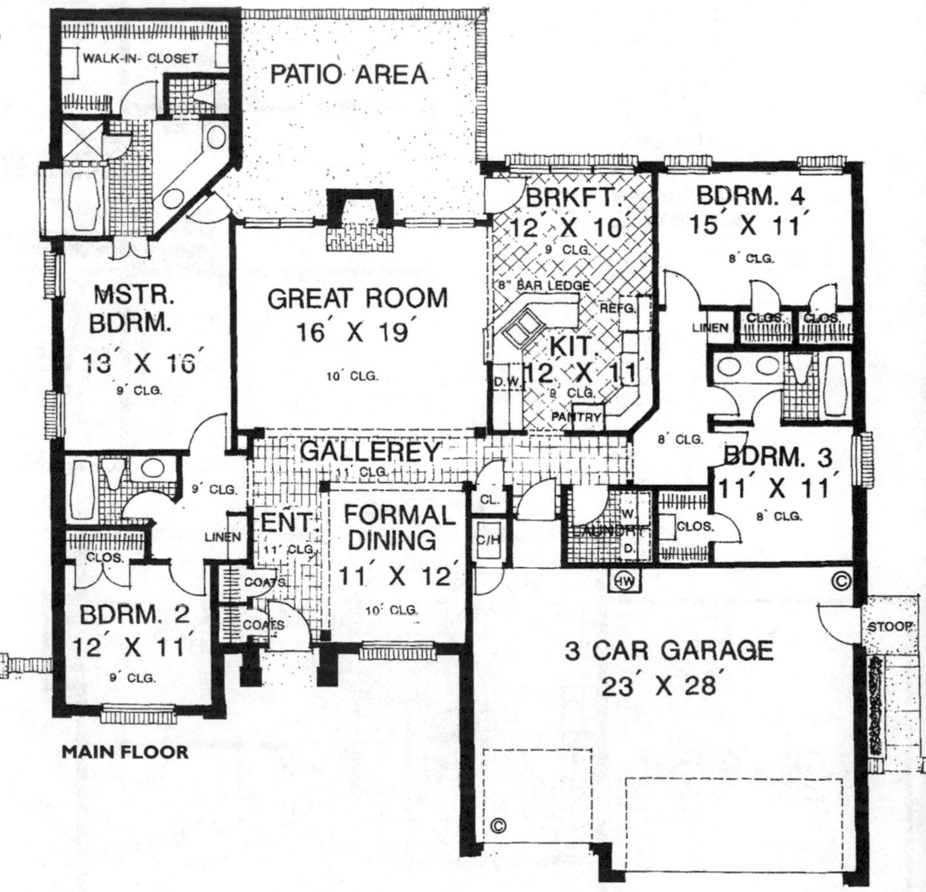

Design 97488

Units	Single
Price Code	D
Total Finished	2,132 sq. ft.
Main Finished	2,132 sq. ft.
Garage Unfinished	763 sq. ft.
Dimensions	72'x58'
Foundation	Basement
Bedrooms	3
Full Baths	2
Main Ceiling	8'
Max Ridge Height	22'
Exterior Walls	2x4

* Alternate foundation options available at an additional charge. Please call 1-800-235-5700 for more information.

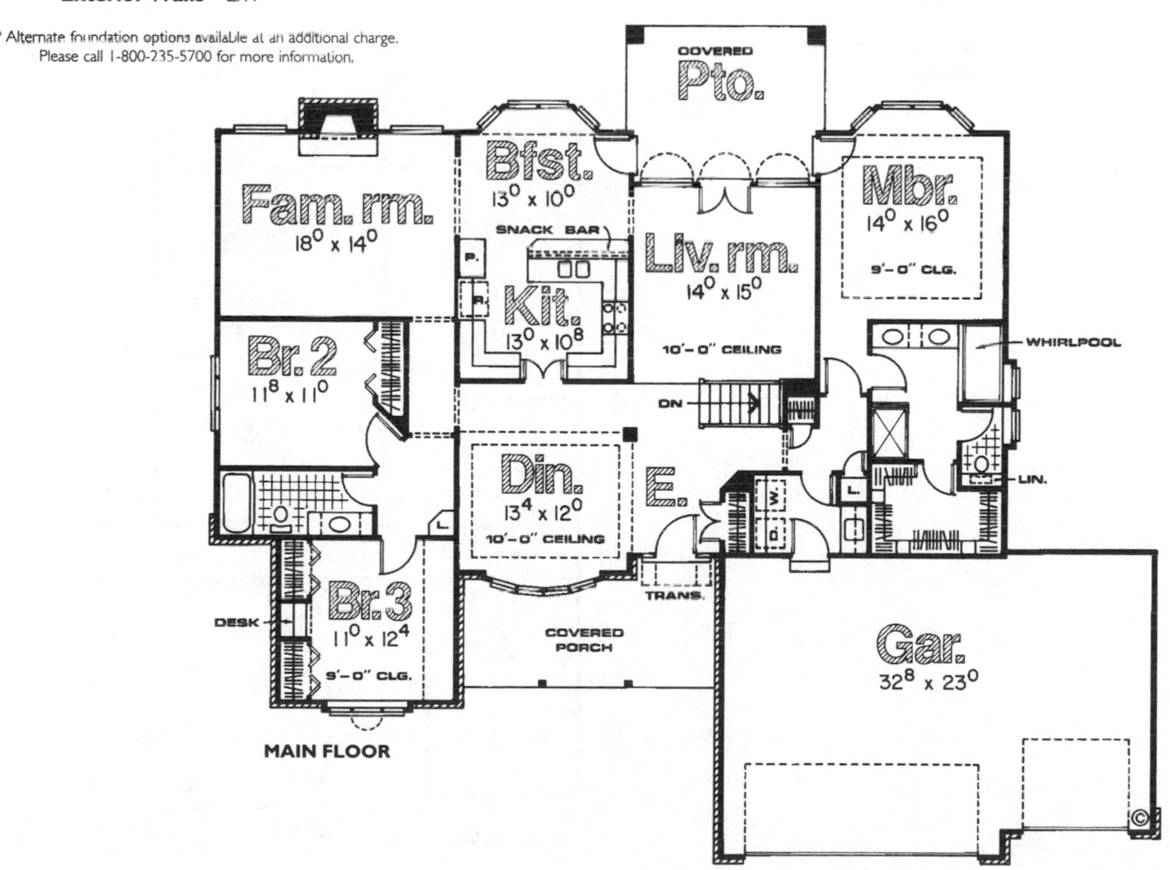

Design 61095

Units	Single
Price Code	D
Total Finished	2,140 sq. ft.
Main Finished	2,140 sq. ft.
Garage Unfinished	394 sq. ft.
Porch Unfinished	235 sq. ft.
Dimensions	40'x84'4"
Foundation	Basement Combo Basement/Crawlspace
Bedrooms	3
Full Baths	2
Main Ceiling	9'
Roof Framing	Stick
Exterior Walls	2x6

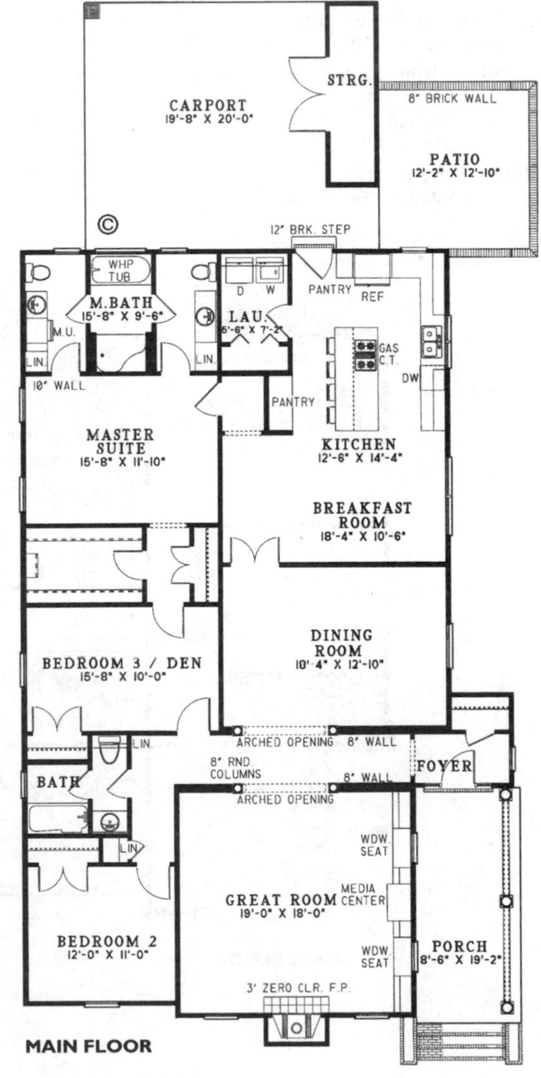

MAIN FLOOR

Design 65391

Units	Single
Price Code	D
Total Finished	2,140 sq. ft.
Main Finished	2,140 sq. ft.
Garage Unfinished	428 sq. ft.
Dimensions	64'x44'1"
Foundation	Basement
Bedrooms	4
Full Baths	2

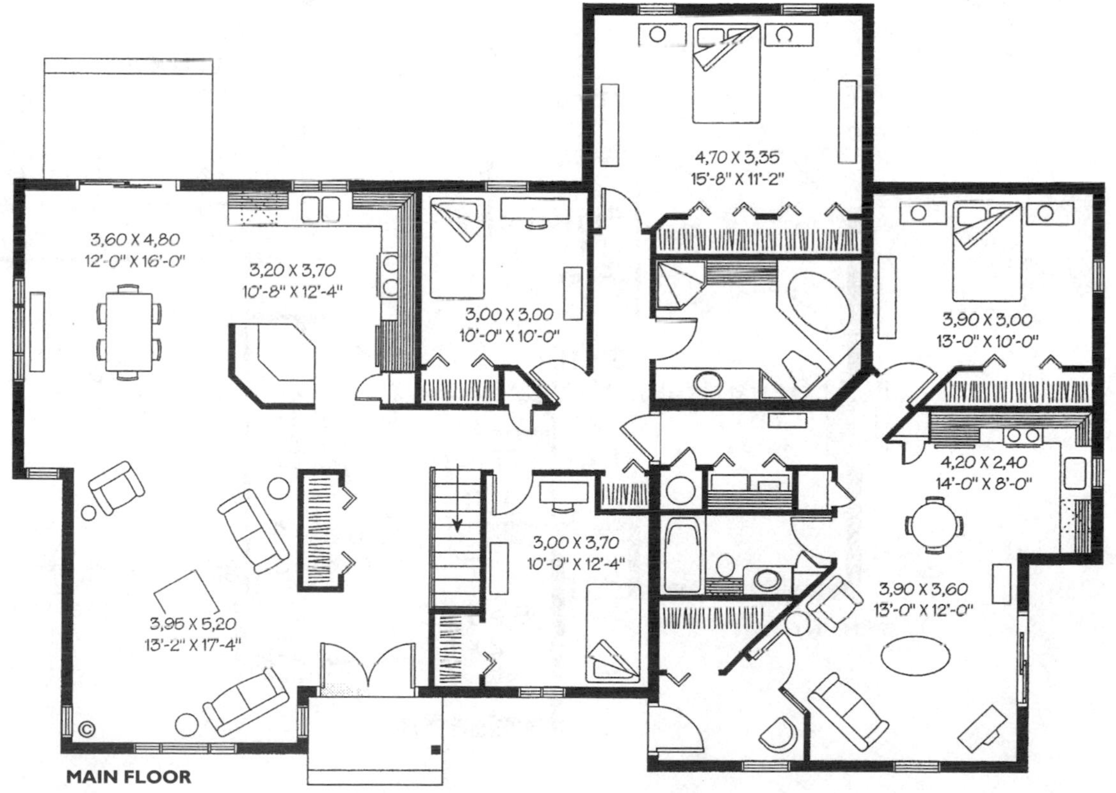

Design 92251

Units	Single
Price Code	D
Total Finished	2,140 sq. ft.
Main Finished	2,140 sq. ft.
Garage Unfinished	409 sq. ft.
Dimensions	65'x54'7"
Foundation	Crawlspace Slab
Bedrooms	3
Full Baths	2
Max Ridge Height	27'
Roof Framing	Stick
Exterior Walls	2x4

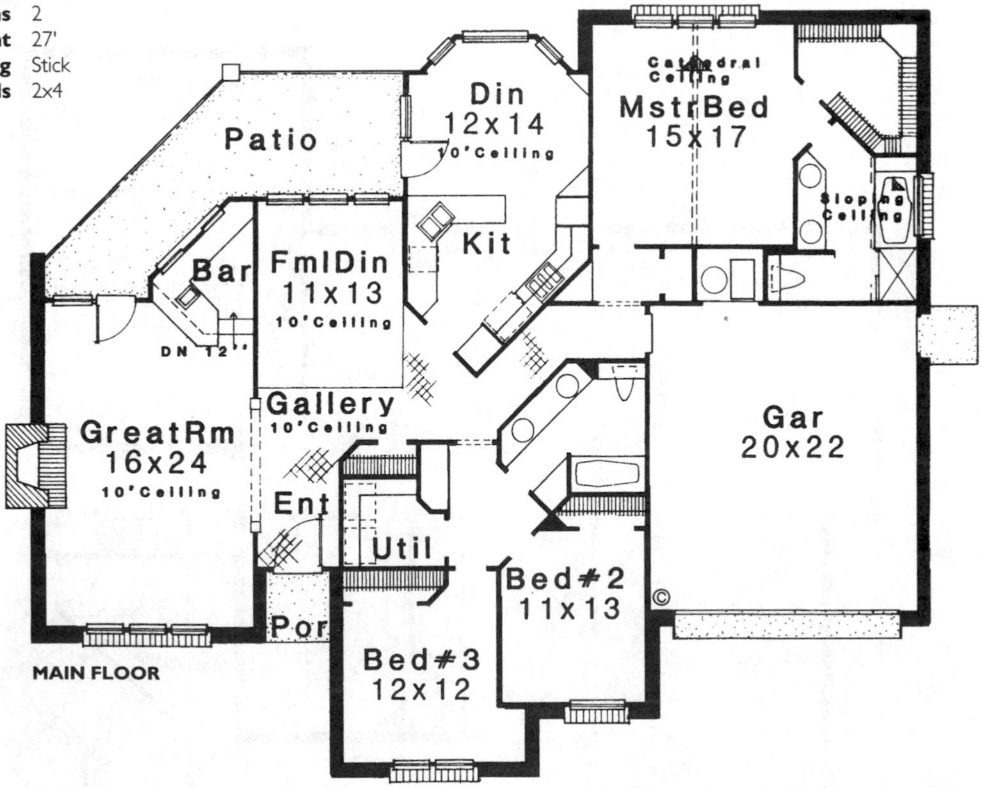

Patio

Din 12x14 10'Ceiling

Cathedral Ceiling

MstrBed 15x17

Sloping Ceiling

Kit

Bar

FmlDin 11x13 10'Ceiling

DN 12''

Gallery 10'Ceiling

GreatRm 16x24 10'Ceiling

Ent

Util

Gar 20x22

Bed#2 11x13

Bed#3 12x12

Por

©

MAIN FLOOR

Design 50037

Units	Single
Price Code	D
Total Finished	2,143 sq. ft.
Main Finished	2,143 sq. ft.
Basement Unfinished	2,143 sq. ft.
Garage Unfinished	529 sq. ft.
Porch Unfinished	217 sq. ft.
Dimensions	76'8"x44'
Foundation	Basement
Bedrooms	3
Full Baths	2
Main Ceiling	9'
Max Ridge Height	26'
Roof Framing	Truss
Exterior Walls	2x4

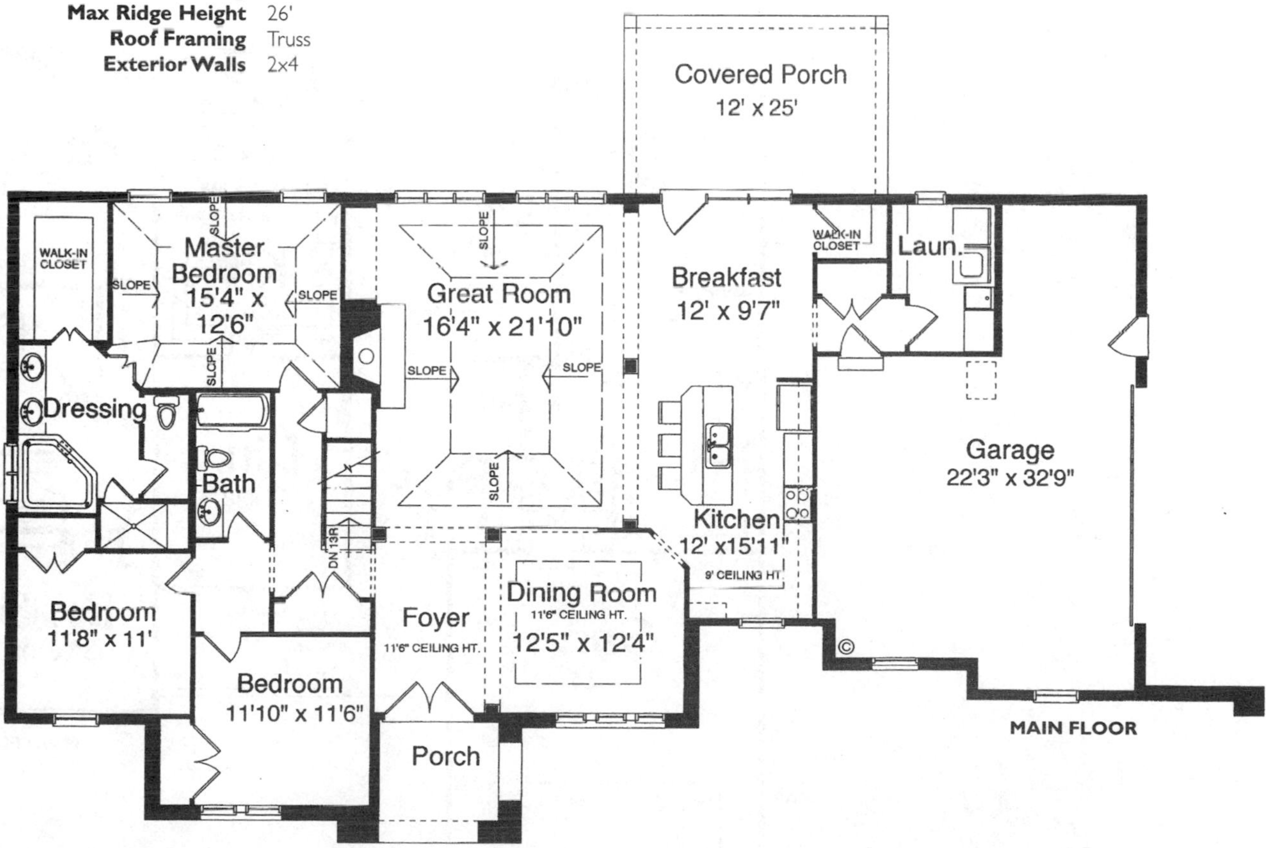

Covered Porch
12' x 25'
WALK-IN CLOSET
Master Bedroom
15'4" x 12'6"
SLOPE
Great Room
16'4" x 21'10"
Breakfast
12' x 9'7"
WALK-IN CLOSET
Laun.
Dressing
Bath
Garage
22'3" x 32'9"
Kitchen
12' x15'11"
9' CEILING HT.
DN 13R
Bedroom
11'8" x 11'
Foyer
11'6" CEILING HT.
Dining Room
11'6" CEILING HT.
12'5" x 12'4"
Bedroom
11'10" x 11'6"
Porch
©

MAIN FLOOR

Design 94983

Units	Single
Price Code	D
Total Finished	2,144 sq. ft.
Main Finished	2,144 sq. ft.
Garage Unfinished	513 sq. ft.
Dimensions	60'8"x58'
Foundation	Basement
Bedrooms	3
Full Baths	2
Max Ridge Height	19'10"
Roof Framing	Stick
Exterior Walls	2x4

* Alternate foundation options available at an additional charge. Please call 1-800-235-5700 for more information.

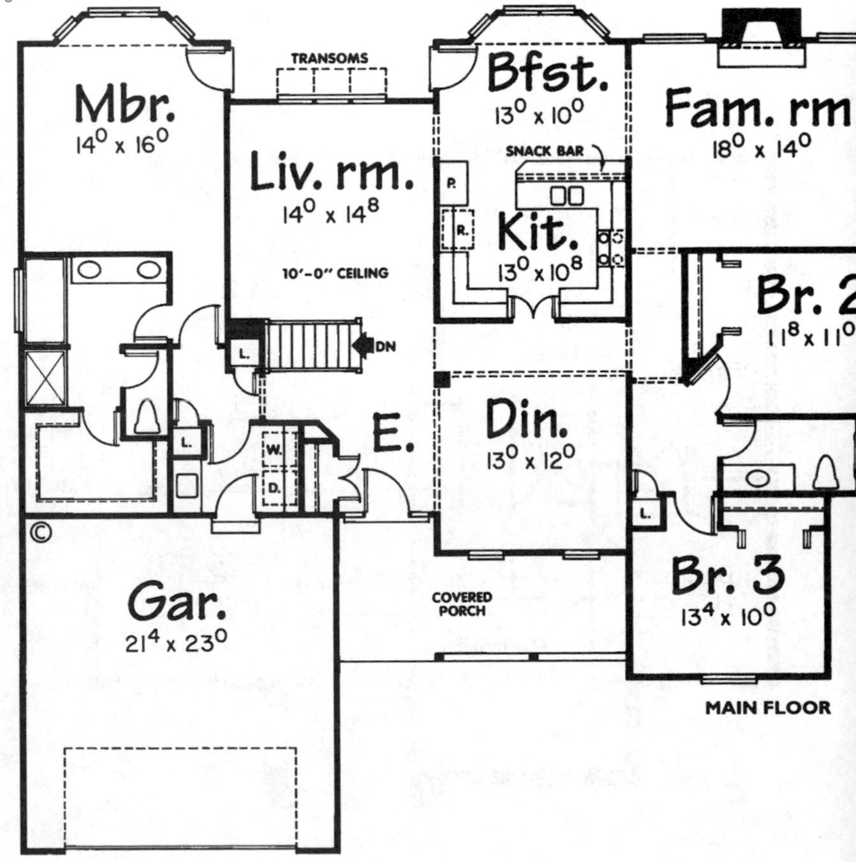

Design 69104

Units	Single
Price Code	D
Total Finished	2,145 sq. ft.
Main Finished	2,145 sq. ft.
Garage Unfinished	647 sq. ft.
Dimensions	60'11"x83'
Foundation	Crawlspace
Bedrooms	3
Full Baths	1
3/4 Baths	1
Main Ceiling	9'
Vaulted Ceiling	18'2"
Max Ridge Height	25'8"
Roof Framing	Truss
Exterior Walls	2x6

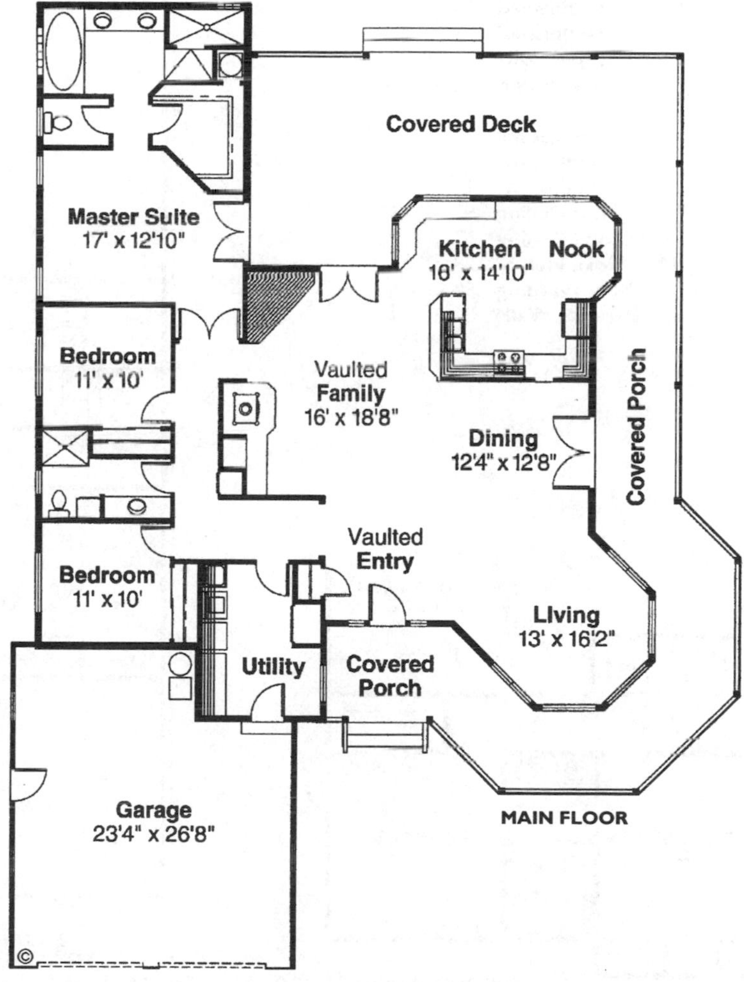

Design 62083

Units	Single
Price Code	D
Total Finished	2,146 sq. ft.
First Finished	1,654 sq. ft.
Second Finished	492 sq. ft.
Garage Unfinished	464 sq. ft.
Porch Unfinished	324 sq. ft.
Dimensions	38'10"x70'4"
Foundation	Crawlspace Slab
Bedrooms	3
Full Baths	2
Half Baths	1
First Ceiling	9'
Second Ceiling	8'
Max Ridge Height	28'10"
Roof Framing	Stick
Exterior Walls	2x4

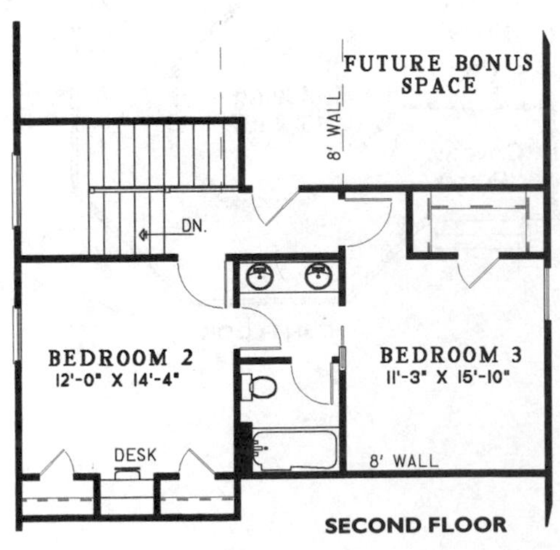

SECOND FLOOR

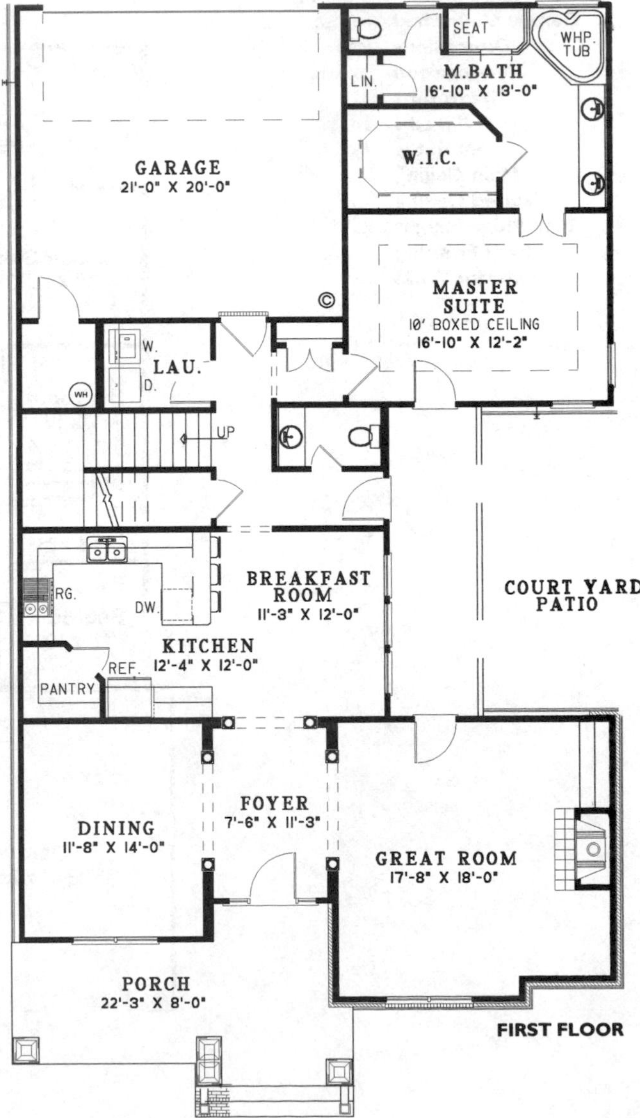

FIRST FLOOR

Design 61096

Units	Single
Price Code	D
Total Finished	2,148 sq. ft.
Main Finished	2,148 sq. ft.
Garage Unfinished	477 sq. ft.
Porch Unfinished	190 sq. ft.
Dimensions	63'x52'8"
Foundation	Crawlspace Slab
Bedrooms	4
Full Baths	2
Main Ceiling	9'
Roof Framing	Stick
Exterior Walls	2x4

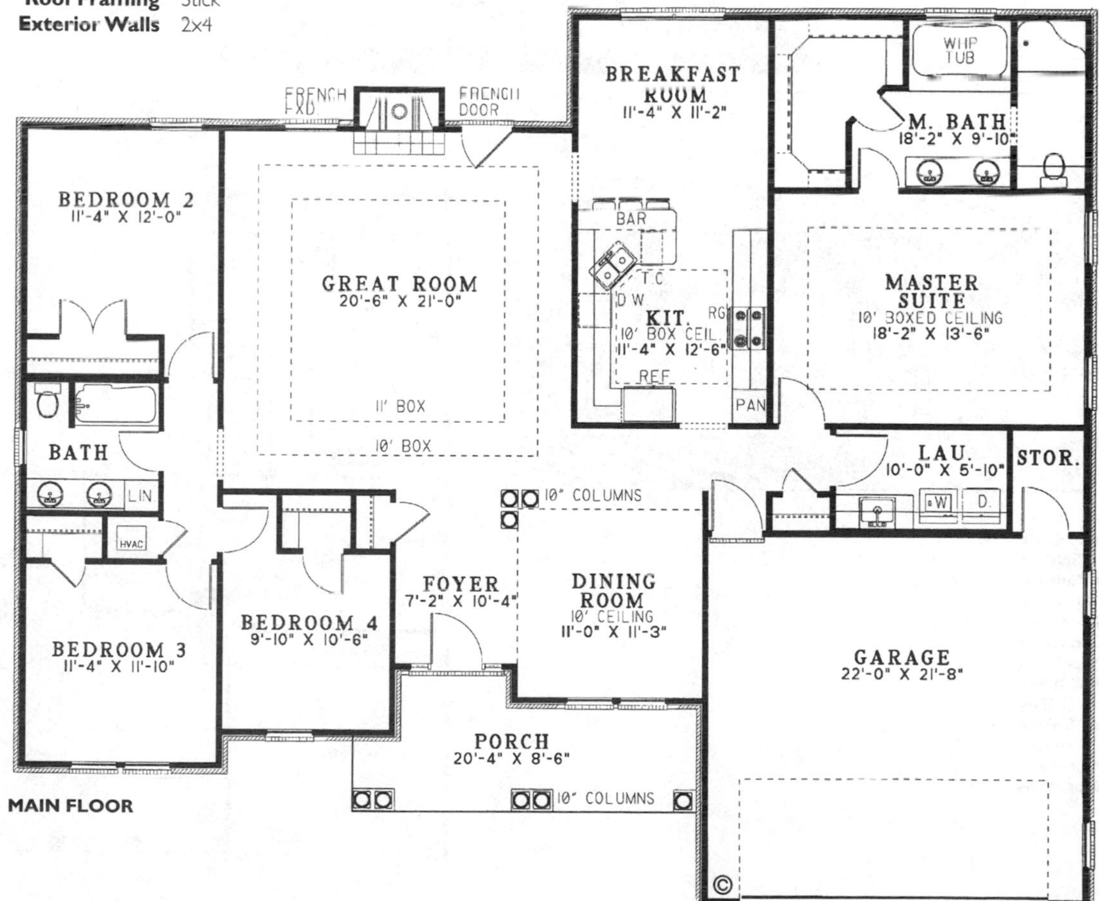

MAIN FLOOR

Design 69155

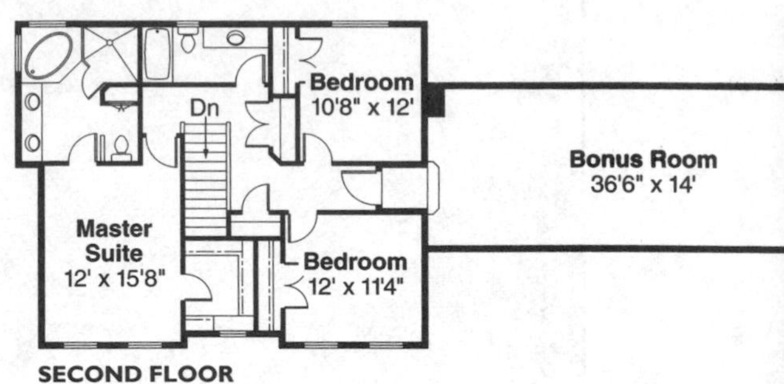

Units	Single
Price Code	D
Total Finished	2,148 sq. ft.
First Finished	1,195 sq. ft.
Second Finished	953 sq. ft.
Bonus Unfinished	570 sq. ft.
Garage Unfinished	959 sq. ft.
Dimensions	77'x45'
Foundation	Crawlspace
Bedrooms	3
Full Baths	2
Half Baths	1
First Ceiling	9'
Second Ceiling	9'
Max Ridge Height	28'
Roof Framing	Truss
Exterior Walls	2x6

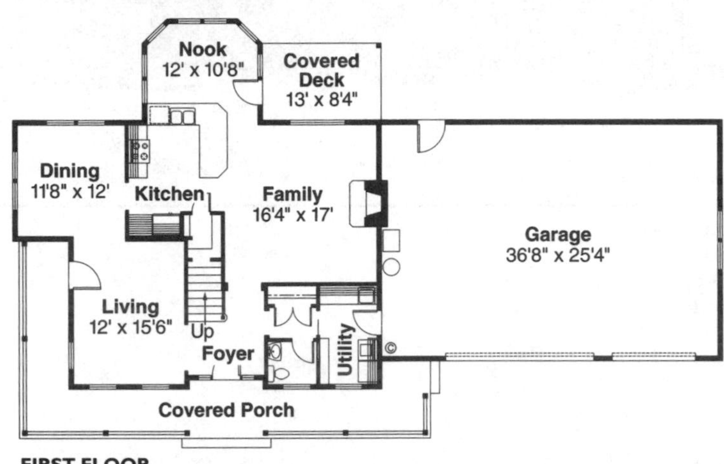

Design 63028

Units	Single
Price Code	D
Total Finished	2,153 sq. ft.
Main Finished	2,153 sq. ft.
Garage Unfinished	434 sq. ft.
Dimensions	61'8"x62'
Foundation	Slab
Bedrooms	4
Full Baths	2
Main Ceiling	10'
Vaulted Ceiling	12'
Max Ridge Height	21'6"
Roof Framing	Truss
Exterior Walls	2x4

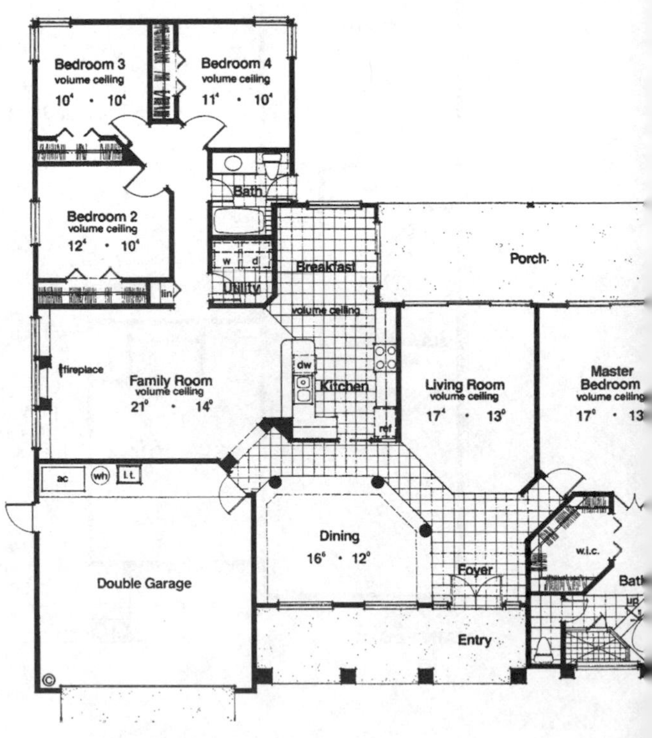

Design 97150

Units	Single
Price Code	D
Total Finished	2,153 sq. ft.
Main Finished	2,153 sq. ft.
Basement Unfinished	2,153 sq. ft.
Garage Unfinished	573 sq. ft.
Dimensions	65'x54'
Foundation	Basement
Bedrooms	3
Full Baths	2
Main Ceiling	9'1⅛"
Max Ridge Height	24'
Roof Framing	Truss
Exterior Walls	2x6

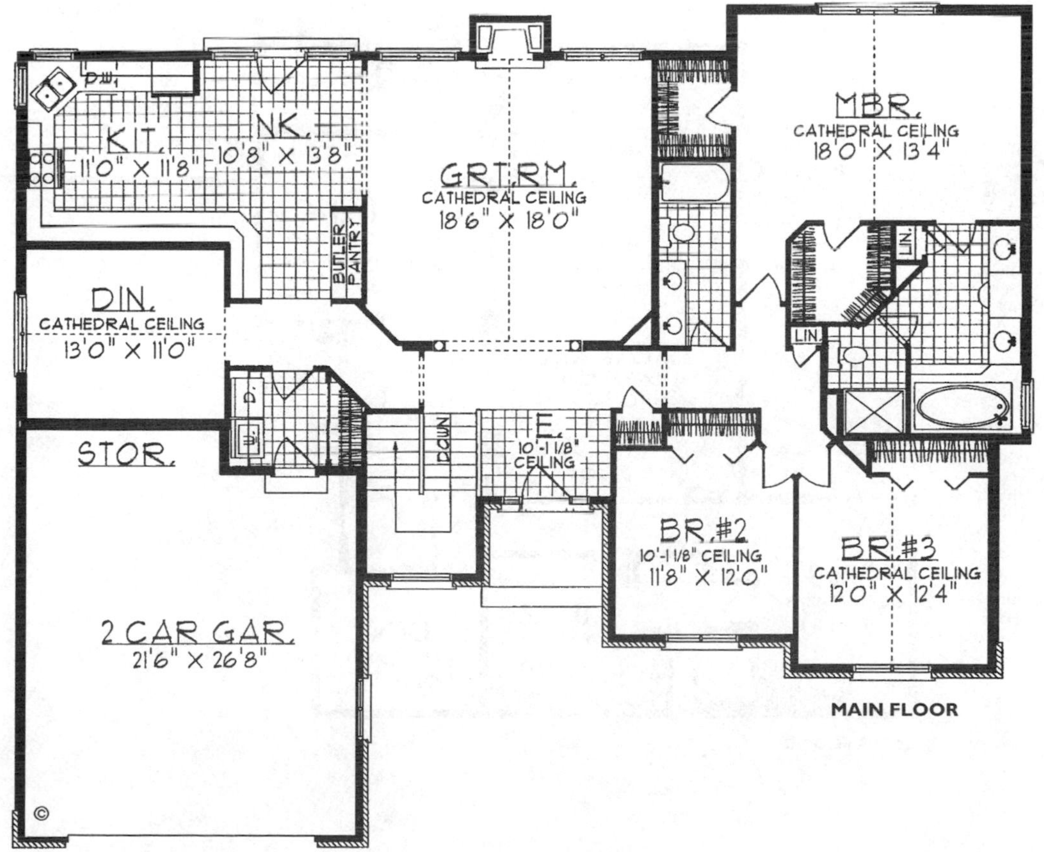

Design 91548

Units	Single
Price Code	D
Total Finished	2,155 sq. ft.
Main Finished	2,155 sq. ft.
Dimensions	60'x79'
Foundation	Crawlspace
Bedrooms	3
Full Baths	2
Half Baths	1
Max Ridge Height	22'
Roof Framing	Truss
Exterior Walls	2x6

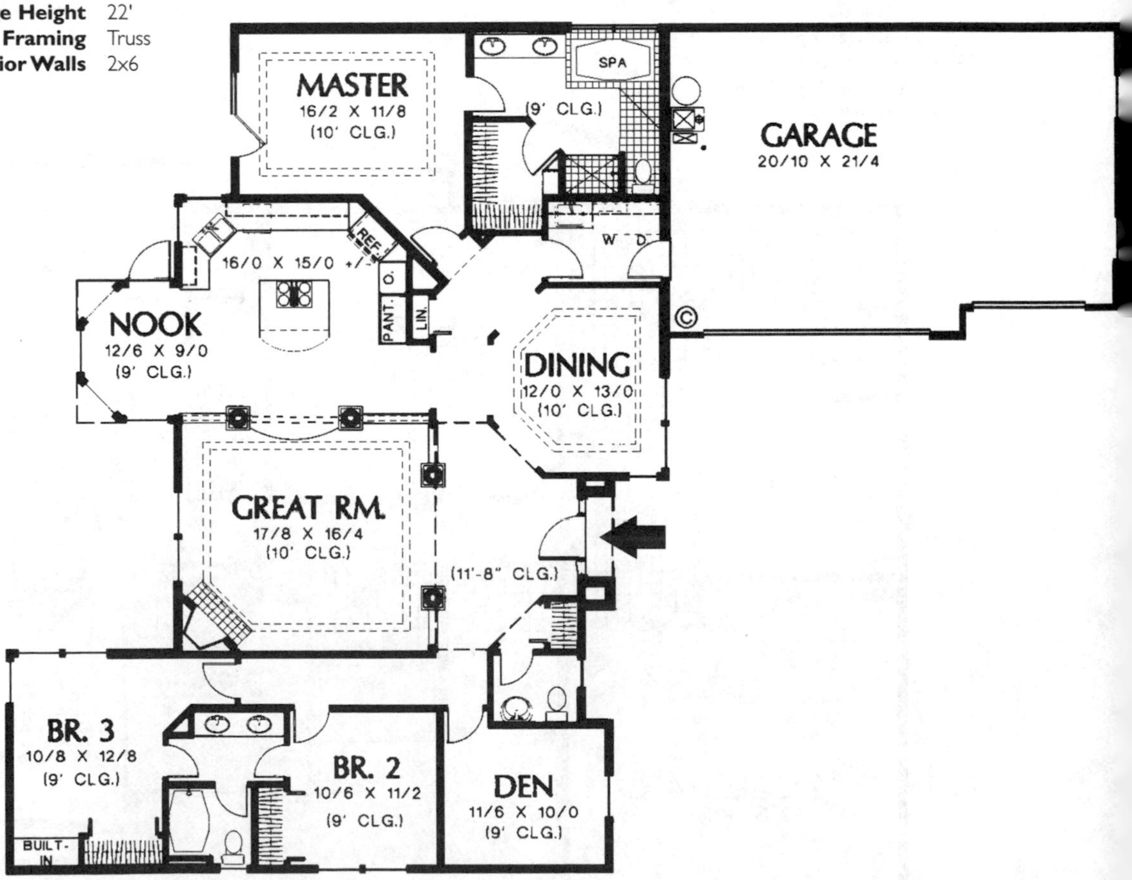

MASTER
16/2 X 11/8
(10' CLG.)

SPA
(9' CLG.)

GARAGE
20/10 X 21/4

16/0 X 15/0 +/-
REF.
O.
PANT.
LIN.
W D

NOOK
12/6 X 9/0
(9' CLG.)

DINING
12/0 X 13/0
(10' CLG.)

GREAT RM.
17/8 X 16/4
(10' CLG.)

(11'-8" CLG.)

BR. 3
10/8 X 12/8
(9' CLG.)
BUILT-IN

BR. 2
10/6 X 11/2
(9' CLG.)

DEN
11/6 X 10/0
(9' CLG.)

MAIN FLOOR

Design 90484

Units	Single
Price Code	D
Total Finished	2,167 sq. ft.
Main Finished	2,167 sq. ft.
Basement Unfinished	2,167 sq. ft.
Garage Unfinished	491 sq. ft.
Deck Unfinished	184 sq. ft.
Dimensions	59'x59'10"
Foundation	Basement Crawlspace Slab
Bedrooms	3
Full Baths	2
Max Ridge Height	26'
Roof Framing	Stick
Exterior Walls	2x4

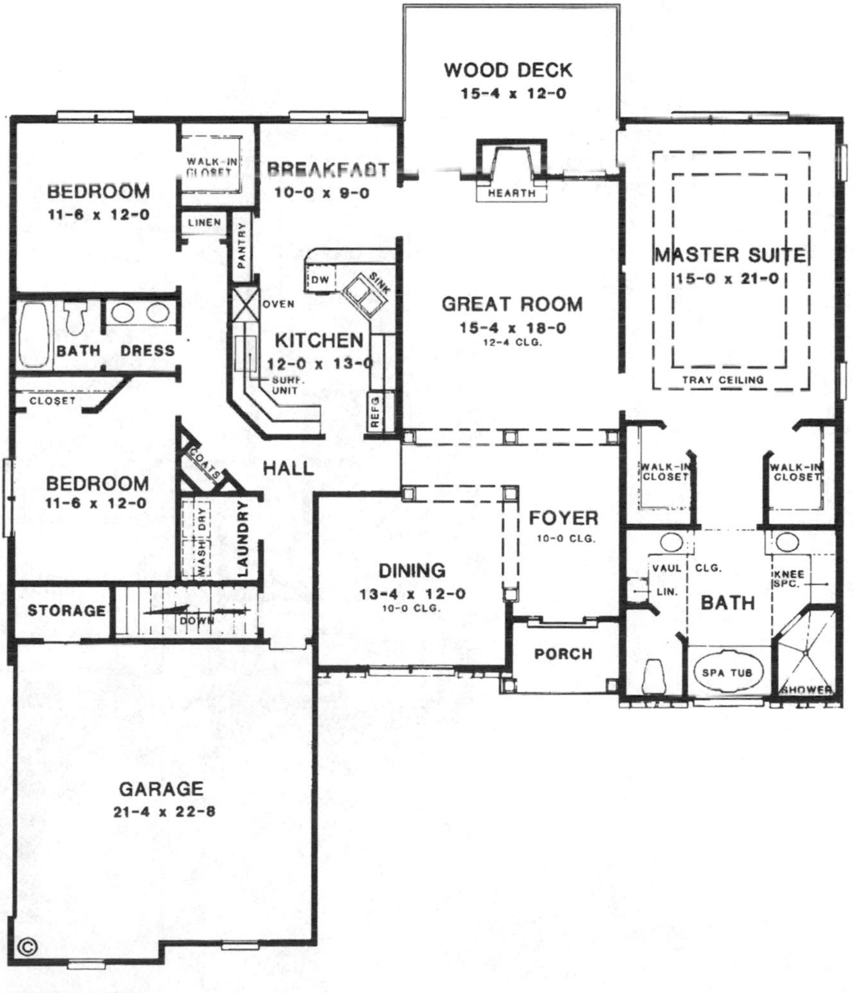

MAIN FLOOR

Design 98512

Units	Single
Price Code	D
Total Finished	2,167 sq. ft.
Main Finished	2,167 sq. ft.
Garage Unfinished	690 sq. ft.
Deck Unfinished	162 sq. ft.
Porch Unfinished	22 sq. ft.
Dimensions	64'x58'1"
Foundation	Slab
Bedrooms	3
Full Baths	2
Main Ceiling	8'-10'
Max Ridge Height	26'3"
Roof Framing	Stick
Exterior Walls	2x4

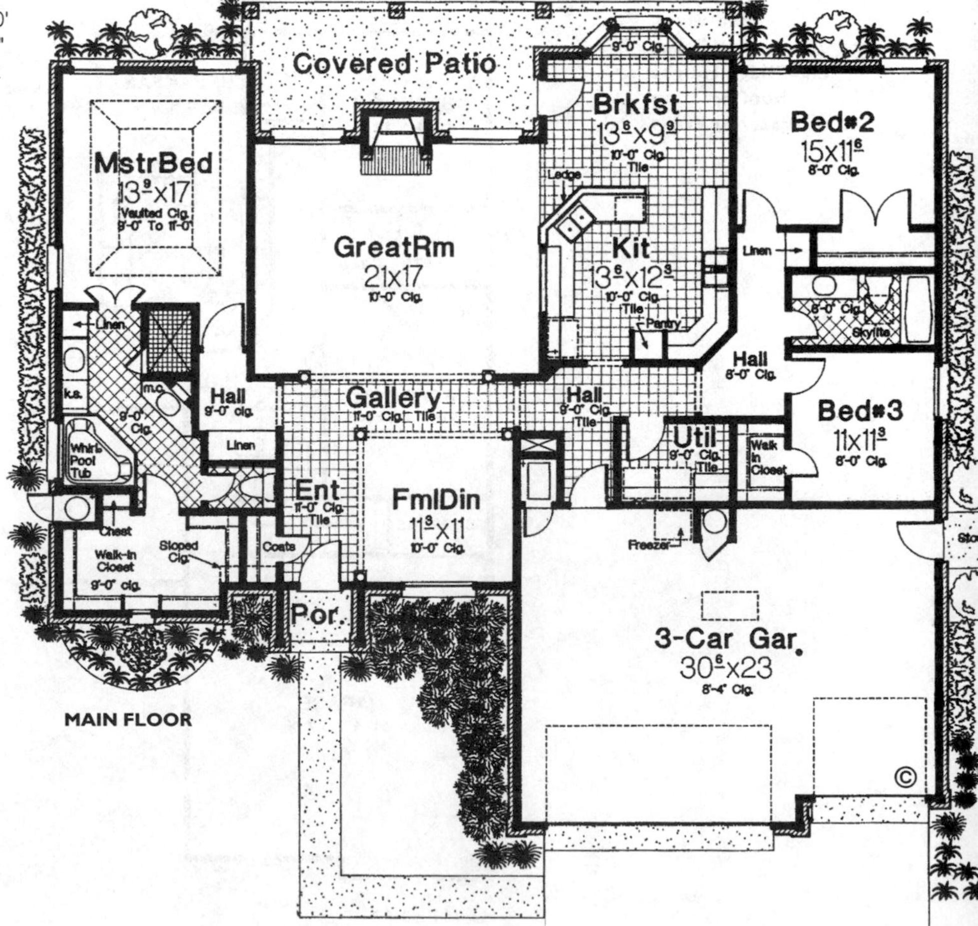

Design 98554

Units	Single
Price Code	D
Total Finished	2,169 sq. ft.
Main Finished	2,169 sq. ft.
Garage Unfinished	542 sq. ft.
Deck Unfinished	160 sq. ft.
Dimensions	76'6"x44'4"
Foundation	Slab
Bedrooms	4
Full Baths	3
Main Ceiling	8'-10'
Max Ridge Height	24'6"
Roof Framing	Stick
Exterior Walls	2x4

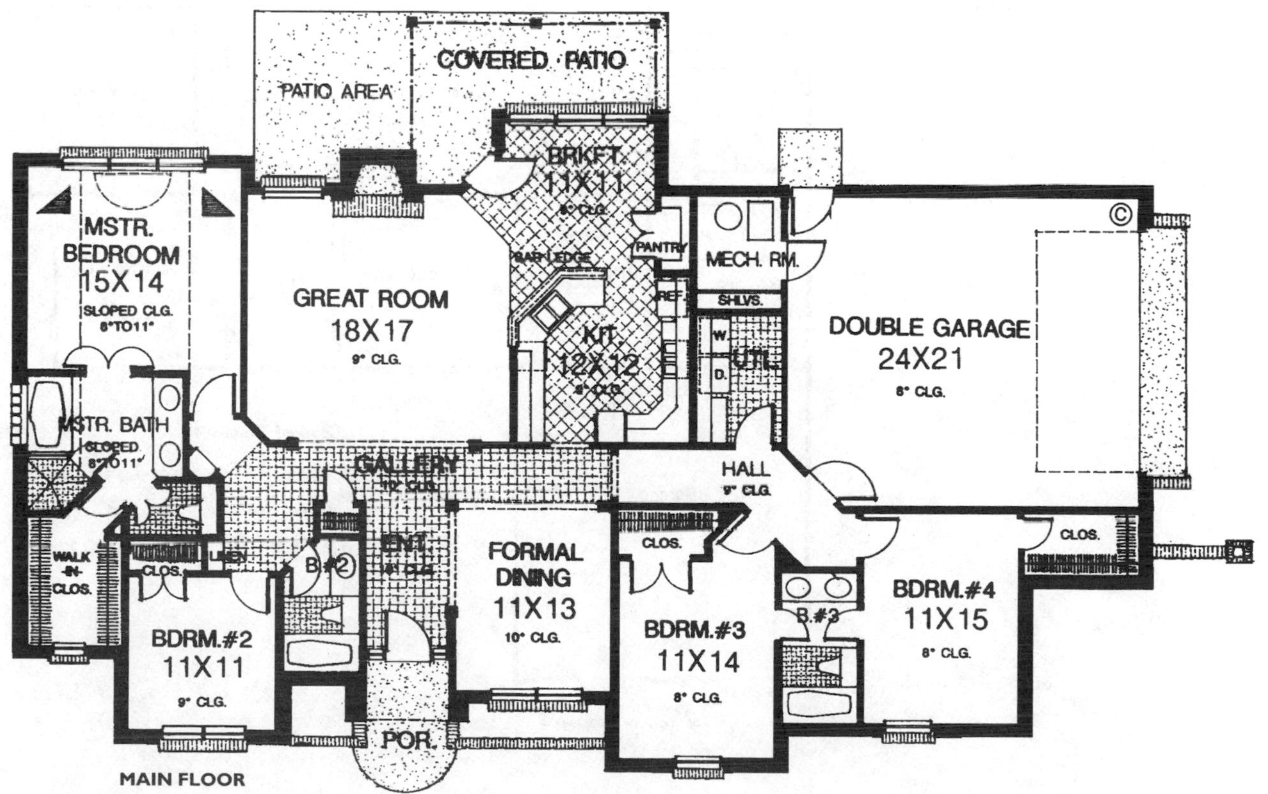

Design 98470

Units	Single
Price Code	D
Total Finished	2,170 sq. ft.
Main Finished	2,170 sq. ft.
Basement Unfinished	2,184 sq. ft.
Garage Unfinished	484 sq. ft.
Dimensions	63'6"x61'
Foundation	Basement Crawlspace
Bedrooms	3
Full Baths	2
Half Baths	1
Main Ceiling	9'
Max Ridge Height	27'
Roof Framing	Stick
Exterior Walls	2x4

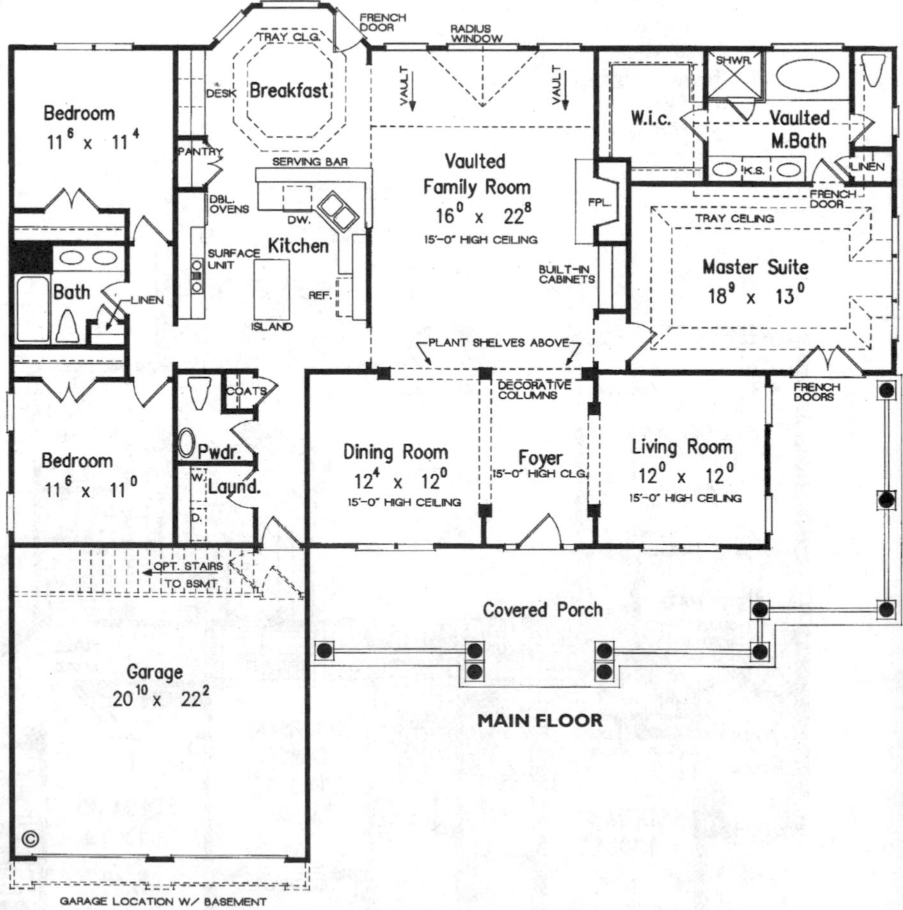

Design 65131

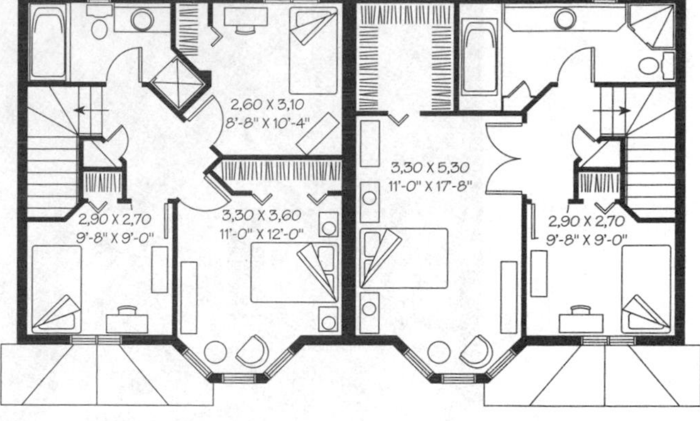

SECOND FLOOR

Units	Duplex
Price Code	D
Total Finished	2,172 sq. ft.
First Finished	1,086 sq. ft.
Second Finished	1,086 sq. ft.
Dimensions	44'x28'8"
Foundation	Basement
Bedrooms	3
Full Baths	1
Half Baths	1
First Ceiling	8'
Second Ceiling	8'
Max Ridge Height	25'11"
Roof Framing	Truss
Exterior Walls	2x6

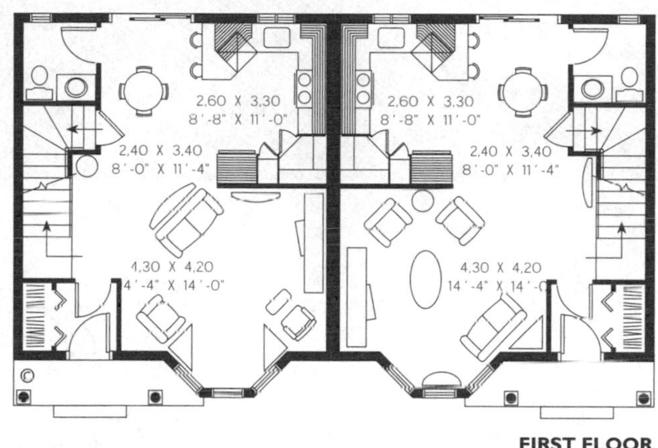

FIRST FLOOR

Design 93145

Units	Single
Price Code	D
Total Finished	2,174 sq. ft.
Main Finished	2,174 sq. ft.
Basement Unfinished	2,174 sq. ft.
Dimensions	67'x51'
Foundation	Basement
Bedrooms	3
Full Baths	2
Max Ridge Height	23'
Roof Framing	Truss
Exterior Walls	2x6

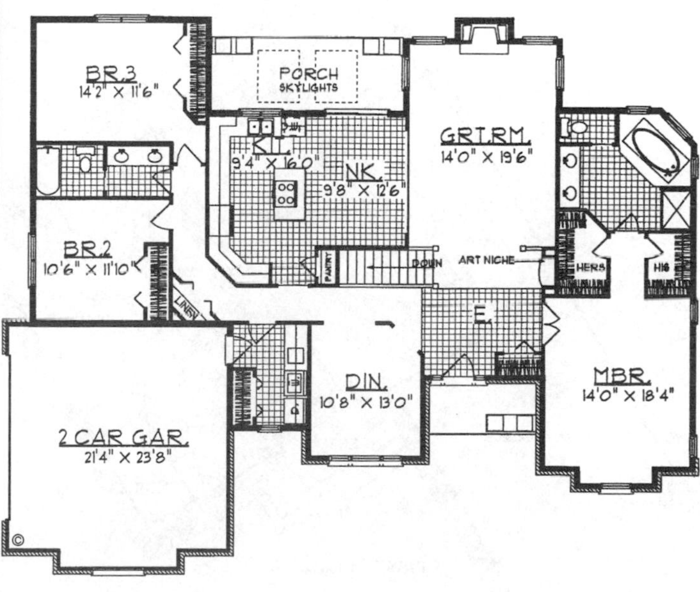

MAIN FLOOR

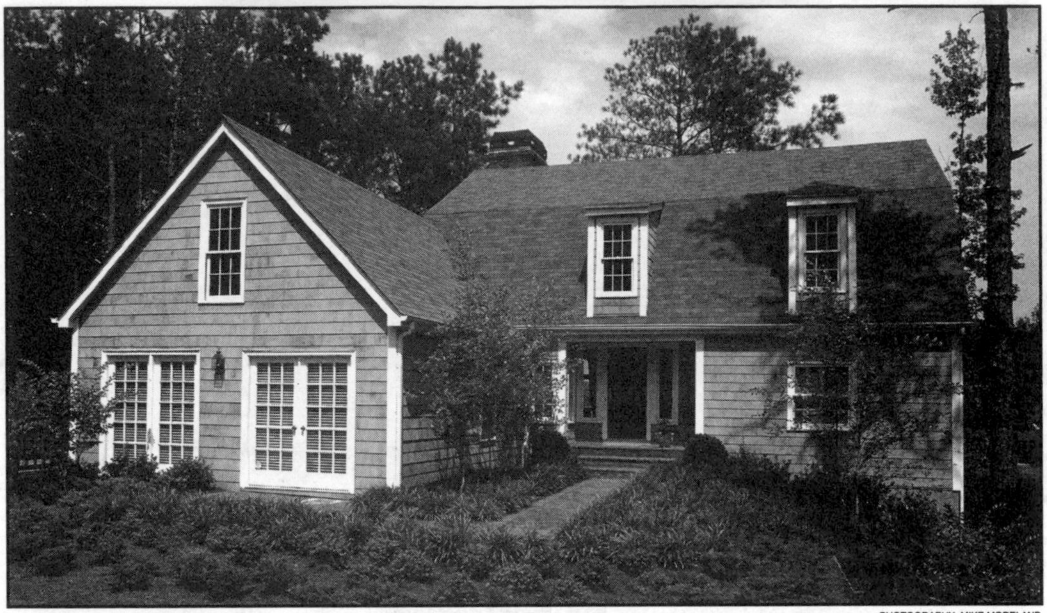

Design 19410

PHOTOGRAPHY: MIKE MORELAND

Units	Single
Price Code	D
Total Finished	2,175 sq. ft.
First Finished	1,600 sq. ft.
Second Finished	575 sq. ft.
Basement Unfinished	1,509 sq. ft.
Garage Unfinished	413 sq. ft.
Dimensions	48'4"x60'
Foundation	Basement
Bedrooms	5
Full Baths	3
Half Baths	1
First Ceiling	8'4"
Second Ceiling	8'4"
Roof Framing	Stick
Exterior Walls	2x4

Please note: The photographed home may have been modified to suit homeowner preferences. If you order plans, have a builder or design professional check them against the photograph to confirm actual construction details.

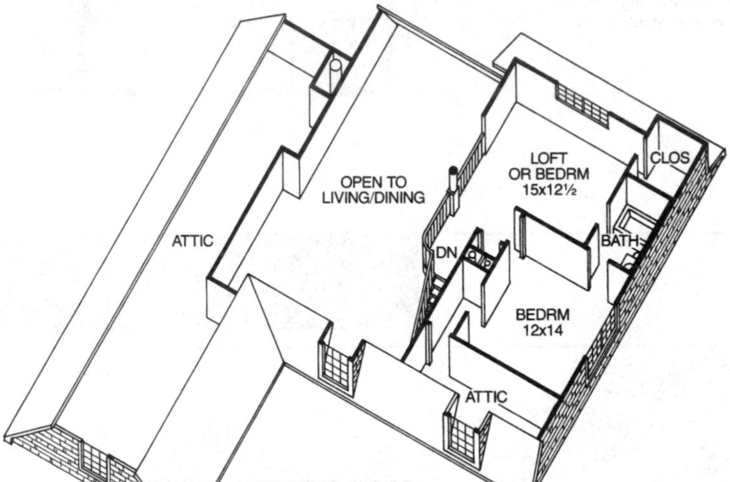

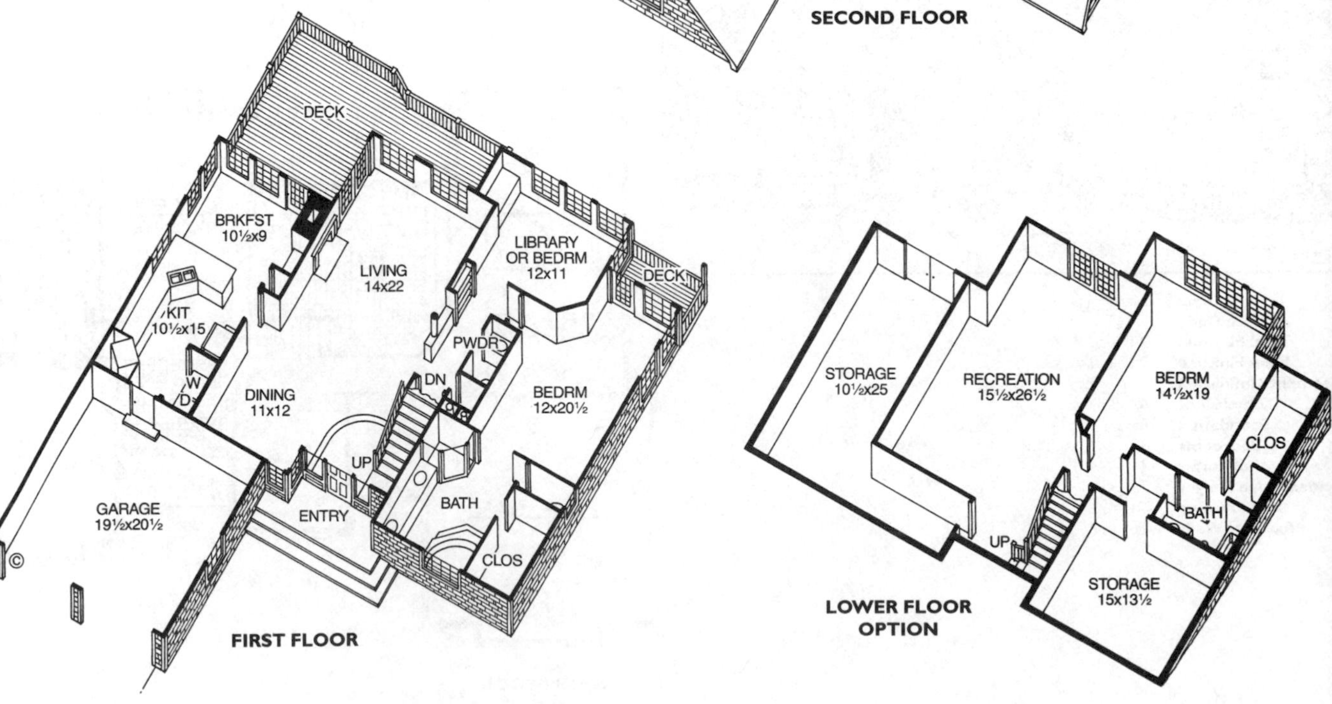

Design 98517

Units	Single
Price Code	D
Total Finished	2,175 sq. ft.
First Finished	1,472 sq. ft.
Second Finished	703 sq. ft.
Garage Unfinished	540 sq. ft.
Deck Unfinished	144 sq. ft.
Porch Unfinished	36 sq. ft.
Dimensions	58'x39'10"
Foundation	Slab
Bedrooms	4
Full Baths	2
Half Baths	1
First Ceiling	9'
Second Ceiling	8'
Max Ridge Height	25'
Roof Framing	Stick
Exterior Walls	2x4

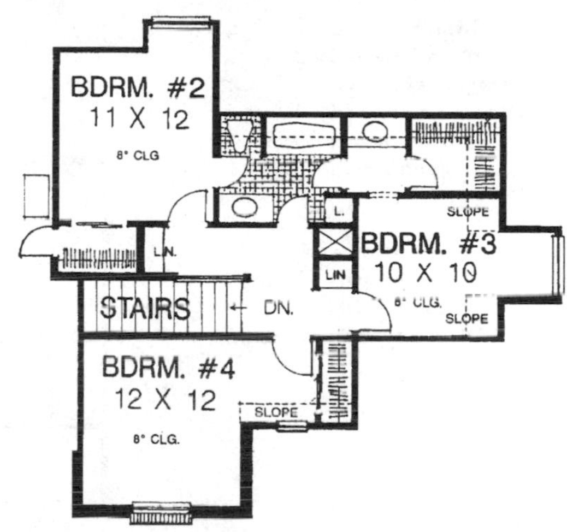

SECOND FLOOR

FIRST FLOOR

Design 61030

Units	Single
Price Code	D
Total Finished	2,180 sq. ft.
Main Finished	2,180 sq. ft.
Garage Unfinished	672 sq. ft.
Porch Unfinished	228 sq. ft.
Dimensions	58'4"x68'6"
Foundation	Basement Crawlspace Slab
Bedrooms	3
Full Baths	2
Half Baths	1
Exterior Walls	2x4

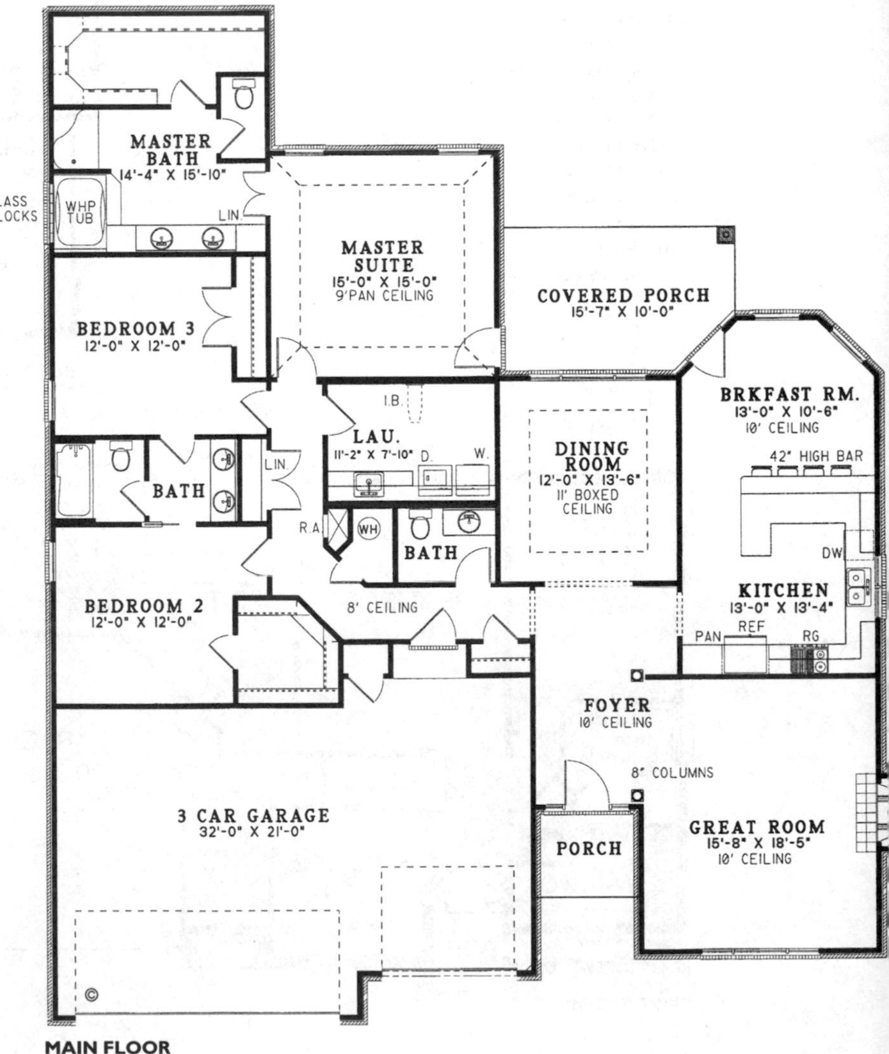

MAIN FLOOR

Design 92443

Units	Single
Price Code	B
Total Finished	1,507 sq. ft.
Main Finished	1,507 sq. ft.
Dimensions	50'x30'
Foundation	Basement
Bedrooms	3
Full Baths	2
Roof Framing	Stick
Exterior Walls	2x4

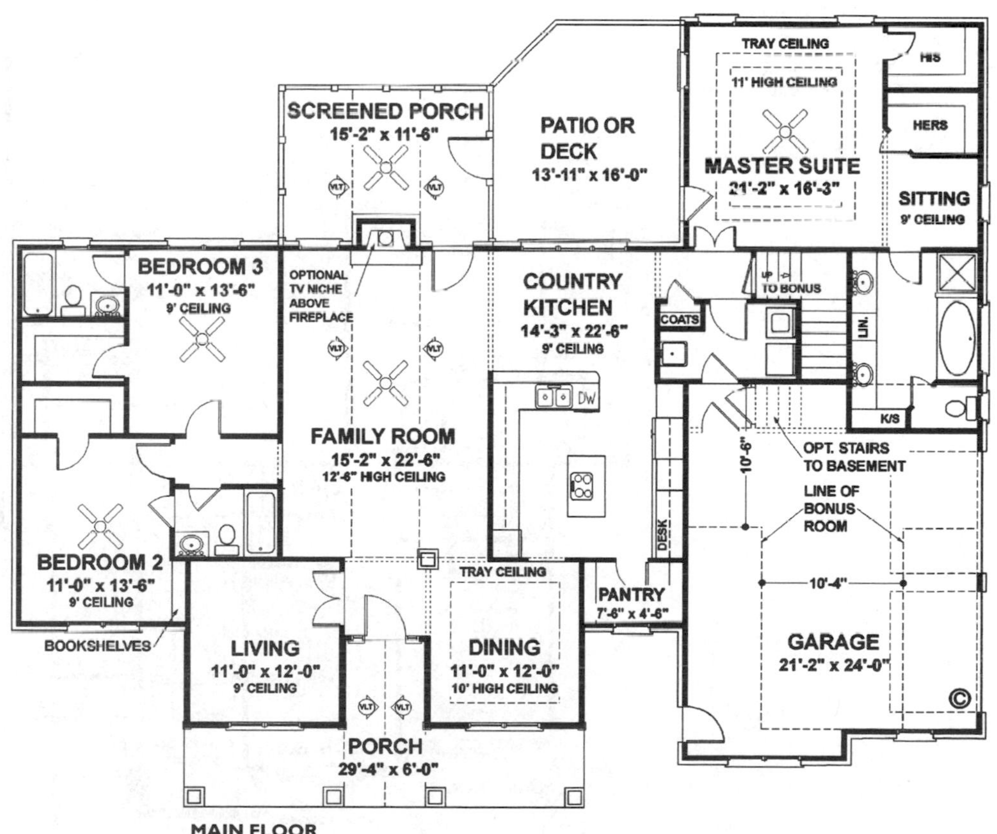

MAIN FLOOR

Design 97494

Units	Single
Price Code	D
Total Finished	2,186 sq. ft.
Main Finished	2,186 sq. ft.
Garage Unfinished	720 sq. ft.
Dimensions	64'x66'
Foundation	Basement
Bedrooms	3
Full Baths	2
Half Baths	1
Main Ceiling	8'
Max Ridge Height	25'
Roof Framing	Stick
Exterior Walls	2x4

* Alternate foundation options available at an additional charge. Please call 1-800-235-5700 for more information.

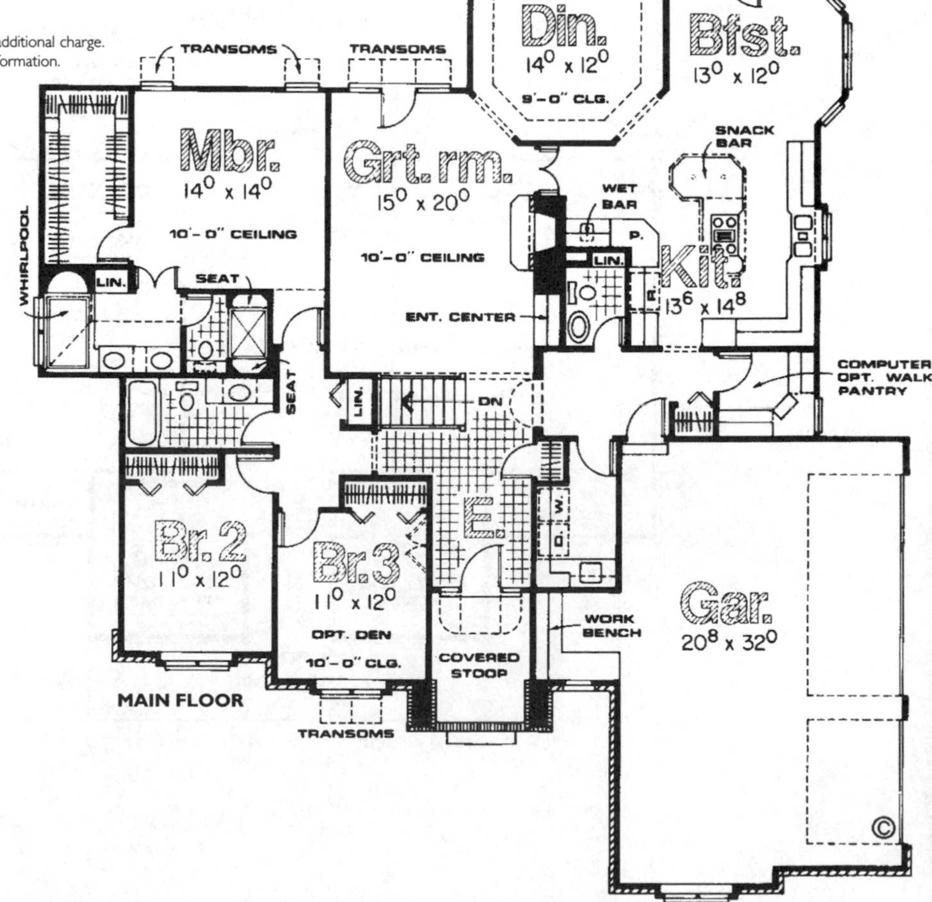

Design 97470

Units	Single
Price Code	D
Total Finished	2,188 sq. ft.
Main Finished	2,188 sq. ft.
Garage Unfinished	704 sq. ft.
Deck Unfinished	269 sq. ft.
Dimensions	71'x49'4"
Foundation	Basement
Bedrooms	3
Full Baths	2
Main Ceiling	9'
Max Ridge Height	28'10"
Roof Framing	Stick
Exterior Walls	2x4

* Alternate foundation options available at an additional charge. Please call 1-800-235-5700 for more information.

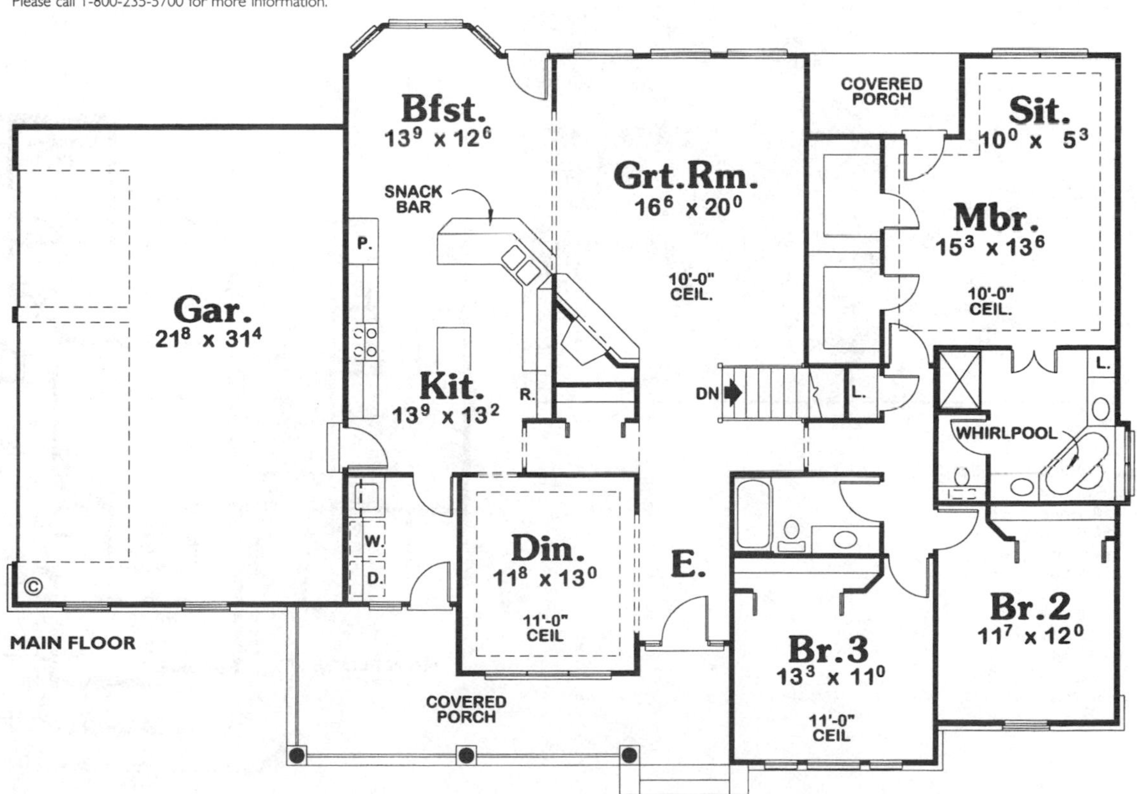

Design 64513

Units	Single
Price Code	D
Total Finished	2,189 sq. ft.
Main Finished	2,189 sq. ft.
Porch Unfinished	360 sq. ft.
Dimensions	62'x40'
Foundation	Crawlspace Slab
Bedrooms	3
Full Baths	2
Half Baths	1
Main Ceiling	8'
Max Ridge Height	24'
Roof Framing	Stick
Exterior Walls	2x4

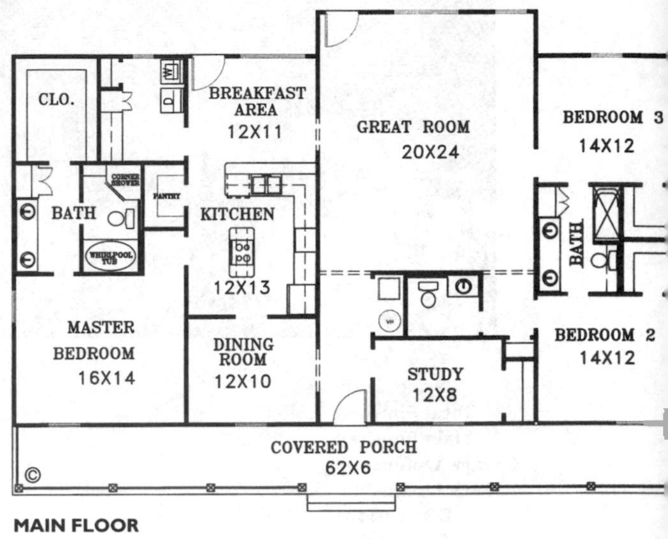

MAIN FLOOR

Design 98555

Units	Single
Price Code	D
Total Finished	2,190 sq. ft.
Main Finished	2,190 sq. ft.
Garage Unfinished	642 sq. ft.
Deck Unfinished	122 sq. ft.
Dimensions	65'x63'
Foundation	Slab
Bedrooms	4
Full Baths	2
Half Baths	1
Max Ridge Height	24'2"
Roof Framing	Stick
Exterior Walls	2x4

MAIN FLOOR

Design 97847

Units	Single
Price Code	D
Total Finished	2,192 sq. ft.
Main Finished	2,192 sq. ft.
Garage Unfinished	642 sq. ft.
Deck Unfinished	75 sq. ft.
Porch Unfinished	40 sq. ft.
Dimensions	54'10"x71'1"
Foundation	Slab
Bedrooms	4
Full Baths	3
Main Ceiling	8'-10'
Max Ridge Height	26'
Roof Framing	Stick
Exterior Walls	2x4

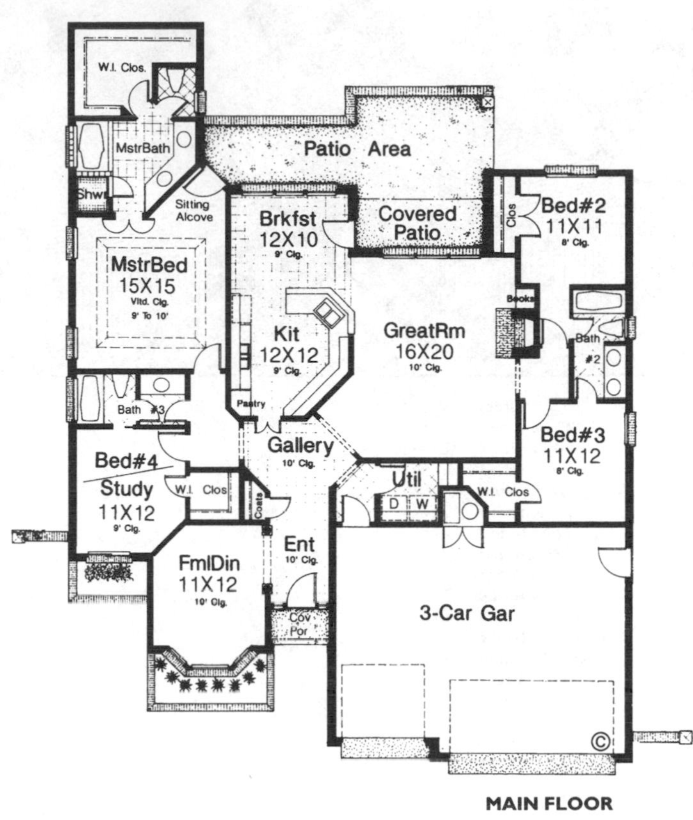

Design 98466

Units	Single
Price Code	D
Total Finished	2,193 sq. ft.
Main Finished	2,193 sq. ft.
Bonus Unfinished	400 sq. ft.
Basement Unfinished	2,193 sq. ft.
Garage Unfinished	522 sq. ft.
Dimensions	64'6"x59'
Foundation	Basement Crawlspace Slab
Bedrooms	4
Full Baths	2
Main Ceiling	9'
Second Ceiling	8'
Max Ridge Height	27'
Roof Framing	Stick
Exterior Walls	2x4

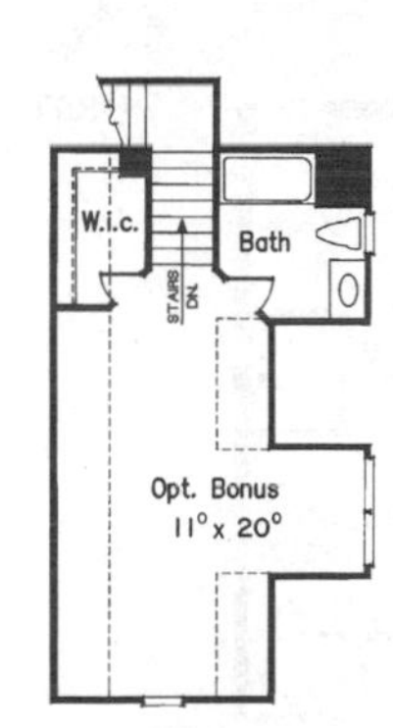

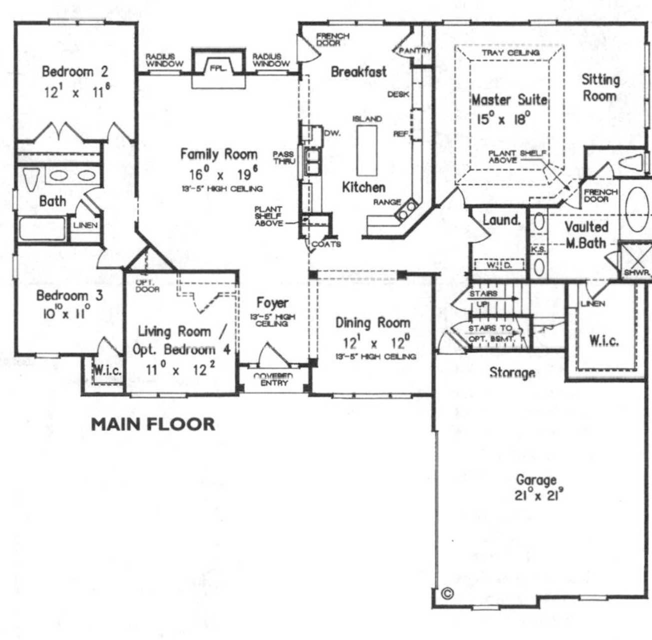

Design 10507

Units	Single
Price Code	D
Total Finished	2,194 sq. ft.
Main Finished	2,194 sq. ft.
Garage Unfinished	576 sq. ft.
Dimensions	76'x75'
Foundation	Crawlspace
Bedrooms	3
Full Baths	1
3/4 Baths	1
Main Ceiling	8'
Max Ridge Height	15'
Roof Framing	Stick
Exterior Walls	2x6

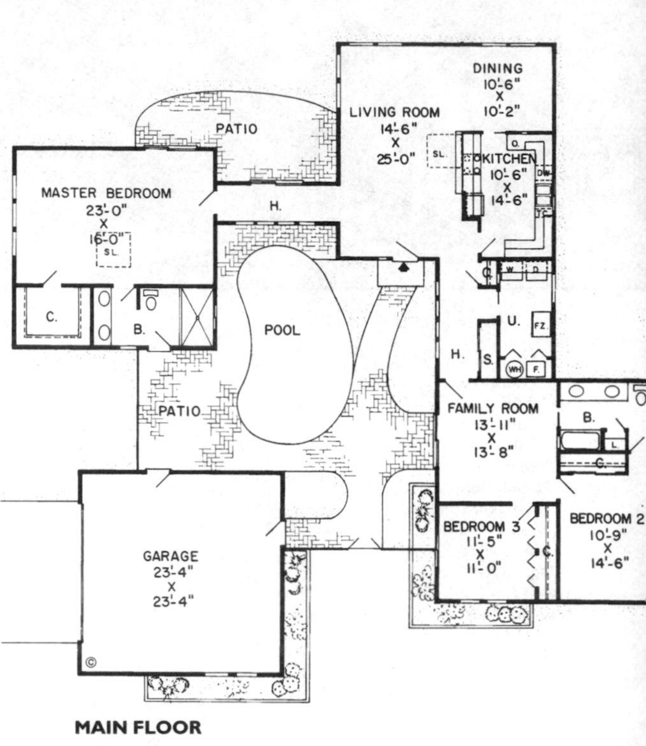

MAIN FLOOR

Design 97710

Units	Single
Price Code	D
Total Finished	2,198 sq. ft.
First Finished	1,706 sq. ft.
Second Finished	492 sq. ft.
Basement Unfinished	1,706 sq. ft.
Deck Unfinished	175 sq. ft.
Porch Unfinished	38 sq. ft.
Dimensions	59'4"x65'
Foundation	Basement
Bedrooms	3
Full Baths	2
Half Baths	1
Max Ridge Height	31'
Roof Framing	Truss
Exterior Walls	2x4

Breakfast 9' x 16'
Kitchen 8'4" x 15'4"
Great Room 16'10" x 21'
Dressing
walk-in closet
Dining Room 13'8" x 11'8"
Hall
Foyer
Master Bedroom 14' x 17'4"
Bath
Porch
Laun.
Two-car Garage 21' x 29'8"

FIRST FLOOR

Bedroom 15' x 10'7"
Great Room Below
Bath
Bedroom 13'10" x 10'7"
Foyer Below

SECOND FLOOR

Design 65666

Units	Single
Price Code	D
Total Finished	2,200 sq. ft.
Main Finished	2,200 sq. ft.
Dimensions	56'x74'
Foundation	Crawlspace Slab
Bedrooms	4
Full Baths	3
Main Ceiling	8'
Max Ridge Height	28'
Roof Framing	Stick
Exterior Walls	2x4

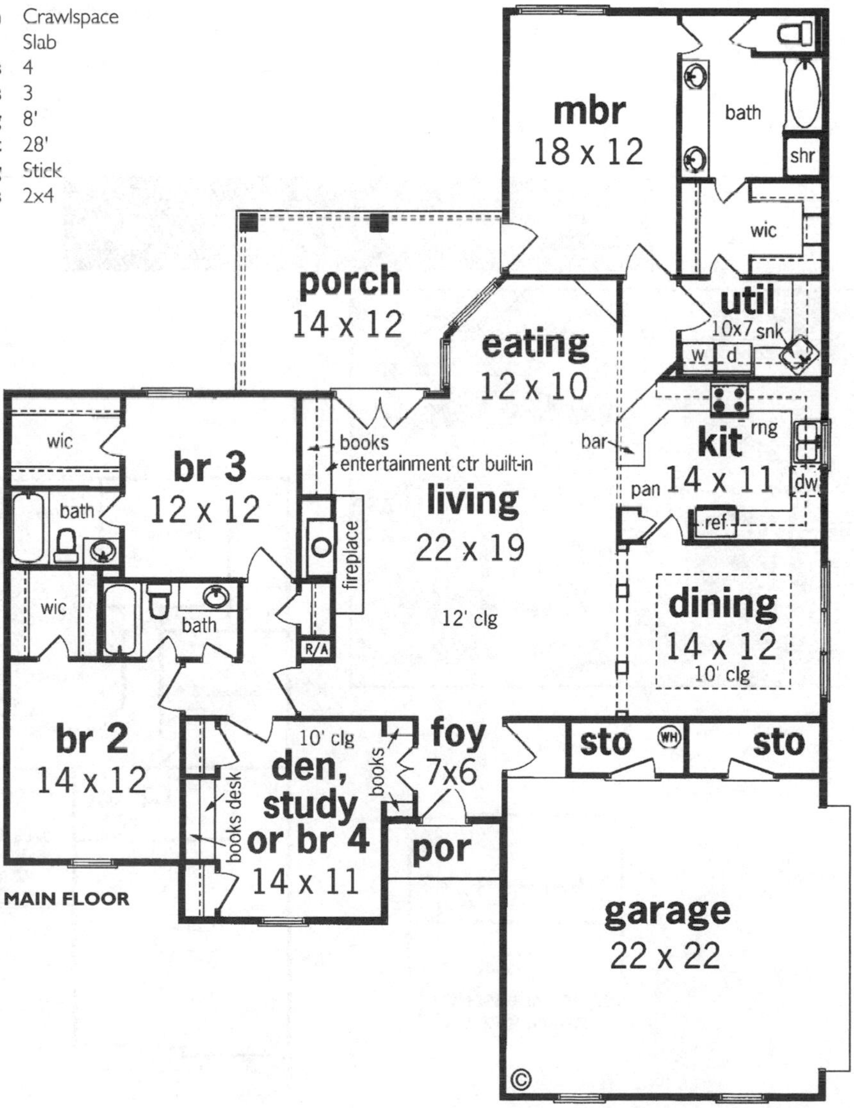

mbr
18 x 12
bath
shr
wic
porch
14 x 12
eating
12 x 10
util
10x7
snk
w
d
rng
kit
14 x 11
bar
pan
dw
ref
wic
br 3
12 x 12
books
entertainment ctr built-in
living
22 x 19
12' clg
bath
fireplace
wic
bath
R/A
dining
14 x 12
10' clg
br 2
14 x 12
10' clg
den,
study
or br 4
14 x 11
books
books desk
foy
7x6
por
sto
WH
sto
garage
22 x 22

MAIN FLOOR

Design 94676

Units	Single
Price Code	D
Total Finished	2,201 sq. ft.
Main Finished	2,201 sq. ft.
Garage Unfinished	853 sq. ft.
Deck Unfinished	222 sq. ft.
Porch Unfinished	240 sq. ft.
Dimensions	71'10"x66'10"
Foundation	Slab
Bedrooms	3
Full Baths	2
Half Baths	1
Main Ceiling	9'
Max Ridge Height	30'9"
Roof Framing	Stick
Exterior Walls	2x4

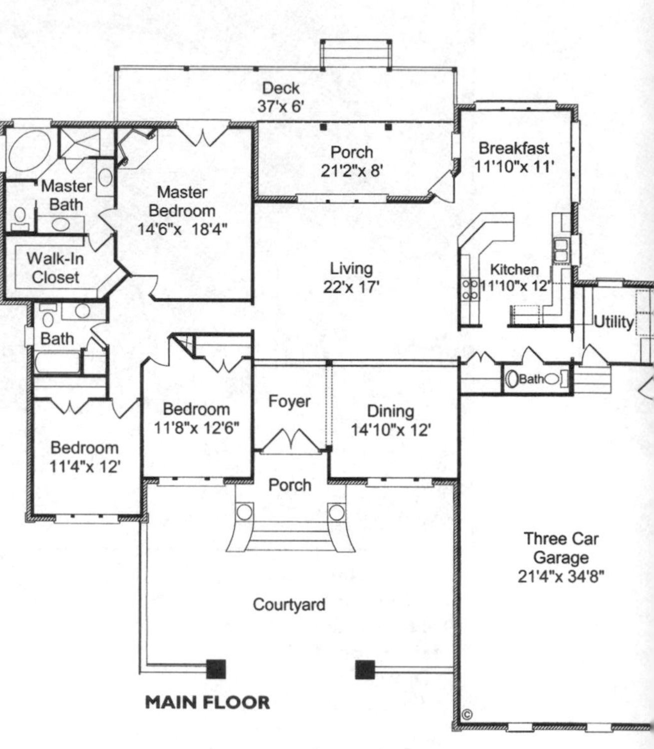

MAIN FLOOR

Design 97228

Units	Single
Price Code	D
Total Finished	2,201 sq. ft.
Main Finished	2,201 sq. ft.
Basement Unfinished	2,201 sq. ft.
Garage Unfinished	452 sq. ft.
Dimensions	59'6"x62'
Foundation	Basement Crawlspace
Bedrooms	3
Full Baths	2
Half Baths	1
Max Ridge Height	25'
Roof Framing	Stick
Exterior Walls	2x4

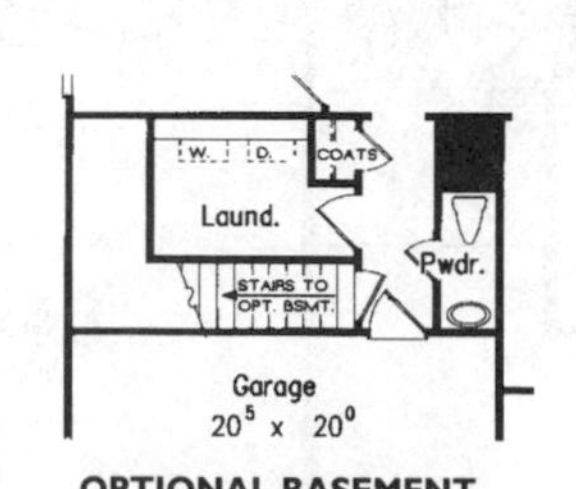

OPTIONAL BASEMENT STAIR LOCATION

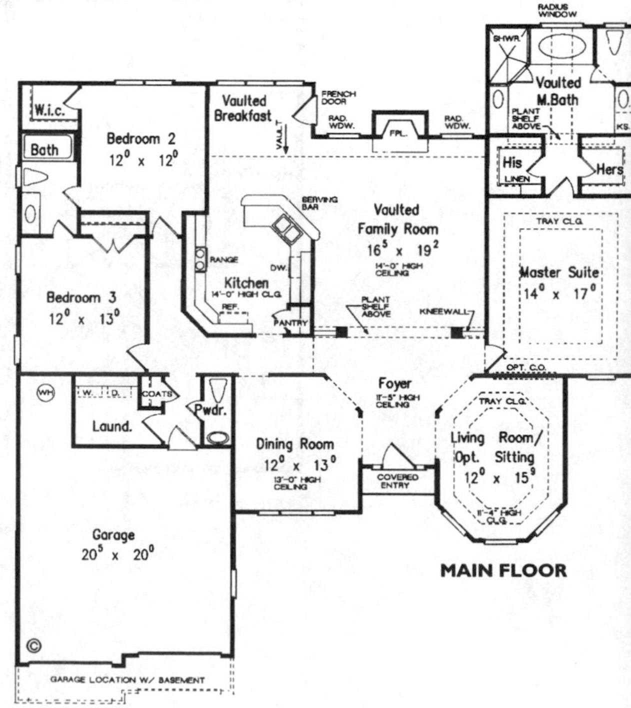

MAIN FLOOR

Design 99130

Units	Single
Price Code	D
Total Finished	2,204 sq. ft.
Main Finished	2,204 sq. ft.
Basement Unfinished	2,204 sq. ft.
Dimensions	64'x56'
Foundation	Basement
Bedrooms	3
Full Baths	2
Max Ridge Height	23'8"
Roof Framing	Truss
Exterior Walls	2x6

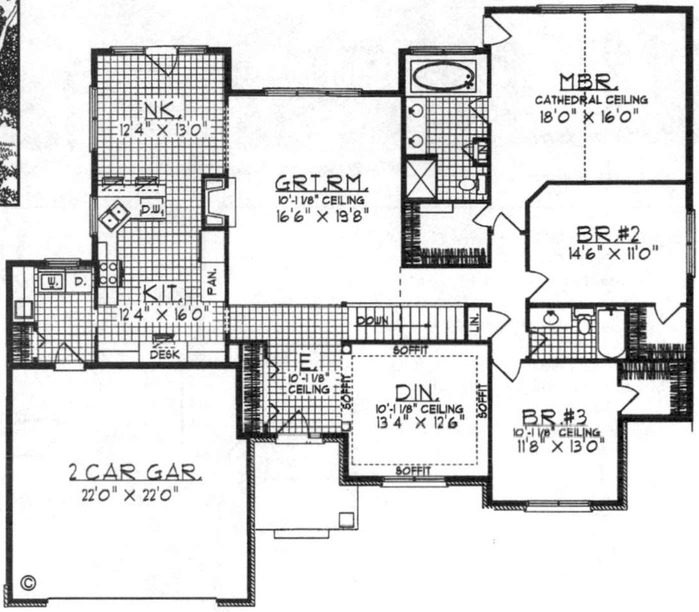

MAIN FLOOR

Design 94658

PHOTOGRAPHY: COURTESY OF THE DESIGNER

Units	Single
Price Code	D
Total Finished	2,205 sq. ft.
First Finished	1,552 sq. ft.
Second Finished	653 sq. ft.
Dimensions	60'x50'
Foundation	Pier/Post
Bedrooms	3
Full Baths	2
First Ceiling	9'
Second Ceiling	9'
Max Ridge Height	37'10"
Roof Framing	Stick
Exterior Walls	2x4

Please note: The photographed home may have been modified to suit homeowner preferences. If you order plans, have a builder or design professional check them against the photograph to confirm actual construction details.

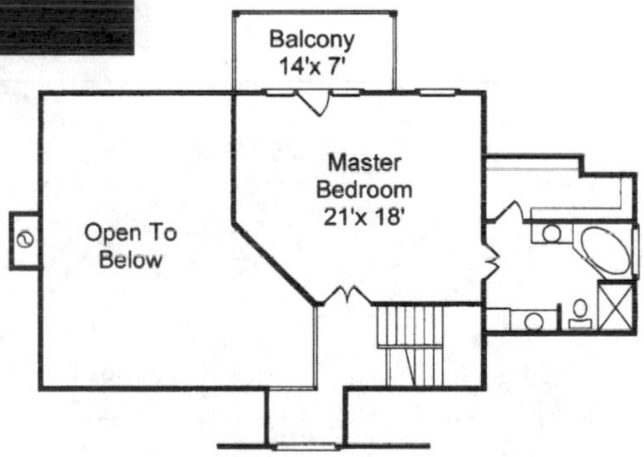

SECOND FLOOR

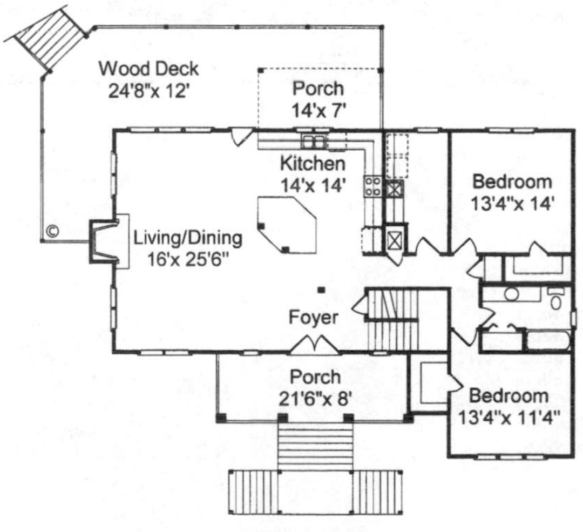

FIRST FLOOR

Design 92643

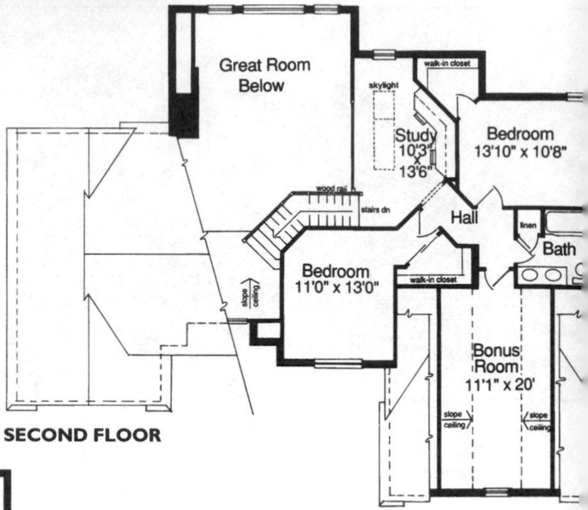

Units	Single
Price Code	D
Total Finished	2,209 sq. ft.
First Finished	1,542 sq. ft.
Second Finished	667 sq. ft.
Bonus Unfinished	236 sq. ft.
Basement Unfinished	1,470 sq. ft.
Garage Unfinished	420 sq. ft.
Dimensions	58'6"x49'
Foundation	Basement
Bedrooms	3
Full Baths	2
Half Baths	1
First Ceiling	8'
Second Ceiling	8'
Max Ridge Height	26'
Roof Framing	Truss
Exterior Walls	2x4

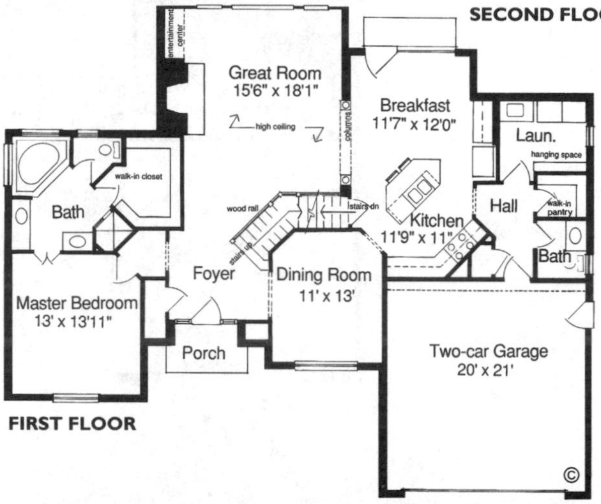

Great Room Below
Study 10'3" x 13'6"
Bedroom 13'10" x 10'8"
Hall
Bath
Bedroom 11'0" x 13'0"
Bonus Room 11'1" x 20'

SECOND FLOOR

Great Room 15'6" x 18'1"
Breakfast 11'7" x 12'0"
Laun.
Bath
Hall
Kitchen 11'9" x 11'
Foyer
Dining Room 11' x 13'
Bath
Master Bedroom 13' x 13'11"
Porch
Two-car Garage 20' x 21'

FIRST FLOOR

Design 97858

Units	Single
Price Code	D
Total Finished	2,214 sq. ft.
Main Finished	2,214 sq. ft.
Garage Unfinished	599 sq. ft.
Deck Unfinished	136 sq. ft.
Porch Unfinished	42 sq. ft.
Dimensions	55'x77'11"
Foundation	Slab
Bedrooms	3
Full Baths	2
Half Baths	1
Main Ceiling	9'-10'
Max Ridge Height	27'
Roof Framing	Stick
Exterior Walls	2x4

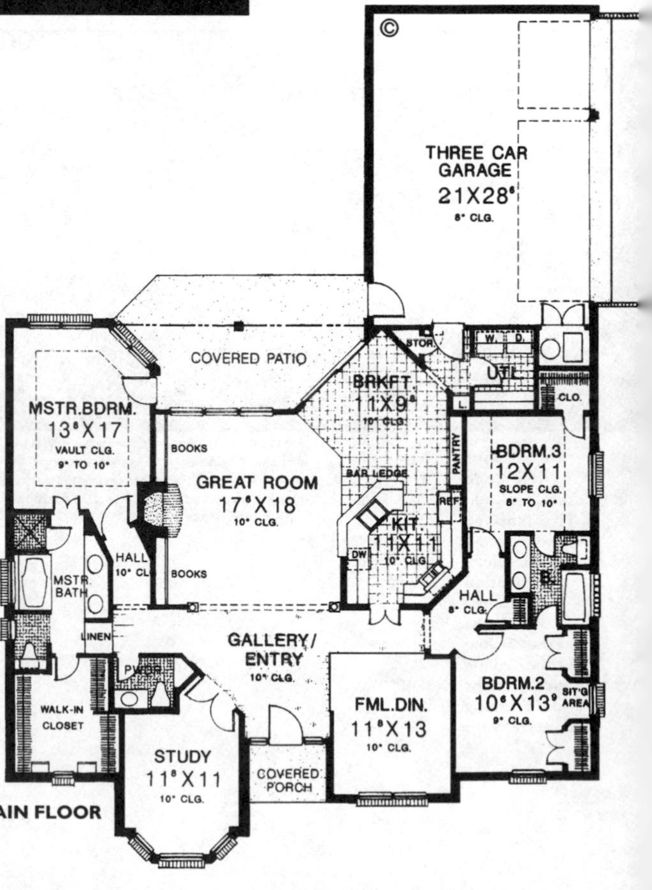

THREE CAR GARAGE 21X28
COVERED PATIO
MSTR.BDRM. 13X17
BRKFT 11X9
GREAT ROOM 17X18
KIT 11X11
BDRM.3 12X11
GALLERY/ ENTRY
FML.DIN. 11X13
BDRM.2 10X13
STUDY 11X11
COVERED PORCH

MAIN FLOOR

Design 63100

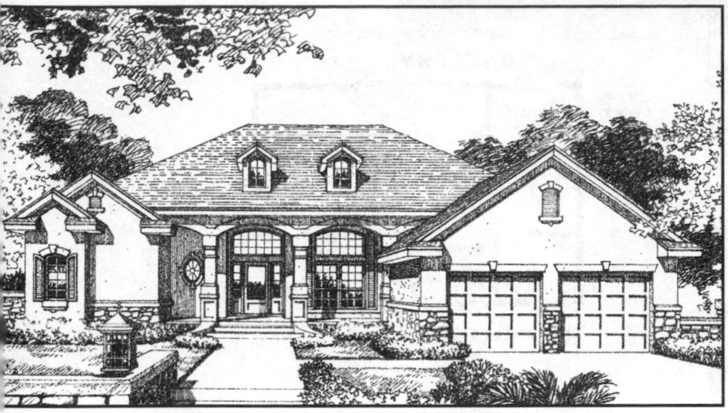

Units	Single
Price Code	D
Total Finished	2,224 sq. ft.
Main Finished	2,224 sq. ft.
Garage Unfinished	554 sq. ft.
Dimensions	58'6"x72'
Foundation	Slab
Bedrooms	4
Full Baths	2
3/4 Baths	1
Max Ridge Height	25'10"
Roof Framing	Truss

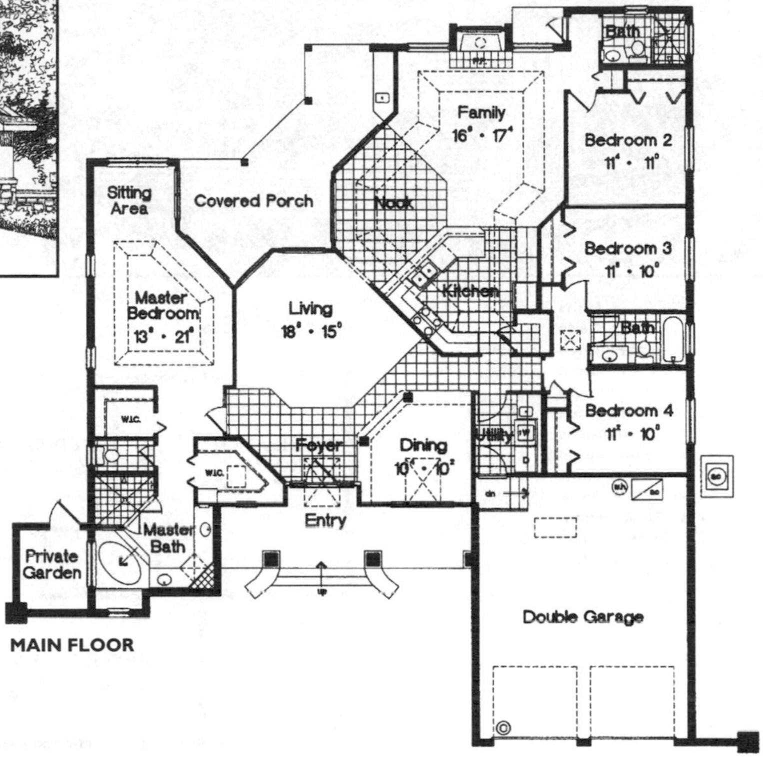

Bath
Family
16⁶ · 17⁴
Bedroom 2
11⁴ · 11⁰
Sitting Area
Covered Porch
Nook
Bedroom 3
11⁰ · 10⁰
Master Bedroom
13⁰ · 21⁶
Living
18⁰ · 15⁰
Kitchen
Bath
Bedroom 4
11⁰ · 10⁰
W.I.C.
Foyer
Dining
10⁶ · 10²
Utility
W.I.C.
Entry
Master Bath
Private Garden
Double Garage

MAIN FLOOR

Design 91591

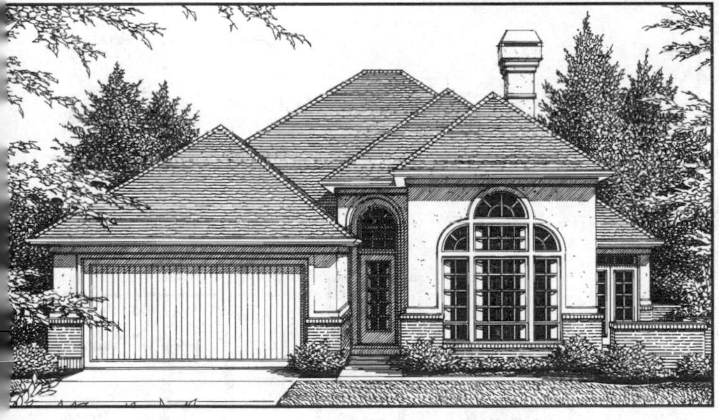

Units	Single
Price Code	D
Total Finished	2,225 sq. ft.
Main Finished	2,225 sq. ft.
Garage Unfinished	420 sq. ft.
Dimensions	45'x73'
Foundation	Crawlspace
Bedrooms	3
Full Baths	2
Max Ridge Height	28'
Roof Framing	Stick
Exterior Walls	2x6

MASTER
12/8 X 15/6
(10'-4" CLG.)
NOOK
11/0 X 11/6
BR 2
11/6 X 11/2
(9' CLG.)
FAMILY
15/0 X 18/0
(10'-4" CLG.)
11/0 X 11/2
(14'-1" CLG.)
DINING
16/2 X 10/8
(10'-4" CLG.)
BR 3
10/4 X 12/0
(9' CLG.)
DEN
10/6 X 12/0
(10'-4" CLG.)
GARAGE
19/4 X 20/8
LIVING
13/0 X 14/6
(15'-4" CLG.)

MAIN FLOOR

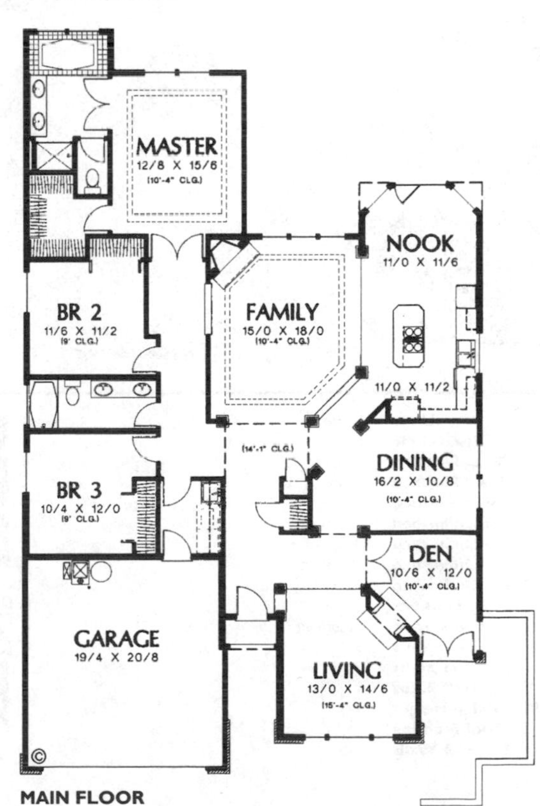

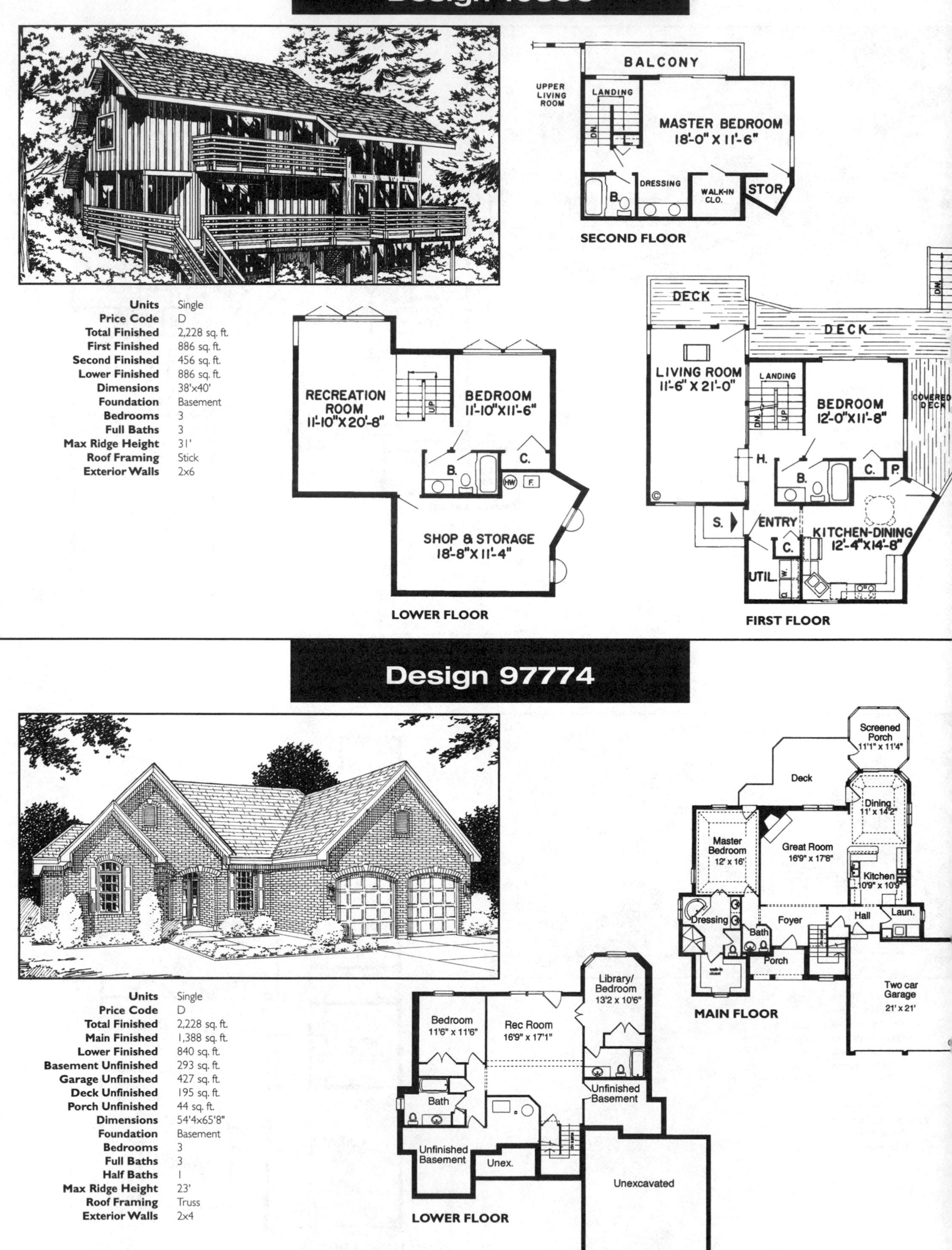

Design 10396

Units	Single
Price Code	D
Total Finished	2,228 sq. ft.
First Finished	886 sq. ft.
Second Finished	456 sq. ft.
Lower Finished	886 sq. ft.
Dimensions	38'x40'
Foundation	Basement
Bedrooms	3
Full Baths	3
Max Ridge Height	31'
Roof Framing	Stick
Exterior Walls	2x6

Design 97774

Units	Single
Price Code	D
Total Finished	2,228 sq. ft.
Main Finished	1,388 sq. ft.
Lower Finished	840 sq. ft.
Basement Unfinished	293 sq. ft.
Garage Unfinished	427 sq. ft.
Deck Unfinished	195 sq. ft.
Porch Unfinished	44 sq. ft.
Dimensions	54'4x65'8"
Foundation	Basement
Bedrooms	3
Full Baths	3
Half Baths	1
Max Ridge Height	23'
Roof Framing	Truss
Exterior Walls	2x4

Design 98329

Units	Single
Price Code	D
Total Finished	2,228 sq. ft.
Main Finished	2,228 sq. ft.
Deck Unfinished	130 sq. ft.
Porch Unfinished	48 sq. ft.
Dimensions	58'4"x61'4"
Foundation	Slab
Bedrooms	3
Full Baths	2
Main Ceiling	10'
Max Ridge Height	22'6"
Roof Framing	Stick
Exterior Walls	2x6

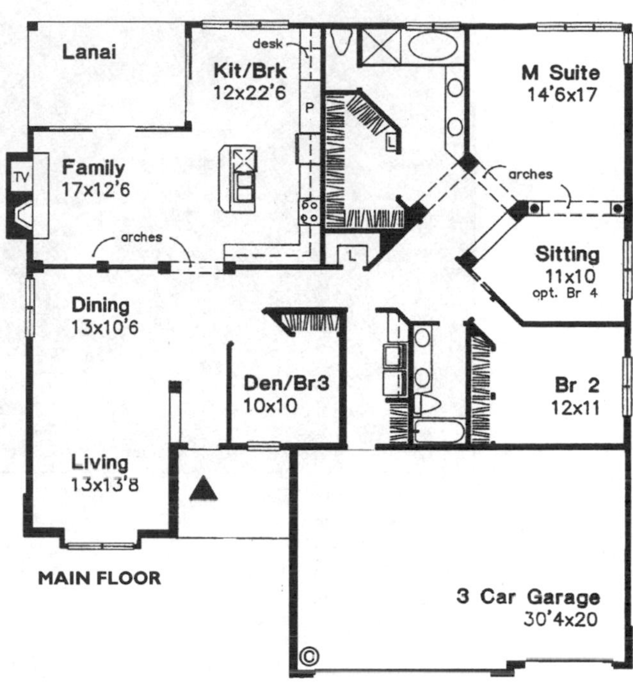

MAIN FLOOR

Design 97135

Units	Single
Price Code	D
Total Finished	2,229 sq. ft.
Main Finished	2,229 sq. ft.
Basement Unfinished	2,229 sq. ft.
Garage Unfinished	551 sq. ft.
Dimensions	65'x56'
Foundation	Basement
Bedrooms	3
Full Baths	2
Max Ridge Height	26'
Roof Framing	Truss
Exterior Walls	2x6

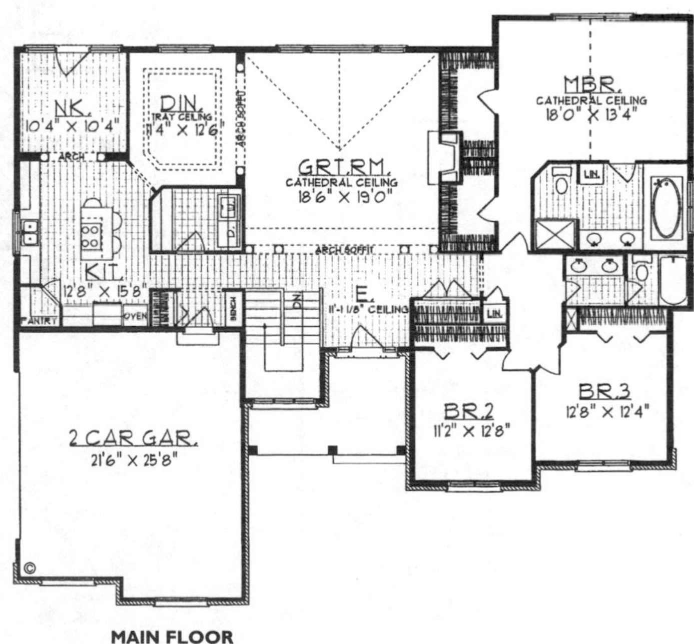

MAIN FLOOR

Design 94673

Units	Single
Price Code	D
Total Finished	2,232 sq. ft.
Main Finished	2,232 sq. ft.
Dimensions	57'6x37'10"
Foundation	Slab
Bedrooms	3
Full Baths	2
Roof Framing	Stick

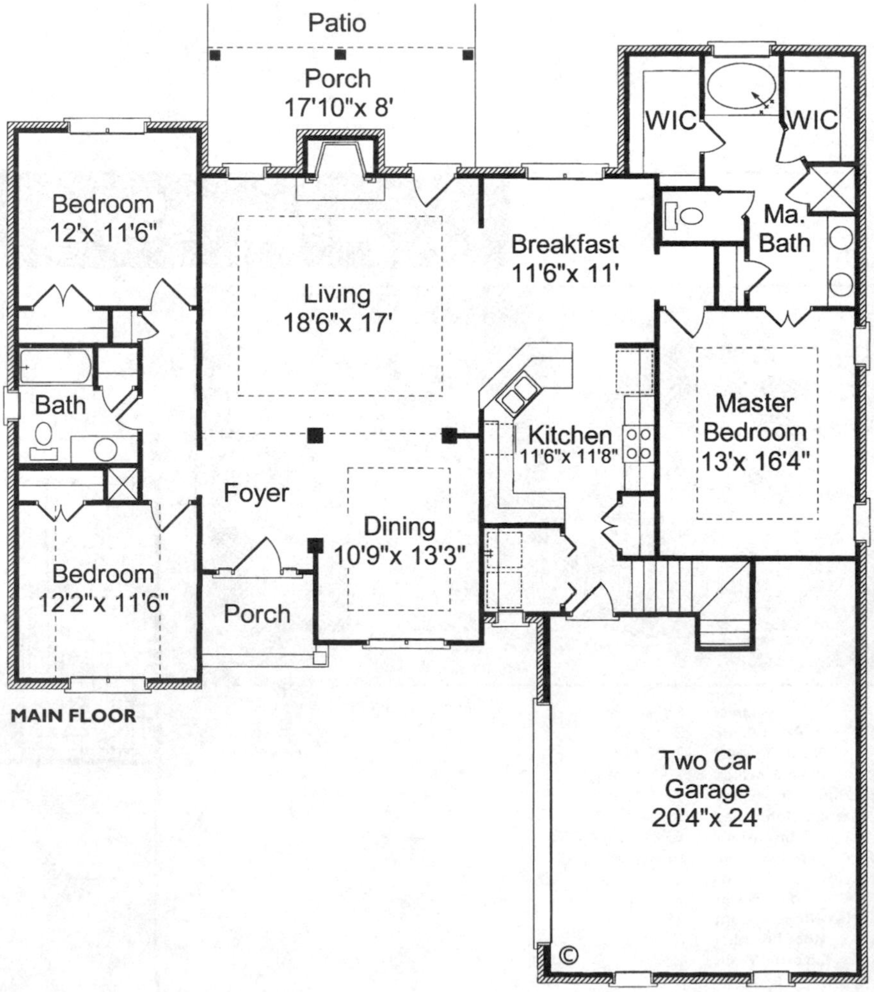

Patio
Porch
17'10"x 8'
WIC
WIC
Bedroom
12'x 11'6"
Ma.
Bath
Breakfast
11'6"x 11'
Living
18'6"x 17'
Master
Bedroom
13'x 16'4"
Bath
Kitchen
11'6"x 11'8"
Foyer
Dining
10'9"x 13'3"
Bedroom
12'2"x 11'6"
Porch
Two Car
Garage
20'4"x 24'
©

MAIN FLOOR

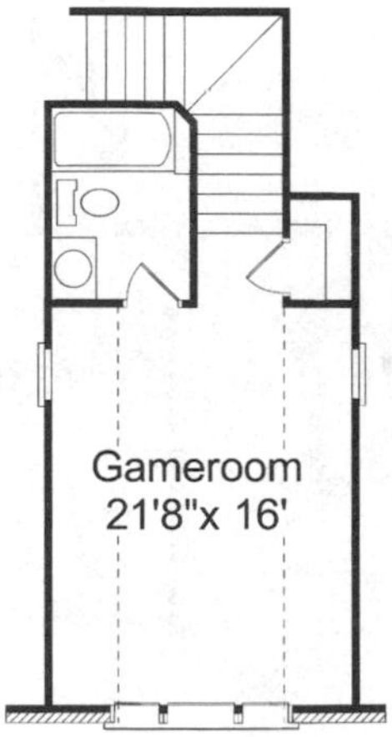

Gameroom
21'8"x 16'

BONUS

Design 69108

Units	Single
Price Code	D
Total Finished	2,234 sq. ft.
Main Finished	2,234 sq. ft.
Bonus Unfinished	489 sq. ft.
Garage Unfinished	755 sq. ft.
Dimensions	76'x56'4"
Foundation	Basement
Bedrooms	3
Full Baths	2
Main Ceiling	9'
Second Ceiling	8'
Vaulted Ceiling	18'
Max Ridge Height	26'
Roof Framing	Truss
Exterior Walls	2x6

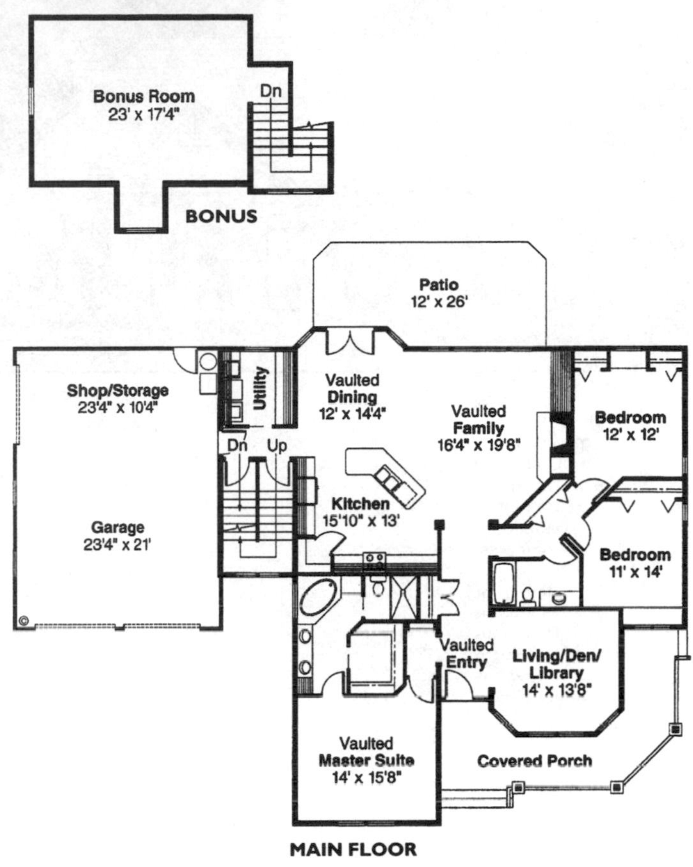

Design 93151

Units	Single
Price Code	D
Total Finished	2,234 sq. ft.
Main Finished	2,234 sq. ft.
Basement Unfinished	2,234 sq. ft.
Dimensions	66'x59'
Foundation	Basement
Bedrooms	3
Full Baths	2
Half Baths	1
Max Ridge Height	22'6"
Roof Framing	Stick
Exterior Walls	2x6

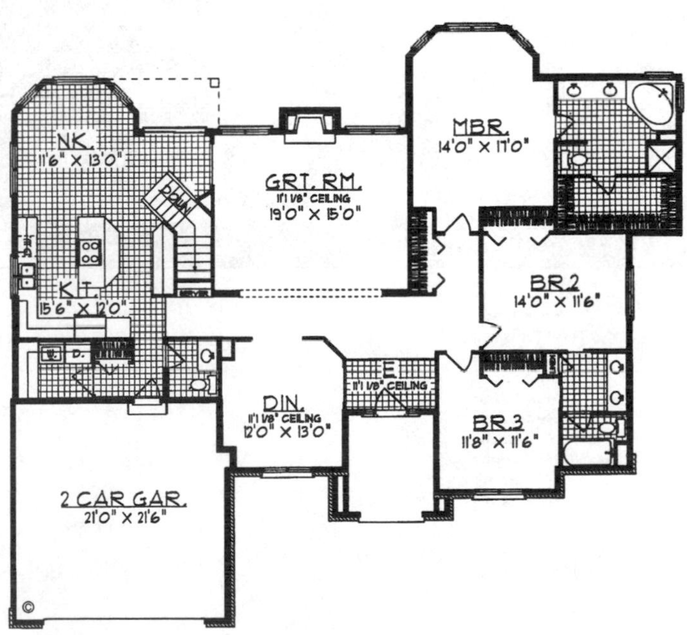

Design 98424

Units	Single
Price Code	D
Total Finished	2,236 sq. ft.
Main Finished	2,236 sq. ft.
Basement Unfinished	2,236 sq. ft.
Garage Unfinished	517 sq. ft.
Dimensions	63'x67'
Foundation	Basement Crawlspace
Bedrooms	3
Full Baths	2
Half Baths	1
Max Ridge Height	25'5"
Roof Framing	Stick
Exterior Walls	2x4

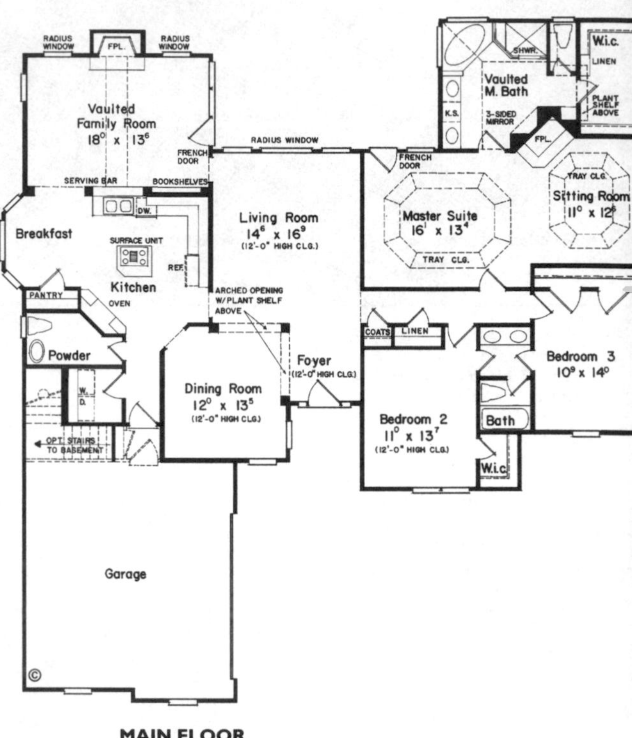

MAIN FLOOR

Design 98544

Units	Single
Price Code	D
Total Finished	2,238 sq. ft.
Main Finished	2,238 sq. ft.
Dimensions	60'x61'1"
Foundation	Slab
Bedrooms	4
Full Baths	3
Max Ridge Height	24'
Roof Framing	Stick
Exterior Walls	2x4

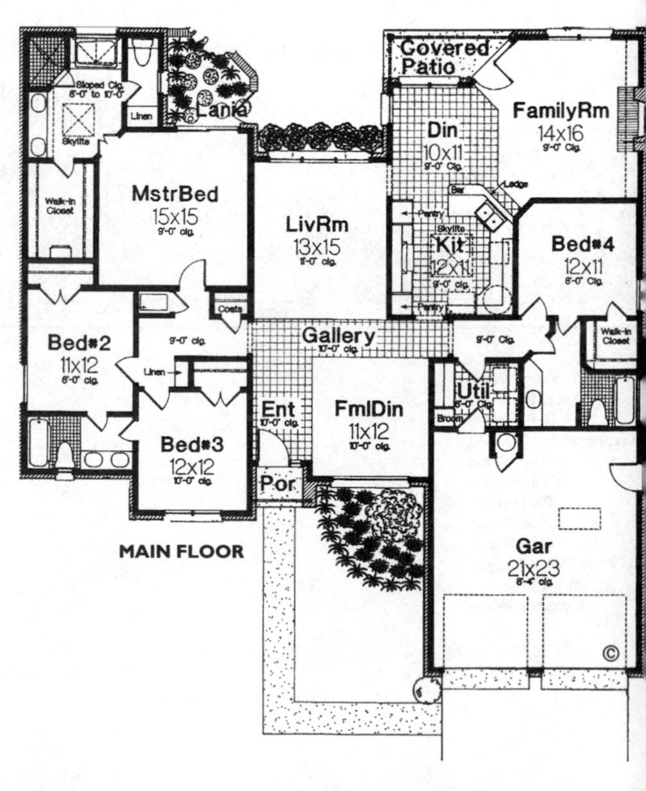

MAIN FLOOR

Design 24964

Units	Single
Price Code	D
Total Finished	2,240 sq. ft.
First Finished	1,195 sq. ft.
Second Finished	1,045 sq. ft.
Bonus Unfinished	429 sq. ft.
Basement Unfinished	1,195 sq. ft.
Garage Unfinished	635 sq. ft.
Deck Unfinished	198 sq. ft.
Porch Unfinished	130 sq. ft.
Dimensions	55'8"x46'
Foundation	Basement Crawlspace Slab
Bedrooms	3
Full Baths	2
Half Baths	1
First Ceiling	9'
Second Ceiling	8'
Max Ridge Height	34'
Roof Framing	Truss
Exterior Walls	2x4

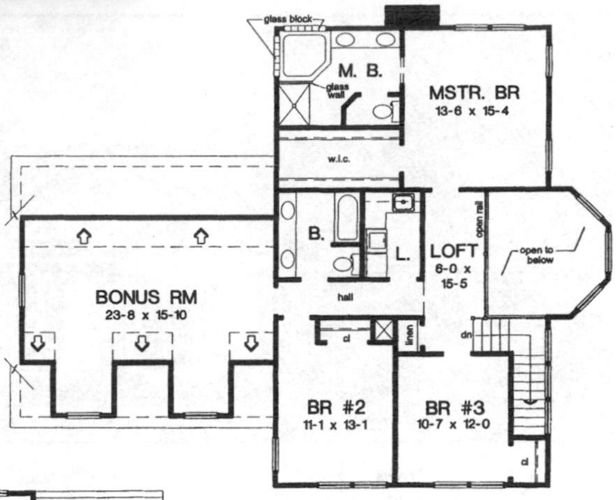

SECOND FLOOR

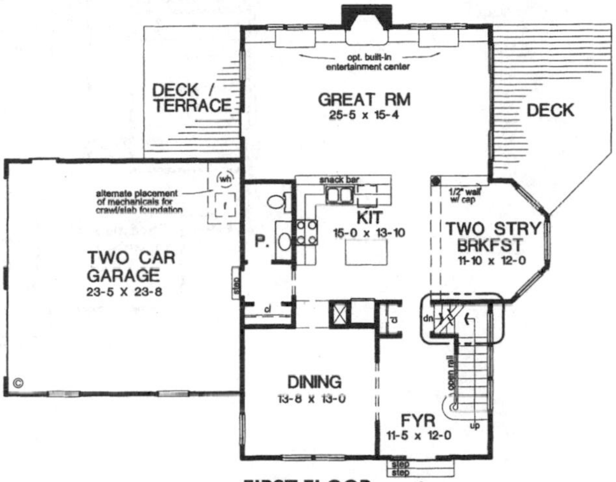

FIRST FLOOR

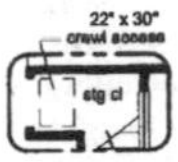

CRAWLSPACE/SLAB FOUNDATION OPTION

Design 68068

Units	Single
Price Code	D
Total Finished	2,242 sq. ft.
Main Finished	2,242 sq. ft.
Bonus Unfinished	613 sq. ft.
Garage Unfinished	525 sq. ft.
Dimensions	63'4"x60'
Foundation	Basement Crawlspace Slab
Bedrooms	2
Full Baths	2
Main Ceiling	9'
Max Ridge Height	26'
Roof Framing	Stick
Exterior Walls	2x4

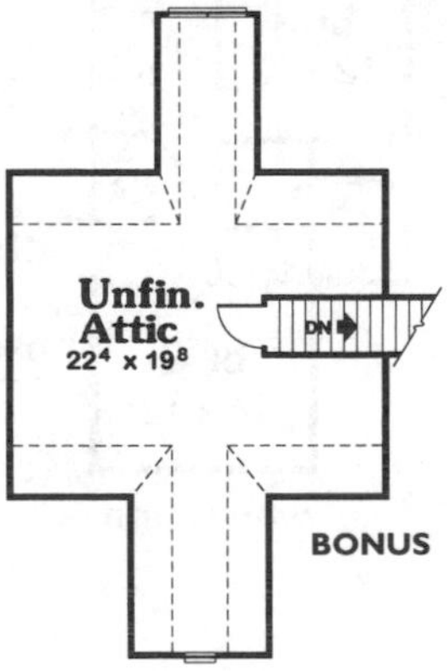

ernate foundation options available at an additional charge.
Please call 1-800-235-5700 for more information.

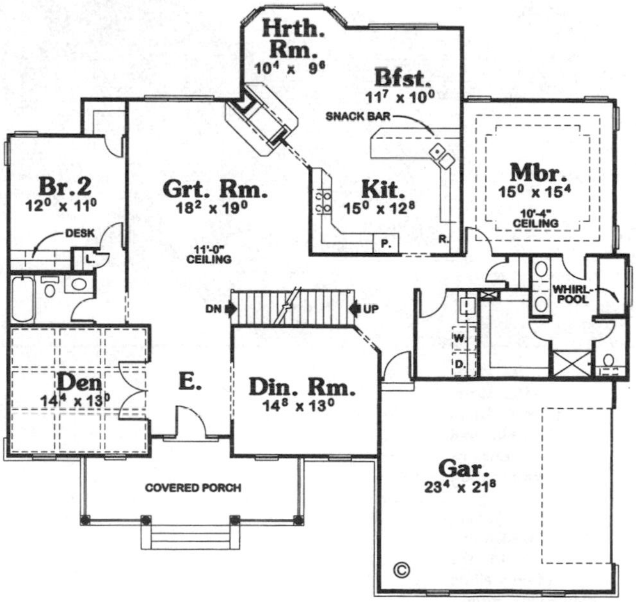

BONUS

MAIN FLOOR

Design 94610

Units	Single
Price Code	D
Total Finished	2,246 sq. ft.
Main Finished	2,246 sq. ft.
Garage Unfinished	546 sq. ft.
Porch Unfinished	195 sq. ft.
Dimensions	61'10"x65'5"
Foundation	Crawlspace Slab
Bedrooms	4
Full Baths	2
Half Baths	1
Main Ceiling	9'
Max Ridge Height	24'
Roof Framing	Truss
Exterior Walls	2x4, 2x6

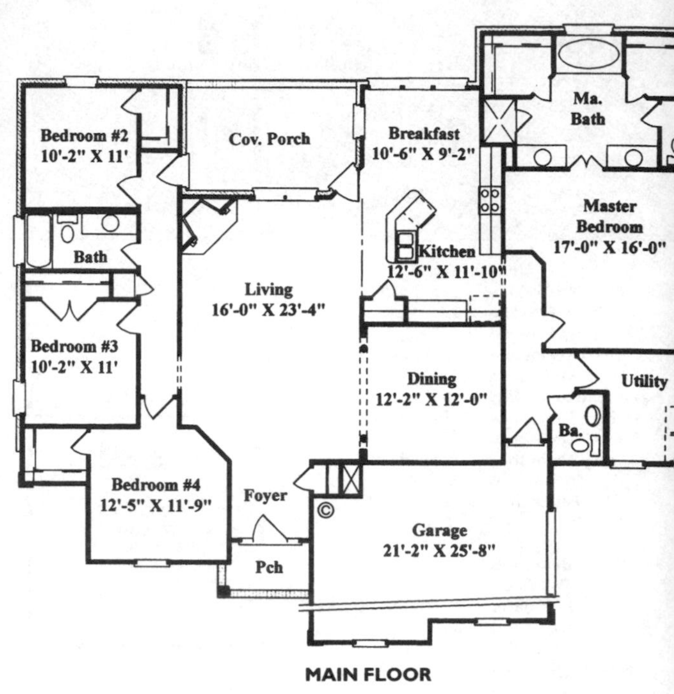

Design 65667

Units	Single
Price Code	E
Total Finished	2,252 sq. ft.
Main Finished	2,252 sq. ft.
Dimensions	72'x60'
Foundation	Basement Crawlspace Slab
Bedrooms	4
Full Baths	2
Main Ceiling	8'
Max Ridge Height	27'
Roof Framing	Stick
Exterior Walls	2x6

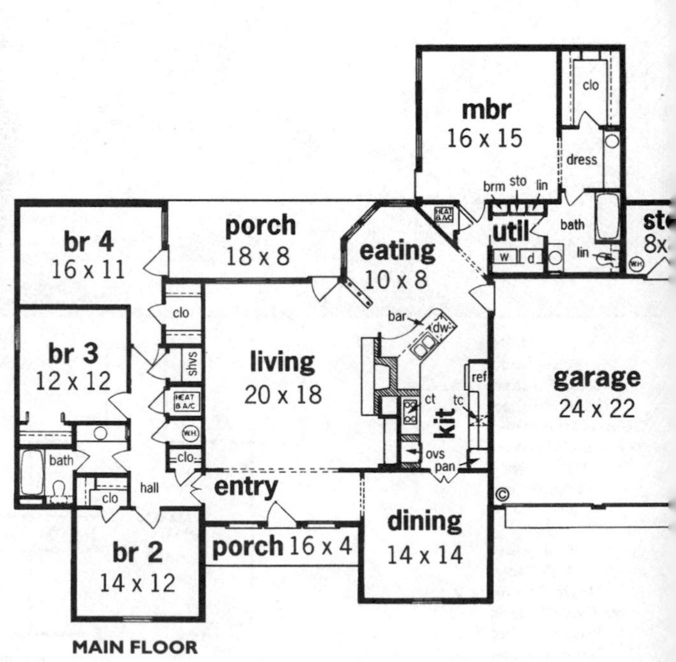

Design 68162

Rear Elevation

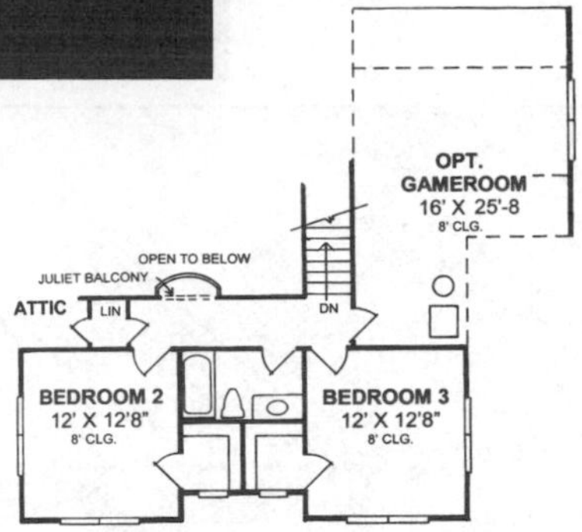

SECOND FLOOR

FIRST FLOOR

Units	Single
Price Code	E
Total Finished	2,252 sq. ft.
First Finished	1,736 sq. ft.
Second Finished	516 sq. ft.
Bonus Unfinished	242 sq. ft.
Garage Unfinished	638 sq. ft.
Porch Unfinished	1,223 sq. ft.
Dimensions	80'x59'
Foundation	Slab
Bedrooms	4
Full Baths	3
First Ceiling	9'
Max Ridge Height	30'
Exterior Walls	2x4

Alternate foundation options available at an additional charge.
Please call 1-800-235-5700 for more information.

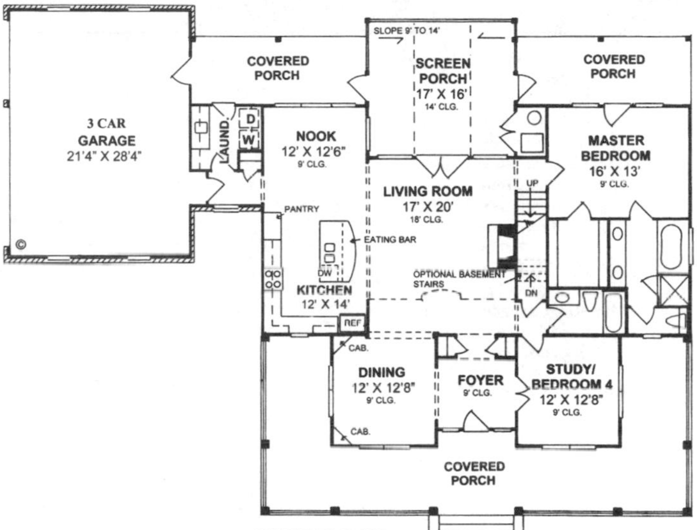

Design 97850

MAIN FLOOR

Units	Single
Price Code	E
Total Finished	2,253 sq. ft.
Main Finished	2,253 sq. ft.
Garage Unfinished	602 sq. ft.
Deck Unfinished	205 sq. ft.
Porch Unfinished	110 sq. ft.
Dimensions	63'x60'3"
Foundation	Slab
Bedrooms	4
Full Baths	2
3/4 Baths	1
Main Ceiling	8'-10'
Max Ridge Height	26'
Roof Framing	Stick
Exterior Walls	2x4

Design 66090

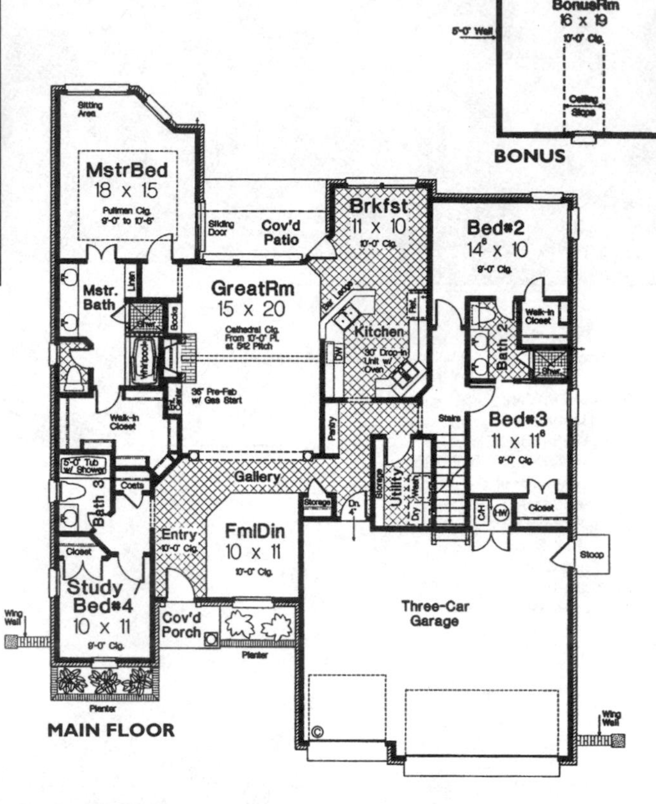

Units	Single
Price Code	F
Total Finished	2,255 sq. ft.
Main Finished	2,255 sq. ft.
Bonus Unfinished	324 sq. ft.
Garage Unfinished	660 sq. ft.
Dimensions	55'x70'
Foundation	Slab
Bedrooms	4
Full Baths	2
3/4 Baths	1
Main Ceiling	8'
Max Ridge Height	24'6"
Roof Framing	Stick
Exterior Walls	2x4

Design 99459

PHOTOGRAPHY: COURTESY OF THE DESIGNER

Units	Single
Price Code	E
Total Finished	2,256 sq. ft.
First Finished	1,602 sq. ft.
Second finished	654 sq. ft.
Dimensions	54'x50'
Foundation	Basement
Bedrooms	4
Full Baths	2
Half Baths	1
Max Ridge Height	26'
Roof Framing	Stick/Truss
Exterior Walls	2x4

Please note: The photographed home may have been modified to suit homeowner preferences. If you order plans, have a builder or design professional check them against the photograph to confirm actual construction details.

* Alternate foundation options available at an additional charge.
Please call 1-800-235-5700 for more information.

Design 20231

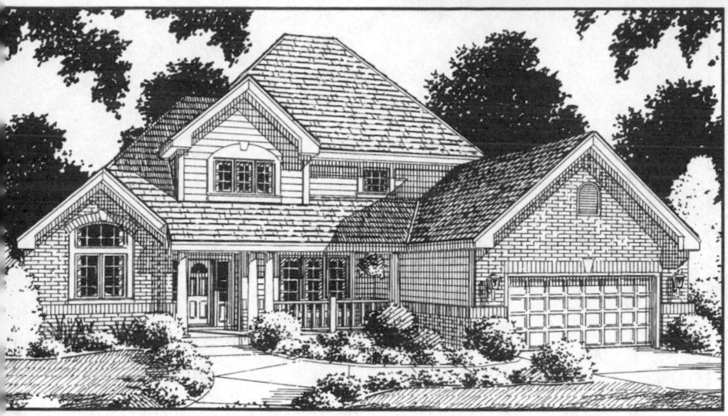

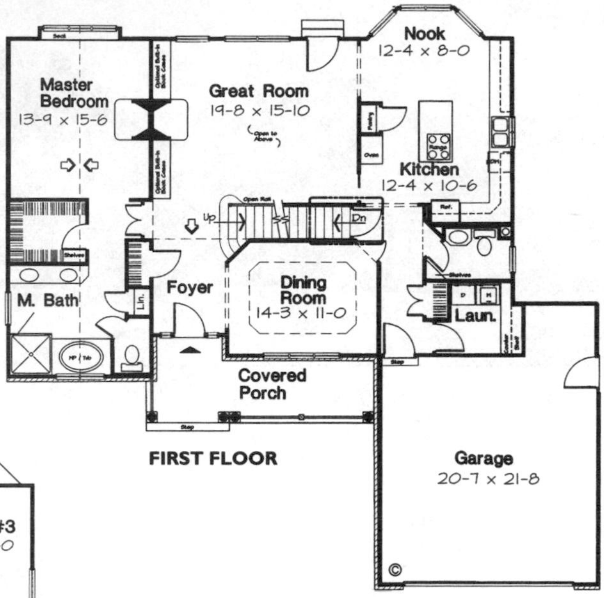

Nook
12-4 x 8-0
Master Bedroom
13-9 x 15-6
Great Room
19-8 x 15-10
Kitchen
12-4 x 10-6
M. Bath
Foyer
Dining Room
14-3 x 11-0
Laun.
Covered Porch
Garage
20-7 x 21-8

FIRST FLOOR

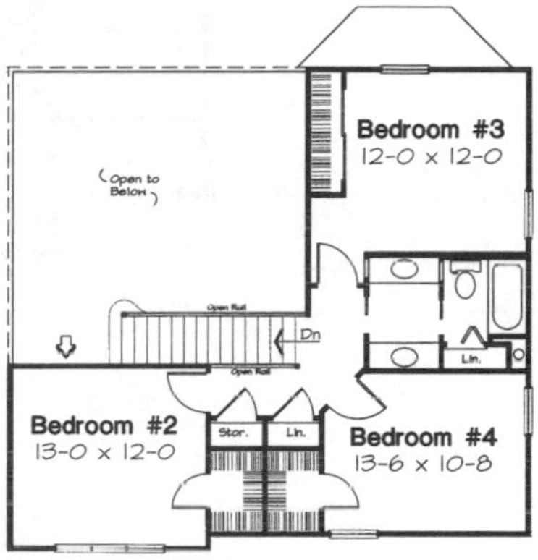

Bedroom #3
12-0 x 12-0
Bedroom #2
13-0 x 12-0
Bedroom #4
13-6 x 10-8
Stor.
Lin.
Dn

SECOND FLOOR

Units	Single
Price Code	E
Total Finished	2,257 sq. ft.
First Finished	1,540 sq. ft.
Second Finished	717 sq. ft.
Basement Unfinished	1,545 sq. ft.
Garage Unfinished	503 sq. ft.
Porch Unfinished	144 sq. ft.
Dimensions	57'x56'8"
Foundation	Basement Crawlspace Slab
Bedrooms	4
Full Baths	2
Half Baths	1
First Ceiling	9'
Second Ceiling	8'
Max Ridge Height	33'6"
Roof Framing	Truss

Design 98548

3-Car Gar
30x19
Patio Area
Covered Patio
Brkfst
11x11
Bed#4
13x11
Great Room
19x20
Kit
12x13
Util
Ent
FmlDin
12x12
Pwdr
MstrBed
14x17
Cov. Porch
Bed#3
11x11
Bed#2
13x13

MAIN FLOOR

Units	Single
Price Code	E
Total Finished	2,257 sq. ft.
Main Finished	2,257 sq. ft.
Garage Unfinished	601 sq. ft.
Porch Unfinished	325 sq. ft.
Dimensions	65'x65'10"
Foundation	Crawlspace Slab
Bedrooms	4
Full Baths	2
Half Baths	1
Main Ceiling	9'-11'
Max Ridge Height	25'
Roof Framing	Stick
Exterior Walls	2x4

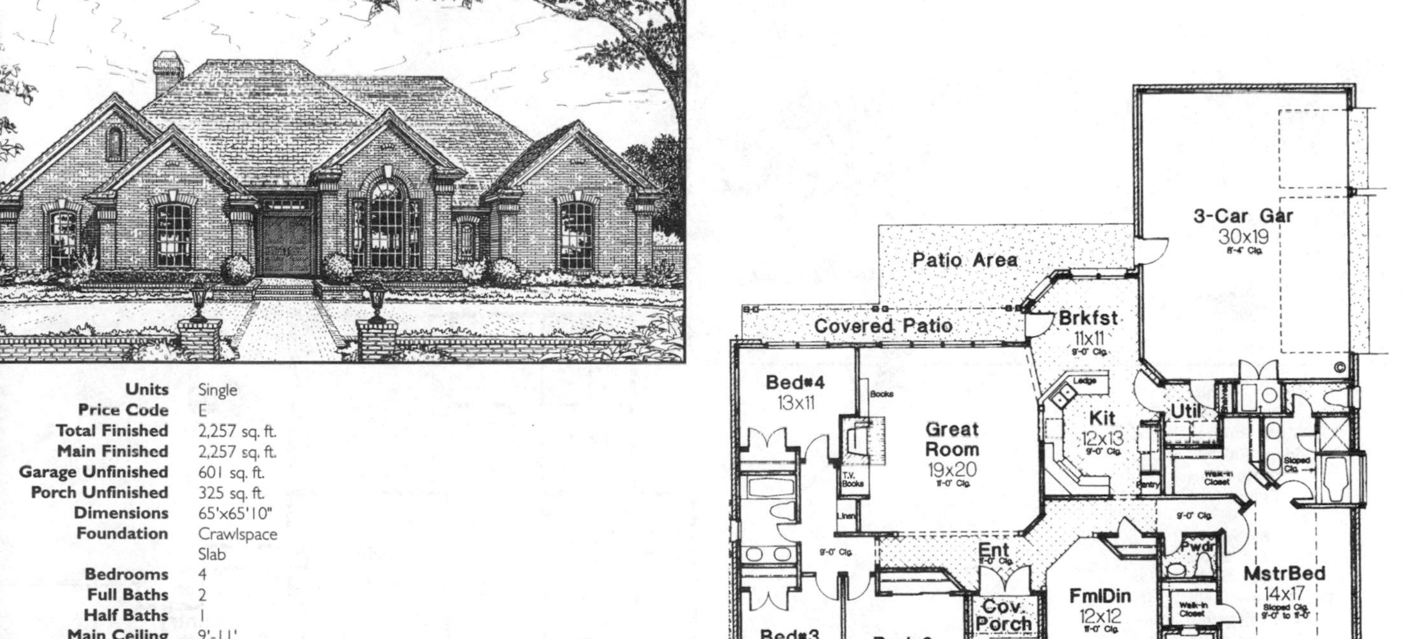

Design 98557

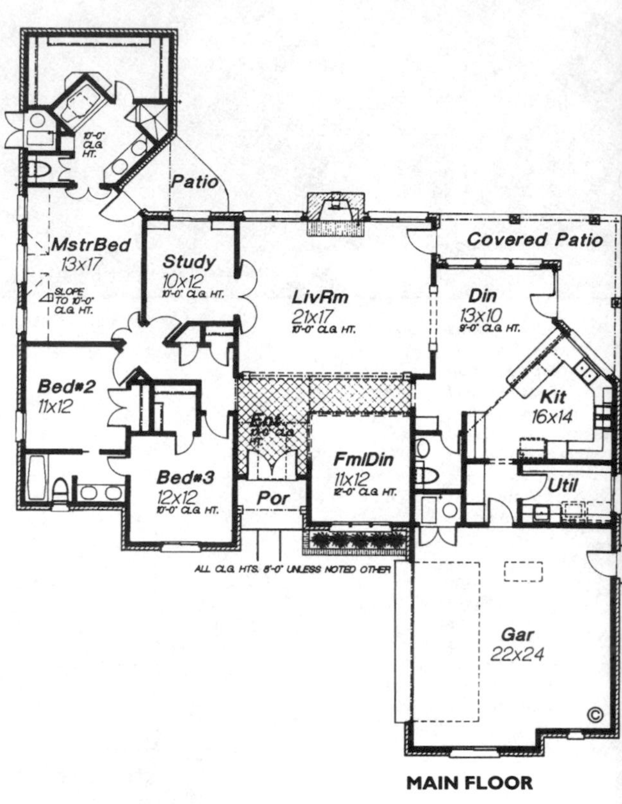

MAIN FLOOR

Units	Single
Price Code	E
Total Finished	2,257 sq. ft.
Main Finished	2,257 sq. ft.
Garage Unfinished	528 sq. ft.
Dimensions	64'7"x77'10"
Foundation	Slab
Bedrooms	3
Full Baths	2
Half Baths	1
Main Ceiling	9'-10'
Max Ridge Height	26'6"
Roof Framing	Stick
Exterior Walls	2x4

Design 65668

Units	Single
Price Code	E
Total Finished	2,259 sq. ft.
Main Finished	2,259 sq. ft.
Dimensions	56'x93'
Foundation	Crawlspace Slab
Bedrooms	3
Full Baths	2
Half Baths	1
Max Ridge Height	32'
Roof Framing	Stick
Exterior Walls	2x6

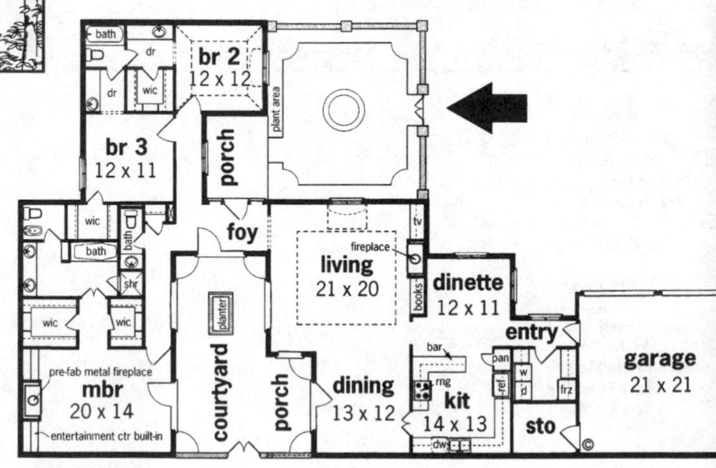

MAIN FLOOR

Design 99457

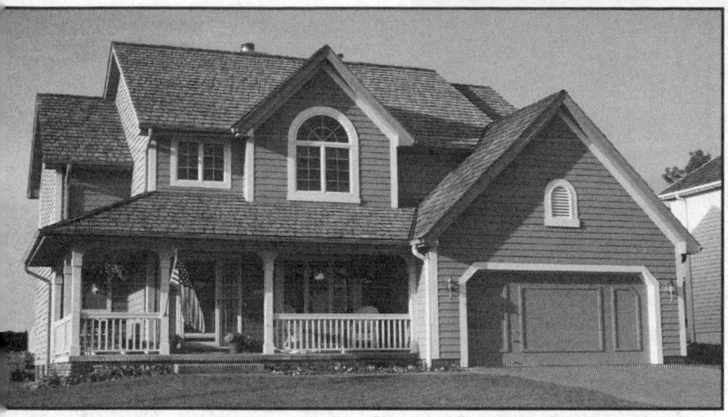

PHOTOGRAPHY: COURTESY OF THE DESIGNER

Units	Single
Price Code	E
Total Finished	2,270 sq. ft.
First Finished	1,150 sq. ft.
Second Finished	1,120 sq. ft.
Basement Unfinished	1,150 sq. ft.
Garage Unfinished	457 sq. ft.
Dimensions	46'x48'
Foundation	Basement
Bedrooms	4
Full Baths	2
Half Baths	1
First Ceiling	8'
Second Ceiling	8'
Tray Ceiling	9'4"
Max Ridge Height	28'
Roof Framing	Stick
Exterior Walls	2x4

ernate foundation options available at an additional charge. Please call 1-800-235-5700 for more information.

Please note: The photographed home may have been modified to suit homeowner preferences. If you order plans, have a builder or design professional check them against the photograph to confirm actual construction details.

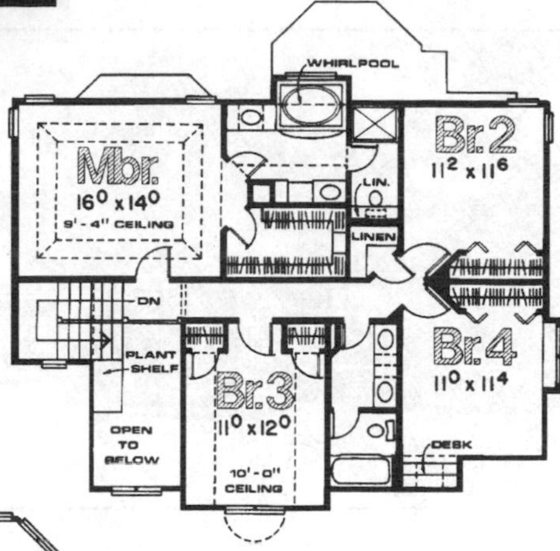

WHIRLPOOL
Mbr.
16⁰ x 14⁰
9'-4" CEILING
Br. 2
11² x 11⁶
LIN.
LINEN
DN
PLANT SHELF
OPEN TO BELOW
Br. 3
11⁰ x 12⁰
10'-0" CEILING
Br. 4
11⁰ x 11⁴
DESK

SECOND FLOOR

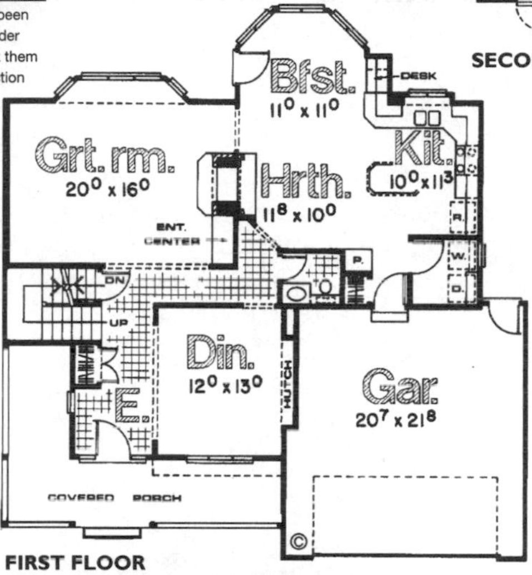

Bfst.
11⁰ x 11⁰
DESK
Grt. rm.
20⁰ x 16⁰
Hrth.
11⁸ x 10⁰
Kit.
10⁰ x 11³
ENT. CENTER
DN
UP
P.
W.
D.
Din.
12⁰ x 13⁰
HUTCH
E.
Gar.
20⁷ x 21⁸
COVERED PORCH

FIRST FLOOR

Design 90485

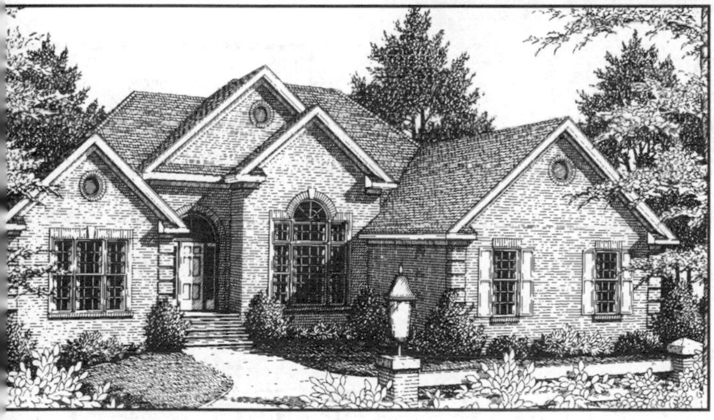

Units	Single
Price Code	E
Total Finished	2,271 sq. ft.
Main Finished	2,271 sq. ft.
Garage Unfinished	484 sq. ft.
Dimensions	61'6"x57'10"
Foundation	Basement Crawlspace Slab
Bedrooms	4
Full Baths	2
Max Ridge Height	25'4"
Roof Framing	Stick
Exterior Walls	2x4

WOOD DECK
32-0 x 12-0
HEARTH
BEDROOM
12-2 x 11-0
CLOSET
BREAKFAST
12-0 x 10-0
DESK
PANTRY
MASTER BEDROOM
13-2 x 16-0
TRAY CEILING
LINEN
BATH
CLOSET
HALL
SLOPE
GREAT ROOM
18-8 x 25-6
CATHEDRAL CEILING
SINK
DW
STOVE
KITCHEN
12-0 x 12-0
REFG
BRM.
COAT
BATH
SPA TUB
SHWR
WASH
DRY
BEDROOM
11-2 x 11-0
FOYER
9-0 x 8-0
13' CLG.
DINING
14-0 x 11-6
13' CLG.
LAUNDRY
WALK-IN CLOSET
DOWN
BEDROOM
12-2 x 11-4
PORCH
GARAGE
21-4 x 21-4

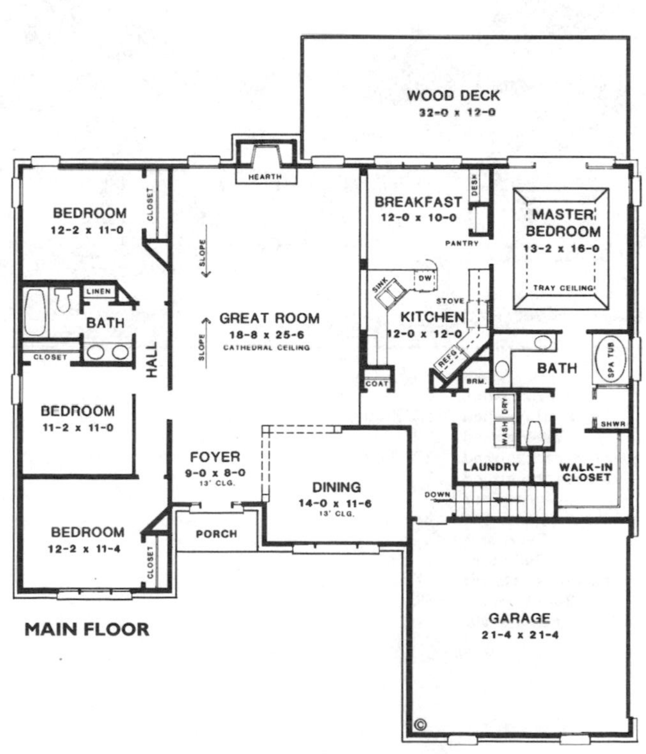

MAIN FLOOR

Design 93172

Units	Single
Price Code	E
Total Finished	2,274 sq. ft.
Main Finished	2,274 sq. ft.
Basement Unfinished	2,274 sq. ft.
Porch Unfinished	232 sq. ft.
Dimensions	77'8"x56'
Foundation	Basement
Bedrooms	3
Full Baths	2
Max Ridge Height	24'6"
Roof Framing	Stick
Exterior Walls	2x6

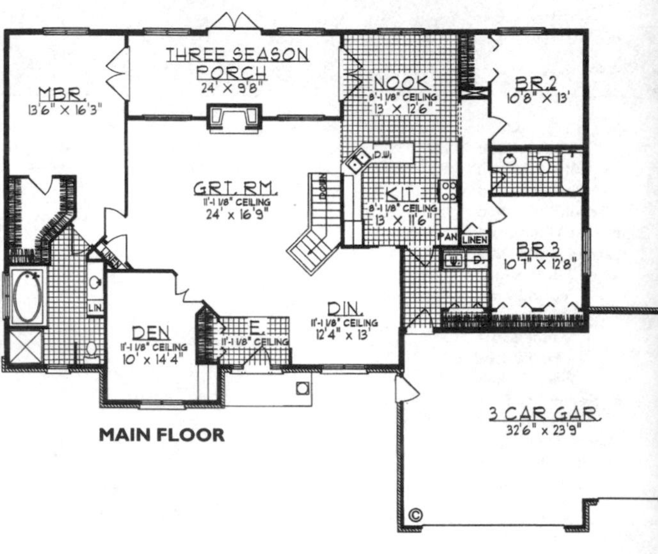

Design 92404

Units	Single
Price Code	E
Total Finished	2,275 sq. ft.
Main Finished	2,275 sq. ft.
Basement Unfinished	2,207 sq. ft.
Garage Unfinished	512 sq. ft.
Dimensions	62'x60'
Foundation	Basement
Bedrooms	3
Full Baths	2
Max Ridge Height	22'
Roof Framing	Stick
Exterior Walls	2x4

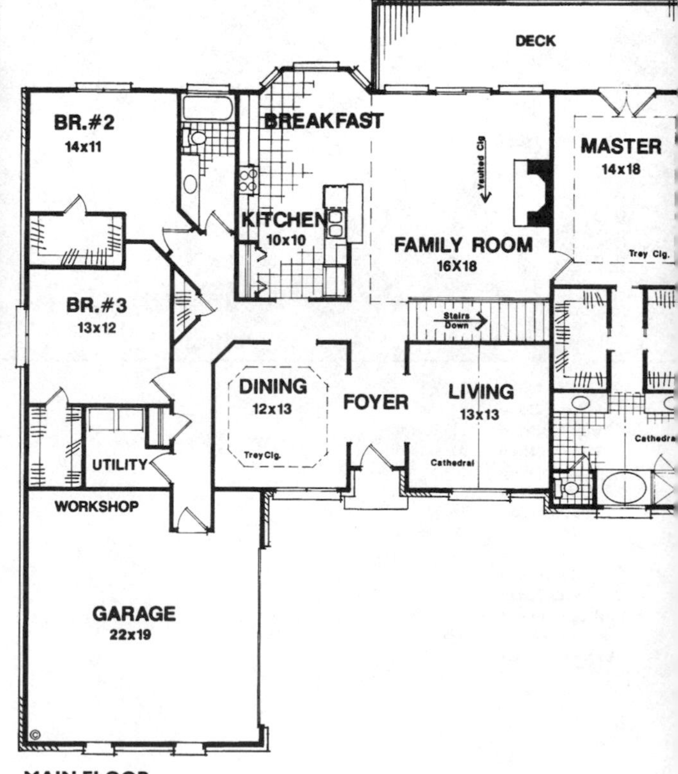

Design 97737

Units	Single
Price Code	E
Total Finished	2,278 sq. ft.
Main Finished	2,278 sq. ft.
Basement Unfinished	2,278 sq. ft.
Garage Unfinished	540 sq. ft.
Porch Unfinished	41 sq. ft.
Dimensions	59'x57'
Foundation	Basement
Bedrooms	3
Full Baths	1
3/4 Baths	1
Main Ceiling	9'
Max Ridge Height	25'
Roof Framing	Truss
Exterior Walls	2x4

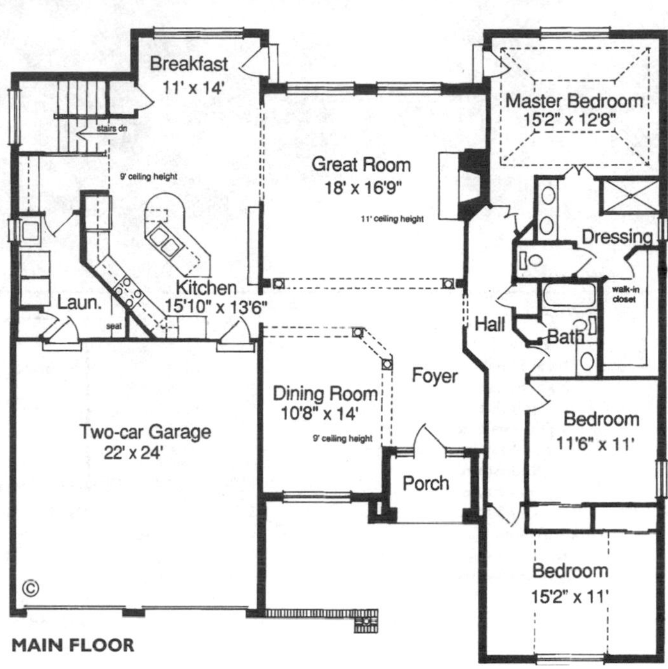

Design 97833

Units	Single
Price Code	F
Total Finished	2,279 sq. ft.
Main Finished	2,279 sq. ft.
Garage Unfinished	588 sq. ft.
Deck Unfinished	120 sq. ft.
Dimensions	60'x63'7"
Foundation	Slab
Bedrooms	4
Full Baths	2
Half Baths	1
Main Ceiling	8'
Max Ridge Height	27'
Roof Framing	Stick
Exterior Walls	2x4

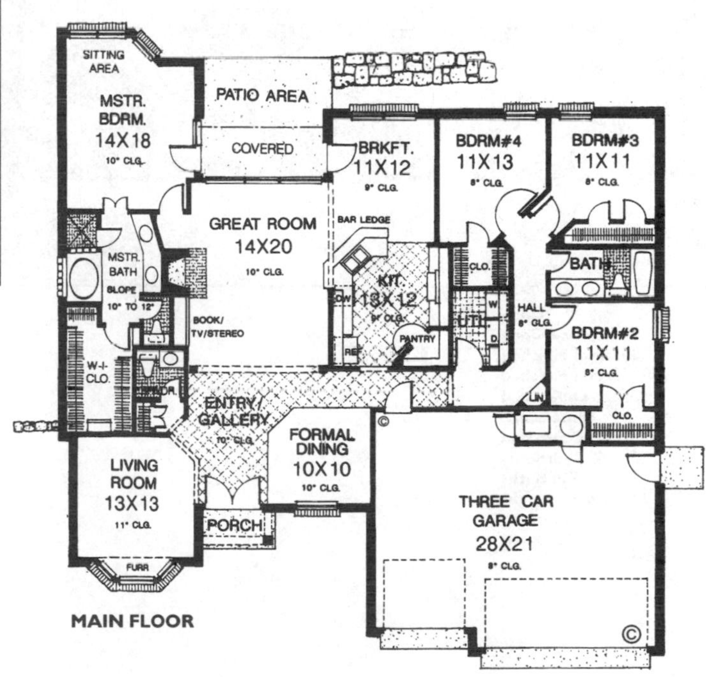

Design 91796

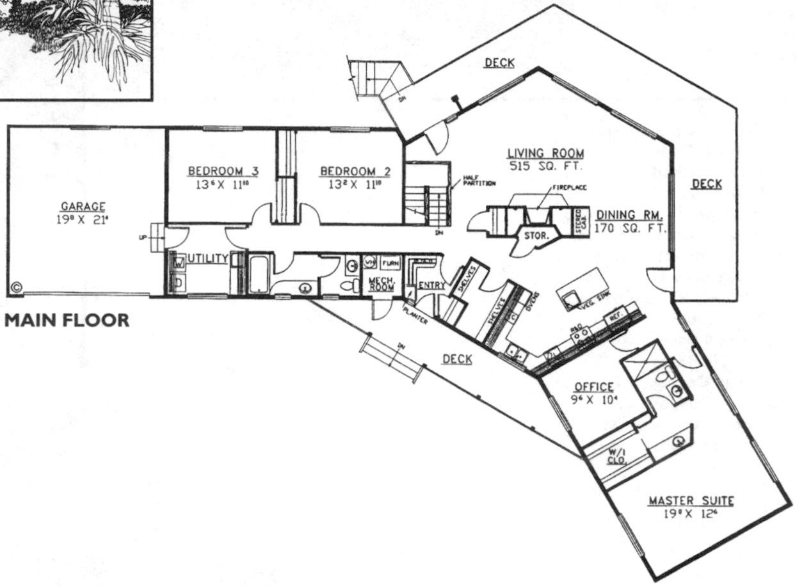

Units	Single
Price Code	E
Total Finished	2,280 sq. ft.
Main Finished	2,280 sq. ft.
Garage Unfinished	440 sq. ft.
Dimensions	99'6"x66'
Foundation	Basement
Bedrooms	3
Full Baths	1
3/4 Baths	1
Max Ridge Height	17'
Roof Framing	Stick/Truss
Exterior Walls	2x6

DECK
LIVING ROOM
515 SQ. FT.
DECK
BEDROOM 3
13⁶ X 11¹⁰
BEDROOM 2
13² X 11¹⁰
GARAGE
19⁸ X 21⁴
DINING RM.
170 SQ. FT.
UTILITY
MECH. ROOM
ENTRY
DECK
OFFICE
9⁶ X 10⁴
MASTER SUITE
19⁸ X 12⁶

MAIN FLOOR

Design 98593

Units	Single
Price Code	E
Total Finished	2,285 sq. ft.
Main Finished	2,285 sq. ft.
Garage Unfinished	653 sq. ft.
Dimensions	74'10"x56'10"
Foundation	Slab
Bedrooms	4
Full Baths	3
Max Ridge Height	22'
Roof Framing	Stick
Exterior Walls	2x4

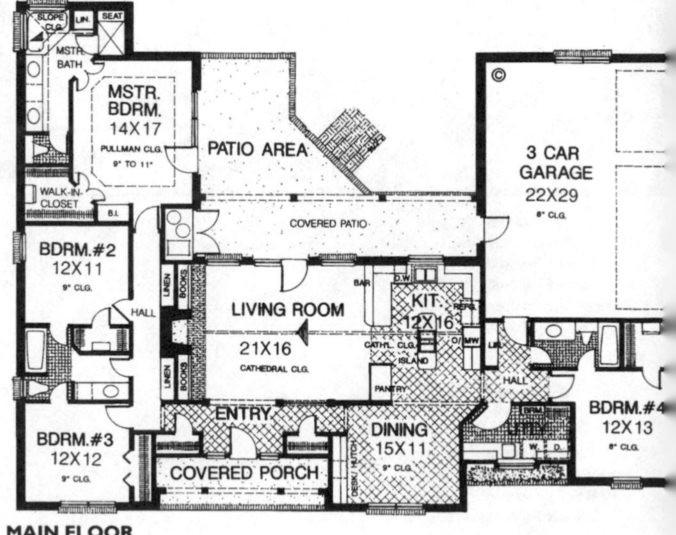

MAIN FLOOR

Design 96530

Units	Single
Price Code	E
Total Finished	2,289 sq. ft.
Main Finished	2,289 sq. ft.
Garage Unfinished	758 sq. ft.
Dimensions	66'x77'
Foundation	Crawlspace Slab
Bedrooms	3
Full Baths	3
Main Ceiling	8'
Max Ridge Height	22'
Roof Framing	Stick
Exterior Walls	2x4

DINING 12x14
VERANDA
LOUNGING 12x10
KITCHEN 12x12
GREAT RM 22x20 12' CEILING
MASTER SUITE 16x14
12' CLG VAULT
UTILITY
SEE-THRU FIREPLACE
CLOSET
CLOSET
RECEIVING RM 23x10
BATH
WHIRLPOOL
SHOWER
BATH
LIN
CLOSET
CLOSET
STO
CLOS
PORCH
STUDY/BEDRM 12x11
BEDRM 16x12
CLOSET
BATH
PORCH
GARAGE 32x22

MAIN FLOOR

Design 93049

Units	Single
Price Code	E
Total Finished	2,292 sq. ft.
Main Finished	2,292 sq. ft.
Garage Unfinished	526 sq. ft.
Dimensions	80'7"x50'6"
Foundation	Crawlspace Slab
Bedrooms	4
Full Baths	2
Half Baths	1
Max Ridge Height	22'
Roof Framing	Stick
Exterior Walls	2x4

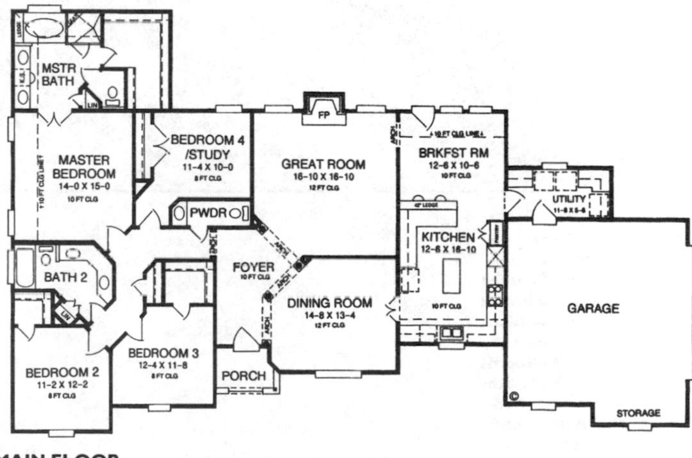

MAIN FLOOR

Design 94947

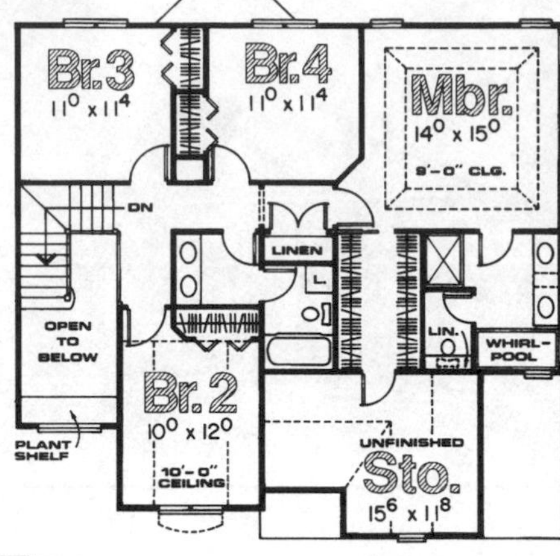

SECOND FLOOR

Units	Single
Price Code	E
Total Finished	2,308 sq. ft.
First Finished	1,273 sq. ft.
Second Finished	1,035 sq. ft.
Basement Unfinished	1,273 sq. ft.
Garage Unfinished	485 sq. ft.
Dimensions	52'x40'
Foundation	Basement
Bedrooms	4
Full Baths	2
Half Baths	1
Max Ridge Height	27'5"
Roof Framing	Stick
Exterior Walls	2x4

* Alternate foundation options available at an additional charge. Please call 1-800-235-5700 for more information.

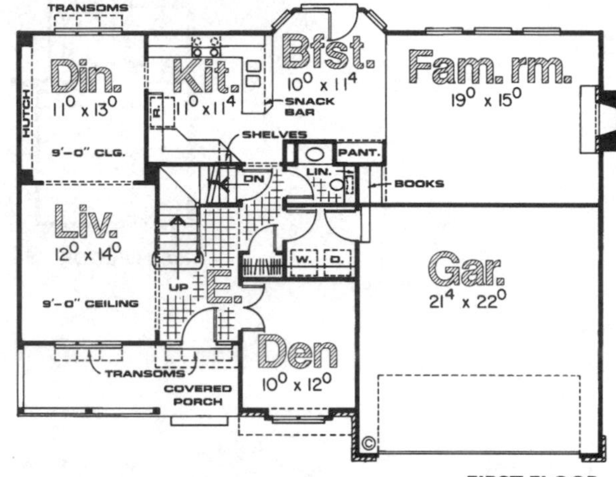

FIRST FLOOR

Design 97503

Units	Single
Price Code	E
Total Finished	2,310 sq. ft.
Main Finished	2,310 sq. ft.
Garage Unfinished	638 sq. ft.
Dimensions	54'6"x97'7"
Foundation	Slab
Bedrooms	3
Full Baths	2
Half Baths	1
Max Ridge Height	25'10"
Roof Framing	Stick
Exterior Walls	2x4

* This home is not to be built 20-mile radius of Madisonville, LA or Baton Rouge, LA.

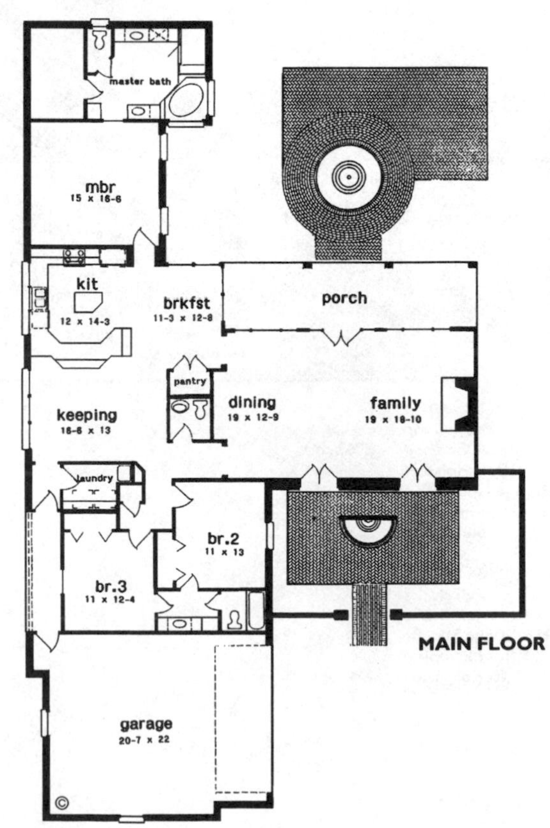

MAIN FLOOR

Design 97246

Units	Single
Price Code	E
Total Finished	2,311 sq. ft.
Main Finished	2,311 sq. ft.
Bonus Unfinished	425 sq. ft.
Basement Unfinished	2,311 sq. ft.
Garage Unfinished	500 sq. ft.
Dimensions	61'x65'4"
Foundation	Basement Crawlspace
Bedrooms	4
Full Baths	2
Half Baths	1
Main Ceiling	9'
Second Ceiling	8'
Max Ridge Height	26'8"
Roof Framing	Stick
Exterior Walls	2x4

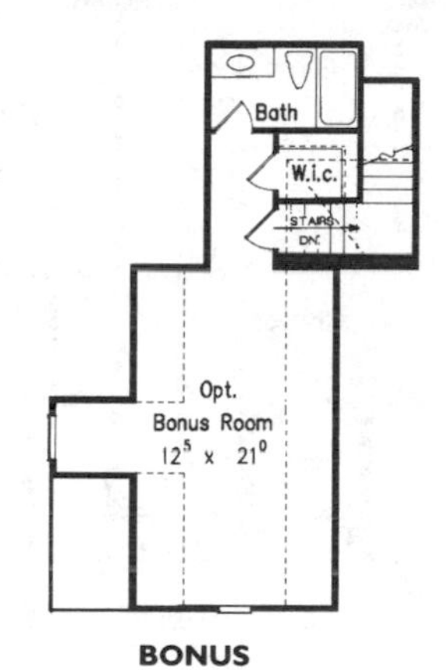

BONUS

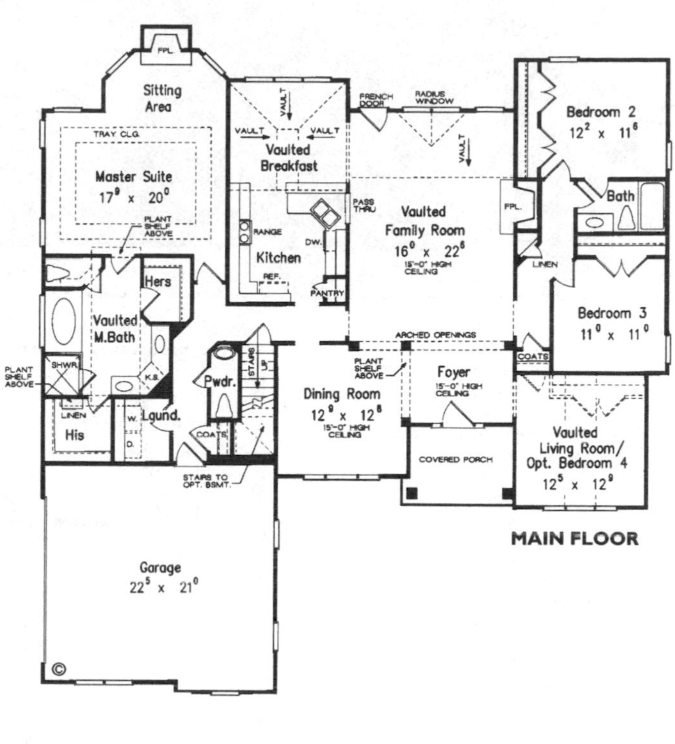

MAIN FLOOR

Design 98571

Units	Single
Price Code	E
Total Finished	2,313 sq. ft.
Main Finished	2,313 sq. ft.
Bonus Unfinished	433 sq. ft.
Garage Unfinished	448 sq. ft.
Deck Unfinished	198 sq. ft.
Porch Unfinished	48 sq. ft.
Dimensions	60'x60'1½"
Foundation	Slab
Bedrooms	3
Full Baths	2
Half Baths	1
Max Ridge Height	25'6"
Roof Framing	Stick
Exterior Walls	2x4

BONUS

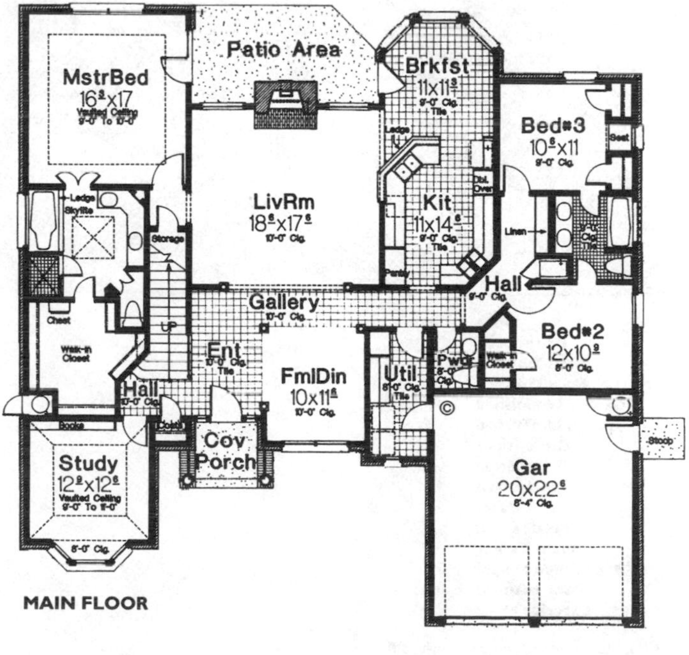

MAIN FLOOR

Design 92646

Units	Single
Price Code	E
Total Finished	2,320 sq. ft.
First Finished	1,595 sq. ft.
Second Finished	725 sq. ft.
Basement Unfinished	1,471 sq. ft.
Garage Unfinished	409 sq. ft.
Dimensions	61'x41'8"
Foundation	Basement
Bedrooms	4
Full Baths	2
Half Baths	1
First Ceiling	8'
Second Ceiling	8'
Max Ridge Height	29'3"
Roof Framing	Truss
Exterior Walls	2x4

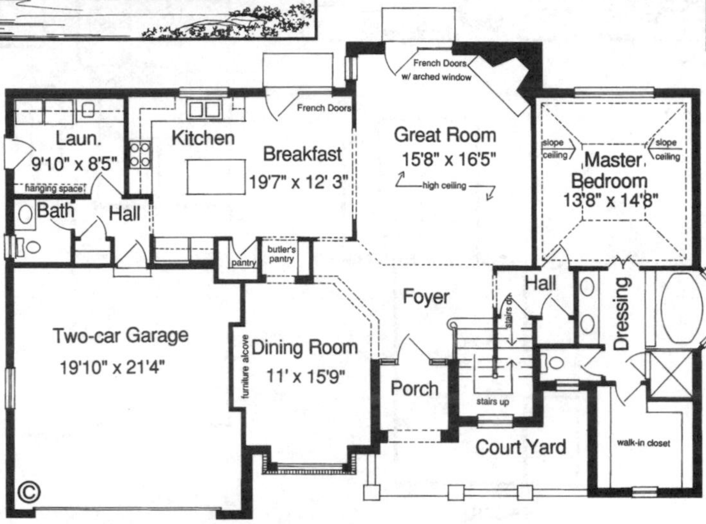

Bedroom 10'8" x 13'5"
Bedroom 10'9" x 10'
Great Room Below
Hall
linen
linen
Bath
Balcony
Bedroom 11' x 11'2"
Porch
desk
bookshelves
stairs dn
slope ceiling
slope ceiling
slope ceiling

SECOND FLOOR

Laun. 9'10" x 8'5"
hanging space
Kitchen
French Doors
Breakfast 19'7" x 12' 3"
French Doors w/ arched window
Great Room 15'8" x 16'5"
high ceiling
slope ceiling
slope ceiling
Master Bedroom 13'8" x 14'8"
Bath
Hall
pantry
butler's pantry
Foyer
Hall
Dressing
Two-car Garage 19'10" x 21'4"
furniture alcove
Dining Room 11' x 15'9"
stairs dn
Porch
stairs up
Court Yard
walk-in closet
©

FIRST FLOOR

Design 97504

Units	Single
Price Code	E
Total Finished	2,322 sq. ft.
Main Finished	2,322 sq. ft.
Garage Unfinished	484 sq. ft.
Porch Unfinished	100 sq. ft.
Dimensions	68'11"x74'
Foundation	Slab
Bedrooms	4
Full Baths	2
Half Baths	1
Main Ceiling	9'-12'
Max Ridge Height	30'
Roof Framing	Stick
Exterior Walls	2x4

*This home is not to be built 20-mile radius of Madisonville, LA or Baton Rouge, LA.

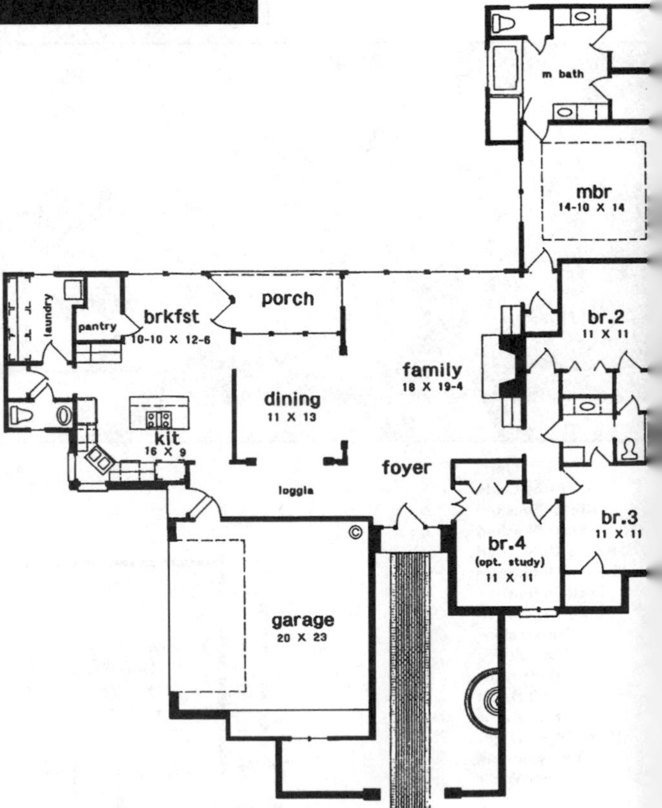

m bath
mbr 14-10 X 14
laundry
pantry
brkfst 10-10 X 12-6
porch
br.2 11 X 11
family 18 X 19-4
dining 11 X 13
kit 16 X 9
foyer
loggia
br.3 11 X 11
br.4 (opt. study) 11 X 11
garage 20 X 23
©

MAIN FLOOR

Design 94633

Units	Single
Price Code	E
Total Finished	2,326 sq. ft.
First Finished	1,261 sq. ft.
Second Finished	1,065 sq. ft.
Porch Unfinished	420 sq. ft.
Dimensions	46'x46'
Foundation	Crawlspace Slab
Bedrooms	3
Full Baths	2
Half Baths	1
First Ceiling	10'
Second Ceiling	9'
Max Ridge Height	30'6"
Roof Framing	Stick
Exterior Walls	2x4

Design 64165

Units	Single
Price Code	H
Total Finished	2,329 sq. ft.
Main Finished	2,329 sq. ft.
Garage Unfinished	528 sq. ft.
Porch Unfinished	215 sq. ft.
Dimensions	72'x73'
Foundation	Crawlspace
Bedrooms	3
Full Baths	2
Half Baths	1
Max Ridge Height	25'4"
Roof Framing	Stick/Truss
Exterior Walls	2x6

ate foundation options available at an additional charge.
Please call 1-800-235-5700 for more information.

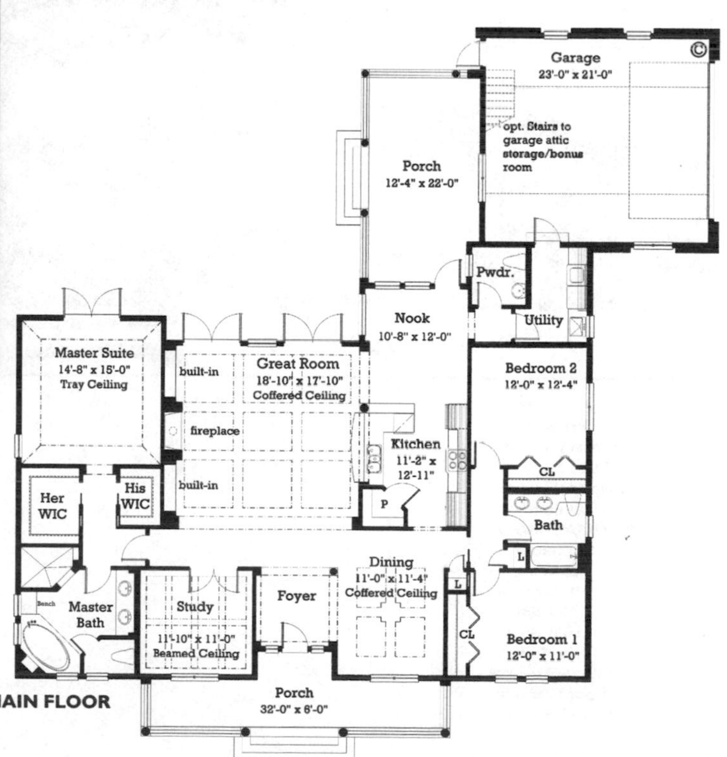

Design 98233

Units	Single
Price Code	E
Total Finished	2,330 sq. ft.
Main Finished	2,330 sq. ft.
Basement Unfinished	2,330 sq. ft.
Garage Unfinished	416 sq. ft.
Deck Unfinished	196 sq. ft.
Dimensions	50'x70'
Foundation	Crawlspace
Bedrooms	3
Full Baths	3
Main Ceiling	9'
Tray Ceiling	14'
Max Ridge Height	32'
Roof Framing	Stick
Exterior Walls	2x4

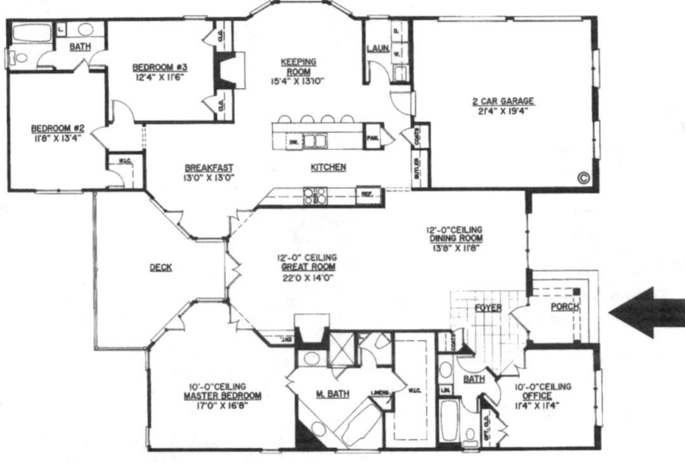

MAIN FLOOR

Design 97857

Units	Single
Price Code	E
Total Finished	2,332 sq. ft.
Main Finished	2,332 sq. ft.
Garage Unfinished	620 sq. ft.
Deck Unfinished	80 sq. ft.
Porch Unfinished	48 sq. ft.
Dimensions	82'3"x86'6"
Foundation	Slab
Bedrooms	3
Full Baths	2
Half Baths	1
Main Ceiling	9'-10'
Max Ridge Height	29'
Roof Framing	Stick
Exterior Walls	2x4

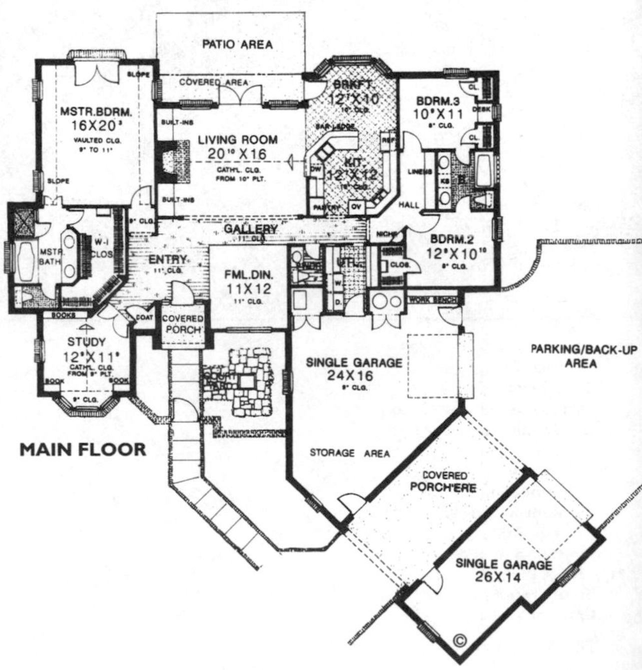

MAIN FLOOR

Design 65316

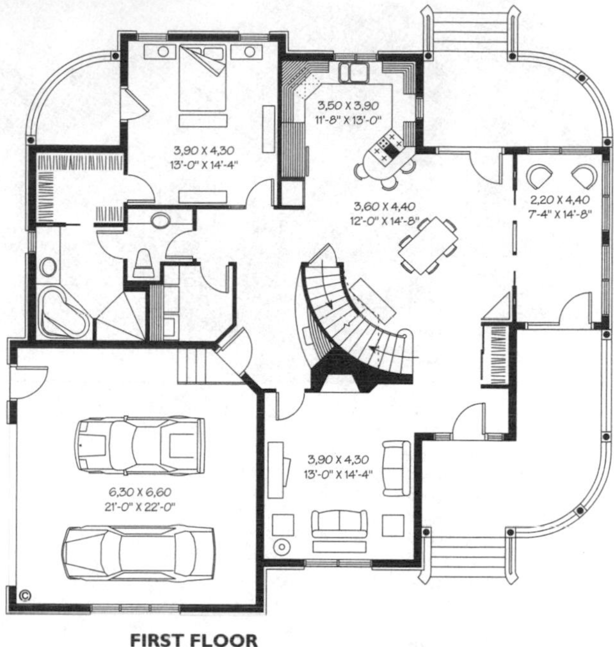

FIRST FLOOR

Units	Single
Price Code	E
Total Finished	2,333 sq. ft.
First Finished	1,472 sq. ft.
Second Finished	861 sq. ft.
Basement Unfinished	1,472 sq. ft.
Dimensions	52'8"x51'
Foundation	Basement
Bedrooms	4
Full Baths	2
First Ceiling	9'
Second Ceiling	8'
Max Ridge Height	31'6"
Roof Framing	Truss
Exterior Walls	2x6

3,00 X 3,10
10'-0" X 10'-4"
2,80 X 3,90
9'-4" X 13'-0"
3,30 X 3,40
11'-0" X 11'-4"
3,90 X 4,30
13'-0" X 14'-4"

SECOND FLOOR

Design 81003

Units	Single
Price Code	E
Total Finished	2,342 sq. ft.
First Finished	1,234 sq. ft.
Second Finished	1,108 sq. ft.
Dimensions	56'x74'6"
Foundation	Crawlspace
Bedrooms	4
Full Baths	2
Half Baths	1
First Ceiling	9'
Second Ceiling	8'
Max Ridge Height	34'6"
Roof Framing	Truss
Exterior Walls	2x6

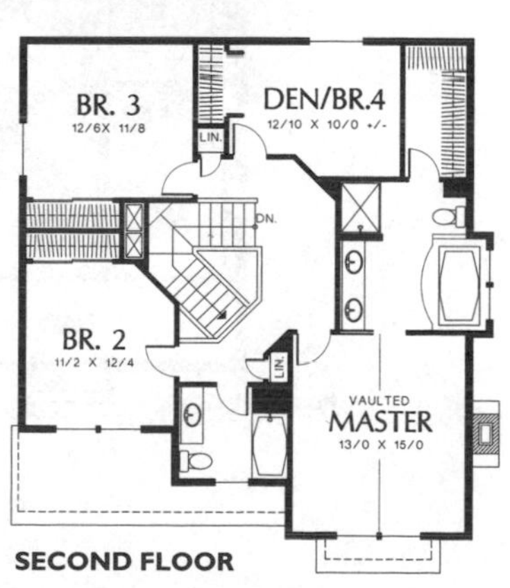

SECOND FLOOR

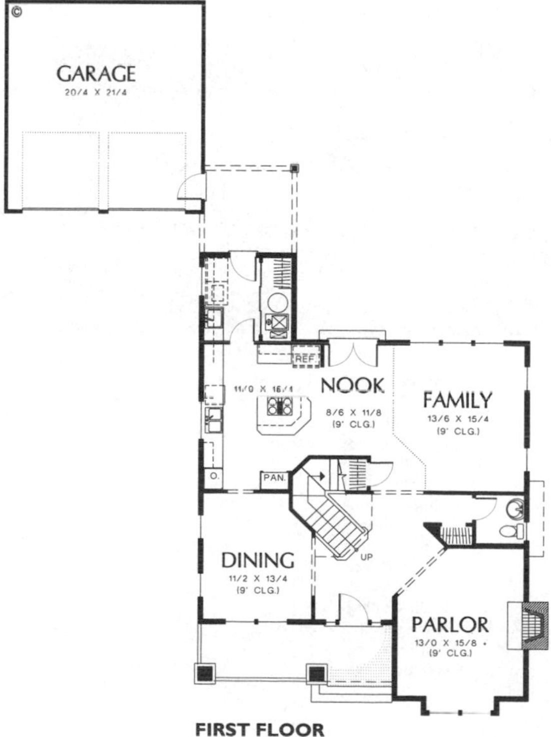

FIRST FLOOR

Design 94639

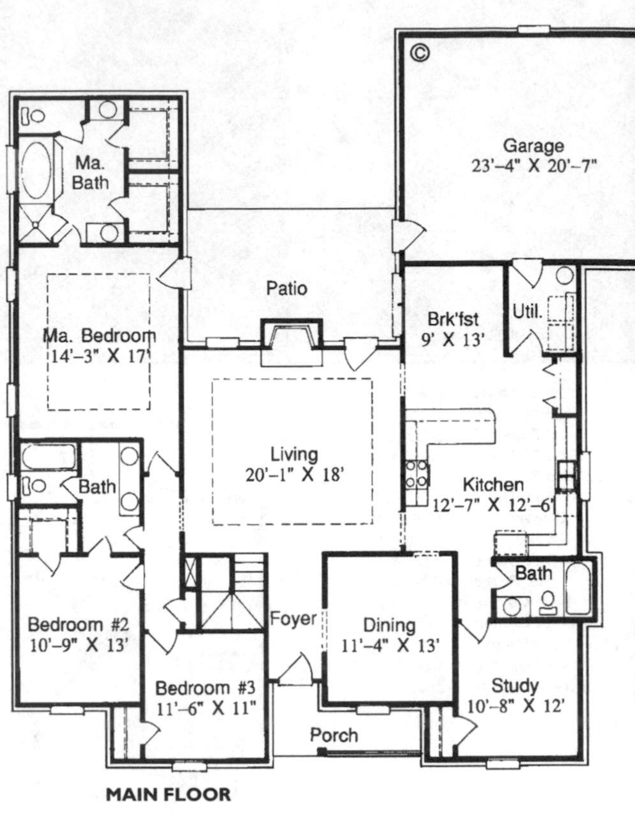

MAIN FLOOR

Units	Single
Price Code	E
Total Finished	2,345 sq. ft.
Main Finished	2,345 sq. ft.
Garage Unfinished	510 sq. ft.
Porch Unfinished	62 sq. ft.
Dimensions	59'10"x66'3"
Foundation	Slab
Bedrooms	3
Full Baths	3
Max Ridge Height	23'
Roof Framing	Stick
Exterior Walls	2x4

Design 66048

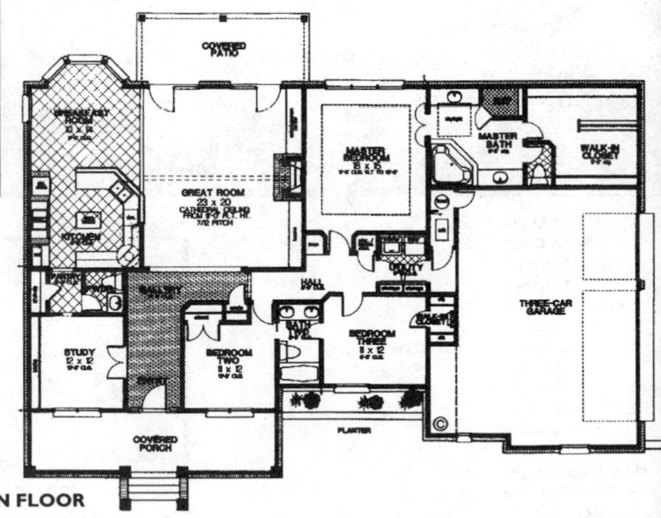

MAIN FLOOR

Units	Single
Price Code	E
Total Finished	2,352 sq. ft.
Main Finished	2,352 sq. ft.
Garage Unfinished	702 sq. ft.
Deck Unfinished	230 sq. ft.
Porch Unfinished	262 sq. ft.
Dimensions	76'x48'4"
Foundation	Slab
Bedrooms	3
Full Baths	2
Half Baths	1
Main Ceiling	9'-10'
Max Ridge Height	26'
Roof Framing	Stick
Exterior Walls	2x4

Design 66047

Units	Single
Price Code	E
Total Finished	2,353 sq. ft.
Main Finished	2,353 sq. ft.
Garage Unfinished	650 sq. ft.
Deck Unfinished	150 sq. ft.
Dimensions	55'x70'7¼"
Foundation	Slab
Bedrooms	4
Full Baths	3
Main Ceiling	9'
Max Ridge Height	27'6"
Roof Framing	Stick
Exterior Walls	2x4

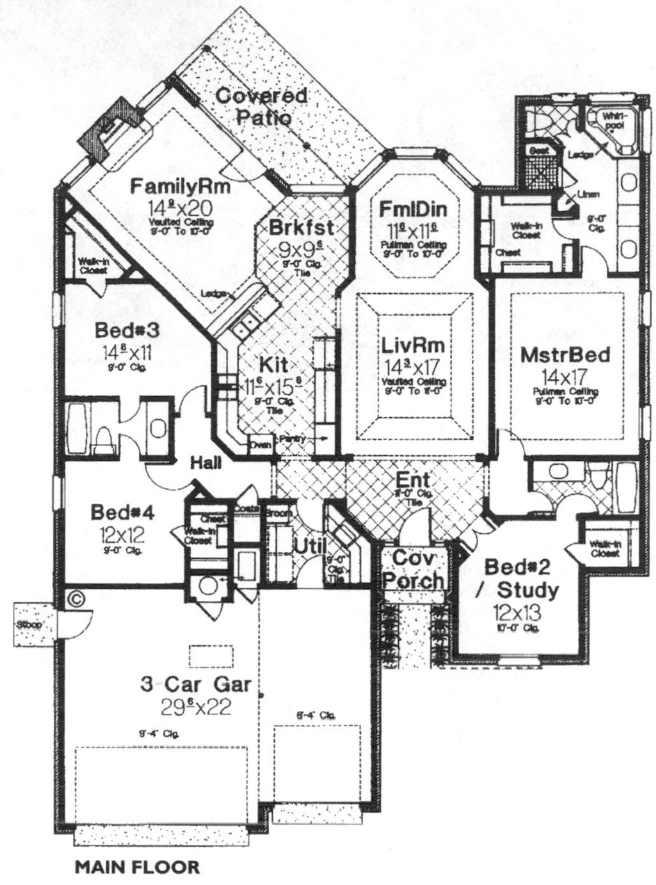

MAIN FLOOR

Design 24404

Units	Single
Price Code	E
Total Finished	2,356 sq. ft.
First Finished	1,236 sq. ft.
Second Finished	1,120 sq. ft.
Dimensions	68'8½"x42'
Foundation	Basement Crawlspace Slab
Bedrooms	5
Full Baths	2
3/4 Baths	1
First Ceiling	9'
Second Ceiling	8'
Max Ridge Height	28'
Roof Framing	Stick
Exterior Walls	2x4

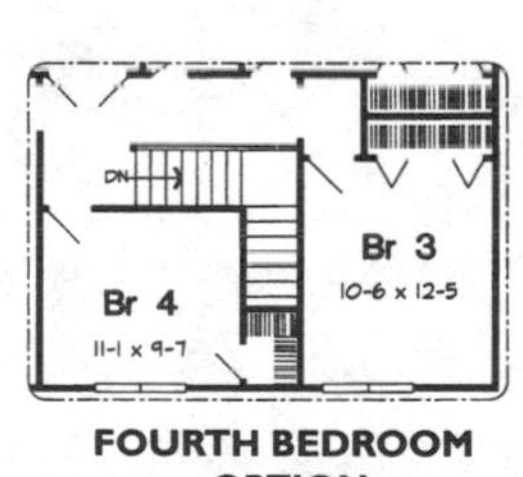

FOURTH BEDROOM OPTION

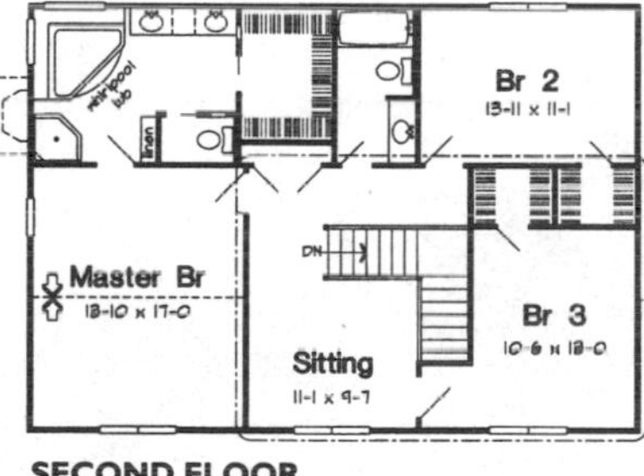

SECOND FLOOR

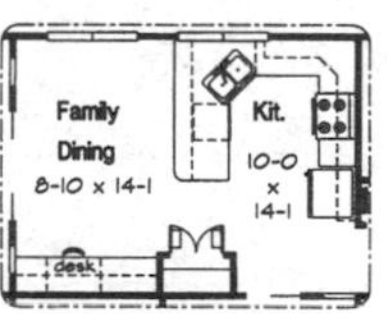

KITCHEN OPTION

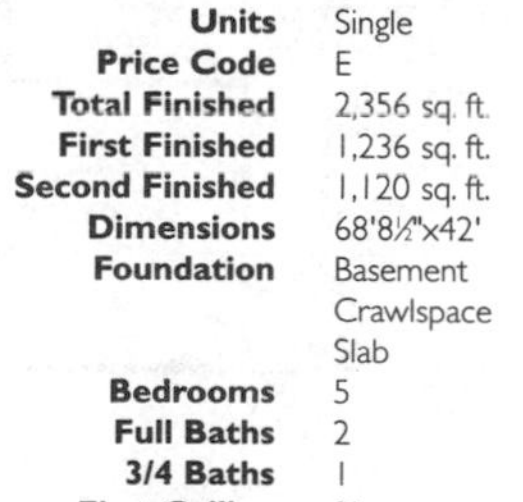

CRAWLSPACE/SLAB FOUNDATION OPTION

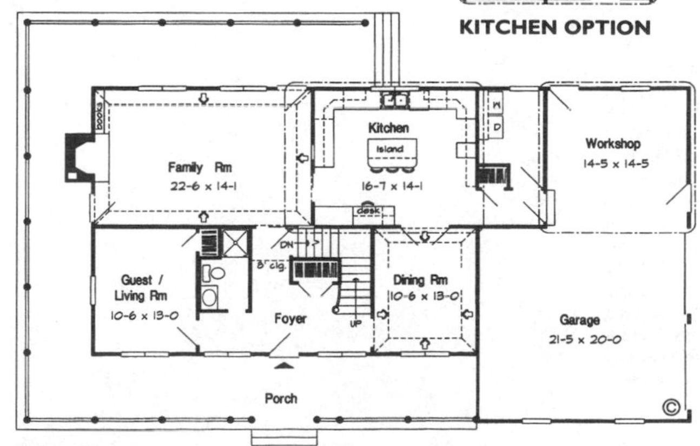

FIRST FLOOR

Design 94613

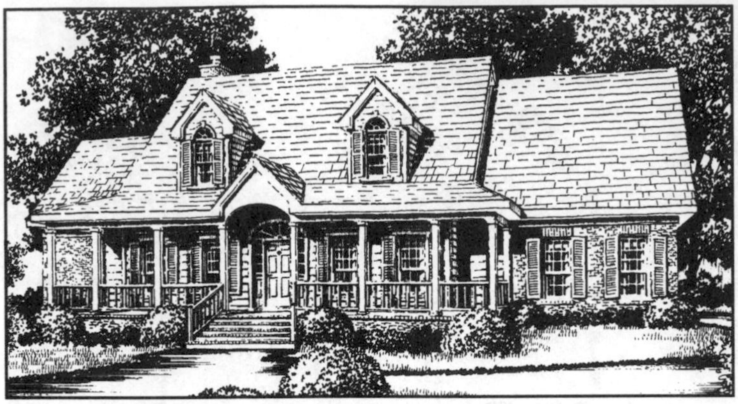

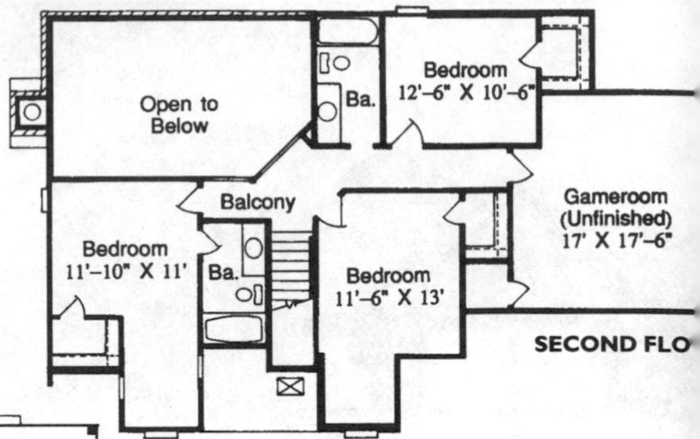

Open to Below
Ba.
Bedroom 12'-6" X 10'-6"
Balcony
Gameroom (Unfinished) 17' X 17'-6"
Bedroom 11'-10" X 11'
Ba.
Bedroom 11'-6" X 13'
SECOND FLO

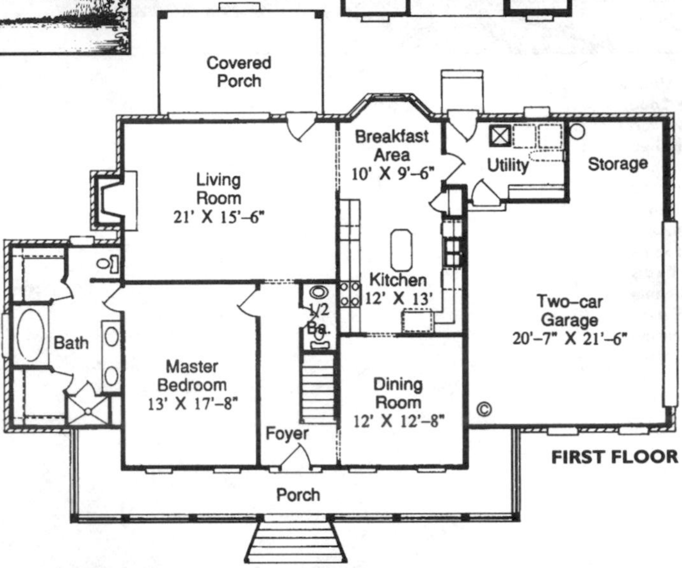

Covered Porch
Breakfast Area 10' X 9'-6"
Utility
Storage
Living Room 21' X 15'-6"
Kitchen 12' X 13'
1/2 Ba.
Bath
Master Bedroom 13' X 17'-8"
Two-car Garage 20'-7" X 21'-6"
Dining Room 12' X 12'-8"
Foyer
FIRST FLOOR
Porch

Units	Single
Price Code	E
Total Finished	2,357 sq. ft.
First Finished	1,492 sq. ft.
Second Finished	865 sq. ft.
Bonus Unfinished	303 sq. ft.
Garage Unfinished	574 sq. ft.
Porch Unfinished	440 sq. ft.
Dimensions	66'10"x49'7"
Foundation	Crawlspace Slab
Bedrooms	4
Full Baths	3
Half Baths	1
First Ceiling	9'
Second Ceiling	8'
Max Ridge Height	29'
Roof Framing	Truss
Exterior Walls	2x4, 2x6

Design 93440

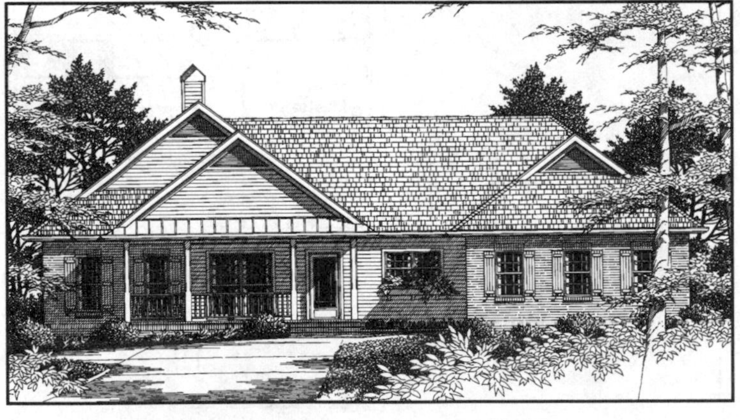

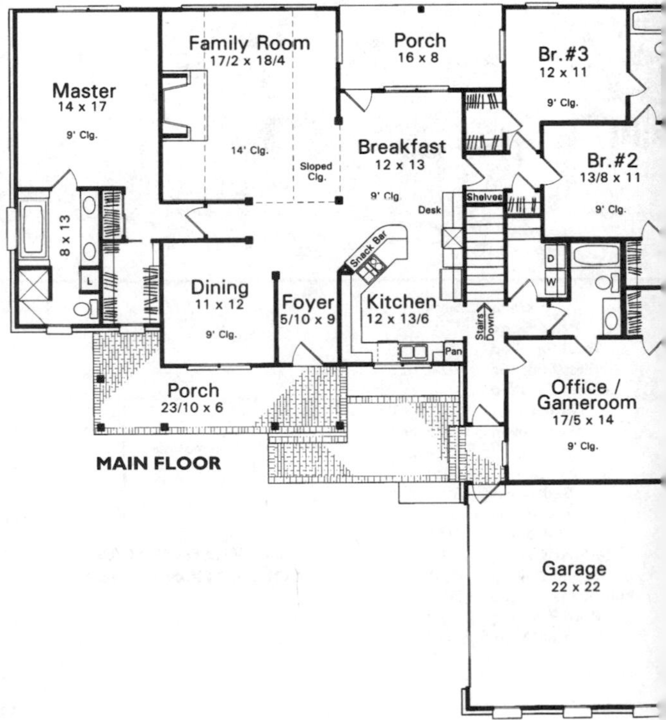

Family Room 17/2 x 18/4
Porch 16 x 8
Br. #3 12 x 11
9' Clg.
Master 14 x 17
9' Clg.
14' Clg.
Sloped Clg.
Breakfast 12 x 13
9' Clg
Br. #2 13/8 x 11
9' Clg.
Desk
Shelves
8 x 13
Snack Bar
Dining 11 x 12
9' Clg.
Foyer 5/10 x 9
Kitchen 12 x 13/6
Stairs Down
Pan
Porch 23/10 x 6
Office / Gameroom 17/5 x 14
9' Clg.
MAIN FLOOR
Garage 22 x 22

Units	Single
Price Code	E
Total Finished	2,361 sq. ft.
Main Finished	2,361 sq. ft.
Basement Unfinished	2,361 sq. ft.
Garage Unfinished	490 sq. ft.
Deck Unfinished	128 sq. ft.
Porch Unfinished	168 sq. ft.
Dimensions	67'x69'6"
Foundation	Basement
Bedrooms	3
Full Baths	3
Main Ceiling	9'
Vaulted Ceiling	14'
Max Ridge Height	22'5"
Roof Framing	Stick
Exterior Walls	2x4

Design 69107

Deck

Vaulted
Great Room
40' x 16'10"

Dining

Living

Vaulted
Kitchen

Bedroom
10' x 13'

Bedroom
13'6" x 11'

Utility

Sitting
Area

Entry

Master Suite
19' x 19'

Covered Porch

Dn

Garage
23'4" x 23'2"

©

MAIN FLOOR

Units	Single
Price Code	E
Total Finished	2,365 sq. ft.
Main Finished	2,365 sq. ft.
Basement Unfinished	2,365 sq. ft.
Garage Unfinished	566 sq. ft.
Dimensions	79'x70'6"
Foundation	Crawlspace
Bedrooms	3
Full Baths	2
Main Ceiling	10'
Second Ceiling	8'
Vaulted Ceiling	21'
Max Ridge Height	24'
Roof Framing	Truss
Exterior Walls	2x6

Design 94632

Units	Single
Price Code	E
Total Finished	2,365 sq. ft.
Main Finished	2,365 sq. ft.
Dimensions	67'6"x73'
Foundation	Crawlspace Slab
Bedrooms	4
Full Baths	2
Main Ceiling	9'
Max Ridge Height	31'6"
Roof Framing	Stick
Exterior Walls	2x4

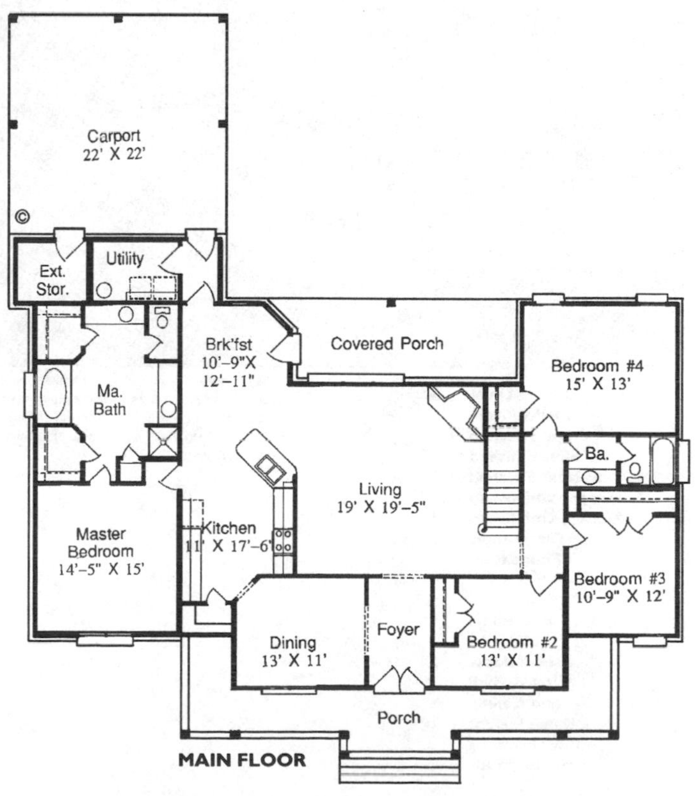

Design 98572

Units	Single
Price Code	E
Total Finished	2,370 sq. ft.
Main Finished	2,370 sq. ft.
Garage Unfinished	638 sq. ft.
Deck Unfinished	132 sq. ft.
Porch Unfinished	30 sq. ft.
Dimensions	55'x63'10"
Foundation	Slab
Bedrooms	4
Full Baths	2
Half Baths	1
Max Ridge Height	26'8"
Roof Framing	Stick
Exterior Walls	2x4

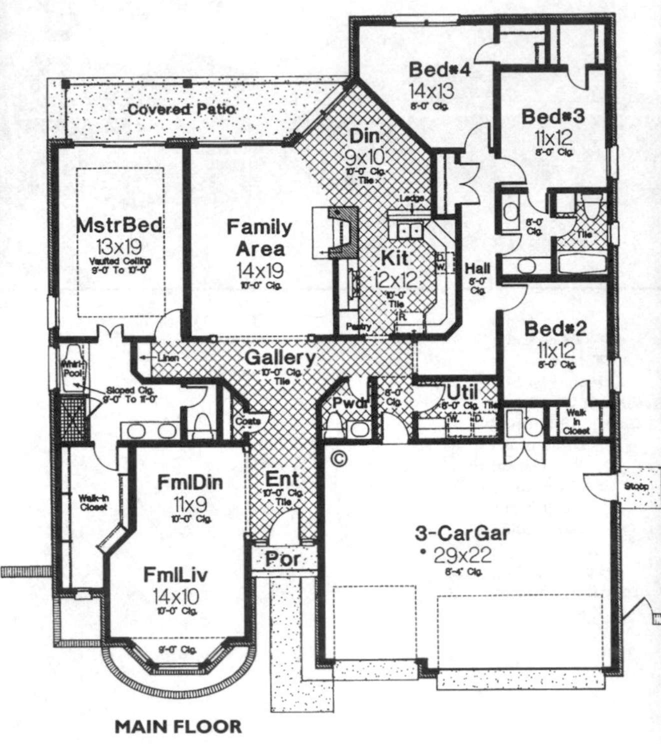

MAIN FLOOR

Design 20368

PHOTOGRAPHY: JOHN EHRENCLOU

Units	Single
Price Code	E
Total Finished	2,372 sq. ft.
First Finished	1,752 sq. ft.
Second Finished	620 sq. ft.
Basement Unfinished	1,726 sq. ft.
Garage Unfinished	714 sq. ft.
Dimensions	64'x52'
Foundation	Basement Crawlspace Slab
Bedrooms	3
Full Baths	2
Half Baths	1
First Ceiling	8'
Second Ceiling	8'
Max Ridge Height	29'6"
Roof Framing	Stick
Exterior Walls	2x4, 2x6

Please note: The photographed home may have been modified to suit homeowner preferences. If you order plans, have a builder or design professional check them against the photograph to confirm actual construction details.

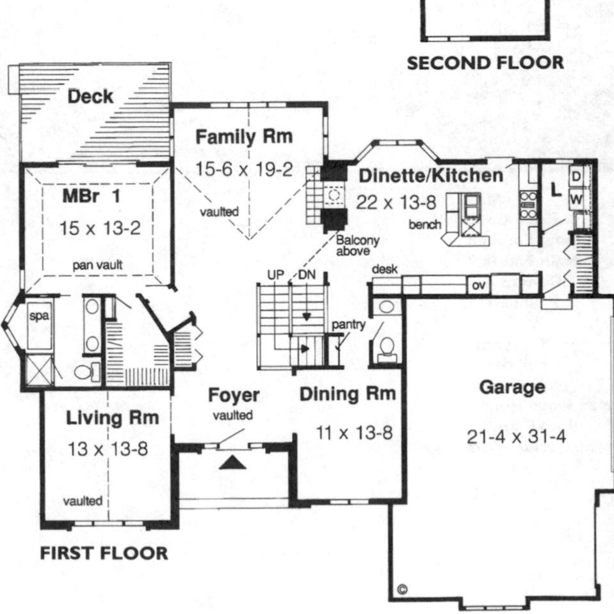

FIRST FLOOR

Design 91503

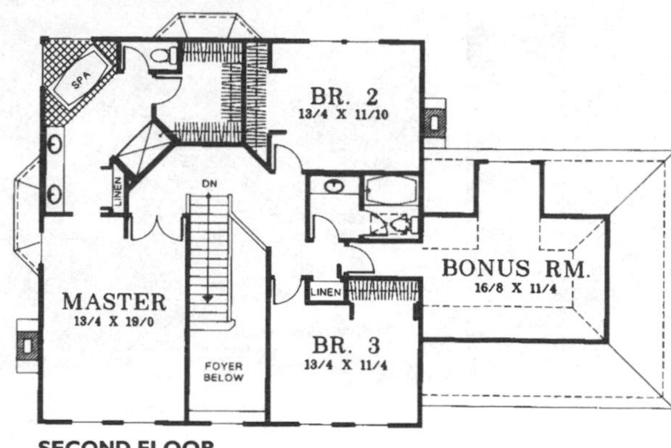

SECOND FLOOR

Units	Single
Price Code	E
Total Finished	2,385 sq. ft.
First Finished	1,285 sq. ft.
Second Finished	1,100 sq. ft.
Bonus Unfinished	238 sq. ft.
Dimensions	59'x38'
Foundation	Basement Crawlspace
Bedrooms	3
Full Baths	2
Half Baths	1
Max Ridge Height	31'
Roof Framing	Stick
Exterior Walls	2x4

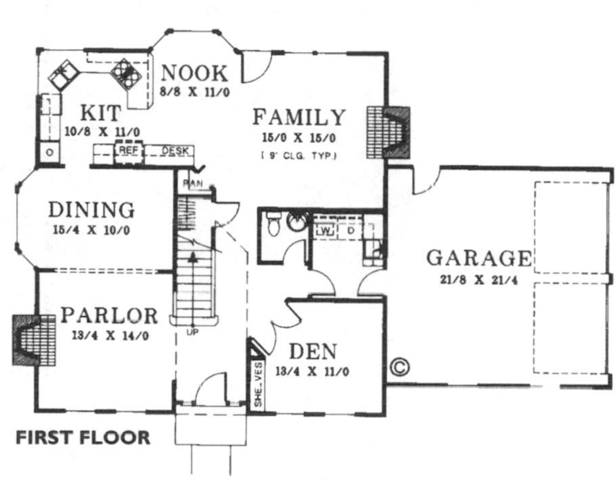

FIRST FLOOR

Design 92546

Units	Single
Price Code	E
Total Finished	2,387 sq. ft.
Main Finished	2,387 sq. ft.
Garage Unfinished	505 sq. ft.
Porch Unfinished	194 sq. ft.
Dimensions	64'10"x54'10"
Foundation	Crawlspace Slab
Bedrooms	4
Full Baths	2
Half Baths	1
Main Ceiling	9'
Max Ridge Height	28'
Roof Framing	Truss
Exterior Walls	2x4

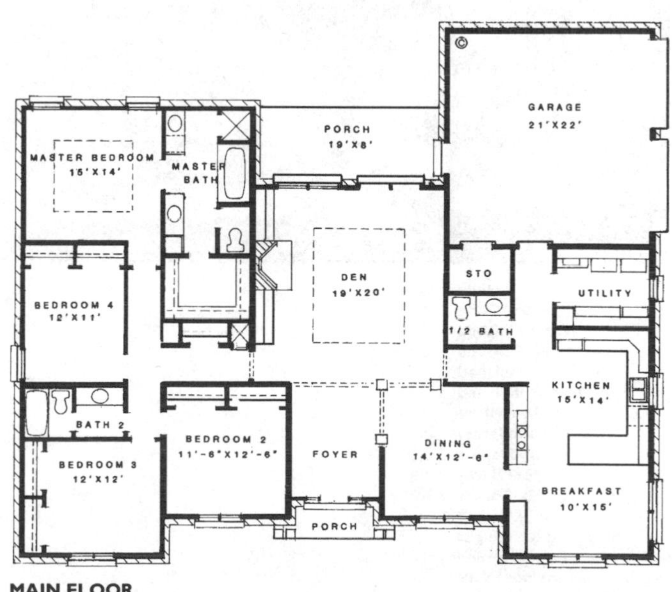

MAIN FLOOR

Design 93033

Units	Single
Price Code	E
Total Finished	2,389 sq. ft.
Main Finished	2,389 sq. ft.
Garage Unfinished	543 sq. ft.
Porch Unfinished	208 sq. ft.
Dimensions	75'2"x61'4"
Foundation	Crawlspace Slab
Bedrooms	4
Full Baths	2
Half Baths	1
Max Ridge Height	22'
Roof Framing	Stick
Exterior Walls	2x4

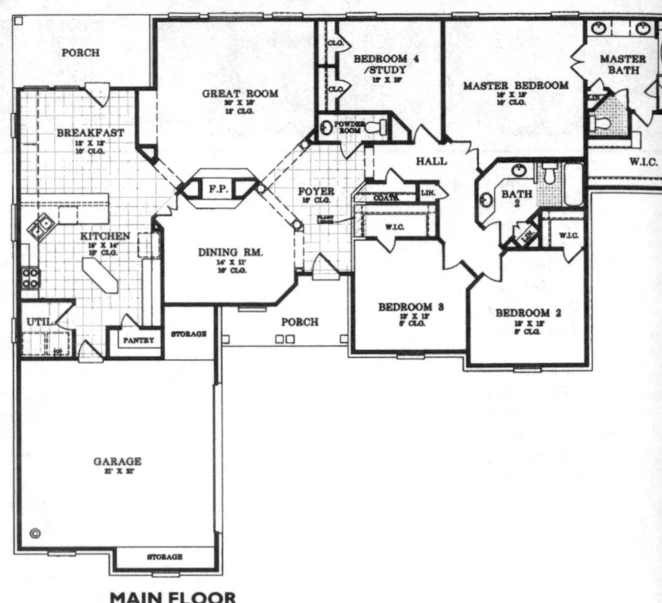

MAIN FLOOR

Design 66039

Units	Single
Price Code	E
Total Finished	2,390 sq. ft.
Main Finished	2,390 sq. ft.
Garage Unfinished	602 sq. ft.
Deck Unfinished	202 sq. ft.
Dimensions	60'x76'
Foundation	Slab
Bedrooms	3
Full Baths	2
Half Baths	1
Main Ceiling	9'-10'
Max Ridge Height	27'6"
Roof Framing	Stick
Exterior Walls	2x4

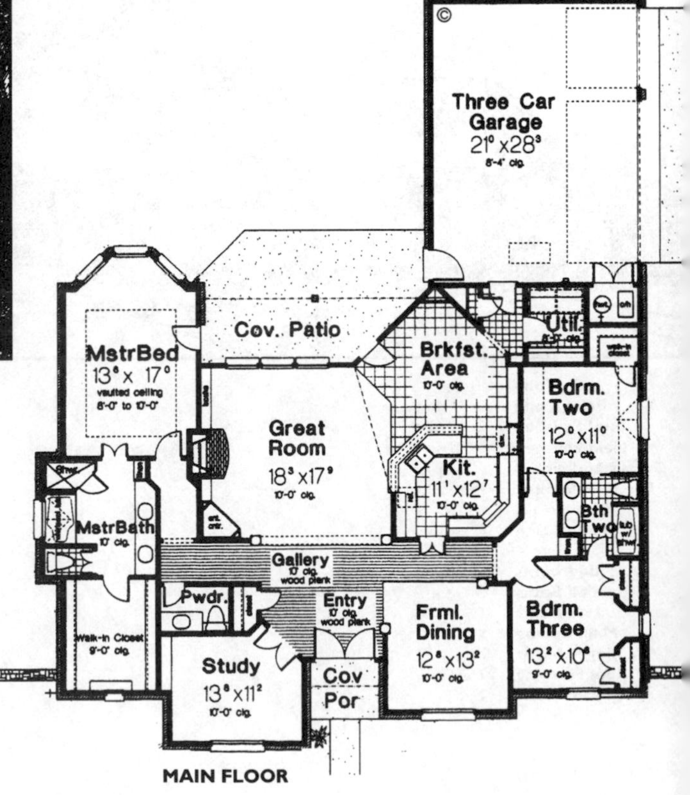

MAIN FLOOR

Design 65629

PHOTOGRAPHY: COURTESY OF THE DESIGNER

Units	Single
Price Code	E
Total Finished	2,396 sq. ft.
Main Finished	2,396 sq. ft.
Dimensions	72'x60'
Foundation	Basement Crawlspace Slab
Bedrooms	4
Full Baths	2
Main Ceiling	9'
Max Ridge Height	28'
Roof Framing	Stick
Exterior Walls	2x6

Please note: The photographed home may have been modified to suit homeowner preferences. If you order plans, have a builder or design professional check them against the photograph to confirm actual construction details.

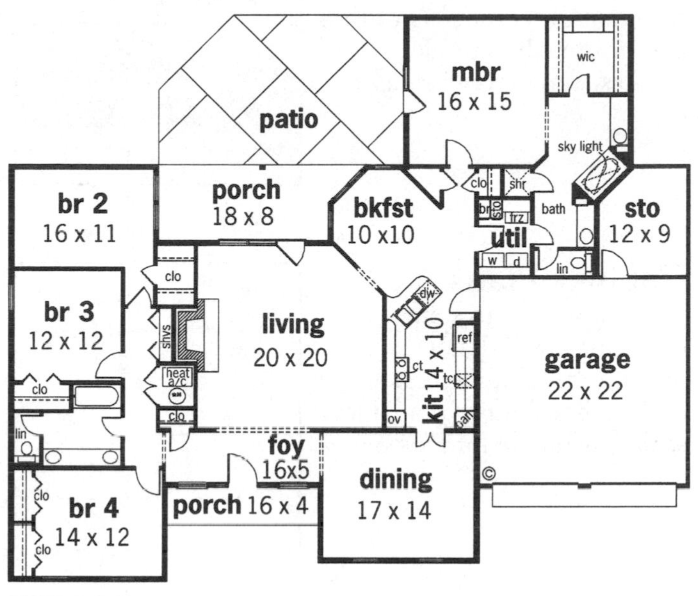

MAIN FLOOR

Design 63108

Units	Single
Price Code	E
Total Finished	2,397 sq. ft.
Main Finished	2,397 sq. ft.
Garage Unfinished	473 sq. ft.
Dimensions	73'2"x73'2"
Foundation	Slab
Bedrooms	3
Full Baths	2
Half Baths	1
Main Ceiling	10'
Tray Ceiling	13'4"
Max Ridge Height	22'8"
Roof Framing	Truss
Exterior Walls	2x4

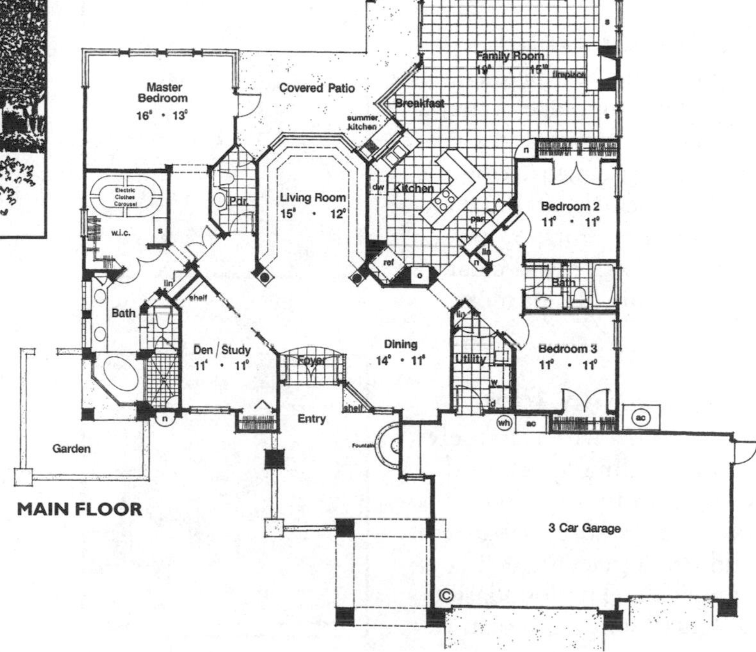

MAIN FLOOR

Everything you need...to Make Your Dream Come True!

Exterior Elevations

Scaled drawings of the front, rear, and sides of the home. Information pertaining to the exterior finish materials, roof pitches, and exterior height dimensions.

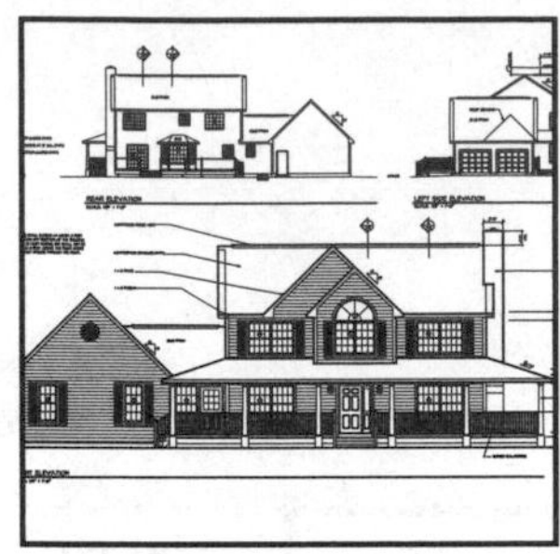

Cabinet Plans

These plans, or in some cases elevations, will detail the layout of the kitchen and bathroom cabinets at a larger scale. Available for most plans.

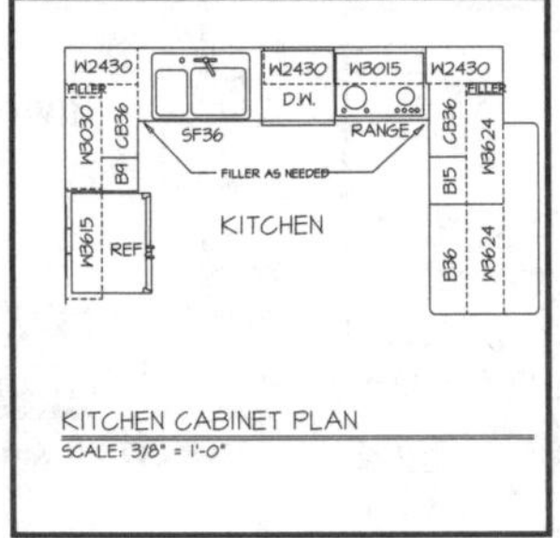

Typical Wall Section

This section will address insulation, roof components, and interior and exterior wall finishes. Your plans will be designed with either 2x4 or 2x6 exterior walls, but if you wish, most professional contractors can easily adapt the plans to the wall thickness you require.

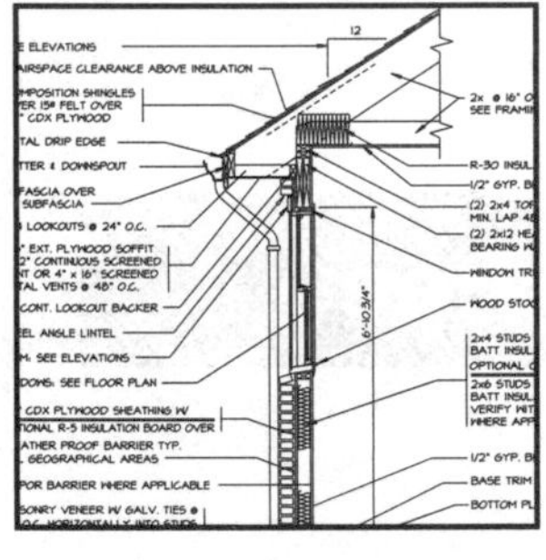

Fireplace Details

If the home you have chosen includes a fireplace, a fireplace detail will show typical methods of constructing the firebox, hearth, and flue chase for masonry units, or a wood frame chase for zero-clearance units. Available for most plans.

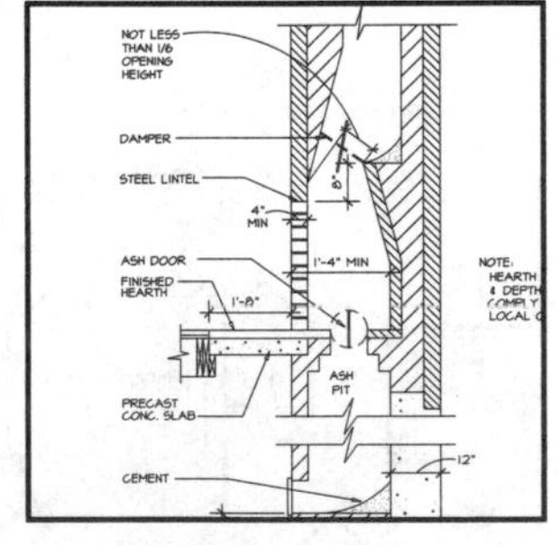

Foundation Plan

These plans will accurately show the dimensions of the footprint of your home, including load-bearing points and beam placement if applicable. The foundation style will vary from plan to plan.

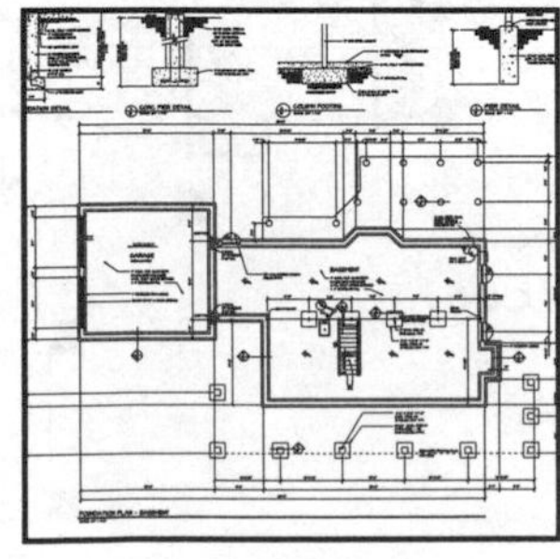

Roof Plan

The information necessary to construct the roof will be included with your home plans. Some plans will reference roof trusses, while many others contain schematic framing plans. These framing plans will indicate the lumber sizes necessary for the rafters and ridgeboards based on the designated roof loads.

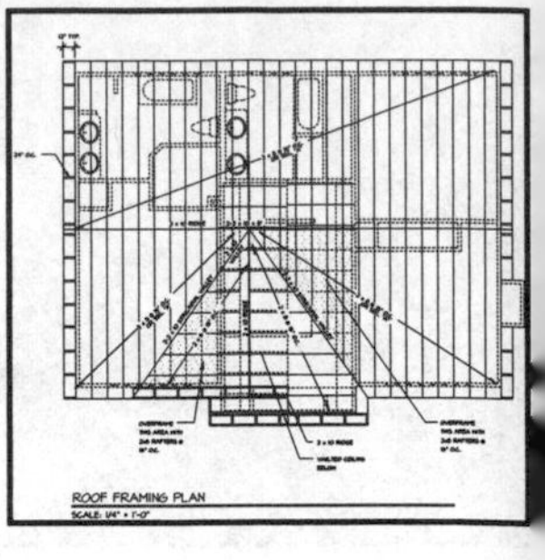

Typical Cross Section

A cut-away cross-section through the entire home shows your building contractor the exact correlation of construction components at all levels of the house. It will help to clarify the load bearing points from the roof all the way down to the basement. Available for most plans.

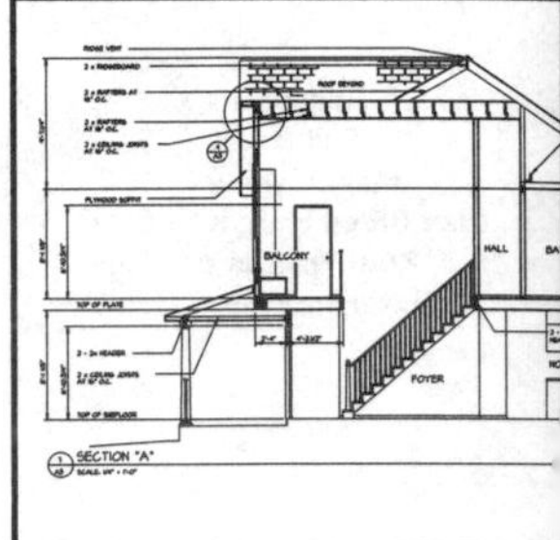

Detailed Floor Plans

The floor plans of your home accurately depict the dimensions of the positioning of all walls, doors, windows, stairs, and permanent fixtures. They will show you the relationship and dimensions of rooms, closets, and traffic patterns. The schematic of the electrical layout may be included in the plan.

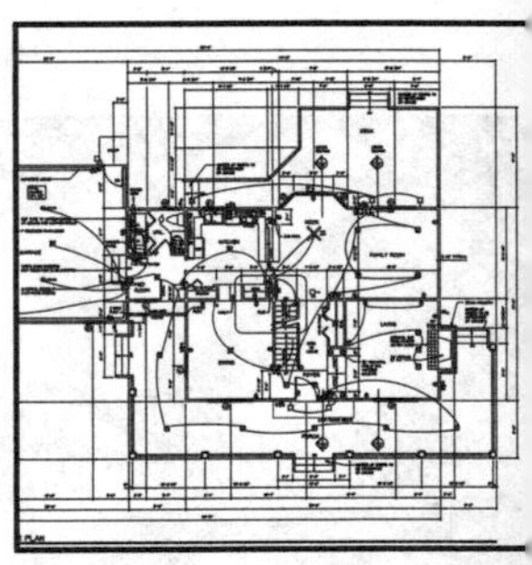

Stair Details

If the design you have chosen includes stairs, the plans will show the information that you need in order to build them either through a stair cross section or on the floor plans.

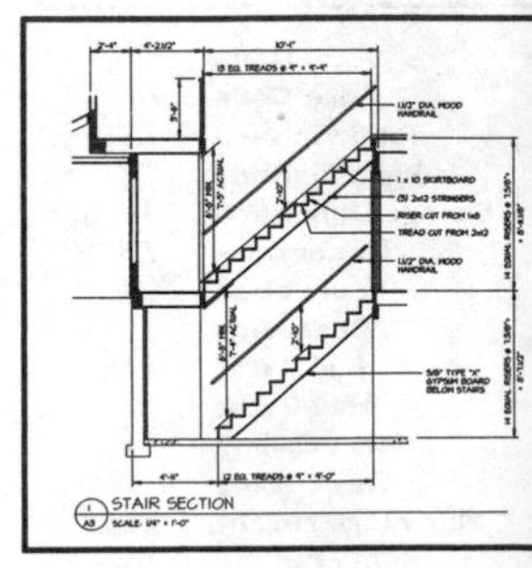

Reversed Plans Can Make Your Dream Home Just Right!

You could have exactly the home you want by flipping it end-for-end. Simply order your plans "reversed." We'll send you one full set of mirror-image plans (with the writing backwards) as a master guide for you and your builder.

The remaining sets of your order will come as shown in this book so the dimensions and specifications are easily read on the job site. Most plans in our collection come stamped "reversed" so there is no confusion.

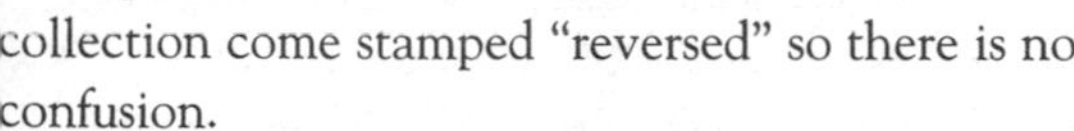

We can only send reversed plans with multiple-set orders. There is a $50 charge for this service.

Some plans in our collection are available in Right Reading Reverse. Right Reading Reverse plans will show your home in reverse, with the writing on the plan being readable. This easy-to-read format will save you valuable time and money. Please contact our Sales Department at 800-235-5700 to check for Right Reading Reverse availability. There is a $135 charge for Right Reading Reverse. RRR

Remember To Order Your Materials List

Available at a modest additional charge, the Materials List gives the quantity, dimensions, and specifications for the major materials needed to build your home. You will get faster, more accurate bids from your contractors and building suppliers—and avoid paying for unused materials and waste. Materials Lists are available for all home plans except as otherwise indicated, but can only be ordered with a set of home plans. Due to differences in regional requirements and homeowner or builder preferences, electrical, plumbing and heating/air conditioning equipment specifications are not designed specifically for each plan. ML

What Garlinghouse Offers

Home Plan Blueprint Package

By purchasing a multiple-set package of blueprints or a Vellum from Garlinghouse, you not only receive the physical blueprint documents necessary for construction, but you are also granted a license to build one (and only one) home. You can also make simple modifications, including minor non-structural changes and material substitutions, to our design, as long as these changes are made directly on the blueprints purchased from Garlinghouse and no additional copies are made.

Home Plan Vellums

By purchasing Vellums for one of our home plans, you receive the same construction drawings found in the blueprints, but printed on vellum paper. Vellums can be erased and are perfect for making design changes. They are also semi-transparent, making them easy to duplicate. But most importantly, the purchase of home plan Vellums comes with a broader license that allows you to make changes to the design (ie, create a hand drawn or CAD derivative work), to make copies of the plan, and to build one home from the plan.

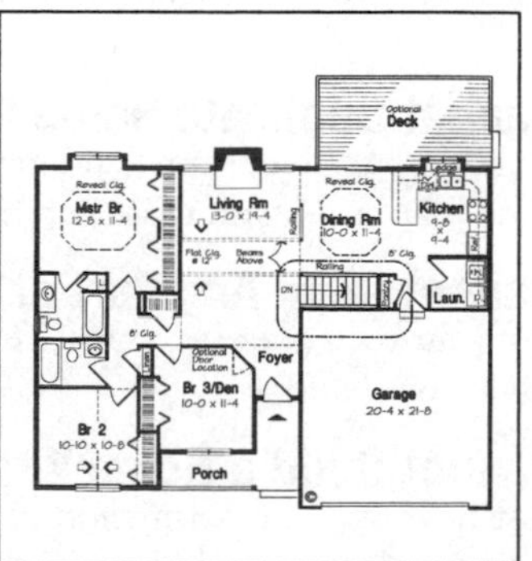

License To Build Additional Homes

With the purchase of a blueprint package or Vellums, you automatically receive a license to build one home and only one home, respectively. If you want to build more homes than you are licensed to build through your purchase of a plan, then additional licenses may be purchased at reasonable costs from Garlinghouse. Inquire for more information.

Modifying Your Favorite Design Made Easy

MODIFICATION PRICING GUIDE

CATEGORIES	ESTIMATED COST
Kitchen Layout Plan and Elevation	$175.00
Bathroom Layout Plan and Elevation	$175.00
Fireplace Plan and Details	$200.00
Interior Elevation	$125.00
Exterior Elevation Material Change	$140.00
Exterior Elevation Add Brick or Stone	$400.00
Exterior Elevation Style Change	$450.00
Non Bearing Walls (interior)	$200.00
Bearing and/or Exterior Walls	$325.00
Wall Framing Change 2x4 to 2x6 or 2x6 to 2x4	$240.00
Add/Reduce Living Space Square Footage	Quote Required
New Materials List	Quote Required
Change Trusses to Rafters or Change Roof Pitch	$300.00
Framing Plan Changes	$325.00
Garage Changes	$325.00
Add a Foundation Option	$300.00
Foundation Changes	$250.00
Right Reading Reverse	$575.00
Architect's Seal (available for most states)	$300.00
Energy Certificate	$150.00
Light and Ventilation Schedule	$150.00

Questions?

Call our customer service department at 1.860.659.5667

#1 Modifying Your Garlinghouse Home Plan

Simple modifications to your dream home, including minor non-structural changes and material substitutions, can be made by you and your builder by marking the changes directly on your blueprints. However, if you are considering making significant changes to your chosen design, we recommend that you use the services of The Garlinghouse Design Staff. We will help take your ideas and turn them into a reality, just the way you want. Here's our procedure:

When you place your Vellum order, you may also request a free Garlinghouse Modification Kit. In this kit, you will receive a red marking pencil, furniture cut-out sheet, ruler, a self-addressed mailing label, and a form for specifying any additional notes or drawings that will help us understand your design ideas. Mark your desired changes directly on the Vellum drawings. NOTE: Please use only a ***red pencil*** to mark your desired changes on the Vellum. Then, return the red-lined Vellum set in the original box to us.

Important: Please roll the Vellums for shipping, ***do not fold***.

We also offer modification estimates. For a $50 fee, we will provide you with an estimate to draft your changes based on your specific modifications before you purchase the vellums. After you receive your estimate, if you decide to have us do the changes, the $50 estimate fee will be deducted from the cost of your modifications. If, however, you choose to use a different service, the $50 estimate fee is non-refundable. (Note: Personal checks cannot be accepted for the estimate.)

Within five days of receipt of your plans, you will be contacted by a member of the design staff with an estimate for the design services to draw those changes. A 50% deposit is required before we begin making the actual modifications to your plans.

Once the design changes have been completed to your vellum plan, a representative will call to inform you that your modified Vellum plan is complete and will be shipped as soon as the final payment has been made. For additional information, call us at 1-860-659-5667. Please refer to the Modification Pricing Guide for estimated modification costs.

#2 Reproducible Vellums for Local Modification Ease

If you decide not to use Garlinghouse for your modifications, we recommend that you follow our same procedure of purchasing Vellums. You then have the option of using the services of the original designer of the plan, a local professional designer, or an architect to make the modifications.

With a Vellum copy of our plans, a design professional can alter the drawings just the way you want, then you can print as many copies of the modified plans as you need to build your house. And, since you have already started with our complete detailed plans, the cost of those expensive professional services will be significantly less than starting from scratch. Refer to the price schedule for Vellum costs.

Ignoring Copyright Laws Can Be A $100,000 Mistake

Recent changes in the US copyright laws allow for statutory penalties of up to $100,000 per incident for copyright infringement involving any of the copyrighted plans found in this publication. The law can be confusing. So, for your own protection, take the time to understand what you can and cannot do when it comes to home plans.

What You Can't Do

You Cannot Duplicate Home Plans

Purchasing a set of blueprints and making additional sets by reproducing the original is illegal. If you need multiple sets of a particular home plan, then you must purchase them.

You Cannot Copy Any Part of a Home Plan to Create Another

Creating your own plan by copying even part of a home design found in this publication without permission is called "creating a derivative work" and is illegal.

You Cannot Build a Home Without a License

You must have specific permission or a license to build a home from a copyrighted design, even if the finished home has been changed from the original plan. It is illegal to build one of the homes found in this publication without a license.

How to obtain a construction cost calculation based on labor rates and building material costs in your zip code area!

Vhat will your eam home cost? P QUOTE as the answer!

Why? Do you wish you could quickly find out the building cost for your new home without waiting for a contractor to compile hundreds of bids? Would you like to have a benchmark to compare your contractor(s) bids against? Well, now you can with the Zip Quote Home Cost lculator. Zip Quote is only available for zip codes within United States.

w? Our Zip Quote Home Cost Calculator will enable 1 to obtain the calculated building cost to construct your v home, based on labor rates and building material costs hin your zip code area, without the normal delays or ssles usually associated with the bidding process. Zip Quote 1 be purchased in two separate formats, either an itemized a bottom line format.

Iow does Zip Quote actually work? When you call to 'er, you must choose from the options available for your cific home in order for us to process your order. Once we eive your Zip Quote order, we process your specific home n building materials list through our Home Cost lculator which contains up-to-date rates for all residential or trades and building material costs in your zip code area. e result? A calculated cost to build your dream home in r zip code area. This calculation will help you (as a sumer or a builder) evaluate your building budget.

ll database information for our calculations is furnished Marshall & Swift, L.P. For over 60 years, Marshall & ft L.P. has been a leading provider of cost data to fessionals in all aspects of the construction and odeling industries.

ion 1 The **Itemized Zip Quote** is a detailed building erials list. Each building material list line item will arately state the labor cost, material cost, and equipment (if applicable) for the use of that building material in construction process. This building materials list will be marized by the individual building categories and will e additional columns where you can enter data from your tractor's estimates for a cost comparison between the erent suppliers and contractors who will actually quote their products and services.

ion 2 The **Bottom Line Zip Quote** is a one line marized total cost for the home plan of your choice. This calculation is also based on the labor cost, material cost, equipment cost (if applicable) within your zip code area. tom Line Zip Quote is available for most plans. Please for availability.

t The price of your Itemized Zip Quote is based upon pricing schedule of the plan you have selected, in addition to the price of the materials list. Please refer to the pricing schedule on our order form. The price of your initial Bottom Line Zip Quote is $29.95. Each additional Bottom Line Zip Quote ordered in conjunction with the initial order is only $14.95. A bottom Line Zip Quote may be purchased separately and does NOT have to be purchased in conjunction with a home plan order.

FYI An Itemized Zip Quote Home Cost Calculation can ONLY be purchased in conjunction with a Home Plan order. The Itemized Zip Quote can not be purchased separately. If you find within 60 days of your order date that you will be unable to build this home, then you may apply the price of the plans and the materials list towards the price of a new set of plans (see order info pages for plan exchange policy). The Itemized Zip Quote and the Bottom Line Zip Quote are NOT returnable. The price of the initial Bottom Line Zip Quote order can be credited toward the purchase of an Itemized Zip Quote order, only if available. Additional Bottom Line Zip Quote orders, within the same order can not be credited. Please call our Sales Department for more information.

An Itemized Zip Quote is available for plans where you see this symbol. ZIP

A Bottom line Zip Quote is available for all plans under 4,000 sq. ft. or where you see this symbol. BL

Please call for current availability.

Some More Information The Itemized and Bottom Line Zip Quotes give you approximated costs for constructing the particular house in your area. These costs are not exact and are only intended to be used as a preliminary estimate to help determine the affordability of a new home and/or as a guide to evaluate the general competitiveness of actual price quotes obtained through local suppliers and contractors. However, Zip Quote cost figures should never be relied upon as the only source of information in either case. **Land, landscaping, sewer systems, site work, contractor overhead and profit, and other expenses are not included in our building cost figures. Excluding land and landscaping, you may incur an additional 20% to 40% in costs from the original estimate.** Garlinghouse and Marshall & Swift L.P. cannot guarantee any level of data accuracy or correctness in a Zip Quote and disclaim all liability for loss with respect to the same, in excess of the original purchase price of the Zip Quote product. All Zip Quote calculations are based upon the actual blueprints and do not reflect any differences or options that may be shown on the published house renderings, floor plans, or photographs.

the Garlinghouse company

BEST PLAN VALUE IN THE INDUSTRY!

Order Code No. **H3BSM**

Order Form

Plan prices guaranteed until 7/7/04. After this date, call for updated pricing.

_____________ *foundation*

____ *set(s) of blueprints for plan #*________	$_____
____ *Vellum & Modification kit for plan #*________	$_____
____ *Additional set(s) @ $50 each for plan #*________	$_____
____ *Mirror Image Reverse @ $50 each*	$_____
____ *Right Reading Reverse @ $135 each*	$_____
____ *Materials list for plan #*________	$_____
____ *Detail Plans @ $19.95 each*	
❑ *Construction* ❑ *Plumbing* ❑ *Electrical*	$_____
____ *Bottom Line Zip Quote @ $29.95 for plan #*________	$_____
____ *Additional Bottom Line Zip Quote*	
*@ $14.95 for plan(s) #*________	$_____
Zip code where building ________	
____ *Itemized Zip Quote for plan(s) #*________	$_____
Shipping	$_____
Subtotal	$_____
Sales Tax *(CT residents add 6% sales tax, IL residents add 7%, WI residents add 5%) (Not required for other states)*	$_____
TOTAL AMOUNT ENCLOSED	$_____

Send your check, money order, or credit card information to:
(No C.O.D.'s Please)

Please submit all United States & other nations orders to:
Garlinghouse Company
174 Oakwood Drive
Glastonbury, CT. 06033
CALL: (800) 235-5700 FAX: (860) 659-5692

VISA MasterCard

Please Submit all Canadian plan orders to:
Garlinghouse Company
102 Ellis Street
Penticton, BC V2A 4L5
CALL: (800) 361-7526 FAX: (250) 493-7526

ADDRESS INFORMATION:

NAME: ____________________

STREET: ____________________

CITY: ____________________

STATE: ____________ ***ZIP:*** ____________

DAYTIME PHONE: ____________________

E-MAIL ADDRESS: ____________________

Credit Card Information

Charge To: ❑ Visa ❑ Mastercard

Card # |_|_|_|_|_|_|_|_|_|_|_|_|_|_|_|_|

Signature ____________________ Exp. ___/___

Payment must be made in U.S. funds. Foreign Mail Orders: Certified bank checks in U.S. funds only

To order your plan on-line now using our secure server, visit:
www.garlinghouse.com/bhg

CUSTOMER SERVICE	TO PLACE ORDERS
Questions on existing orders?	• To order your homeplans • Questions about a plan
➡ **1-800-895-3715**	➡ **1-800-235-5700**

Privacy Statement (please read)

Dear Valued Garlinghouse Customer,

Your privacy is extremely important to us. We'd like to take a little of your time to explain our privacy policy.

As a service to you, we would like to provide your name to companies such as the following:

- Building material manufacturers that we are affiliated with, who would like to keep you current with their product line and specials.
- Building material retailers that would like to offer you competitive prices to help you save money.
- Financing companies that would like to offer you competitive mortgage rates.

In addition, as our valued customer, we would like to send you newsletters to assist in your building experience. *We* would also appreciate *your* feedback by filling out a customer service survey aimed to improve our operations.

You have total control over the use of your contact information. You let us know exactly how you want to be contacted. Please check all boxes that apply. Thank you.

☐ Don't mail
☐ Don't call
☐ Don't E-mail
☐ Only send Garlinghouse newsletters and customer service surveys

In closing, we hope this shows Garlinghouse's firm commitment to providing superior customer service and protection of your privacy. We thank you for your time and consideration.

Sincerely,

The Garlinghouse Company

BEFORE ORDERING PLEASE READ ALL ORDERING INFORMATION

For Our USA Customers:
Order Toll Free: 1-800-235-5700
onday-Friday 8:00 a.m. to 8:00 p.m. Eastern Time
or FAX your Credit Card order to 1-860-659-5692
All foreign residents call 1-860-659-5667

CUSTOMER SERVICE	TO PLACE ORDERS
Questions on existing orders?	• To order your homeplans • Questions about a plan
➡ 1-800-895-3715	➡ 1-800-235-5700

For Our Canadian Customers:
Order Toll Free: 1-800-361-7526
Monday-Friday 8:00 a.m. to 5:00 p.m. Pacific Time
or FAX your Credit Card order to 1-250-493-7526
Customer Service: 1-250-493-0942

Please have ready: 1. Your credit card number 2. The plan number 3. The order code number ➪ **H3BSM**

Garlinghouse 2003 Blueprint Price Code Schedule

1 Set	4 Sets	8 Sets	Vellums	ML	Itemized ZIP Quote
$345	$385	$435	$525	$60	$50
$375	$415	$465	$555	$60	$50
$410	$450	$500	$590	$60	$50
$450	$490	$540	$630	$60	$50
$495	$535	$585	$675	$70	$60
$545	$585	$635	$725	$70	$60
$595	$635	$685	$775	$70	$60
$640	$680	$730	$820	$70	$60
$685	$725	$775	$865	$80	$70
$725	$765	$815	$905	$80	$70
$765	$805	$855	$945	$80	$70
$800	$840	$890	$980	$80	$70

Shipping — (Plans 1-59999)	1-3 Sets	4-6 Sets	7+ & Vellums
Standard Delivery (UPS 2-Day)	$25.00	$30.00	$35.00
Overnight Delivery	$35.00	$40.00	$45.00

Shipping — (Plans 60000-99999)	1-3 Sets	4-6 Sets	7+ & Vellums
Ground Delivery (7-10 Days)	$15.00	$20.00	$25.00
Express Delivery (3-5 Days)	$20.00	$25.00	$30.00

International Shipping & Handling	1-3 Sets	4-6 Sets	7+ & Vellums
Regular Delivery Canada (10-14 Days)	$30.00	$35.00	$40.00
Express Delivery Canada (7-10 Days)	$60.00	$70.00	$80.00
Overseas Delivery Airmail (3-4 Weeks)	$50.00	$60.00	$65.00

Additional sets with original order $50

IMPORTANT INFORMATION TO READ BEFORE YOU PLACE YOUR ORDER

ow Many Sets of Plans Will You Need?

e Standard 8-Set Construction Package

*Our experience shows that you'll speed up every step of construction and avoid costly building errors by ordering enough sets to go around. Each desperson wants a set—the general contractor and all subcontractors: foundation, electrical, plumbing, heating/air conditioning, and framers. Don't forget ur lending institution, building department, and, of course, a set for yourself. * Recommended For Construction **

e Minimum 4-Set Construction Package

*If you're comfortable with arduous follow-up, this package can save you a few dollars by giving you the option of passing down plan sets as work ogresses. You might have enough copies to go around if work goes exactly as scheduled and no plans are lost or damaged by subcontrators. But for only $60 re, the 8-set package eliminates these worries. * Recommended For Bidding **

e Single Study Set

We offer this set so you can study the blueprints to plan your dream home in detail. They are stamped "study set only—not for construction" and you cannot ld a home from them. In pursuant to copyright laws, it is illegal to reproduce any blueprint.

Reorder Call 800-235-5700

If you find after your initial purchase that you require additional sets of plans, you may purchase them from us at special reorder prices (please call for pricing details) vided that you reorder within six months of your original order date. There is a $28 reorder processing fee that is charged on all reorders. For more information on rdering plans, please contact our Sales Department.

stomer Service/Exchanges Call 800-895-3715

If for some reason you have a question about your existing order, please call 800-895-3715. Your plans are custom printed especially for you once you place your er. For that reason we cannot accept any returns. If for some reason you find that the plan you have purchased from us does not meet your needs, then you may hange that plan for any other plan in our collection. We allow you 60 days from your original invoice date to make an exchange. At the time of the exchange, you will be rged a processing fee of 20% of the total amount of your original order, plus the difference in price between the plans (if applicable), plus the cost to ship the new plans ou. Call our Customer Service Department for more information. Please Note: Reproducible Vellums can only be exchanged if they are unopened.

portant Shipping Information

Please refer to the shipping charts on the order form for service availability for your specific plan number. Our delivery service must have a street address or al Route Box number—never a post office box. (PLEASE NOTE: Supplying a P.O. Box number only will delay the shipping of your order.) Use a work address if no is home during the day. Orders being shipped to APO or FPO must go via First Class Mail. Please include the proper postage.

For our International Customers, only Certified bank checks and money orders are accepted and must be payable in U.S. currency. For speed, we ship international orders Air Parcel Post. Please refer to the chart for the correct shipping cost.

portant Canadian Shipping Information

To our friends in Canada, we have a plan design affiliate in Penticton, BC. This relationship will help you avoid the delays and charges associated with shipments n the United States. Moreover, our affiliate is familiar with the building requirements in your community and country. We prefer payments in U.S. Currency. If you, vever, are sending Canadian funds please add 45% to the prices of the plans and shipping fees.

Important Note About ilding Code Requirements

All plans are drawn to conform to one or more of the industry's major national building standards. However, due to the variety of local building regulations, your n may need to be modified to comply with local requirements—snow loads, energy loads, seismic zones, etc. Do check them fully and consult your local building cials.

A few states require that all building plans used be drawn by an architect registered in that state. While having your plans reviewed and stamped by such an hitect may be prudent, laws requiring non-conforming plans like ours to be completely redrawn forces you to unnecessarily pay very large fees. If your state has h a law, we strongly recommend you contact your state representative to protest.

The rendering, floor plans, and technical information contained within this publication are not guaranteed to be totally accurate. Consequently, no information n this publication should be used either as a guide to constructing a home or for estimating the cost of building a home. Complete blueprints must be purchased such purposes.

Option Key

BL Bottom-line Zip Quote **ML** Materials List Available **ZIP** Itemized Zip Quote **RRR** Right Reading Reverse **DUP** Duplex Plan

Option Key

BL Bottom-line Zip Quote ML Materials List Available ZIP Itemized Zip Quote RRR Right Reading Reverse DUP Duplex Plan

TOP SELLING
GARAGE PLANS

Save money by Doing-It-Yourself using our Easy-To-Follow plans. Whether you intend to build your own garage or contract it out to a building professional, the Garlinghouse garage plans provide you with everything you need to price out your project and get started. Put our 90+ years of experience to work for you. Order now!!

No. 06016C $24.95

Apartment Garage With One Bedroom

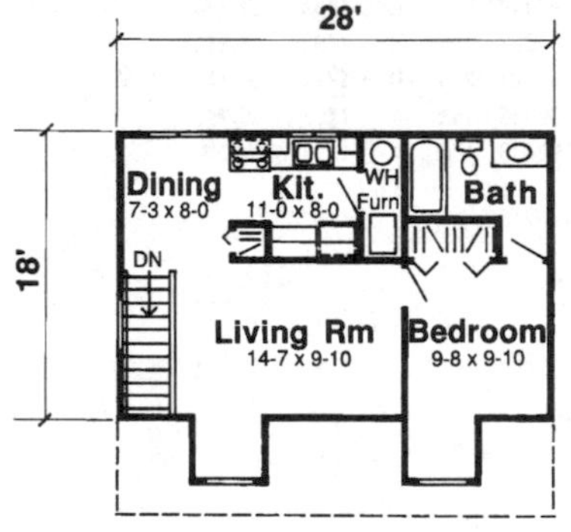

- 24' x 28' Overall Dimensions
- 544 Square Foot Apartment
- 12/12 Gable Roof with Dormers
- Slab or Stem Wall Foundation Options

No. 06015C $24.95

Apartment Garage With Two Bedrooms

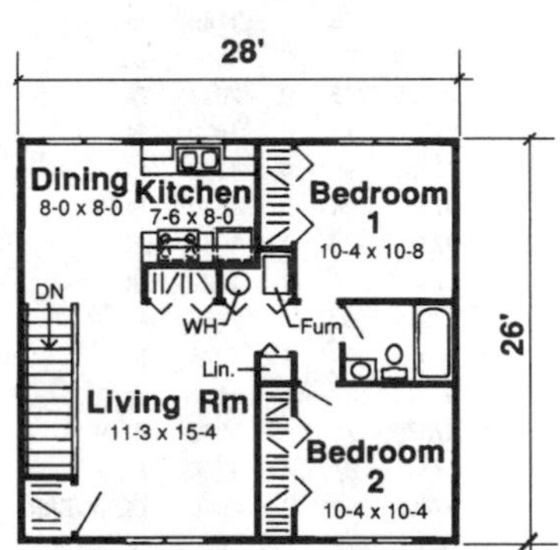

- 26' x 28' Overall Dimensions
- 728 Square Foot Apartment
- 4/12 Pitch Gable Roof
- Slab or Stem Wall Foundation Options

No. 06012C $16.95

30' Deep Gable &/or Eave Jumbo Garages

- 4/12 Pitch Gable Roof
- Available Options for Extra Tall Walls, Garage & Personnel Doors, Foundation, Window, & Sidings
- Package contains 4 Different Sizes
- 30' x 28' • 30' x 32' • 30' x 36' • 30' x 40'

No. 06013C $16.95

Two-Car Garage With Mudroom/Breezeway

- Attaches to Any House
- 24' x 24' Eave Entry
- Available Options for Utility Room with Bath, Mudroom, Screened-In Breezeway, Roof, Foundation, Garage & Personnel Doors, Window, & Sidings

No. 06001C $14.95

12', 14' & 16' Wide-Gable 1-Car Garages

- Available Options for Roof, Foundation, Window, Door, & Sidings
- Package contains 8 Different Sizes
- 12' x 20' Mini-Garage • 14' x 22' • 16' x 20' • 16' x 24'
- 14' x 20' • 14' x 24' • 16' x 22' • 16' x 26'

No. 06003C $14.95

24' Wide-Gable 2-Car Garages

- Available Options for Side Shed, Roof, Foundation, Garage & Personnel Doors, Window, & Sidings
- Package contains 5 Different Sizes
- 24' x 22' • 24' x 24' • 24' x 26'
- 24' x 28' • 24' x 32'

No. 06007C $16.95

Gable 2-Car Gambrel Roof Garages

- Rear Stairs to Loft Workshop
- Front Loft Cargo Door With Pulley Lift
- Available Options for Foundation, Garage & Personnel Doors, Window, & Sidings
- Package contains 5 Different Sizes
- 22' x 26' • 22' x 28' • 24' x 28' • 24' x 30' • 24' x 32'

No. 06006C $16.95

22' & 24' Deep Eave 2 & 3-Car Garages

- Can Be Built Stand-Alone or Attached to House
- Available Options for Roof, Foundation, Garage & Personnel Doors, Window, & Sidings
- Package contains 6 Different Sizes
- 22' x 28' • 22' x 32' • 24' x 32'
- 22' x 30' • 24' x 30' • 24' x 36'

No. 06002C $14.95

20' & 22' Wide-Gable 2-Car Garages

- Available Options for Roof, Foundation, Garage & Personnel Doors, Window, & Sidings
- Package contains 7 Different Sizes
- 20' x 20' • 20' x 24' • 22' x 22' • 22' x 28'
- 20' x 22' • 20' x 28' • 22' x 24'

No. 06008C $16.95

Eave 2 & 3-Car Clerestory Roof Garages

- Interior Side Stairs to Loft Workshop
- Available Options for Engine Lift, Foundation, Garage & Personnel Doors, Window, & Sidings
- Package contains 4 Different Sizes
- 24' x 26' • 24' x 28' • 24' x 32' • 24' x 36'

Order Code No: **H3BSM**

Garage Order Form

Please send me 1 complete set of the following GARAGE PLAN BLUEPRINTS:

Item no. & description ____________ Price $ ________

Additional Sets

(@ $10.00 EACH) $ ________

Garage Vellum

(@ $200.00 EACH) $ ________

Shipping Charges: **UPS Ground (3-7 days within the US)** $ ________

1-3 plans $7.95
4-6 plans $9.95
7-10 plans $11.95
11 or more plans $17.95

Subtotal: $ ________

Resident sales tax: $ ________

(CT residents add 6% sales tax, IL residents add 7%, WI residents add 5%) (Not required for other states)

Total Enclosed: $ ________

My Billing Address is:

Name: ________________________

Address: ________________________

City: ________________________

State: ____________ Zip: ____________

Daytime Phone No. (   ) ____________

My Shipping Address is:

Name: ________________________

Address: ________________________
(UPS will not ship to P.O. Boxes)

City: ________________________

State: ____________ Zip: ____________

For Faster Service...Charge It!
U.S. & Canada Call
1(800)235-5700

All foreign residents call 1(860)659-5667

MASTERCARD, VISA

Card # | | | | | | | | | | | | | | | | |

Signature ________________ Exp. ___/___

If paying by credit card, to avoid delays:
billing address must be as it appears on credit card statement

or FAX us at (860) 659-5692

Here's What You Ge

- Three complete sets of drawings for each plan orde
- Detailed step-by-step instructions with easy-to-follo diagrams on how to build your garage (not available with apartment garages)
- For each garage style, a variety of size and garage door configuration options
- Variety of roof styles and/or pitch options for most garages
- Complete materials list
- Choice between three foundation options: Monolith Slab, Concrete Stem Wall or Concrete Block Stem W
- Full framing plans, elevations and cross-sectionals f each garage size and configuration

Garage Plan Blueprints

All blueprint garage plan orders contain one complete s of drawings with instructions and are priced as listed n to the illustration. **These blueprint garage plans can r be modified.** Additional sets of plans may be obtained $10.00 each with your original order. UPS shipping used unless otherwise requested. Please include t proper amount for shipping.

Garage Plan Vellums

By purchasing vellums for one of our garage plans, y receive one vellum set of the same construction drawir found in the blueprints, but printed on vellum pap Vellums can be erased and are perfect for making des changes. They are also semi-transparent making th easy to duplicate. But most importantly, the purchase garage plan vellums comes with a broader license t allows you to make changes to the design (ie, creat hand drawn or CAD derivative work), to make copies the plan and to build one garage from the plan.

Send your order to:
(With check or money order payable in U.S. funds only)

The Garlinghouse Company
174 Oakwood Drive
Glastonbury, CT 06033

No C.O.D. orders accepted; U.S. funds only. UPS will not ship to Pos Office boxes, FPO boxes, APO boxes, Alaska or Hawaii.

Canadian orders:

UPS Ground (5-10 days within Canada)
1-3 plans $15.95
4-6 plans $17.95
7-10 plans $19.95
11 or more plans $24.95

Prices subject to change without notice.